INFORMATION AND COMPUTATION

Essays on Scientific and Philosophical Understanding of Foundations of Information and Computation

World Scientific Series in Information Studies
(ISSN: 1793-7876)

Series Editor: Mark Burgin *(University of California, Los Angeles, USA)*

World Scientific Series in Information Studies — **Vol. 2**

INFORMATION AND COMPUTATION

Essays on Scientific and Philosophical Understanding of Foundations of Information and Computation

Gordana Dodig-Crnkovic

Mälardalen University, Sweden

Mark Burgin

University of California, Los Angeles, USA

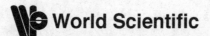
World Scientific

NEW JERSEY · LONDON · SINGAPORE · BEIJING · SHANGHAI · HONG KONG · TAIPEI · CHENNAI

Published by

World Scientific Publishing Co. Pte. Ltd.

5 Toh Tuck Link, Singapore 596224

USA office: 27 Warren Street, Suite 401-402, Hackensack, NJ 07601

UK office: 57 Shelton Street, Covent Garden, London WC2H 9HE

British Library Cataloguing-in-Publication Data
A catalogue record for this book is available from the British Library.

World Scientific Series in Information Studies — Vol. 2
INFORMATION AND COMPUTATION
Essays on Scientific and Philosophical Understanding of Foundations of Information and Computaiton

ISBN-13 978-981-4295-47-5
ISBN-10 981-4295-47-7

Printed in Singapore by B & Jo Enterprise Pte Ltd

CONTENTS

PREFACE

INFORMATION AND COMPUTAITON – OMNI PRESENT AND PERVASIVE

The world is full of information. Information is everywhere. It is in us and outside us. Information connects us to other people and it separates and alienates us. Information makes us happy and sad. It brings joy, satisfaction, grief, delight, pain, and consolation. In order for anything to exist for an individual, the individual must get information on it, either by means of perception or by re-organization of the existing information into new patterns and networks in the brain. With the advent of World Wide Web and a prospect of semantic web, the ways of information supply for individuals, networks of humans and machines and for humanity as a whole are becoming strategically important in a number of ways. Information becomes pivotal for communication, research, education systems, government, businesses and basic functioning of everyday life. Information architecture can rightly be characterized as the backbone of our civilization, as our essential supporting mechanism.

Information has developed into the leading factor in the world's economy as the following quotation demonstrates:

"Today, we need to look at what investments – and investment philosophies – will position us for success in the 21st century, when information, not manufacturing, will be the spark and engine of economic leadership.

The forces we face are massive – a global recession, climate change, an explosion of information that is reshaping how we conduct our business and personal lives. I believe that IT can transform these increasingly intersecting challenges into opportunities." (Banerjee, 2009).

Hope is put into information technology development such as the cloud – the next stage of the internet - a huge, intelligent, sustainable infrastructure where everything will be delivered as services: computing power, business processes and personal interactions.

However, in spite of all strategic importance and omnipresence of information, scientists have not come to the decisive conclusion about the essence and nature of information. There are hundreds of opinions and dozens of theories (cf., for example (Adriaans and van Benthem, 2008; Burgin, 2010)), but still the information concept is evasive and vague although correct knowledge about information is necessary for our understanding of the world we live in.

Information is related to everything and every thing is related to information. However, the most intimate relations exist between information and energy. On the one hand, principles of the general theory of information developed in (Burgin, 2003; 2005a; 2010) demonstrate that energy is a kind of information in the broad sense. This correlates with the von Weizsäcker's idea (1995/2006) that *energy might in the end turn out to be information*. In essence, all physical characteristics become different kinds of information obtained about physical systems and processes. According to one of the outstanding physicists of the 20th century John Archibald Wheeler, it means that every physical quantity derives its ultimate significance and meaning from information (Wheeler, 1990; 1994).

The most fundamental approach to physics based on information, the, so-called, *ur*-theory, has been developed in the school of von Weizsäcker (von Weizsäcker, 1958; von Weizsäcker, Scheibe and Süssmann, 1958; Castell, *et al*, 1975-1986; Lyre, 2002). The main idea is that what physicists learn about nature comes from observation and experiments through measurement. According to von Weizsäcker, measurement is information extraction from physical objects and processes. Thus, physical objects and processes are entirely characterized by the information that can be acquired from them. In such a way, physics reduces to predicting measurement outcomes.

Frieden (1998) also developed a new approach to physics based on Fisher information, explaining that physics as a knowledge system about the universe is built from knowledge acquired through information reception and processing. According to this conception, the observer is included into the phenomenon of measurement as his properties as an information receiver influence what data are collected and how they are collected and interpreted. The basic contention of Frieden is that physicists think that they study material systems as they are, while they actually study information that they are able to get from these systems.

On the other hand, according to the general theory of information, information is energy in the structural world, e.g., in the world of knowledge and data, while conventional energy is energy in the physical world, i.e., the world of material objects. At the physical level of reality, relations between information and energy are considered by Umpleby (2007) who comes to a conclusion that at the level of data signal processing "difference" is more elementary than information. Information is what the universe is, in some sense, made of, while the difference is a trait in a structure of a cognitive agent.

A grounded analysis of this statement by some researchers shows that actually any difference is accessible only through information reception. Consequently, information is a more basic (and in some sense, more elementary) phenomenon than "difference."

However, many other researchers believe that data are basic elements of which information is made, and information is stuff of which knowledge is made. This approach finds its structural representation in the, so-called, Data-Information-Knowledge Pyramid.

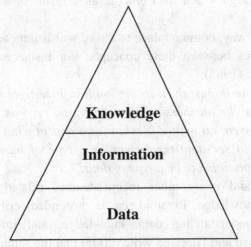

Fig. 1. The Data-Information-Knowledge (DIK) Pyramid

There are different interpretations of the levels from this pyramid (cf., for example, (Stenmark, 2002; Boisot and Canals, 2004; Burgin, 2010)). The most popular of them tells:

Information is structuring of data (or structured data)

Knowledge is structuring of information (or structured information)

However, another approach (cf., for example, (Meadow and Yuan, 1997)) suggests a different picture:

Data usually means a set of symbols with little or no meaning to a recipient.

Information is a set of symbols that does have meaning or significance to their recipient.

Knowledge is the accumulation and integration of information received and processed by a recipient.

This and many other definitions show absence of consensus on the meaning of these terms. For instance, in many books and papers, the terms *knowledge* and *information* are used interchangeably, even though the two entities, being intertwined and interrelated concepts, are far from identical. While some researchers define knowledge and/or data in terms of information, others define information in terms of data and knowledge. For instance, Kogut and Zander (1992) conceive information as "knowledge which can be transmitted without loss of integrity," while Tuomi (1999) argues that data emerge as a result of adding value to information.

In a similar way, commonplace usage of words *data* and *information* blurs differences between these concepts. For instance, Machlup and Mansfield write (1983):

"*Data are the things given to the analyst, investigator, or problem-solver; they may be numbers, words, sentences, records, assumptions - just anything given, no matter in what form and of what origin... Many writers prefer to see data themselves as a type of information, while others want information to be a type of data.*"

All these and many other inconsistencies related to the Data-Information-Knowledge Pyramid cause grounded criticism of this approach to understanding data, knowledge, and information. For instance, Capurro and Hjorland write (2003) that the semantic concept of information, located between data and knowledge is not consistent with the view that equates modern information management with information technology. Boisot and Canals (2004) criticize distinctions that have been drawn between data, information, and knowledge by those who analyzed the Data-Information-Knowledge Pyramid. Fricke (2008) also offers valid arguments that the hierarchy is unsound and methodologically undesirable. In addition, researchers criticized various implications of the Data-Information-Knowledge Pyramid. For instance, Tuomi (1999) argues that in contrast to the conventional estimation that knowledge is more valuable than information, while information is superior to data, these relations have to be reversed.

Problems with the Data-Information-Knowledge Pyramid are resolved in the general theory of information where relations between data, information and knowledge are represented by the Knowledge-Information-Matter-Energy (KIME) Square.

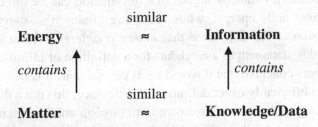

Fig. 2. The Knowledge-Information-Matter-Energy (KIME) Square

The KIME Square visualizes and embodies the following principle:
Information is related to knowledge and data as
energy is related to matter.

It means that knowledge and data contain information as matter (material bodies) contains energy. As it is possible to convert matter into energy, extract energy from material bodies and convert energy into material things, e.g., into subatomic particles, it is doable to convert knowledge and data into information and information into knowledge and data. When people are learning, they receive information and then transform it into knowledge and data (Burgin, 2001; 2010). As a result we come to a clear understanding of roles that teachers and student play in the educational process: a teacher cannot put knowledge into the heads of her students, she is able only to provide information and students themselves have to convert this information into knowledge.

In addition, the KIME Square tells us that while data and knowledge belong to the same type of objects, the essence of information is very different (Burgin, 2005a). Like energy gives dynamics to substance, information produces dynamics of data and knowledge.

Some may be confused that data and knowledge are considered as similar entities. We can explain their relations in a metaphorical way. The first metaphor elucidates that data and knowledge are like different types of molecules: data are like molecules of water, which has two atoms, while knowledge is like molecules of DNA, which contains billions of atoms. One more metaphor provides another analogy: data and knowledge are like living beings, but data are like bacteria, while knowledge is like a human being.

In addition, Umpleby argues that information can be directly related to matter and energy while adopting Bateson's statement that *information is the difference that makes a difference* (Bateson, 1972). Taking this statement as a candidate for a definition of information, some researchers conceive that it would be as deceptive as it is beautiful. First, without sufficiently exact definition of difference, this not a definition as it is wrong to define one unknown term through another unknown term. This is a logical fallacy. Second, even if we take the mundane meaning of the word *difference*, we may come to a conclusion that anything is a difference because anything is different from something else. Besides, being different, any thing makes this difference and thus, we have to logically conclude that anything is information. This makes the concept of information void from a scientific point of view. Fortunately, this is not true and the concept of information is not only meaningful but is becoming one of the pillars of contemporary science.

At the same time, other researchers (Dodig Crnkovic, 2009) believe Bateson's statement reflects the way information functions in physics, cybernetics, biology and number of other fields and take for granted that *difference* is a clear concept. This belief is based on the assumption that the *difference* is what a specific cognizing system is capable of detecting as difference. So, the *difference* is receiver specific.

In its existence, information is related to many things, such as data, knowledge or difference. It is also intrinsically related to computation. Information is a basic essence of the world, while computation is a process of the dynamic change of information (Dodig Crnkovic, 2006). Indeed, any computation is information processing. However, not any information processing is computation. According to the general theory of information, there are three basic types of information processing (Burgin, 1997; 2010):

- information transmission;
- information transformation;
- information storage.

In *information transmission*, information changes its place in space.

In *information transformation*, information itself and/or its representation are changed.

In *information storage*, information changes its place in time.

There are three reasonable levels of generality in understanding the phenomenon of computation:

On the top level, *computation* is perceived as any transformation of information and/or information representation.

On the middle level, *computation* is distinguished as a discrete process of transformation of information and/or information representation.

On the bottom level, *computation* is recognized as a discrete process of symbolic transformation of information and/or symbolic information representation.

It is necessary to remark that if we do not go beyond the bottom level and insist on discreteness, we would loose continuous time computation realized by general dynamical systems (Bournez, 1999), hybrid systems (Gupta, *et al*, 1999), and special computing devices, such as the differential analyzer (Shannon, 1941; Moore, 1996).

It looks natural to define *computation* as transformation of information representation. This is the traditional approach of computationalism (cf., for example, (Kelemen, 2006)). It is also natural to assume that transformations can be discrete, continuous and partially continuous.

As there are different representations of information, this definition results in separation of *substantial types* of computations:

1. Symbolic computation when information is represented by symbols.
2. Material *computation* when information is represented by material things. This can be a biological cell or an atom and can be continuous as there is continuum in many branches of physics.

Artificial devices, such as computers and calculators, perform material computation, representing symbolic computation, which is pivotal. The same process of symbolic computation can be realized by different material computations, e.g., on different computers. Quantum computation is a kind of symbolic computations embodied in material computation where symbols are represented by quantum states.

It is an open problem whether symbolic computation is possible without material computation although the majority of researchers (Dodig-Crnkovic 2009) cannot even imagine such a situation, believing that there is no information without physical representation and there is no computation without information.

At the same time, a broader view of computation reflected by the middle level results in three *operational types* of computation (Burgin, 2005):

1. Discrete computation when digital or symbolic operations are performed in elementary separated steps.
2. Continuous or analogue computation when operation goes without breaks in time.
3. Piecewise continuous computation, which combines both discrete computation and continuous computation.

In addition, we have three *temporal types* of computation (Burgin, 2005):

1. Sequential computation, which is performed in linear time.
2. Parallel or branching computation, in which separate steps (operations) are synchronized in time.

3. Concurrent computation, which does not demand synchronization in time.

Note that while parallel computation is completely synchronized, branching computation is not completely synchronized.

Existence of various types and kinds of computation, as well as a variety of approaches to the concept of computation, shows complexity of understanding computation in the holistic picture of the world.

In this volume, a number of leading researchers and philosophers study problems of information and computation treating information in its dynamical context - time changes of informational structures, their interaction, and impact. From this perspective, we need much better understanding of information processing and its primary form – computation than we have now. As there is no information without (physical) representation, the dynamics of information is implemented on different levels of granularity by different physical processes, including the level of computation performed by computing machines and living organisms. There are a lot of open problems related to the nature of information and essence of computation, as well as to their relationships. How is information dynamics represented in computational systems, in machines, as well as in living organisms? Are computers processing only data or information and knowledge as well? How is information processing related to knowledge management and sciences, especially to science of information itself? What do we know of computational processes in machines and living organisms and how these processes are related? What can we learn from natural computational processes that can be useful for information systems and knowledge management? These and similar problems associated with information and computation are treated in the book.

In Chapter 1, "Cybersemiotics and the Question of Knowledge", Søren Brier treats the paninformationalism as a kind of informational structural realism, according to which the "fabric of the universe" is the informational structure, and pancomputationalism (natural computationalism) is the idea that the universe is a computational system, which by physical processes "computes" its own next state. Based on this understanding, he advances the argument that paninformationalism and pancomputationalism, seen together as a paradigm for information, cognition and communication, are not enough to explain the role of the first-person conscious embodied social awareness. Arguing in the framework of *cybersemiotics*, Brier emphasizes importance of the production of signification and meaning, for which science currently lacks a detailed understanding in the framework of *info-computationalism*. Besides, he proposes a cybersemiotic theory of knowledge based on Peirce's semiotic framework as a step towards a more realistic theory of knowing, which is important for technological applications.

In Chapter 2, "Information Dynamics in a Categorical Setting", Mark Burgin builds a categorical models for information and information processes based on the general theory of information, which is a synthetic approach that organizes and encompasses all main directions in information theory. On the methodological level, the general theory of information is formulated as system of principles, explaining what information is and how to measure information. The goal of this chapter is to build a mathematical stratum of the general theory of information based on category theory. Abstract categories allow the author to develop flexible models for information and its flow, as well as for computers, networks and computation. In this context, portions of information are modeled by operators in system representation spaces.

There are two types of representation of information dynamics in categories: the categorical representation and functorial representation. The categorical representations of information dynamics preserve internal structures of information spaces associated with infological systems as their state or phase spaces, modeling portions of information by categorical information operators. The functorial representations of information dynamics preserve external structures of information spaces associated with infological systems as their state or phase spaces, modeling portions of information by functorial information operators. Properties of these types of representations are studied. In particular, sequential, concurrent and parallel compositions of categorical information operators are defined and analyzed. Obtained results facilitate building a common framework for information and computation. Now category theory is also used as a unifying framework for physics, biology, topology, and logic, as well as for the whole mathematics. This provides a base for analyzing physical and information systems and processes by means of categorical structures and methods. In addition, categorical models of computation are discussed, demonstrating relations between information and computation on the level of their mathematical models in the categorical setting. In Conclusion, the author formulates various open problems in the mathematical theory of information.

Chapter 3, "Mathematics as a biological process", presents Greg Chaitin's comparative analysis of complexity in mathematics, physics and biology. Complexity is one the main characteristics of any process (cf., for example, (Chaitin, 1987; Li and Vitanyi, 1997; Burgin, 2005)). This characteristic discriminates simple processes from complex ones and shows that processes in living organisms are especially complex. In contrast to this, Chaitin starts his chapter by pointing out that his algorithmic complexity does not apply to biology. On the other hand, he conjectures that the idea of complexity that comes from biology can be used to find the limits of mathematics. As an example, Chaitin describes Hilbert's program aimed at complete mechanization and automatization of mathematics. As we know, Gödel demonstrated that no finite set of axioms can allow derivation of all true sentences even in such a basic system as the formal (Peano) arithmetic. In essence, any finite set of axioms for arithmetic is either incomplete or inconsistent. So, the Hilbert program was to stay unfinished. Incompleteness discovered by Gödel is also reflected in the work of Turing (1936), who showed that there are basic things in mathematics which cannot be computed. Chaitin explains incompleteness and incomputability using the notion of algorithmic complexity. In algorithmic complexity, something has N bits of complexity if you need an N-bit program to calculate it, irrespective how long this N-bit program takes to run. Unlike physics, biology is fundamentally complex and biological processes cannot be explained in simple equations. According to Chaitin, pure mathematics is even worse than biology when it comes to complexity, as it is provably infinitely complex.

Chaitin argues that the bits of the number Ω give maximally unknowable information in pure mathematics. This might be true if mathematicians would acquire information only by logical deduction. Applying more powerful methods, such as induction, mathematics can go beyond the number Ω (cf. (Burgin, 2005)). It is also necessary to understand that Ω is not a number in the conventional sense because it depends on the choice of a universal Turing machine or universal partial recursive function.

Even though biology is enormously complex, its algorithmic complexity, according to Chaitin, is finite, while pure mathematics has infinite algorithmic complexity. Gödel alleged that his theorems did not affect human mathematicians because humans have a "divine spark which enables them to directly intuit mathematical truth" helping them to decide undecidable problems. Turing, on the other hand, thought humans are not basically different from machines. Chaitin himself believes that people might be a mix of both. The connection between computation, information and biology is a recurrent theme in this chapter.

In Chapter 4, "Information, Causation and Computation", John Collier, starts with two basic assumptions:

1. All information takes a physical form.
2. Everything physical can be explained in dynamical terms.

This allows Collier to infer that information must be explicable in terms of forces and flows. As forces and flows are physical phenomena and physics can be expressed in terms of information (cf., for example, (Frieden, 1998) or (von Weizsäcker, 1985; Lyre, 2002)), this approach looks like information reverse engineering. Collier's explication is done in order to study causation and is based on Bateson's definition of information as the difference (Bateson, 1972). The chapter shows that bringing together causation (which makes a dynamical difference) with the logic of information flow makes possible to see causation as a sort of computation. This view is compatible with natural computationalism which sees the whole of the universe as a computing physical system.

In Chapter 5, "From Descartes to Turing: The Computational Content of Supervenience", Barry Cooper uses the notion of definability in a structure and the concept of a Turing machine with an oracle as a model of interactive computation to address the problem of supervenience of mental properties on physical ones. According to Kim (1993), supervenience represents the idea that mentality is, at the bottom, physically based, and there is no free-floating mentality unanchored in the physical nature of objects and events in which it is manifested.

It is necessary to remark that a Turing machine with an oracle treated by Cooper as a model of interactive computation is as interactive as a simple a Turing machine introduced in 1936 (Turing, 1936) where there is interaction between the head and tape of the machine. In essence any computation is interactive when the computing device receives input and gives output. The notions of input and output imply interaction with the environment. However, the first explicitly interactive model of computation was *neural network*, the simplest case of which appeared in the work of McCulloch and Pitts (1943) being a precursor of nowadays connectionism.

Cooper also shows how to give a computational content to emergence, use emergence to link functions of the brain to higher mental activity, and apply definability to recursions involving mental representations. This leads to presenting the organism with a coherence and organic unity.

Chapter 6 presents "A Dialogue Concerning Two World Systems, Info-Computational Vs. Mechanistic." In it Gordana Dodig-Crnkovic and Vincent Müller compare the classical mechanistic world view, where Church-Turing thesis takes Turing Machines to be capable of modeling all possible computations, with the new emerging info-computationalism which takes the dynamics of the universe to be a process of computation, be it digital or analog, symbolic or sub-symbolic, technological or of the type known as natural computation (cf., for example (Ballard, 1997; MacLennan, 1999)). The argument is advanced so that for the first time in history of science, a scientific framework has a grounded capacity of embracing the biotic (living) world into the domain of computer science, and in particular, including the ability to rekindle the computational models of mind, based on natural computing. Of course, if the science is to remain "objective", which may be interpreted as "inter-subjective", this new understanding of life and mind would also have to be the third person view, comprising knowledge of what happens in the world when a human or an animal has conscious experience. In this context, the subjective experience, such as *qualia*, must be addressed by other scholarly, intellectual and artistic fields.

In Chapter 7, "Does Computing Embrace Self-Organization?", Wolfgang Hofkirchner analyzes the rise of the computer as man-made machine for processing information, the spread of PCs, the diffusion of

ICTs and the penetration of social life including the natural environment as well as human bodies with "intelligent" devices. The author explores possibilities of computation and its relations to information and self-organization. It is demonstrated what happens if computers and computation would be treated from the position of technically oriented, mechanistic thinking. In this case, it is easy to show that computing in this restricted sense does not encompass self-organization.

The mechanistic way of thinking about computation brings researchers to the statements that "information generation defies being formalized, expressed by a mathematical function, or carried out by a computer" and "the generation of information escapes algorithmization, in principle." In reality, there is a big and flourishing area called algorithmic information theory, which is based on algorithmic, and thus, computational approach and which successfully studies information (cf., for example, (Chaitin, 1987; Li and Vitanyi, 1997; Burgin, 2005)).

In the chapter, mechanistic computation is also contrasted to emergence. At the same time, existing computational processes, which are much broader than their mechanistic counterpart, include a big and flourishing area called evolutionary computations (cf., for example, (Koza, 1992; Fogel, 1995; Michalewicz, 1996; Eberbach, 2005; Burgin and Eberbach, 2008; Burgin and Eberbach, 2009)). The basic idea of evolutionary computations is computational emergence in a form of evolution. One of the examples of such emergence is the Game of Life (cf., (Langton, 1989)).

Besides, theory of algorithms and computation has models, such as non-deterministic and probabilistic finite automata and non-deterministic and probabilistic Turing machines, which perform computations, but go far beyond strictly mechanistic procedures (cf., for example, (Hromkovic, 2005; Burgin, 2005)).

This demonstrates that the understanding of computing and information processing depends on the made assumptions, serving as litmus test, which indicates whether or not this understanding amounts to a really adequate paradigm.

In Chapter 8, "Analysis of Information and Computation in Physics Explains Cognitive Paradigms: From Full Cognition to Laplace Determinism to Statistical Determinism to Modern Approach", Vladik

Kreinovich, Roberto Araiza, and Juan Ferret analyze the problem of prediction in physics from the computational viewpoint. They explicate the three main physical paradigms in understanding physical reality: Laplace determinism, statistical determinism, and information accessibility, which they call the Modern Approach. *Laplace determinism* means that knowing the initial conditions, it is possible to predict future behavior of the system that is observed. *Statistical determinism* means that knowing the initial conditions, it is possible to predict probabilities of different future events in the system that is observed. *Information accessibility* (Modern Approach) means that knowing the initial conditions, it is possible to predict the system behavior that is observed.

The authors show how these paradigms can be naturally explained by their computational analysis. To achieve this goal, they use concepts from the algorithmic information theory, such as Kolmogorov complexity, which was introduced by Ray Solomonoff, Andrey Kolmogorov and Gregory Chaitin, and algorithmic randomness (cf., for example, (Chaitin, 1987; Li and Vitanyi, 1997; Burgin, 2005)), as well as the novel, more physics-oriented versions of these concepts developed by the authors.

Chapter 9, "Bodies - Both Informed and Transformed Embodied Computation and Information Processing," by Bruce MacLennan is dedicated to an analysis of embodied computing. It emphasizes the importance of the development of physical computing or "embodied computing" for the future of computational technology, including the control of processes at nano-scales.

MacLennan observes the essential interrelationships between information processing and physical processes and discusses relationships between function, structure, regulation, causation, and the definition of computation. The chapter concludes with the claim that in order to fully exploit embodied computation, we need robust and powerful theoretical tools, but according to MacLennan the theory of Church-Turing computation, performed by an abstract logical machine is not suitable for the study of embodied computing. It is possible to add that by its essence, embodied computing is super-recursive and thus, its theory is a part (subtheory) of the theory of super-recursive algorithms (Burgin, 2005).

In Chapter 10, "Computation on Information, Meaning and Representations: An Evolutionary Approach", Christophe Menant interprets computation as "a process of the dynamic change of information," which does not independently exist but is generated by the system that uses it for a definite purpose. This is in a good agreement with the general theory of information, where computation is regarded as information transformation, while information is understood as potency for changes (Burgin, 2003; 2005). According to the author, "information can be meaningless like thunderstorm noise or it can be meaningful like an alert signal. However, even thunderstorm noise participates to the generation of meaningful information about coming rain. Thus, it becomes important to analyze the relations between information, its meaning and representation. To make these relations explicit and constructive, the author uses the concept of the Meaning Generator System (MGS), which connects systems and their environment.

In Chapter 11, "Interior Grounding, Reflection, and Self-Consciousness," Marvin Minsky explores the problem of consciousness, emphasizing the view on the mind as a multi-level system of processes. He describes how researchers recognize consciousness and what might be happening when a person thinks consciously. The next question of interest is about how our mental levels develop and grow. Minsky criticizes the popular view of "grounding in experience" when the mental development is assumed to proceed by beginning with learning low-level reactions, waiting for each stage to consolidate before people can learn to think more abstractly. Subjective experience, ever so often emphasized by philosophers, is nothing really direct, but a complex process based on the "n-th hand reports" that have gone through many kinds of transformations. For example the visual system in a human brain includes dozens of different processing centers. Sensations are complex reflective activities, sometimes involving cascades in which parts of the brain are affected by signals whose origins we cannot detect and thus hard to explain. In agreement with Kant (cf., (Kant, 1902-1956)), Minsky states that our empirical knowledge is a combination of that which we receive through sensory impressions (experience), and knowledge which the cognition supplies from within, by different mechanisms like associations, reasoning, analogical thinking, and similar. This brings

Minsky to the problem of knowledge representation. In contrast to the most popular approaches where researchers advocate one form of knowledge representation, e.g., logic or semantic networks, Minsky argues that knowledge in the brain forms a hierarchy of different levels of representation, from micronemes, neural networks, k-lines and k-trees, semantic networks, frames, picture frames, trans-frames to narrative stories – each of the levels having specific dedicated role in knowledge representation. Methodological analysis of knowledge also supports this conjecture, separating three basic levels of knowledge: the micro-level, macro-level and mega-level (cf., (Burgin, 2010)). Each of these levels comprises several specific forms of knowledge representation.

In Chapter 12, "A Molecular Dynamic Network: Minimal Properties and Evolutionary Implications," Walter Riofrio is proposing a hypothesis addressing the problem of the emergence and self-maintenance of protocellular organization, describing a kind of evolutionary mechanism before the life as we understand it today appeared. Riofrio builds his approach on the observation that for biological systems, robustness and evolvability are in continuous tension.

In order to understand the basic properties of life, it is crucial to understand the first forms that developed much earlier than previously thought. This chapter indicates that the development of interconnected molecular processes is possible evolving from random initial conditions.

In Chapter 13, "Super-recursive Features of Evolutionary Processes and the Models for Computational Evolution," Darko Roglic is developing a computational approach based on biological information processing, *computational evolution* in the sense of (Banzhaf, *et.al.*, 2006), and *inductive Turing machines*, a computational model introduced by Burgin and approved by Kolmogorov (Burgin, 1983). The goal is using ideas that reflect natural biological system functioning, to develop new kinds of computational evolutionary systems. Roglic describes and analyzes information processing in biological systems, as well as computation by biologically oriented computers. As the author writes, to build systems that can adapt to their environments and learn from their experience is the long-standing goal, attracting researchers from many fields. Giving an overview of biological information processing, Roglic comes to a grounded conclusion that even evolvable capabilities of bacteria for adaptation in rapidly changing and extremely hostile environment are not achievable for modern computational systems working in the paradigm of the Church-Turing thesis. To overcome limitations of recursive algorithms working in the boundaries of the Church-Turing thesis, super-recursive evolutionary information processing is used.

In addition, conventional Turing machines cannot change their instructions (rules of computation) in the process of computation because their instructions are separated from the processed data. Discussing ideas of a learning machine, Turing (1950) insisted that the rules of computation have to be time-invariant. At the same time, self-adaptation demands changing the rules. This brings Roglic to the idea of self-modification in computing systems.

Reflexive Turing machine was suggested by Burgin (1992) as a generic model for programs or automata that change (improve) themselves while they are working. Kleene (1960) formulated a conjecture that an algorithm that changes (improves) itself while working can have higher computational/decision power that Turing machines. In (Burgin, 1992), it is proved that a Turing machine can simulate any reflexive Turing machine. This disproved the Kleene conjecture and gave more evidence in support of the Church-Turing Thesis, although at that time it was known (Burgin, 1987) that the Church-Turing Thesis in its strong form (equating all possible computations with Turing machines) is invalid.

However, it was proved (Burgin, 1993) that reflexive Turing machines can be much more efficient than Turing machines, essentially reducing time of computation. This result supports the approach of Roglic who uses ideas from natural biological systems in developing new kinds of computational evolution systems. To this end, Roglic describes a EC machine, bacteria-like EC(BL-EC) machine and Sequencer machine as four-dimensional patterns of horizontal-vertical computation, which reflects the structure, functioning and ontogenetic development of a living organism. BL-EC machine has two basic modules: Interactor program as a part of input and output information processing system and Processor as a part of working information processing system.

In Chapter 14, "Towards a Modeling View of Computing," Oron Shagrir presents a general characterization of a computing system, building on the observation that computation operates with information or over representations that does not require structural constraint in a sense of an algorithmic or rule-governed process. Shagrir provides an example from computational neuroscience: the modeling account of computing of the oculomotor integrator, which models certain mathematical relations "in the world" by the mathematical relations defined for the cellular electric activity. In general, there is an "isomorphism" between the formal or mathematical relations that represent actual relations between the states of the modeled system, and mathematical relations between the states of the modeling system. The idea of computation as modeling can be traced back to analog computers.

This correspondence shows that modeling knowledge has the form of the basic element of knowledge described in (Burgin, 2010). This modeling knowledge is represented by the following diagram

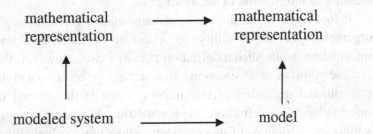

Shagrir provides a general characterization of a computing system, which is both semantic and formal. The semantic feature consists of information-processing, which maps one set of representations to another, while the formality refers to functional relations between the ccomputing system states, being similar to the mathematical relations between the entities that are represented.

In Chapter 15, "What's Information, for an Organism or Intelligent Machine? How Can a Machine or Organism Mean?", Aaron Sloman studies problems of information and meaning with the emphasis on clarifying the concept of information, providing a profound methodological analysis of the current situation. Giving reasonable arguments, he asserts that the concept "information" cannot be defined explicitly in terms of simpler concepts, including "matter" and "energy". Instead, the meanings of such basic phenomena are defined implicitly in part by the structure of the theories in which they occur, and in part by the way those theories are used in practice. Sloman gives persuasive evidence and explains why it is impossible to define information without circularity in such a way that the definition would encompass diverse uses and interpretations of the term *information*. Several other researchers share this opinion (cf., for example, (Capurro, *et al*, 1999; Melik-Gaikazyan, 1997)).

At the same time, a comprehensive definition of information in the general theory of information (Burgin, 2010) does not have circularity and encompasses a host of diverse definitions of information, either making them specializations of the general definition or assigning a more adequate meaning to those definitions. For instance, information entropy $H(m)$ is often called Shannon's information. However, as it is explained in the general theory of information, $H(m)$ is not information but a measure of information in the message m.

It looks like a paradox: several authoritative researchers give valid arguments for impossibility to elaborate a concise definition of information, while such a definition already exists. However, there is no contradiction in this situation. Researchers reject a possibility of a conventional definition of information, while in the general theory of information the definition is parametric, depending on a system parameter. Variations of this parameter allow one to obtain the diversity of all meanings and interpretations (sometimes in a more adequate form) of the term *information*.

However, to understand and use more efficiently information and information processes, it is necessary to specify different kinds and types of information, describing essential properties of the studied phenomena. To do this, Sloman elucidates and studies three basic aspects of information: *content*, *function* (or *use*, or *causal role*) and the *medium* (or *representation*, or *carrier*) in which information is expressed. It is possible for the same information content to be put to different uses, to be conveyed by different media and to play different roles. Thus, when information is used, it is natural to distinguish the content of the information, which Sloman calls *phrastic* following (Hare, 1952), from the use that is being made of it, which Sloman calls *neustic* also following (Hare, 1952). Besides, as Sloman rightly notes, from the earliest days of AI and software engineering, it was clear that choice of information representation could make a large difference to the success of a particular information processing system. This perfectly correlates with the basic principles of the general theory of information (Burgin, 2010).

The main goal of Chapter 16, "Inconsistent Knowledge as a Natural Phenomenon", by Kees de Vey Mestdagh and Jaap Henk Hoepman is ranking of reasonable inferences as a computational approach to naturally inconsistent (legal) theories. At first, the authors give a broad perspective on problems of inconsistent knowledge and inconsistent information, concentrating on the natural inconsistency, which results from the distributed character of information processing and variation between information content in different carriers of information. The bounded character of information and information processing allows for natural inconsistency (in the sense of inconsistency being the result of the different perspectives as opposed to faulty perception or other forms of faulty processing like processing on the basis of incomplete knowledge). Natural inconsistency constitutes no general problem. It only generates a specific practical problem if a common perspective is needed. However, a common perspective is frequently required for a variety of reasons ranging from the demand for making a decision (on a common perspective or action) to the need for a decidable logic or for a finite algorithm. There are three main approaches to solve the problem of common perspective: universalism, utilitarianism and contractarianism. Universalism claims that there are universal decisive principles (cf., for example, Kant's *categorical imperative* (Kant, 1902-1956)). Utilitarism promoted by philosophers, such as David Hume, Jeremy Bentham, John Stuart Mill, claims that it is possible to make a decisive cost-benefit analysis (cf., for example, Kant's *hypothetical imperative* (Kant, 1902-1956)). Contractarianism avoids the semantic problems of utilitarism by introducing a purely formal decisive criterion (*pacta sunt servanda*). None of these approaches have ever been made computationally tractable. Inconsistency as a natural phenomenon explains why they never will. The core of the problem is that there is not only natural inconsistency at the level of perspectives on the actual situation, but also natural inconsistency at the level of the principles used to decide for a common perspective. There is no universal preferential ordering of perspectives at both levels, because there is no (known, let alone a universally recognized) universal processor and because there is no exhaustive or non contradictory set of universal or utilitarian principles or contracts available.

Each domain of knowledge is more or less affected by this problem, but the domain of legal knowledge is affected by it intensely, since it consists of the rules and procedures used to describe and to solve legal conflicts, that presuppose contradictory and hence inconsistent perspectives. An analysis of the solution of the problem of common perspective found in the legal domain can most likely be used to solve the problem in other domains.

Human processors of legal knowledge follow formal and informal problem solving methods to reduce the number of valid (legitimate) legal perspectives and eventually to decide, temporally and within a specific context, to a common perspective. The formal methods are based on universal properties of formally valid legal argument. The informal methods are based on legal heuristics consisting in tentative decisive legal principles.

The first category can be formalized by logic because it applies peremptory to all legal perspectives. The second category can not be fully formalized by logic because, although it applies commonly, it always can be refuted by a contradictory decisive principle and even by the mere existence of an underlying contradictory argument.

The authors develop the Logic of Reasonable Inferences that formalizes the reduction of all actual legal perspectives to all formally valid legal perspectives. This logic is a legal logical variety in the sense of (Burgin, 1995; 2004). In the process of the logic development, decisive legal principles are categorized into three classes. The properties of the three classes are used to define the semantics of meta-predicates, which can be used to rank the remaining perspectives computationally. This approach is very perspective because logical varieties represent the natural development of logical calculi and thus, they show the direction in which mathematical logic will inevitably go.

In the last part of the chapter, the authors illustrate the behavior of the Logic of Reasonable Inferences in combination with the meta-predicates by a complex legal example.

In Chapter 17, "On the Algorithmic Nature of the World", Hector Zenil and Jean-Paul Delahaye try to identify evidence in support of or in contravention of the claim that the world is algorithmic in nature. The idea that nature functions exclusively in the form of computation has been taken increasingly seriously following the lead of some authors, such as Fredkin, Schmidhuber, and Wolfram. However, any scientific hypothesis has to be verified by experiments and observation. In contrast to this, there has been no way to either verify or refute the idea of the algorithmic nature of the world. The authors describe a test for this hypothesis based on mathematical statistics, the theory of algorithmic (Kolmogorov) complexity and an experimental evaluation of Levin's universal distribution. To achieve their goal, Zenil and Delahaye perform statistical comparisons of the frequency distributions of data samples from physical sources, such as repositories of information in the form of images from the web, data stored in a hard drive, computer programs and DNA sequences, and the output frequency distributions generated by purely algorithmic means, e.g., by running abstract computing machines, such as Turing machines, cellular automata and Post Tag systems. The authors find some indications of correlations having weak to strong significance. This is the case with distributions from the chosen abstract devices, as well as with data from the chosen physical sources. Each of these sources separately turned out to show several degrees of correlation. At the same time, while the correlation between the two sets is partial, each distribution is correlated with, at least, one other distribution produced by an abstract model of computation.

To conclude, it is our hope that the research presented in this volume will bring us a significant step closer to understanding the phenomena of information and computation and their relationships, making a difference that makes a difference. Obviously, at this stage we do not want to claim that we have a "final theory of everything" in front of us (even if such a theory would be possible), but the ideas developed and results obtained in this book provide a grounded proof of deep and profoundly important research going on in the foundations of information and computation.

Last but not least we want to express our sincere gratitude to the authors both for their highly interesting chapters, each of them addressing an important topic for the future development of the research field, and for their contributions in forming the book as a whole. This book presents a substantially collaborative project, where authors even helped in the reviewing process, taken part in discussing topics and contributed with suggestions about the way of presentation of the book. We would also like to thank Kaj Børge Hansen, Patrick Allo, Luciano Floridi and Ruth Hagengruber for reviewing parts of the book.

References

Adriaans, P. and van Benthem, J. (Eds) (2008) *Handbook on the Philosophy of Information*, North Holland

Ballard, D.H. (1997) *An Introduction to Natural Computation*, MIT Press, Cambridge

Banerjee, P. Technology critical to turning mass of data into useful insight, *FT.com*, April 8, 2009

Banzhaf, W.,Beslon, G., Christensen, S., Foster, A.J, Kepes, F., Lefort, V., Miller, F.J., Radman, M. and Ramsden, J. (2006) Guidelines: From artificial evolution to computational evolution: a research agenda, *Nature Reviews Genetics*, v. 7, pp. 729–741

Bateson, G. (1972) *Steps to an Ecology of Mind*, Ballantine Books, New York

Boisot, M. and Canals, A. (2004) Data, Information, and Knowledge: Have we got it right, *Journal of Evolutionary Economics*, v. 14, pp. 43–67

Bournez, O. (1999) Achilles and the tortoise climbing up the hyper-arithmetical hierarchy, *Theoretical Computer Science*, v. 210, No.1, pp. 21–71

Burgin, M. S. (1983) Inductive Turing Machines, *Notices of the Academy of Sciences of the USSR*, v. 270, No. 6, pp. 1289–1293   (translated from Russian, v. 27, No. 3)

Burgin, M. (1987) The Notion of Algorithm and the Turing-Church Thesis, In *Proceedings of the VIII International Congress on Logic, Methodology and Philosophy of Science*, Moscow, v. 5, part 1, pp. 138–140

Burgin, M.S. (1992) Reflexive Calculi and Logic of Expert Systems, in *Creative processes modeling by means of knowledge bases*, Sofia, pp. 139–160

Burgin, M. (1993) Reflexive Turing Machines and Calculi, *Vychislitelnyye Sistemy (Logical Methods in Computer Science)*, No. 148, pp. 94–116, 175–176   (in Russian)

Burgin, M. (1995) Logical Tools for Inconsistent Knowledge Systems, *Information: Theories & Applications*, v.3, No. 10, pp.13–18

Burgin, M. (1997) Information Algebras, *Control Systems and Machines*, No.6, pp. 5–16 (in Russian)

Burgin, M. (2001) Information in the Context of Education, *Journal of Interdisciplinary Studies*, v. 14, pp. 155–166

Burgin, M. (2003) Information Theory: A Multifaceted Model of Information, *Entropy*, v. 5, No. 2, pp. 146–160

Burgin, M. (2004) Logical Tools for Program Integration and Interoperability, in *Proceedings of the IASTED International Conference on Software Engineering and Applications*, MIT, Cambridge, pp. 743–748

Burgin, M. (2005) *Super-recursive Algorithms*, Springer, New York/Heidelberg/Berlin

Burgin, M. (2005a) Is Information Some Kind of Data? *Proceedings of the Third Conference on the Foundations of Information Science* (FIS 2005), Paris, France, July, pp. 1–31 (electronic edition: http://www.mdpi.net/fis2005/proceedings.html)

Burgin, M. (2010) *Theory of Information: Fundamentality, Diversity and Unification*, World Scientific, New York/London/Singapore

Burgin, M. and Eberbach, E. (2008) Cooperative Combinatorial Optimization: Evolutionary Computation Case Study, *BioSystems*, v. 91, no.1, pp. 34–50

Burgin, M. and Eberbach, E. (2009) On Foundations of Evolutionary Computation: An Evolutionary Automata Approach, in *Handbook of Research on Artificial Immune Systems and Natural Computing: Applying Complex Adaptive Technologies*, Section II: Natural Computing, Section II.1: Evolutionary Computing, Chapter XVI, Medical Information Science Reference/IGI Global, Hershey, New York, pp. 342–360

Capuro, R., and Hjorland, B. (2003) The Concept of Information, *Annual Review of Information Science and Technology*, v. 37, No. 8, pp. 343–411

Capurro, R., Fleissner, P., and Hofkirchner, W. (1999) Is a Unified Theory of Information Feasible? In *The Quest for a unified theory of information*, Proceedings of the 2nd International Conference on the Foundations of Information Science, pp. 9-30

Castell, L., Drieschner, M., and von Weizsäcker, C.F. (Eds.) (1975–1986) *Quantum Theory and the Structures of Time and Space* (6 volumes), Hanser, Munich

Chaitin, G.J. (1987) *Algorithmic Information Theory*, Cambridge University Press, Cambridge

Dodig-Crnkovic, G. (2006) *Investigations into Information Semantics and Ethics of Computing*, Mälardalen University Press (http://urn.kb.se/resolve?urn=urn:nbn:se:mdh: diva-153)

Dodig-Crnkovic, G. (2009) *Information and Computation Nets. Investigations into Info-computational World*, VDM Verlag

Eberbach, E. (2005) Toward a theory of evolutionary computation, *BioSystems*, v. 82, pp. 1–19

Frieden, R.B. (1998) *Physics from Fisher Information*, Cambridge University Press, Cambridge

Fricke, M. (2008) *The Knowledge Pyramid: A Critique of the DIKW Hierarchy*, Preprint (electronic edition: http://dlist.sir.arizona.edu/2327/)

Fogel D.B. (1995), *Evolutionary Computation: Toward a New Philosophy of Machine Intelligence*, IEEE Press

Gupta, V., Jagadeesan, R., and Saraswat, V.A. (1999) Computing with Continuous Change, *Science of Computer programming*, v. 30, No. 1/2, pp. 3–49

Hare, R. (1952) *The language of Morals*, Oxford University Press, Oxford

Hromkovic, J. (2005) *Design and Analysis of Randomized Algorithms*, Springer, New York

Kant, E. (1902–1956) *Gessamelte Schriften*, Der Preussischen Akademie der Wissenschaften, de Gruyter, Berlin/New York

Kelemen, J. (2006) On a Possible Future of Computationalism, 7th *International Symposium of Hungarian Researchers on Computational Intelligence*, pp. 51–56

Kim, J. (1993) Mind and Supervenience, Cambridge University Press, Cambridge

Kleene, S.C. Mathematical logic: constructive and non-constructive operations, in *"Proceedings of the International Congress of Mathematicians*, 1958", Cambridge University Press, New York, 1960, pp. 137–153

Kogut, B. and Zander, U. (1992) Knowledge of the Firm: Combinative Capabilities, and the Replication of Technology, *Organization Science*, v. 3, No. 3, pp. 383–397

Koza, J. (1992) *Genetic Programming*, I, II, III, MIT Press, 1992, 1994, 1999

Langton, C. G. (1989) Artificial Life, in *Artificial Life*, pp. 1–47

Li, M., and Vitanyi, P. (1997) *An Introduction to Kolmogorov Complexity and its Applications,* Springer-Verlag, New York

Lyre, H. (2002) Quanten der Informationtheorie: Eine philosophisch-naturwissenschaftliche Einfürung, Fink, Munich

Machlup, F. and Mansfield, U. (Eds.) (1983) *The Study of Information*: *Interdisciplinary Messages*, Wiley, New York

MacLennan, B.J. (1999) Field computation in natural and artificial intelligence, *Information Sciences*, v. 119, pp. 73–89

McCulloch, W. S., and Pitts, E. (1943) A Logical Calculus of the Ideas Immanent in Nervous Activity, *Bulletin of Mathematical Biophysics*, v. 5, pp.115–133

Meadow, C. T. and Yuan, W. (1997) Measuring the impact of information: Defining the concepts, *Information Processing and Management*, v. 33, No. 6, pp. 697–714

Melik-Gaikazyan, I. V. (1997) *Information processes and reality*, Nauka, Moscow (in Russian, English summary)

Michalewicz, Z. (1996) *Genetic Algorithms + Data Structures = Evolution Programs*, Third edition, Springer-Verlag

Moore, C. (1996) Recursion Theory on the Reals and Continuous-time Computation: Real numbers and computers, *Theoretical Computer Science*, v. 162, No. 1, pp. 23–44

Shannon, C. (1941) Mathematical Theory of the Differential Analyzer, *J. Math. Physics*, MIT, v. 20, pp. 337–354

Stenmark, D. (2002) The Relationship between Information and Knowledge and the Role of intranets in Knowledge Management, in *Proceedings of the 35th Annual Hawaii International Conference on System Sciences* (*HICSS-35*), v. 4, IEEE Press, Hawaii (http://csdl2.computer.org/comp/proceedings/hicss/2002/1435/04/14350104b.pdf)

Tuomi, I. (1999) Data is More Than Knowledge: Implications of the Reversed Knowledge Hierarchy for Knowledge Management and Organizational Memory, *Journal of Management Information Systems*, Vol. 16, No. 3, pp. 107–121

Umpleby, S.A. (2007) Physical relationships among matter, energy and information, *Systems Research and Behavioral Science Systems Research*, v. 24, pp. 369–372

von Weizsäcker, C.F. (1985) *Aufbau der Physik*, Hanser, Munich, Germany (Eglish translation: *The Structure of Physics*, Springer, Berlin/Heidelberg/New York, 2006)

von Weizsäcker, C.F., Scheibe, E., and Süssmann, G. (1958) Komplementarität und Logik, III (Mehrfache Quantelung), *Zeitschrift für Naturforschung*, v. 13, pp. 705–721

M. Burgin

G. Dodig-Crnkovic

CHAPTER 1

CYBERSEMIOTICS AND THE QUESTION OF KNOWLEDGE

Søren Brier

http://www.brier.dk/SoerenBrier/index.htm

The introduction of this book states its purpose and paradigmatic view point as follows: "The book focuses on relations between information and computation. Information is a basic structure of the world, while computation is a process of the dynamic change of information. In order for anything to exist for an individual, the individual must get information on it, either by means of perception or by re-organization of the existing information into new patterns and networks in the brain."

Though I am supportive of this transdisciplinary endeavor, I will argue that it is only possible if the informational and computational view of what Dodig-Crnkovic (2006) calls the pancomputational/ pan-informational view is integrated with a Peircean semiotic insight. This needs to be done in order to relate an evolutionary theory of information more realistically to the actual phenomenologically experienced knowing processes and functions in the human social world. It is my view that in order to make such an integration, one needs to include a theory of first person awareness, qualia, signification and the communication of meaning integrated with cybernetic informational and computational theories. I will argue that there is no way to bypass the crucial role of naturally developed and culture-born self-conscious embodied awareness if one wants to arrive at a transdisciplinary theory of information, cognition and communication including language. In short, this is the ambition of making a scientific theory of knowing and knowledge in the form of a cybersemiotics. The question is, if science as we know it can encompass self-consciousness and meaning as causal agents in nature or, rather, encompass the reality that the synergy between nature, living systems, consciousness and intersubjective communication produces.

The Basic Problems a Transdisciplinary Research Program has to Deal with

The cybernetic computational informative view is based on universal and abstract (un-embodied) conceptions of information and computation that

1

are the foundation of "the information processing paradigm", which is foundational for much cognitive science and its latest developments in brain function and linguistics (Brier 2008a). It claims that "information" is the objective knowledge form of the structure of the world. Furthermore, it claims that information can be objectively divided into pieces of "data", and that humans, brains, computers and organizations process them basically in the same way. This process is called "computation" (See Gardner 1985). Computation, in a further development of this vision (Dodig-Crnkovic 2006), is seen as a basic – not really well-defined concept – of information processing in nature that goes beyond the Turing computer definition.

All these concepts are therefore metaphorical to a certain degree, as they extend our knowledge of the computer's functioning in computer science into a general epistemology (a philosophy of knowledge and knowing) which it is not possible to make without stipulating an ontology as well (a world view and an anthropology). Such an ontology must have the following premises:

1. The world view sees the universe as a computer.
2. The anthropological aspect of this ontology sees humans as dynamic systems producing and guided by information processed by a computationally functioning brain and body.
3. Language is seen as a sort of culturally developed program for social information processing between brains.
4. Knowledge is seen as information structures and structural information processing first and foremost based on algorithmic processes.

Based on the currently used definitions of computing understood as the Turing machine and Wiener or Shannon's information concepts, this is still too narrow a view to offer a full understanding of human cognition and communication. A Turing machine is the ultimate abstract programmable machine without a particular embodiment. Penrose (1995) argues via the known incompleteness of consistent logical systems that a person is not a Turing machine. So does Searle (1989).

It might be that it is the inability to extract human persons from their embodiment and the cultural programming of language that makes a science of consciousness so difficult. We do not know if the brain works like a computer, or rather from a bio-psychological view we are pretty sure it doesn't. Searle points to the biology of the body and brain as holding the secret of how to produce consciousness. The way to understand consciousness goes through the understanding of life and the processes that make living systems so different from machines. As far as we know there is no phenomenological awareness in computers. It only develops in biological systems. But we do not really know why! Contrary to Dennett (1991) I do not think that consciousness has been explained from the present biological knowledge of the brain and by viewing conscious awareness as self-deceptive when it comes to causal influence on what our body does.

To be convinced of how difficult it is to theoretically connect the informational and the experiential, one only has to read Chalmers' *The Conscious mind: In Search of a Fundamental Theory* (1996). He collects nearly all the material in science and philosophy we had on the subject at that time, except Peirce's semiotic philosophy. Still I do not think Chalmers manages to make a transdisciplinary fundamental theory that is convincing in his attempt to unite the informational with the experiential as he falls back on a type of double aspect theory, where the experiential is the inside of information in the brain. But there is the deep troublesome problem lying in the obvious observation that I am not my brain. My brain is mine. So who or what is phenomenological me? Is it possible that it is something before and outside scientific explanations as we know them? Furthermore, what role does it play in cognition and communication?

Another problem lies with the phenomenon of intersubjectivity, language communication and the creation of common knowledge in a society. This phenomenon is the foundation of science. It is based on intersubjectively well-functioning communication in a field of meaning, coordinating knowledge and practise in the real world. In some strange way we do embody each other, and this is part and parcel of our ability to communicate.

It is my thesis that we might need to add a foundation even broader than the present computational one to the information processing paradigm, as a transdisciplinary research program has to deal with several lacunae in our knowledge:

1. We need to know a lot more about the relation between human meaningful information and the meaningless algorithmic processing of information in order to make a transdisciplinary theory of cognition and communication that can include meaningful communication and perception.
2. We need to know much more about how humans embody information to make meaning, and how embodied and un-embodied information differ in order to make a much broader concept of computation, if that is going to be the paradigmatic ground concept for a new transdisciplinary paradigm.
3. We need to know more about the nature of our perception and knowledge. Human knowledge is embodied and is therefore rooted in our evolution and genetic makeup and our ecological interactions, preserving our body and its procreation. But how does consciousness appear and become formed by these circumstances, and how does language come into play here?
4. Finally, we need to know more about the interaction between culture and embodied knowledge. Knowledge seems to be both in the body, in the mind, and in the conscious use of language. These three levels seem to interact. But how does language bind them all together and create our culturally influenced meaning, creating self-consciousness and the existential perspective? The embodied minds of individuals, linguistically speaking, seem to be like cyborgs, because the individual minds of people putatively become programmed with language and culture that enable a person (an individual)/ makes a subject able to operate in the social and cultural domain that makes up a civilisation and its rationality, and thereby obtain the specific self-reflective human consciousness. What seems to be lacking is an understanding of how to integrate our knowledge of the role of first person experience, qualia, meaning and signification in our scientific knowledge of the evolution of life and the human nervous system, and how it has developed language, society and culture. Science is an important product of those developments, and is therefore in a strange double position also here.

That may be one of the problems we have to confront, and the way to do this maybe by making new distinctions about different types of sciences.

The Intentional and the Cenoscopic Sciences

It seems to be a very fundamental problem that behind the workings of the specific sciences such as information and computer science there is another type of more general "science" that has to do with the general foundation of human knowing, or rather what condition makes human knowing possible. This is not a problem that can be addressed by the sciences in themselves in the form they have now. It needs to include a philosophical reflection. Cantwell Smith (1998) suggest to call the more general meta- and philosophical sciences *Intentional Science*. He rightly points out that the basis of what we call science is an observer who is observing a world from the outside of that world. Yet, this is paradoxical since physical laws are assumed only to function as universal under the condition of a closed universe. Thus the philosophical frame supporting the special sciences is a dualistic and rationalist "view from nowhere" made by un-embodied observers, where the knower is viewed as external to the known.

As Merleau-Ponty writes, there is another way to look at the world, which his tradition calls phenomenological, and which produces another type of knowledge than science. He writes:

> *Science has not and never will have, by its nature, the same significance qua form of being as the world which we perceive, for the simple reason that it is a rationale or explanation of that world. I am, not a 'living creature' nor even a 'man', nor again even 'a consciousness' endowed with all the characteristics which zoology, social anatomy or inductive psychology recognize in these various products of the natural or historical process – I am the absolute source, my existence does not stem from my antecedents, from my physical and social environment; instead it moves out towards them and sustains them, for I alone bring into being for myself (and therefore into being in the only sense that the word can have for me) the tradition which I elect to carry on, or the horizon whose distance from me would be abolished – since that distance is not one of its properties – if I were not there to scan it with my gaze.*"

(Merleau-Ponty (1966) p. ix)

Phenomenology defines an experiential "life world" of conscious experience as more basic than the "universe" that science built out of the integration of its theories. Phenomenology claims to represent a lived experiential unified world before the distinction between subject and object on which science build, is made. Science has primarily dealt with the objects of its dualistic world view, but is now trying to encompass the self-same subject, on which its whole epistemological process is founded. In doing so it is making a strange loop as Douglas Hofstadter points out in the title of his book *I Am a Strange Loop*.

But information and computer science is a development based on the 'view from nowhere'. They are rational explanatory sciences that build up an observer-independent "universe" that is opposed to my "life world" as observer or scientist. The collective social life world is pretty much the "place" from where "common sense" is shaped through interaction with other life worlds, as the phenomenological sociologist Alfred Schutz (1967) showed us in his *Phenomenology of the Social World*.

Some physicists seem to think that the world view built out of science's results is pretty much continuous with the public life worlds of common sense. This is far from the case. As Cantwell Smith (op. cit.) points out, the world of modern physics is very far from our common sense view of "the material world". Quantum physics, relativity theory and thermodynamics – even classical Newtonian mechanicism — has very little to do with our practical view of "things" and their possible processes. One could point out that this also goes for evolutionary and ecological theory in biology, plate tectonics in geology, as well as the functioning of the organs in our body that we normally never feel, such as the liver and the brain. The latter cannot feel itself and can have no representation of its own workings in our self-consciousness other than what we make up in fantasies.

Cantwell Smith defines intentional systems as those systems that are subject to norms, not least dynamical norms, such as survival (1998 p.9). Adaptation to surrounding conditions is favourable if it leads to long term survival of the species. This may be sufficient on a primitive biological level of living systems; but in human life much more than survival is foregrounded at any one time. What counts is what Aristotle called "the good life", which is so complicated that no final theory in the form of episteme — understood as knowledge of universal laws — could be coined for it. In this phronetic knowledge — as Aristotle called it — one had to rely heavily on human socially lived experience to cope with how to make good decisions in the always new and often unexpected situations that keep coming up in human social lives. This has vast consequences. Cantwell Smith writes:

> *In sum, taking on full-fledged dynamic normativity is an unimaginably consequential move. It implies that any viable account of intentionality — any transformation of science broad enough to incorporate intentional systems, and thus to treat meaning along with matter and mechanism — will also, thereby, have to address mattering as well. Put it this way: in spite of what the logical tradition may have suggested, you can't just bite off truth and reference, and glue them, piecemeal, onto physical reality, without eventually taking on the full range of other norms: ethics, worth, virtue, value, beauty. By analogy, think of how computer science once thought it could borrow time from the physical world, without having to take on space and energy. It worked for a bit, but soon people realised what should anyway have been predictable: that time is not ultimately an isolable fragment (not an "independent export") of physics. By the same token, it would be myopic to believe that the study of intentional systems can be restricted to some "safe" subset of the full ethical and aesthetic dimension of the human condition — and especially myopic to believe that it can traffic solely in terms of such static notions as truth and reference, or limit itself to a hobbled set of dynamic norms (such as survival). To believe that would be to be an ostrich, not a hero.*

(Cantwell Smith 1998 p. 11)

The other basic problem that Cantwell Smith also points out is that the world is not an "other" or an object. This is so because we are part of it. The world is the ground that hosts the on-living systems such as rock as well as life, symbols, meaning and consciousness. The world is one and does not have an other! It cannot be two and be "a world" at the same time. Thus, in the intentional sciences we have to work with embodied human observers making knowledge inside the world! This is very much the conception that second order cybernetics — the cybernetics of observing systems of von Foerster (1984) and the autopoiesis theory of Maturana and Varela (1980 and 1988) — is based on. Thus the task has become that of describing a knowing system's operation within its own domain of description (Brier 2009), and accounting for the constitution of its identity and the conditions of its persistence in its own terms.[1] Cantwell Smith writes:

> *In order to abstract anything as an object, that is — in order to construct material ontology — we have to be committed to that out of which, and that in which, we objectify. It follows that, in order to say anything at all — in order to refer, in order to stabilise an object as an object — an agent must literally be committed to that which cannot be "said." For the "world," in this sense, is not the "post-intentional" world of thereby-arrayed materiality. It is something prior and more profound. Something like the "ground of being" that, in our faulty, partial, perspectival, self-interested way, we take to host the rock. The transcendental grounds for the possibility of objects — if one likes Kantian language. Or the world of "no-thing-ness," if one's preferences run Buddhist (remember: the gauntlet is to develop a global perspective). Perhaps it is a noumenal world, except that to cleave phenomenal appearance from noumenal reality sounds suspiciously like one of those formal distinctions we have been at such pains to eschew. Whatever: it is a world of norms as much as of objects, a world of mattering as well as of matter.*
>
> (Cantwell Smith 1998 p. 18)

Actually both Peirce and Spencer-Brown in their philosophies of semiosis and "making a distinction" end up with a foundation of no-

---

[1] This is for instance what Maturana and Varela (1980 and 1988 as well as Maturana 1988 a & b) attempt to do for biological systems with their theory of autopoiesis, but not managing to encompass a theory of conscious meaning. Niklas Luhmann (1990, 1992, 1995 and 1999) has attempted to generalize this theory and use for human socio-communicative systems by introducing two more types of autopoiesis system, namely a psychic one and a socio-communicative. He writes that they operate in the medium of meaning and the biological system in the medium of life. But only communication communicates. I have criticized his theory of meaning and his claim to have based it on Husserl's phenomenology in Brier (2007b)

thing-ness or emptiness (Brier 2007b, 2008c, 2009). Put it in another way, the purpose of the intentional sciences is to find a theoretical explanatory way of putting the knower into a known — the world — that is constructed so as to keep the knower viable in practice. This is not what the sciences have done so far, and the computational and informational sciences are no exception to this. But maybe they are developing such a role. However, this is limited insofar as their view does not deal with life, consciousness, feeling and qualia. Therefore Cantwell Smith points out that "we are leaving the age of (purely mechanistic or physicalistic) science, and entering an age of signification "(p.16). I could not agree more!

I have agreed with this analysis for the last 25 years although I only found it expressed in this way during the last six months and have been searching for such a new foundation that can contain both the sciences and the intentional sciences. Autopoiesis theory, Luhmann's system theory and second order cybernetics lack a foundation in first person awareness such as the one Merleau-Ponty described (Brier 2008a), but which I found in C. S. Peirce's pragmaticist semiotic philosophy. Furthermore, from the start Peirce actually attempted new ways of classifying sciences in order to be able to give a name to the new work he was doing. We cannot go through how he developed those classifications here, but will concentrate on what he called the Sciences of Discovery. Peirce divided the Sciences of Discovery into:

> (I) **mathematics** (which draws necessary conclusions about hypothetical objects);
> (II) **cenoscopy** or philosophy (about positive phenomena in general, such as confront a person at every waking moment, rather than special classes, and not settling theoretical issues by special experiences or experiments), and
> (III) **idioscopy**, or the special sciences (about special classes of positive phenomena, and settling theoretical issues by special experiences or experiments).

Peirce writes:

> *Class II is philosophy, which deals with positive truth, indeed,*
> *yet contents itself with observations such as come within the range*
> *of every man's normal experience, and for the most part in every*

waking hour of his life. Hence Bentham calls this class,
coenoscopic. *These observations escape the untrained eye
precisely because they permeate our whole lives, just as a man
who never takes off his blue spectacles soon ceases to see the blue
tinge. Evidently, therefore, no microscope or sensitive film would
be of the least use in this class. The observation is observation in a
peculiar, yet perfectly legitimate, sense. If philosophy glances now
and then at the results of special sciences, it is only as a sort of
condiment to excite its own proper observation.*

(Peirce CP 1.241)

I believe that this is another way of characterizing what Cantwell Smith
calls the intentional sciences. Now, with respect to what we normally call
sciences Peirce has the following description:

Class III is Bentham's **idioscopic;** *that is, the special
sciences, depending upon special observation, which travel or
other exploration, or some assistance to the senses, either
instrumental or given by training, together with unusual
diligence, has put within the power of its students. This class
manifestly divides itself into two subclasses, the physical and the
psychical sciences;*

(Pierce CP 1.242)

Thus, to carry through a transdisciplinary paradigm for information,
cognition and communication, we need to make a cenoscopic foundation
for the ideoscopic sciences since they cannot make such a foundation
themselves. This is why Kuhn (1970) points out that the making of new
paradigms and the choosing among candidates for a new paradigm to solve
problems the old paradigm could not, and for which we really need a new
paradigm, is not in itself a totally rational scientific process. Thus I am
arguing for my choice whilst knowing that there are also values in play.

Theoretically Integrating Consciousness, Meaning and Nature

As Chalmers (1996) argues, we have every reason to believe that — as a
natural phenomenon — consciousness is subject to natural laws. But this

is not to say that the natural laws concerning consciousness will be *physical* laws or even informational laws! They may be quite different in kind and we might need to expand our view of nature in order to encompass the emergence of the semiotic capability of human experiences, perception and communication. In that case we need to integrate, as far as we can, law-like understanding of signification, cognition and communication into our scientific understanding of the evolution of the universe and life on earth.

In my opinion, this is what the chemist and logician and founder of evolutionary triadic semiotics C.S. Peirce worked on, 100 years ahead of his time. It is also what a group of researchers have now attempted to upgrade and integrate into a modern evolutionary and ecological conception of signification by creating what is now called biosemiotics (Brier 1998 a and b, 1999, 2001 a and b, 2002, 2003, 2005, 2008 a and b, Emmeche 1998 and 2007, Favareau 2008, Hoffmeyer 1996, 2008). It is this paradigm, which I have attempted to integrate with the informational and computational sciences in the framework of Cybersemiotics.

In the making of a transdisciplinary theory of signification and communication in nature, man, machine and animals, I have argued (Brier 2008a) that it seems necessary to add semiotics in order to encompass both nature, human and machine in a theory of signification and cognition. I have, over the years, contributed to an attempt to make such a foundation through development of Peirce's pragmaticist semiotics in biosemiotics. This is founded on a phenomenological view of the experience and perception of all living embodied systems and is an attempt to combine them with the sciences through a process-oriented paradigm that transcends mechanical physics. Thus it is neither an externalist nor an internalist approach; nor is it both; but it is an attempt to transcend such dualism through Peirce's triadic philosophical semiotics.

As Peirce's semiotics is the only semiotics that deals systematically with non-intentional signs of the body and of nature at large, it has become the main source for semiotic contemplations of the similarities and differences of signs of inorganic nature, signs of living systems (biosemiotics), and the cultural and linguistic signs of humans living together in a society (Brier 2008b) as well as in computational technology. The cybersemiotic approach (Brier 2008) explains this further through a semiotized version of Luhmann's triple autopoietic theory of communication combined with pragmatic theories of meaning as an embodied social evolutionary process. Cybersemiotics see the effect of evolution as the development of what Hoffmeyer (2008) calls "semiotic freedom" and what Peirce considers a growth in rationality. It is an attempt to make an explicit theory of how the life world of an organism is constituted and, therefore, how first person views are possible and just as real as matter is. This is carried out by means of a new triadic concept of sign-interaction and signification, where signs are not passive instruments but have a certain life of their own through the ways they make qualities emerge from Firstness through Secondness into the Thirdness of semiotic processes. It is not possible to explain that theory in full in this short chapter and I have already done that in multiple articles (see reference list) and in the book *Cybersemiotics. Why information is not enough* (Brier 2008a). Here I will argue more for the necessity and depth of the project, and why it should become a huge new transdisciplinary research program that would be the next step in the development of cognitive science. In addition, I will look into how the project ties in with several other scientist-philosophers' views on the crisis in which our 'knowledge about knowing' finds itself.

Historical Perspective

European- and American-based culture stands at a watershed when it comes to taking the final step into a knowledge culture. Either we can stay with our dualistic understanding of knowledge and rationality, which we developed through the Renaissance and made central to our civilization and culture during the Enlightenment; or we can deepen the foundation with integrating knowledge of human embodiment, first person experience, semiosis and life world practice. From the Greeks we inherited the idea of a well-ordered and mathematically beautiful Cosmos on which we — for instance Galileo — in the Renaissance built the foundation of the new mechanical physics. It was the belief that rationality and the order of the world fitted a divine order of logic and mathematics. As Prigogine (Prigogine & Stengers 1984, Prigogine 1980 and 1996) shows, from Laplace forward the belief was that the physical world could be explained in one mathematical formula — a "world formula". This was what Laplace culled from Enlightenment thinking (D'Alambert was his teacher). That is one of the reasons that Russell and Whitehead tried to unite logic and mathematics in their *Principia* — and why Gödel's incompleteness proof was such a shock for Hilbert's mathematical view.

Physics has continued the search for the world formula. Steven Hawking is one of the most well known exponents of it and has, with his book *A Brief History of Time* (1988), produced the most-bought popular science book in the history of man. The paradigm has "spilled over" into the search for the genetic algorithms and artificial intelligence. As Lakoff (1987) has shown, it has created a myth of abstract un-embodied intelligence as the highest goal of knowledge. The Greeks considered mathematics to be divine, and the heavenly bodies to move in perfect circles, and classical physics hoped to find exact, deterministic context free of eternal laws of nature. This led for a period to a worship of computers as being the ideal of intelligence, and later the idea that the personal consciousness of a human could be transmitted on the Internet and live there forever as a 'pure intelligence'. The idea is that our brains are organic hardware or wetware and, furthermore, that our intelligence and cognitive abilities, as well as our personalities, are the informational programs that run on that wetware. Most famous is William Gibson's groundbreaking cyberpunk *Sprawl Trilogy*, starting with the book *Neuromancer* (1984). It promotes the idea of "jacking in" to the Net, fastening electrodes of your Web-connected computer directly onto brain switches on your skull, your mind travelling into the three-dimensional informational world of cyberspace. The idea was probably taken from the prevailing belief that robots can be intelligent in the same way as humans, but in an un-embodied way that makes their "self" transferrable between hardwares. The most famous example is "Data" in the *Star Trek: The Next Generation* TV series and movies. In the movie *Enigma*, his intelligence is transferred to another robot some days before he is destroyed on a mission, and the concluding point in the film is that it will develop his personality in this "body". There is also the idea of an "emotion chip" that somehow will add emotions to his completely rational mind which cannot understand humour. The movies also play with the possibilities of adding tactile experiences to Data's senseless body, which the Borg do by grafting human skin onto the robot with

nerve connections to his "brain". Just movies, some would say; but not
just "just": They are based on a mechanical approach to the living that
Descartes especially stands for, and the dualism that was a result of his
philosophy. These are important ways of thinking about mind,
knowledge and computer technology permeating our culture. (See for
instance the arguments in Hayles 1999). It is now time to unite the two
opposites of mechanicism and organicism into a new synthesis and at the
same time unite Snow's two cultures into a third culture (Brier 2005).

The idea of intelligence and knowledge based on the Turing machine
has carried us a long way. It is now called *the information processing
paradigm of cognitive science*. The research project presented here is
based on the hypothesis that the usefulness of the paradigm has run out
for the modern complicated problems and systems we have to deal with
(Brier 1996) unless it is updated with semiotic knowledge. Therefore a
new cognitive semiotics is under development, marked by its own
journal, as well as the burgeoning of biosemiotics. I have attempted to
unite the two disciplinary fields in Brier (2009b). A crucial problem is, of
course, human interaction with computers and how to integrate the
computer, Internet and robots in our culture in ways that support human
development, social as well as existential production of meaning, so that
it will not destroy the centre of democratic culture with its respect for the
uniqueness and rights of the individual human being.

The Post-modern Government of World Formula Technology

Artificial Intelligence (AI), biotechnology and environmental science can
be seen as prime examples of the increasing problematization of science
and technology development within areas as diverse as social sciences,
policy processes and the public, where scientific accountability as well as
public acceptability of science have become central issues. The
governance of AI, genetic technology and sustainability technology can
thus be seen as a continuing process of negotiation in a complex network
involving social systems as diverse as science, politics, law, and mass
media, as well as the general public.

How will the post-modern, democratic knowledge society handle the
fact that three pure basic research programs — namely foundational

physics, cognitive science's information processing paradigms (including AI) and genetics — have turned into applied programs creating new industries and technologies that deeply affect our self-understanding in modern democratic society (Brier 1994)?

We seem to be at the end of the usefulness of Enlightenment thinking (Luntley 1995. Brier 2008a), at least in the way it was picked up and developed by logical positivism and turned into logical empiricism. The Enlightenment's concepts of a universal God and a universal scientific rationality, side by side as a guarantee of stability behind cultural changes and relativities, cannot be upheld anymore. In the West we have to analyse the limitations in our cultural concepts of knowledge, meaning, and world view and self-understanding, which make it difficult for us to incorporate genetic engineering, artificial intelligence and ecological thinking in our democratic, scientific and Christian culture based on Enlightenment thinking. We need to analyse how limitations in the previous paradigmatic frameworks of science and meaning have formed our theories of computational intelligence, genetic algorithms and ecological wholeness in such a way that they are bound to be incompatible with most paradigms of mind, communication and meaning in the humanities and social sciences.

It is difficult to prove that scientific methods can cover all aspects of reality in our attempt to get trustworthy knowledge. Personal existential knowledge (the conscious life world of a person), tacit knowledge, practice in itself, and the meaning of life, could very well be such areas where scientific methods cannot penetrate, and where more ideographic methods are needed. Behaviourism, different forms of eliminative materialism, information science, cognitive science now in its information processing paradigm form, when developed as "grand narratives", attempt to explain human communication from outside, without respecting the phenomenological and hermeneutical aspects of existence. Winograd and Flores (1986) pointed out the lack of an experiential aspect in these paradigms long ago, and made an attempt at a more comprehensive framework. Thus something important of human "nature" is missing in these systems and the technologies developed on their bases (Fodor 2001).

In my view, to attempt to understand human beings, their communication and interpretation and efforts to make meaning of the world and their own lives, from frameworks which, at their foundation, are unable to fathom basic human features such as consciousness, free will, meaning and interpretation, is reductionistic in a deeply inadequate way relating to this question. They have proved their worth in other ways in science and technology. This is because a purely informational and computational approach without concepts of interpretation and signification attempts to explain away basic human conditions of existence, and thereby reduces or even ruins what it attempts to explain. This is — incidentally — the main argument in Gadamer's (1975) book *Truth and Method* on the hermeneutical foundation of science. Scientific method alone is not the way to truth. All basic scientific concepts are based on qualitative and meaningful interpretation as they are constructed in any paradigm — as Cantwell Smith indeed points out with his concept of intentional sciences, and Peirce with his cenoscopic sciences.

Life, as human embodiment, is fundamental to the understanding of human understanding, including ecological and evolutionary perspectives and their connection to Cosmology. Within these perspectives, Deely (1990 with still new enlarged editions being published), Emmeche (1998), Hoffmeyer (1996 and 2008) and Brier (2003) are, among others, working on the basis of meaning generated by the embodied minds of individuals. Thus, the concepts of information and meaning in the form of signification in signs are competing to claim foundational statues; but they are actually complementary to each other if we want to make a transdisciplinary science of information, cognition and communication.

Information in Etymology

The word information is derived from Latin *informare,* which means "give form to". In the Oxford English Dictionary definition of the word it is connected both to knowledge and communication.

Knowledge communicated concerning some particular fact, subject or event; that of which one is apprised or told; intelligence, news.

The double notions of information as both facts and communication are also inherent in one of the foundations of information theory: *cybernetics* introduced by Norbert Wiener (1948).

The cybernetic theory was derived from the new findings in the 1930s and 1940s regarding the role of bioelectric signals in biological systems, including the human being. The full title of Wiener's book was:

Cybernetics or Control and Communication in the Animal and the Machine. Cybernetics was thus from the beginning attached to biology as well as to feedback and control. Wiener (1948) connects information and entropy with organization and therefore evolution. He writes on p. 18:

> *The notion of the amount of information attaches itself very naturally to a classical notion in statistical mechanics: that of entropy. Just as the amount of information in a system is a measure of its degree of organisation, so the entropy of a system is a measure of its degree of disorganisation.*

How is information then measured? Wiener defines it as a probability: here he describes the amount of information mathematically as an integral, i.e. an area of probability measurements, where he defines information as negentropy inspired by Schrödinger, on p. 76:

> *The quantity that we here define as amount of information is the **negative** of the quantity usually defined as entropy in similar situations.*

Wiener's view of information is thus that it contains a structure. Many researchers attempt to build up a concept of meaning on this foundation. The structure in itself has meaning, some researchers suggest. But such a concept of meaning may be used on computer systems but does not have much to do with that upon which living systems and human beings operate in cognition and communication.

System theorists build further on this concept and see information as something that is used by a mechanism or organism, a system which is seen as a "black box", for steering the system towards a predefined goal. The goal is compared with the actual performance, and signals are sent back to the sender if the performance deviates from the norm. This concept of negative feedback has proven to be a powerful tool in most control mechanisms, relays etc.

Information According to Shannon

The other scientist connected with information theory is Claude Shannon, who was a contemporary of Wiener. As an AT&T

mathematician he was primarily interested in the limitations of a channel in transferring signals, and the cost of information transfer via a telephone line. He developed a mathematical theory for such communication in *The Mathematical Theory of Communication*, (Shannon & Weaver 1949). Shannon defines information as a purely quantitative measure of communicative exchanges.

Weaver (in Shannon & Weaver 1949), links Shannon's mathematical theory to the second law of thermodynamics and states that it is the entropy of the underlying stochastic process in the information source that determines the rate of information generation (p.103):

The quantity which uniquely meets the natural requirements that one sets up for "information" turns out to be exactly that which is known in thermodynamics as entropy.

Shannon defines the amount of information as the negative of the logarithm of a sum of probabilities. The minus sign in this formula means the opposite of Wiener's minus sign. It is there because the amount of information according to Shannon is equal to entropy and deals with meaning. According to Weaver's explanation of Shannon's theory in the same book, Information is a measure of one's freedom of choice in selecting a message. The greater this freedom of choice, the greater the information, the greater the uncertainty that the message actually selected is a particular one. Greater freedom of choice, greater uncertainty, and greater information go hand in hand. Thus, whereas Wiener sees information as negative entropy, i.e. a "structured piece of the world", Shannon's information is the same as (positive) entropy. This makes Shannon's "information" the opposite of Wiener's "information".

Wiener's "information" presumes an observer with a meaning of his/her own outside the system, who determines the goal of the system. The observer may be another machine but in the end (or perhaps beginning) there must be a human being somewhere with an intention or purpose. But primacy of first person experience to the whole concept of observer in cybernetics is never really contemplated in Wienerian first order cybernetics, but only starts in second order cybernetics. The observer's meaning is then seen as interrelated with the system's meaning.

Wiener's concept of information relates both to man-made systems and to living subsystems like the liver or even the brain as a tissue of neurons. These systems use signals in a way that cybernetic theory seems to explain.

Meaning in Shannon's Sense

One of the conclusions from Shannon's theory is that entropy contains more information than structure. Shannon presumes something/someone outside the transmission chain with a message which corresponds to "information". However, it is not information that is transmitted, but signals. There is a sender and a receiver of these signals. The sender's meaning must be interpreted by the receiver outside the transmission itself. In order to do this, both sender and receiver must have something in common — at least a code of meaningful interpretation otherwise they will not understand each other. To have a sign or language game in common one usually also needs to have roughly the same kind of consciousness and body and in full-blown human natural language, a culture. Logic and understanding are two different sides of meaning. One has to learn about the culture and its mentality if one wants to understand a new language.

Thus all meaning is interpreted outside the transmission of signals. "Information" according to Shannon, must therefore not be confused with meaning. Shannon's information relates not so much to what you do say as to what you could say (or do not say). The problems of interpreting signals into a "message" are left outside the theoretical space within which Shannon's definition is formed. Not so with Wiener, since he assumes some meaning at least for the system level. It is tempting to see Shannon's signals as "data" and the meaning of the signals as "information", but this would be wrong.

Shannon's information cannot be transmitted, like the system theorists assume. The problem is that although the concepts of Information theory cover only the technical level of communication, they were developed for humans in human communication. Especially cybernetic theory claims its closeness to the human brain. But, humans do not communicate with electric signals from the brain (yet?). They communicate with meaningful signs between embodied minds.

Human communication involves a very complex interpretation by the "receiver". The meaning of a text or a sign does not exist independently of the receiver as a fixed state. It enters as a percept through our senses and clashes with our mind. A percept is the result of our interaction with what is exterior. Peirce writes:

> *Our logically initial data are percepts. Those percepts are undoubtedly purely psychical, altogether of the nature of thought. They involve three kinds of psychical elements, their qualities of feeling, their reaction against my will, and their generalizing or associating element*
>
> (Peirce CP 8.144, 1900)

According to Peirce's ways of using his three categories the process of the percept is a pure 'Second': a clash between two different phenomena. Thus, it does include Firstness but not Thirdness as there is no interpretation of any kind of regularity or meaning yet. Peirce writes:

> *The direct percept [...] has no generality; [...] it appears under a physical guise [...] it does not appear as psychical. The psychical, then, is not contained in the percept*
>
> (Peirce CP 1.253, 1902)

Thirdness in perception emerges with the construction of perceptual fact or a cognition, which is the intellect's fallible account of making meaning of precepts through a generalization operated upon a series of percepts. The perceptual judgment gives propositional form to the perceptual coalescence. It constitutes an irresistible hypothesis with regards to percepts.

Percepts are not, strictly speaking, objects of experience. Though the percept makes knowledge possible, it offers no information as it does not contains any Thirdness. Experience, understood as the knowing process imposed upon us in or by the course of living, is "perfused" with Thirdness in the form of generality and continuity as fallible account of percepts. "Meaning" must somehow be constructed by the receiver, within certain frames. There is a theoretical lack of agreement in finding a basis for determining meaning between informational and semiotic paradigms. Along with this, there is no theory of the existence of first person experience and qualia in most informational and computational approaches. There is thus a lack of theoretical framework regarding what consciousness is, and regarding the question of how what goes on in consciousness can have causal influence on the material world, such as the body.

Possible Transdisciplinary Frameworks

What kind of framework, then, is necessary to develop a theory of signification in the age of science, when science thought that it had finally conquered religion and spirituality? There seem presently to be three basic frameworks for understanding signification:

1. A framework based on a cybernetic informational world view of which Norbert Wiener was the founder and of which Gregory Bateson represented the most advanced views. It was the idea of an ecological cybernetic mind based on the concept of information as a difference that makes a difference in circular systems.

2. A second framework derived from the autopoiesis (organizationally closed systems) of Maturana and Varela, which is in opposition to the cybernetically informational world view built on thermodynamics. The argument in autopoiesis is that there is a radical shift from open chemical systems to autopoietic ones because of closure. It is also through this closure that individuals — a concept not distinguishable at the level of physics and chemistry — are created. Individuals cannot be identified at a molecular level. There will be some downward causation from the new boundary conditions controlling for instance the environment that determines how proteins are folded. Autopoiesis theory in Maturana and Varela's original version is a kind of bio-constructivism, saying important things about the conditions for systems to be living, but there is no theory of mind as first person experience with qualia, emotions and will.

3. The third framework is some version of general system theory inspired by Ludwig von Bertallanffy. Today many researchers seem to adhere to an organicist philosophy based on complexity science or the theory of complex adaptive systems (CAS). One can here seemingly still adhere to a kind of physicalistic basic ontology, then postulate that the increase of complexity drives the emergence of life

as well as cognition that, in the end, makes consciousness, qualia and feelings possible. I do not find that the present theories of emergence offer us any mechanism to understand the emergence of life — not to mention experiential mind — from matter in these theories. This is especially true if our basic definition of matter is that it is something dead and inert, even though it is combined with an information science approach that sees information as objective structural differences in matter or between parts of matter. It does not solve the problem of how experience and meaningful cognition and communication come into the world. To say that it is "emergence" is just to give the deep problem a name, not an explanation.

4. The fourth framework is Niklas Luhmann's system theory (Luhmann 1990, 1992, 1995 and 1999) in which he has made a serious attempt to solve the above problem (4) by accepting the psyche and the socio-communicative system as autopoietic systems on top of the biological one in a generalized version of the autopoiesis theory. He accepts the psyche as an autopoietic system, but makes no attempt to explain its creation or ontological status. He then understands information in Bateson's terms as a difference that makes a difference, and then integrates Bateson's cybernetic theory with Husserl's phenomenology in such a way that a message consists of information, utterance and interpretation. I find Luhmann's threefold autopoietic view fruitful. But I think that the embodiment of knowing in living systems is a prerequisite for the psychological as well as for the socio-communicative as they provide the field of meaning that the socio-communicative level feeds on and manipulates! The epistemology and a vague ontology in this paradigm is taken from Spencer Brown "Laws of form", where the observer is basic in making the first distinction. Consciousness is accepted in an open ontology, but the unification of the various frameworks of Wiener, Bateson, Maturana, Spencer Brown, Bertalanffy's general system theory and Husserl's phenomenology seem not to be carried through in a manner that is philosophically consistent. I do not think Luhmann manages to produce an ontology for, and a definition of, experientially-based meaning. He is a systemic sociologist, not a philosopher and only use philosophy to the extend it helps solving his sociological problems.

The Phaneroscopic Approach

To sum up the problems we have encountered above and which are still prevalent in the three paradigms, I cannot see how there can be any direct connection between negentropy and meaning per se. I argue that it is only living systems that can attach meaning to information patterns because they can experience emotions. This is done because living systems are individuals with an interest in surviving, procreation and pleasure. This is the first level of meaning. Peirce talks about signification when an organism gets meaning out of non-intentional signals and turns them into signs by giving them meaning in relation to its form of life.

In the making of a transdisciplinary theory of signification and communication for living, human, social and technological systems I argue that C. S. Peirce's semiotics is the only sign theory that deals systematically with non-conscious intentional signs of the body as well as with language in an evolutionary perspective. Thus, contrary to the information processing paradigm of cognitive science and any form of computational theory, Peirce starts which the experienced world, which he calls the *phaneron*. Peirce writes, in the Adirondack Lectures,

> *Phaneroscopy is the description of the phaneron; and by the phaneron I mean the collective total of all that is in any way or in any sense present to the mind, quite regardless of whether it corresponds to any real thing or not. If you ask present when, and to whose mind, I reply that I leave these questions unanswered, never having entertained a doubt that those features of the phaneron that I have found in my mind are present at all times and to all minds. So far as I have developed this science of phaneroscopy, it is occupied with the formal elements of the phaneron.*

(CP 1.284, 1905)

Peirce even puts logic into his evolutionary semiotic framework and claims that logic is semiotic. Thus he includes logic in a non-mechanistic framework basis that includes signification. Therefore the basis of the pragmaticistic view he developed is semiotic. The fact is that our present conceptions of science have raised consistency problems for developing a natural evolutionary theory of awareness and signification involving levels of semiosis up to full language capacity. A crucial question for some is whether it is possible to develop a transdisciplinary framework where a scientific theory of nature and a phenomenological-hermeneutic theory of interpretation and meaning can be integrated with an evolutionary theory of levels of semiosis.

As mentioned above some researchers (see for instance Emmeche 2007, Dodig-Crnkovic, 2006 and also in this volume) have stressed the organicist view, with its theory of emergence based on so-called *Complexity Science* with its concept of CAS (Complex Adaptive System) as a solution. The term CAS means an open system in a thermodynamic gradient (far from equilibrium, in what Prigogine calls dissipative structures) with many strongly-coupled degrees of freedom, non-linear connections and feedback mechanisms. They often exhibit hysteresis and therefore have pre-stages to memory functions; they often have a hierarchical or heterarchical complexity, dynamic networks, locally differentiating, and have emergent and holistic properties. Complexity science has moved science away from a linear mechanistic view of the world to a view based on non-linear dynamics, evolutionary development and systems thinking.

Like cognitive information science one of the basic problems is that the theory simply crosses the line between non-living, living, conscious and social systems without concern about the qualitative differences in them. This is very much in the tradition of cybernetics, systems science, and information science on which it draws (if we neglect radical forms of holism). The basic problem of life, mind and signification is simply ignored on the basis that they are presumed to be explained with reference to the scientific foundation. But this is never spelled out. However, we do need to make a conscious and well-argued choice of where and how to place von Neumann's famous epistemic cut. In his most famous paper he wrote:

> That is, we must always divide the world into two parts, one being the observed system, the other the observer. In the former, we can follow up all physical processes (in principle at least) arbitrarily precisely. In the latter, this is meaningless. The boundary between the two is arbitrary to a very large extent... but this does not change the fact that in each method of description, the boundary

must be placed somewhere, if the method is not to proceed vacuously, i.e. if a comparison with experiment is to be possible.

(von Neumann, 1955, p. 419)

There seems just to be a vague idea that life and consciousness are emergent qualities of basically physical/material systems, and in this way: it is not challenged by the received view of physical sciences. If life is a new organization of dead matter as physics describes it, we have a problem. It seems that all research up to the present indicates that it is not possible to distinguish the living from the lifeless on the atomic as well as on the chemical level. Pattee writes:

It is not possible to distinguish the living from the lifeless by the most detailed "motion of inorganic corpuscles" alone. The logic of this answer is that life entails an epistemic cut that is not distinguishable by microscopic (corpuscular) laws. As von Neumann's argument shows, any distinction between subject and object requires a description of the constraints that execute measurement and control processes, and such a functional description is not reducible to the dynamics that is being measured or controlled.

(Pattee 2001 p. 16)

Today it is generally accepted that humans, their consciousness, language, communication and culture are a product of the same reality as all the other natural objects created through the evolution of the universe and its content. This means that the cut we have made between material nature and culturally born human consciousness has become too absolute to provide a basis for the solving of our present problems of producing a general theory of information, cognition and communication. Nature cannot be purely mechanical in its essence. Material mechanicism works well as a paradigm for some limited types of system in equilibrium (Prigogine and Stengers 1984), but it is not a sufficient model to base the description of how living systems were developed inside our universe and how they became conscious and became symbol-users. Howard Pattee writes:

This illusion of isolation of symbols from matter can also arise from the apparent arbitrariness of the epistemic cut. It is the essential function of a symbol to "stand for" something — its referent — that is, by definition, on the other side of the cut. This necessary distinction that appears to isolate symbol systems from the physical laws governing matter and energy allows us to imagine geometric and mathematical structures, as well as physical structures and even life itself, as abstract relations and Platonic forms. I believe this is the conceptual basis of Cartesian mind–matter dualism. This apparent isolation of symbolic expression from physics is born of an epistemic necessity, but ontologically, it is still an illusion.

(Pattee 2001 p. 17)

So, how can we turn the basic theory of computers and AI's manipulation of material symbols into an understanding of how living and conscious systems process symbolic meaning?

Information and Semiosis

As already argued, there is a lack of a basis for determining meaning in the cybernetic, autopoietic, systemic and informational-computational theories. Along with this there is no theoretical foundation established for the existence of first person experience and qualia and its causal influence on both the material and the informational world. Dennett (1991), for instance, denies that consciousness has any causal influence on matter and as such it can neither be the initiator of the movement of our bodies nor the initiator of speech.

The informational realm is proto-semiotic seen from a biosemiotic point of view, whose theory assumes that you need a living system and its individuality to produce a fully fledged Interpretant in the process of signification. I have used autopoiesis to try to characterize this shift from dead to living systems, the crucial point being that living systems differ from things by being individuals in the world, and therefore have "a point of view". Thus they are true interpreters. As individuals with an interest in survival, growth and procreation they produce meaning by relating events to their survival, growth and procreation. As they develop, the feeling of good experience becomes more guiding and when they as humans become self-conscious through language and culture, the existential level of the question of meaning arises and produces philosophy, humanities, sciences and religion.

Wiener is famous for writing that "Information is information, neither matter nor energy". Shannon is ambiguous about how the meaning concept enters his information concept. I would say that both information concepts presuppose the human mind and its social, embodied and existential concept of meaning. Thus they are not able to deliver a reflective theory of meaning.

The great question here is whether we can represent meaning in bits at all. Do all human brains have their own common universal language based on bits before it is translated into the various natural human languages developed by the various cultures that exist on earth, since all children have the capability to learn any language? If so, symbols would get their meaning from (subconscious?) thought, which would then have to have its own universal language, in which we think before translating it to a natural language? If this is so, a neuro-cognitive computational information science has a real chance of establishing a universal theory of information, cognition and communicative meaning. Jerry Fodor (1987) postulates such a universal language of thought, which he calls *Mentalese*. Fodor imagines that Mentalese might be a form of interaction between three-dimensional forms. Pinker (1995) expresses the same kind of theories. But, as far as I know, we have not invented an artificial meaning processing system close to natural language as yet. I am aware that Lotfi Zadeh (inventor of Fuzzy Logic) is trying to make an approximation, by extending his basic idea of fuzzyness. He calls it "computing with words". Still, that very complicated system is very limited in its representation of meaning (see http://www-bisc.cs.berkeley.edu). It is an abstract model that has very little to do with Mentalese as far as I can see and does not claim to attempt to be anything like that.

If we stay with Wiener's definition of information, then we can have information without meaning, but not meaning without information. Shannon's information is based on the identification of a set of possible states that the system can be in given a specific context, such as communication with the alphabet. So it is dependent on a system too. Shannon's focus was on making technology for human communication. Meaningful human communication was always the context for his engineering work; hence the ambiguity I mentioned earlier.

I doubt that we can formalize meaning. It is a human social concept involving linguistic, embodied, self-conscious beings with emotions, will and qualia. Meaning is what makes the difference make a difference. By this action of signification we include the difference as a significant thing or invention in what I call a 'signification sphere' (Brier 2008a). Thus we return to the phaneron of Peirce to look for another foundation of meaning.

It is important to notice that the phaneron is not a group of percepts, since these, as we have discussed above, percepts are pure Seconds. The phaneron always includes Thirdness. It does not limit itself to the brutal irruption in our consciousness of something exterior like the percept, which "knocks on the door" of our awareness. That is to say, the percept is still standing outside as long as it is not interpreted, and is thus not meaningfully present to the mind. It is like when one is sleeping and dreaming, and then one realizes that something not identified is disturbing the dream. That is the percept. When one's mind suddenly identifies the disturbance with the ringing of an alarm clock and realizes "It is my alarm clock, which I set in order to get up in order to be able to attend an important meeting", then it enters the phaneron.

Thus it is by the formation of a perceptual judgment that percepts are allowed to enter our mind as actual experiences and then come to belong to the lived phaneron. When objectified, the perceptual judgment can be understood as a unit of experience. To produce signs and signification you need Firstness, Secondness as well and Thirdness. This analysis is what brought Peirce to his three basic categories:

> So, then, there are these three modes of being: first, the being of a feeling, in itself, unattached to any subject, which is merely an atmospheric possibility, a possibility floating in vacuo, not rational yet capable of rationalization; secondly, there is the being that consists in arbitrary brute action upon other things, not only irrational but anti-rational, since to rationalize it would be to destroy its being; and thirdly, there is living intelligence from which all reality and all power are derived; which is rational necessity and necessitation.
>
> A feeling is what it is, positively, regardless of anything else. Its being is in it alone, and it is a mere potentiality. A brute

force, as, for example, an existent particle, on the other hand, is
nothing for itself; whatever it is, it is for what it is attracting and
what it is repelling: its being is actual, consists in action, is
dyadic. That is what I call existence.

A reason has its being in bringing other things into connexion
with each other; its essence is to compose: it is triadic, and it
alone has a real power.

Signs, the only things with which a human being can, without
derogation, consent to have any transaction, being a sign
himself, are triadic; since a sign denotes a subject, and signifies
a form of fact, which latter it brings into connexion with the
former [. . .]

(Peirce CP 6.341 - 344)

Every sign process comes about by combining Firstness with
Secondness and Thirdness created through the tendency to take habits.
The assumption is that this basic sign process is the common foundation
for mind and nature, not matter, energy and physical information alone. I
see no way that we can explain or give a good model for signification
and communication from a mechanistic view of nature that sees nature as
a basic independent reality which, through self-organization, develops
forms that interact as information, *and then* life and meaning "emerges".

Conclusion

Meaning processing and information processing remain structurally
coupled in systems which are able to process meaning. Not all systems
are able to do so, and for these systems one expects information
processing without meaning processing. The point is that all living
systems also produce meaning, even if they do not have a well
differentiated psychic and /or a social system.

Whatever happens in the material world all processes produce
entropy from dissipated gradients. But already at the biological level we
find several possible other purposes (final causes). For example,
Darwinians say that whatever happens serves to increase the "fitness" of
populations. At the socio-cultural level, one agency's order may be
another's disorder. Parsing events into order or disorder from an

individual or social point of view requires a system of interpretation to make the decision. Thus this must already have a foundation in our biological making as the theory of autopoiesis see it.

From a thermodynamic point of view we are feeding on entropy production because, being part of the self-organizing material ecological systems on the surface of the earth, we are shunting some of the Sun's energy rather than letting it be serenely reflected off into space as heat radiation. Living systems are built out of neg-entropy, as Schrödinger saw it, as a sort of dissipative structure, which Prigogine described in mathematic terms. The expanding universe absorbs all the entropy-energy which the Earth radiates and creates irreversibility, physical time and thereby also drive evolution.

But in such a view there is a lack of a basis for determining meaning. This is because it is an ideoscopic view only and lacks its cenoscopic foundation in a theory of the existence of first person experience and qualia and how the knowledge that is the basis of the ideoscopic science is produced. Humans — the necessary prerequisites for producing science — are interpreting and meaning-making social communicative creatures who find themselves, as products of a universe they are bound to, trying to understand, by the very essence of their nature as Gadamer describes it in *Truth and Method*. Gadamer is not *against* scientific knowledge, as he is sometimes interpreted to be: he just holds a view compatible to Cantwell Smith and Peirce's.

The Peircean view presented here of course makes me shy away from the idea that we should be able to define meaning on any pure mathematical or algorithmic level, as I see meaning as embodied pragmaticist signification attached to the evolutionary fight for existence, good experiences among other things in the form of sensual gratification and a meaningful life. This leads to discussions of values, the good life, the meaning of life, religion and philosophy in the social conscious human. Functionalist meaning can probably be described for certain primitive uses as an operator. But, I do not think it is fruitful to claim that meaning is an operator in itself. It is my point of view that all meaning and value comes from our existential awareness of being embodied living beings in an ecological web of signs.

Then there is the problem of levels of meaning. A male seagull, that has as part of its mating ritual bringing a morsel of food to the female as it would if she were a young or nesting, makes a coded message. Actually ethologists interpret it as a sign of non-hostile intentions because those other situations, which the feeding 'symbolizes', are caring and non-threatening situations. Ethologists call it ritualization. Many of us would say that the fish is a symbol or a metaphor, on a very low level that is not conscious. We would further say that these "sign plays" (a Cybersemiotic concept) are the prerequisite for socio-communication. The often discussed meaning and pragmatic functioning of the concept 'bachelor' in human society is based on ritualized seeking for a mate. Thus meaning is biologically embodied, psychologically experienced and socially expressed and ritualized in language.

The meaning-processing in discourse is much richer than the lower-order systems. While the individual (psychology) is still facing the problems of life, the next-order level of culture is also supra-individual and proliferating with a meaning dynamic above the sum of the psychological ones.

To me this is the field of meaning, and it is generated by the embodied mind in living systems. Un-embodied systems like the computer cannot really produce meaning through signification that means anything to and by themselves, therefore. So it is the biological and the psychological autopoietic systems that produce this "substance" of meaning that the socio-communicative systems then operate through language, then modulate and develop to still more sophisticated levels, for instance in ideoscopic sciences.

Acknowledgements

I want to thank Paul Cobley and Wolfgang Hoffkirschner for their useful critical comments on the draft versions of the text and Cobley for suggesting so many good improvement of the language.

Bibliography

Brier, S. (1992). Information and Consciousness: A Critique of the Mechanistic Foundation of the Concept of Information, *Cybernetics & Human Knowing*, Vol.1, no. 2/3, pp 71-94.

Brier, S. (1998a). Cybersemiotics: a transdisciplinary framework for information studies, *BioSystems*, 46 (1998) 185–191.

Brier, S. (1998b). The Cybersemiotic Explanation of the Emergence of Cognition: The Explanation of Cognition, Signification and Communication in a non-Cartesian Cognitive biology, *Evolution, and Cognition*, Vol. 4, no.1, pp. 90–102.

Brier, S. (1999). Biosemiotics and the foundation of cybersemiotics. Reconceptualizing the insights of Ethology, second order cybernetics and Peirce's semiotics in biosemiotics to create a non-Cartesian information science, *Semiotica*, 127-1/4, 1999, 169–198.

Brier, S. (2001a). Cybersemiotics and Umweltslehre, *Semiotica*, 134-1/4 (2001), 779–814.

Brier, S. (2001b). Ecosemiotics and Cybersemiotic, *Sign Systems Studies*, 29.1, 107–120.

Brier, S. (2002). Intrasemiotics and Cybersemiotics, *Sign System Studies* 30.1, 113–127.

Brier, S. (2003). The Cybersemiotic model of communication: An evolutionary view on the threshold between semiosis and informational exchange, *TrippleC* 1(1): 71–94. http://triplec.uti.at/articles/tripleC1(1)_Brier.pdf

Brier, S (2005). Third Culture: Cybersemiotic's inclusion of a Biosemiotic Theory of Mind, *Axiomathes*, 15:211–228.

Brier, S, (2006). The necessity of Trans-Scientific Frameworks for doing Interdisciplinary Research, *Kybernetes*, no. 3-4: 403–425.

Brier, S. (2007a). The Cybersemiotics Framework as a means to conceptualize the difference between computing and semiosis, Gordana Dodig Crnkovic and Susan Stuart: *Computation, Information, Cognition: The Nexus and the Liminal*, CSP, pp. 178–195. Proceedings E-CAP 2005 Västeraas Universitet, Sverige.

Brier, S. (2007b). Applying Luhmann's system theory as part of a transdisciplinary frame for communication science, *Cybernetics & Human Knowing*, Vol. 14, no. 2-3. pp. 29–65.

Brier, S. (2008a). *Cybersemiotics: Why Information Is Not Enough,* Toronto Studies in Semiotics and Communication, University of Toronto Press, pp. 477.

Brier, S. (2008b),A Paradigm for Biosemiotics, *Signs* 2008 pp. 30–81. http://vip.db.dk/signs/artikler/Brier%20(2008)%20the%20paradigm%20of%20peircean%20biosemiotics.pdf

Brier, S. (2008c), Bateson and Peirce on the pattern that connects and the sacred, Chapter 12 pp- 229–255 in Hoffmeyer, J. (ed.)(2008). *A Legacy for Living Systems: Gregory Bateson as a precursor for biosemiotic thinking*, Biosemiotics 2. London: Springer Verlag.

Brier, S. (2009a). Cybersemiotic Pragmaticism and Constructivism, *Constructivist Foundations* Vol. 5, No. 1, pp. 19–38. http://www.univie.ac.at/constructivism/journal/articles/5/1/019.brier.pdf

Brier, S. (2009b). Levels of Cybersemiotics: Possible Ontologies of signification, *Cognitive Semiotics*, Issue 4 (Spring 2009), pp. 28–62.

Cantwell Smith, B. (1998). *God, Approximately • 4,* http://www.ageofsignificance.org/people/bcsmith/print/smith-godapprox4.pdf. , visited July 2009.

Gardner, H. (1985). *The Mind's New Science: A History of the Cognitive Revolution,* - New York: Basic Books, Inc., Publishers.

Chalmers, D. J. (1996). *The Conscious mind: In Search of a Fundamental Theory.* New York and Oxford: Oxford University Press.

Deely, J. (1990). *Basics of Semiotics.* Bloomington, Indiana University Press.

Dennett, D. C. (1991). *Consciousness Explained,* Back Bay Books

Dodig-Crnkovic, D. (2006). *Investigations into Information Semantics and Ethics of Computing,* PhD Thesis, Mälardalen University Press, September 2006.

Emmeche, C. (1998). Defining Life as a Semiotic Phenomenon, *Cybernetics & Human Knowing,* Vol. 5, No. 1, pp. 33–42.

— (2007). On the Biosemiotic nature of Embodiment and our Cyborg Nature, *Body, Language and Mind. Vol 1. Embodiment,* Ziemke, T., Zlatev, J. and R. Frank (eds.), 379–410. Berlin: Mouton.

Favareau, D. (2008). The Biosemiotic Turn: a Brief history of the Sign Concept in Pre-Modernist Science, *J. of Biosemiotics* 1:5–23.

Fodor, J. A. (1987). *Psychosemantics: the Problems of Meaning.* Cambridge, MA: MIT Press.

Fodor, J. (2001). *The Mind Does not Work that Way: The Scope and Limits of Computational Psychology,* The MIT Press, Cambridge Massachusetts.

Foerster, H. von (1984). *Observing Systems,* (The Systems Inquiry Series), California, USA: Intersystems Publications.

Gadamer, H-G. (1975), *Truth and Method.* New York, Seabury Press.

Gardner, H. (1985). *The Mind's New Science: A History of the Cognitive Revolution,* - New York:,Basic Books, Inc., Publishers.

Hawking, S. (1988). *A Brief History of Time,* Bantam Books.

Hayles, N.K. (1999). *How we became Posthuman: Virtual Bodies in Cybernetics, Literature, and Informatics,* Chicago; University of Chicago Press.

Hoffmeyer, J. (1996). *Signs of Meaning in the Universe,* Bloomington: Indiana University Press.

Hoffmeyer, J. (2008). Biosemiotics: An Examination into the Signs of Life and the Life of Signs. Scranton, USA, Scranton University Press.

Hoffmeyer, J. & Emmeche, Claus (1991). Code-Duality and the Semiotics of Nature, Anderson, Myrdene; Merrell, Floyd (eds.). *On Semiotic Modeling.* Berlin: Mouton de Gruyter, 117–166.

Kuhn, T. (1970). *The Structure of Scientific Revolutions,* 2nd enlarged ed. Chicago: The University of Chicago Press.

Lakoff, G. (1987). *Women, Fire and Dangerous Things: What Categories Reveal about the Mind,* Chicago and London: The University of Chicago Press.

Luhmann, N. (1990). *Essays on Self-Reference,* New York: Colombia University Press.

— (1992). What is communication? *Communication Theory,* Vol. 2. No. 3, August 1972. pp. 251–258.

— (1999). Sign as Form, *Cybernetics & Human Knowing* V. 6 No. 3. Special Issue: Luhmann: Cybernetics, Systems and Semiotics. pp. 21–37.

Luntley, M. (1995). *Reason, Truth and the Self: The Postmodern Reconditioned*, London: Routledge.

Maturana, H.R. (1988a). Ontology of observing: The Biological Foundation of Self Consciousness and the Physical Domain of Existence, *The Irish Journal of Psychology*, Vol. 9, no. 1, pp. 25–82.

— (1988b). Reality: The Search for Objectivity, or the Quest for a Compelling Argument, *Irish Journal of Psychology*, Vol. 9, 1, pp. 25–82

— & Varela, F. (1980). *Autopoiesis and Cognition: The Realization of the Living*, London: Reidel,

— & Varela, F (1986). *Tree of Knowledge: Biological Roots of Human Understanding*, London: Shambhala Publishers.

Merleau-Ponty, M. (1966). *Phenomenology of Perception,* Translated by C. Smith. London: Routledge & Kegan Paul. Originally published as *Phenomenologie de la Perception* (Paris, Gallimard, 1945).

von Neumann, J. (1955). *The Mathematical Foundations of Quantum Mechanics*, Princeton University Press, Princeton, NJ.

Pattee, H. (2001). The physics of symbols: bridging the epistemic cut", *Biosystems*, Volume 60, Issues 1-3, May 2001, Pages 5–21

Penrose, R. (1995). *Shadows of the Mind: A Search for the Missing Science of Consciousness*, London: Oxford University Press.

Peirce, C.S. (1931–58). CP *Collected Papers vol. I-VIII.* Cambridge MA: Harvard University Press. Used here is Peirce (1994 [1866–1913]): *The Collected Papers of Charles Sanders Peirce.* Electronic edition reproducing Vols. I-VI ed. Charles Hartshorne & Paul Weiss (Cambridge: Harvard University Press, 1931-1935), Vols. VII-VIII ed. Arthur W. Burks (same publisher, 1958). Charlottesville: Intelex Corporation.

Pinker, S. (1995). *The Language Instinct: How the Mind Creates Language*, New York: Harper Perennial.

Prigogine, I. (1980). *From Being to Becoming*, San Francisco: W.H. Freeman.

— (1996). The End of Certainty. Time, Chaos, and the New Laws of Nature, New York: The Free Press.

— and Stengers, I. (1984). *Order Out of Chaos: Man's New Dialogue with Nature,* New York: Bantam Books.

Schrödinger, E. (2006/1967). *What is Life?*, Cambridge: Cambridge University Press.

Schutz, A.(196..) *The Phenomenology of the Social World,* Evanston, IL: Northwestern University Press, (Original in German 1932).

Searle, J. (1989). *Minds, Brains and Science*. London: Penguin Books.

Shannon, C.E. & Weaver, W. (1949). *The Mathematical Theory of Communication*, Urbana: The University of Illinois Press.

Wiener, N. (1965/1948). *Cybernetics or Control and Communication in the Animal and the Machine,*New York: The MIT Press and John Wiley & Sons, 2nd. Ed. (org. 1948).

CHAPTER 2

INFORMATION DYNAMICS IN A CATEGORICAL SETTING

Mark Burgin

Department of Mathematics
University of California, Los Angeles
405 Hilgard Ave.
Los Angeles, CA 90095

The general theory of information is a synthetic approach, which organizes and encompasses all main directions in information theory. On the methodological level, it is formulated as a system of principles, explaining what information is and how to measure information. The goal of this chapter is to build a mathematical stratum of the general theory of information based on category theory. Abstract categories allow us to develop flexible models for information and its flow, as well as for computers, networks and computation. There are two types of representations information dynamics in categories: Categorical representation and functorial representation. The categorical representations of information dynamics preserve internal structures of information spaces associated with infological systems as their state or phase spaces. Functorial representations of information dynamics preserve external structures of information spaces associated with infological systems as their state or phase spaces. Properties of these types of representations are studied. Obtained results facilitate building a common framework for information and computation. Now category theory is also used as unifying framework for physics, biology, topology, and logic, as well as for the whole mathematics. This provides a base for analyzing physical and information systems and processes by means of categorical structures and methods.

1. Introduction

The general theory of information is a synthetic approach, which organizes and encompasses all main directions in information theory. On the methodological level, it is formulated as a system of principles, explaining what information is and how to measure information. The goal of this chapter is to build a mathematical stratum of the general theory of information based on category theory. Abstract categories allow us to develop flexible models for information and its flow, as well as for computers, networks and computation. Information is intrinsically related to transformations (Burgin, 1998/1999). That is why portions of information are modeled by operators in system representation spaces. There are two types of representation of information dynamics in categories: the categorical representation studied in Section 4 and functorial representation studied in Section 5. The categorical representation of information dynamics preserves internal structures of information spaces associated with infological systems as their state or phase spaces. In it, portions of information are modeled by categorical information operators. The functorial representation of information dynamics preserves external structures of information spaces associated with infological systems as their state or phase spaces. In it, portions of information are modeled by functorial information operators. Properties of these types of representations are studied. In particular, sequential, concurrent and parallel compositions of categorical information operators are defined and analyzed. Here we pay more attention to the categorical representation. Obtained results facilitate building a common framework for information and computation. Now category theory is also used as unifying framework for physics (cf., for example (Baez and Stay, 2009)), for biology (cf., for example (Ehresmann and Vanbremeersch, 1987; 2007; Levich and Solov'yov, 1999)), for computation (cf., for example (Anderson, 1975; Arbib and Manes, 1975; Ehrig and Kreowski, 1975; Manes, 1975; Manin, 1999; Moggi, 1991; Power and Robinson, 1997; Scott, 2000)), for topology, and for logic Mor_C (A, B). Elements form Hom_C (A, B) are called (cf., for example (Johnstone, 1977; Barr and Wells, 1983; Lambek and Scott, 1986; Abramsky and Duncan, 2005)), as well as for the whole mathematics (cf., for example (Johnstone, 1977; Goldblatt, 1979)). This provides a base for analyzing physical and information systems and processes by means of categorical structures and methods.

Section 2 provides the reader with knowledge on categories that is necessary for understanding results obtained in this work. Section 3 gives a compressed description of the phenomenological stratum of the general theory of information. Categorical information operators are studied in

Section 4 and functorial information operators are studied in Section 5. In Section 6, categorical models of computation are discussed, demonstrating relations between information and computation on the level of their mathematical models. Section 7 (Conclusion) contains open problems in the mathematical theory of information.

The author is grateful to Gordana Dodig-Crnkovic and Kaj Børge Hansen for many useful remarks.

2. Elements of Category Theory

There are two approaches to the mathematical structure called a *category*. One approach treats categories in the framework of the general set-theoretical mathematics. Another approach establishes categories independently of sets and uses them as a foundation of mathematics different from set theory. It is possible to build the whole mathematics in the framework of categories. For instance, such a basic mathematical concept as a binary relation is frequently studied in categories (cf., for example, (Burgin, 1970)). Toposes allow one to reconstruct set theory as a subtheory of category theory (cf., for example, (Goldblatt, 1979)). According to the first approach, we have the following definition of a category.

Definition 2.1. A *category* **C** consists of two collections Ob **C**, the *objects* of **C**, and Hom **C**, the *morphisms* (also called *arrows*) of **C** that satisfy the following three axioms:

A1. For every pair A, B of objects from Ob **C**, there is a set $\mathrm{Hom}_C(A, B) \subseteq$ Hom **C**, also denoted by $\mathrm{H}_C(A, B)$ or $\mathrm{Mor}_C(A, B)$. Elements from $\mathrm{Hom}_C(A, B)$ are called morphisms from A to B in **C**. When f is a morphism from A to B, it is denoted by $f\colon A \to B$. The object A is called the domain of f and object B is called the codomain of f.

A2. For every three objects A, B and C from Ob **C**, there is a binary partial operation, which is a partial function from pairs of morphisms that belong to the direct product $\mathrm{Hom}_C(A, B) \times \mathrm{Hom}_C(B, C)$ to morphisms in $\mathrm{Hom}_C(A, C)$. In other words, when $f\colon A \to B$ and $g\colon B \to C$, there is a morphism $g \circ f\colon A \to C$, which is also denoted by gf and called the composition of morphisms g and f in **C**. This composition is associative, that is, if $f\colon A \to B$, $g\colon B \to C$ and $h\colon C \to D$, then $h \circ (g \circ f) = (h \circ g) \circ f$.

A3. For every object A from Ob **C**, there is a morphism 1_A in $Hom_C(A, A)$, called the identity on A, for which if $f: A \rightarrow B$, then $1_B \circ f = f$ and $f \circ 1_A = f$.

Example 2.1. The category of sets **SET**: objects are arbitrary sets and morphisms are mappings of these sets.

Example 2.2. The category of groups **GRP**: objects are arbitrary groups and morphisms are homomorphisms of these groups.

Example 2.3. The category of topological spaces **TOP**: objects are arbitrary topological spaces and morphisms are continuous mappings of these topological spaces.

Remark 2.1. In the case when a category **C** has a set of objects, it may be treated as a graph where objects are vertices and morphisms are edges.

Definition 2.2. A morphism $f: A \rightarrow B$ from the category **C** is called:

a) A *monomorphism* if for all morphisms h and k in **C** such that the compositions $f \circ h$ and $f \circ k$ exist and are equal, it follows that $h = k$.

b) An *epimorphism* if for all morphisms h and k in **C** such that the compositions $h \circ f$ and $k \circ f$ exist and are equal, it follows that $h = k$.

c) A *bimorphism* if it is both a monomorphism and epimorphism.

d) A *section* if there is a morphism $g: B \rightarrow A$ from the category **C** such that $g \circ f = 1_A$.

e) A *retraction* if there is a morphism $g: B \rightarrow A$ from the category **C** such that $f \circ g = 1_B$.

f) An *isomorphism* if it is both a section and retraction.

An *initial object* also called a *coterminal object* of the category **C** is an object I in **C** such that for every object X in **C**, there exists a single morphism $I \rightarrow X$. A *terminal object* also called a *final object* of the category **C** is an object T in **C** such that for every object X in **C** there exists a single morphism $X \rightarrow T$. Initial objects and terminal objects are dual concepts.

A *zero object* in the category **C** is an object 0 that is both an initial object and a terminal object.

Mapping of categories that preserve their structure are called functors. There are functors of two types: covariant functors and contravariant functors.

Definition 2.3. A *covariant functor* F: **C** $\to$ **K**, also called a *functor*, from a category **C** to a category **K** is a mapping that is stratified into two related mappings F_{ObC} : Ob **C** $\to$ Ob **K** and F_{MorC} : Mor **C** $\to$ Mor **K** , i.e., F_{ObC} associates an object $F(A)$ from the category **K** to each object A from the category **C** and F_{MorC} associates a morphism $F(f)$: $F(A) \to F(B)$ from the category **K** to each morphism f: $A \to B$ from the category **C**. In addition, F satisfies the following two conditions:

1. $F(1_A) = 1_{F(A)}$ for every object A from the category **C**;
2. $F(f \circ g) = F(f) \circ F(g)$ for all morphisms f and g from the category **C** when their composition $f \circ g$ exists.

That is, functors preserve identity morphisms and composition of morphisms.

Definition 2.4. A *contravariant functor* F: **C** $\to$ **K** from a category **C** to a category **K** consists of two mappings F_{ObC} : Ob **C** $\to$ Ob **K** and F_{MorC} : Mor **C** $\to$ Mor **K**, i.e., F_{ObC} associates an object $F(A)$ from the category **K** to each object A from the category **C** and F_{MorC} associates a morphism $F(f)$: $F(A) \to F(B)$ from the category **K** to each morphism f: $A \to B$ from the category **C**, that satisfy the following two conditions:

1. $F(1_A) = 1_{F(A)}$ for every object A from the category **C**;
2. $F(f \circ g) = F(g) \circ F(f)$ for all morphisms f and g from the category **C** when their composition $f \circ g$ exists.

It is possible to define a contravariant functor as a covariant functor on the dual category $\mathbf{C}^{\text{op}}$. In what follows, we consider only covariant functors.

Definition 2.5. A functor F: **C** $\to$ **K** is called:

a) an *endofunctor* if **C** = **K**;
b) *dense*, or *representative*, if for each object $A \in$ Ob **K**, there is some object $B \in$ Ob **C** such that $F(B)$ is isomorphic to A;
c) *full* if each Hom-set restriction $F|_{\text{Hom}(A,B)}{}^{\text{Hom}(F(A),F(B))}$ of F is surjective.
d) *faithful* if each Hom-set restriction $F|_{\text{Hom}(A,B)}{}^{\text{Hom}(F(A),F(B))}$ of F is injective.

It is possible to read more about categories, functors and their properties, for example, in (Herrlich and Strecker, 1973; Goldblatt, 1979).

3. The Phenomenological Stratum of the General Theory of Information

The general theory of information is built on an axiomatic base, which consists of two classes of principles and their relations. The first class contains ontological principles, which bring to light general properties and regularities of information and its functioning. Principles from the second class explain how to measure information and are called axiological principles. The first ontological principle determines a perspective for information definition, i.e., in what context information is defined.

Ontological Principle O1 (the *Locality Principle*). It is necessary to separate information in general from information (or a portion of information) for a system R.

In other words, empirically, it is possible to speak only about information (or a portion of information) for a system.

Definition 3.1. The system R with respect to which some information is considered is called the *receiver*, *receptor* or *recipient* of this information.

Such a receiver/recipient can be a person, community, class of students, audience in a theater, animal, bird, fish, computer, network, database and so on.

The Locality Principle explicates an important property of information, but says nothing what information is. This is done by the second principle, which has several forms.

Ontological Principle O2 (the *General Transformation Principle*). In a broad sense, *information* for a system R is a capacity to cause changes in the system R.

Thus, we may understand information in a broad sense as a capacity (ability or potency) of things, both material and abstract, to change other things. Information exists in the form of *portions of information*. Informally, a portion of information is such information that can be separated from other information. Information is, as a rule, about something. What information is about is called an *object* of this information.

The Ontological Principle O2 has several consequences. First, it demonstrates that information is closely connected to transformation. Namely, it means that information and transformation are functionally similar because they both point to changes in a system. At the same time, they are different because information is potency for (or in some sense, cause of) change, while transformation is the change itself, or in other words, transformation is an operation, while information is what induces this operation.

Second, the Ontological Principle O2 explains *why* information influences society and individuals all the time, as well as why this influence grows with the development of society. Namely, reception of information by individuals and social groups induces transformation. In this sense, information is similar to energy. Moreover, according to the Ontological Principle O2, energy is a kind of information in a broad sense. This well correlates with the Carl Friedrich von Weizsäcker's idea (cf., for example, (Flükiger, 1995)) that *energy might in the end turn out to be information.*

Third, the Ontological Principle O2 makes it possible to separate different kinds of information. For instance, people, as well as any computer, have many kinds of memory. It is even supposed that each part of the brain has several types of memory agencies that work in somewhat different ways, to suit particular purposes (Minsky, 1986). It is possible to consider each of these memory agencies as a separate system and to study differences between information that changes each type of memory. This might help to understand the interplay between stability and flexibility of mind, in general, and memory, in particular.

In essence, we can see that all kinds and types of information are encompassed by the Ontological Principle O2.

However, the common usage of the word *information* does not imply such wide generalizations as the Ontological Principle O2 implies. Thus, we need a more restricted theoretical meaning because an adequate theory, whether of the information or of anything else, must be in significant accord with our common ways of thinking and talking about what the theory is about, else there is the danger that theory is not about what it purports to be about. To achieve this goal, we use the concept of an *infological system* IF(R) of the system R for the information definition, which is constructed in two steps. At first, we make the concept of information relative and then we choose a specific class of infological systems to specify information in the strict sense. That is why it is impossible and, as well as, counterproductive to give an exact and thus, too rigid and restricted definition of an infological system. Indeed, information is a very rich and widespread phenomenon to be reflected by a restricted rigid definition (cf., for example, (Capurro, *et al*, 1999; Melik-Gaikazyan, 1997)).

The concept of *infological system* plays the role of a free parameter in the general theory of information, providing for representation of different kinds and types of information in this theory. That is why the concept of *infological system*, in general, should not be limited by boundaries of exact definitions. A free parameter must really be free. Identifying an infological system IF(R) of a system R, we can define information relative to this system. This definition is expressed in the following principle.

Ontological Principle O2g (the *Relativized Transformation Principle*). *Information* for a system R *relative to the infological system* IF(R) is a capacity to cause changes in the system IF(R).

As a model example of an infological system IF(R) of an intelligent system R, we take the system of knowledge of R. In cybernetics, it is called the *thesaurus* Th(R) of the system R. Another example of an infological system is the memory of a computer. Such a memory is a place in which data and programs are stored and is a complex system of diverse components and processes.

Elements from IF(R) are called *infological elements*.

There is no exact definition of infological elements although there are various entities that are naturally considered as infological elements as they allow one to build theories of information that inherit conventional meanings of the word *information*. For instance, knowledge, data, images, algorithms, procedures, scenarios, ideas, values, goals, ideals, fantasies, abstractions, beliefs, and similar objects are standard examples of infological elements.

When we take a physical system D as the infological system and allow only for physical changes, we see that information with respect to D coincides with energy.

Taking a mental system *B* as the infological system and considering only mental changes, we find that information with respect to *B* coincides with mental energy.

These ideas are crystallized in the following principle.

Ontological Principle O2a (the *Special Transformation Principle*). *Information in the strict sense* or *proper information* or, simply, information for a system *R*, is a capacity to change structural infological elements from an infological system IF(*R*) of the system *R*.

To better understand how infological system can help explicating the concept of information in the strict sense, we consider cognitive infological systems.

An infological system IF(*R*) of the system *R* is called *cognitive* if IF(*R*) contains (stores) cognitive elements or constituents, such as knowledge, data, ideas, fantasies, abstractions, beliefs, etc. A cognitive infological system of a system *R* is denoted by CIF(*R*) and is related to cognitive information.

In the case of a cognitive infological system, it looks like it is possible to give an exact definition of cognitive information. However, now cognitive sciences do not know all structural elements involved in cognition. A straightforward definition specifies cognition as activity (process) that gives knowledge. At the same time, we know that knowledge, as a rule, comes through data and with data. So, data are also involved in cognition and thus, have to be included in cognitive infological systems. Besides, cognitive processes utilize such structures as ideas, images, beliefs, values, measures, problems, tasks, etc. Thus, to comprehensively represent cognitive information, it is imperative to include all such objects in cognitive infological systems.

For those who prefer to have an exact definition contrary to a broader perspective, it is possible to define a cognitive infological system as the system of knowledge. This approach was used by Shreider (1967) and Mizzaro (2001).

Cognitive infological systems are standard examples of infological systems, while their elements, such as knowledge, data, images, ideas, fantasies, abstractions, and beliefs, are standard examples of infological elements. Cognitive infological systems are very important, especially, for intelligent systems as the majority of researchers believe that information is intrinsically connected to knowledge.

Ontological Principle O2c (**the** *Cognitive Transformation Principle*). *Cognitive information* for a system R, is a capacity to cause changes in the cognitive infological system $CIF(R)$ of the system R.

As the cognitive infological system contains knowledge of the system it belongs to, cognitive information is the source of knowledge changes.

It is useful to understand that in the definition of cognitive information, as well as of other types of information in the strict sense, it is assumed that an infological system $IF(R)$ of the system R is a part (subsystem) of the system R. However, people have always tried to extend their cognitive means using different objects. In ancient times, people made marks on stones and sticks. Then they used paper. Now they use computers and computer networks.

There are two ways to take this peculiarity into consideration. In one approach, it is possible to consider extended infological systems that do not completely belong to the primary system R. Another approach allows one to treat R as a cognitive system, including all objects used for cognitive purposes. In this case, when we regard an individual A as a cognitive system R, we have to include (in R) all cognitive means used by A. The second approach does not demand to consider extended infological systems. All of them are parts (subsystems) of the primary system R.

Let I be a portion of information for a system R.

Ontological Principle O3 (**the** *Embodiment Principle*). For any portion of information I, there is always a carrier C of this portion of information for a system R.

Really, people get information from books, magazines, TV and radio sets, computers, and from other people. To store information people use their brains, paper, tapes, and computer disks. All these entities are carriers of information.

For adherents of the materialistic approach, the Ontological Principle O3 must be changed to its stronger version.

Ontological Principle OM3 (**the** *Material Embodiment Principle*). For any portion of information I, there is some substance C that contains I.

The substance C that is a carrier of the portion of information I is called the *physical*, or *material*, *carrier* of I.

Ontological Principle O4 (the *Representability Principle*). For any portion of information I, there is always a representation C of this portion of information for a system R.

As any information representation is, in some sense, its carrier the Ontological Principle O4 implies the Ontological Principle O3.

The first three ontological principles ((O1)-(O3) or (O1)-(OM3)) imply that information connects the carrier C with the system R and thus, information I is a component of the following fundamental triad (Burgin, 1997)

$$(C, I, R)$$

People empirically observed that for information to become available, the carrier must interact with a receptor that was capable of detecting information the carrier contained. This empirical fact is represented by the following principle.

Ontological Principle O5 (the *Interaction Principle*). A transaction/transition/transmission of information goes on only in some interaction of the carrier C with the system R.

Ontological Principle O6 (the *Actuality Principle*). A system R accepts a portion of information I only if the transaction/transition/transmission causes corresponding transformations.

For instance, if after reading this paper, your knowledge remains the same, you do not accept cognitive information from this text. In a general case, when the recipient's knowledge structure was not changed, there is no cognitive information reception.

Ontological Principle O7 (the *Multiplicity Principle*). One and the same carrier C can contain different portions of information for one and the same system R.

The last three principles reflect only situations when transformation of an infological system takes place. However, it is important to know and predict properties of these transformations, for example, to evaluate the extent or measure of transformations.

4. Categorical Representation of Information Dynamics

To build a categorical representation of information dynamics, at first, we construct categorical representation of the information receptor/receiver R because according to the Principles O1 and O2, information is determined by its action on the information receptor/receiver. When we are interested in information in the strict sense, we consider only an infological system $IF(R)$ of R.

Let us take a category $\mathbf{C}$.

Definition 4.1. A categorical representation of the system $IF(R)$ (or R) assigns objects from $\mathbf{C}$ to the states of $IF(R)$ (correspondingly, R) and morphisms from $\mathbf{C}$ to transformations of $IF(R)$ (or R).

In this case, $\mathrm{Mor}_{IF(R)} \mathbf{C}$ ($\mathrm{Mor}_R \mathbf{C}$) denotes the set of all morphisms from $\mathbf{C}$ that represent transformations of $IF(R)$ (correspondingly, R) and if $A, B \in \mathrm{Ob}\ \mathbf{C}$, then $\mathrm{Hom}_{IF(R)}(A, B) = \mathrm{Mor}_{IF(R)} \mathbf{C} \cap \mathrm{Hom}_{\mathbf{C}}(A, B)$ ($\mathrm{Hom}_R (A, B) = \mathrm{Mor}_R \mathbf{C} \cap \mathrm{Hom}_{\mathbf{C}}(A, B)$).

Example 4.1. Objects of the category $\mathbf{C}$ are linear spaces, while morphisms are linear mappings (linear operators) of these spaces.

Example 4.2. Objects of the category $\mathbf{C}$ are sets, e.g., sets of knowledge items, such as considered in (Mizzaro, 2001), or of propositions, such as considered in (Bar-Hillel and Carnap, 1958; Halpern and Moses, 1985), while morphisms are mappings (transformations) of these sets.

Example 4.3. Words, or more generally, texts are information carriers, as well as information representations. Thus, it is natural to take words (or texts) as objects of the category $\mathbf{C}$. Then morphisms of this category are computations that transform one word (system of words) into another one. These computations may be restricted to computations of some class of abstract automata, such as finite automata, Turing machines, inductive Turing machines or neural networks (cf., for example, (Burgin, 2005)). It is possible to consider information automata in the sense of Cooper (1978) as devices that perform computations.

Example 4.4. Thesaurus is a natural infological system (Burgin, 2003; 2003a). An efficient representation of a thesaurus is a set of words, or more generally, of texts, which are information carriers, as well as information representations (Shreider, 1967). Thus, it is natural to take sets of words (or texts) as objects of the category **C**. Then morphisms of this category are multiple computations (Burgin, 1983) performed by systems/automata from some class, e.g., Turing machines, inductive Turing machines or finite automata.

Example 4.5. Classifications, which are also infological systems, and their infomorphisms in the sense of (Barwise and Seligman, 1997) form a category in which classifications are objects and infomorphism are morphisms.

Informally, a portion of information I is a potency to cause changes in (infological) systems, i.e. to change the state of this system (cf. Section 3). Assuming that all systems involved in such changes are represented in a category **C**, we see that a change in a system may by represented by a morphism from this category. This gives us a transformation of the system. As a result, I is represented by a categorical information operator $Op(I)$. When it does not cause misunderstanding, it is possible to denote the information portion I and the information operator $Op(I)$ by the same letter I.

Let us consider a categorical representation of the system $IF(R)$ in a category **C**.

Definition 4.2. A *categorical information operator* $Op(I)$ over the category **C** is a mapping $Op(I)$: Ob **C** $\to$ Mor **C** such that for any $A \in$ Ob **C**, $Op(I)(A) \in$ $Hom_{IF(R)}$ (A, X) for some $X \in$ Ob **C**. The morphism $Op(I)(A)$ is called the *component* of the categorical information operator $Op(I)$ at A.

Informally, a categorical information operator shows how each object (infological system) changes when a portion of information is received.

Note that it is possible that the object X coincides with the same object A. When $Op(I)(A) = 1_A$, it means that the information portion I does not change the object (state) A.

Example 4.6. Taking the category **C** from the Example 4.1, in which objects of the category **C** are linear spaces and morphisms are linear operators in these spaces, we can build categorical information operators. These operators assign a linear operator to each linear space from **C**. Such operators represent, for example, information extraction by measurement in physics (cf., for example (Rocchi and Panella, 2007)).

Example 4.7. Taking the category **C** from the Example 4.3, in which words (or texts) are objects and morphisms are computations performed by automata from some class, e.g., Turing machines, inductive Turing machines or finite automata, we obtain computational information operators. These operators assign a computation to each word (text) where this word (text) is the input.

Example 4.8. Taking the category **C** from the Example 4.4, in which an object is a thesaurus, e.g., represented by systems of words (or texts), and morphisms are transformations of these thesauruses, we obtain a cognitive information operator, which assigns to each thesaurus its transformation. There are different types of cognitive information operators:

1. computational cognitive information operators;
2. analytical cognitive information operators;
3. matrix cognitive information operators;
4. set-theoretical cognitive information operators;
5. named-set-theoretical cognitive information operators.

For instance, transformations of knowledge states studied by Mizzaro (2001) form set-theoretical cognitive information operators, while infomorphisms studied by Barwise and Seligman (1997) shape named-set-theoretical cognitive information operators and transformations studied by Shreider (1967) bring into being analytical cognitive information operators

Definition 4.3. A categorical information operator Op(I) is called:

a) *Monoperator* if all morphisms Op(I)(A) with $A \in$ Ob **C** are monomorphisms.

b) *Epoperator* if all morphisms Op(I)(A) with $A \in$ Ob **C** are epimorphisms.

c) *Bimoperator* if all morphisms Op(I)(A) with $A \in$ Ob **C** are bimorphisms.

d) *Secoperator* if all morphisms Op(I)(A) with $A \in$ Ob **C** are sections.

e) *Retroperator* if all morphisms Op(I)(A) with $A \in$ Ob **C** are retractions.

f) *Isoperator* if all morphisms Op(I)(A) with $A \in$ Ob **C** are isomorphisms.

Informally, we have the following interpretation of the introduced types of information operators:

Information monoperators preserve distinctions between previously accepted information portions.

Information epoperators preserve distinctions between next coming information portions.

Information bimoperators are both information monoperators and information epoperators.

Information retroperators represent such information portions I the impact of which can be erased from system state by another information impact, i.e., there is another information portions J that moves the infological system $IF(R)$ back to the previous state.

Information secoperators represent such information portions I that act like an eraser of some previously received information.

Information isooperators are both information retroperators and information secoperators.

Example 4.9. Taking a category **C** from Example 4.2 where objects are sets of propositions More generally, knowledge items) and morphisms are transformations of these sets, we define the categorical information operator O so that for each set A of propositions, the corresponding morphism $O(A)$ is a deduction in a monotone logic. As we know, deduction in a monotone logic only adds new propositions to the initial set. Thus, O is a categorical information monoperator.

Example 4.10. Let us take a category **C** where objects are collections of books that some library L has at different periods of time and morphisms are transformations of these collections that go from time to time. Assuming that this library never discards books, we see that any categorical information operator O in **C** is a categorical information monoperator.

Example 4.11. Let us take a category **C** where objects are collections of software systems that some software depositary L has at different periods of time and morphisms are transformations of these collections that go from time to time. We define the categorical information operator O so that for each set A of software systems, the corresponding morphism $O(A)$ is validation of programs from A and exclusion of invalid systems and copies of the same system. As software systems are never added by the morphism $O(A)$, we see that any categorical information operator O in **C** is a categorical information epoperator.

Information is a dynamic essence and its processing involves different operations with information and its representations and carriers. In the mathematical setting of categories, operations with information are represented by operations with information operators. One of the most important information operations is the (sequential) composition of categorical information operators.

Definition 4.4. The *sequential composition* (often called simply *composition*) of categorical information operators $\text{Op}(I)$ and $\text{Op}(J)$ is a mapping $\text{Op}(I) \circ \text{Op}(J)$: Ob **C** $\to$ Mor **C** such that for any $A \in$ Ob **C**, if $\text{Op}(J)(A) \in \text{Hom}_C (A, B)$, then $[\text{Op}(I) \circ \text{Op}(J)](A) = \text{Op}(I)(B) \circ \text{Op}(J)(A)$.

By definition, the sequential composition of categorical information operators also is a categorical information operator.

We do not use the shorter name *composition* instead of the name *sequential composition* because there are other types of compositions of categorical information operators, for example, parallel composition of categorical information operators or concurrent composition of categorical information operators.

Let us find some properties of the sequential composition of categorical information operators.

Proposition 6.4 from (Herrlich and Strecker, 1973) implies the following result.

Proposition 4.1. The sequential composition of categorical information monoperators $\text{Op}(I)$ and $\text{Op}(J)$ is a categorical information monoperator.

Proposition 6.5 from (Herrlich and Strecker, 1973) implies the following result.

Proposition 4.2. If the sequential composition $\text{Op}(I) \circ \text{Op}(J)$ of categorical information operators $\text{Op}(I)$ and $\text{Op}(J)$ is a categorical information monoperator, then $\text{Op}(J)$ is a categorical information monoperator.

Proposition 6.12 from (Herrlich and Strecker, 1973) implies the following result.

Proposition 4.3. The sequential composition of categorical information epoperators $\mathrm{Op}(I)$ and $\mathrm{Op}(J)$ is a categorical information epoperator.

Propositions 4.1 and 4.2 imply the following result.

Corollary 4.1. The sequential composition of categorical information bimoperators $\mathrm{Op}(I)$ and $\mathrm{Op}(J)$ is a categorical information bimoperator.

Proposition 6.13 from (Herrlich and Strecker, 1973) implies the following result.

Proposition 4.5. If the sequential composition $\mathrm{Op}(I) \circ \mathrm{Op}(J)$ of categorical information operators $\mathrm{Op}(I)$ and $\mathrm{Op}(J)$ is a categorical information epoperator, then $\mathrm{Op}(I)$ is a categorical information epoperator.

Proposition 5.4 from (Herrlich and Strecker, 1973) implies the following result.

Proposition 4.5. The sequential composition of categorical information secoperators $\mathrm{Op}(I)$ and $\mathrm{Op}(J)$ is a categorical information secoperator.

Proposition 5.5 from (Herrlich and Strecker, 1973) implies the following result.

Proposition 4.6. If the sequential composition $\mathrm{Op}(I) \circ \mathrm{Op}(J)$ of categorical information operators $\mathrm{Op}(I)$ and $\mathrm{Op}(J)$ is a categorical information secoperator, then $\mathrm{Op}(J)$ is a categorical information secoperator.

Proposition 5.10 from (Herrlich and Strecker, 1973) implies the following result.

Proposition 4.7. The sequential composition of categorical information retroperators $\mathrm{Op}(I)$ and $\mathrm{Op}(J)$ is a categorical information retroperator.

Propositions 4.5 and 4.7 imply the following result.

Corollary 4.2. The sequential composition of categorical information isoperators $\mathrm{Op}(I)$ and $\mathrm{Op}(J)$ is a categorical information isoperator.

Proposition 6.13 from (Herrlich and Strecker, 1973) implies the following result.

Proposition 4.8. If the sequential composition $\mathrm{Op}(I) \circ \mathrm{Op}(J)$ of categorical information operators $\mathrm{Op}(I)$ and $\mathrm{Op}(J)$ is a categorical information retroperator, then $\mathrm{Op}(I)$ is a categorical information retroperator.

Obtained results are used to prove the following theorem.

Theorem 4.1. a) All categorical information operators over the category **C** form a monoid $\mathbf{CIO_C}$ where the categorical information operator $\mathrm{Op}(\varnothing)$ over the category **C** corresponding to the empty information $\varnothing$ for which $\mathrm{Op}(\varnothing)(X) = 1_X$ for any $X \in \mathrm{Ob}\ \mathbf{C}$ is the identity of this monoid.

b) All categorical information monooperators over the category **C** form a monoid $\mathbf{CIMO_C}$, which is a submonoid of the monoid $\mathbf{CIO_C}$.

c) All categorical information epoperators over the category **C** form a monoid $\mathbf{CIPO_C}$, which is a submonoid of the monoid $\mathbf{CIO_C}$.

d) All categorical information bimoperators over the category **C** form a monoid $\mathbf{CIBO_C}$, which is a submonoid of the monoid $\mathbf{CIO_C}$.

e) All categorical information secoperators over the category **C** form a monoid $\mathbf{CISO_C}$, which is a submonoid of the monoid $\mathbf{CIO_C}$.

f) All categorical information retroperators over the category **C** form a monoid $\mathbf{CIRO_C}$, which is a submonoid of the monoid $\mathbf{CIO_C}$.

g) All categorical information isoperators over the category **C** form a monoid $\mathbf{CIIO_C}$, which is a submonoid of the monoid $\mathbf{CIO_C}$.

Let us consider a categorical representation of an infological system $\mathrm{IF}(R)$ in a category **C**. It determines the category IFC where $\mathrm{Ob}\ \mathrm{IFC} = \mathrm{Ob}\ \mathbf{C}$ and $\mathrm{Hom}_{\mathrm{IFC}}(A, B) = \mathrm{Hom}_{\mathrm{IF}(R)}(A, B)$ for any $A, B \in \mathrm{Ob}\ \mathbf{C}$ where $\mathrm{Hom}_{\mathrm{IF}(R)}(A, B)$ consists of those morphisms that represent transformations of the infological system $\mathrm{IF}(R)$. Functors defined in the category **C** induce functors defined in the category IFC.

Let us take two infological systems $\mathrm{IF}(R)$ and $\mathrm{IF}(Q)$ and categorical representations of the infological system $\mathrm{IF}(R)$ in a category **C** and of the infological system $\mathrm{IF}(Q)$ in a category **K**.

Proposition 4.9. A functor F: IFC $\to$ IFK associates categorical information operators over **K** to categorical information operators over **C** and preserves their sequential composition.

Indeed, to each object A from **C** the functor F assigns the object $F(A)$ from **K**, and if O is a categorical information operator, then F assigns the morphism $F(O(A))$ from Mor **K** to each morphism $O(A)$ from **C**. By definition (cf. Section 2), functors preserve sequential composition. Thus, sequential composition of categorical information operators is also preserved.

This result is used to prove the following theorem.

Theorem 4.2. A functor F: IFC $\to$ IFK induces a homomorphism F_{CIO}: **CIO**$_C$ $\to$ **CIO**$_K$ of monoids.

Informally, functors preserve the structure of information transformations. Proposition 4.9 and Theorem 4.2 show that functors are mappings between categories of states of different infological systems that are compatible with actions of information. Functors allow one to study how the same information operates act in different infological systems.

The set of categorical information operators also has the structure of a polygon or S-set (cf., for example, (Shevrin, 1991; Weinert, 1980)).

Corollary 4.3. The monoid **CIO**$_C$ is a polygon over the monoid Func(IFC, IFC) of all endofunctors in the category IFC.

Let us take a property P of categorical information operators.

Definition 4.5. A functor F: IFC $\to$ IFK :

a) *preserves* the property P if for any categorical information operator A over **C** with the property P, its image $F(A)$ is a categorical information operator over **K** with the property P.

b) *reflects* the property P if for any categorical information operator A over **C**, if its image $F(A)$ has the property P, then A also has the property P.

Proposition 12.2 from (Herrlich and Strecker, 1973) implies the following result.

Theorem 4.3. Every functor F: IFC $\to$ IFK preserves categorical information secoperators, categorical information retroperators, and categorical information isoperators over the category **C**.

Corollary 4.4. Any functor F: IFC $\to$ IFK induces the following homomorphisms of monoids:

$$F_{\text{CIO}}: \mathbf{CISO_C} \to \mathbf{CISO_K}$$

$$F_{\text{CIO}}: \mathbf{CIRO_C} \to \mathbf{CIRO_K}$$

$$F_{\text{CIO}}: \mathbf{CIIO_C} \to \mathbf{CIIO_K}$$

Theorem 12.10 from (Herrlich and Strecker, 1973) implies the following result.

Theorem 4.4. Every dense full and faithful functor F: IFC $\to$ IFK preserves categorical information monooperators, categorical information epoperators, categorical information bimoperators over the category **C**.

Corollary 4.5. A dense full and faithful functor F: IFC $\to$ IFK induces the following homomorphisms of monoids:

$$F_{\text{CIO}}: \mathbf{CIMO_C} \to \mathbf{CIMO_K}$$

$$F_{\text{CIO}}: \mathbf{CIPO_C} \to \mathbf{CIPO_K}$$

$$F_{\text{CIO}}: \mathbf{CIBO_C} \to \mathbf{CIBO_K}$$

$$F_{\text{CIO}}: \mathbf{CISO_C} \to \mathbf{CISO_K}$$

$$F_{\text{CIO}}: \mathbf{CIRO_C} \to \mathbf{CIRO_K}$$

$$F_{\text{CIO}}: \mathbf{CIIO_C} \to \mathbf{CIIO_K}$$

Proposition 12.9 from (Herrlich and Strecker, 1973) implies the following result.

Theorem 4.5. Every full faithful functor F: IFC $\to$ IFK reflects categorical information secoperators, categorical information retroperators, and categorical information isoperators over the category **C**.

In addition to sequential composition, it is possible to define concurrent and parallel compositions of categorical information operators.

Let us consider a category **C** with pushouts (Herrlich and Strecker, 1973).

Definition 4.6. A categorical information operator O over **C** is called the *free sum* of categorical information operators O_1 and O_2 over **C** if for any $A \in$ Ob **C**, there is the pushout (1) where $q = g \circ O_1(A) = f \circ O_2(A)$ and $O(A) = q$.

$$
\begin{array}{ccc}
B & \xrightarrow{\;g\;} & D \\
{\scriptstyle O_1(A)}\big\uparrow & \nearrow{\scriptstyle q} & \big\uparrow{\scriptstyle f} \\
A & \xrightarrow{\quad} & C \\
& {\scriptstyle O_2(A)} &
\end{array}
\tag{1}
$$

The free sum of categorical information operators O_1 and O_2 over **C** is denoted by $O_1 \circledast O_2$.

By properties of pushouts (Herrlich and Strecker, 1973) the free sum of categorical information operators is defined uniquely up to an isomorphism.

On the level of information processes, the free sum of categorical information operators represents consistent integration of information. Now when people and databases receive information from diverse sources, information integration has become an extremely important cognitive operation. Information integration plays a mission critical role in a diversity of applications from life sciences to E-Commerce to ecology to disaster management. These applications rely on the ability to integrate information from multiple heterogeneous sources.

Operationally, Definition 4.3 means that the free sum of two categorical information operators O_1 and O_2 is constructed by taking pushouts for couples of actions of O_1 and O_2 on each object in **C**. It models concurrent information processing (e.g., integration and composition of information).

Theorem 4.6. The free sum of any two categorical information operators is a categorical information epoperator.

Proof. Let us take the free sum O of two categorical information operators O_1 and O_2 over **C**. Then for any object $A \in$ Ob **C**, there is the pushout (1). To prove that O is a categorical information epoperator, we need to show that q always is an epimorphism.

Let us consider two morphisms $k, h \in \text{Hom}_{\text{C}}(D, Q)$ such that $k \circ q = h \circ q$. Then we have

$$k \circ q = k \circ f \circ O_2(A) = k \circ g \circ O_1(A) = h \circ q = h \circ f \circ O_2(A) = h \circ g \circ O_1(A)$$

It gives us the commutative diagram (2).

$$\begin{array}{ccc} & k \circ g & \\ B & \longrightarrow & Q \\ O_1(A) \uparrow k \circ q = h \circ q & & \uparrow h \circ f \\ A & \longrightarrow & C \\ & O_2(A) & \end{array} \qquad (2)$$

By the definition of a pushout (cf., for example, (Herrlich and Strecker, 1973)), we have a morphism $p\colon D \to Q$, which is defined in a unique way and for which

$$p \circ f \circ O_2(A) = p \circ g \circ O_1(A) \qquad (3)$$

As the equality (3) is also true for morphisms k and h and morphism p is unique, we have $k = h = p$.

Theorem is proved because the object $A \in \mathrm{Ob}\ \mathbf{C}$ and morphisms k and h were chosen in an arbitrary way.

Theorem 4.7. Every dense full and faithful functor $F\colon \mathrm{IFC} \to \mathrm{IFK}$ preserves the free sum of categorical information operators.

<u>Proof.</u> Let us take an arbitrary object $A \in \mathrm{Ob}\ \mathbf{C}$, and consider the commutative diagram (4) that corresponds to the free sum of categorical information operator O_1 and O_2 over $\mathbf{C}$.

$$\begin{array}{ccc} & g & \\ B & \longrightarrow & D \\ O_1(A) \uparrow & \nearrow p & \uparrow f \\ A & \longrightarrow & C \\ & O_2(A) & \end{array} \qquad (4)$$

The functor F maps the diagram (4) into the commutative diagram (5). To prove the theorem, we show that this diagram is a pushout in the category $\mathbf{K}$.

$$\begin{array}{ccc} & F(g) & \\ F(B) & \longrightarrow & F(D) \\ F(O_1(A)) \big\uparrow & & \big\uparrow F(f) \\ F(A) & \longrightarrow & F(C) \\ & F(O_2(A)) & \end{array} \qquad (5)$$

Let us consider the commutative square (6) where H is some object from the category $\mathbf{K}$.

$$\begin{array}{ccc} & k & \\ F(B) & \longrightarrow & H \\ F(O_1(A)) \big\uparrow & & \big\uparrow h \\ F(A) & \longrightarrow & F(C) \\ & F(O_2(A)) & \end{array} \qquad (6)$$

As F is a dense functor, there is an object $M \in$ Ob $\mathbf{K}$, such that $M = F(X)$ for some object $X \in$ Ob $\mathbf{C}$, and there is an isomorphism $u: H \to M$. This gives us commutative diagrams (7) and (8) in the category $\mathbf{K}$.

$$\begin{array}{ccccc} & k & & u & \\ F(B) & \longrightarrow & H & \longrightarrow & M \\ F(O_1(A)) \big\uparrow & & h \big\uparrow & & \\ F(A) & \longrightarrow & F(C) & & \\ & F(O_2(A)) & & & \end{array} \qquad (7)$$

$$\begin{array}{ccc} & u{\circ}k & \\ F(B) & \longrightarrow & F(X) \\ F(O_1(A)) \big\uparrow & u{\circ}h & \big\uparrow \\ F(A) & \longrightarrow & F(C) \\ & F(O_2(A)) & \end{array} \qquad (8)$$

As F is a full functor, there are morphisms $l \in \mathrm{Hom}_{\mathbf{C}}(B, X)$ and $t \in \mathrm{Hom}_{\mathbf{C}}(C, X)$ such that $f(l) = u \circ k$ and $f(t) = u \circ h$. It gives us the square (9) in the category $\mathbf{C}$.

$$
\begin{array}{ccc}
B & \xrightarrow{\ l\ } & X \\
{\scriptstyle O_1(A)}\big\uparrow & & \big\uparrow{\scriptstyle t} \\
A & \xrightarrow[\ O_2(A)\ ]{} & C
\end{array}
\qquad (9)
$$

By construction, $F(l \circ O_1(A)) = (u \circ k) \circ F(O_1(A)) = (u \circ h) \circ F(O_2(A)) = F(t \circ O_2(A))$ as (8) is a commutative square. Thus, the square (7) is also commutative because F is a faithful functor. Indeed, if $l \circ O_1(A) \neq t \circ O_2(A)$, then it implies $(u \circ k) \circ F(O_1(A)) \neq (u \circ h) \circ F(O_2(A))$. However, the square (8) is commutative.

As the square (4) is a pushout in $\mathbf{C}$, we obtain the commutative diagram (10).

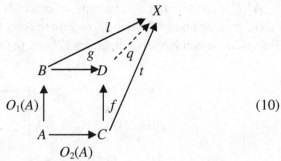

$$\qquad (10)$$

The functor F maps the diagram (10) into the commutative diagram (11).

$$\qquad (11)$$

As a result, we obtain the commutative diagram (12) because u is an isomorphism and it has the inverse $u^{-1}: M \to H$.

$$
\begin{array}{c}
\end{array}
$$

F(X) = M \overset{u^{-1}}{\longrightarrow} H

$F(l)$

$F(g)$ $F(q)$

$F(B) \longrightarrow F(D)$ $F(t)$

$F(O_1(A)) \uparrow$ $F(f) \uparrow$

$F(A) \longrightarrow F(C)$

$F(O_2(A))$

(12)

As the commutative square (6) is arbitrary in the category $\mathbf{K}$, it means that (5) is a pushout in the category $\mathbf{K}$. Consequently (cf. Definition 4.4), the morphism $F(p)$ where morphism $p = g{\circ}O_1(A) = f{\circ}O_2(A)$ defines the free sum of categorical information operators FO_1 and FO_2 over $\mathbf{K}$.

Theorem is proved as A is an arbitrary object in the category $\mathbf{C}$.

Informally, Theorem 4.7 means that functors, i.e., systems of mappings between categories of states of different infological systems that are compatible with actions of information, preserve consistent information integration when these functors do not violate differences between information transformations, isomorphically cover these transformations and represent all system states.

Let us consider a category $\mathbf{C}$ with finite products (Herrlich and Strecker, 1973).

Given an object $A \in$ Ob $\mathbf{C}$, categorical information operators O_1 and O_2 over $\mathbf{C}$ produce to the following diagram

$$
\begin{array}{c}
B \\
O_1(A) \uparrow \\
A \longrightarrow C \\
O_2(A)
\end{array}
$$

(13)

Building the product $B \times C$ of objects B and C and using properties of products (cf., for example, (Herrlich and Strecker, 1973)), we obtain the commutative diagram (14), in which the morphism q is defined in a unique way.

$$
\begin{array}{ccc}
 & p_B & \\
B & \longleftarrow & B \times C \\
O_1(A) \Big\uparrow & q \quad \nearrow & \Big\downarrow p_C \\
A & \longrightarrow & C \\
 & O_2(A) &
\end{array}
\qquad (14)
$$

Performing these amendments for all objects from the category $\mathbf{C}$, we obtain a categorical information operator O over $\mathbf{C}$, which is called the *direct sum* of categorical information operators O_1 and O_2. The formal description is given in the following definition.

Definition 4.7. The *direct sum* of categorical information operators O_1 and O_2 over $\mathbf{C}$ is the categorical information operator O over $\mathbf{C}$ defined for any $A \in \mathrm{Ob}\ \mathbf{C}$, by Diagram (14) where $O(A) = q$.

The direct sum of categorical information operators O_1 and O_2 over $\mathbf{C}$ is denoted by $O_1 \oplus O_2$. It models parallel information processing, e.g., parallel information reception, composition and independent information integration.

By properties of products (Herrlich and Strecker, 1973) the free sum of categorical information operators is defined uniquely up to an isomorphism.

Theorem 4.8. The direct sum of any two categorical information operators one of which is a monoperator is a categorical information monoperator.

<u>Proof.</u> Let us take the direct sum O of two information operators, a categorical information monoperator O_1 and a categorical information operator O_2 over $\mathbf{C}$. Then for any object $A \in \mathrm{Ob}\ \mathbf{C}$, there is the commutative diagram (14), in which the morphism q is defined in a unique way.

To prove that O is a categorical information monoperator, we need to show that q always is a monomorphism.

Let us consider two morphisms $k, h \in \mathrm{Hom}_{\mathbf{C}}(Q, A)$ such that $q \circ k = q \circ h$. Then we have

$$O_1(A) \circ k = p_B \circ q \circ k = p_B \circ q \circ h = O_1(A) \circ h$$

As O_1 is a categorical information monoperator, $O_1(A)$ is a monomorphism. Consequently, we have $k = h$. Thus, $O(A)$ is also a monomorphism.

Theorem is proved because the object $A \in \mathrm{Ob}\ \mathbf{C}$ and morphisms k and h were chosen in an arbitrary way.

The result of Theorem 4.8 has the following interpretation. If a portion of information preserves distinctions between previously received information portions, then its independent integration (parallel composition) with any portion of information also preserves distinctions between previously received information portions.

Theorem 4.9. Every dense full functor $F: \mathbf{IFC} \to \mathbf{IFK}$ preserves the direct sum of categorical information operators.

<u>Proof</u>. Let us take an arbitrary object $A \in \mathrm{Ob}\ \mathbf{C}$, and consider the commutative diagram (15) that corresponds to the direct sum of categorical information operator O_1 and O_2 over $\mathbf{C}$.

$$
\begin{array}{ccc}
 & p_B & \\
B & \longleftarrow & B{\times}C \\
O_1(A) \Big\uparrow \; {\diagup}O(A) & & \Big\downarrow p_C \\
A & \longrightarrow & C \\
 & O_2(A) &
\end{array}
\qquad (15)
$$

The functor F maps the diagram (15) into the commutative diagram (16). To prove the theorem, we show that $F(B{\times}C)$ is the product $F(B){\times}F(C)$ in the category $\mathbf{K}$.

$$\begin{array}{ccc}
& F(p_B) & \\
F(B) & \longleftarrow & F(B{\times}C) \\
\uparrow F(O_1(A)) \quad \nearrow F(O(A)) & & \downarrow F(p_C) \\
F(A) & \longrightarrow & F(C) \\
& F(O_2(A)) &
\end{array} \tag{16}$$

Let us consider the diagram (17) where H is some object from the category $\mathbf{K}$.

$$\begin{array}{c}
F(B) \\
f \uparrow \\
H \xrightarrow{\;\;g\;\;} F(C)
\end{array} \tag{17}$$

As F is a dense functor, there is an object $M \in \mathrm{Ob}\ \mathbf{K}$, such that $M = F(X)$ for some object $X \in \mathrm{Ob}\ \mathbf{C}$, and there is an isomorphism $u: M \to H$. This gives us Diagram (18) in the category $\mathbf{K}$.

$$\begin{array}{c}
F(B) \\
f{\circ}u \uparrow \\
F(X) \xrightarrow{\;\;g{\circ}u\;\;} F(C)
\end{array} \tag{18}$$

As F is a full functor, there are morphisms $k \in \mathrm{Hom}_{\mathbf{C}}(X, B)$ and $h \in \mathrm{Hom}_{\mathbf{C}}(X, C)$ such that $F(k) = f{\circ}u$ and $F(h) = g{\circ}u$. It gives us Diagram (19) in the category $\mathbf{C}$.

$$\begin{array}{c}
B \\
k \uparrow \\
X \xrightarrow{\;\;h\;\;} C
\end{array} \tag{19}$$

Using properties of products (cf., for example, (Herrlich and Strecker, 1973)), we transform Diagram (19) into Diagram (20), in which the morphism q is defined in a unique way.

$$
\begin{array}{ccc}
& p_B & \\
B \xleftarrow{\hspace{1cm}} & & B \times C \\
k \uparrow & \nearrow{q} & \downarrow p_C \\
X \xrightarrow[\hspace{1cm}]{} & & C \\
& h &
\end{array}
\tag{20}
$$

The functor F maps Diagram (20) into the commutative diagram (21).

$$
\begin{array}{ccc}
& F(p_B) & \\
F(B) \xleftarrow{\hspace{1cm}} & & F(B \times C) \\
F(k) \uparrow & \nearrow{F(q)} & \downarrow F(p_C) \\
F(X) \xrightarrow[\hspace{1cm}]{} & & F(C) \\
& F(h) &
\end{array}
\tag{21}
$$

As u is an isomorphism, it is possible to extend Diagram (21) to Diagram (22).

$$
\begin{array}{ccc}
& F(p_B) & \\
F(B) \xleftarrow{\hspace{1cm}} & & F(B \times C) \\
F(k) \uparrow & \nearrow{F(q)} & \downarrow F(p_C) \\
f \nearrow F(X) \xrightarrow[F(h)]{} & & F(C) \nearrow \\
u^{-1} & g & \\
H & &
\end{array}
\tag{22}
$$

By construction, Diagram (22) is commutative and we have two equalities: $F(p_B) \circ v = f$ and $F(p_C) \circ v = g$ where $v = F(q) \circ u^{-1}$. Indeed,

$$F(p_B) \circ v = F(p_B) \circ F(q) \circ u^{-1} = F(p_B \circ q) \circ u^{-1}$$
$$= F(k) \circ u^{-1} = f \circ u \circ u^{-1} = f$$

as $u \circ u^{-1} = 1_H$.

In a similar way, we have

$$F(p_C) \circ v = F(p_C) \circ F(q) \circ u^{-1} = F(p_C \circ q) \circ u^{-1}$$
$$= F(h) \circ u^{-1} = g \circ u \circ u^{-1} = g$$

Thus, for any object H from the category $\mathbf{K}$, morphisms $f\colon H \to F(B)$ and $g\colon H \to F(C)$ are extended to the morphism $v\colon H \to F(B{\times}C)$. To prove that $F(B{\times}C)$ is the product $F(B){\times}F(C)$ in the category $\mathbf{K}$, we have to demonstrate that the morphism v is uniquely determined by the pair f and g.

Let us assume that there is another morphism $r\colon H \to F(B{\times}C)$ such that $F(p_B) \circ r = f$ and $F(p_C) \circ r = g$. It gives us the commutative diagram (23) in the category $\mathbf{K}$, which is presented below.

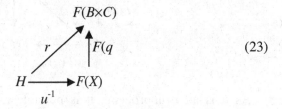

$$(23)$$

As $r \neq F(q) \circ u^{-1}$, we have $r \circ u \neq F(q)$. At the same time, there is a morphism $t\colon X \to B{\times}C$ such that $F(t) = r \circ u$, $p_B \circ t = k$ and $p_C \circ t = h$ because F is a full functor. Uniqueness of the morphism $q\colon X \to B{\times}C$ implies $t = q$. Consequently, $F(t) = r \circ u = F(q)$ and $r = F(q) \circ u^{-1}$. Thus, the morphism v is uniquely determined by the pair f and g. As H is an arbitrary object from the category $\mathbf{K}$, $F(B{\times}C)$ is the product $F(B){\times}F(C)$ in $\mathbf{K}$. This means that Diagram (21) defines the direct sum of categorical information operator FO_1 and FO_2 over $\mathbf{K}$.

Theorem is proved.

The categorical representation of information dynamics allows many interpretations, including computational formalisms, in which morphisms represent computational processes. Models of computations in categories are considered in Section 6.

5. Functorial Representation of Information Dynamics

Let us take a categorical representation of the system IF(R) in a category **C**. Objects from **C** stand for states/phases of IF(R) and morphisms from **C** represent relations between states/phases of IF(R). Functorial information operators describe transitions between states/phases of IF(R) with preservation of relations.

Definition 5.1. A *functorial information operator* Opf(I) over the category **C** is an endofunctor in IF**C**.

Functorial information operators give a model of information that reflects not only changes of the infological system (as categorical information operators do) but also alterations in information processing after some portion of information is received and accepted. For instance, let us consider a person A who knows only one language – English. Then she learns Spanish. Learning is naturally represented by information reception (Burgin, 2001). In the formal model, learning acquires the form of information operator action. This action changes the system of knowledge of A, namely, knowledge of Spanish is added. Due to these changes, A begins understanding Spanish texts, i.e., information processing of A also changes are modeled by functorial information operators.

Definition 5.1 and properties of functors imply the following result.

Theorem 5.1. All functorial information operators over the category **C** form a monoid **FIO$_C$** where the identical endofunctor is the identity of this monoid.

Corollary 5.1. The monoid **CIO$_C$** is a polygon over the monoid **FIO$_C$**.

Proposition 12.2 from (Herrlich and Strecker, 1973) implies the following result.

Proposition 5.1. A functorial information operator preserves identities, isomorphisms, sections, retractions, and commutative triangles.

Proposition 12.8 from (Herrlich and Strecker, 1973) implies the following result.

Proposition 5.2. A faithful functorial information operator reflects monomorphisms, epimorphisms, bimorphisms, constant morphisms, coconstant morphisms, zero morphisms, and commutative triangles.

Proof of Theorem 4.9 gives us the following result.

Proposition 5.3. A dense full functorial information operator preserves products.

Having two types of information operators, it is natural to look for relations between these types.

Definition 5.2. A categorical information operator O over the category $\mathbf{C}$ is called *f-categorical* if there is a mapping FO: Mor $\mathbf{C} \to$ Mor $\mathbf{C}$ such that $FO(1_A) = 1_A$ for any object A from $\mathbf{C}$ and for any morphism $f: A \to C$ from $\mathbf{C}$, $FO(f)$ is the unique morphism that makes the following diagram commutative.

$$
\begin{array}{ccc}
 & FO(f) & \\
B & \longrightarrow & D \\
O(A) \uparrow & & \uparrow O(C) \\
A & \longrightarrow & C \\
 & f &
\end{array}
\qquad (24)
$$

Theorem 5.2. Any *f*-categorical information operator O over a category $\mathbf{C}$ induces a functorial information operator FO over the category $\mathbf{C}$.

Proof. We need only to show that the second condition from the definition of a covariant functor is true (cf. Section 2).

Let us consider an *f*-categorical information operator O over the category $\mathbf{C}$ and two morphisms $f: A \to C$ and $k: C \to H$. By Definition 5.2, it gives us the commutative Diagram (25).

$$
\begin{array}{ccccc}
 & FO(f) & & FO(k) & \\
B & \longrightarrow & D & \longrightarrow & G \\
O(A) \uparrow & & O(C) \uparrow & & \uparrow O(H) \\
A & \longrightarrow & C & \longrightarrow & H \\
 & f & & k &
\end{array}
\qquad (25)
$$

At the same time, we also have the commutative Diagram (26).

$$FO(k \circ f)$$
$$B \longrightarrow G$$

$$O(A) \uparrow \qquad O(H) \uparrow \qquad\qquad (26)$$

$$A \longrightarrow H$$
$$k \circ f$$

It is possible to transform Diagram (25) into Diagram (27).

$$FO(k) \circ FO(f)$$
$$B \longrightarrow G$$

$$O(A) \uparrow \qquad\qquad O(H) \uparrow \qquad\qquad (27)$$

$$A \longrightarrow H$$
$$k \circ f$$

Comparing commutative squares (26) and (27), we see that uniqueness of $FO(k \circ f)$ implies that $FO(f \circ k) = FO(f) \circ FO(k)$. Thus, FO is an endofunctor.

Theorem is proved.

It is interesting to find conditions when a categorical information operator also is a functorial information operator. Let us consider a category **C** with pushouts and the following condition (**PO**):

If O is a categorical information operator and Diagram (28) is a pushout square, then it is possible to extend Diagram (28) to the commutative Diagram (29) where u is an isomorphism.

$$g$$
$$B \longrightarrow D$$

$$O(A) \uparrow \qquad\qquad \uparrow h \qquad\qquad (28)$$

$$A \longrightarrow C$$
$$f$$

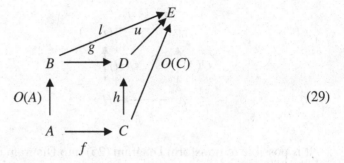

$$(29)$$

By properties of pushouts, the external square in Diagram (29) is also a pushout.

Theorem 5.3. A categorical information epoperator O over the category **C** is also (or more exactly, induces) a functorial information operator FO over **C** if O satisfies the condition (PO).

Proof. Taking a categorical information operator O, we know that it is defined for objects of the category **C**. To make it a functorial information operator FO over the category **C**, we need to define it for morphisms of the category **C** and show that this operator preserves sequential composition of morphisms and identity morphisms.

Let us consider a morphism $f: A \to C$. Then the categorical information operator O determines a morphism $O(A): A \to B$. This gives us the following diagram.

$$
\begin{array}{c}
B \\
O(A) \uparrow \\
A \xrightarrow{\ \ f\ \ } C
\end{array}
\qquad (30)
$$

Properties of the category **C** allow us to build the pushout (31) for Diagram (30).

$$
\begin{array}{ccc}
B & \xrightarrow{\ g\ } & D \\
O(A) \uparrow & & \uparrow h \\
A & \xrightarrow{\ f\ } & C
\end{array}
\qquad (31)
$$

By Property PO, Diagram (31) allows us to obtain Diagram (32).

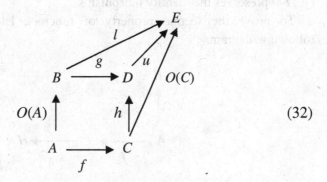

$$(32)$$

This makes it possible to define the mapping $FO_{ObC} : \mathrm{Ob}\ \mathbf{C} \to \mathrm{Ob}\ \mathbf{C}$ and the mapping $FO_{MorC} : \mathrm{Mor}\ \mathbf{C} \to \mathrm{Mor}\ \mathbf{C}$ such that $FO_{ObC}(A) = B$, $FO_{ObC}(C) = E$, and $FO_{MorC}(f) = u \circ g$. It gives us the commutative Diagram (33).

$$
\begin{array}{ccc}
FO(A) = B & \xrightarrow{\;FO(f) = u \circ g\;} & FO(C) = D \\
\uparrow{\scriptstyle O(A)} & & \uparrow{\scriptstyle h} \\
A & \xrightarrow{\quad f \quad} & C
\end{array}
\tag{33}
$$

Now it is necessary to check for $FO = (FO_{ObC} , FO_{MorC})$ properties that define functors (cf. Section 2, Definition 2.3).

In the case when $C = A$ and $f = 1_A$, we have the following diagram.

$$
\begin{array}{ccc}
B & \xrightarrow{\;1_A\;} & B \\
\uparrow{\scriptstyle O(A)} & & \uparrow{\scriptstyle O(A)} \\
A & \xrightarrow{\;1_A\;} & A
\end{array}
\tag{34}
$$

It is easy to check that Diagram (34) is a pushout. Thus, $FO(1_A) = 1_A$, i.e., FO preserves the identity morphisms.

To prove the second property of functors, let us consider the following diagram.

$$
\begin{array}{c}
B \\
O(A) \uparrow \\
A \xrightarrow{\ f\ } C \xrightarrow{\ k\ } H
\end{array}
\tag{35}
$$

By Condition (PO), there is the pushout (36) for the pair of morphisms $(O(A), f)$.

$$
\begin{array}{ccc}
B & \xrightarrow{FO(f)} & E \\
O(A) \uparrow & & \uparrow O(C) \\
A & \xrightarrow{\ f\ } & C
\end{array}
\tag{36}
$$

Diagrams (35) and (36) give us Diagram (37).

$$
\begin{array}{c}
E \\
O(C) \uparrow \\
C \xrightarrow{\ k\ } H
\end{array}
\tag{37}
$$

By Condition (PO), there is the pushout (38) for the pair of morphisms $(O(C), h)$.

$$
\begin{array}{ccc}
 & FO(k) & \\
E & \longrightarrow & D \\
O(C) \uparrow & & \uparrow O(H) \\
C & \longrightarrow & H \\
 & k &
\end{array}
\qquad (38)
$$

In a similar way, we build the pushout (39) for the pair of morphisms $(O(A), h{\circ}f)$.

$$
\begin{array}{ccc}
 & FO(k{\circ}f) & \\
B & \longrightarrow & G \\
O(A) \uparrow & & \uparrow O(H) \\
A & \longrightarrow & H \\
 & k{\circ}f &
\end{array}
\qquad (39)
$$

Combining Diagrams (36) and (38), we obtain commutative Diagram (40).

$$
\begin{array}{ccccc}
 & FO(f) & & FO(k) & \\
B & \longrightarrow & D & \longrightarrow & Q \\
O(A) \uparrow & & O(C) \uparrow & & \uparrow O(H) \\
A & \longrightarrow & C & \longrightarrow & H \\
 & f & & k &
\end{array}
\qquad (40)
$$

As (39) is a pushout, we can build the following commutative diagram.

$$
\begin{array}{ccc}
 & & Q \\
FO(k) \circ FO(f) & \quad r & \\
B & \longrightarrow & G \quad O(H) \\
 & FO(k{\circ}f) & \\
O(A) \uparrow & \uparrow O(H) & \\
A & \longrightarrow & H \\
 & k{\circ}f &
\end{array}
\qquad (41)
$$

From Diagram (41), we have $G = Q$ and $r \circ O(H) = O(H) = 1_G \circ O(H)$. By the initial conditions, O is a categorical information epoperator. Thus, $O(H)$ is an epimorphism. By properties of epimorphisms, $r = 1_G$. Consequently, $FO(f) \circ FO(k) = FO(k \circ f)$. It means that FO is a covariant functor because f and k are arbitrary morphisms from the category $\mathbf{C}$.

Theorem is proved.

6. Computations and Automata in Categories

There are several approaches to representing computation in the categorical setting. Here we consider two of them. In the first one, a categorical model of such a theoretical computational structure as λ-calculus is constructed and studied. The second approach is based on the concept of an automaton in a category.

One of the classical models of algorithms is the λ-calculus constructed by Church (1932/33). While Turing machine has served for many years as a model for computers (cf., for example (Burgin, 2005)), the λ-calculus has been used as a theoretical tool for building programming languages. For instance, such a popular programming language as LISP (McCarthy, 1960) and its dialects, such as Scheme (Abelson, et al, 1996)), are based on the λ-calculus. In essence, these and other functional programming languages, such as ML, Erlang or Haskell, explicitly reflect the structure of the λ-calculus. Moreover there are also connections between the λ-calculus and such a popular in 1960s programming language as ALGOL (cf., (Landin, 1965)).

However, functional programming languages use more developed structures than the λ-calculus. Namely, the λ-calculus was oriented by its creator on working only with one type of information representation – terms of the λ-calculus. At the same time, to be computationally efficient, functional programming languages allow working with different types of data. Church (1940) introduced the typed λ-calculus, in which terms have types, to get around the problem of Russel's paradox in the case of Frege's logic. To make the λ-calculus closer to computational practice, the typed λ-calculus is used now (cf., for example (Barendregt, 1992)).

Usually types are considered as objects in the category modeling the typed λ-calculus, while terms, which represent programs or algorithms, play the role of morphisms. This brought researchers to a Cartesian closed category (Lambek, 1980). However, it is more natural to take data of one and the same type as objects in the category modeling typed λ-calculus because computation transforms data and not necessarily types.

Categorical representation of the typed λ-calculus allowed researchers to study semantics of programming languages or specification languages.

The automaton approach to the categorical modeling in the theory of computation has three versions. In one of them, the automaton is the whole category, in the second approach a category of automata as objects and their homomorphisms as morphisms is built, while in the third approach, the automaton is constructed using elements of the category.

In the traditional approach, an accepting finite automaton **A** is considered as a system $\langle \Sigma, Q, F \, q_0 \,, \delta \rangle$ that consists of three sets where Σ is a finite set of *input symbols* called the alphabet of **A**, Q is a finite *set of states*, and F is a subset of Q called the set of *final* (in some cases, *accepting*) states of **A**, one element q_0 from Q called the *initial* or *start state* of **A**, and one binary relation or function $\delta: \Sigma \times Q \to Q$ called the transition function/relation of **A**. In the context of category theory, it is possible to treat **A** as a category in which objects are states that belong to Q and morphisms/arrows are triples (p, σ, q) in $Q \times \Sigma \times Q$ or relations $\sigma : Q \to Q$. This allows one to study automata by methods of category theory.

On the other hand, we can define homomorphism of finite automata as pairs of mappings of the sets Σ and Q such that preserve final and initial states, as well as the transition function/relation. Taking automata as objects and their homomorphisms as morphisms we build a category of finite automata. This also allows one to study automata by methods of category theory.

One more way to immerse automata into categories is to take an abstract category **C** with direct products and to define an automaton **A** in the category **C** as a system $\langle \Sigma, Q, F \, q_0 \,, \delta \rangle$ that consists of objects Σ as the *input object*, Q as the *state object*, and a subobject F of Q as the *final object*, a subobject q_0 of Q as the *initial object* of **A**, and a morphism $\delta: \Sigma \times Q \to Q$ called the transition morphism of **A**. This also allows one to study automata by methods of category theory.

Moreover, modeled by a physical system R, an abstract automaton (state transition machine) becomes an information automaton because it performs information operations and produces information. Indeed, when a symbol comes to the system R, it has to recognize this symbol (the first information operation), to find whether the symbol belongs to the alphabet of the automaton (the second information operation), and if it is true, to make a corresponding state transition, which also includes information operations. To recognize a symbol means to get correct information about this symbol's type. Finding whether a symbol belongs to some set, e.g., to the alphabet of the automaton, is also information production. In this context, the states of the automaton are naturally interpreted as states of an infological system because the whole system R plays the role of this infological system.

One more connection between categories and computations is studied by Burstall and Rydeheard (1985). They interpret constructions in categories as computer programs and such constructions are often abstract and not related to a particular category, but valid for all categories equipped with certain properties, e.g., for categories having products or pushouts.

Several conferences on categories and computer science were organized (cf., (Gray and Scedrov, 1989; Fourman, *et al*, 1992; Moggi and Rosolini, 1997)). Walters (1992) worte a textbook on category theory and its applications in computer science.

7. Conclusion

Obtained results bring us to the following open problems.

1. In Theorem 5.2, conditions for a categorical information operator to be a functorial information operator are found. It would be interesting to find other conditions when a categorical information operator is a functorial information operator, as well as conditions when a functorial information operator is a categorical information operator.

2. Functorial information operators form a category with natural transformations of endofunctors as morphisms. An interesting direction in the categorical information theory is to study properties of categories of functorial information operators.

3. Categorical information operators form a category with operator transformations as morphisms. An interesting direction in the categorical information theory is to study properties of categories of categorical information operators.

4. One more interesting problem is to find conditions when a categorical information operator preserves (reflects) definite classes of objects. For instance, in this paper, it is done for products in categories.

5. In this paper, it is demonstrated that under definite conditions, functorial information operators preserve products in categories. Thus, an appealing problem is to find conditions when a functorial information operator preserves (reflects) definite classes of objects.

6. In this paper, it is demonstrated that under definite conditions, functorial information operators preserve identities, isomorphisms, sections, retractions, and commutative triangles. Thus, a worthy of note problem is to find conditions when a functorial information operator preserves definite classes of diagrams.

7. In this paper, it is demonstrated that faithful functorial information operators reflect monomorphisms, epimorphisms, bimorphisms, constant morphisms, coconstant morphisms, zero morphisms, and commutative triangles. Thus, a worthy of note problem is to find conditions when a functorial information operator reflects definite classes of diagrams.

8. In this paper, we studied three operations with categorical information operators: sequential composition, free sum, and direct sum. However, there are much more natural operations with information (Burgin, 1997a). Many of them are used in information processing. Thus, an important problem is to construct other natural information operations with categorical information operators and to study their properties.

9. Similarly, an important problem is to construct different natural information operations with functorial information operators and to study their properties.

10. It is possible to use the category-theoretical model of information constructed in this paper for mathematical representation and

study of various information processes, such as information transmission, processing and storage. Discovery of general laws of information processes on the level of abstract categories would allow researchers to find important regularities in the diversity of information systems, applying these regularities to the further development of information technology.

References

Abelson, H., Sussman, G.J. and Sussman, J. (1996) *Structure and Interpretation of Computer Programs*, MIT Press

Abramsky, S. and Duncan, R. (2005) A categorical quantum logic, Preprint in Physics quant-ph/0512114 (electronic edition: http://arXiv.org)

Anderson, B. D. O. (1975) A control theorist looks at abstract nonsense, in *Proceedings of the First International Symposium, Lecture Notes in Computer Science*, v. 25, Springer, pp. 35–50

Arbib, M.A. and Manes, E. G. (1975) A categorist's view of automata and systems, in *Proceedings of the First International Symposium, Lecture Notes in Computer Science*, v. 25, Springer, pp. 51–64

Baez, J. and Stay, M. (2009) Physics, Topology, Logic and Computation: A Rosetta Stone, Preprint in Physics gr-qc/ 0903.0340 (electronic edition: http://arXiv.org)

Barendregt, H. (1992) Lambda Calculi with Types, *J. Functional Programming*, v. 2, No. 3, pp. 367–374

Bar-Hillel, Y. and Carnap, R. (1958) Semantic Information, *British J. of Philosophical Sciences*, v. 4, No. 3, pp. 147–157

Barr, M. and Wells, C. (1983) *Toposes, Triples and Theories*, Springer Verlag, Berlin,

Barwise, J. and Seligman, J. (1997) *Information Flow: The Logic of Distributed Systems*, Cambridge Tracts in Theoretical Computer Science 44, Cambridge University Press, Cambridge Tracts in Theoretical Computer Science

Burgin, M. (1970) Categories with involution and relations in γ-categories, *Transactions of the Moscow Mathematical Society*, v. 22, pp. 161-228 (translated from Russian)

Burgin, M. (1983) Multiple computations and Kolmogorov complexity for such processes, *Notices of the Academy of Sciences of the USSR*, v. 27, No. 2, pp. 793–797

Burgin, M. (1995) Algorithmic Approach in the Dynamic Theory of Information, *Notices of the Russian Academy of Sciences*, v.342, No. 1, pp. 7–10

Burgin, M. (1997) *Fundamental Structures of Knowledge and Information*, Academy for Information Sciences, Kiev (in Russian)

Burgin, M. (1997a) Information Algebras, *Control Systems and Machines*, No.6, pp. 5–16 (in Russian)

Burgin, M. (1998/1999) Information and Transformation, *Transformation*, No.1, pp. 48–53 (in Polish)

Burgin, M. (2001) Information in the Context of Education, *The Journal of Interdisciplinary Studies*, v. 14, pp. 155–166

Burgin, M. (2003) Information Theory: A Multifaceted Model of Information, *Entropy*, v. 5, No. 2, pp. 146–160

Burgin, M. (2003a) Information: Problem, Paradoxes, and Solutions, *TripleC*, v. 1, No.1, pp. 53–70

Burgin, M. (2004) Data, Information, and Knowledge, *Information*, v. 7, No.1, pp. 47–57

Burstall, R.M. and Rydeheard, D. (1985) Computing with Categories, *LNCS*, v. 240, pp. 506–517

Capurro, R., Fleissner, P., and Hofkirchner, W. (1999) Is a Unified Theory of Information Feasible? In *The Quest for a unified theory of information*, Proceedings of the 2nd International Conference on the Foundations of Information Science, pp. 9–30

Church, A. (1932/33) A Set of Postulates for the Foundations of Logic, *Annals of Mathematics*, v. 33, pp. 346–366; v. 34, pp. 839–864

Church, A. (1940) A formulation of the simple theory of types, *Journal of Symbolic Logic*, v. 5, pp. 56–68

Cooper, W.S. (1978) *Foundations of Logico-Linguistics*, D. Reidel P.C., Dordrecht/Boston

Ehresmann, A.C. and Vanbremeersch, J.-P. (1987) Hierarchical Evolutive Systems: A mathematical model for complex systems, *Bull. of Math. Biology*, v. 49, No.1, pp. 13–50

Ehresmann, A.C. and Vanbremeersch J.P. (2007) *Memory Evolutive Systems: Hierarchy, Emergence, Cognition*, Elsevier Science

Ehrig, H. and Kreowski, H.-J. (1975) Power and initial automata in pseudoclosed categories, in *Proceedings of the First International Symposium, Lecture Notes in Computer Science*, v. 25, Springer, pp. 144–150

Fourman, M. P., Johnstone, P. T. and Pitts, A. M. (Eds.) (1992) *Applications of categories in computer science*, Proceedings of the London Mathematical Society Symposium, Durham, LMSLNS, v. 177, Cambridge University Press, Cambridge, 1991

Flükiger, D.F. (1995) *Contributions towards a Unified Concept of Information*, Doctoral Thesis, University of Berne

Goldblatt, R. (1979) *Topoi: The Categorical analysis of Logic*, North-Holland P.C., Amsterdam

Gray, J.W. and Scedrov, A. (Eds.) (1989) Categories in Computer Science and Logic, Contemporary Mathematics, v. 92, AMS

Halpern, J.Y. and Moses, Y. (1985) Towards a theory of knowledge and ignorance, in *Logics and Models of Concurrent Systems*, Springer-Verlag, New York, pp. 459–476

Herrlich, H. and Strecker, G.E. (1973) *Category Theory*, Allyn and Bacon Inc., Boston

Johnstone, P.T. (1977) *Topos Theory*, Academic Press, London/New York/ San Francisco

Lambek, J. (1980) From λ-calculus to Cartesian closed categories, in *Essays on Combinatory Logic, Lambda Calculus and Formalism*, Academic Press, New York, pp. 375–402

Lambek, J. and Scott, P.J. (1986) *Introduction to Higher-order Categorical Logic*, Cambridge University Press, Cambridge

Landin, P. (1965) A correspondence between ALGOL 60 and Church's lambda-notation, Comm. ACM, v. 8 , 89–101, 158–165

Levich, A. P., and Solov'yov, A.V. (1999) Category-Functor Modeling of Natural Systems, *Cybernetics and Systems*, v.30, No.6, pp.571–585

McCarthy, J. (1960) Recursive functions of symbolic expressions and their computation by machine, *Communications of the ACM*, v. 4 , pp. 184–195

Manes, E. G. (Ed.) (1975) Category Theory Applied to Computation and Control, in *Proceedings of the First International Symposium, Lecture Notes in Computer Science*, v. 25, Springer

Manin, Y.I. (1999) *Classical computing, quantum computing, and Shor's factoring algorithm*, preprint in Quantum Physics, (arXiv:quant-ph/9903008)

Melik-Gaikazyan, I. V. (1997) *Information processes and reality*, Nauka, Moscow (in Russian, English summary)

Minsky, M. (1986) *The Society of Mind*, Simon and Schuster, New York

Mizzaro, S. (2001) Towards a theory of epistemic information, Information Modelling and Knowledge Bases, v. 12, *IOS Press*, Amsterdam, pp. 1–20

Moggi, E. (1991) Notions of computation and monads, *Information and Computation*, v. 93 , No. 1, pp. 55 - 92

Moggi, E. and Rosolini, G. (Eds.) (1997) *The seventh biennial conference on categories and computer science*, Lect. Notes in Comp. Science, v. 1290, Springer

Power, J. and Robinson, E. (1997) Premonoidal categories and notions of computation, *Mathematical Structures in Computer Science*, v. 7, No. 5, pp. 453 - 468

Rocchi, P. and Panella, O. (2007) Acquisition of Information is Achieved by the Measurement Process in Classical and Quantum Physics, in *AIP Conf. Proceedings*, v. 962, pp. 206–214

Scott, P. (2000) Some aspects of categories in computer science, in *Handbook of Algebra*, v. 2, Elsevier, Amsterdam, pp. 3–78

Shevrin, L.N. (1991) Semigroups, in *General Algebra*, v.2, pp. 11–191 (in Russian)

Shreider, Y. A. (1967) On Semantic Aspects of Information Theory, *Information and Cybernetics*, Moscow, Radio, pp. 15–47 (in Russian)

Vanbremeersch, J.P. Chandler, J. and Ehresmann, A.C. (1996) Are interactions between different time-scales a characteristic of complexity? in *Actes du Symposium ECHO*, Amiens (pp. 162–167).

Walters, R. F. C. (1992) *Categories and computer science*, Cambridge University Press, Cambridge

Weinert, H.J. (1980) S-sets and semigroups, *Semigroup Forum*, v. 19, No. 1, pp. 1–78

CHAPTER 3

MATHEMATICS AS A BIOLOGICAL PROCESS

G. J. Chaitin

http://www.umcs.maine.edu/~chaitin

This paper is the transcript of a talk given 5 June 2007 in Boston at the Wistar Retrospective Symposium.

I've been learning some biology at this meeting, but what can I contribute to the discussion? The answer is, not much. I do discrete mathematics, in fact, metamathematics. In my work I use a notion of complexity, and it would be great if this complexity concept had something to do with biology. Unfortunately it doesn't.

Biology deals with very complicated systems, but I don't think my work on complexity can be applied to biology. Instead I've taken the idea of complexity from biology and I'm using it to try to understand what mathematics can and cannot achieve. That's called metamathematics. So in this talk you are going to see an idea from biology applied in an unexpected way.

My story begins about a century ago with David Hilbert, a famous German mathematician, who believed that mathematical truth is absolutely rigorous, completely black or white, never gray. And he wanted to demonstrate that in the most clear-cut, straightforward possible way. He wanted to formalize all of mathematics.

Hilbert was responding to problems in the foundations of mathematics provoked by Cantor's theory of infinite sets. There were many paradoxes, paradoxes discussed by such people as Bertrand Russell and Frege and many others. Hilbert's proposal for dealing with this crisis was formalism.

Hilbert's plan for avoiding contradictions and paradoxes in mathematics was to make mathematical reasoning extremely precise. He believed that mathematics is absolute truth, totally black or white. Therefore, he reasoned, it ought to be possible for us all to agree on a finite set of axioms to use as the basis for all of math. And we should use symbolic logic, not a natural language, because natural languages are ambiguous.

In other words, Hilbert's goal was to formalize mathematics completely, to set up an axiomatic system in the style of Euclid, but for **all** of mathematics. His plan was to write down a list of axioms, using formal logic, for all of mathematics. And once we all agree on the rules of logic and on the axioms, then this will once and for all clarify what mathematics is, and how things should be done. Math will consist of everything you can prove from those axioms using these rules of logic.

The goal was to make everything completely **objective**, and to eliminate all subjectivity from mathematics. If somebody claims that they have a proof, done in this very formal way, with no missing steps, then it's completely mechanical to check whether the proof is correct or not. A machine can do it. You don't need any human referees. Well, you do need referees to say if the result is worth publishing, but you don't need anybody to check whether the proof is correct or not.

So this was Hilbert's idea. And once he found the correct rules of logic and the right list of axioms, he would then have to convince people that this was a good system that we should all use, and that it avoids all the paradoxes. So Hilbert's project was rather ambitious. But it starts with the simple idea that if mathematics really provides absolute truth, then it ought to be possible to formalize everything in precisely this way.

Some people really hated David Hilbert's idea. Since Hilbert was a German, you will not be surprised to hear that one of his severest critics was a Frenchman, Henri Poincaré. Poincaré compared Hilbert's proposal with that mythical Chicago machine — this was when Chicago had enormous slaughterhouses — where pigs go in one end of the machine and out come neatly wrapped sausages at the other end. Is mathematics just a sausage-making machine? Poincaré didn't think that it was, not at all.

But Poincaré's caustic remarks didn't deter Hilbert and his disciples.

So what happened next?

Well, for about thirty years it looked like Hilbert was making progress and would eventually succeed in carrying out this project. Then disaster struck...

Let me say, by the way, that Hilbert's formalist, axiomatic style survives in the Bourbaki school, which even though Bourbaki is now gone, is still very influential. Bourbaki was a group of French mathematicians who were traitors to French mathematics, because they preferred Hilbert's Prussian approach to Poincaré's. Even though Bourbaki has now disbanded, formalization's icy grip still rules mathematics, and this comes from Hilbert. The current fashion is that ideally a math paper should have **no** words, no diagrams, no examples, and no discussion of history or motivation, a very formalist view indeed.

Okay, so this was Hilbert's idea. But it was initially viewed as a **good** idea, because Hilbert didn't say that people should actually work in a logical language and publish machine-checkable proofs. The real goal was to make mathematics absolutely certain, completely rigorous. And most mathematicians thought that this ought to be possible since mathematical arguments are much more convincing than arguments in physics or in law.

So despite Poincaré's remarks, Hilbert's project sounded like a good idea, and a number of mathematicians worked on it for about thirty years. And then in 1931 in Vienna, Kurt Gödel, who initially was working to carry out Hilbert's program, showed that it couldn't be done. This is the famous 1931 **incompleteness** theorem of Kurt Gödel. The basic idea is that "I'm unprovable" is provable if and only if it's false.

I have only thirty minutes, so I'm not going to be able to explain Gödel's proof. It shows that Hilbert's program can't work, because the first step was to come up with an axiomatic system for all of math (and then to convince people to use it by showing that you don't get the contradictions and paradoxes that were bothering mathematicians). But what Gödel showed is that no finite set of axioms, no formal axiomatic theory, can include everything — there is no **theory of everything** for pure mathematics. That's what Gödel showed.

This was quite a shock, and in 1936 Alan Turing made things even worse. Turing found a much deeper reason for incompleteness. This is in Turing's famous 1936 paper "On computable numbers, with an

application to the *Entscheidungsproblem*." In a way, Turing's 1936 paper
creates the computer industry, because it talks about flexible, universal
machines and the idea of hardware and software. And besides
constructing a primitive kind of computer called a Turing machine, this
paper introduces the idea of the computer to pure mathematics as a
fundamental new concept.

However, I think that the most interesting thing about this paper isn't
its positive aspect, it's its negative aspect. The negative aspect of the
paper is that Turing shows that there are very basic things which cannot
be computed. And from uncomputability — from the existence of
mathematical questions where you cannot calculate the answers
systematically — Turing deduces a form of incompleteness, a new kind
of incompleteness theorem.

You see, if Hilbert had been right, and you had a formal axiomatic
system for all of math, you could systematically run through the tree of
all possible proofs. This would be very slow, but in principle you could
systematically look at all one-step proofs, two step proofs, three step
proofs, and that way you could mechanically generate all the theorems
starting from the axioms. And if you wanted to see whether something is
true or not, you just do that until either you find a proof that the result
you're interested in is true, or you find a proof that the result you're
interested in is false. This is why Poincaré mocked Hilbert's project
saying that it would make mathematics into a sausage machine.

What Turing showed in 1936 is that there can't be such a sausage
machine, because there are mathematical questions where you can't
systematically calculate the answer, and therefore you can't prove what
the answer is either, not in all individual cases. Because if you **could**,
then you could run through all possible proofs until you either find a
proof that the answer is "yes" or that the answer is "no," and this would
give you a mechanical procedure, an algorithm, for always calculating
the answer, which however cannot exist because of uncomputability. So
incompleteness is a corollary of uncomputability.

Turing's work is wonderful because it makes incompleteness much
more solid. Gödel's proof was too paradoxical: "I'm unprovable" is too
much like "This statement is false." Gödel's proof looks too close to the

paradoxes which were upsetting everybody. But Turing found a more basic reason that you can't have a formal theory for all of mathematics.

What about my own work? I haven't mentioned that yet.

What I've tried to add to this discussion of incompleteness is some kind of a notion of complexity. What's complexity? Well, there's certainly a lot of complexity in biological systems. At this meeting we've seen lots of examples of how amazingly complex some basic biological mechanisms are. But how do you define complexity? Well, there's lots of ways of defining complexity. And in fact you biologists don't give a precise definition, you just sort of know. You can recognize it when you see it.

But I'm a mathematician, so my idea was a definition of complexity that may not be useful in biology, but which I can use in metamathematics. I just look at the size of computer programs. I say that something has N bits of complexity if you need an N-bit program to calculate it. This is a very straightforward definition. I don't care how long this N-bit program takes to run. If the smallest program that calculates something is exactly a thousand bits long, I don't care if that program goes on working for billions and billions of years, as long as it finally yields the thing I'm interested in.

This is a very simple-minded measure of complexity that is not intended for use in practical applications. It's intended to apply in pure math. So what can you do with this idea, with this toy notion of complexity? I think it enables you to compare biology and mathematics. But first let me compare physics and biology, they're two extremes.

Theoretical physics is very beautiful because it's based on a small bunch of simple, elegant equations for the laws of physics. And most physicists hope to someday find a theory of everything, a set of equations which you can put on a T-shirt, otherwise what's the point, right? So that's what fundamental physics looks like.

Now let's contrast this with the situation in biology. Biology is very complicated and fascinating and full of surprises. You are never going to find a simple equation for your wife, for a human society, for the global economy, or for that enormous table of the catalytic reactions in the metabolism in every single cell. Biology is not at all like fundamental physics. In biology there are no simple equations. Biology is complicated, it's messy, it works.

Now let's look at pure mathematics, and see how it compares with physics at one extreme, a simple fundamental theory that applies to everything, and with biology, where things are very complicated, very surprising, very diverse, very messy. Well, obviously mathematics co-evolved with physics, right? Normally, you'd think that mathematics must be like theoretical physics, and that's what Hilbert thought. You know, one of the reasons I'm a pure mathematician rather than a biologist is that I don't have a good memory. French was my worst subject, but I could do well whenever there are a few fundamental principles and then in each individual case you have to derive the consequences. I could do that on the spot, but I was awful at remembering things.

But is mathematics really simple and elegant like physics? Surprisingly enough, using this idea of complexity that I sort of borrowed from biology, I can not only show that pure math is like biology, in fact it's even worse than biology, because it's **infinitely** complex, provably infinitely complex.

To repeat, physics, that's the idea of a simple theory for the entire universe, that's the idea that the universe looks complicated but is really very simple. And you show that by giving the equations, and presumably simple initial conditions, and then the big bang takes off, so in principle you can calculate the time-evolution of the entire universe step by step using the laws of physics. But in biology you don't expect things to be simple, you expect things to be wonderfully rich, complicated, frozen accidents, *bricolage*, things patched on top of other things.

How can I show that mathematics is closer to biology than to physics? Well, like this. Turing considers a problem that's called the **halting problem**. This is actually the basic idea in his 1936 paper. The halting problem is to decide in advance if a self-contained computer program will eventually stop. And the fundamental mathematical result in Turing's 1936 paper is that there is no general algorithmic solution to the halting problem. (This is how Turing shows that there are important things which can't be calculated.)

There's no way to calculate in advance whether a computer program will go on forever or will eventually stop. Of course, you can start running the program, and if it stops, you know it's stopped. But there is no general way to know at what point to give up and decide that you already gave it enough time, and if it hasn't halted yet, it's never going to. I'm talking about self-contained computer programs.

This is Turing's fundamental result. Now I'm going to change things a little bit. Instead of talking about individual computer programs, consider all possible computer programs, put them all in a bag, shake it well, close your eyes, pick a random computer program, and ask, what is the probability this computer program eventually halts. I call this number the halting probability Ω. It's a number between zero and one.

If every computer program halts, then the halting probability Ω is one. If no computer program halts, if they all search endlessly, then the halting probability Ω is zero. And since in actual fact some computer programs halt and some never halt, the halting probability is greater than zero and less than one.

This number Ω is very simply defined, it's just a probability, not a big deal. But it turns out that you cannot know the numerical value of Ω, you can't calculate it, because it's extremely valuable information and would enable you to answer many, many important mathematical questions.

I always think of writing out Ω in binary, in base-two, and of the infinite sequence of bits that come after the decimal point. These bits turn out to be incredibly valuable, because you can show that they are the most compressed way of giving answers to the halting problem. The bits of Ω are the best possible oracle for the halting problem.

What does Ω have to do with oracles? Well, supposing you could ask God yes/no questions, and you want to bother him as little as possible, the best thing to do is not to ask about individual cases of the halting problem. The best way to get answers to the halting problem is to ask what are the initial bits of the halting probability. Ω is the diamond you get by compressing the coal of Turing's halting problem. Once you get rid of all the redundancy, it's not surprising that what comes out looks random, because once you eliminate all the redundancy from anything, what's left doesn't have any structure. If it had any structure, then we could compress it some more.

In the definition of the halting probability Ω, how do I pick a program at random? Well, the computer programs are written in binary, and for every bit of the program you do an independent toss of a fair coin. So each N-bit program that halts contributes 2^{-N} to the halting probability Ω. And for this to work and give a finite sum instead of diverging to infinity, it's important to use self-delimiting programs. In other words, no extension of a valid program is a valid program. But this is rather technical and I don't have time to explain it.

Okay, so this number Ω, its bits look completely random. In fact, according to classical Shannon information theory, anything that's been compressed as much as possible seems structureless or random, for example, Gaussian noise. Because if there were any structure, you could use that to compress the information more. In fact, if you use a file-compression program on a computer, for example, LZW compression, the stuff that comes out may be your precious file, but it looks pretty meaningless once you've compressed it, because if it didn't, that means the compression program didn't do a good job.

Now I come to the punch line of my talk. The point of all this is that the bits of the number Ω are an example of irreducible complexity. They are maximally unknowable information in pure mathematics itself. In a way the bits of Ω are the DNA for all of mathematics. And they're the proof that mathematics is infinitely complex, and therefore even worse than biology. Biology is enormously complex, but it has **finite** complexity. But pure math, I can prove that that has **infinite** complexity.

Let me explain this better. Let's say you want to calculate, you want to know the numerical value of Ω with a certain degree of precision, say, N bits of precision. You want to know the first N bits after the decimal point, which amounts to knowing the numerical value of Ω to one part in 2^N. To be able to calculate those first N bits, you unfortunately will need to use an N-bit program. So you might as well just write them out from a table without doing any calculating.

If I wanted to misuse Kantian terminology, I would say "the thing in itself" is the only way to comprehend the bits of Ω. You can exhibit them, but you can't really calculate them.

Let me explain this differently. Why are the bits of Ω maximally unknowable and infinitely complex? Well, let's say that you have a formal mathematical theory which enables you to prove that, say, the tenth bit of Ω is a 1, or that the ninety-ninth bit of Ω is a 0. Well, any mathematical theory that enables you to prove what are the values of the first N bits of the halting probability, has to have N bits of axioms.

Of course, you can have an axiom that directly tells you what the first N bits of the halting probability are. Anything can be proved if you are willing to add it as a new axiom. But in the case of Ω, that's the only way to proceed, that's the only way to be able to use mathematical proof to determine the first N bits. In other words, Ω has irreducible complexity. The only way to get N bits of Ω out of a mathematical theory is to put all that complexity in, which means you're not using reasoning. You can prove anything by adding it as a new axiom, and in this case that is the very best you can do.

Every one of these bits is an independent atomic mathematical fact, it's one bit of mathematical creativity. Every one of these bits is a complete surprise. It's a mathematical fact which has no connection with any other mathematical fact, or at least with any other bit of Ω. In other words, if you knew the first million bits of the halting probability, it wouldn't help you to get the next bit. If you knew all the even bits, it wouldn't help you to get any of the odd bits. It's very much like independent tosses of a fair coin, even though Ω is mathematically defined in a very straightforward way.

So this is a place where mathematical truth is irreducible. What I've basically done is I've gotten irreducible complexity by compressing all the redundancy out of individual cases of Turing's halting problem. Once you remove all the redundancy, it's not surprising that what you have left cannot be compressed any more and is irreducibly complex. What this all shows is that if you're interested in the value of individual bits of Ω, then you're in big trouble.

Of course, one possible reaction to all of this is "Well, I don't care about the halting probability!" But since Ω is part of pure math and is irreducibly complex, and it's an infinite number of bits, this shows that pure math as a whole is infinitely complicated, and therefore in a sense even worse than biology.

Okay, how has the world of mathematics adjusted to all of this? Well, the basic answer is that nobody wants to hear this message, and pure mathematicians go on as if Hilbert were right, and as if Bourbaki were still in fashion.

What about Gödel and Turing? What do they think are the consequences of their own work? What do they think all this says about the human mind and human capabilities?

Gödel himself did not think that the incompleteness theorem limits the capability of human mathematicians. Gödel's view is that human beings have a divine spark which enables them to directly intuit mathematical truth, to directly perceive the Platonic world of mathematical ideas. Gödel has faith that if a mathematical question is important, using this divine spark, mathematicians will eventually be able to settle it. He disagrees with the standard interpretation of his result, as showing limitations on what human beings can achieve. Rebecca Goldstein explains this very well in her book on Gödel called *Incompleteness*.

What about Turing? Turing is a very different kettle of fish. Turing wrote one of the famous papers on artificial intelligence, in fact, one of the first papers on artificial intelligence. Turing believed that human beings are machines, and that computers can be programmed to think like a human being. No divine spark, none at all!

I don't know whether we have a divine spark or we're just machines, I think maybe there's a little bit of **both**. And therefore I think that it's important that each individual make a decision, you know, which do you prefer, and does their best to do something about it.

References

Goldstein R. (2005) *Incompleteness: The Proof and Paradox of Kurt Gödel*, Norton, New York.

Malone D. (2007) *Dangerous Knowledge*, TV program on Cantor, Boltzmann, Gödel and Turing broadcast in the UK by BBC 4, *http://video.google.com/videoplay?docid=-5122859998068380459#*

Byers W. (2007) *How Mathematicians Think: Using Ambiguity, Contradiction, and Paradox to Create Mathematics*, Princeton University Press.

Chaitin G. (2007) *Thinking about Gödel and Turing: Essays on Complexity, 1970–2007*, World Scientific, Singapore.

CHAPTER 4

INFORMATION, CAUSATION AND COMPUTATION

John Collier

Durban, South Africa
collierj@ukzn.ac.za

Causation can be understood as a computational process once we understand causation in informational terms. I argue that if we see processes as information channels, then causal processes are most readily interpreted as the transfer of information from one state to another. This directly implies that the later state is a computation from the earlier state, given causal laws, which can also be interpreted computationally. This approach unifies the ideas of causation and computation. A complication is the irreducible nature of many complexly organized systems. I offer a solution to this problem for the information transfer interpretation of causation.

1. Introduction

I make two basic assumptions. First, all information has a physical form, and second, that everything that is real is dynamical or can be explained in dynamical terms. Something is dynamical only if it involves nothing but forces and flows. Mathematically, dynamical systems are ones that involve a delta function or a time derivative. I assume a somewhat stronger assumption that dynamical systems must involve some physical properties that can be interpreted as forces or flows. From the dynamical assumption of the physical basis of information, it follows that information must be explicable in terms of forces and flows. At first this is counterintuitive, since information is typically thought of as a cognitive, computational or logical notion. However it is possible to bring logic and causation together through a specific analysis if the logic of information flow and a reasonable definition of what it is to make a physical difference, given that information is well characterized as "a distinction that makes a difference" (MacKay 1969), or "a difference that makes a difference" (Bateson 1973: 428). Unlike energy flow, information has to do with the constraints on the boundary conditions of energy flow. It has to do with the form, grounded in the symmetries and asymmetries of a given structure, and their relations to each other that can be given a physical interpretation in terms of the flows of information from one form to another, Information is thus neither a measure of energetic relations, or of transfers of matter (Weiner 1948) Information theory, then, is fundamentally the rigorous study of distinctions and their relations, inasmuch as they make a difference. The physicalist assumption implies that these distinctions are physical, and the dynamical assumption implies that they make a difference to forces and/or flows. Fundamentally, information is a constraint on energy flows. In some systems, such as biological and cognitive systems, these constraints (boundary conditions) are much more significant than the energetic and material relations. Such systems are information systems. However, more generally, all systems can be understood from this perspective, and all causal systems can be understood or interpreted as information systems.

By bringing together causation (which makes a dynamical difference) with the logic of information flow, it becomes possible to see causation as a sort of computation. Inasmuch as there are regular relations between an initial state and a later state of a system, the relations are interpretable in computational terms. There may be random relations between the two states as well, but there is not much we can say about these relations except for there expected size.

2. Information

Causation can be understood as the transfer of information, if information is understood in the proper way as a physical mode (Collier 1999). In order to do this, we need a clear notion of the information in a thing[1], a notion of transfer of information, and what it is for information to be physical. I start with the information in a thing.

In the static case, the information in an object or property can be derived by asking a set of canonical questions that classify the object uniquely (possibly up to some error factor for continuous or vague objects) with yes or no answers, giving a 1-1 mapping from the questions and object to the answers. This gives a string of 1s and 0s (see figure).

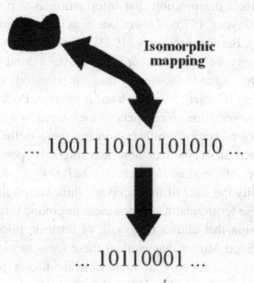

Isomorphic mapping

... 1001110101101010 ...

... 10110001 ...

Fig. 1. Information in a structure.

There are standard methods to compress these strings (though whether we have the maximally compressed string is in general non-computable). The compressed form is a line in a truth table, and is a generator of everything true of the thing required to classify it. There need not be a unique shortest string, but the set will be a linear space of logically equivalent propositions. The dimensionality of this space is the amount of information in the original object. The equivalence class of propositions in this space is the factual content of the object. This is reminiscent of Wittgenstein in the *Tractatus*, except that he thought there was a basic set of propositions that constitute the facts of the world,

---

[1] By 'thing' I mean anything objective, including properties, systems, states of systems, and objects. See (Ladyman et al 2007).

propositions being distinguished by their form. I would say that there is just basic factual content about things, which would, and usually does, generate multiple equivalent propositions, if one prefers to consider propositions as by their encoding rather than their content.

It has often been claimed, and I think that this is the most widespread view, that the information in something is relative to interests, or at least to interactions with other things. For example, the great information theorist Jaynes took the position that information is a property of an epistemic state (Jaynes 1975). Others, such as Carnap and Bar-Hillel (Bar-Hillel 1964), Barwise and Perry (1983) Israel and Perry 1990 would make it a property of sentences or statements, a kind of semantic property. I have argued, however, that information originates in symmetry breaking (Collier 1996), a physical process. Prior to this I had argued that representation (and hence measurement, or detection) requires that there be intrinsic information out there in the world to be detected, and gave an account of how this might be possible (Collier 1990). Although information transfer is relative to a channel and a receiver (especially the state of the receiver), information itself need not be defined in these terms, and it is convenient to ground information in a non-relative version that allows us to talk of intrinsic information. My former student, Scott Muller, has worked these ideas out in careful and original detail to give a reply to Jaynes, while taking over most of Jaynes' formalism and basic ideas, using the resources of group theory to provide a mathematical basis for the study of symmetry and symmetry breaking (Muller 2007).

The dynamic case is more general, the static case being a special version, but we seem to find it easier to start with the static case. In principle Fig. 1 also describes how we could treat the dynamical case, but obviously there is something more going on: information isn't merely there; it flows. We need an account not just of information in a state, but of information flow in an interconnected system.

So how does it work? First, we need an account of information flow. I start with Barwise and Seligman (1997) *Information Flow: The Logic of Distributed Systems*. I use it because it is the best worked out account available, and avoids the mistakes many have made by taking the Shannon formulation of information theory as canonical and fundamental, which ignores semantic aspects of information. Barwise and Seligman developed a theory of information channels, something missing from most other accounts of information. Shannon invokes channels, but does not explain what they are, or what their properties are. Barwise and Seligman give a formal definition of information channels. Ironically, the basic ideas, grounded in the idea of distributed systems, were developed in the 1930s, well before Shannon;s work. Perhaps he was taking these ideas for granted.[2] Measures of the quantity (and quality) of information follow naturally from their approach.

Their model of information flow is based on four principles. It is a mathematical model, and thus should apply to anything that can be represented according to the principles. Their examples are primarily from the cognitive and biological world, and they make no mention of causation as a form of information flow, but they do mention information in "every fluctuation of the natural world" (Barwise and Seligman 1997: 4). However, they use causation in examples given in the preliminary discussion of their model. This presents a potential for circularity in any application of the model to causal connection, so I will have to state their approach so as to be sure to avoid any vicious circularity. As they say, their model "is not an analysis of all and sundry accounts of information and information flow", but it is well adapted to my purposes.

The Four Principles of Information Flow

Principle 1: Information flow results from regularities in a distributed system.

Principle 2: Information flow crucially involves both types and their particulars.

Principle 3: It is by virtue of regularities among connections that information about components of distributed system carries information about the other components.

Principle 4: The regularities of a given distributed system are relative to its analysis in terms of information channels.

---

[2] Attempts to combine Shannon information measures with the Barwise-Seligman approach can be found in (Awien 2004, Moskowitz et al 2004, and Seligman 1991).

The first principle of information flow

Note that information flow requires a distributed system. Information flow occurs in a context in which the parts are connected. Furthermore, the connections must be regular. Note that this does not require invoking causality, since the regularity can be determined from redundancies in the information system itself. On the other hand, the distribution of the system seems to require causality. In a sense it does, but I will argue below that causality does not have to be invoked explicitly. The connections, I will argue, can be understood as the identical information. Given other conditions, this identity can be understood as a causal relation. The regularities can be nomic, conventional, abstract, or of some other form, depending on the sort of system involved. The principle is completely general. Furthermore, the parts of the distributed system can be of any kind. The kind will determine the type of connection required.

Accidental relations cannot carry information. Generally, the more random a system, the less information it can carry (this is not to be confused with the fact that an equiprobable code carries maximal information in a Shannon coding – the coding is part of the system, and there must be some regularity between the coding and uncoding for information to be carried by a channel). Even if there are statistical regularities between A and B, if these are chance, no information is carried by these regularities between A and B (though, by chance, the result may be useful).

The second principle of information flow

Mathematics and theories deal with types (i.e. classes, or categories or other abstract kinds). For example, if we consider the information that two dice were rolled, then we might consider the probability of getting a seven. Mathematically this is the outcome which has six possible forms, and the probability is 1/6. The information that a seven was rolled therefore is $1/6\log_2 6$, or about .43 bits. On the other hand, information is carried by particulars, or tokens. A token is an instantiation of something that is classified, and a type is a particular classification. Specifically, a classification A is an ordered triple $<A, \Sigma_A, \models_A>$ of a set A of objects to be classified (the tokens of A), a set of objects used for classification and binary relation between the two Σ_A, that tells which tokens are classified as which type, $\models_A$. For the dice example, the classification is made up of the total of each possible roll from two to twelve, the particular rolls, and the assignment of each roll to a number. The classification $\models_A$ constrains the assignment of tokens through constraints if and only if the classification assigns some token a in the set of interest A to a type α within a set of types Σ_A in the classification. The complete set of constraints is called the theory of the classification, Θ_A. It represents all the regularities of the system modeled by classification A. An infomorphism is a pair f of functions $<f^\wedge, f^\vee>$ between two classifications A and B, one from the set of objects used to classify A to the set of objects used to classify B, and the other from B to A, such that the biconditional relating the second function to the inverse of the first function holds for all tokens b of B and all types of A, $f^\vee(c) \models_A \alpha$ if and only if $c \models_C f^\wedge(\alpha)$. The biconditional is called the *fundamental property of infomorphisms.*

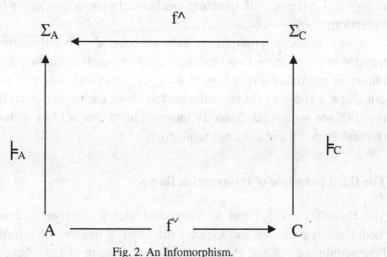

Fig. 2. An Infomorphism.

An information channel for a distributed system is an indexed family of infomorphisms with a common core codomain C. The infomorphisms allow information to be carried from one part of the system to another.

For example, in a flashlight, the components might be a bulb, battery, switch and case. The channel is basically a connected series of infomorphisms from switch to bulb through the mediation of battery and case. A channel, perhaps obviously, does not need to be sequential as a whole, but various parts do, e.g., the switch sends information to allow the flow of electricity through the case to the bulb, so that the bulb has information about the state of the switch. In this case, if the channel is sound (functioning), the switch also has information about the bulb, but this sort of converse relationship need not hold. For example the relation between a nuclear reactor and its control room should be a channel, so that the control room gives information about the state of the reactor. The reactor, however, does not have information about the state of the control room, except through (we hope) certain switch that should control activities in the reactor. If the reactor, however, gets outside of certain parameters, all hope of controlling it is lost. The readings on the dials and indicators of the control room might still record faithfully the state of the reactor, but the converse channel has become unsound. Many channels are of this one way sort (for example, in typical measurements of physical systems, with quantum mechanical systems *perhaps* a bizarre exception).

If any of the infomorphisms fails in some distributed system, the transfer of information fails (redundancy of channels could help to avoid failure of information transfer). Note that a common cause c of a and b can allow a and b to contain information about each other, even though they are not sequential. Thus an infomorphism can hold by virtue of a channel even if a and b are not sequential.

The third principle of information flow

The classification $\models_C$, and its associated theory Θ_C give us a way to model the regularities and capture the basic principles of information flow within the system. Θ_C is just the classification of the tokens under the infomorphisms of the channel, such that each token relation is classified under the relations required by the channel. Again, note that the regularities can be determined by the redundancies in the system, and the connections, to be empirically determined, depend on the specific system, or at least its type. For example, a Newtonian and a general relativistic system will share many classifications, but some will be different. For example, spatial movement in a Newtonian space merely by configuration changes is impossible (no information can be conveyed spatially by this means alone), but in general relativistic spacetime, it is possible, no doubt surprisingly (Guéron 2009). The infomorphisms for the two theories are different.

The first principle focuses attention on distributed systems, while the second focuses on their tokens. The tokens allow us to track which things are connected to which.

Here is Barwise and Seligman's *First proposal* for the third principle. I'm not going to get into the refinements, but this simplified version deals with the simplest nontrivial case in which there are two components a and b. Supposing a is of type α and it carries the information that b is of type β relative to a certain channel if a and b are connected in the channel, and the translation α′ of α entails the translation β′ of β in the theory of C where C is the core of the channel.

This proposal ensures veridicality (the information is entailed), and also the *Xerox principle*:

Xerox Principle: If r being F carries the information that s is G, and s is G carries the information that t is H, then r being F carries the information that t is H (small letters indicate tokens, large, their types).

These are both virtues because they guarantee that information that is transferred is reliable, and that information about something can be chained, permitting chains of veridical information. This is quite useful for epistemology, but that is not my concern here. Two shortcomings of the proposal are, first, that it does not directly identify the regularities of the components of the system (this can be resolved by using the inverse function mapping the questions to the answers). A more substantial problem is that the first proposal requires complete information about the system, *i.e.*, a complete theory of the classification, which we seldom have. This will not be a concern in the application to causation, since it deals with ontology, with only the requirement that the ontology be epistemologically accessible.

The fourth principle of information flow

This principle is designed to deal with exceptions by introducing a relativity to channel of information. For example, what you consider noise on your TV might be a signal to a TV repairman. Notice that this does not imply a relativity of information to interests, but that interests can lead to paying attention to different channels. The information in the respective channels is objective in each case, the noise relative to the (non-functioning or poorly functioning television channel, and the noise as a product of a noise producing channel – the problem for the TV repairman is to diagnose the source of the noise via its channel properties). This sort of relativity might appear to be of little importance in what follows, though it is useful in separating the different laws a causal system might obey, and I also use it to restrict causal channels to dynamical channels to ensure dynamical realism.

3. Causation

The proposal I made in (Collier 1999) was that P is a causal connection in a system from time t_0 to t_1 if and only if some particular part of its form is preserved between states s_0 and s_1 from t_0 to t_1. For physical systems, I restrict the form to structural (roughly, invariant) information as determined by isomorphic mapping and compression described at the beginning of this section, which I call *enformation*. The restriction to enformation is motivated by the requirement that chance regularities cannot carry information. Furthermore I constrain physical information with the Negentropy Principle of Information in order to rule out connected series of preserved information like the trace of a light beam across the face of the moon.

Negentropy Principle of Information

$$\text{NPI:} \qquad I_P = H_{MAX} - H_{ACT}$$

H_{ACT} is the actual entropy; whereas H_{MAX} is the entropy the system would have if its microstates are all equally probable (this is not generally the same as the entropy a system will reach as it approaches equilibrium). This is a definition.[3]

The enformation of a state will be some past of its I_P. NPI rules out cases like the light beam case, since they will not satisfy the Second Law of Thermodynamics, which is presupposed by NPI. In the light beam case, for example, the temperature (and thus the entropy) will vary as it moves across the moon. This means that the information in the light beam is not conserved, even though other aspects of its form are conserved. There may be possible counterexamples to my use of the NPI Principle, but if there are, I am not clear enough about them to be able to evaluate them. In most cases (such as light beam across a suitable curved perfect mirror) the conditions are unrealistic. In other cases it seems that there must have been a connivance that is more probable than that some noncausal relation holds.

The result notion of causal process is: P is a physical causal process in system over a series of states s_i from time t_0 to t_1 if and only if some part of the enformation is transferred from t_0 to t_1, consistent with NPI, and over every intermediate state. The light beam is a special case of common cause rather than direct causation. NPI rules out all cases of such indirect causation (except for a very small number of cases in which the entropies fit NPI, but by chance only. Basically, NPI is a principle that describes the force conditions relevant to information flow in a causal process.

Physical states are tokens of the types of a state space such that each state s is a token of exactly one type. Macrostates are types of states (microstates) that are equivalent for certain state properties, such as energy, pressure and other properties that are insensitive to the specific state (microstate) of the system. Macrostates are relevant for the computation and/or measurement of entropy. The Ω_is in Fig. 3 can be taken to be macrostates without loss of generality (the macrostates are more general, at the very least) to give a macroscopic theory of the system. I will have bit to say about their reality in my conclusion below.

---

[3] Details on the motivation for the use of NPI as a sort of operational definition in the sense of Mach's (1960: 264–271) definition of mass are given in (Collier 1999).

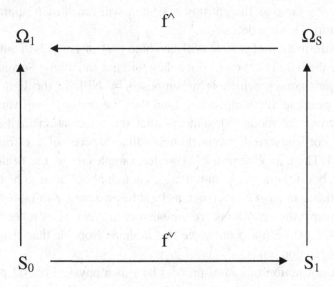

Fig. 3. Infomorphism between states.

With these considerations in mind, the original statement of causal connection can by rephrased in Barwise and Seligman's terms as P is a causal connection in a system from time t_0 to t_1 if and only if there is an channel between s_0 and s_1 from t_0 to t_1 that preserves some part of the information in the first state. Furthermore, P is a physical causal process in system over a series of states s_i from time t_0 to t_1 if and only there is a channel through the states from t_0 to t_1, consistent with NPI, and over every intermediate state.

The conditions on a causal process are much more severe than on a mere causal connection, and are therefore easier to verify. In fact it is unclear how we would check that there is a causal connection when there is no underlying causal process or processes. The connection between several discrete spots of light in succession across the surface of the moon, if there were no causal processes like a pulsating laser beam reflecting off the moon connecting them, would be very mysterious, even if they satisfied NPI. If we did discover such a thing, perhaps looking at the constraints (force) of how NPI applies would help us to understand what is going on. In the case of nonphysical causes, if there are such things, we don't even know where to begin. This does not, however, mean that the causal connection principle does not apply. It might still be that in some mysterious way that there is an infomorphism between s_0 and s_1 from t_0 to t_1, in which case there would be a causal connection (the connection would not be coincidental because of the no accidents condition on infomorphisms). Such possibilities are remote to our experience, however. Causal processes, however, under the channel characterization, are eminently discoverable and investigatable because they involve unbroken channels through continuous space and time that must conform to the Second Law of Thermodynamics.

The problem now is to show how the above accounts of causal connection and causal process relate to the four principles of Barwise and Seligman, and then to show why we should accept that all information flow is either dynamical or else explicable in dynamical terms. **Principle 1**: a causal system involves regularities (the enformation) in a distributed system, satisfying the first principle. **Principle 2**: causation involves both types and particulars. The particulars in this case are the tokens of information. The types are specific to the cases, but the most fundamental type is dynamical. **Principle 3**: the connection in this case is identity, which is perhaps the strongest connection one can have, and requires information transmission across time: it is the identical token of information. Epistemologically, we can infer this, since it is much more parsimonious to infer one identical instance of information rather than a series of similar tokens. Again, the regularities are determined by the redundancy of the information token. This is enough to establish that the basic theory of causation fits the Barwise/Seligman model. Note that their first proposal ensures veridicality as well as transitivity of the information in causal events.

The **fourth principle** is of considerable interest. I have already invoked it by using the specific type dynamical, but further classification can allow one to take a particular causal process or interaction and classify it more specifically to allow for specific causal laws. This relativisation is useful for scientific investigation, and also at least mitigates Nancy Cartwright's (1983) arguments about the laws of physics lying. It is legitimate to look at specific channels, or types of interactions. For example, inasmuch as the theories of gravitation and electrodynamics are separate, we can separate the gravitational and electrodynamic information in a system. More complex material that I have not introduced allows the additivity of channels to get a net effect.

4. Computation

There is a simple sense in which causation on the above account is like a computation: the information in a later state contains information in the earlier state of the system, entailment depending precisely on the causal influence of the earlier state on the later. Inasmuch as entailment by way of a physical process is a computation, then the account guarantees that causation is computational.

Things are not quite so simple, however. There are dynamical systems whose solutions are not analytically computable, including ones as simple as three-body gravitational systems. Bertalanffy (1968: 20), following Franks, breaks down the classification of dynamical systems as shown in Fig. 4 below. Large numbers of real systems have nonlinear equations and many parameters, making their solution analytically impossible, though some such systems can be modelled with numerical computer models. Things are more difficult, however, when there is self-organization and multiple attractors, in which case divergent solutions to the equations of motion cannot be isolated to spatiotemporally local conditions.

Robert Rosen (1991) distinguished between analytic and synthetic systems. Synthetic systems are ones in which the observational basis can be combined in some linear way to obtain and analytic model (thus making the analytic models reducible to their evidence), whereas analytic models are ones having a mathematical dynamical form.[4] They need not be reducible. In other words, there are analytic models whose solutions are not computable. An important case of nonreducible models are those of living systems. They are typified by loops of what Rosen called *efficient causation*. Such systems, I maintain, are exactly those that cannot be fully dealt with via analytical computations or numerical approximations, in particular where they are not in steady state, but show the sort of bifurcations typical of growth and development. These are the complexly organized systems (Collier and Hooker 1999).

---

[4] Rosen's use of analytic here is somewhat confusing and idiosyncratic.

Equation:	Algebraic	Ordinary Differential	Partial Differential
Linear Equations One Parameter	Trivial	Easy	Difficult
Several Parameters	Easy	Difficult	Intractable
Many Parameters	Intractable	Intractable	Impossible
Nonlinear Equations One Parameter	Very Difficult	Very Difficult	Impossible
Several Parameters	Very Difficult	Impossible	Impossible
Many Parameters	Impossible	Impossible	Impossible

Fig. 4. Classification of mathematical difficulty After Bertalanffy 1968: 20.

How can this be reconciled with the view that causation is like a computation? Firstly, the causal networks typical of causally organized systems can be represented by a device introduced by Rosen (1991), though the basic idea seems to go back to Leibniz (1969, see Collier 1999 for discussion). Rosen noted that theoretical models, if accurate, reflect the causal relations in the system modelled, so that the logical relations of the theory are reflected in the causal relations of the system modelled. Understanding causation as information flow implies that the causal relations actually are logical relations, and that the distributed network of information flow can mirror precisely the logical relations of some analytic model, even if that model is not reducible. However, the distributed network flow of information in such systems still fits the Barwise and Seligman approach.

This raises a bit of a paradox. If the system states are sequential, and are information states with entailments between them, is this not a computational relationship? If so, how can the system equations themselves be noncomputable? I think the answer is that we need to distinguish two notions of computability, sequential computability and analytic computability. There are Turing functions that do not terminate. These functions are not analytically computable. Yet each state is determined by the previous state. The sequential states of systems with no synthetic models are similar to these nonanalytic Turing functions (though unlike Turing functions new information can arise in later states due to stochastic processes and information creation via symmetry breaking) in that the information that is transferred is entailed by the earlier state, so causation is accounted without requiring analytic solutions to the system equations.

Conclusions

Information flow in distributed systems can be given an interpretation in dynamical terms. This gives us an account of causation in information theoretic terms. The relations between information theory and logic can then help us to understand the relations between causation and computation. The relations are complicated by the existence of nonreducible models of real systems for which there are no complete analytical solutions. These systems correspond to those having organized complexity (both complex and well-organized) that are the usual subject of complexity theory. The information theoretic account of causation can be seen to fit these systems through an analogue to the distinction between sequentially computable (stepwise computable) Turing functions and analytic (computable) Turing functions.

References

Allwein, Gerard. (2004) A qualitative framework for Shannon information theories. In *Proceedings of the 2004 workshop on New security paradigms,* 23–31. Nova Scotia, Canada: ACM, 2004.

Barwise, J. and J. Perry (1983) *Situations and Attitudes.* Cambridge, MA: MIT Press.

Barwise, J. and J. Seligman (1997) *Information Flow: The Logic of Distributed Systems.* Cambridge: Cambridge University Press.

Bateson, G. (1973) *Steps to an Ecology of Mind.* Paladin. Frogmore: St. Albans.

Bar-Hillel, Y. (1964) *Language and Information.* Reading, MA: Addison-Wesley.

Cartwright, Nancy (1983) *How the Laws of Physics Lie.* Oxford: Oxford University Press.

Collier, John (1990) Intrinsic Information. Philip Hanson (ed) *Information, Language and Cognition: Vancouver Studies in Cognitive Science, Vol. 1.* Oxford: University of Oxford Press: 390–409.

Collier, John (1996) Information originates in symmetry breaking. *Symmetry: Culture & Science* **7** (1996): 247–256.

Collier, John (1999) Causation is the Transfer of Information. Howard Sankey (ed) *Causation and Laws of Nature*. Dordrecht: Kluwer: 279–331.

Collier, John and C.A. Hooker (1999) Complexly organised dynamical systems. *Open Systems and Information Dynamics*, **6**: 241–302.

Guéron, Eduardo (2009) Adventures in curved spacetime. *Scientific American* **301**, no 2: 26–33.

Israel, D. and J. Perry (1990) What is information? Philip Hanson (ed) *Information, Language and Cognition: Vancouver Studies in Cognitive Science, Vol. 1*. Oxford: University of Oxford Press: 1–19.

Jaynes, E.T. (1978) Where do we stand on Maximum Entropy? R.D. Levin and M. Ritbus (eds) *The Maximum Entropy Principle*. Cambridge, MA: MIT Press.

Ladyman J., Rooss, D, Spurrett, D and Collier J. (2007) *Every Thing Must Go: Metaphysics |Naturalized*, Oxford: Oxford University Press.

Leibniz, W.G. (1969). *The Yale Leibniz*, translated by G.H.R. Parkinson. New Haven: Yale University Press.

MacKay, Donald M. (1969) *Information, Mechanism and Meaning*. Cambridge, MA: MIT Press.

Moskowitz, I. S., L. W. Chang, and G. T. Allwein. (2004) A new framework for Shannon information theory. Storming Media.Muller, Scott J. (2007) *Asymmetry: The Foundation of Information*. Berlin: Springer.

Rosen, Robert (1991) *Life Itself: A Comprehensive Inquiry into the Nature, Origin, and Fabrication of Life*. New York: Columbia University Press.

Seligman, Jerry. (1991) Physical situations and information flow. In Situation theory and its applications: Volume 2 (Center for the Study of Language and Information - Lecture Notes) , vol. 2 ed. Jon Barwise, Jean Mark Gawron, Gordon Plotkin, Syun Tutiya. Stanford: Center for the Study of Language and Information.

Von Bertalanffy, Ludwig (1968) *General Systems Theory, revised edition*. New York: Goerge Braziller.

Wiener, Norbert, (1948) *Cybernetics or Control and Communication in the Animal and the Machine*. Hermann & Cie Editeurs, Paris, *The Technology Press*, Cambridge, Mass: John Wiley & Sons *Inc*.

CHAPTER 5

FROM DESCARTES TO TURING: THE COMPUTATIONAL CONTENT OF SUPERVENIENCE

S. Barry Cooper*

University of Leeds, Leeds LS2 9JT, U.K.

pmt6sbc@leeds.ac.uk

Mathematics can provide precise formulations of relatively vague concepts and problems from the real world, and bring out underlying structure common to diverse scientific areas. Sometimes very natural mathematical concepts lie neglected and not widely understood for many years, before their fundamental relevance is recognised and their explanatory power is fully exploited. The notion of definability in a structure is such a concept, and Turing's [77] 1939 model of interactive computation provides a fruitful context in which to exercise the usefulness of definability as a powerful and widely applicable source of understanding. In this article we set out to relate this simple idea to one of the oldest and apparently least scientifically approachable of problems — that of realistically modelling how mental properties supervene on physical ones.

Mathematics can provide precise formulations of relatively vague concepts and problems from the real world, and bring out underlying structure common to diverse scientific areas. Sometimes very natural mathematical concepts lie neglected and not widely understood for many years, before their fundamental relevance is recognised and their explanatory power is fully exploited. Previously we have argued that the notion of definability in a structure is such a concept, and pointed to Turing's [77] 1939 model of interactive computation as providing a fruitful context in which to exercise the usefulness of definability as a powerful and widely applicable source of understanding.

Research supported by EPSRC research grant No. EP/G000212 Computing with Partial Information: Definability in the Local Structure of the Enumeration Degrees.

Below, we relate this simple idea to one of the oldest and apparently least scientifically approachable of problems — that of realistically modelling how mental properties supervene on physical ones. We will first briefly review the origins with René Descartes of mind-body dualism, and the problem of mental causation. We will then summarise the subsequent difficulties encountered, and their current persistence, and the more recent usefulness of the concept of *supervenience* in providing a philosophical workspace in which to make mind-body connections — and the parallel recognition of *emergence* as a tool for giving supervenience a non-reductive physical content. The rise and fall of the British emergentists will provide a salutary warning of the pitfalls of working with too vague a formulation of emergence, and of the need for a test for emergence.

Following on from this, we will further clarify emergence by looking at mathematical analogues, and at approaches to emergence — such as synergetics — with a strong mathematical or scientific content. This will move us away from the empirical quest for emergent phenomena as something surprising towards formalisations of self-organisation in terms of the two-way interaction between physical phenomena, and their descriptions and representations. We will point to the important role of representation in building computationally complex systems with the capability to transcend the Turing barrier. Finally, we will argue for the fundamental role of causality and that of the extended Turing model of the algorithmic content of nature. What we know about the theory of this model will then lead to a clarifying return to the problems of fragmentation and coherence first highlighted by Descartes. In doing so, we will point to the existence of different levels of 'causality', and to give mathematical substance to the common distrust of causality as a term in everyday usage.

1. Substance Dualism, and the Problem of Mental Causation

In general, Descartes aimed at explanations in terms of strictly mechanical principles and mathematical models. But living with an experience of mental phenomena for which there is no obvious underlying mechanism, he proclaimed the essential non-physicality of the mind — for instance, in the Discourse on Method, Part IV, from 1637:

> I [am] a substance the whole essence or nature of which is to think, and for its existence there is no need of any place, nor does it depend on any material thing; so that this me, that is to say, the soul by which I am what I am, is entirely distinct from body ...

Whereas, regarding the body itself (Discourse on Method, Part V), he says:

> ... this will not seem strange to those, who, knowing how many different *automata* or moving machines can be made by the industry of man, without employing in so doing more than a very few parts in comparison with the great multitude of bones, muscles, nerves, arteries, veins, or other parts that are found in the body of each animal. From this aspect the body is regarded as a machine which, having been made by the hands of God, is incomparably better arranged, and possesses in itself movements which are much more admirable, than any of those which can be invented by man.

So Descartes views the body as a very complicated and well-designed machine, and thought and free will as being quite separated from it in nature. As is well-known, Descartes' 'substance dualism' was not well-received, even at the time. Though notwithstanding this, the historical and current failure to build man-made machines to even rival animals (whom Descartes thought certainly would be mechanical in nature), suggests that there is *something* in need of further explanation — and not just in terms of the cleverness of God at constructing automata.

There are various problems connected with such a dualist reading of the relationship between mind and body. The chief of these is the problem of mental causation: How can mentality have a causal role in a world that is fundamentally physical? And then there is the related problem of 'overdetermination' — the problem of phenomena having, according to how one views them, both mental and physical causes. According to Jaegwon Kim [35, p. 156]: "What has become increasingly evident over the past thirty years is that mental causation poses insuperable difficulties for all forms of mind-body dualism ...". Unless of course one takes the epiphenomenalist view, its origins associated with T.H. Huxley [32], and partly supported by neuroscience research over the years, which holds that mental phenomena, though physically caused, do not themselves have a causal impact on the physical world. Otherwise, these problems outlined by Kim persist, in different guises, even within all but the most openly reductive attempts at materialist interpretations. Here is Kim [35, p. 1] again:

> ... the problem of mental causation is solvable only if mentality is physically reducible; however, phenomenal consciousness resists physical reduction, putting its causal efficacy in peril.

And more explicitly [35, p. 1]:

> How can the mind exercise its causal powers in a causally closed physical world? Why is there, and how can there be, such a thing as the mind, or consciousness, in a physical world? ... these two problems, mental causation and consciousness, are intertwined, and that, in a sense, they make each other insoluble.

In fact, Descartes opened up a Pandora's (black) box of more-or-less weird and wonderful takes on the question of how to characterise the mind-body relationship in a scientifically constrained world. How do we characterise the link between mind and physical world? And achieve this in a way that respects the complexities involved?

The spectrum of subtle differences in approach is largely contained within the reductive–nonreductive physicalism spectrum. But the more one tries to clarify the notions involved, the more difficulties one encounters. One is reminded of the old Indian tale of a group of blind men who separately touch different parts of an elephant to learn what it is like, each coming up with very different conclusions based on their particular relationship to the elephant, and on what they were previously familiar with. The version captured in John Godfrey Saxe's 19th century poem *The Blind Men and the Elephant* concludes:

MORAL.

So oft in theologic wars,
The disputants, I ween,
Rail on in utter ignorance
Of what each other mean,
And prate about an Elephant
Not one of them has seen!

Donald Davidson's anomalous monism (see, for example, [17]) establishes just one outpost of this unruly debate. While this is not the right place to discuss this in detail, it is worth remarking that it exploits the tension between events being causally connected, and their being explainable in terms of well-understood laws governing the causal relationship. This distinction is familiar to the computationally-minded, and re-emerges below when we try to extract the computational content of such elusive processes as those governing the mind.

Towards the other end of the spectrum, one finds Saxe's 'MORAL' used to downplay the existence of such entities as consciousness and qualia, which continue to bother observers such as Kim. Here is Daniel Dennett [21, pp. 369-370]:

> It's not hard to see how philosophers have tied themselves into such knots over qualia. They started where anyone with any sense would start: with their strongest and clearest intuitions about their own minds. Those intuitions, alas, form a mutually self-supporting closed circle of doctrines, imprisoning their imaginations in the Cartesian Theater. Even though philosophers have discovered the paradoxes inherent in this closed circle of ideas — that's why the literature on qualia exists — they haven't had a *whole alternative vision* to leap to, and so, trusting their still-strong intuitions, they get dragged back into the paradoxical prison.

But then, as John Searle [65, p. 102] observes, "If Dennett denies the existence of conscious states as we usually think of them, what is his alternative account? Not surprisingly, it is a version of Strong AI." In this way, the relevance of suitably modelling the computational content underlying such controversies is strikingly brought home to us.

2. Supervenience as Workspace

Dennett's view of consciousness is often described as being a *functionalist* one. In the context of the philosophy of mind, a functionalist will look for explanations of mental states in terms of the underlying causal relationships of the system, rather than in the particular physics or biology of its constitution. It is an approach to mental properties which underpins most of cognitive science, and is specially associated with the logician Hilary Putnam (see [55], [56]). Particularly influential was Turing's 1950 paper [79], replacing the question "Can machines think?" with that of whether it is possible for a machine to pass the Turing Test.

More recently, within computer science the virtual machine paradigm, going back to the 1974 paper [51] of Popek and Goldberg, is seen to be very relevant. As commented by Aaron Sloman (private communication):

> ... the relations between (a) running virtual machines in computers and (b) the processes in underlying physical machines, ... at one level ... are well understood as they are created, debugged, extended, and documented by human engineers, yet they have many of the features (including causal over-determination) that have caused puzzlement when noticed in much more complex systems produced by biological evolution (e.g. human minds and brains) and others (e.g. socio-economic systems implemented in psychological systems or the underlying physical processes: a credit crunch seems to be a process in a socio-economic virtual machine distributed over the surface of the earth.)

Sloman has written interestingly on the relations between running virtual machines and the physical implementations, recently taking issue with the Brooks' well-known paper [10] in [68].

What is attractive about functionalism is the freedom it gives to us to seek aspects of mentality beyond the human context, for example in animals or machines. On the other hand, as an explanation of qualia or our experience of consciousness its abstractions seem inadequate to many, based on failures of modelling of the structural complexities involved — or, to put it more simply, a lack of respect for the real world. Functionalism is certainly an attractive perspective for the computer scientist, appearing to free the computational process from a dependence on the medium hosting it. The functionalist may validly draw useful support for a computational perspective on mental phenomena. But in its assumption of the primacy of the functional relationship, it makes it harder to model the infrastructure of such relationships, an understanding of which the character of the physical remains the key. The potential consistency of functionalism with different ends of the materialism-dualism spectrum seems to signal that something is missing from its explanatory power. This how William Hasker expresses it [28, p. 32]:

> ... either the causal-functional states identified by functionalism characteristically involve conscious "feels" (in the case of qualia) and "aboutness" (in the case of intentional states) or they do not. If they do not, then functionalism is not a theory about the mental at all; the name remains, but the subject has

been changed. If they do, then functionalism may indeed be a theory (possibly even a true theory) about the mental, but it does nothing to explain two of the most salient features of the mental states in question, namely subjective consciousness and intentional reference. In this case, there seems to be a need for a theory that more directly addresses the key issue concerning the relationship between consciousness and its physical embodiment.

The problem is that functionalism, much as it *fits* with what follows, does not *provide a workspace* for addressing its own explanatory deficiencies. And this is where the notion of supervenience, as understood in current philosophical usage, comes in. According to Kim [34, 14-15], supervenience:

> ... represents the idea that mentality is at bottom physically based, and that there is no free-floating mentality unanchored in the physical nature of objects and events in which it is manifested.

There are different ways of formalising the notion, but we can say that:

> A set of properties A supervenes upon another set B just in case no two things can differ with respect to A-properties without also differing with respect to their B-properties. (Stanford Encyclopedia of Philosophy)

Then the question becomes: If mental properties supervene on physical properties – how do the complexities of the physical world match those of the mental – and, potentially, of the mirroring process? To quote Aaron Sloman (private communication) again:

> Unfortunately, most philosophers discussing supervenience of mind on matter don't pay detailed attention to the variety of coexisting, enduring, interacting structures and processes that exist in a mind (as in virtual machines in computers), so they ignore most of the complexity in the problem of supervenience.

The rest of this article goes some way to support this viewpoint.

3. The Roots of Reductive Physicalism

Newton himself would probably have been surprised at the way he changed the way people, and particularly scientists, viewed the world. In *Isaac Newton – The Last Sorcerer* [82], Michael White describes the key role alchemy and religion played in Newton's thinking, and Newton's obsession with biblical prophecy as found in his *Observations upon the Prophecies of Daniel.* He comments:

> This demonstrates ... the radical difference between the intellectual perspectives of the seventeenth and twentieth centuries ...

Newton set new standards of descriptive control over natural phenomena, which were to fuel great scientific advances, as well as a distrust of the power and validity of less precise ways of thinking. From Galileo and Newton onwards, the overarching aim of science became the extraction of the mechanical content of the world — a 'clockwork universe'. This development was very much in tune with the various shades of materialism espoused earlier by Descartes, Bacon and Hobbes (most notably in *The Leviathan* from 1651), amongst others. But it was Newton who substantiated the mathematical drive to describe the world in terms of well-defined relations over the continuum, in such a way that predictions emerged as computable functions or simulations, so powerfully dispelling a large range of natural mysteries.

On the other hand, it is well-known that the algorithmic content of a mathematical description involving quite a small number of quantifiers can be largely lost to us. A faith in the descriptive counterpart of nature being logically simple enough to be universally subject to straightforward empirical test is not very scientific, but then the logic that tells us this is less than a hundred years old. When theories such as general relativity and quantum field theory present empirical and mathematical problems of a new kind, one needs to face the fact that our scientific model is in need of an upgrade.

This model, built on the striking success of Newton in predicting such events as the motions of the planets, we recognise in Laplace's description (in [39]) of his 'predictive demon':

> Given for one instant an intelligence which could comprehend all the forces by which nature is animated and the respective situations of the beings who compose it – an intelligence sufficiently vast to submit these data to analysis – it would embrace in the same formula the movements of the greatest bodies and those of the lightest atom; for it, nothing would be uncertain and the future, as the past, would be present to its eyes.

There was very little precision to this model, and there would not be for more than a hundred years after the death of Pierre-Simon, Marquis de Laplace. But there is little doubt that Laplace's demon became in a very real sense an aspirational model for generations of scientists, and one which still holds a strong grip over the thinking of not just scientists, but people from many different walks of life. One can even detect it in the wider social context, when one finds [24] Engels writing in 1880:

> ...modern materialism sees in [history] the process of evolution of humanity, and aims at discovering the laws thereof. ... [it] embraces the more recent discoveries of natural science, according to which Nature also has its history in time, the celestial bodies, like the organic species that, under favorable conditions, people them, being born and perishing. ......[with] two great discoveries, the materialistic conception of history and the revelation of the secret of capitalistic production through surplus-value ...Socialism became a science. The next thing was to work out all its details and relations.

So the aim was to work out the "details and relations", the assumption being that the result would provide a possibly complicated, but mechanistic, model of the real world. And that the predictive power contained therein would allow one to not just understand the course of history, but to manipulate and predict it — the machine would be programmable. This would allow no room for an interactive Cartesian dualism. Echoing Gilbert Ryle's dismissal of any such thing — "I shall often speak of it, with deliberate abusiveness, as the dogma of the Ghost in the Machine" [63, ch. 1] — the machine would be effectively 'ghost-free'.

The first appearance of a mathematical model of such a machine was in two independent and almost simultaneous papers, by Emil Post [52] and Alan Turing [76], describing equivalent, and remarkably similar, formulations of the standard Turing machine model of computation. Such machines only deal with discrete data, so need a little extra work for them to model computation over continuous data, or in a scientific context. Nevertheless, they play an important conceptual role in buttressing the Laplacian model of a potentially deterministic, and predictably so, real world. And, given that the essentials of many computational contexts can be captured perfectly well with approximated data, they provide a model of computable natural processes with a wide range of valid application.

However, any structure with algorithmic content entails some infinitary mathematics, which may involve new relations with physical significance. Turing's Universal Machine first seen in his 1936 paper [76] not only anticipated today's stored program computer, even feeding into von Neumann's thinking on computer design — there was also a very significant 'ghost in the machine', that of *in*computability. Turing's coding up of computing machines, in such a way that they could be used as input-data, also enabled a simple and quite effective diagonalisation leading to an incomputable real number.

4. Nature as Discipline Problem

There was no real evidence though that incomputability was any more than a mathematical curiosity — and for many people, there still isn't. How does one distinguish a computational task which is very complicated, to the point where it outstrips the capabilities of our most powerful computers and mathematical resources, from one for which there is an absolute theoretical barrier to it being computationally captured?

Philosophically this is an important question, since its answer will bring with it mathematical baggage; and how we characterize the *material* nature of the world will need to reflect and accommodate the underlying *mathematical* constraints. In practice, though, one can still argue that the *predictive* power of the mathematics is zero, so that despite the philosophy, it remains a curiosity. This view could only be challenged by a development of the theory of incomputability to a point where it can fill a need for a new explanatory framework; a framework with predictive power. And even then, the Laplacian model brings with it a strong syzygial relationship between machine and material which is hard to break. In fact, the survival of the model depends on this. And moving from the security of the Laplacian model requires a whole Kuhnian shift of paradigm, made harder when the new paradigm appears difficult to understand. At first sight, this is not strictly relevant to the problem of characterising the link between mind and brain; that is, until one recognises that the mathematics of different scenarios necessarily brings with it differing material avatars with correspondingly different functionalities an properties — at some level.

There are many examples of non-trivial reductions of phenomena to the Turing model. This works best when one has an agreed model for the phenomenon in question, which enables something close to a mathematical proof which one can share with others. A well-known example is the 1985 [23] reduction by David Deutsch of the standard model of quantum computation to the Turing model, while proposing the first universal quantum Turing machine. But for Deutsch, this reduction seems to be part of a wider reductive programme, when we see in *Question and Answers with David Deutsch*, on the New.Scientist.com News Service, December, 2006:

> I am sure we will have [conscious computers], I expect they will be purely classical, and I expect that it will be a long time in the future. Significant advances in our philosophical understanding of what consciousness is, will be needed.

Another well-known reductionist – paradoxically, most famous for his part in showing how simple high-school mathematics leads to a diversity of incomputability – is Martin Davis. Here is another far-reaching claim, taken from his article [20]:

> The great success of modern computers as all-purpose algorithm-executing engines embodying Turing's universal computer in physical form, makes it extremely plausible that the abstract theory of computability gives the correct answer to the question What is a computation?, and, by itself, makes the existence of any more general form of computation extremely doubtful.

But back in the real world, one sees persistent problems of prediction, and even of description: how does one get beyond the probabilities governing quantum phenomena associated with measurements; how does one capture emergent phenomena in a general predictive framework; and related to this, how to improve our understanding of chaotic/turbulent contexts and their 'strange attractors'; or to reduce relativistic systems such as black holes to suitably Turing-like models. Even at the level of practical computation, there is a growing interest in non-standard computational models, including a renewed interest in analog and hybrid computing machines – presumably arising from a view, put in writing by J. van Leeuwen and J. Wiedermann [81] that:

... the classical Turing paradigm may no longer be fully appropriate to capture all features of present-day computing.

How does one mathematically deconstruct such apparently complex
physical examples? A pointer to the underlying simplicity of the mathematics involved is found in comments of Georg Kreisel [37] from 1970,
where he proposes a collision problem related to the 3-body problem, which
might result in "an analog computation of a non-recursive function". What
is important in Kreisel's example is his notion of *co-operative phenomenon*,
where the apparent simplicity masks a nonlinearity and an unavoidably
infinitary mathematical analysis, a prerequisite for the mathematics of incomputability to play a role. A more recent example, in which the infinitis-
tic nature of physical phenomena emerges much more explicitly, is provided
by the solution to the Painlevé Problem from 1895, asking whether non-
collision singularities exist for the N-body problem for N 4. For N 5, Jeff
Xia showed in 1988 that the answer is Yes (see Saari and Xia [64]). Other
work in a classical Newtonian setting includes recent papers by Tucker and
Beggs and their collaborators (see, for example, [3], [4]).

Of course, Kreisel thought deeply about extensions of the Church-Turing
thesis, and one can find a more than twenty-page discussion related to his
thinking on this [46, pp.101–123] in volume 1 of Piergiorgio Odifreddi's book
on Classical Recursion Theory. A valuable and more detailed account of
Kreisel's views can be found in Odifreddi's article [47] on *Kreisel's Church*.

5. Chaos and its Analogues

In situations where we find it hard to mathematically capture natural phenomena, we can sometimes learn a lot from reasonably well-understood
mathematical analogues of them. Chaos theory typically deals with situations where the generation of informational complexity is via quite simple
rules, but is accompanied by the emergence of new and surprising regularities. A classic example is that of Robert Shaw's dripping taps (see [67], [66]).
What could be dynamically simpler, we think? But the emergent 'strange
attractors' are interesting and have a less-than-simple relationship to the
underlying basic laws, certainly not one that is known to be practically
computable.

There is a familiar metaphorical link between complexity arising from basic laws in nature, and between mathematical objects, such as the Mandelbrot and Julia sets. The mathematics attached to such well-defined structures may not be directly applicable to the rather messier physical situations, but the parallel between the basic elements on each side — the simple basic laws, the complexity arising from them, the surprising *emergence* (a key notion) of new formal regularities — is close enough for a mathematical overview of the 'toy complexity' to add important new elements to our understanding of what is happening in nature. In particular, there are basic questions concerning the computability or otherwise of the Mandelbrot and Julia sets, which have attracted the attention of high-profile figures, such as Stephen Smale and Roger Penrose, who arrive with impressive track-records as researchers in areas not directly related to computability theoretic questions. This is how Penrose sets the scene in *The Emperors New mind* [49] for the basic question about computability:

> Now we witnessed ... a certain extraordinarily complicated looking set, namely the Mandelbrot set. Although the rules which provide its definition are surprisingly simple, the set itself exhibits an endless variety of highly elaborate structures.

Blum and Smale [6] have actually used the BSS model of computation over arbitrary commutative rings (described in [5]) to show the Mandelbrot set to be incomputable; but as Brattka [7] points out, the BSS model gives the incomputability of such intuitively computable sets as the epigraph of the exponential function.

Of course, one gets the Mandelbrot set as the set of all complex numbers c for which the corresponding transform $z \to z^2 + c$ stays finite, despite unbounded iterations starting with $z = 0$. So at first sight the recognition of a c in the set involves a two-quantifier expression. But on closer inspection, one finds that the complement of the Mandelbrot set can be expressed using just an existential quantifier (a fact that the generation of computer-screen images of the set depends on), so that this complement is intuitively 'computably enumerable'. Put in this light, it is not so surprising that we are looking at possible incomputability.

What we learn from this is to take the logical structure of scientific descriptions a little more seriously, and to look for implications for the computational — and hence predictive — content of particular theories and their applications in the real world. These may be crude projections we are constructing; but arguably less crude than those widely used to prop up the Laplacian model of science, and related extensions of the Church-Turing thesis. And we will see that they contain enough explanatory power to add to the impression that we have what Thomas Kuhn describes as a 'period of tension' characteristic of a prospective paradigm change.

Another important observation is that there seems to be an association between the logical complexity of the description of the Mandelbrot set and the incomputability it promises. And a further observable symptom of these mathematically abstract characteristics, in the form of *emergent* visually beautiful and endlessly unfolding inner structure. This is why such examples are more useful than, say, those provided by the negative solution to Hilbert's Tenth Problem, and its delivery of diophantine expressions for all computably enumerable sets. It is the memory of the very visual emergence exhibited by the Mandelbrot and Julia sets that gives us pause for thought as we watch the endless variety of wave formations breaking on the shore, or the patterns of clouds morphing across the sky. We now have a very detailed understanding of the scientific laws acting locally within, say, the Cat's Eye Nebula, but we look with some wonder and a sense of humility at the intricate global structure observed via sufficiently large and well-placed telescopes. Emergence occurs everywhere, and it presents important conceptual and mathematical challenges.

These challenges take on a new dimension in the next section, when one attempts to apply our lessons the task in hand, that of clarifying the link between mental properties and and their physical host, the brain. But for Daniel Hillis (Chief Technology Officer of Applied Minds, Inc., and ex-Vice President, Research and Development at Walt Disney Imagineering) even the basic and very down-to-earth task of building intelligent machines involves an intimate relationship with emergence (from *Red Herring Magazine*, April 2001):

> I used to think we'd do it by engineering. Now I believe we'll evolve them. We're likely to make thinking machines before we understand how the mind works, which is kind of backwards.

6. Rise and Fall of British Emergentism

In recent years, emergence has figured increasingly in attempts to develop a non-reductive physicalist explanation of our experience of higher mental functionality. But there were earlier anticipations of this contemporary trend, particularly those associated with people working around the end of the nineteenth and beginning of the twentieth century, who became grouped under the heading of 'British emergentism'. The earliest and best-known of these was John Stuart Mill. Although the term 'emergence' was yet achieve its later currency, the developing sense of its meaning and scope is evident in this quote from John Stuart Mill (*A System of Logic*, Bk.III, Ch. 6, 1):

> All organised bodies are composed of parts, similar to those composing inorganic nature, and which have even themselves existed in an inorganic state; but the phenomena of life, which result from the juxtaposition of those parts in a certain manner, bear no analogy to any of the effects which would be produced by the action of the component substances considered as mere physical agents. To whatever degree we might imagine our knowledge of the properties of the several ingredients of a living body to be extended and perfected, it is certain that no mere summing up of the separate actions of those elements will ever amount to the action of the living body itself.

For a full account of the history of the British emergentists one should consult Brian McLaughlin's fascinating survey [44] *The rise and fall of British emergentism*. In the context of this article, the history becomes not just a pointer to the robustness of the intuitions involved, but – more importantly – a cautionary tale centred on an awareness of the reasons for the early emergentists' decline.

In regard to the former, one finds Samuel Alexander reaching for the sort of explanatory power we see in more recent work, when he talks [1, p. 45] about "the emergence of the quality of consciousness from a lower level of complexity", or again [1, p. 14]:

> The argument is that mind has certain specific characters to which there is or even can be no neural counterpart ... Mind is, according to our interpretation of the facts, an 'emergent' from life, and life an emergent from a lower physico-chemical level of existence.

One of the more modern figures in the group active around the 1920s was C.D. Broad, his views finding full expression in his 1923 book [8] on *The Mind and Its Place In Nature*. Here is his take on what emergence has to contribute to the physicalist agenda [8, p. 623]:

> ...the mental properties of those events which do have mental properties are completely determined by the material properties which these events also have ... it is certainly not ... a form of *Reductive* Materialism; it is a form of the theory ... of *Emergent* Materialism.

Within their differing approaches, the emergentists of the 1920s, such as Broad, Samuel Alexander, and C. Lloyd Morgan, conceived of emergence in ways we would recognise today. Schematically, they had identified some of the distinctive characteristics of an emergent property or phenomenon, and had a recognisably modern check list of explanatory tasks they wanted emergence to perform. In particular, Broad and others saw it as being relevant to a number of reductive failures in science, from the mind-body problem to the apparent irreducibility of the 'special sciences' to more basic sciences, and the nature of the relationship of biology to chemistry, and of these to physics. Emergence supported a familiar hierarchical, 'layered' view of nature and its science.

But there was no precise *test* for emergence, neither via practical observation, nor via analysis of a mathematically valid modelling. Emergence was a useful term for those who shared a common appreciation of the existence of what it referred to, but, within the then state of scientific theory, could be misapplied. Here is Broad explaining what emergence is, and trying to convince the reader that it really does exist, and is something non-reductive and different [8, p. 59]:

> ...the characteristic behaviour of the whole [system] *could* not, even in theory, be deduced from the most complete knowledge of the behaviour of its components, taken separately or in other combinations, and of their proportions and arrangements in this whole. This ...is what I understand by the "Theory of Emergence". I cannot give a conclusive example of it, since it is a matter of controversy whether it actually applies to anything ...I will merely remark that, so far as I know at present, the characteristic behaviour of Common Salt cannot be deduced from the most complete knowledge of the properties of Sodium in isolation; or of Chlorine in isolation; or of other compounds of Sodium, such as Sodium Sulphate ...

So, as we start reading the above quotation, we are nodding our heads in agreement; we are then mildly interested to see Broad's acknowledgement that in his time it was 'a matter of controversy whether [emergence] actually applies to anything', and approve of his philosophical etiquette in allowing this fact; but we finish our reading with everything in ruins, as Broad points to the formation of salt crystals as an example of this powerful and mysterious phenomenon of emergence in operation! Here he is [8, p. 62] on the 'emergence' of water from hydrogen and oxygen:

> Oxygen has certain properties and Hydrogen has certain other properties. They combine to form water, and the proportions in which they do this are fixed. Nothing that we know about Oxygen by itself or in its combinations with anything but Hydrogen would give us the least reason to suppose that it would combine with Hydrogen at all ... Here we have a clear instance of a case where, so far as we can tell, the properties of a whole composed of two constituents could not have been predicted from a knowledge of the properties of these constituents taken separately ...

Unfortunately, this was not an error peculiar to Broad. Part of the vitality of the emergentist movement at that time derived from such scientific examples. But within a very short time, increased understanding of how chemical reactions could be explained in terms of (reduced to) subatomic physics was to undermine this key component of emergentist thinking, and play a key role in the subsequent decline of the movement's influence. As McLaughlin puts it [44, pp. 89-90]:

> In a span of roughly one hundred years, British Emergentism enjoyed a great rise and suffered a great fall. ...It is one of my main contentions that advances in science, not philosophical criticism, led to the fall of British Emergentism ... In their quest to discover "the connexion or lack of connexion of the various sciences" (Broad 1923, pp. 41–42), the emergentists left the dry land of the a priori to brave the sea of empirical fortune ... and for a while winds of evidence were in their sails; but the winds gradually diminished, and eventually ceased altogether to blow their way. Without these winds in its sail, the British Emergentist movement has come to an almost complete halt.

Abstracting features of the real world can be a dangerous, even reckless, occupation. The abstractions need to be clearly defined, and applied to well-understood real contexts. Emergence should not be used too loosely as a repository for things we do not yet understand. On the other hand, we will see that the identification of true emergence arguably depends on an analysis of definability in the real world. And given the number of intractable problems the notion of definability throws up even in the 'safer' mathematical context, it is no surprise that mistakes will inevitably occur.

7. The Mathematics of Emergence

Things have not changed that much in the eighty years since the heyday of British emergentism. One knows exactly what Ronald Arkin is referring to when he says ([2, p. 105]):

> Emergence is often invoked in an almost mystical sense regarding the capabilities of behavior-based systems. Emergent behavior implies a holistic capability where the sum is considerably greater than its parts. It is true that what occurs in a behavior-based system is often a surprise to the system's designer, but *does the surprise come because of a shortcoming of the analysis of the constituent behavioral building blocks and their coordination, or because of something else?* (My emphasis)

The success of the Turing Test for machine intelligence inspired the devising of an observer-based Test for Emergence, by Ronald, Sipper and Capcarrère [62]. Here is an outline of the basic criteria they list for the validation of emergence within a given system – where the the key player here, the observer, may also be the system designer:

(1) **Design**: The system has been constructed by the designer, by describing local elementary interactions between components (e.g., artificial creatures and elements of the environment) in a language $\mathfrak{L}_1$.

(2) **Observation**: The observer is fully aware of the design, but describes global behaviors and properties of the running system, over a period of time, using a language $\mathfrak{L}_2$.

(3) **Surprise**: The language of design $\mathfrak{L}_1$ and the language of observation $\mathfrak{L}_2$ are distinct, and the causal link between the elementary interactions programmed in $\mathfrak{L}_1$ and the behaviors observed in $\mathfrak{L}_2$ is non-obvious to the observer – who therefore experiences surprise.

In other words, there is a cognitive dissonance between the observer's mental image of the system's design stated in $\mathcal{L}_1$ and his contemporaneous observation of the system's behavior stated in $\mathcal{L}_2$.

There is a parallel between the Turing Test context and that of the Emergence Test, in that the role of observer is reflects a practical reality. On the other hand, the element of peer review, so appropriate to the task of recognising machine intelligence, does not fit the emergence-recognition task so well, even for emergence related to mental processes. What the test does do is clarify somewhat that practical reality mentioned above. A nice touch is the formal distinguishing of the difference between the languages pertaining to different levels of observation, preparing the way for mathematical analysis of relationships between these languages, and comparisons of relative complexities.

There are already a number of areas in which putative emergence has been approached via mathematical frameworks in which the theory necessarily delivers descriptions framed in explicit and concise language. What is usually apparent in such cases is the presence of non-linearity and an associated presence of mathematically generated infinities and of implicit quantifiers.

In the 1950s, Alan Turing followed through on an old interest in the origin of patterns in nature, proposing a simple reaction-diffusion system describing chemical reactions and diffusion to account for morphogenesis, i.e., the development of form and shape in biological systems. Some of his best-known work in this direction relates to phyllotaxis and the relationship of the standard Fibonacci series to the arrangement of leaves or petals etc. in plants. Typical of Turing, his work on this seems to combine detailed formalisation of concepts and working out of unexpected mathematical relationships in particular cases, with much more far-reaching and visionary ambitions. In a letter to the leading physiologist Professor J.Z. Young, dated 8th February, 1951, Turing talks of working on:

> ...my mathematical theory of embryology ...This is yielding to treatment, and it will so far as I can see, give satisfactory explanations of
>
> i) Gastrulation.
>
> ii) Polygonally symmetrical structures, e.g., starfish, flowers.
>
> iii) Leaf arrangement, in particular the way the Fibonacci series (0,1,1,2,3, 5,8,13,...) comes to be involved.

iv) Colour patterns on animals, e.g., stripes, spots and dappling.

v) Patterns on nearly spherical structures such as some Radio-lara, but this is more difficult and doubtful.

I am really doing this now because it is yielding more easily to treatment. ...

Turing goes on to mention connections with more difficult questions related to brain structure, leading Hodges to speculate that Turing's eventual aim was a logical description of the nervous system. It is this overall vision of drawing out the mathematical underpinnings of nature, ones basic enough to have application to the human brain, which is specially relevant to the topic of this article.

See the webpage on Alan Turing and Morphogenesis maintained by Jonathan Swinton [72] for a wealth of further information.

Under the *synergetics* label comes a whole body of mathematically framed approaches to emergence, associated with the physicist Hermann Haken. Another key figure in the area is Ilya Prigogine, whose work on the mathematical modelling of nonlinear and irreversable processes and dissipative structures brought him the 1977 Nobel Prize in Chemistry. Michael Bushev's book [11] *Synergetics - Chaos, Order, Self-Organization* gives a useful overview of the area.

While drawing technically on the analysis of phase-transitions in thermodynamics, synergetics has grown into an interdisciplinary field dealing with the origins and evolution of macroscopic patterns and spacio-temporal structures in interactive systems. The emphasis is on mapping out *self-organisational* processes in science and the humanities – e.g., autopoiesis.

Synergetics, with its focus on the notion of self-organisation, shifts the viewpoint on emergent phenomena. We switch from interested and surprised observer, to proactive participant groping for the descriptive framework in which to express the connection between microscopic and macroscopic structure. This is the perspective we will maintain throughout the remainder of this article.

8. Definability and Emergent Structure

For the most part, our relationship with emergence involves observation, surprise, and attempts to describe the link between a basic, well understood interactive local structure, and observed emergent patterns of behaviour and more advanced formations. For the most part we follow the familiar route from empirical data to theory — where even a two-way, dialectical interaction between the two does not disturb the essential dominance of the real world in the process. For instance, this is what Turing did for the role of Fibonacci numbers in relation to the sunflower etc.

Theoretically, the element of surprise may arise from the elegance or cleverness of the description discovered. And if the character of the description produces an emotional response in the mathematician or scientist, it is a reasonable guess that the close relationship between the material phenomenon and its description may mean that the character of the description has a key role in in constraining that phenomenon in observably surprising ways. In mathematics, it is well-known that complicated descriptions may take us beyond what is computable — so we certainly have here a potential source of surprise in emergence.

We are now close to capturing an important intuition concerning the relationship between descriptions and the real world, whereby descriptions come to assume the dominant role; the intuition is that entities *exist because of, and according to,* mathematical laws. This is what Leibniz [40] wrote in *The Monadology*, section 32, explaining his *principle of sufficient reason*:

> ... by virtue of which there can be found no fact that is true or existent, or any true proposition, without there being a sufficient reason for its being so and not otherwise, although we cannot know these reasons in most cases.

We can think of 'sufficient reason' as being in a broad sense a *description* of how something arises from a given context, and 'fact' as something we observe to have a real-world validity or existence. It then follows that natural phenomena not only generate descriptions, but arise and derive form from them. The picture is of a world in which basic structure gives rise to further structure describable from below. We then have two important observations: One is that this is redolent of the emergentists' layering of scientific fields; and secondly, that it connects with a useful abstraction —

the concept of mathematical definability, which formalises what we mean by describability in a mathematical structure. The payoff is a new precision to our experience of emergence as a potentially non-algorithmic determinant of events.

Of course, definability is relatively undervalued as a useful mathematical concept. Unlike, say, 'consistency', which has long since been usefully assimilated into the culture, and is no longer recognised as coming out of the logicians toolbox — definability plays a fairly minor role in everyday discourse. Definability is a key concept for those trying to formulate theories about the real universe, with foundational work in this context going back to Hans Reichenbach [58] in 1924, and somewhat later, Carl Gustav Hempel [29]. The mathematical framework within which definability is discussed nowadays was formulated over a period of years, and first appeared in Alfred Tarski's 1931 paper [73] (translated, and reprinted, in [74]).

When one considers definability in relation to how the universe provides 'sufficient reason' for the existence and uniqueness of its own component entities, one needs to deal with the fact that language is a human invention. On the other hand, the elements of logical structure underlying descriptions in a formal first-order language one is fairly safe in assuming to be features of any recognisable universe. It is basic causal relationships which we must consider to be essential ingredients of any universe with enough regularities to be subjected to scientific analysis, and those from which logical structure is derived are arguably the simplest. This leads us to the reasonable assumption that descriptions, giving rise to observed structure in the universe, are not dependent on man-made language, quite the reverse.

There is a language-free approach to identifying those relations on a structure which are fixed uniquely by its basic relations, involving looking at the *automorphisms* of the structure. We say that a relation on a structure is *invariant* if and only if it remains fixed under all automorphisms of the structure. Under the foregoing assumptions about language capturing fundamentals of a structure, invariance is a generalisation of the notion of definability. This does highlight the fact that in a language-dependent expression of 'sufficient reason' in a real context, the particular character of the language used to frame descriptions is very important — in fact, it is well-known that invariance can be characterised as a definability notion in a suitably extended language.

Associating emergence with precise notions of definability immediately leads us to expect a higher level of robustness of emergent phenomena than might otherwise expect. Replicating an interactive environment would lead one to expect the emerging phenomena, captured via definable relations, to be somewhat the similar in the distinct but similar contexts. And this is very much what one finds in practice: this is an intuition supported by experience. Here is Martin Nowak (Director, Program for Evolutionary Dynamics, Harvard University) writing in John Brockman's edited volume of distinguished scientists confessing to *What We Believe But Cannot Prove* [9]:

> I believe the following aspects of evolution to be true, without knowing how to turn them into (respectable) research topics.
>
> Important steps in evolution are robust. Multicellularity evolved at least ten times. There are several independent origins of eusociality. There were a number of lineages leading from primates to humans. If our ancestors had not evolved language, somebody else would have.

In the present context, our universe is that of the human brain. And here, as in the wider physical universe, we have a very good picture of the basic interactions within the brain. What we need is to compare our refined model of emergence with what we know about the brain and the higher mental functionality we would like to relate it to.

9. Supervenience and Emergence in focus

According to Jaegwon Kim [34, pp. 14–15], supervenience:

> ...represents the idea that mentality is at bottom physically based, and that there is no free-floating mentality unanchored in the physical nature of objects and events in which it is manifested.

There are different ways of expressing this more formally, but the informal notion will serve us well enough for now.

The hope is for a clarified notion of emergence helping us pin down the nature of supervenience, and so, of intelligent thought and other aspects of human mentality. The aim is a model which reconciles the pressing and apparently inconsistent claims of physicalism and dualism on our intuitions about the mind. These post-Cartesian expectations include:

- Achieving a non-reductive physicalism, delivering –
- Mind-body supervenience;
- The physical irreducibility of the mental – including consciousness, qualia;
- And the causal efficaciousness of the mental;
- With definability removing conflict between vertical determination and horizontal causation.

But in doing this, we have a number of tasks. One is to identify a role for emergence in mental activity, given the warnings we encountered earlier concerning too loose an application of the criteria for emergence. Another is to examine the extent to which emergence equips our abstraction of mentality, and to isolate phenomena needing further explanation. And, having done this, to fill out, however schematically we allow ourselves to work, the mathematical model within which we want our appropriate notion of definability to be operative.

For our first task we should enlist the help of the Emergence Test. The basic design of the brain is by now well understood. The local interactivity has even been mathematically modelled, and we return to this below; on the other hand, there are mental phenomena which involve non-local activities, which could well point to emergence at work, but whose content, and qualifications for passing the surprise criterion 3 of the Emergence Test, are, in this context, definitely best assessed by us as observers of mentality. (The need for different modes of description for the different levels here — corresponding to languages $\mathcal{L}_1$ and $\mathcal{L}_2$ of the test — is not in question.)

A rich source of such observations is Jacques Hadamard's 1945 book [27] on *The Psychology of Invention in the Mathematical Field*. Hadamard's conversations with Poincaré, who also had a special interest in mental creativity, provided much of the material for the book. In mathematical thinking, there is clearer division than usual between the exercise of pure reason and of more creative thinking. A striking instance of this is seen in the following account of Hadamard:

> At first Poincaré attacked [a problem] vainly for a fortnight, attempting to prove there could not be any such function ...

[quoting Poincaré]:
'Having reached Coutances, we entered an omnibus to go some place or other. At the moment when I put my foot on the step, the idea came to me, without anything in my former thoughts seeming to have paved the way for it ... I did not verify the idea ... I went on with a conversation already commenced, but I felt a perfect certainty. On my return to Caen, for conscience sake, I verified the result at my leisure.'

What is most striking about this anecdote is not so much the surprise ingredient, required by part 3 of the Emergence Test, although the hidden origin of Poincaré's solution to his problem is just what we are looking for in an emergent event. There is a *robustness* to Poincaré's unexpected idea, a 'perfect certainty'. He did not need to write anything down, he was able to carry on a conversation, and carry his valuable solution home entire, for later verification. This is just what we would expect from our refined model of emergence in terms of definability. Definability had given the idea a memetic quality.

Just to be sure this was not just a one-off inexplicably bizarre incident, here is Hadamard again quoting Poincaré:

'Then I turned my attention to the study of some arithmetical questions apparently without much success ... Disgusted with my failure, I went to spend a few days at the seaside and thought of something else. One morning, walking on the bluff, the idea came to me, with just the same characteristics of brevity, suddenness and immediate certainty, that the arithmetic transformations of indefinite ternary quadratic forms were identical with those of non-Euclidian geometry.'

Of course, most mathematicians have had some such experience, even if not so often as Poincaré. Alan Turing seems to have had something like this in mind when he gave the following interpretation of his 1939 attempt [77] to transcend the theoretical constraints presented by Gödel's incompleteness theorem:

Mathematical reasoning may be regarded ... as the exercise of a combination of ... intuition and ingenuity ... In pre-Gödel times it was thought by some that all the intuitive judgements of mathematics could be replaced by a finite number of ... rules. The necessity for intuition would then be entirely eliminated. In our discussions, however, we have gone to the opposite extreme and eliminated not intuition but ingenuity, and this in spite of the fact that our aim has been in much the same direction.

Logicians will know that the device Turing had tried to use to go beyond Gödel was a *representational* one, using recursive ordinals; and that the obstacle encountered was the inaccessibility of particular ordinals to algorithmic grasp.

10. Is that all there is? - Representation

Now let's return to the question of design featuring in parts 1 and 2 of the Emergence Test. How exactly do we bridge the gap between 'emergent' higher mental functionality and ... *what* algorithmic 'design'? Answering is difficult. As Rodney Brooks points out in *Nature* in 2001:

> ... neither AI nor Alife has produced artifacts that could be confused with a living organism for more than an instant.

The alarm bells ringing do not just concern getting the right underlying model. The modellers have done their best and met with limited success, making us ask if emergence is sufficient to explain what we observe in intelligent thought ... *is that all there is?*

And what about connectionist models of computation? They certainly seem to promise exciting things, including the delivery of more than a Turing machine does, as observed by 2005 David E. Rumelhart Prize recipient, Paul Smolensky, in an article [69] in 1988:

> There is a reasonable chance that connectionist models will lead to the development of new somewhat-general-purpose self-programming, massively parallel analog computers, and a new theory of analog parallel computation: they may possibly even challenge the strong construal of Church's Thesis as the claim that the class of well-defined computations is exhausted by those of Turing machines.

Obviously, connectionist models have come a long way since Turing's discussion [78] of 'unorganised machines' — see Christof Teuscher's fascinating book [75] on *Turing's Connectionism* for a full account of how Turing "was the first person to consider building artificial computing machines out of simple, neuron-like elements connected together into networks in a largely random manner" — and the McCulloch and Pitts [43] early paper on neural nets.[†] Despite disputes about the adequacies of neural network model – the dissenting work of Minsky and Papert [45] had a big effect on the area – the approach is still responsible for numerous innovative and exciting developments (see the by now classic contribution of McClelland and Rumelhart [42]).

But for Steven Pinker "... neural networks alone cannot do the job". And focussing on our elusive higher functionality, Pinker points to a "kind of mental fecundity called recursion". By this he seems to have in mind the re-use of *emergent* mental images within mental processes which are responsible for such emergence. This clearly goes beyond the sort of standard recursions one can commonly find neural nets performing. Here is an illustrative example from Pinker [50]:

> We humans can take an entire proposition and give it a role in some larger proposition. Then we can take the larger proposition and embed it in a still-larger one. Not only did the baby eat the slug, but the father saw the baby eat the slug, and I wonder whether the father saw the baby eat the slug, the father knows that I wonder whether he saw the baby eat the slug, and I can guess that the father knows that I wonder whether he saw the baby eat the slug, and so on.

The new element in such recursions is *representation* of non-local collections of data, and again one can identify definability as providing a key concept here. The non-locality is something familiar to neuroscientists, as is the reaching for a physical mechanism for implementing that representation process which feeds into the recursions apparent at the mental level. Making a similar point in the following passage [16, p. 170] from his book on *The Feeling Of What Happens*, the neurologist Antonio Damasio gives a nice description of the hierarchical development of a particular instance of consciousness within the brain, interacting with some external object:

> ... both organism and object are mapped as neural patterns, in first-order maps; all of these neural patterns can become images ... The sensorimotor maps pertaining to the object cause

---

[†]It is an interesting observation on the history of computability after Turing, that even Stephen Kleene, sometimes held responsible for computability (or 'recursive function theory' as he called it) becoming a niche technical area with little connection with the real world, was himself interested in McCulloch and Pitts' paper. Out of this interest grew his own 1956 paper [36] on neural nets (a paper which one will search for in vain in the standard texts on recursion theory).

> changes in the maps pertaining to the organism ... [These]
> changes ... can be re-represented in yet other maps (second-
> order maps) which thus represent the relationship of object and
> organism ... The neural patterns transiently formed in second-
> order maps can become mental images, no less so than the
> neural patterns in first-order maps.

The picture is one of re-representation of neural patterns formed across some region of the brain, in such a way that they can have a computational relevance in forming new patterns. The key conception is that of computational loops incorporating, in a controlled way, these 'second-order' aspects of the computation itself. This reminds us of the layering scenario C.D. Broad, but there is something more complicated going on.

11. Definability in What Structure?

There are, in addition to neural nets, other computational models expressing metaphors for natural processes. Examples include quantum and molecular computing, membrane computing, cellular automata, L-systems, DNA computing, swarm and evolutionary computation, and relativistic computing. Many of these have basic algorithmic content which gives rise to new emergent forms, but none of them seem to have the power shown by the human mind to represent these forms in such a way as to convert them into fodder for their own algorithmic appetites. Here is Damasio again [16, p. 170]:

> As the brain forms images of an object – such as a face, a
> melody, a toothache, the memory of an event – and as the
> images of the object affect the state of the organism, yet another
> level of brain structure creates a swift nonverbal account of
> the events that are taking place in the varied brain regions
> activated as a consequence of the object-organism interaction.
> The mapping of the object-related consequences occurs in first-
> order neural maps representing the proto-self and object; the
> account of the causal relationship between object and organism
> can only be captured in second-order neural maps ... one might
> say that the swift, second-order nonverbal account narrates a
> story: *that of the organism caught in the act of representing its*
> *own changing state as it goes about representing something else.*

In order to get at the essence of what is happening ,here, one needs to get at the essential computational content of definability. One needs to strip away the particularities of diverse natural contexts, and abstract from nature a model which will reveal to us the theoretical constraints on emergence and definability — in the same way that Gödel, working with formal systems, revealed to us basic constraints on algorithmically accessed knowledge. The outcome in prospect is not just a schematic understanding of mental processes, but a model of very general applicability.

Models based closely on particular aspects of nature may deliver very important practical computational benefits, even though there is always the difficulty of developing a *range* of algorithms implementable within a particular model. The benefits of abstraction are well-known. It facilitates depth of theory. It can put apparently diverse contexts within a common framework, enabling one to get an overview. This is important when one is trying to suitably locate emergent phenomena, in that the 'special sciences' which the early emergentists sought to arrange hierarchically do impinge on each other. One needs a model in which emergent entities can be both differentiated, and at the same time can keep their essential character as information transferable across scientific fields. It is true that the division into 'special sciences' is an empirical reality, and makes a lot of sense from the point of view of providing work-spaces within which Thomas Kuhn's 'normal science' (the bread and butter of scientific research) can take place. But given the complexity of the brain and its mental attributes, in which the sort of recursions highlighted by Pinker and Damasio feature, there is a need for a corresponding level of theory which is not yet current. Such a theory needs to capture the abundant descriptive material relating many different contexts, but give it a precision and technical content which will clarify many of the current confusions and controversies. It may not provide us with the sort of practically useful reductions which people are commonly drawn to, but it may provide us with a better idea of the value and limitations of such reductions.

Looking to lessons from other areas, there are a number of fundamental problems facing physicists, for example. A number of these can be expressed as definability problems. High on the list of such problems relates to the standard model of particle physics. As Peter Woit describes it in the introduction to his book *Not Even Wrong: The Failure of String Theory and the Continuing Challenge to Unify the Laws of Physics*:

> By 1973, physicists had in place what was to become a fantastically successful theory of fundamental particles and their interactions, a theory that was soon to acquire the name of the standard model. Since that time, the overwhelming triumph of the standard model has been matched by a similarly overwhelming failure to find any way to make further progress on fundamental questions

Later in the book, he explains: "One way of thinking about what is unsatisfactory about the standard model is that it leaves seventeen non-trivial numbers still to be explained, ... ". How does the universe *define* its own basic components, its laws and entities? There are a number of more-or-less unsatisfactory ways of skirting round this question, in the main appealing to outside assistance from God or Many Worlds (with the addition of the anthropic principle), but the best answer would be an explanation of how the material universe *does it for itself*. Lee Smolin in his recent book *The Trouble With Physics* [70] lists 'Five Great Problems in Theoretical Physics', all of which can be related to basic questions of how and why certain observable features of the real universe arise, or, from our perspective, how the universe *defines* itself. Or, equally important, how it fails to define things. Here are two of Smolin's problems, slightly paraphrased:

- Combine general relativity and quantum theory into a single theory that can claim to be the complete theory of nature.
- Resolve the problems in the foundations of quantum mechanics

For the former, definability considerations in a suitable model might lead one to a negative answer: No such theory exists. And for the latter, allowing that the universe might *fail* to define entities uniquely a basic levels might clarify a lot.

But to return to our question: Definability in what structure? For Smolin, it is causality which is fundamental, and one has to admit that it is hard to say anything about a universe without causal relations. Or to put it another way, if one were to design a universe from nothing, and do it in as simple and incremental way as possible, one would need to have in mind a blueprint in which basic entities, involving simple mathematical relations, were stipulated. This how Smolin [70, p. 241] argues the case:

> It is not only the case that the spacetime geometry determines
> what the causal relations are. This can be turned around:
> Causal relations can determine the spacetime geometry ... Its
> easy to talk about space or spacetime emerging from some-
> thing more fundamental, but those who have tried to develop
> the idea have found it difficult to realize in practice. ... We now
> believe they failed because they ignored the role that causality
> plays in spacetime. These days, many of us working on quan-
> tum gravity believe that causality itself is fundamental - and is
> thus meaningful even at a level where the notion of space has
> disappeared.

So, to paraphrase Smolin, not only do global features of the universe constrain its causal structure; it is also the case that causal relations have
comprise a structure which may determine the nature of the global relations on that structure. We are back with the basic mathematical notions
of definability and invariance needed to express such notions. What Smolin
has in mind is a range of approaches, associated with 'early champions of
causality' such as Roger Penrose, Rafael Sorkin, Fay Dowker, and Fotini
Markopoulou.

Of course, the notion of causality has been discussed since at least the
time of Aristotle, while it was David Hume (in [31], for example) who most
memorably brought out the need for more clarity. For us, causal relations
are not just observed successions of contiguous events inductively extended;
they involve some necessary connection, which, since the time of Newton,
we have expected to be mathematical in nature. Even Hume [31, p. 56]
asserts:

> Shall we rest contented with these two relations of contiguity
> and succession? By no means ... there is a NECESSARY CON-
> NEXION to be taken into consideration.

There are now two important observations concerning the mathematical modelling of causal relationships. The first is the obvious one that ever
since Newton, we have tried, and to a large extent succeeded, in characterising *basic* causal relations in terms of functions over the real numbers
(sometimes this real domain being implicit, and needing some coding to
coax out); and that these functions tend to have a high degree of continuity and accessibility to computer processing. And the second observation
is that there are other causal relations which are still within the scientific

domain, and describable in terms of real numbers, but which do not appear to produce *computable* relationships. We saw examples of the latter earlier.

The scenario we have been building is one in which relations in science are those subject to descriptions, and, in fact, in terms or real numbers. And that these relations are subject to hierarchical classification in terms of their logical complexity in some appropriate formal language. The claim is that in each area of science, the basic relations are computable ones; that the limitation to such relations still gives us a very good correspondence between science and 'reality'; and that these basic relations are truly basic in that the more complicated causality we encounter is somehow associated with — is in fact definable in terms of — our basic computable causal relations. Maybe the simplest example is Krcisel's three-body situation. One can try and reduce the problem of predicting the motion to the computable two-body situation, but then the underlying infinitary nature of the non-linear mathematics produces something closely akin to an emergent phenomenon. The physical context is not obviously 'global' in the sense that the large-scale formations in the Cat's Eye Nebula are, but there is a mathematical dimension to the causality which serves a similar role in making description more difficult, and prediction not computable.

In the next section we give a brief introduction to the Turing model of computation with real inputs, designed to capture the basic causal relations of Newton and science more generally. And the final section will look at what we can extract from what we know so far about about Turing invariance and definability.

12. The Turing Model Extended

The oracle Turing machine, which made its first appearance in Turing [77], should be familiar enough. The details are not important, but can be found in most reasonable introductions to computability (see for instance [13]).

The basic form of the questioning permitted is modelled on that of everyday scientific practice. This is seen most clearly in today's digital data gathering, whereby one is limited to receiving data which can be expressed, and transmitted to others, as information essentially finite in form. But with the model comes the capacity to collate data in such a way as enable us to deal with arbitrarily close approximations to infinitary inputs and hence outputs, giving us an exact counterpart to the computing scientist working with real-world observations. If the different number inputs to the oracle machine result in 0-1 outputs from the corresponding Turing computations, one can collate the outputs to get a binary real computed from the oracle real, the latter now viewed as an input. This gives a partial computable functional Φ, say, from reals to reals.

As usual, one cannot computably know when the machine for Φ computes on a given natural number input, so Φ may not always give a fully defined real output. So Φ may be partial. One can computably list all oracle machines, and so index the infinite list of all such Φ, but one cannot computably sift out the partial Φ's from the list.

Anyway, put $\mathbb{R}$ together with this list, and we get the Turing Universe. Depending on one's viewpoint, this is either a rather reduced scientific universe, or a much expanded one. The familiar mathematical presentation of it is due to Emil Post [53], in his search for the informational underpinnings of computational structure.

Post's first step was to gather together binary reals which are computationally indistinguishable from each other, in the sense that they are mutually Turing computable from each other. Mathematically, this delivered a more standard mathematical structure to investigate — the familiar upper semi-lattice of the *degrees of unsolvability*, or *Turing degrees*.

Schematically, as we have argued, any causal context framed in terms everyday computable mathematics can be modelled in terms of Turing reductions. In particular, viewing scientific observations as causal events, one can model these computations with oracles, as

Anyway, emergence can now be formalised as definability over the appropriate substructure of the Turing universe; or more generally, as invariance under automorphisms of the Turing universe. Any computable causal relation will be found amongst those listed by Turing and forming part of the Turing universe.

This brings us to a well-known research programme, initiated by Hartley Rogers in his 1967 paper [60], in which he drew attention to the fundamental problem of characterising the Turing invariant relations. Again, the intuition is that these are key to pinning down how basic laws and entities emerge as mathematical constraints on causal structure. It is important to notice how the richness of Turing structure discovered so far becomes the raw material for a multitude of non-trivially definable relations, matching in its complexity what we attempt to model.

Unfortunately, the current state of Rogers' programme is in some disarray. For a number of years research in this area was dominated by a proposal originating with the Berkeley mathematician Leo Harrington, which can be (very) roughly stated:

Bi-interpretability Conjecture: *The Turing definable relations are exactly those with information content describable in second-order arithmetic.*

Most importantly, bi-interpretability is not consistent with the existence of non-trivial Turing automorphisms. Despite decades of work by a number of leaders in the field, the exact status of the conjecture is still a matter of controversy. For those of us who have grown up with Thomas Kuhn's 1962 book [38] on the structure of scientific revolutions, such tensions can be seen as signs that something scientifically important is at stake.

There are other computational reducibilities with good claims to model particular causal contexts. Particularly important is the generalisation of Turing reducibility in which non-deterministic computations are permitted. This provides a natural model of environments where computations call on auxiliary information which is possibly incomplete, so that an oracle would be forced to remain silent, possibly stalling the computation permanently while the machine waited for a non-existent reply from the oracle. In this situation, 'guessing' at certain points in a computation might enable one to avoid using information one cannot access. There are everyday examples of such situations. Mathematically (see [13, ch. 11]), the model is usually presented in terms of *enumeration reducibility*.

The bi-interpretability conjecture can be applied to other models of relative computation, but is quite sensitive to the way information is accessed. Turing reducibility and enumeration reducibility, which have strong claims to having captured the most general mode of effective computation from real information, including that involved in basic natural laws, human observation, and currently feasible computer functionality, seem to have a peculiarly complex theory. For them, there is a rich body of definable relations (as one would expect in a candidate model for aspects of real-world complexity), but relations definable in everyday language (by which we mean here second-order arithmetic) may still turn out to be undefinable in these models. Constrain the information-gathering capacity of the reducibility, and definability in the resulting structure becomes less interesting – for instance, in the structure of the *many-one* degrees, the zero degree consisting of the outright computable objects is the only one definable. But, moving towards the other end of the spectrum, if we allow a computation to call on (uncoded) infinitary information before completion, and one may get bi-interpretability, ruling it out as a route to modelling of the sort of ambiguity one sees at the quantum level, or in mental activity at the subconscious level. For instance, the hyperdegrees admit bi-interpretability.

13. Mental Causation Revisited

The test of any mathematical model is its success in providing persuasive explanations for natural phenomena for which previously there were at best conflicting interpretations. For better understanding of the relationship between brain and mentality, we still have the basic questions:

- How can mentality have a causal role in a world that is fundamentally physical?
- And what about overdetermination – the problem of phenomena having both mental and physical causes?

As Jaegwon Kim [35] concisely puts it:

> ... the problem of mental causation is solvable only if mentality is physically reducible; however, phenomenal consciousness resists physical reduction, putting its causal efficacy in peril.

What we have outlined above is how we can give computational content to emergence, use emergence to link functions of the brain to higher mental activity, use definability to contribute substance to recursions involving mental representations, and hence present the whole organism with a new coherence and organic entity.

Let us summarise what we now have at hand.

Firstly, it is clear that the notion of causality can be a misleading concept in this context. This is certainly true in relation to overdetermination — that is, the problem of mental phenomena having both physical and mental causes. As we have seen, causality in the everyday sense can be substantiated through the existence of mathematical relationships between events, which provide a definite mathematical connection from the caused to the causing. But when one looks at emergent phenomena, one can have both emergent objects *and* emergent relationships. The emergent relationships, at the newly emergent level, may be computable in the classical sense, whilst the relationship between the emergent phenomenon and the substratum on which it rests may be more complex, to the point of being beyond computation. There is clearly a causal relationship between emergent phenomenon and substratum, and we may have a definition of it, so that the mathematical qualification for vertical causality exists. But the computable relations at the emergent level may be much more in evidence, to the point where they become the basis for a scientific field, with its own mathematical relations and attending causality. Where is the *real* causality here? We need to recognise that the old notions are unhelpful, and that a full description of the mathematics involved is the best we can do. Further, we need to recognise that the different levels can interact in quite complex ways, and that some of these interactions, connecting emergent and basic levels can be quite basic and mechanistic themselves. This, of course, is the basis for the success of modern psychiatry, employing mechanistic interventions to modify the emergent mentality. What we are seeing here is a renewed dualism, but a more mature version of it. This is implicit in a recent paper [15] of Antonella Corradini, which has had an influence on the development of this article.

Kim comments [35, p. 15]:

> Mind-body supervenience has been embraced by some philosophers as an attractive option because it has seemed to them a possible way of protecting the autonomy of the mental domain without lapsing back into antiphysicalist dualism.

But goes on:

> how [is] it ... possible, on such a picture, for mentality to have causal powers, powers to influence the course of natural events.

This forms part of a section [35, pp. 13–22] on "The Supervenience/Exclusion Argument", which can be used as an exercise (see particularly p. 19) in applying our more coherent conception of causality.

So – recognisable 'causality' occurs at different levels of the model, connected by relative definability. But this causality may occur in the form of relations with identifiable algorithmic content, this content at higher levels being emergent. The diverse levels form a unity, with the 'causal' structure observed at one level reflected at other levels — with the possibility of both computable and incomputable 'feedback' between levels.

One striking feature of the current debate about supervenience and non-reductive physicalism, is the extensive (and often very perceptive) contribution from those with a theological interest. The aim of setting the human mind free from the scientific cage of physicalism is a demanding and worthy project which melds well with a religious agenda. This is William Hasker, writing in *The Emergent Self* [28, p. 175]:

> The "levels" involved are levels of organisation and integration, and the downward influence means that the behavior of "lower" levels – that is, of the components of which the "higher-level" structure consists – is different than it would otherwise be, because of the influence of the new property that emerges in consequence of the higher-level organisation.

This is consistent with our model. Our model does preserve determinism through all levels, but is not Laplacian. There is no predictive demon permitted, there is no limit to the potential richness of information involved. The mathematical blueprint for mental attributes and activities may well be contained within the actuality of the physical brain. But cut open the brain, or subject it to less intrusive inspection, and you will see only imperfect evidence of the content of these levels. "We" are participants according to the newly emergent rules and entities, and our mentality is part of the organism. And there is no omniscient god even consistent with this model; we have at best a "self-evolving god".‡

Although the mathematical model discussed here might not be to the total satisfaction of, say, Samuel Alexander (whose emergent phenomena were held to be of quite mysterious origin), it does go some way towards rescuing consciousness, qualia and free will from the reductionists' dead hand. For instance, mental causality is given the sort of status that the person in the street would accept, along with consciousness and qualia. These do 'exist'. And the ubiquitous incomputability consequent on logically com-

---

‡A description due to my wife, I should say.

plex definitions raises the sort of everyday judgements we make above the level of what a computer does. There really can be adventure in thinking, involving hidden agendas in which the whole organism participates, and which certainly gives the feeling of free will, and allows us to live with a very valid assumption of the importance of human mental activity.

References

1. S. Alexander. *Space, Time, and Deity* Vol. 2, 1927.
2. R.C. Arkin. *Behaviour-Based Robotics.* MIT Press, 1998.
3. E.J. Beggs and J.V. Tucker. *Experimental computation of real numbers by Newtonian machines.* Proceedings Royal Society Series A, **463** (2007), 1541–1561.
4. E.J. Beggs, J.F. Costa, B. Loff and J.V. Tucker. *Computational complexity with experiments as oracles.* Proceedings Royal Society Series A, **464** (2008), 2777–2801.
5. L. Blum, F. Cucker, M. Shub and S. Smale. *Complexity and Real Computation.* Springer, 1997.
6. L. Blum and S. Smale. *The Godel incompleteness theorem and decidability over a ring.* In *From Topology to Computation: Proceedings of the Smalefest (Berkeley, CA, 1990),* Springer, New York, 1993, pp.321–339.
7. V. Brattka. *The emperors new recursiveness: the epigraph of the expo- nential function in two models of computability.* In *Words, languages & combinatorics, III (Kyoto, 2000).* World Sci. Publishing, River Edge, NJ, 2003, pp.63–72.
8. C.D. Broad. *The Mind and Its Place In Nature.* Kegan-Paul, London, 1923.
9. J. Brockman (ed.). *What We Believe but Cannot Prove: Today's Leading Thinkers on Science in the Age of Certainty,* Harper Perennial, New York, 2006.
10. R. A. Brooks. *Elephants Dont Play Chess.* Robotics and Autonomous Systems, **6** (1990), 3–15.
11. M. Bushev. *Synergetics – Chaos, Order, Self-Organization.* World Scientific, 1994.
12. S.B. Cooper. *Clockwork or Turing U/universe? – remarks on causal determinism and computability.* In *Models and Computability* (S. B. Cooper and J. K. Truss, eds.), London Mathematical Society Lecture Note Series 259, Cambridge University Press, Cambridge, 1999, pp. 63–116.
13. S.B. Cooper. *Computability Theory.* Chapman & Hall/CRC, Boca Raton, London, New York, Washington, D.C., 2004.
14. S.B. Cooper and P. Odifreddi. *Incomputability in Nature.* In S.B. Cooper and S.S. Goncharov. *Computability and Models.* Kluwer Academic/Plenum, New York, Boston, Dordrecht, London, Moscow, 2003, pages 137–160.
15. A. Corradini. *The emergence of mind. A dualistic understanding.* In

A. Carsetti (ed.), *Causality, Meaningful Complexity and Knowledge Construction*, Springer, 2009.

16. A.R. Damasio. *The Feeling Of What Happens: Body and Emotion in the Making of Consciousness*, Harcourt Brace, 1999.

17. D. Davidson. *Mental Events*. In *Experience and Theory* (Foster and Swanson, eds.), Duckworth, London, 1970. Reprinted in Davidson, 2001.

18. D. Davidson. *Essays on Actions and Events*, 2nd ed. Oxford University Press, Oxford, 2001.

19. M. Davis. *The Universal Computer: The Road from Leibniz to Turing*. W.W. Norton, New York, London, 2000.

20. M. Davis. *The myth of hypercomputation*. In *Alan Turing: Life and legacy of a great thinker* (C. Teuscher, ed.), Springer-Verlag, Berlin, Heidelberg, 2004, pp. 195–212.

21. D.C. Dennett. *Consciousness Explained*. Little, Brown & Company, 1991.

22. R. Descartes. *Discourse on Method*. Paris, 1637.

23. D. Deutsch. *Quantum theory, the Church Turing principle, and the universal quantum computer*. Proc. Roy. Soc., A 400 (1985), 97–117.

24. F. Engels. *Socialism: Utopian and Scientific*. In *Revue Socialiste*, 1880. Reprinted in *Marx/Engels Selected Works* (trans. from the French by Paul Lafargue in 1892), vol. 3, pp.95–151.

25. Yu.L Ershov, S.S. Goncharov, A. Nerode, J.B. Remmel (Editors). *Handbook of Recursive Mathematics*, Volumes 1 and 2. Elsevier, Amsterdam, New York, Oxford, Tokyo, 1998.

26. E.R. Griffor (Editor). *Handbook of Computability Theory*. Elsevier, Amsterdam, New York, Oxford, Tokyo, 1999.

27. J. Hadamard. *The Psychology of Invention in the Mathematical Field*. Princeton Univ. Press, Princeton, 1945.

28. W. Hasker. *The Emergent Self*. Cornell University Press, Ithaca, London, 1999.

29. C.G. Hempel. *Fundamentals of Concept Formation in Empirical Science*. University of Chicago Press, Chicago, 1952.

30. A. Hodges. *Alan Turing: The Enigma*. Vintage, London, Melbourne, Johannesburg, 1992.

31. D. Hume. *A Treatise of Human Nature* (1740). Reprinted by Oxford University Press, Oxford, 1967.

32. T.H. Huxley. *On the Hypothesis that Animals are Automata, and its History*. The Fortnightly Review, n.s. **16** (1874), 555–580. Reprinted in *Method and Results: Essays by Thomas H. Huxley*, D. Appleton and Company, New York, 1898.

33. J. Kim. *Mind and Supervenience*. Cambridge University Press, Cambridge, 1993.

34. J. Kim. *Mind in a Physical World*. MIT Press, 1998.

35. J. Kim. *Physicalism, or Something Near Enough*. Princeton University Press, Princeton, Oxford, 2005.

36. S.C. Kleene. *Representation of events in nerve nets and finite automata*. In C. Shannon and J. McCarthy (eds.), *Automata Studies*, Annals of mathematics

studies, no. 34, Princeton University Press, Princeton, N.J., 1956, pp. 3–42.

37. G. Kreisel *Church's Thesis: a kind of reducibility axiom for constructive mathematics*. In *Intuitionism and proof theory: Proceedings of the Summer Conference at Buffalo N.Y. 1968* (A. Kino, J. Myhill and R. E. Vesley, eds.), North-Holland, Amsterdam, London, 1970, pp. 121–150.

38. T.S. Kuhn. *The Structure of Scientific Revolutions*. Third edition 1996, University of Chicago Press, Chicago, London.

39. P.S. de Laplace. *Essai Philosophique sur les Probabilités*. English trans. by F.W. Truscott and F.L. Emory, Dover, New York, 1951.

40. G.W. Leibniz. *La Monadologie* (1714). English translation by G.M. Ross, 1999.

41. Y. Matiyasevich. *Hilbert's Tenth Problem*. MIT Press, Cambridge, Mass., London, 1993.

42. J.L. McClelland and D.E. Rumelhart. *Parallel Distributed Processing: Explorations in the Microstructure of Cognition*. MIT Press, Cambrige, MA, 1986.

43. W. McCulloch and W. Pitts. *A logical calculus of the ideas immanent in nervous activity*. Bull. Math. Biophys. **5** (1943), 115–133.

44. B.P. McLaughlin. *The Rise and Fall of British Emergentism*. In *Emergence or Reduction? – Essays on the Prospects of Nonreductive Physicalism* (A. Beckermann, H. Flohr, J. Kim, eds.), de Gruyter, Berlin, 1992, pp. 49–93.

45. M. Minsky and S. Papert. *Perceptrons: An Introduction to Computational Geometry*, MIT Press, Cambridge MA, 1969.

46. P. Odifreddi. *Classical Recursion Theory*. North-Holland/Elsevier, Amsterdam, New York, Oxford, Tokyo, 1989.

47. P. Odifreddi. *Kreisel's Church*. In *Kreiseliana: About and Around Georg Kreisel* (ed. P. Odifreddi). A K Peters, 1996. Reprinted in Olszewski, Wolenski and Janusz, pp.353–382.

48. A. Olszewski, J. Wolenski and R. Janusz (eds.). *Church's Thesis After 70 Years*. Ontos Verlag, 2006.

49. R. Penrose. *The Emperor's New Mind: Concerning Computers, Minds, and the Laws of Physics*. Oxford University Press, Oxford, New York, Melbourne, 2002.

50. S. Pinker. *How the Mind Works*. W.W. Norton, New York, 1997.

51. G.J. Popek and R.P. Goldberg. *Formal requirements for virtualizable third generation rchitectures*. Communications of the ACM **17** (1974), 412–421.

52. E.L. Post. *Finite combinatory processes – Formulation 1*. J. of Symbolic Logic **1** (1936), 103–105; reprinted in Post (1994).

53. E. L. Post. *Degrees of recursive unsolvability: preliminary report*. (abstract). Bull. Amer. Math. Soc. **54** (1948), 641–642.

54. E.L. Post. *Solvability, Provability, Definability: The Collected Works of Emil L. Post* (Martin Davis, Editor). Birkhäuser, Boston, Basel, Berlin, 1994.

55. H. Putnam. *Minds and Machines*, reprinted in Putnam (1975).

56. H. Putnam. *The Nature of Mental States*, reprinted in Putnam (1975).

57. H. Putnam. *Mind, Language, and Reality*. Cambridge University Press, Cambridge, 1975.

58. H. Reichenbach. *Axiomatik der relativistischen Raum-Zeit-Lehre*, 1924. English translation: *Axiomatization of the theory of relativity*. University of California Press, 1969.

59. C. Reid. *Hilbert*. Springer-Verlag, Berlin, Heidelberg, New York, London, Paris, Tokyo, 1986 (paperback edition).

60. H. Rogers, Jr. *Some problems of definability in recursive function theory*. In *Sets, Models and Recursion Theory* (J.N. Crossley, ed.), Proceedings of the Summer School in Mathematical Logic and Tenth Logic Colloquium, Leicester, August–September, 1965, North-Holland, Amsterdam, pp. 183–201.

61. H. Rogers, Jr. *Theory of Recursive Functions and Effective Computability* (1967). Reprinted by MIT Press, Cambridge, Mass., London, 1987.

62. E.M.A. Ronald, M. Sipper and M.S. Capcarrère. *Design, observation, surprise! A test of emergence*. Artificial Life, **5** (1999), 225–239.

63. G. Ryle. *The Concept of Mind*. University of Chicago Press, Chicago, 1949.

64. D. G. Saari and Z. Xia. *Off to Infinity in Finite Time*. Notices of the Amer. Math. Soc. **42** (1995), 538–546.

65. J.R. Searle. *The Mystery of Consciousness*. Granta, London, 1997.

66. R. Shaw. *Strange attractors, chaotic behaviour, and information flow*. Z. Naturforsch, **36A** (1981), 80–112.

67. R. Shaw, *The dripping faucet as a model chaotic system*, The Science Frontier Express Series, Aerial Press, Santa Cruz, CA, 1984.

68. A. Sloman, *Some requirements for human-like robots: Why the recent overemphasis on embodiment has held up progress*. In : Creating Brain-Like Intelligence: From Basic Principles to Complex Intelligent Systems (B. Sendhoff, E. Körner, O. Sporns, H. Ritter, K. Doya, Eds.). Lecture Notes in Computer Science Vol. 5436, Springer 2009, pp. 248–277.

69. P. Smolensky. *On the proper treatment of connectionism*. Behavioral and Brain Sciences **11** (1988), 1–74.

70. L. Smolin. *The Trouble With Physics: The Rise of String Theory, the Fall of a Science and What Comes Next*. Houghton Mifflin, 2006.

71. R.I. Soare. *Recursively Enumerable Sets and Degrees*. Springer-Verlag, Berlin, Heidelberg, New York, London, Paris, Tokyo, 1987.

72. J. Swinton. *Alan Turing and morphogenesis*. Part of Jonathan Swinton's homepage: http://www.swintons.net/jonathan/turing.htm.

73. A. Tarski. *Sur les ensembles définissables de nombres réels. I*. Fundamenta Mathematicae, 17 (1931), 210–239.

74. A. Tarski. *On Definable Sets of Real Numbers*, translation of Tarski (1931) by J.H. Woodger. In A. Tarski, *Logic, Semantics, Metamathematics*, second edition, ed. by J. Corcoran. Hackett, Indianapolis, 1983, pp. 110–142.

75. C. Teuscher. *Turing's Connectionism: An Investigation of Neural Network Architectures*. Springer-Verlag, London, Berlin, Heidelberg, 2002.

76. Turing A. M. (1936) *On computable numbers, with an application to the Entscheidungsproblem*. Proc. London Math. Soc. (2) **42** (1936–7), pp. 230–265. Reprinted in A. M. Turing, *Collected Works: Mathematical Logic*, pp. 18–53.

77. A.M. Turing. *Systems of logic based on ordinals*. Proc. London Math. Soc. (2) **45** (1939), pp. 161–228. Reprinted in A. M. Turing, *Collected Works: Mathematical Logic*, pp. 81–148.

78. A. M. Turing. *Intelligent machinery*. National Physical Laboratory Report (1948). In *Machine Intelligence 5* (B. Meltzer and D. Michie, eds.), Edinburgh University Press, Edinburgh, 1969, pp. 3–23. Reprinted in A. M. Turing, *Collected Works: Mechanical Intelligence* (D. C. Ince, ed.), North-Holland, Amsterdam, New York, Oxford, Tokyo, 1992, pp. 107–127.

79. A.M. Turing. *Computing machinery and intelligence*. Mind **59** (1950), 433–460. Reprinted in A. M. Turing, *Collected Works: Mechanical Intelligence* (D. C. Ince, ed.), North-Holland, Amsterdam, New York, Oxford, Tokyo, 1992.

80. A.M. Turing. *Collected Works: Mathematical Logic* (R.O. Gandy and C.E.M. Yates, Editors). Elsevier, Amsterdam, New York, Oxford, Tokyo, 2001.

81. J. van Leeuwen and J. Wiedermann. *The Turing Machine Paradigm in Contemporary Computing*. In *Mathematics Unlimited – 2001 and Beyond* (eds. B. Enquist and W. Schmidt), LNCS, Springer, 2000.

82. M. White. *Isaac Newton – The Last Sorcerer*. Fourth Estate, London, 1997.

CHAPTER 6

A DIALOGUE CONCERNING TWO WORLD SYSTEMS: INFO-COMPUTATIONAL VS. MECHANISTIC

Gordana Dodig-Crnkovic and Vincent C. Müller

Mälardalen University & Anatolia College/ACT
www.idt.mdh.se/personal/gdc & www.typos.de

The dialogue develops arguments for and against adopting a new world system – info-computationalist naturalism – that is poised to replace the traditional mechanistic view. We try to figure out what the info-computational paradigm would mean, in particular its pancomputationalism. We discuss steps towards developing the new generalized notion of computing that is necessary here which includes both symbolic and sub-symbolic information processing, and its relation to traditional notions. We investigate whether pancomputationalism can possibly provide the basic causal structure to the world, whether the overall research programme of info-computationalist naturalism appears productive, especially when it comes to new rigorous approaches to the living world and whether it can revigorate computationalism in the philosophy of mind.

It is important to point out that info-computational naturalism does not invalidate mechanistic approach within the domains where it has shown its soundness, but it extends the domain of research to the classes of phenomena which were not possible to adequately address in terms of mechanistic approaches. The relationship is like the one between relativistic and classical physics or between non-Euclidean and Euclidian geometry, i.e. the new paradigm includes and generalizes the old one, making the older mechanistic paradigm a special case of the more general framework.

1. Introduction

1.1. *Galileo, Ptolemy, Mechanicism and Systèmes du Monde*

In his 1632 *Dialogue Concerning the Two Chief World Systems (Dialogo sopra i due massimi sistemi del mondo)*, Galileo contrasts two different world views: the traditional Ptolemaic geocentric system where every-

thing in the Universe circles around the Earth, vs. the emerging Coperni-
can system, where the Earth and other planets orbit the Sun. Even though
the question whether the Earth was the center of the Universe or not was
important in itself, the real scientific revolution was going on in the
background; the transition from qualitative Aristotelian physics to the
Galileo-Newtonian quantitative mechanistic physics necessary to support
the new worldview. The new model with equations of motion for celes-
tial bodies following Newton's laws set the standard for all of physics to
come. This mechanistic paradigm accommodates even for Quantum Mechanics and Theory of Relativity, two theories that are both part of the
classical mechanical "Clockwork Universe" and question its basic intuitions about a perfectly intuitive, regular and predictable "World-
Machine" *(Machina Mundi)*.

The mechanistic world view is based on the following principles:

(M1)   The ontologically fundamental entities of the physical reality
       are physical structures *(space-time & matter)* and change of
       physical structures *(motion)*.

(M2)   All the properties of any complex physical system can be de-
       rived from the properties of its components.

(M3)   Change of physical structures is governed by laws.

(M4)   The observer is outside of the system observed.

Mechanistic models assume that the system is closed, isolated from the
environment, and laws of conservation (energy, mass, momentum, etc.)
thus hold. Environment, if modelled at all, is treated only as a perturba-
tion for the steady state of the system.

1.2. Info-Computational Naturalism (ICON)

What we begin to see at present is a fundamentally new paradigm of not
only sciences but even a more general paradigm of the universe, comparable in its radically novel approach with its historical predecessors the
Mytho-poetical Universe and the Mechanistic Universe. We identify this
new paradigm as Info-Computational Universe.

According to info-computational naturalism (ICON) the physical universe is fundamentally an informational structure whose dynamics are identified as computational processes [Dodig-Crnkovic, 2006; 2008]. This computation process is Natural computing; see Bruce MacLennan's article in this volume. Mark Burgin's article, "Information Dynamics in a Categorical Setting", presents a common framework for information and computation, building a mathematical stratum of the general theory of information based on category theory.

A remarkable feature of info-computationalism is its ability to unify living and nonliving physical world and to provide clues to mental capacities in humans and animals. Of all grand unifications or *systèmes du monde* as Greg Chaitin says in his *Epistemology as Information Theory: From Leibniz to Ω* [Chaitin, 2007a] this is the first one holding promise to be able to explain and simulate in addition to non-living universe even the structure and behavior of living organisms, including the human mind.

Complexity is important for many physical phenomena, and is an essential characteristic of life, the domain in which the info-computational approach best shows its full explanatory power. Living organisms are complex, goal-oriented autonomous information-processing systems with ability of self-organization, self-reproduction (based on genetic information) and adaptation. They (we) evolved through pre-biotic and biological evolution from inanimate matter. The understanding of basic info-computational features of living beings has consequences for many fields, especially information sciences, cognitive science, psychology, neuroscience, theory of computing, artificial intelligence and robotics but also biology, sociology, economics and other fields where informational complexity is essential.

Being on the edge of a brand new era we have a good enough reason to follow Galileo's example and try to contrast two world systems – the existing and well established mechanistic framework with the new emerging unfinished but promising info-computational one.

The info-computational world view is based on the following principles:

(IC1)   The ontologically fundamental entities of the physical reality are *information* (structure) and *computation* (change).

(IC2) Properties of a complex physical system cannot be derived solely from the properties of its components. Emergent properties must be taken into account.

(IC3) Change of informational structures is governed by laws.

(IC4) The observer is a part of the system observed.

Info-computational models comprise *open systems* in communication with the environment. The environment is a constitutive element for an open complex info-computational system. A *network* of interconnected parts is a typical configuration, where understanding is sought on the meta-level with respect to constituent parts. Info-computational models include mechanistic ones as a special case when interaction of the system with the environment may be neglected.

In what follows we will try to contrast the mechanistic and info-computational positions. This dialogue between Müller (VCM) and Dodig-Crnkovic (GDC) is the result of a series of discussions on the topic we had on different occasions over the last couple of years.

2. Pancomputationalist Claims

VCM

When both authors were invited to contribute a debate to a conference in 2008[1], we jointly submitted an abstract that included the following characterization:

> Info-computationalism is the view that the physical universe can be best understood as computational processes operating on informational structure. Classical matter/energy in this model is replaced by information, while the dynamics are identified as computational processes. In this view the universe is one gigantic computer that continuously computes its next states, following physical laws.

Info-computationalism here appears as a conjunction of two theses: one

---

[1] "Philosophy's Relevance in Information Science" at the University of Paderborn, 3.-4.10.08, organized by Ruth Hagengruber. http://groups.uni-paderborn.de/hagengruber/pris08

about processes (computation) and one about structure (information). In this dialogue, I want to focus on the first one, that all processes are computational, which I shall call "pancomputationalism".[2] In any case, if this pancomputationalism fails, the stronger thesis of info-computationalism fails with it.

Our first task is to gain a better understanding of the thesis involved. I shall propose some alternative readings that will be further elucidated and evaluated in this dialogue. I will start with the strongest thesis and move to weaker ones; so if one agrees with a particular thesis on this list, one will probably agree with all that follow further down.

One reading of the basic thesis in the above quote is:

P1: The universe is a computer

This seems to be the strongest version, so I shall call it *"strong pancomputationalism"*. Perhaps I should mention that this view normally includes the thesis that the universe is physical, something that we shall just assume in the following. A bit more restricted is the reduction to changes or 'processes' in the universe:

P2: All processes are computational processes

This thesis is the main target of our discussion here, so I shall just call it *"pancomputationalism"*. Very often, the point of the theory in question, however, is not what processes *are* (whatever that may mean, exactly), but how they can be *described*, so this suggests another formulation:

P3: All processes can be described as computational processes

Weak pancomputationalism. This formulation, however is ambiguous as it stands, and I shall thus avoid it. Its ambiguity stems from the fact that – as I will explain presently - there are very different reasons to claim that processes can be described in this way; reasons concerning the theory of computing and reasons concerning the nature of the universe. Whether one wants to take a realist or an anti-realist view of computing will be decisive here. Reasons concerning the nature of the universe (realist reasons) might be formulated as follows:

---

[2] The term "pancomputationalism" was probably coined by [Floridi, 2004, 566].

P4: All processes can be described as computational processes because we discovered that they are computational

This theory can justly bear the title of a pancomputationalism because it claims to have discovered a fundamental fact about the world. It is, in fact, just the pancomputationalism of P2 plus the claim that this feature has been discovered, so I think P4 can be disregarded; it is just 'pancomputationalism'. Another possible explanation of P3 that relies on a particular (anti-realist) notion of computation is:

P5: All processes can be described as computational processes because there is nothing more to being a computational process than being described as such

Anti-realist weak pancomputationalism. This theory does not claim that the universe has a particular structure; in fact it is often used to argue *against* a theory that a part of the world (the mind) is computational in any substantial sense. Instead, it stems from the anti-realist view that it is our description as such that makes a process into a computational one. Versions of this tradition are represented, for example, by David Chalmers [Chalmers, 1993; 1994; 1996] John Searle [Searle, 1980; 1990; 1992, 207f] and Oron Shagrir [Shagrir, 2006]. While P5 thus has a lot of support in the literature, I would suggest that it is too weak for a substantial pancomputationalism in the sense envisaged by Dodig-Crnkovic.

What we need in our development of P3 is a realist formulation, like this one:

P6: All processes can be described as computational processes because this happens to be a useful way of describing them in scientific theory

Realist weak pancomputationalism. This thesis takes a realist view of computation and then claims that all the actual processes of the universe are such that they can be described as computational in a scientific theory of the universe (while some processes in other possible worlds might not have this feature). It is 'weak' because it only talks about ways of description, not about realist ontology – unlike P2.

If we wanted to regard the issue just in terms of how things may be described without claiming that this description is or should be part of a scientific theory, then we would descend to what is really just a metaphorical remark, and thus the end of our sequence:

P7: All processes can be described as if they were computational processes

Metaphorical pancomputationalism. This thesis is probably true and it looks like it might be extremely useful in areas as different as economics and microbiology. It does not say anything about the world, however, but that things may be described *as if* they were computational – be that scientific or not.

A further question is whether the claim of pancomputationalism, in one of the versions above, is meant to be a claim about 'everything' or 'everything deep down'; i.e. is computation a fundamental property of the universe ('deep down') and other properties relate to it systematically, e.g. they reduce to it? Or is literally everything in the universe computational? Against the latter, stronger, claim there are many areas of the universe (social, aesthetic, mental) that do not seem computational at all.[3] Are they, or are they 'deep down'?

GDC

P1: The universe is a computer

As all subsequent theses P2-P6 are just the weaker versions of P1 let me focus on the strongest claim, P1 in the first place. The pancomputationalist original claim is exactly P1. *Of that which is universe we say that it is a computer.* What pancomputationalists[4] actually aim for is not only giving the universe just another name ("computer") but they suggest that universe *computes*.

It is pretty obvious that universe computer is not of the same sort as my PC, as it contains stars, rocks, oceans, living organisms and all the rest (including PC's). So *we talk about a more general idea of computing and a computer.* This question of computing in real world, the nature of compu-

---

[3] Here are some examples of social, aesthetic or mental facts that do not seem computational: "The struggle over copyright in the digital age is really a power struggle", "Her hair curled beautifully", "My breath was taken away by the sight".
[4] http://en.wikipedia.org/wiki/Pancomputationalism

ting as implemented in physics, is addressed in this volume by MacLennan and Shagrir. Cooper and Sloman discuss questions of the relationship between computing, information and mind. Needless to say, in the pancomputational universe, mind is a result of natural computation that our brains supported by bodily sensors and actuators constantly perform.

In sum, I would say that all of proposed pancomputational claims P1-P6 are correct. The universe is a computer, but an unconventional (natural) one; its dynamics (temporal evolution) best can be understood as computation and it can be described as such. There is nothing more to being computational process but being used as computation.[5]

For the last claim P7, however, I propose it to be modified. Metaphor is a figure of speech while pancomputationalism concerns the physical world. I would say that pancomputationalism is a metaphor in the same sense as Niels Bohr's liquid drop model is a metaphor of atomic nucleus. In sciences we are used to talk about *models* and for a good reason. We use model as a tool to interact with the world. So if you agree to call it *model* instead of a *metaphor*, I would agree even with P7. I propose the following:

P7': All physical processes can be *modeled* as computational processes

which I recognize as pancomputationalist claim. We will have several occasions in this dialogue to return to the question of what is computing and to discuss unconventional (natural) computing that is going on in computational universe. In principle, there seems to be no ontological hindrance to our including the system or process we try to compute among the models we use. We then get what I take to be the fundamental idea of pancomputationalism: The function governing a process is calculated by the process itself[6]. The following remark by Richard Feynman lucidly explains the idea:

> It always bothers me that according to the laws as we understand them today, it takes a computing machine an infinite number of logi-

---

[5]As Kaj Børge Hansen puts it, "A computation is a thought experiment. We often increase our power and ability to do thought experiments by aiding our limited memory and imagination by symbolic representations, real and virtual models, and computers." (Personal communication.)

[6] For this formulation I thank KB Hansen.

cal operations to figure out what goes on in no matter how tiny a region of space and no matter how tiny a region of time… I have often
made the hypothesis that ultimately physics will not require a mathematical statement, that in the end the machinery will be revealed
and the laws will turn out to be simple.

[Feynman, 1965, 57][7]

3. Are There any Arguments for Pancomputationalism?

VCM

As far as I can tell the arguments in favor of pancomputationalism have
been largely intuitive, indicating that this view is useful and offers an elegant all-encompassing view of the world in terms that are well understood.
This feature it shares, however, with any number of all-encompassing ideologies (like pantheism or vulgar liberalism). These intuitive arguments
apply to all of P1-P7 without offering any particular support for the
stronger versions. What is missing is a positive argument that out of the
many overall theories *this one* is true and in *one version* of it.

GDC

Pancomputationalism apart from being universal has nothing to do with
pantheism which is not based on scientific methods. I don't think that
vulgar liberalism either should be mixed in here as it is not a theory
about the universe in its entirety, so I would suggest comparison with
atomism as a good example of universal theory. In natural sciences the
most general theories are the best ones. Universal laws are the best laws.
Being universal is nothing bad, just on the contrary! It is expected of a
theory of nature to be universal.

The central question is how *epistemologically productive* this paradigm is, as it really is a research programme (on this I share the view
presented by Wolfgang Hofkirchner in this volume) whose role is to mo-
bilize researchers to work in the same direction, within the same global

---

[7] Used as the motto for the 2008 Midwest NKS Conference,
http://www.cs.indiana.edu/~dgerman/2008midwestNKSconference/index.html

framework. The majority of natural sciences, formal sciences, technical sciences and engineering are already based on computational thinking, computational tools and computational modeling [Wing, 2008].

Allow me to list some arguments for paradigm change, since it was said that these are missing. Following are some of the promises of info-computationalism:

The synthesis of the (presently alarmingly disconnected) knowledge from different fields within the common info-computational framework which will enrich our understanding of the world. Present day narrow specialization into different isolated research fields has gradually led into impoverishment of the common world view.

Integration of scientific understanding of the phenomena of life (structures, processes) with the rest of natural world helping to achieve "the unreasonable effectiveness of mathematics" such as in physics (Wigner) even for complex phenomena like biology that today lack mathematical effectiveness (Gelfand).[8]

Understanding of the semantics of information as a part of data-information-knowledge-agency sequence, in which more and more complex relational structures are created by computational processing of information. An evolutionary naturalist view of semantics of information in living organisms is based on interaction (information exchange) of an organism with its environment.

A unified picture of fundamental dual-aspect information/computation phenomenon is applicable in natural sciences, information science, cognitive science, philosophy, sociology, economy and number of others.

Relating phenomena of information and computation understood in interactive paradigm makes it possible for investigations in logical pluralism of information produced as a result of interactive computation.[9] Of special interest are open systems in communication with the environment and related logical pluralism including paraconsistent logic.

Advancement of our computing methods beyond the Turing-Church paradigm, computation in the next step of development becoming able to

---

[8] See Chaitin, "Mathematics, Biology and Metabiology" (Foils, July 2009)
http://www.umcs.maine.edu/~chaitin/jack.html
[9] This logical pluralism is closely related to phenomena of consistency and truth; see also de Vey Mestdagh & Hoepman in this volume.

handle complex phenomena such as living organisms and processes of life, knowledge, social dynamics, communication and control of large interacting networks (as addressed in *organic computing* and other kinds of *unconventional computing*), etc.

Of all manifestations of life, mind seems to be information-theoretically and philosophically the most interesting one. Info-computationalism (pancomputationalism + paninformationalism) has a potential to support (by means of models and simulations) our effort in learning about mind.[10]

4. What is Computing? (I) The Fragile Unity of Pancomputational-ism

VCM

There are several theories about what constitutes a "computation", the classical one being Turing's, which identifies computation with a digital algorithmic process (or "effective procedure"). If, however, pancomputa-tionalism requires a larger notion of computing that includes analog computing and perhaps other forms, it would seem necessary to specify what that notion is – while making sure that Turing's notion is included. It is far from clear that there is a unifying notion that can cover all that the pancomputationalist wants, and therefore there is a danger that the advertised elegance of a single all-encompassing theory dissolves under closer inspection into a sea of various related notions.

It should be noted for fairness, however that while it is clearly a de-sideratum to specify the central notions of one's theory, pancomputation-alism can hardly be faulted for failing to achieve what is generally re-garded as a highly demanding task, namely a general specification of computation.

---

[10] On the practical side, understanding and learning to simulate and control functions and structures of living organisms will bring completely new medical treatments for all sorts of diseases including mental ones which to this day are poorly understood. Understanding of information-processing features of human brain will bring new insights into such fields as education, media, entertainment, cognition etc.

One possible response to this challenge deserves a mention here, namely the response that relies on the traditional use of mathematical or formal tools in science. This could be condensed into the following thesis:

F: All physical processes can be described formally

I suspect that sympathies for this view stand behind much of the support for pancomputationalism. However, F is not identical to strong pancomputationalism and not even easy to reconcile with it, for three reasons: a) F talks about the possibility to *describe* things, i.e. it does not make any claim to a realist reading [unlike P1 and P2], b) its use would identify computing with formal description and c) it explicitly talks about processes and thus forbids any swift moves from P2 to P1 – in case that P1 is the desired thesis. What is the logical relation between pancomputationalism and thesis F?

GDC

Actually the lack of understanding for what computing is may be a good argument for starting this whole research programme. At the moment, the closest to common acceptance is the view of computing as information processing, found in Neuroscience, Cognitive science and number of mathematical accounts of computing; see [Burgin, 2005] for exposition. For a process to be a computation a model must exist such as algorithm, network topology, physical process or in general any mechanism which ensures definability of its behavior.

The three-dimensional characterization of computing can be made by classification into orthogonal types: digital/analog, interactive/batch and sequential/parallel computation. Nowadays digital computers are used to simulate all sorts of natural processes, including those that in physics are described as continuous. In this case, it is important to distinguish between the mechanism of computation and the simulation model. It is interesting to see how computing is addressed in the present volume, especially Barry Coopers account of definability and Bruce MacLennans embodied computing. We will mention symbolic vs. sub-symbolic computing as important in this context. So symbolic part is what is easily recognized as thesis F[11]. In a sense we may say that F applies even to sub-symbolic computing on a meta-level. What is described formally is not the computational process step by step, but the mechanism that will produce that process.

Information processing[12] is the most general characterization of computing and common understanding of computing in several fields. In the info-computational approach information is a structure and computation is a process of change of that structure (Dodig Crnkovic, 2006). I have used the expression "dynamics of information" for computation. No matter if your data form any symbols; computation is a process of change of the data/structure. On a fundamental quantum-mechanical level, the universe performs computation on its own (Lloyd, 2006). Symbols appear on a much higher level of organization, and always in relation with living organisms. Symbols represent something for a living organism, have a function as carriers of meaning.[13] (See Christophe Menant in this volume).

5. What is Computing? (ii) discrete Vs. Continuum or Digital vs. Analog

VCM

I used to believe that what a computational process is was nicely defined by Church and Turing in the 1930ies, namely that these are the "effective" procedures", just the algorithms that can be computed by some Turing machine. This does, at least, provide something like a 'core' notion.

---

[11] As already pointed out, we have two different types of computation: physical substrate sub-symbolic and symbolic which also is based on physical computation. In Mark Burgin's words: "However, we can see that large physical computations can give a futile symbolic result, while extended and sophisticated symbolic computations sometimes result in meager physical changes. Pancomputationalism actually cannot exist without accepting the concept of physical computation. Discovery of quantum and molecular computing shows that the same symbolic computation may result from different kinds of physical computation." (From e-mail exchange with Mark Burgin, 26.07.2009)

[12] A popular account in Wikipedia http://en.wikipedia.org/wiki/Computation

[13] Douglas Hofstadter has already addressed the question of a symbol formed by other symbols in his *Gödel, Escher, Bach*. [Taddeo and Floridi, 2005] present a critical review of the symbol grounding problem with a suggestion that symbols must be anchored in sub-symbolic level.

It can be expanded in several ways, but any notion of computing should include this 'core'. One expansion is 'hypercomputing'; the idea that there can be algorithmic procedures that compute what no Turing machine could compute (typically by carrying out infinitely many computing steps). Now, I do not think that a machine can carry out infinitely many steps in finite time and come up with an output [Müller, 2008a] – but I would grant, of course, that hypercomputing is computing, if only it were physically possible in this world, or indeed in any possible world.

There might be a set of computing procedures that is larger than the one defined by Church-Turing – and there is certainly a mathematical set of computable functions larger than that computable by Turing machine (e.g. that computable by Turing's idea of his machine plus "oracle"). This is still quite far from saying that the universe is a computer (P1 above), however. So pancomputationalism probably has to add 'analog computers' as well, machines who's processing is not digital steps and who's output thus requires measurement to a degree of accuracy (if there is any 'output' at all).[14] My understanding of 'computer', as suggested by [Turing, 1936], is that such machines characteristically go beyond mere *calculators* (like those already invented by Leibniz and Pascal) in that they are *universal*; they can, in principle, compute *any* algorithm, because they are programmable – in this sense, Zuse's Z3 was the first computer (1941). If this feature of universality is a criterion for being a computer, then analog machines do not qualify because they can only be programmed in a very limited sense. This is a question of conventional terminology, however, so if we want to call such analog devices 'computers', we can. What is not clear to me is how this relates to the notion of 'symbol', traditionally a central one for computing. Presumably, analog computers do not use symbols, or digital states that are interpreted as symbols.

So, if we grant that computing includes digital hypercomputing and analog computing, this raises two questions: First, how can you guarantee that the notion of 'computing' you are using here is in any sense uni-

---

[14] This extension to 'analog computers' is not necessary if pancomputationalism adds the thesis of 'digital physics', that the world is fundamentally digital; something that I find rather implausible - though there are arguments about this issue [Müller, 2008b] [Floridi, 2009].

fied, i.e. *one* notion? (The question raised above.) And second, how does this broadening of the notion help to support the notion that everything is computing, beyond providing an ad hoc answer to the obvious challenge that not everything is a digital computer?

GDC

In the above, you identify hypercomputing as one way to expand the notion of computing, by carrying on infinitely many computational steps in a finite time, so we can focus our discussion for a while on the analysis of that statement. We can translate this question in its turn into Chaitin's question about the existence of real numbers; see Chaitin *How real are real numbers?* [in Chaitin, 2007b, 276]. For Chaitin real numbers are chimeras of our own minds, they just simply do not exist! He is in good company. Georg Leopold Kronecker's view was that, while everything else was made by man, the natural numbers were given by God. The logicists believed that the natural numbers were sufficient for deriving all of mathematics. In the above, you seem to suggest this view.

Even though pragmatic minded people would say that discrete set can always be made dense enough to mimic continuum for all practical purposes, I think on purely principal grounds that one cannot dispense with only one part in a dyadic pair and that continuum and discrete are mutually defining.[15]

Here I would just like to point out that the discrete – continuum problem lies in the underpinning of calculus and Bishop George Berkeley in his book *The analyst: or a discourse addressed to an infidel mathematician*, argued that, although calculus led to correct results, its foundations were logically problematic. Of derivatives (which Newton called fluxions) Berkley wrote:

---

[15] I suppose that this dyadic function comes from our cognitive apparatus which makes the difference in perception of discrete and continuous. It is indirectly given by the world, in a sense that we as a species being alive in the world have developed those dyadic/binary systems for discrete (number) and continuous (magnitude) phenomena as the most effective way to relate to that physical world.

Much of our cognitive capacities seem to have developed based on vision, which has on its elementary level the difference between: signal/no signal.

And what are these fluxions? The velocities of evanescent increments. And what are these same evanescent increments? They are
neither finite quantities, nor quantities infinitely small, nor yet nothing. May we not call them ghosts of departed quantities?[16]

Philosophical problems closely attached to the idea of infinity in mathematics are classical ones.

From physics on the other hand, there are persistent voices, such as
[Lesne, 2007] witnessing for the necessity of continuum in physical
modeling of the world. Here is the summary:

This paper presents a sample of the deep and multiple interplay between discrete and continuous behaviours and the corresponding
modellings in physics. The aim of this overview is to show that discrete and continuous features coexist in any natural phenomenon,
depending on the scales of observation. Accordingly, different models, either discrete or continuous in time, space, phase space or con-
jugate space can be considered. [Lesne, 2007]

[Floridi, 2009] proposes the Alexandrian solution to the above Gordian
knot by cutting apart information from computation, and expressing everything in terms of information. This would be analog to describing a
verb with a noun; it is possible but some information gets lost. It is nevertheless true that informational structure of the universe is richer than
what Turing Machines as a typical mechanical/mechanistic model can
produce.[17]

... digital ontology (the ultimate nature of reality is digital, and the
universe is a computational system equivalent to a Turing Machine)
should be carefully distinguished from informational ontology (the
ultimate nature of reality is structural), in order to abandon the for-

---

[16] http://www.maths.tcd.ie/pub/HistMath/People/Berkeley/Analyst/Analyst.html Berkeley
talks about *the relationship between the model and the world*, not about the inner structure of the model itself. Worth noticing is KB Hansen's remark that "problems observed
by Berkeley have been solved by Bolzano, Cauchy, Riemann, Weierstrass, and Robinson.
Modern mathematical analysis rests on solid foundations."
[17] For we talk about computational processes that not only calculate functions but are able
to interact with the world, posses context-awareness, ability of self-organization, self-
optimization and similar.

mer and retain only the latter as a promising line of research. Digital vs. analogue is a Boolean dichotomy typical of our computational paradigm, but digital and analogue are only "modes of presentation" of Being (to paraphrase Kant), that is, ways in which reality is experienced or conceptualised by an epistemic agent at a given level of abstraction. A preferable alternative is provided by an informational approach to structural realism, according to which knowledge of the world is knowledge of its structures. The most reasonable ontological commitment turns out to be in favour of an interpretation of reality as the totality of structures dynamically interacting with each other. [Floridi, 2009, 151]

What info-computationalist naturalism wants is to understand that dynamical interaction of informational structures as a computational process. It includes digital and analogue, continuous and discrete as phenomena existing in physical world on different levels of description and digital computing is a subset of a more general natural computing.

The question of continuum vs. discrete nature of the world is ages old and it is not limited to the existing technology. Digital philosophy as well as Turing machine has been epistemologically remarkably productive (see Stephen Wolframs work, e.g. [Wolfram, 2002] along with Ed Fredkin and number of people who focused on the digital aspects of the world). Digital is undoubtedly one of the levels we can use for the description, but from physics it seems to be necessary to be able to handle continuum too (as we do in Quantum Mechanics). For a very good account, see [Lloyd, 2006].

6. What is computing? (III) Natural Computing as a Generalization of the Traditional Notion of Computing

GDC

We have already discussed *hypercomputing* as the possibility of carrying on infinitely many (computational) steps in a finite time as a question of our understanding of the nature of the world (continuous, discrete) and our idea of infinity. There is however yet another possibility to approach the question of computing beyond the Turing model which goes under

different names and has different content: *natural computing, unconventional computing, analog computing, organic computing, sub-
symbolic computing*, etc.

In order to expound the present understanding of computing, and its
possible paths of development we study the development of the computing field in the past half a century, driven by the process of miniaturiza-
tion with dramatically increased performance, efficiency and ubiquity of
computing devices. However, this approach based on the understanding
of computation as symbol manipulation performed by a Turing Machine
is rapidly approaching its physical and conceptual limits.

Ever since Turing proposed his machine model identifying computation with the execution of an algorithm, there have been questions about
how widely the Turing Machine model is applicable. Church-Turing
Thesis establishes the equivalence between a Turing Machine and an algorithm, interpreted as to imply that *all of computation must be algorithmic*. Hector Zenil and Jean-Paul Delahaye in this volume investigate
the question of the evidence of the algorithmic computational nature of
the universe.

With the advent of computer networks, the model of a computer in
isolation, represented by a Turing Machine, has become insufficient; for
an overview see (Dodig Crnkovic 2006). Today's software-intensive and
intelligent computer systems have become huge, consisting of massive
numbers of autonomous and parallel elements across multiple scales. At
the nano-scale they approach programmable matter; at the macro scale,
multitude of cores compute in clusters, grids or clouds, while at the plan-
etary scale, sensor networks connect environmental and satellite data.
The common for these modern computing systems is that they are *en-
semble-like* (as they form one whole in which the parts act in concert to
achieve a common goal like an organism is an ensemble of its cells) and
physical (as ensembles act in the physical world and interact with their
environment through sensors and actuators).

A promising new approach to the complex world of modern autonomous, intelligent, adaptive, networked computing has successively
emerged. Natural computing is a new paradigm of computing (MacLennan, Rozenberg, Calude, Bäck, Bath, Müller-Schloer, de Castro, Paun)
which deals with computability in the physical world such as biological

computing/organic computing, computing on continuous data, quantum computing, swarm intelligence, the immune systems, and membrane computing, which has brought a fundamentally new understanding of computation.

Natural computing has different criteria for success of a computation. The halting problem is not a central issue,[18] but instead the adequacy of the computational response. Organic computing system e. g. adapts dynamically to the current conditions of its environment by self-organization, self-configuration, self-optimization, self-healing, self-protection and context-awareness. In many areas, we have to computationally model emergence not being algorithmic (Aaron Sloman, Barry Cooper) which makes it interesting to investigate computational characteristics of non-algorithmic natural computation (sub-symbolic, analog). Interesting to observe is epistemic productiveness of natural computing as it leads to a significantly bidirectional research (Rozen); as natural sciences are rapidly absorbing ideas of information processing, field of computing concurrently assimilates ideas from natural sciences.

VCM

P$\neq$NP. Or, to be a bit more explicit: I really suspect that Turing was right about his set of digitally computable functions, no matter how long it might take to compute them. All of the fashionable 'beyond Turing' computing (small, networked, natural, adaptive, etc. etc.) is either just doing what a Turing machine does or it is not digital computing at all. If it is not digital computing, then my question (notorious by now) is: Why call it computing? In what sense of that word?

GDC

Let me remind that for a process to be a computation a model must exist such as algorithm, network topology, physical process or *in general any mechanism which ensures definability of its behavior*. So we distinguish computation models and physical implementations of computation.

---

[18] In the Turing model a computation must halt when execution of an algorithm has finished.

Talking about *models of computation* beyond Turing model, super-recursive algorithms are an instructive example. They represent computation which can give a result after a finite number of steps, does not use infinite objects, such as real numbers, and nevertheless is more powerful than any Turing machine. *Inductive Turing machines* described in [Burgin, 2005] have all these properties. Besides, their mode of computation is a kind of a natural computation, as demonstrated with respect to evolutionary computations.

When it comes to *physical implementations*, natural computing presents the best example of the more general computational process than that used in our present days computers. In what sense of the word is that computing? In the sense of computation as a physical process, see Feynman's remark about physical computing from 2.2 above.

Physical processes can be used for digital and analog computation. It is true that historical attempts to build analog computers did not continue because of the problem with noise. In a new generation of natural computers we will use features organic computing possess in order to control complexity. Organic systems are very good at discerning information from noise.

This leads us to the next important characteristics of natural computers. They will not be searching for a perfect (context free) solution, but for a good enough (context dependent) one. This will also imply that not all computational mechanisms will be equivalent, but we will have classes of equivalence of computational devices in the same sense as we have different types of computational processes going on at different levels of organization.

Why call it computation?

Simply because it is a generalization of present day computation from discrete symbol manipulation to any sort of (discrete, continuous) manipulation of symbols or physical objects (discrete, continuous), which follow physical or logical laws.

7. Computation and Causation

VCM

As we already saw, pancomputationalism seems to rely on an understanding of computation that is rather unconventional. Conventional understanding investigates a physical process and then says about that process that it computes (a function). *Which* processes in the world are the ones that are computing is a thorny question that hinges on the criteria; on whether one regards computing as a matter of discovery or a matter of perception; etc. So, even if one says things like that the universe is information processing [Wiener, 1961, 132 etc.], this is still meant in the sense that there is some 'stuff' in the world that is undergoing processes which are information processing – not that the universe *is* a computer.

No matter which processes are regarded as computational ones (i.e. how narrow or wide the notion of computing is taken to be), a usual assumption is that the same computation can be carried out by different physical processes – one example of this is the remark that the same software can 'run' on different hardware, even on hardware that is structurally quite different. What this underlines is that the output of a computation, e.g. "0", is a different entity from the outcome of the physical process, e.g. a switch being in "position A" (which stands for "0"). The computation is not the cause of the position of the switch, but the physical process is. The same computational process on different hardware would have resulted in "0", but quite possibly *not* in a switch in "position A". In fact, a computation cannot cause anything, it is just a syntactic event, or perhaps the syntactic description of an event (out of the massive literature on this issue, see [Piccinini, 2008]). If this is right, then computation cannot be used as an overall empirical theory, as I indicated in my paper for the Paderborn meeting [Müller, 2009].

GDC

Pancomputationalism indeed often (but not necessarily) relies on an understanding of computation that is unconventional. Exactly that unconventional computation is one of the most exciting innovations that pancomputationalism supports. Not all adherents of unconventional computation (computation beyond Turing limit) are pancomputational-ists. Unconventional computation will be found all over this volume (Cooper, MacLennan, Shagrir, ...) based on different arguments and approaches. There are conferences and journals on unconventional computing, organic computing, and natural computing. I see it as a good sign of coherence coming from different, often completely unre-lated fields. A good overview on non-classical computation may be found in [Stepney, 2005].

When it comes to the issue of causal inefficacy of computation, that is really not a problem for control systems or robotics where you indeed see computation causing an artifact to interact with the envi-ronment. Info-computationalism has no problem with computation not being causally connected with the physical world. As the world com-putes its own next state, it means that computation has causal power. Not only spontaneous computation of the universe in form of natural computation is causally effective, even human-designed (constructed) devices controlled by computational processes show that computation is what directly connects to the world.

In the same way as there is no information without (physical) rep-resentation [Karnani, et al., 2009], there is no computation without information (which must have physical representation). So any output of a computation performed by a computer (say "0" from your exam-ple) can in principle be used as an input for a control system that launches a rocket or starts any sort of machine controlled by a com-puter. Today we have numerous examples of embedded computers and even embodied ones (see MacLennan in this volume) where computa-tional processes control or in other ways impact physical world.

8. Is Pancomputationalism Vacuous or Epistemically Productive?

VCM

Presumably, pancomputationalism is an empirical theory, so it should indicate which empirical evidence it will count as supportive and make predictions about empirical findings that – if they do not materialize – would count as evidence *against* the theory, perhaps even as falsification.

The absence of such links to empirical findings would increase suspicion that the theory is actually devoid of content. Has the theory produced any new testable hypotheses?

GDC

> "Theories are nets: only he who casts will catch." Novalis

Novalis is quoted by Karl Popper in the introduction to *The Logic of Scientific Discovery*. In the third chapter, Popper elaborates:

> Theories are nets cast to catch what we call "the world": to rationalize, to explain, and to master it. We endeavor to make the mesh ever finer and finer.[19] [Popper, 1959]

Not only so that no theory, however general, can capture all aspects of the universe simultaneously (and thus we have a multitude of different general scientific theories valid in their specific domains, on specific level of abstraction), but even more importantly: pancomputationalism is not a single monolithic theory but *a research programme*. We talk about *système du monde*. This volume provides examples and shows how things happen to develop more in the spirit of *Let a Thousand Flowers Bloom*. The process of consolidation, purification, formalization is the next step. We are still in a discovery phase.

In order to understand the development of a *research programme* let us return to the analogy of pancomputationalism with atomism[20], the belief that all physical objects consist of *atoms* and *void* (Leucippus and Democritus). We can equally ask how atomism could have possibly been falsified. I don't think it could. Because atomism (and in a similar way pancomputationalism) is not to be understood as a single hypothesis but as a research programme. In the strict sense atomism has already been

---

[19] This example can be paraphrased to say that not only that our nets are getting finer, but maybe altogether different methods of fishing and not only the finer-grained mesh nets can be devised.

[20] I have used this analogy with atomism for many years, only recently to see in a Documentary/Drama "Victim of the brain" (on Hofstadter/Dennett's "The Mind's I" [Hofstadter and Dennett, 1981] featuring Daniel Dennett and Marvin Minsky), that Douglas Hofstadter uses exactly that argument in a very elegant way, see http://www.mathrix.org/liquid/#/archives/victim-of-the-brain

falsified because atoms are not indivisible (but made of nucleus made of nucleons made of quarks made of ...) and void (vacuum) is not empty (but full of virtual particles that pop up into being and disappear again). The process of the development of atomist research project has both changed the original idea about atoms and void and what we identify as their counterparts in the physical world.

The fundamental question thus does not seem to be about the "truth" of a singular statement such as: Is it true that there are only atoms and void? But as we use atoms and void as a net to catch the structure of the physical reality, those ideas are instrumental to our understanding, and in the interaction with the world, both our concepts and what we are able to reach to in the world change concurrently. What is fundamental is *construction of meaning*, or *epistemological productiveness* of a paradigm, or how much we can learn from the research programme.

You [Müller, 2008c, 38] rightly use Kant to suggest the way to address the question of how to define *Computing and Philosophy*, namely by answering the following questions:

> What can we hope for (from Computing and Philosophy)?
> What should we do (with Computing and Philosophy)?
> What can we know (about Computing and Philosophy)?

Equivalent questions can be asked about info-computationalist programme. A theory (or a paradigm) is an epistemic tool, that very tool Novalis and Popper use to catch (or extract as Cooper in this volume says) what for us is of interest in the world. Compared to mytho-poetic and mechanistic frameworks the emerging info-computational paradigm is the most general one and the richest in expressive repertoire developed through our interaction with the world.[21] When the dominating interaction with the world was mechanistic, the most general paradigm was mechanistic. The world in itself/for itself is simply a reservoir/resource [Floridi, 2008] of possible interactions for a human. We know as much of the world as we explore and "digest" (as a species or as a community of praxis).

---

[21] Our nets are global computer networks of connected computational, information processing devices. The classic era of mechanism was focused on matter and energy. Our own info-computational paradigm focuses on information and computation.

Since we wish to devise an intelligible conceptual environment for ourselves, we do so not by trying to picture or photocopy whatever is in the room (mimetic epistemology), but by interacting with it as a resource for our semantic tasks, interrogating it through experience, tests and experiments. Reality in itself is not a source but a resource for knowledge. Structural objects (clusters of data as relational entities) work epistemologically like constraining affordances: they allow or invite certain constructs (they are affordances for the information system that elaborates them) and resist or impede some others (they are constraints for the same system), depending on the interaction with, and the nature of, the information system that processes them. They are exploitable by a theory, at a given Level of Abstraction, as input of adequate queries to produce information (the model) as output. [Floridi, 2008]

All we have are constructs made for a purpose, and so is even the case with pancomputationalism: let's say world is a computer, what sort of computing is it then? It is not a vacuous tautology but a proposal for exploration, a research programme. It presupposes a dynamical reflexive relationship between our understanding of the physical world and our theoretical understanding of computation or what a computer might be.

The worst thing which can happen is that some of the world is impossible to use for learning of any new principles or building any new smart machines. That may happen if physical processes are irreducible and if we want to know the result of computation we have to use the replica of a system, which is not very useful. But that is not the major issue. First of all even in case or randomness [Chaitin, 2007a] when no information compression is possible the physical world shows remarkable stability and we can expect it to repeat the same behavior under same circumstances, so we don't have to actually repeat all computations, but remember recurring behaviors.

9. Pancomputationalism and the Mind

VCM

The view that the human mind is a computer has been a cornerstone of the cognitive sciences from their beginning, supported by the philosophical position of 'machine functionalism'. It has come under increasing pressure in recent years, and under the impression of the main arguments many have been lead to abandon it.[22] Is there any substantial sense in which info-computationalism relieves this pressure and blows some life into the notion that the mind is a computer beyond saying that everything is?

GDC

Yes, I would say so. I would like to claim that info-computationalism (info-computationalist naturalism) has something essentially new to offer and that is *natural computation/organic computation,* which applies to our brains too.

    The classical critique of old computationalism based on abstract, syntactic notion of computation represented by Turing Machine model does not apply to the dynamic embodied physical view of computing that new natural computational models support. [Scheutz, 2002] has the right diagnosis:

> Instead of abandoning computationalism altogether, however, some researchers are reconsidering it, recognizing that real-world computers, like minds, must deal with issues of embodiment, interaction, physical implementation, and semantics.

Scheutz similarly to Shagrir in this volume concludes that according to all we know brain computes, but the computation performed is not of in the first place a Turing Machine type. Several papers in this issue contribute to the elucidation of earlier misunderstandings; from Marvin Min-

---

[22] A quick indication of some main points: The problem of meaning in a computational system (Chinese room and symbol grounding), the critique of encodingism (Bickhard), the stress on non-symbolic or sub-symbolic cognition, the integration of cognition with emotion and volition, the move away from a centralized notion of cognition and towards 'embodiment', etc.

sky's analysis of the hard problem of consciousness to Aaron Sloman's approach to mind as virtual machine. This book presents an effort to build the grounds for understanding of computing in its most general form and to use it in addressing real world phenomena, including life and mind, those topics mechanistic models are not suitable to deal with.

Part of our previous discussion about discrete vs. continuum is relevant for the argument about computational nature of mind. If computation is allowed to be continuous, then the mind can be computational:

> Brains and computers are both dynamical systems that manipulate symbols, but they differ fundamentally in their architectures and operations. Human brains do mathematics; computers do not. Computers manipulate symbols that humans put into them without grounding them in what they represent. Human brains intentionally direct the body to make symbols, and they use the symbols to represent internal states. The symbols are outside the brain. Inside the brains, the construction is effected by spatiotemporal patterns of neural activity that are operators, not symbols. The operations include formation of sequences of neural activity patterns that we observe by their electrical signs. The process is by neurodynamics, not by logical rule-driven symbol manipulation. The aim of simulating human natural computing should be to simulate the operators. In its simplest form natural computing serves for communication of meaning. Neural operators implement non-symbolic communication of internal states by all mammals, including humans, through intentional actions. (...) I propose that symbol-making operators evolved from neural mechanisms of intentional action by modification of non-symbolic operators. [Freeman, 2009]

The above shows nicely the relationship between symbolic and non-symbolic computing. All that happens inside our heads is non-symbolic computing. (Freeman claims it is non-symbolic while Shagrir with neuroscientists claims it is computing.) Our brains use non-symbolic computing internally to manipulate relevant external symbols!

If we learn to interpret life as a network of information processing structures and if we learn how our brains (and bodies) perform all that information processing then we will be able to make new computers which will smoothly connect to our information processing cognitive apparatus.

To summarize, we can choose digital description but then we will be able to see the world in that "digital light". If we choose continuum, we will capture different phenomena. Pancomputationalism does not exclude any of the (discrete, continuum, digital or analog) computing (information processing). Info-computational naturalism, being a general unifying approach connects natural information processes with corresponding informational structures.

10. Concluding remarks

VCM

What I think this exchange shows is that a lot of work remains to be done before we can say that pancomputationalism is a well-understood and evaluated position (not to mention info-computationalism, which involves further claims). I am therefore not of the view that the position is refuted, but that we need to clarify its claims, its fruitfulness and its possible problems – it is to this program that we hoped that our discussion would contribute (and to my mind it did).

It is in this intention that I suggested a list of possible theses at the outset. It might be useful to list them here again (where P4-P6 are possible readings of P3):

P1: The universe is a computer *(strong pancomputationalism)*

P2: All processes are computational processes *(pancomputationalism)*

P3: All processes can be described as computational processes *(weak pancomputationalism)*

P4: All processes can be described as computational processes because we discovered that they are computational (= P2)

P5: All processes can be described as computational processes because there is nothing more to being a computational process than being described as such *(anti-realist weak pancomputation-alism)*

P6: All processes can be described as computational processes because this happens to be a useful way of describing them in scientific theory *(realist weak pancomputationalism)*

P7: All processes can be described as if they were computational processes *(metaphorical pancomputationalism)*

In response, we were told in no uncertain terms that, out of the various theses, strong pancomputationalism (P1) is the intended reading. Fine, in this strong realist reading the answer to my first question becomes even more urgent: What *would be* the case if the theory were false, i.e. what *would* a counterexample look like? My suggestion (in good Popperian tradition, since his name was invoked), is that there is a danger for very general ideologies that seem to explain everything, but really are empty and explain nothing. If classical atomism is still a useful or true theory (unlike pantheism), there must be a sense in which it can be interpreted as such.

In the defense of the theory, it was stressed that pancomputationalism should be viewed as a 'research program', a 'paradigm' that it is 'epistemologically productive', and that in any case theories should not be viewed as statements but as nets. All of this looks like P6, rather than P1. As long as it is granted that these two are different theses, this strategy might be accused of claiming the stronger thesis but defending the weaker one. I see several instances of this problem here.

One example is the response to the problem of the apparent causal inefficacy of computing, countered by examples of computers that do things. As an indication to show how this is not the same, let us look at Sloman's suggestion that there are 'virtual machines' active in the human brain that causally generate aspects of conscious experience [Sloman, 2009]. This looks like he is saying that computing has causal power – but not quite, since he says that virtual machines are mathematical objects that do nothing, only *running* virtual machines have causal powers (since they run on physical hardware, I would add). He makes the crucial distinction. My problem did not consist in the strange suggestion that computers do not have causal powers (mine certainly has) but in the question whether the computational processes *qua computational processes* have these powers (since their output is only the "0" in my example, not the position of a physical switch). In pancomputationalism, the stronger thesis about computing processes per se is claimed, and the weaker about running/actual/realized computing processes is defended.

A further example of this strategy is the defense of the stronger P1 via the weaker claim that the universe is processing information. It may well be true that information processing is an elementary feature of the universe, but information processing is information processing; computing is computing. Perhaps computing is one species of information processing among others (in some sense of 'information' it is), but why expand the one notion into the other? If we really want to say that all information processing is computational, is that a definitional remark or is this a discovery about information processing? If it is definitional, I might adopt my understanding of the thesis proposed here but I would then note that we now identify one unclear notion (computing) with another even less clear one (information processing); which does not look like a good strategy. In any case, all problems that beset the pancomputationalist approach also beset that of info-computationalism, plus the new ones associated with 'information'. If the remark is expressing a discovery, I would like to see the evidence for the claim that there is non-computational information processing does not exist. (In other words, I would come back to my first remark and wonder what a non-computational process would be, on the pancomputationalist account.)

Last but not least, the claim that the universe is computational looked quite strong when that term was understood as Turing computation, but then computation was dissolved into a much wider notion, the borders of which I cannot quite discern (I keep coming back to this issue). My worry about apparently non-computational processes in the world could not be countered because "everything is computing" is a priori, and we do not even want to take it as a reductionist claim ("everything is computing, deep down").

One example of my confusion is the interpretation of the remark by Feynman quoted above to support pancomputationalism. "In what sense of the word is that computing? In the sense of computation as a physical process, see Feynman's remark about physical computing from 2.2." This sounds circular and Feynman's remark does not help. I think it can well be read as *opposing* the idea that the universe computes (disregarding any context). He could be taken to say: Since it would take a computing machine infinite time, the "machinery" that is revealed in the end is not computational.

It truly is not clear to me how much can be explained with a wide notion of computing that somehow incorporates digital and analog, formal and physical, Turing and dynamic systems, etc. etc. I have nothing against these proposals, indeed my feeling is that some processes can usefully be described as computational (though even P6 in its generality is false) and many more as if they were. I also suspect that the metaphorical power of info-computationalism is strong enough to support an entire research program which will generate many interesting insights. Having said that, we have seen what happened to fruitful and successful research programs like classical AI or computationalism in the philosophy of mind that rested on weak foundations – they eventually hit the wall. I suspect that this will be the fate of info-computationalism also.

GDC

First let us go back to Feynman. It is not a coincidence that this quote was used as the motto for the 2008 Midwest NKS Conference which gathered most prominent pancomputationalists. They interpret Feynman as saying that nature computes much more effective than any of our present machines. Moreover Feynman seems to imply that our going via mathematical models of physical phenomena might be the reason for that ineffectiveness.

Now the question of what is reasonable to understand as computation. For the nascent field of natural computation, we can apply the well known truth that our knowledge is in a constant state of evolution. Ray Kurzweil would even warn: Singularity is near, singularity where knowledge production exceeds our ability to learn [Kurzweil, 2005]. Moreover, by integrating/assimilating new pieces of knowledge, the whole existing knowledge structure changes. Atomism has changed substantially from the Democritus' original view. And yet it has not been refuted but only modified. Why? Because it was epistemically productive! Simply put, atomism has helped us to think, helped us to build new knowledge and to interact in different way with the physical world.

That is exactly what we expect from info-computationalism – to provide us with a good framework which will help our understanding of the world, including life and ourselves and our acting in that world. It is basically about learning and making sense of the world. Having history of several major paradigm shifts behind us, we have no reason to believe that info-computational framework is the absolutely perfect answer to all questions we may ask about the life, universe and everything but it seems to be the best research framework we have right now.

If pancomputationalism claims that the entire universe computes, a discovery of a process in the world which is impossible to understand as computational would falsify the pancomputational claim. Something changes, but we have no way to identify that process as computation. A stereotypical claim would be: writing a poem. That cannot possibly be a computational process! On which level of organization? I want to ask. On a level of neuroscience all that happens in the world while someone writes a poem is just a sequence of computational processes. Poets might find that level uninteresting, as well as they might find uninteresting the fact that the beautiful lady they sing of is made of atoms and void. But there are cases where we really want to know about how things work on a very basic level.

As a research program info-computationalism will either show to be productive or else it will die out. The only criterion for survival is how good it will be compared with other approaches. That development of a research programme is a slow but observable process. Following the number of articles, journals, conferences etc. dealing with unconventional computing, organic computing, or natural computing we can assess how active the field is. Subsequently we will also be able to follow its results.

Here is again a summary of what makes info-computationalist naturalism a promising research programme:

-   Unlike mechanicism, info-computationalist naturalism has the ability to tackle as well fundamental physical structures as life phenomena within the same conceptual framework. The observer is an integral part of the info-computational universe.

- Integration of scientific understanding of the structures and processes of life with the rest of natural world will help to achieve "the unreasonable effectiveness of mathematics" (or computing in general) even for complex phenomena of biology that today lack mathematical effectiveness (Gelfand) – in sharp contrast to physics (Wigner).

- Info-computationalism (which presupposes pancomputationalism and paninformationalism) presents a unifying framework for common knowledge production in many up to know unrelated research fields. Present day narrow specialization into various isolated research fields has led to the alarming impoverishment of the common world view.

- Our existing computing devices are a subset of a set of possible physical computing machines, and Turing Machine model is a subset of envisaged more general natural computational models. Advancement of our computing methods beyond the Turing-Church paradigm will result in computing capable of handling complex phenomena such as living organisms and processes of life, social dynamics, communication and control of large interacting networks as addressed in *organic computing* and other kinds of *unconventional computing*.

- Understanding of the semantics of information as a part of the data-information-knowledge-wisdom sequence, in which more and more complex relational structures are created by computational processing of information. An evolutionary naturalist view of semantics of information in living organisms is given based on interaction/information exchange of an organism with its environment.

- Discrete and analogue are both needed in physics and so in physical computing which can help us to deeper understanding of their relationship.

- Relating phenomena of information and computation understood in interactive paradigm will enable investigations into logical pluralism of information produced as a result of interactive computation. Of special interest are open systems in communication with the environment and related logical pluralism including paraconsistent logic.

- Of all manifestations of life, mind seems to be information-theoretically and philosophically the most interesting one. Info-computationalist naturalism (pancomputationalism + paninformationalism) has a potential to support, by means of models and simulations, our effort in learning about mind and developing artifactual (artificial) intelligence in the direction of organic computing.

The spirit of the research programme is excellently summarized in the following:

"In these times brimming with excitement, our task is nothing less than to discover a new, broader, notion of computation, and to understand the world around us in terms of information processing." [Rozenberg and Kari, 2008]

Acknowledgements

The authors want to thank Ruth Hagengruber, Kaj Børge Hansen, Luciano Floridi and Mark Burgin for useful comments on earlier versions of this paper.

References

Burgin, M. (2005). *Super-recursive algorithms.* Berlin: Springer.
Chaitin, G. (2007a). 'Epistemology as information theory: From Leibniz to Ω'. In Dodig-Crnkovic, G. & Stuart S., (Eds.), *Computation, information, cognition: The nexus and the liminal.* Newcastle: Cambridge Scholars Publishing pp. 27–51.
Chaitin, G. (2007b). *Thinking about Gödel and Turing: Essays on Complexity, 1970-2007.* Boston: World Scientific.
Chalmers, D.J. (1993). 'A computational foundation for the study of cognition', in.
Chalmers, D.J. (1994). 'On implementing a computation'. *Minds and Machines,* 4, pp. 391–402.
Chalmers, D.J. (1996). 'Does a rock implement every finite-state automaton?' *Synthese,* 108, pp. 309–333.
Dodig-Crnkovic, G. (2006). *Investigations into information semantics and ethics of computing.* Västerås: Mälardalen University Press.
Dodig-Crnkovic, G. (2008), 'Semantics of Information as Interactive Computation', in Moeller, M., Neuser W. & Roth-Berghofer T. (Eds.), *Fifth international workshop on philosophy and informatics, Kaiserslautern 2008.* Berlin: Springer.
Feynman, R.P. (1965). *The character of physical law.* Boston: MIT Press 2001.

Floridi, L. (2004). 'Open problems in the philosophy of information'. *Metaphilosophy*, 35, pp. 554–582.

Floridi, L. (2008). 'The method of levels of abstraction'. *Minds and Machines*, 18, pp. 303–329.

Floridi, L. (2009). 'Against digital ontology'. *Synthese*, 168, pp. 151–178.

Freeman, W. (2009). 'The Neurobiological Infrastructure of Natural Computing: Intentionality''. *New Mathematics and Natural Computation*, 5, pp. 19–29.

Hofstadter, D.R. & Dennett D.C. (Eds.). (1981). *The mind's I: Fantasies and reflections on self and soul.* New York: Basic Books.

Karnani, M., Pääkkönen K. & Annila A. (2009). 'The physical character of information'. *Proceedings of the Royal Society A: Mathematical, Physical and Engineering Science*, 465, pp. 2155–2175.

Kurzweil, R. (2005). *The singularity is near: When humans transcend biology.* London: Viking.

Lesne, A. (2007). 'The discrete versus continuous controversy in physics'. *Mathematical Structures in Computer Science*, 17, pp. 185–223.

Lloyd, S. (2006). *Programming the Universe: A Quantum Computer Scientist Takes on the Cosmos.* New York: Alfred A Knopf.

Müller, V.C. (2008a). 'On the possibility of hypercomputing supertasks'. *Minds and Machines*, resubmission under review.

Müller, V.C. (2008b). 'Representation in digital systems'. In Briggle, A., Waelbers K. & Brey P., (Eds.), *Current issues in computing and philosophy*. Amsterdam: IOS Press pp. 116–121.

Müller, V.C. (2008c). 'What a course on philosophy of computing is not'. *APA Newsletter on Philosophy and Computers*, 8, pp. 36–38.

Müller, V.C. (2009). 'Pancomputationalism: Theory or metaphor?' In Hagengruber, R., (Ed.), *The relevance of philosophy for information science*. Berlin: Springer p. forthcoming.

Piccinini, G. (2008). 'Computation without representation'. *Philosophical Studies*, 134, pp. 205–241.

Popper, K. (1959). *The logic of scientific discovery.* New York: Basic Books.

Rozenberg, G. & Kari L. (2008). 'The many facets of natural computing'. *Communications of the ACM*, 51.

Scheutz, M. (2002). 'Computationalism: the next generation'. In Scheutz, M., (Ed.), *Computationalism: new directions.* Cambridge: Cambridge University Press.

Searle, J.R. (1980). 'Minds, brains and programs'. *Behavioral and Brain Sciences*, 3, pp. 417–457.

Searle, J.R. (1990). 'Is the brain a digital computer?' *Proceedings and Addresses of the American Philosophical Association*, pp. 21–37.

Searle, J.R. (1992). *The rediscovery of mind.* Cambridge, Mass.: MIT Press.

Shagrir, O. (2006). 'Why we view the brain as a computer'. *Synthese*, 153, pp. 393–416.

Sloman, A. (2009). 'What Cognitive Scientists Need to Know about Virtual Machines'. *Proceedings of CogSci 2009, The Annual Meeting of the Cognitive Science Society*, 31, p. forthcoming.

Stepney, S.e.a. (2005). 'Journeys in non-classical computation I: A grand challenge for computing research''. *The International Journal of Parallel, Emergent and Distributed Systems,* 20, pp. 5–19.

Taddeo, M. & Floridi L. (2005). 'Solving the symbol grounding problem: A critical review of fifteen years of research'. *Journal of Experimental and Theoretical Artificial Intelligence,* 17, pp. 419–445.

Turing, A. (1936). 'On computable numbers, with an application to the Entscheidungsproblem'. *Proceedings of the London Mathematical Society,* pp. 230–256.

Wiener, N. (1961). *Cybernetics: or control and communication in the animal and the machine.* Cambridge, Mass.: MIT Press.

Wing, J. (2008). 'Five deep questions in computing'. *CACM,* 51, pp. 58–60.

Wolfram, S. (2002). 'A new kind of science', in, Champaign, Il.: Wolfram Media.

CHAPTER 7

DOES COMPUTING EMBRACE SELF-ORGANIZATION?

Wolfgang Hofkirchner

Unified Theory of Information Research Group
c/o Institute of Design and Technology Assessment,
Vienna University of Technology .
Favoritenstraße 9, A-1040 Vienna, Austria
wolfgang.hofkirchner@tuwien.ac.at

It is a widely held assumption that computers process information. When finding out that natural systems manifest information processes, it is hypothesised that natural systems too are computers. This can be called the quintessence of the "computational turn", however, it is a *non sequitur*. This chapter draws upon the ontological distinction of strict determinism and less-than-strict determinism. It contends that artificial devices like computers work on the basis of strict determinism, while natural systems to the extent as they self-organise work on the basis of less-than-strict determinism. Strict determinism is a derivative of less-than-strict determinism. Thus the chapter concludes that concerning computers and natural, self-organising systems the assumption of the computational turn is wrong. It is the other way round: computers play a restricted, though essential and indispensable, part within self-organising (natural and social) contexts.

1. Introduction

The rise of the computer as man-made machine for processing information, the spread of PCs, the diffusion of ICTs and the penetration of social life including the natural environmment as well as human bodies with "intelligent" devices on our way to pervasive computing all seem to justify a "computational turn" – the assumption that the nature of social and natural information processes is identical to the nature of information processing in artifacts and a research programme that aims at devising smooth tools that connect to persons better because of the convergence of

185

social and natural information processes with artificial information processing. Often, e.g., in fields like "emergent computing" and "organic computing", it is asserted that the new paradigm of the computational turn is different from preceding paradigms like, e.g., cognitivism. This assertion, however, was heard already when connectionism tried to overcome cognitivism. It might be doubted whether connectionism was a replacement of technically oriented, mechanistic thinking (which might become clear in the course of the argumentation below).

In order to be able to contrast the new assumption against those which it is set out to replace it is necessary to enter the field of ontological considerations and deliberations – assumptions on how the world is, how it functions, how things, properties and relations populate it. The most decisive question in that context is how causal relations are viewed. Do causes determine effects and, if so, to which extent?

This question is important to answer because

(1) the understanding of computing and information processing depends on the answer;
(2) it serves as litmus test indicating whether or not this understanding amounts to a really new paradigm.

2. Determinism

Determinism is the view of determinacy and indeterminacy in real-world causal relationships. The mechanistic view is associated with the names of Newton and Laplace. Another view that is emerging goes hand in hand with research in self-organisation.

It is worth noting that the notion of "determinism" used here might differ from the commonly used term. It seems a common habit not to distinguish between "determinism" and the "principle of causality" and thus to conflate both. The principle of causality tells us that there is no event that is not caused, that is, every event is held to be an effect of a cause. Thus it is assumed there exists a closed chain of causes and effects. However, "causality" signifies the direct interaction between events. "Determinism", on the other hand, is about interaction between events, be it a direct one or an "indirect" one. So-called "indirect" interaction refers to laws that regards that part of interaction that is universal and necessary and to chance that regards that part of interaction that is not universal but particular and not necessary but random. If you cut free chance from the principle of causality, then you get indeterminism. Otherwise you can talk about random events that are nevertheless caused (see Hörz 1962, Hörz 1971, 208, Fuchs-Kittowski 1976, 178–187).

Hence determinism is, primarily, about how entities are related to each other in an ontological sense. It's only in a second sense about predictability. Unpredictability might be due to lack of intelligibility (then it is an epistemological issue) or to fortuitous factors (then it is an ontological issue).

2.1. *The Clockwork View*

Newton's mechanical perception of the world was based on three principles (see Gerthsen et al. 1995, 13, Fleissner et al. 1997):

(1) The principle of inertia: a body on which no forces are exerted moves constantly in a straight line.
(2) The principle of action: If a force F is exerted on a body of mass m and velocity v, the impulse of the body, mv, is changed, such that $d/dt\,(mv) = F$.
(3) The principle of reaction: If the force F which is acting on a body has its origin in another body, exactly the opposite force $-F$ is acting on the latter.

Newton's classical mechanics used the concept of causality in an elementary way. If a force is acting on a body, by the principle of action the velocity of the body is changed in a unique way. The body is accelerated proportionately to the force exerted.

These principles imply the unique determination of the effect on the basis of a known cause.

This mechanistic worldview was made explicit by the well-known idea of Laplace that a demon who knew the world formula plus all data describing a certain state of the universe would be capable of predicting and retrodicting any state of the universe, and which in Popper's terms may be called the clockwork view of the universe (Popper 1966).

The thesis of strict determinism, in terms of systems, can be characterised as follows (see Heylighen 1990, Weingartner 1996, 187–189):

(1) Given a system, inputs and outputs are related in such a way that each input is related to one, and only one, output. The system transforms the input into the output by way of a mechanism which can be conceived of as a bijection. If you call the input "cause", and the output "effect", you may state that equal causes have equal effects and distinct causes have distinct effects.
(2) Little changes in the causes lead to little changes in the effects.
(3) There are only repetitions. Each state of a system will return in the future.

In this sense *causa aequat effectum*, or – as Newton's dictum was interpreted elsewhere (Fleissner et al. 1997) – *actio est reactio*. Due to the mathematical function, a tool is provided by which calculable results seem to be guaranteed.

2.2. *Less-Than-Strict Determinism*

Now there is a paradigm shift from classical physics towards self-organisation theories, and from the mechanistic world view which originally laid the foundations for classical physics, towards a view which allows for processes that produce emergent properties, relations and entities (see Kanitscheider 1993, Coveney et al. 1990, Goerner 1994). It is worth recalling the remarkable words of Sir James Lighthill (1986), who regretted that so many scientists had for so many centuries trailed what, in the sixties of the twentieth century, was proven definitely false. He felt obliged to apologise publicly for this.

As science has unravelled the natural world, mechanical relations and strict determinism which are prevalent in the clockwork view of the universe hold for systems at or near at thermodynamic/chemical equilibrium only. But they do not hold for systems exposed to fields in which the uneven distribution of energy density exceeds a critical level.

Such field potentials force energy to flow in non-linear and interdependent ways. And here the systems are showing self-organisation, that is the build-up of order out of fluctuations via dissipation of entropy.

In case of less-than-strict determinism and emergentism causality, in terms of system-theoretical considerations, in contradistinction to the description of a mechanical universe, must be described as follows (Hofkirchner 1998):

(1) Inputs and outputs are not related in a way which can be plotted as bijective mapping. There are no transformation mechanisms which unambiguously turn the causes into the effects; causes and effects are coupled in a way that allows different causes to have the same effect and the same cause to have different effects.

(2) Little changes in the causes may lead to big changes in the effects.

(3) The more complex a system, the less probable the return of a certain state in the future.

This is what ensues ontologically from findings in self-organisation research. Thus *causa non aequat effectum, actio non est reactio.* Due to mathematical short cuts not being applicable, emergent phenomena cannot be predicted in detail. There is no mechanistic transformation which turns the cause into the effect. There is an activity of the system itself which selects one of the several possible ways of reacting. There remains a gap in quality between cause and effect which cannot be bridged in a mechanical way.

Hence, standing on the base of the concept of emergence, we have on the one hand the opportunity to stick to the principle of causality, which means that there is nothing which was created out of nothing (let's leave the question of the coming into being of the universe out), and on the other hand there remains enough openness to let novelties arise which did not exist before.

Less-than-strict determinism is not to say that there is no determinism at all or that the clockwork view has to be replaced with a clouds view. It does not mean that anything goes. It only admits that nature itself is capable of spontaneously producing events which are not describable in a mechanistic way and that besides and beyond clear-cut one-to-one cause-effect-relations there are more flexible causal connections in the real world, too, which seem to be more important and more in number. These connections are due to the fact that self-organising systems have the freedom to choose between several alternatives which make up a non-devoid space of possibilities, compared with mechanical systems where there is only one possibility. Seen this way, strict determinacy is but a special case of causality. It applies if, and only if, the system is deprived of the freedom to choose between several alternatives and the space of possibilities is narrowed down to one trajectory only.

In that way the thesis of less-than-strict determinism not only opposes the thesis of strict determinism but also leads to a new understanding of determinism which includes strictness as correct under certain conditions only.

The common feature of all non-mechanical causation is that the cause is an event which plays the role of a mere trigger of processes, which themselves depend on the nature of the system, at least inasmuch as they are dependent on the influence from the system's environment, and that the effect is an event in which this very self-organisation process finally ends up.

3. Information Processing, Computation

Let's apply now the mechanistic worldview and the thesis of less-than-strict determinism to the case of information generation.

A clockwork universe offers no room for information. If we presume that information has something to do with novelty, information is not possible in a mechanistic universe because there is nothing new to this universe. There is also no need for a concept of information. Everything can be explained in terms of matter. Specific conditions of matter instantiate universal laws of matter. The only place where information could enter the stage is the case of human knowledge about these laws. Science would then be the historical process by which absolute truth is revealed – an idea definitely out-of-date.

This is in sharp contrast to what findings in self-organisation research render obvious.

Self-organisation may be looked upon as the way evolutionary systems come into existence or change their structure, state or behaviour and the way they maintain themselves (their structure, state or behaviour). In either case it is a process in which a difference is produced or reproduced, in that a quality, which differs from the qualities that existed before a certain point of time is made to appear or, from that point on, is sustained vís-a-vís and by virtue of co-existing qualities from which it differs. Hence, in either case emergence is the underlying process.

Thus a philosophy of emergence seems the proper background theory of evolutionary systems thinking. Emergentist philosophy, as developed for instance by Lewis Morgan and summed up by David Blitz (1992) in a book on Emergent Evolution, holds that effects which do not "result" from causes, that is, which are not "resultant" but "emergent", cannot be "reduced" to their causes. In this case causation is only a necessary constraint, but not a sufficient one as it is in mechanistic causation.

By that, self-organisation inheres a touch of spontaneity, that is, a touch of indeterminacy, since the order that is built up is not fully determined. Bifurcations mark possibilities for the system to go one way or another in building up its order. But there is no condition outside the system that compels the system to go this way or that way. It is, so to say, up to the system itself. Determined is that the system has to go one way or another, but it is not determined which way to go.

Actually, with the paradigm shift from the mechanistic worldview cognisant of objects only towards a more inclusive view of a less-than-strict, emergent, and even creative universe inhabited by subjects too, we have got everything required to connect the notion of information to the idea of self-organisation; it is the very idea of systems intervening between input/cause and output/effect and thus breaking up the direct cause-effect-relationships of the mechanistic worldview that facilitates, if not demands, the notion of information, for information is bound to the precondition of subjects and their subjective agency. Self-organising systems that transform the input into an output in a non-mechanical way, that is, in the context of an amount of degrees of freedom undeniably greater than that of a one-option only, are subjects. And each activity in such a context, each acting vís-a-vís undeniable degrees of freedom, is nothing less than the generation of information because the act to discriminate, to distinguish, to differentiate, is information.

Self-organisation stands therefore at the beginning of all information, insofar as the system selects one of a number of possible responses to a causal event in its environment, as it shows preference for the particular option it chooses to realise over a number of other options, as it "decides" to discriminate.

Information is involved in self-organisation. Every system acts and reacts in a network of systems, elements and networks, and is exposed to influences mediated by matter and/or energy relations. If the effects on the system are fully derivable from, and fully reducible to, the causes outside the system, no informational aspects can be separated from matter/energy cause-effect relations. However, as soon as the effects become dependent on the system as well (because the system itself contributes to them), as soon as the influences play the role of mere triggers for effects being self-organised by the system, as soon as degrees of freedom intervene and the reaction of the system is unequal to the action it undergoes, the system produces information (see Haken 1988). Information is created, if there is a surplus of effects exceeding causes in a system. Information occurs during the process in which the system exhibits changes in its structure, or in its state, or in its behaviour (Fenzl et al. 1996), i.e., changes which are due to the system. Information is created by a system, if it is organising itself at any level. Information is that part of the process of self-organisation that is responsible for generating new features in the system's structure, state, or behaviour. In a figurative sense, information can be looked upon as the result of this process, as what is new in the structure, state, or behaviour. And insofar as this new feature in system A may serve to stimulate self-organising (and therefore informational) processes to produce new features in system B, we can speak of information in a metaphoric sense as if it were something to be sent from one system to another.

Summing up, we can speak of information in the following situations: where the deterministic connection between cause and effect is broken up; where a system's own activity comes into play, and the cause becomes the mere trigger of self-determined processes in the system, which finally lead to the effect; where the system makes a decision and a possibility is realised by an irreducible choice.

Since information generation is a process that allows novelty to emerge, it is worth noting that information generation is not a mechanical process and thus defies being formalised, expressed by a mathematical function, or carried out by a computer. It is only in the case of a mechanical process, that methods of mental transformation apply so as to unequivocally lead from a model of the cause to the model of the effect. These intellectual methods are provided by formal sciences like formal logic, mathematics, or computer science; they involve the deduction of a conclusion from its premises or the calculation of a result or a computer operation (Krämer 1988). Mechanical processes can be mapped onto algorithmic procedures that employ clear-cut and unambiguous instructions capable of carrying out by the help of computers as universal machines. But the generation of information escapes algorithmisation, in principle.

Having said this, it follows that a claim of algorithmic information theory to study information based upon algorithmic and computational approaches is, according to the definition of information given above, to be considered a too ambitious one. For this approach does not cover the whole range of what the phenomenon of information embraces. In particular, it must fail to reflect novelty as essential quality of information. Deductions, by definition, don't yield novelties, algorithms, by definition, can't do it either, nor can computation, by definition, do it.

The distinction between the property "deterministic" and the property "probabilistic" concerning automata is, in this context, misleading. Also probabilistic machines rely completely on strict deterministic mechanisms in the sense defined above and are thus mechanistic despite their inclusion of, e.g., "random numbers" which are, in fact, pseudo-random numbers produced by strict deterministic mechanisms (Fuchs-Kittowski 1976, 193). Machines don't choose. To claim this would blur the distinction between the way mechanical devices work and the way systems endowed with subjectiveness (evolutionary systems, i.e., self-organising systems) act. At best we can say that probabilistic computing is a way to simulate less-than-strict deterministic processes of real-world systems but it is not exactly the way these processes work in real world.

This holds for evolutionary computing too. Apart from using the same computer mechanisms, there seems to be a mechanistic misinterpretation of Darwinian theory (see e.g. Peter Corning 2003 who is one of the critics) underlying the computation of evolutionary processes that makes it, at best, a simulation of real-world evolutionary processes but not identical to them or an evolution itself. As Mario Bunge (2003, 152) puts it, "things are not the same as their artificial simulates. In particular, a computer simulation of a physical, chemical, biological, or social process is not equivalent to the original process: at most, it is similar to some aspects of it." Susan Oyama (2000) collected a many literature dealing with that problem with regard to biology.

The argument here that stresses novelty and thus emergence is an ontological one but not an epistemological one (Hofkirchner 2001). It is worth noting that Heinz von Foerster who is known as the first who at the end of the fifties of the last century introduced the notion of self-organising systems to the scientific community (see v. Foerster 1960 and v. Foerster et al. 1962) and who is known for his distinction between trivial and nontrivial systems himself used an epistemological argument. According to von Foerster, a nontrivial system is nontrivial, finally, because the observer is faced with a nontrivial problem when trying to find out how the system works. A nontrivial system differs from a trivial one in that "a response once observed for a given stimulus may *not* be the same for the same stimulus given later," due to the fact that it has at least one internal state z "whose values co-determine its input-output relation (x,y). Moreover, the relationship between the present and subsequent internal states (z, z') is co-determined by the inputs (x)" (v. Foerster 1984, 10). Ontologically, however, there is no difference between trivial and nontrivial systems. Both kinds of systems can behave strictly deterministically. Once the mechanism of the function f_y and f_z of a nontrivial system is fixed, its output y, given an input x, is unambiguously determined (Hügin 1996, 128). Thus, Foerster's hidden ontology turns out to be mechanistic.

The same holds for the case of deterministic (*sic!*) chaos. You can't predict the next state of a chaotic system since there is no formula that helps you compute whatever step you like, while the next step the real-world system in question will take is strictly determined. This means there are restraints in epistemology, while ontologically there is no difference in determination.

4. Paradigms

There is an intricate relation between the ontic and the epistemic, between reality and method. Furthermore, we have to add a "praxic" dimension, that is, praxis, to this relationship which altogether yield a praxio-onto-epistemological perspective (Hofkirchner et al. 2005).

Thus a paradigm can be looked upon as a body of interrelated praxiological, ontological and epistemological assumptions formed along a particular way of thinking.

The mechanistic paradigm is made up of praxiological, ontological and epistemological assumptions shaped according to the reductionist way of thinking. The new paradigm, if it is to deserve the attribute "new", has to be shaped according to a different way of thinking that is set up to confront complexity.

Let's first deal with the relationship of praxis, reality and method, then explain ways of thinking and, finally, employ these findings to the paradigms in question.

4.1. *Praxis, Reality, Method*

Praxio-onto-epistemology is a stance that builds upon onto-epistemology as coined by Hans Jörg Sandkühler (1990, 1991, 34–37, 353–369) and shaped by Rainer E. Zimmermann (e.g. 2002, 147–167). Onto-epistemology tries to reconcile realism with constructivism. Praxio-onto-epistemology tries to complement the interrelationship of ontology and epistemology by the relation to ethics, aesthetics and axiology all of which we propose to include in so-called praxiology (Hofkirchner et al. 2005).

In terms of subjects and objects, praxis is the totality of the human subject-object-dialectic, reality is what is, so to say, objecting to becoming subject to humans, and method is the subjective way of casting objects and making them subject to humans. It becomes clear from that order of definitions that praxis builds upon reality and that reality builds upon method. Anyway, there is relative autonomy of each of the domains (praxis may shape reality but reality gives the scope of possible practices, while reality may shape method but method gives the scope of possible realities).

The rationale for defining subject matters in such a concatenated way is to give an appropriate sketch of the following: particular interests (that reflect particular practices) define the sphere of intervention (that is made up of objects in which subjects are interested and is characterised by a boundary beyond which there are no real objects since there is no subject interested in them) and particular spheres of intervention (that reflect particular realities) define the scope of instruments (that is made up of means which are useful for intervention and is characterised by a boundary beyond which there are no real means since they do not fit the object); and, in turn, particular instruments (that reflect particular methods) can help construct a particular sphere of intervention that excludes different realities and particular spheres of intervention can meet a particular bunch of interests that exclude different interests.

4.2. *Ways of Thinking*

A way of thinking is the way how identity and difference are thought to relate to each other. Relating identity and difference may be presumed to be the most basic function of thinking. That is, practical problems that come to thought, entities that are investigated, phenomena that have to be cognised, may be identical in certain respects but may differ from each other in other respects..

Regarding identity and difference, given complexity, that is, provided that which differs is more complex than that from which it differs, but, by the same token, instaurates an integrated whole, the question arises as to how the simple does relate to the complex, that is, how less complex problems or objects or phenomena do relate to more complex ones.

The first way of thinking, in terms of ideal types, establishes identity by eliminating the difference for the benefit of the less complex side of the difference and at the cost of the more complex side; it reduces "higher complexity" to "lower complexity"; this is known as reductionism. Reductionism is manifested by the main stream of natural and engineering science.

The counterpart of the reductive way of thinking is what might be called projective. Projective thinking too establishes identity by eliminating the difference, albeit for the benefit of the more complex side of the difference and at the cost of the less complex side; it takes the "higher" level of complexity as its point of departure and extrapolates or projects from there to the "lower" level of complexity. It overestimates the role of the whole and belittles the role of the parts. This is one trait of many humanities.

Both the reductive and the projective way of thinking yield unity without diversity.

To go on, there is a third way opposed to both reductionism and projectivism in that it eliminates identity by establishing the difference for the sake of each manifestation of complexity in its own right; it abandons all relationships between all of them by treating them as disjunctive; it dissociates one from the other, it dichotomises and yields dualism (or pluralism) in the sense of diversity without unity. Let's call it disjunctivism. In fact, this is a description of the state of the scientific adventure as a multiplicity of monodisciplinary approaches that are alien and deaf towards each other.

Eventually, there is a fourth way of thinking that negates all three ways together. This is a way of thinking that establishes identity as well as difference favouring neither of the manifestations of complexity; it establishes identity in line with the difference; it integrates both sides of the difference (yielding unity) and it differentiates identity (yielding diversity); it is a way of thinking that is based upon integration and differentiation; it is opposed to both dissociation and unification and yields unity and diversity in one. It integrates "lower" and "higher complexity" by establishing a dialectical relationship between them.

4.3. *Mechanicism vs. Emergentism*

Let us distinguish between objects of praxis (the praxic dimesnion), objects of reality (the ontic dimension) and objects of method (the epistemic dimension) (Hofkirchner 2004). Objects of praxis O_p are the ones which are acted upon. Objects of reality O_o are the ones existing as such. And objects of method O_e are the ones in our heads. According to the way we (assume to) act on objects O_p, we assume how they exist independently of our actions as O_o. And according to the way (we assume) the objects O_o exist, we assume methods of investigation and representation by which we manipulate the objects O_e in our heads. And according to the way we (assume to) link objects O_p in praxis, (we assume) they are able to be linked as objects O_o in reality, and it is according to the latter that (we assume) they have to be linked by our method as objects O_e.

Let O_x^{t1} and O_x^{t2} indicate the same object O_x at the point of time t_1 and t_2 respectively whereby x = {p, o, e} and let the arrow $\rightarrow$ indicate an unambiguous transformation while the sign $\underline{\uparrow}$ shall signify a transformation that involves ambiguity.

Then we can describe the mechanistic paradigm as follows:

(1) on the praxic level we have $O_p^{t1} \rightarrow O_p^{t2}$; that is, the action applicable is a "brute force" operation which leads unambiguously from the object in an initial state to the object in a well-determined final state; humans can apply this operation only when functionalising cause-effect-relationships that rest upon the ontic level;

(2) thus on the ontic level we have $O_o^{t1} \rightarrow O_o^{t2}$; that is, the object at t_1 is causally transformable into the object at t_2 by pure necessity; this is the case with strict determinism; objects transform in this manner only when embodying on the ontic level deductive logic or computable functions or algorithmic precriptions that are located on the epistemic level;

(3) thus on the epistemic level we have $O_e^{t1} \rightarrow O_e^{t2}$; that is, the object at time t_2 is derivable from the object at time t_1, given particular conditions; the outcome is necessitated in a compelling way: a conclusion is drawn from premises in an inference and there is no way to evade that, a mathematical solution results from inputs in formulae and there is no way to evade that, and data is processed by algorithmic computer programmes and there is no way to evade that.

That is to say, first, the mechanistic paradigm is reductionistic, since the output, be it praxic, ontic, or epistemic, to which higher complexity is ascribed is leveled down to the respective input to which lower complexity is ascribed, and, second, information processing within the confines of this paradigm cannot generate information, since the transformations under consideration are by definition devoid of self-organisation, emergence and novelty. In deductive transformations the truth value is transferred from the input to the output and cannot give room to leaps in quality, in algebraic transformations the output explicates what is implicit in the input and cannot give room to leaps in quality, in algorithmic transformations each step is determined by the preceding step and cannot give room to leaps in quality.

The mechanistic paradigm must fail, if applied to processes other than mechanistic. The generation of information is not a mechanistic process. It is bound to self-organisation which is open for leaps in quality. Thus another paradigm has to be cast to fit information processes. We have to replace transformations of that rigid, fixed character with another kind of transformations that are open for openness so as to yield:

(1) on the praxic level $O_p^{t1} \uparrow O_p^{t2}$; according to evolutionary systems design, human intervention is a mere nudge that when intelligently deployed may trigger a transformation by which the desired outcome may emerge; evolutionary systems design takes advantage of the self-organisation capacity of the objects of reality in that it aims at facilitating or dampening those processes and not at constructing them *ab novo* nor getting rid of them;

(2) on the ontic level $O_o^{t1} \uparrow O_o^{t2}$; according to evolutionary systems modeling, the starting point of the transformation builds the base upon which a contingent reality will emerge; the transformation may inhere bifurcations and thus not "obey natural laws" as viewed in a mechanicist concept but rather adhere to propensities our cosmos is displaying (see late Popper 1977);

(3) on the epistemic level $O_e^{t1} \uparrow O_e^{t2}$; according to evolutionary systems methodology, the base from wich the transformation on the ontic level starts has to be codified on the epistemic level as necessary condition only but not as sufficient one (as is the case with the mechanistic paradigm) in order to do justice to the emergent character of the "result" of the transformation which represents a new quality; dialectical logic with its sublation scheme is a good candidate for grasping this relationship.

Having said all this, the question remains whether or not, in the computationalist perspective, computation equals information-processing equals transformations in the mechanistic, reductionistic, deterministic sense. Only if computation is meant as a self-organising process involving emergence in a non-epistemological sense, it can do justice to the generation of information.

Actually, computers compute according to the mechanistic paradigm and thus cannot bring about new information. But this is not to say that they are expandable. Though they are bound to algorithmic procedures they are of advantage to and a needful link in human information generation. Inmidst the overarching cycles of human information processes, including cognition, communication and cooperation, they play their role and carry out the task that is distributed to them and is not *per se* generation of information. The situation can be compared to the field of logic. We certainly make use of deductive logic but are aware of the power of the unformalisable.

5. Conclusion

The computational turn resulting eventually in pan-computationalism equates computation and information-processing. If information-processing as it is done in computers is considered to be the role-model for information processes going on in the universe, then information generation is impossible, since information generation involves the phenomenon of emergence on the ontic level. Hence the need for the paradigm of self-organising real-world systems. Current computations find their *raison d'etre* in assisting, augmenting, supporting human information generation.

References

Blitz, D. (1992). *Emergent evolution: qualitative novelty and the levels of reality* (Kluwer, Dordrecht)
Bunge, M. (2003). *Emergence and Convergence* (University of Toronto Press, Toronto).
Corning, P. (2003). *Nature's Magic* (Cambridge University Press, Cambridge).
Coveney, P., and Highfield, R. (1990). *The Arrow of Time* (Allen, London).

Fenzl, N., and Hofkirchner, W. (1997). Information Processing in Evolutionary Systems. An Outline Conceptual Framework for a Unified Information Theory. In: *Self-Organization of Complex Structures: From Individual to Collective Dynamics,* Schweitzer, F., ed., Foreword by Hermann Haken (Gordon & Breach, London), pp. 59–70.

Fleissner, P., and Hofkirchner, W. (1997). Actio non est reactio. An Extension of the Concept of Causality towards Phenomena of Information. *World Futures,* 3–4(49) & 1–4(50)/1997, pp. 409–427.

Foerster, H. v. (1960). On Self-Organizing Systems and Their Environments. In: *Cybernetics of Cybernetics,* Foerster, H. v., ed. (Future Systems, Minneapolis), pp. 220–230.

Foerster, H. v. (1984). Principles of Self-Organization – In a Socio-Managerial Context. In: *Self-Organization and Management of Social Systems,* Ulrich, H. and Probst, G. J. B., eds. (Springer, Berlin), pp. 2–24.

Foerster, H., and Zopf, G. W., eds. (1962). *Principles of Self-Organization* (Pergamon Press, Oxford).

Fuchs-Kittowski, K. (1976). *Probleme des Determinismus und der Kybernetik in der molekularen Biologie* (Gustav Fischer Verlag, Jena).

Gerthsen, C., Kneser, H. O., and Vogel, H. (1995). *Physik* (Springer, Berlin).

Goerner, S. J. (1994). *Chaos and the Evolving Ecological Universe* (Gordon & Breach, Amsterdam).

Haken, H. (1988). *Information and self-organization.* (Springer, Berlin).

Heylighen, F. (1990). Autonomy and Cognition as the Maintenance and Processing of Distinctions. In *Self-Steering and Cognition in Complex Systems, Toward a New Cybernetics,* Heylighen, F., Rosseel, E., and Demeyere, F., eds. (Gordon & Breach, New York), pp. 89–106.

Hofkirchner, W. (1998). Emergence and the Logic of Explanation – An Argument for the Unity of Science. *Acta Polytechnica Scandinavica, Mathematics, Computing and Management in Engineering Series,* 91, pp. 23–30.

Hofkirchner, W. (2001). The Hidden Ontology: Real World Evolutionary Systems Concept as Key to Information Science. *Emergence* 3/3, pp. 22–41.

Hofkirchner, W. (2004). A New Way of Thinking and a New World View: On the Philosophy of Self-Organisation I. *Cybernetics & Human Knowing,* Vol. 11, No. 1, pp. 63–78

Hofkirchner, W., Fuchs, C., and Klauninger, B. (2005). Informational Universe. A praxeo-onto-epistemological Approach. In *Human Approaches to the Universe, Interdisciplinary Studies,* Martikainen, E., ed. (Academic Bookstore, Helsinki), pp. 75–94.

Hörz, H. (1962). *Der dialektische Determinismus in Natur und Gesellschaft* (Deutscher Verlag der Wissenschaften, Berlin).

Hörz, H. (1971). *Materiestruktur* (Deutscher Verlag der Wissenschaften, Berlin).

Hügin, U. (1996). *Individuum, Gemeinschaft, Umwelt. Konzeption einer Theorie der Dynamik anthropogener Systeme* (Peter Lang, Bern).

Kanitscheider, B. (1993). *Von der mechanistischen Welt zum kreativen Universum. Zu einem neuen philosophischen Verständnis der Natur* (Wissenschaftliche Buchgesellschaft, Darmstadt).

Krämer, S. (1988). *Symbolische Maschinen*. (Wissenschaftliche Buchgesellschaft, Darmstadt).

Lighthill, J. (1986). The Recently Recognized Failure of Predictability in Newtonian Dynamics. *Proc. R. Soc.* A 407, p. 38.

Oyama, S. (2000). *The Ontogeny of Information. Developmental Systems and Evolution* (Duke University Press, Durham NC).

Popper, K. R. (1966). *Of clouds and clocks: An approach to the problem of rationality and the freedom of man. The Arthur Holly Compton memorial lecture* (Washington University, Washington).

Popper, K. R. (1997). *A World of Propensities* (Thoemmes Press, Bristol).

Sandkühler, H. J. (1990). Onto-Epistemologie. *Europäische Enzyklopädie zu Philosophie und Wissenschaften* (Meiner, Hamburg), pp. 608–615.

Sandkühler, H. J. (1991). *Die Wirklichkeit des Wissens, Geschichtliche Einführung in die Epistemologie und Theorie der Erkenntnis* (Suhrkamp, Frankfurt).

Weingartner, P. (1996). Müssen wir unseren Gesetzesbegriff revidieren? In *Gesetz und Vorhersage*, Weingartner, P. , ed. (Alber, Freiburg im Breisgau), pp. 179–222.

Zimmermann, R. (2002), *Kritik der interkulturellen Vernunft* (mentis, Paderborn).

CHAPTER 8

ANALYSIS OF INFORMATION AND COMPUTATION IN PHYSICS EXPLAINS COGNITIVE PARADIGMS: FROM FULL COGNITION TO LAPLACE DETERMINISM TO STATISTICAL DETERMINISM TO MODERN APPROACH

Vladik Kreinovich[1], Roberto Araiza[1] and Juan Ferret[2]

Departments of [1]Computer Science and [2]Philosophy
University of Texas at El Paso, El Paso, Texas 79968, USA
vladik@utep.edu, raraiza@miners.utep.edu, jferret@utep.edu

In this chapter, we analyze the problem of prediction in physics from the computational viewpoint. We show that physical paradigms like Laplace determinism, statistical determinism, etc., can be naturally explained by this computational analysis. In our explanations, we use the notions of the Algorithmic Information Theory such as Kolmogorov complexity and algorithmic randomness, and the novel, more physics-oriented variants of these notions.

1. Introduction

Computability in theoretical computer science: traditional approach. Traditionally, the theoretical analysis of computations is mainly concentrated on analyzing which *mathematical* functions can be computed, which can be efficiently computed, etc.

Computability: a practical problem. It is desirable to take into account that from the practical viewpoint, computing mathematical functions (and solving precisely formulated mathematical problems) is an auxiliary task.

One of the main objectives of computations is to predict the behavior of different processes in the real (*physical*) world. In view of this objective, it is important to distinguish between:

- general *data* and
- data that represents *knowledge* – i.e., that helps in this prediction.

It is also important to analyze what can be computably predicted and what cannot be predicted.

Predictability in physics: different paradigms. The understanding of what can be predicted has changed throughout the history of physics (see, e.g., Reference [2]). Usually, a new paradigm appears when for some real-life processes, the previous paradigm turns out to be too optimistic; examples will be given below.

First paradigm: Full Cognition. In the beginning, the understanding was that science can potentially describe all the details of the process "from scratch". For example, Kepler was not only predicting how the planets move, he was also trying to predict the fate of princes by looking at the positions of the stars.

At present, we understand that it is possible to predict how the stars and the planets move, but it does not seem to be possible to predict human behavior and human fate. However, in Kepler's time, there seems to have been no understanding of this difference: science was supposed to be able to explain and predict everything. Yes, it is easier to predict how the planets move, it is more difficult to predict how people will behave, but both were considered legitimate science.

Similarly, now we know that it is not possible to make long-term (even yearly) weather predictions. However, even in the early 18 century, many weather almanacs were published that tried to predict weather for one (or more) years ahead – and these almanacs were actively bought by practicing farmers.

Limitations of the Full Cognition (FG) paradigm. The inability to predict such things as weather and human behavior led scientists to realize that a universal prediction "from scratch" is not always possible.

Laplace Determinism (LD). It turned out that while we cannot predict these phenomena based on *general principles* and ideas, we can often get reasonable predictions if we know the current state of the system.

For example, it is impossible to predict the fate of the newborn child based on the locations of stars and planets at the time when the child was born. However, when we observe the behavior of a person, when we find out his or her strengths, weaknesses, and behavior patterns, we can often reasonably well predict this person's fate. Similarly, when we observe the weather pattern in a given location, we can usually predict, e.g., that May will be dry and warm, that August will be rainy, etc.

The idea that if we know the current state ("initial conditions") then we can predict the future behavior of the system was first explicitly formulated by Pierre-Simon Laplace, the 19 century mathematician and astronomer. Because of this, the corresponding paradigm is usually called *Laplace Determinism*.

Laplace Determinism: successes. Laplace Determinism has been the major paradigm of 19 century physics. Newton's mechanics, Maxwell's electrodynamics, many other physical theories – they are all formulated in terms of systems of differential equations, equations that enable us to go from the initial conditions to the predictions of the future states.

Even now, Laplace Determinism covers a significant portion of practical applications of physics.

Laplace Determinism: limitations. At the end of the 19 century, several new processes were discovered in which prediction turned out to be impossible. The most well known of these processes was radioactivity, i.e., the ability of atoms to spontaneously turn into other atoms.

All atoms of a radioactive material are absolutely identical, i.e., have practically identical initial conditions. So, from the viewpoint of the Laplace Determinism, they should all behave in exactly the same way – in particular, they should all undergo radioactive decay at the same time.

In reality, different atoms decay at different times, and all attempts to predict these times were unsuccessful.

Another limitation of Laplace Determinism comes from the analysis of decisions made by humans (and by other living beings). The famous Buridan's ass paradox considers a donkey placed between two absolutely identical bales of hay. Since these bales are absolutely identical, there is no reason for select one of them and not the other. Thus, a deterministic decision-making donkey will not be able to select one of these bales – and thus, the poor donkey may eventually starve to death. In practice, this will never happen – because a donkey would select one of the bales at random.

The need to take into account such random selections makes deterministic predictions impossible.

Statistical Determinism (SD).   The physicists started collecting data about individual radioactive decay events. While they were unable to predict the time of individual events, they found out that the *frequencies* with which different atoms decay at different moments of time can be predicted.

In other words, while we cannot predict the exact future states, we can predict the *probabilities* of different future states.

At first, it was assumed that this need to restrict ourselves to statistical predictions was only typical of *some* exotic events like radioactivity. However, the successes of quantum physics have shown that a similar phenomenon holds for *all* physical predictions – at least those predictions in which we must take into account the properties of microobjects like atoms or elementary particles. Equations of quantum mechanics do not predict the values of the future location or velocity of a particle, they only describe the so-called *wave function* $\psi(x)$. Once we know the wave function, we can estimate the probability of finding a particle at a location x (as $|\psi(x)|^2$).

From the modern viewpoint, this need to consider probabilities is a well-known textbook fact. However, in the 1920s and even in the 1930s, the idea that the Laplace Determinism paradigm must be replaced was very controversial: even Einstein famously said that he did not believe that God plays dice.

The paradigm in which, once we know the initial conditions, we can predict the probabilities of different future events, is usually called *Statistical Determinism*.

Statistical Determinism is still the prevailing paradigm in most areas of fundamental physics.

Limitations of Statistical Determinism and the emergence of a new paradigm.   Starting with the 1960s, it turned out that for many real-life phenomena, even predicting probabilities is not always possible.

This phenomenon is best known for *chaotic systems*, i.e., systems in which a minor (practically non-observable) deviation in the initial conditions can lead to a drastic qualitative change in the future behavior of a system.

This phenomenon was first observed on the example of a simplified system of equations for predicting weather, and it has since been observed in numerous real-life phenomena.

Since even predicting probabilities is not always possible, the modern paradigm of physics – which we would call the Modern Approach (MA) – claims simply that if we know the initial conditions, then we can predict *some information* about the probabilities of different future states.

Physics paradigms: computational challenge. We have described the past and current physical paradigms. We have described them in a purely empirical way. Since these paradigms are about predictions – i.e., in effect, about prediction-related *computations* – it is desirable to understand these paradigms (and their relations and transitions) from the computational viewpoint.

What we do in this paper. In the paper, we will show that an appropriate computational analysis of predictability naturally explains the appearance of these different physical paradigms. We will also describe how this analysis can be used in working physics. As an example, we will give a recent unusual result from computational cosmology.

Comment. From the mathematical viewpoint, our analysis uses the notions of Algorithmic Information Theory such as Kolmogorov complexity and algorithmic randomness, as well as the novel, more physics-oriented variants of these notions.

2. Algorithmic Information Theory: How It Naturally Arises from Physical Paradigms

The need to describe randomness. As we have mentioned, in Statistical Determinism, we predict the probabilities of different future states. For example, we predict the probabilities that an atom decays at different moments of time. We are unable to predict when each individual atom decays.

For example, if we start with a given set of n atoms $a_1, \ldots, a_n$, and we know that at a certain moment of time, half of these atoms decay. We can describe the final state of this system by describing which atoms decayed and which did not. This can be naturally done by describing an n-bit sequence in which the i-bit is 1 if the i-th atom decayed and is 0 if it did not. For example, 101... means that the 1st and the 3rd atoms decayed, but the 2nd atom did not. We cannot predict which of the n atoms decayed. The actual sequence of decayed atoms is *random*, in the sense that all the information it contains is that half of the atoms decayed.

The fact that we cannot predict which atoms decay means that regular sequences like 010101... are not physically possible – because in such a sequence, we will be able to easily predict which atoms will decay and which atoms will not.

How can we describe this notion of randomness in precise terms?

Kolmogorov's original definition of randomness. In the 1960s, A. N. Kolmolgorov and his student P. Martin-Löf used the difficulty-to-predict as a formal definition of randomness.

They started by observing that when a binary sequence s is regular, i.e., has the form 010101..., then even when this sequence is long, we can write a short (and simple) program p that generates this sequence. For example, to generate a sequence consisting of 1,000 pairs 01, we can write a simple for-loop:

```
for (i = 0; i < 1000; i++)
  print("01");
```

Vice versa, if a short program can generate a long sequence, this means that this sequence s is regular.

The fact that a sequence is random means that it is not regular, i.e., that it is not possible to have a short program that generates this sequence.

Of course, we are dealing with finite sequences, and a finite sequence $s = 11001\ldots$ can always be generated by a program that prints this sequence bit by bit:

```
print("11001...");
```

However, if we use this idea to generate a sequence consisting of 1,000 symbols, we will need a program of the same length of 1,000 symbols (even a little bit longer, because we also need a print command).

Thus, the difference between regular sequences and random sequences is that

- regular sequences can be generated by programs which are much shorter, while
- random sequences can only be generated by programs of approximately the same length.

To capture this difference, Kolmogorov and Martin-Löf defined *Kolmogorov complexity* $K(s)$ of a finite sequence s as the shortest length of a program that generates the sequence s.

We can always generate a given sequence s by simply printing it bit by bit. We have already mentioned that the length of this program is equal to the length $\text{len}(s)$ of the sequence s plus a small number of bits C needed to describe the print statement. Thus, the Kolmogorov complexity $K(s)$ of an arbitrary sequence s – which is defined as the shortest length of the program that generates s – cannot exceed the length $\text{len}(s) + C$ of this bit-by-bit program: $K(s) \leq \text{len}(s) + C$.

For random sequences, no significantly shorter programs are possible. Thus, for a random sequence s, its Kolmogorov complexity $K(s)$ – the length of the shortest program for generating s – cannot be much smaller than its length. This idea is behind the definition of randomness of a binary sequence.

Let C be an integer. A finite binary sequenced is called *C-random* if $K(s) \geq \text{len}(s) - C$.

Comment. Strictly speaking, to make this definition precise, we need to fix a (universal) programming language, i.e., a programming language in which every algorithm can be programmed (like C or Java). However, it turned out that all the languages are, in some reasonable sense, equivalent: namely, the choice of a language only changes the length by a additive constant.

Beyond regular and random sequences: a useful consequence of Kolmogorov's formalization of randomness. In the previous paragraphs, we only considered two types of sequences: regular sequences and random sequences.

What about generic sequences? For an arbitrary sequence s, we can also describe its Kolmogorov complexity as the length of the shortest program p that generates this sequence s. Once we know the program p, we can easily generate s – by simply running a compiler from the corresponding programming language.

The important point is that, as we will show, the program p is itself random in the Kolmogorov-Martin-Löf sense. Indeed, if we could generate p by running a much shorter program q with $\text{len}(q) \ll \text{len}(p)$, then we would be able to generate x from q as well: by first generating the code p, and then by running this code to generate x. The fact that p is the shortest program for generating x means that q cannot be much shorter than p – i.e., that the Kolmogorov complexity $K(p)$ must be approximately equal to the length $\text{len}(p)$ of this sequence p.

By definition, sequence for which $K(p) \approx \text{len}(p)$ are called random. Thus, p is indeed a random sequence.

So, we arrive at a somewhat non-intuitive conclusion: that an arbitrary binary sequence s can be obtained by applying a simple algorithm to some auxiliary random sequence p.

Comment. For a mathematician or for a physicist, the fact that an arbitrary sequence can be obtained by applying an appropriate algorithmic process to a random sequence may sound novel. While mathematics behind Kolmogorov's complexity is indeed reasonably novel, the possibility to represent an arbitrary signal as a combination of deterministic and random effects is well known and well established in statistical data and signal processing. There, the main objective – usually attainable – is to to find an approximate deterministic dependence for which the approximation error is purely random.

What we do in this paper. In this paper, we use the Kolmogorov complexity ideas to show that many physicists' paradigms can be explained by the need for algorithmically feasible predictions.

3. Explanation of Main Cognitive Paradigms of Physics

Need for prediction: reminder. Our objective is to predict the state $s(t)$ of the Universe at future moments of time.

To be more precise, we would like to predict *as much as possible* about the state of the Universe at the future moments of time.

Ideal situation. In the ideal situation, we should have an algorithm that, given a future moment t, a location x, and the quantity f, would predict the value $f(x, t)$ of the quantity f at the given location at the given moment of time.

This ideal situation corresponds to what we called *full cognition*.

Algorithm that uses measurement results. Since it turned out that no such universal algorithm is possible, the next natural idea is to use the initial conditions – i.e., the current values of the physical quantities – to predict the future state of the Universe. This is what we called *Laplace Determinism*.

Where is the beef? At this point, a reader may rightfully ask: what is the point of simply repeating the paradigms that we have already covered in the introduction? Up to now, there was indeed no point yet, but non-so-trivial consequences will start in the next paragraph.

Interesting consequence: initial conditions should be random. What does this mean that we are unable to predict the state of the universe without using initial conditions? It simply means that initial conditions cannot be predicted "from scratch" – otherwise, we would be able to combine the two algorithms:

- algorithm for computing these initial conditions, and
- the algorithm for predicting the suture state of the world based on these initial conditions

and thus, get an (assumed impossible) algorithm for full cognition.

In algorithmic terms, what does it mean for a sequence to be unpredictable? In Kolmolgorov's formalization, unpredictability simply means that the initial conditions are *random*.

Why is this consequence physically interesting? The fact that initial conditions are random may be an interesting mathematical observation, but does it have physical consequences? Yes, it does.

These physical consequences are related to the seeming contradiction between the physical equations and common sense about the direction of time.

From the purely mathematical viewpoint, Newton's laws do not change it we simply replace the original time coordinate t with a new coordinate $t' = -t$ – i.e., if we change the direction of time. If we videotape a purely mechanical motion and then show the motion backwards, the resulting motion will still make perfect sense.

However, when we turn from a system consisting of a few bodies to a system consisting of a large number of molecules, this time symmetry somehow disappears. Examples of this obvious (and mysterious) time asymmetry are well known.

For example, it is easy to observe that if we prepare a vessel with two separate compartments, place smoke in one compartment, leave clean air in another compartment, and then remove the separation, the gases will mix. The equations all remain time-invariant. Strictly speaking, if at the moment when the two gases have mixed, we simply invert the directions of all the velocities, we should see the same process reverting itself – and gases separating. A mathematician may say that this reversion is still physically possible but its probability is very low. However, a physicist would usually make a much stronger statement: the separation is simply not possible.

Let us give another example in which this impossibility is even more clear. If I drop a breakable cup on the hard floor, it will break into pieces. Theoretically, it may seem possible to imaging the reverse phenomenon: that the broken pieces magically fall back into place – but from the common sense viewpoint, everyone will agree that this magical recovery of the whole cup from pieces is not possible.

How do physicists explain this impossibility? Clearly this impossibility does not come from equations – since all the equations do not change if we simply replace t with $-t$. A usual physicists' explanation is that the hypothetic cup recovery process is not stable. We never know the exact values of the initial locations and initial velocities, and if we change these initial conditions a little bit, the magic recovery of a broken cup will simply not occur.

In precise terms, what the physicists are saying is that for a cup to recover, we need to have very special, very well-defined initial conditions. However, since there are many unpredictable effects, the actual initial conditions cannot be predictable and exact.

In other words, what the physicists are saying is that it is not sufficient to describe the equations describing physical dynamics, we must also postulate that the initial conditions are *random*.

Our claim is that there is actually no need for a special new postulate – the very fact that we went from Full Cognition to Laplace Determinism means, in effect, that the initial conditions should be random.

Towards explaining other physical ideas within the Laplace Determinism paradigm. The fact that the randomness of initial conditions seems to follow naturally from our analysis of cognition makes us wonder that maybe other physical ideas within Laplace Determinism can also be naturally explained by a similar analysis.

Indeed, the general idea of Laplace Determinism is that we predict the values $f(x, t)$ of different physical quantities f at difference locations x and at different future moments of time t based on the initial conditions $g(x, t_0)$. In the worst-case scenario,

- to predict each value $f(x, t)$, we need to have full information about all the initial conditions, i.e., to have all the values $f(y, t_0)$ corresponding to all possible spatial locations y;
- each quantity can attain all possible numbers as its values, so, e.g., to get the value with accuracy 2^{-k}, we need to actually generate all k bits from this sequence;
- finally, once we have succeeded in predicting the value of one physical quantity f at a certain location, this prediction will not in any way help in predicting the values of other quantities at different spatial locations.

The resulting computations require a large amount of input (all the initial conditions), produce the large size output (all bits need to be produced), and cannot utilize other previous predictive computations. In this worst case, the success of these predictive computations is thus in doubt. To make successful predictions, it is therefore reasonable to look for physical systems in which at least some of these complexities are relaxed.

Let us describe possible relaxations and let us show that they indeed correspond to fundamental physical ideas.

Relaxing input complexities: the notion of causality. Let us first consider what will happen is we relax the need for the value $f(x,t)$ to depend on the initial values $g(y,t_0)$ for *all* possible spatial locations y. Relaxing this need means that we assume that the value $f(x,t)$ of a physical field only depends on the values $g(y,t_0)$ for *some* spatial locations.

The values of $g(y,t_0)$ at other spatial locations y do not affect the values $f(x,t)$ at all.

Since physical fields are interconnected, it is reasonable to expect that since the value $f(x,t)$ of the physical field f does not depend on $g(y,t_0)$, the values of all other physical fields at the location x at moment t are also not affected by the values $g(y,t_0)$. Thus, this limitation does not depend on the specific fields, it depends only on the space-time points (x,t) and (y,t_0).

Thus, we have space-time moments (x,t) $(t > t_0)$ which are affected by the moments (y,t_0) and space-time moments which are nor affected. In other words, we naturally arrive at the notion of *causality*, the notion that – in this space-time form – only appeared in the mainstream physics in the early 20 century, with Einstein's Special Relativity Theory.

What we have shown is that from the algorithmic viewpoint, this notion can be very naturally derived.

Relaxing output limitations: bounds on physical quantities, quantization, conservation laws. The output complexity comes from the fact that, in general, all real values are possible for each physical quantity. In the worst case scenario,

- arbitrarily large and arbitrarily small values are possible, and
- once two real values are possible, all intermediate values are possible too.

Thus, to relax these limitations, it is reasonable to consider the possibility that

- there are bounds on the values of physical properties – from above and/or from below, and
- not all intermediate values are possible, there is only a discrete set of possible values.

Such possibilities are well known in physics. For example, there are bounds on the possible values of the velocities (bounded by the speed of light), distance (bounded by the size of the Universe), entropy's rate of change (bounded by 0 from above), etc.

It is also well known that some quantities like electric charge can only take values from a certain discrete of values.

For some quantities, possible future values are limited to a single value – these are properties described by *conservation laws* such as energy conservation.

Relaxing the independence limitations: the emergence of symmetry. Finally, the relaxation of the third complication – that predicting one values $f(x, t)$ does not help in predicting other values – means that once we know the value $f(x, t)$, this will help us predict the values of some other quantities at some other spatial locations and moments of time.

The possibility to use the values at some points to make predictions about the values at other points is related to the notion of *symmetry*, one of the most fundamental notions of modern physics.

These physical consequences are not always independent. In our informal description, all these physical consequences seem independent from each other. However, a detailed analysis has shown that they these consequences are actually interrelated.

For example, an accurate Kolmogorov complexity-based formalization of the idea that initial conditions should be random leads to the need to bound the values of physical quantities (see, e.g., Reference [6]).

To be more precise, this interrelation is based not only on the original notion of Kolmogorov randomness but also on it physics-related modification. This modification [3, 6] is based on the fact that according to physicists, events with sufficiently small probabilities cannot occur. This means, in particular, that once we have a definable sequence of events $A_1 \supseteq A_2 \supseteq \ldots \supseteq A_n \supseteq \ldots$ with an empty intersection $\cap A_n = \emptyset$, we have $p(A_n) \to 0$ and therefore, for some N, this probability becomes so small that this event does not occur.

We can thus require that the set E of actually possible events has the following property: for every definable monotonic sequence $A_n \supseteq A_{n+1}$ with the empty intersection, there exists an integer N for which $A_N \cap E = \emptyset$.

To show that this definition leads to boundedness of a physical quantity q, we can simply take, as A_n, the set of all the events in which the value of q is outside the interval $[-n, n]$: $|q| > n$. Clearly, this sequence is monotonic, and the intersection of all the sets A_n is empty: since a real number cannot be larger than all possible integers n.

Thus, there exists a value N for which no events from the set A_N can occur. By definition of the event A_N, this means that values q with $|q| > N$ are impossible – and thus, that all the physical values of the quantity q are bounded by the bound N.

Comment.   This argument sounds *simple* – and it is simple. However, this simplicity is based on a rather *complex* proof that the above requirement on the set E of actual events is indeed physically possible; for details of this proof, see, e.g., Reference [6] (and references therein).

What if we still cannot predict everything?   In the previous paragraphs, we describe possible physical ideas that can be helpful in predicting the future state of the physical world – i.e., in effect, the future values of different physical quantities.

But what if, even with all these physical ideas, we are still unable to make predictions? According to our Kolmogorov complexity analysis, this would simply mean that the resulting values $f(x, t)$ cannot be algorithmically determined based on the initial conditions – i.e., that there are some random events that also determine these future values.

In such situation, we cannot predict the actual values of the future quantities, but we can predict the *probabilities* of different values. This is the situation that we called *Statistical Determinism*.

Beyond Statistical Determinism. At first glance, according to our analysis, the algorithms operating on random sequences cover all possible measurement results. Since this representation corresponds to Statistical Determinism, why do we need to go beyond this physical paradigm?

The main reason is that in the original Kolmogorov's analysis, he only took into account the *length* of the corresponding program, but not its *running time*. For physical predictions, running time can be crucial: if we can predict the future, but these predictions will continue way after these events occur, then these predictions are useless. Alas, this possibility is not purely theoretical: there are many important real-life prediction problems – such a predicting where a tornado will go – for which the only known predicting algorithms require running time which goes way past the actual tornado motion.

For such algorithms, even probabilities are difficult to predict. A typical example of such situations are chaotic systems. Chaotic systems are usually deterministic, there is a simple program generating this sequence – but the actual predictions are nevertheless not computationally possible.

In mathematical terms, these situations are described by *resource-bounded Kolmogorov complexity*, versions of Kolmogorov complexity that take into account not only the length of the program, but also its running time – and maybe other characteristics like the number of processors needed to run the corresponding algorithms. At present, applications of resource-bounded Kolmogorov complexity to physics are much less developed that for the traditional Kolmogorov complexity. We hope that future developments in this area will pour some light on what we called Modern Approach paradigm of physics.

4. Case Study: A Recent Cosmological Breakthrough as an Example of a Successful Prediction

Prediction in cosmology: a brief description of the problem. Cosmology studies how the Universe as a whole evolves, it studies the large-scale structure of the Universe.

For cosmology, we can also formulate a usual prediction problem: how can we predict the future state of the Universe? What will happen in the next ten billion years? These questions are of great fundamental importance. However, because of the large-scale structure of the corresponding processes, these predictions cannot be directly verified – unless we are willing to wait for several more billion years.

What we can try to "predict" – and where we can check our predictions – is what happened in the past. We have numerous observations about the past, for two reasons:

- first, observations from distant galaxies actually come from the distant past, simply due to the fact that, e.g., to traverse a distance of one billion light years, light has to travel one billion years;
- second, we often observe physical processes that have "frozen" in time, remain largely unchanged since the distant past; the most well known phenomenon of this type is 3K radiation that comes from the early stage of the Universe; there are other such phenomena as well.

Prediction in cosmology: challenges.   One of the main problems with prediction in general is that for many physical systems, small deviations increase exponentially with time. Thus, with the advent of time, even the small uncertainty in the initial condition translates into an enormous uncertainty at prediction time, so enormous that the prediction becomes practically useless.

Such a situation occurs in meteorology, where, because of this exponential growth, we are unable to predict weather for periods exceeding a few days or weeks. This problem is especially serious in cosmology, where dynamics involves time periods of more than ten billion years.

The fact that in cosmology, fluctuations grow exponentially, is well known. Indeed, from observing the 3K radiation, the remainder of the original state of the world, we can conclude that at that time, the state was almost perfectly isotropic and homogeneous, inhomogeneities were extremely small, barely distinguishable. However, these small homogeneities have led to the whole modern structure of the Universe, with all the rich structure of galaxies, clusters, stars, planets, etc.

From the purely theoretical viewpoint, in cosmology, we are in an enviable situation: in addition to knowing the state $s(t_0)$ of the Universe at the current moment of time t_0, we also know (via the 3K radiation) the state at a moment t_r close to the beginning of the Universe. We know how the Universe evolves, so theoretically, we can use both known states as initial conditions to predict the phenomena at some past times t:

- we can start with the current state $s(t_0)$ and integrate the known dynamical equations back into the past, or
- we can start with the original state of the Universe $s(t_r)$, and integrate the same dynamical equations into the future.

However, in practice, due to the exponential growth of fluctuations, both methods do not lead to reasonable predictions.

A recent breakthrough: description. A few years ago, a group of cosmologists and mathematicians came up with a novel idea: to use *both* the current state $s(t_0)$ and the original state $s(t_r)$ when predicting the past states $s(t)$. This idea has led to successful predictions: specifically, at the large-scale level, they succeeded in using the 3K state and current locations of the galaxy clusters to "predict" (reconstruct) the velocities of these clusters (see, e.g. [1, 4, 8]; see also Reference [5]).

A recent breakthrough: methodological challenge. From the physical viewpoint, the above result is spectacular. However, this result raises a natural methodological question: how did the above idea overcome the challenge of exponential growth of fluctuations, a challenge that seems to make all long-term predictions impossible?

What we do in this section. In this section, we show that the above novel approach can indeed lead to successful predictions, even in situations with exponentially growing fluctuations.

Thus, in other physical areas, exponential growth of fluctuations does not necessarily means that predictions are completely impossible: when we supplement the current state $s(t_0)$ with the additional knowledge about the past, we can indeed get very good predictions.

Exponential growth of fluctuations: reminder. Before we present our explanations, let us recall where the exponential growth of fluctuations comes from.

We want to trace how small deviations $x(t)$ from a current state change with time. In general, the change in these deviations is described by a dynamical equation $\dfrac{dx}{dt} = f(x)$ for an appropriate function $f(x)$. Since the deviations are small, we can expand the function $f(x)$ in Taylor series and keep only linear terms in this expansion. Thus, we get a system of equations $\dfrac{dx}{dt} = a + Ax$ for some appropriate vector a and a matrix A.

Since x are deviations from the given state, if we start with the current state (i.e., with $x(t_0) = 0$), we should end up with the current state as well, i.e., with $x(t) = 0$ for all t. Thus, the value $x(t) = 0$ corresponding to the unperturbed state must satisfy the above equations. Substituting $x(t) = 0$ into these equations, we conclude that $a = 0$. Thus, the dynamical equations take the following form

$$\frac{dx}{dt} = Ax.$$

Solutions to these equations are well known. To describe these solutions, we can use the eigenvectors of the matrix A. In the non-degenerate case, when all the eigenvalues of the matrix A are different, we can simplify the above system if we use the eigenvectors e_i of the matrix A, i.e., unit vectors for which $Ae_i = \lambda_i \cdot e_i$ for the corresponding eigenvalues λ_i.

It is well known that the eigenvalues form a basic, in the sense that an arbitrary vector $x(t)$ can be described as a linear combination of these eigenvectors:

$$x(t) = c_1(t) \cdot e_1 + \ldots + c_n(t) \cdot e_n.$$

Substituting this expression into the above dynamical system and using the fact that $Ax_i = \lambda_i \cdot x_i$, we conclude that

$$\sum_{i=1}^{n} \frac{dc_i(t)}{dt} \cdot e_i = \sum_{i=1}^{n} \lambda_i \cdot c_i(t) \cdot e_i.$$

Since the vectors e_i form a basis, the fact that the vectors on the left-hand side and on the right-hand side of the above equation coincide means that the coefficients at e_i at both sides must coincide too, i.e., that for every i, we must have

$$\frac{dc_i(t)}{dt} = \lambda_i \cdot c_i(t).$$

This simple differential equation has a known solution $c_i(t) = C_i \cdot \exp(\lambda_i \cdot t)$ for some constant C_i. Thus, the general solution to the above dynamical system has the form

$$x(t) = \sum_{i=1}^{n} C_i \cdot \exp(\lambda_i \cdot t) \cdot e_i.$$

When we know the state $x(t_0)$, we thus know the coefficients $c_i(t_0)$. Thus, in principle, from the value $c_i(t_0) = C_i \cdot \exp(\lambda_i \cdot t_0)$, we can conclude that $C_i = c_i(t_0) \cdot \exp(-\lambda_i \cdot t_0)$ and thus, that for every other moment t, we have

$$c_i(t) = C_i \cdot \exp(\lambda_i \cdot t) = c_i(t_0) \cdot \exp(\lambda_i \cdot (t - t_0)).$$

Theoretically, this is the desired predicting formula, but in practice, predicting is difficult:

- when we predict from the moment t_0 into the past, the factor

$$\exp(\lambda_i \cdot (t - t_0))$$

grows exponentially for eigenvalues with negative real part; thus, negligible uncertainty in the current values $c_i(t_0)$ lead to huge uncertainty in the past state;

- on the other hand, when we predict from the moment t_r into the future, the factor $\exp(\lambda_i \cdot (t - t_r))$ grows exponentially for eigenvalues with positive real part; thus, negligible uncertainty in the current values $c_i(t_r)$ lead to huge uncertainty in the future state.

For cosmological systems it is well known that such an exponential increase indeed occurs – meaning that the corresponding matrix has both eigenvalues with positive real parts and eigenvalues with negative real parts.

Comment. In the degenerate case, the general solution is similar, with the exception that we can also have additional solutions of the type $t^k \cdot \exp(\lambda_i \cdot t)$. In this case, the dynamic equations are slightly different, but the exponential growth of fluctuations remains.

What happens when we use both the current state and the past state for predictions. If we use both the current state $x(t_0)$ and the past state $x(t_r)$ for predictions, then, for each i, we have both values $c_i(t_0)$

and $c_i(t_r)$. In this case, for a given moment of t between t_r and t_0, we can predict the values $c_i(t)$ as follows:

- for the eigenvalues λ_i with negative real parts, we can predict the values $c_i(t)$ as $c_i(t) = c_i(t_r) \cdot \exp(\lambda_i \cdot (t - t_r))$;
- on the other hand, for the eigenvalues λ_i with non-negative real parts, we can predict the values $c_i(t)$ as

$$c_i(t) = c_i(t_0) \cdot \exp(\lambda_i \cdot (t - t_0)).$$

Once we know the values $c_i(t)$, we can reconstruct the state

$$x(t) = \sum_{i=1}^{n} c_i(t) \cdot e_i.$$

In both cases (of eigenvalues with negative real parts and of eigenvalues with non-negative real parts), the absolute values of the coefficients at $c_i(t_0)$ and $c_i(t_r)$ remain bounded by 1. Thus, fluctuations do not grow with time, and we can predict the values at all intermediate moments of time t with the same accuracy with which we know the current and the past states.

Thus, prediction based on past and future values is indeed possible.

Comment. The difference between predicting based only on the current state or only on the past state – and the prediction based on both states – is similar to the known difference between extrapolation and interpolation:

- extrapolation means predicting values outside the interval on which the values are known, while
- interpolation means predicting values inside the interval on which the values are known – filling the gaps.

It is known that interpolation is often practically possible, while extrapolation is often not possible – especially if we want to extrapolate far away from the known values. This is exactly what we observe now:

- prediction only from the present or only from the past – an analogue of extrapolation – is, for cosmology, not practically possible;
- on the other hand, prediction of the values $x(t)$ based on the values $x(t_r)$ and $x(t_0)$ for which $t_r < t < t_0$ – an analogue of interpolation – is practically possible.

Acknowledgments

This work was supported in part by the National Science Foundation grant HRD-0734825, by Grant 1 T36 GM078000-01 from the National Institutes of Health, and by Grant MSM 6198898701 from MŠMT of Czech Republic.

References

1. Y. Brenier, U. Frisch, M. Hénon, G. Loeper, S. Matarrese, R. Mohayaee, and A. Sobolevskii, Reconstruction of the early Universe as a convex optimization problem, *Monthly Notices of the Royal Astronomical Society* **346**, pp. 501–524, (2003).
2. R. Feynman, R. Leighton, and M. Sands, *The Feynman Lectures on Physics* (Addison Wesley, Boston, Massachusetts, 2005).
3. A. M. Finkelstein and V. Kreinovich, Impossibility of hardly possible events: physical consequences, In: *Abstracts of the 8 International Congress on Logic, Methodology, and Philosophy of Science*, Moscow, 1987, **5**, Part 2, pp. 23–25.
4. U. Frisch, S. Matarrese, R. Mohayaee, and A. Sobolevsky, A reconstruction of the initial conditions of the Universe by optimal mass transportation, *Nature* **417**, pp. 260–262, (2002).
5. V. Kreinovich, Interval computations and their possible use in estimating accuracy of the optimization-based reconstruction of the early Universe, *Abstracts of the International Workshop "At the Interface of Dynamical and Statistical Cosmology and Transport Optimization"*, Haifa, Israel, March 22–26, 2009.
6. V. Kreinovich and A. M. Finkelstein, Towards applying computational complexity to foundations of physics, *Notes of Mathematical Seminars of St. Petersburg Department of Steklov Institute of Mathematics* **316**, pp. 63–110 (2004); reprinted in *Journal of Mathematical Sciences*, **134**, 5, pp. 2358–2382, (2006).
7. M. Li and P. Vitányi, *An introduction to Kolmogorov Complexity and its Applications* (Springer Verlag, New York, 2008)
8. R. Mohayaee and A. Sobolevskii, The Monge-Ampére-Kantorovich approach to reconstruction in cosmology, *Physica D* **237**, pp. 2145–2150, (2009).

CHAPTER 9

BODIES — BOTH INFORMED AND TRANSFORMED EMBODIED COMPUTATION AND INFORMATION PROCESSING

Bruce J. MacLennan

Department of Electrical Engineering & Computer Science
University of Tennessee, Knoxville
E-mail: maclennan@utk.edu

Post-Moore's Law computing will require an assimilation between computational processes and their physical realizations, both to achieve greater speeds and densities and to allow computational processes to assemble and control matter at the nanoscale. Therefore, we need to investigate "embodied computing," which addresses the essential interrelationships of information processing and physical processes in the system and its environment in ways that are parallel to those in the theory of embodied cognition. We briefly discuss matters of function and structure, regulation and causation, and the definition of computation. We address both the challenges and opportunities of embodied computation. Analysis is more difficult because physical effects must be included, but information processing may be simplified by dispensing with explicit representations and allowing massively parallel physical processes to process information. Nevertheless, in order to fully exploit embodied computation, we need robust and powerful theoretical tools, but we argue that the theory of Church-Turing computation is not suitable for the task.

1. Post-Moore's Law Computation

Although estimates differ, it is clear that the end of Moore's Law is in sight; there are physical limits to the density of binary logic devices and to their speed of operation. This will require us to approach computation in new ways, which present significant challenges, but can also broaden and deepen our concept of computation in natural and artificial systems.

In the past there has been a significant difference in scales between computational processes and the physical processes by which they are realized. For example, there are differences in spatial scale: the data with which programs operate (integers, floating point numbers, characters, pointers, etc.) are represented by large numbers of physical devices comprising even larger numbers of particles. Also, there are differences in time scale: elementary computational operations (arithmetic, instruction sequencing, memory access, etc.), are the result of large numbers of state changes at the device level (typically involving a device moving from one saturated state to another). However, increasing the density and speed of computation will force it to take place on a scale (spatial and temporal) near that of the underlying physical processes. With fewer hierarchical levels between computations and their physical realizations, and less time for implementing computational processes, computation will have to become more like the underlying physical processes. That is, post-Moore's Law computing will depend on a greater assimilation of computation to physics.

In discussing the role of physical embodiment in the "grand challenge" of non-classical computing, Stepney writes,

> Computation is physical; it is necessarily embodied in a device whose behaviour is guided by the laws of physics and cannot be completely captured by a closed mathematical model. This fact of embodiment is becoming ever more apparent as we push the bounds of those physical laws. [Stepney, 2004, p. 29]

Traditionally, a sort of Cartesian dualism has reigned in computer science; programs and algorithms have been conceived as idealized mathematical objects; software has been developed, explained, and analyzed independently of hardware; the focus has been on the *formal* rather than the *material*. Post-Moore's Law computing, in contrast, because of its greater assimilation to physics, will be less idealized, less independent of its physical realization. On one hand, this will increase the difficulty of programming since it will be dependent on (or, some might say, contaminated by) physical concerns. On the other hand, as I will argue here, it also presents many opportunities that will contribute to our understanding and application of information processing in the future. To understand them, I will make a brief digression through non-Cartesian developments in philosophy and cognitive science.

2. Embodied Cognition

Johnson and Rohrer trace the theory of *embodied cognition* to its roots in the pragmatism of James and Dewey, both of whom stressed the importance of understanding cognition as an embodied biological process [Johnson, Rohrer, 2007]. Dewey's *Principle of Continuity* asserts that there is no break from our highest, most abstract cognitive activities, down through our sensory and motor engagement with the physical world, to their foundation in biological and physical processes. Cognition is the emergent pattern of purposeful interactions between the organism and its environment (including other organisms). Psychologists, such as Piaget and Gibson, and philosophers, such as Heidegger, Polanyi, and Merleau-Ponty, have made similar points.

Hubert Dreyfus and others have stressed the importance and benefits of embodiment in cognition. As Dreyfus observed, there are many things that we (implicitly) know simply by virtue of having a body [Dreyfus, 1979, pp. 248–250, 253]. Therefore, in embodied cognition, embodiment is not incidental to cognition (or to information processing), but essential to it. For representative recent work see [Clark, 1997; Pfeifer, Scheier, 1999; Iida, Pfeifer, Steels, Kuniyoshi, 2004; Pfeifer, Bongard, 2007]. Finally, from [Brooks, 1991] onward there has been increasing understanding of the value and exploitation of embodiment in AI and especially in robotics [Iida, et al., 2004].

3. Embodied Computation

Pfeifer, Lungarella, and Iida provide a concise definition of *embodiment*: "the interplay of information and physical processes" [Pfeifer, Lungarella, Iida, 2007, p. 1088]. On this basis we define *embodied computation* as information processing in which the physical realization and the physical environment play an unavoidable and essential role.

3.1. *Physics for Computational Purposes*

Embodied computing can be understood as a natural consequence of the decreasing size and cost of computing devices. Historically, *offline* computer applications were most common. Interaction with the environment could be characterized as *input—process—output*. That is, physical input (e.g., punched cards, magnetic tape) was presented to the computer and converted into internal, computational representations, and in this effectively abstract form it was processed. As abstract results were generated they were converted into specific physical representations (e.g., printed paper, punched cards, magnetic tape) for use after the program terminated. It is easy to see offline computation as the evaluation of a mathematical function on an argument, which is the way it is treated in the traditional theory of computation.

As computers became smaller and less expensive, it became feasible to embed them as controllers in larger systems. *Embedded computations* are in ongoing interaction with their environments, are typically non-terminating, and have to be of a physical size and real-time speed compatible with the physical systems in which they are embedded. Their basic structure is *sensors—controller—actuators*, in which, however, there are critical real-time feedback loops through the physical environment from the actuators back to the sensors. Nevertheless, the basic model is similar to offline computing in that the sensors and actuators perform the conversions to and from the computational medium, which is effectively abstract (largely independent of specific physical realization). Physical considerations are confined to the embedding device and its environment, the transducers (sensors, actuators), and basic physical characteristics of the control computer (size, weight, electrical requirements, clock rate, memory capacity).

The difference between *embedded computing* and *embodied computing* is that in the latter there is little or no abstract computation; the computation must be understood as a physical system in continuing interaction with other physical systems (its environment). The strength of embodied computing, like the strength of embodied cognition, resides in the fact that information representation is often implicit in the computation's physical realization and in its environment.

Representations and information processes emerge as regularities in the dynamics of the physical systems that allow the computational system to fulfill its function.

Another significant advantage of embodied computing is that many computations are performed "for free" by the physical substrate. For example, diffusion occurs naturally in many fluids, such as liquids and gases, and in other media. It can be used for many computational processes, including broadcasting of information and massively parallel search, such as in path planning through mazes, optimization, and constraint satisfaction [Khatib, 1986; Miller, Roysam, Smith, O'Sullivan, 1991; Rimon, Koditschek, 1989; Steinbeck, Tóth, Showalter, 1995; Ting, Iltis, 1994]. Diffusion is expensive to implement by conventional computation, but it comes for free in many physical systems.

As is well known, many artificial neural networks are based on matrix-vector multiplications combined with simple nonlinear functions, such as the *logistic sigmoid*, $1/[1 + \exp(-x)]$. Also, many universal approximation theorems are based on linear combinations of sigmoids and similar functions [Haykin, 1999, pp. 208–94]. Computing a sigmoid on a conventional computer requires computing a series approximation to a transcendental function (e.g., exp, tanh) or approximating the sigmoid by table look-up and linear interpolation. However, sigmoidal behavior is typical of many physical systems, for it results from an exponential growth process that gradually saturates. For example, available chemical receptors may become occupied or the supply of signaling molecules may become exhausted. In general, sigmoidal response comes for free because physical resources become saturated or depleted. In embodied computing we do not need to program sigmoid functions explicitly; we can exploit common physical processes with the required behavior.

Further, many self-organizing systems depend on positive feedback for growth and extension and on negative feedback for stabilization, delimitation, separation, and the creation of structure (in space or time). In embodied computation negative feedback may be implemented by naturally occurring physical processes such as evaporation, dispersion, and degradation of chemicals. These processes will occur anyway; embodied computation makes productive use of them.

One final example must suffice. Many algorithms, such as simulated annealing [Kirkpatrick, Gelatt, Vecchi, 1983] and stochastic resonance [Benzi, Parisi, Sutera, Vulpiani, 1982], use randomness for productive purposes, including escape from local optima, symmetry breaking, deadlock avoidance, exploration, etc. Such randomness comes for free in physical systems in the form of noise, uncertainty, imprecision, and other stochastic phenomena.

In summary, with conventional computing technology we often "torture" the physical substrate so that it implements desired computations (e.g., using continuous electronic processes to implement binary logic), whereas embodied computation "respects the medium," conforming to physical characteristics rather than working against them.[a] The goal in embodied computation is *to exploit the physics, not to circumvent it* (which is costly).

3.2. *Computation for Physical Effect*

We have seen how embodied computation exploits physical processes for the sake of information processing, but embodied computation also uses information processing to govern physical processes. That is, typically we think of computation as a physical system in which the physical states and processes represent (perhaps imperfectly) certain abstract states and processes, which constitute a desired information system. In mathematical terms, there is a (perhaps imperfect) homomorphism from the concrete physical system onto the abstract information system [MacLennan, 1994 a; MacLennan, 2004]. But we can look at computation from a different perspective, since an information system (and, in a general-purpose computer, the program) governs the flow of matter and energy in the physical computer (subject, of course, to the computer's structure and the laws of physics). This is in fact an essential function in natural embodied computation (including embodied cognition), which governs physical processes (e.g., growth, metabolism) in an organism's body and its physical interactions with other organisms and their environment. Often,

---

[a] The metaphors of "torturing" and "respecting the medium" were suggested to me by Christof Teuscher and Peter Dittrich, respectively.

the result of embodied computation is not information, but *action*, and even self-action, self-transformation, and self-construction.

When our purpose is information processing, then the goal is often to represent the information with as small a quantity of energy or matter (e.g., electrical charge) as possible — consistent with reliable operation — so that state changes will require as small a movement of energy or matter as possible, for the sake of minimizing state-transition time and heat dissipation. Indeed, the (unattainable) goal has been a sort of *disembodied* computation and communication, in which pure form is represented, transmitted, and transformed without need of material realization. On the other hand, when embodied computation is applied to the control of matter and energy, we may want to move *more* rather than *less*. This is because, in contrast to conventional embedded computers, in embodied computation there may be no clear distinction between the processors and the actuators; the physical effects may be a direct consequence of the computational process (as opposed to being *controlled* by them). Therefore embodied computation may involve the movement of relatively large amount of matter or energy compared to traditional computation, such as large molecules, large electrical quantities, etc. For example, in *algorithmic assembly* DNA computation is used to assemble nanostructures [e.g., Barish, Rothemund, Winfree, 2005; Rothemund, Papadakis, Winfree, 2004; Rothemund Winfree, 2000; Winfree, 1998], and our own work explores the use molecular computation based on combinator reduction for nanostructure synthesis and control [MacLennan, 2003 a].

Further, embodied computation can be applied to the implementation of active materials, that is, materials that have a complex behavioral repertoire. Thus, embodied computation might be used to implement an artificial tissue that can recognize environmental conditions and open or close channels in response to them, or otherwise transport matter or energy across the membrane, perhaps transforming it in the process. Embodied computation might be used to implement a material, analogous to cardiac tissue, capable initiating and controlling organized patterns of contraction.

Much current nanotechnology has a materials orientation, by which I mean that it is most successful at producing bulk materials with a desired nanostructure or microstructure; to create macroscopic structure we must resort to more traditional manufacturing methods. Yet morphogenesis and pattern formation in embryological development show us that embodied computational processes can coordinate the proliferation, movement, and disassembly of cells, macromolecules, and smaller molecules to produce highly complex systems with elaborate hierarchical structure from the nanoscale up to the macroscale. This is an inspiring model for future nanotechnology: using embodied computation to control the multistage self-organization of complex, functional, and active hierarchical systems, that is, *artificial morphogenesis* [MacLennan, 2009 a, 2010].

4. Related Work

Several authors have discussed embodied computation and related concepts. There is not space here for a complete review (which, in any case, would be premature at this point in time), so I will limit myself to a few similarities and differences.

According to Hamann and Wörn an *embodied computation system* consists of at least two levels, with adaptive self-organization and collective behavior at the higher levels resulting from spatially local interactions among "microscopic control devices," which are embodied devices comprising sensors, actuators, a processor, and memory [Hamann, Wörn, 2007]. There are several aspects to their embodiment, including a lack of separation between processor and memory and an essential dependence of the computation on the physical world (e.g., spatial position). They name simple robots, cells, and molecules as examples of microscopic control devices. Their definition has much in common with our own, but seems to conflate embodiment with issues of adaptation, self-organization, robustness, loose coupling, etc., which are related to embodiment, but not essential to it.

Stepney discusses the ideas of *material computation* and *in materio* computers, that is, systems in which the physical substrate "naturally" computes [Stepney, 2008]. These concepts are very similar to embodied computation as I have presented it, with perhaps two differences. First, she advises that we focus on non-living substrates in order to understand material computation, since biological systems are so much more complicated. Second, it appears that she is primarily concerned with the use of physical materials to implement computations, and less concerned with the use of computational processes to organize and control matter and energy. (Indeed, this difference is suggested by the terms *material* computation and *embodied* computation, since the latter connotes a self-organizing, self-regulating body and an organicist approach.) Stepney considers a variety of physical media that might be used for computation. She also cautions us against an ill-advised application to material computation of notions from Turing computation, a topic that I address later (Secs. 9–10).

5. Computation and Information Processing

An obvious question is whether embodied computation is a kind of computation at all, that is, whether it is appropriate to apply the terms *computation* and *information processing* to these physical processes. A brief consideration of the usage of these terms may prove helpful.

We may begin with *computation*, which — like *calculation* — originally referred to a human activity. Calculation was an embodied human activity performed primarily with concrete objects (Lat., *calculi* = pebbles). Computation was more abstract (Lat., *computare*, referring to the reckoning of accounts, etc.), but even *putare* (to think over, reckon, etc.) has a primary sense of tidying up physically [*OLD*, s.vv. computo, puto]. As is well known, before the middle of the twentieth century, a *computer* was a human occupation, which was later extended to certain artificial systems, *automatic computers* [*OED*]. More recently the term has been transferred back to natural systems, and we use *natural computation* to refer to computation occurring in nature or inspired by it. What are the features common to human and non-human natural computation and to artificial computers? I will address this later.

The ordinary sense of *information* is derived from the verb *to inform*, which means to give *form* to something or to oneself [*OED*, s.vv.]. That is, it is the shape or configuration that is relevantly altered, not its substance or material. Like computation, the activity of *informing* (another or oneself) and the abstraction *information* refer originally to human activities. By extension they are naturally applied to non-human animals. In both cases the effect of information is to reshape the pattern of (internal or external) activity of an organism or group of organisms. Also like computing, the ideas of information and information processing have been transferred to artifacts. Shannon (and before him, Hartley) facilitated this extension in part by taking human relevance and meaning out of the definition of information.

In order to expand our concepts of embodied computation and information processing it is especially fruitful to understand natural (non-technological) information processing systems. In addition to teaching us information processing paradigms distinct from binary digital logic, they can show us how to exploit embodiment for more effective information processing. This raises a demarcation issue: how do we discriminate information processing (and computation) from other natural processes? To decide, we must look to the function (or purpose) of the process, a topic to which I now turn.

6. Function and Structure

6.1. *Function*

Function, purpose, and other teleological notions are problematic in science, but I will argue that they are largely unproblematic in the context of computation and information processing.

On one hand, the function of an artifact is generally easy to determine: ask the designer. That is, artifacts are designed for a purpose, which is often explicitly stated or easy to determine in a contemporary or historical cultural context. The function of some specific historical and prehistoric artifacts may be unclear, but that fact does not invalidate the general principle.

Similarly, although teleological notions, such as purpose and function, are problematic in a biological context, and are ultimately grounded in inclusive fitness, they are unproblematic in the context of particular biological subsystems. For example, biologists routinely and objectively investigate and describe the functions of the digestive, reproductive, immune, and nervous systems. Therefore, we can, in principle at least, establish criteria for whether or not the function of a biological system is information processing and computation, or something else.

However, in biology, but also in technology, structures and processes may serve multiple functions. Although such combinations of function may interfere with our understanding of the system, they improve system efficiency. (In an engineering context it is called the *Shanley Principle*; see Sec. 9).

I believe that the fundamental criterion distinguishing information processing from other physical processes is that only the abstract form is relevant to the purpose; it could as well be realized by other physical systems. This is the root of the *multiple realizability* commonly taken to be characteristic of computation. Furthermore, information, as formalized by Shannon, depends on contrasts and distinctions, that is, on *form*, and is independent of the physical substrate supporting the contrasts.

In order to explore the essence of information processing, especially in the context of embodiment, it will be convenient to use the Aristotelian notions of *form* (Grk. *eidos*, Lat. *forma*) and *matter* (Grk. *hulê*, Lat. *materia*) which correspond, in more modern terms, to organization and energy. That is, it is the abstract shape or structure that is relevant to information processing, and its physical substrate is relevant only insofar as its suitability to support the form.

Computation is a physical process and therefore it takes place in a physical medium, a substratum supporting its formal structures and their transformations. For computation qua computation, the specific properties of the medium are relevant only insofar as they support the formal organization and process that constitutes the computation or information process.[b] If we abstract away from these irrelevant specific properties, we are left with a kind of generic matter, or neutral substrate, not infinitely malleable or indeterminate, but able to support the formal structures and processes that fulfill the computational system's purpose. For example, any modern computer architecture can be understood as a

---

[b] Obviously, the specific instantiation may be relevant to non-computational issues, such as physical robustness, energy requirements, physical compatibility with the rest of the system (e.g., a biological computational medium in a living organism, an electronic computational medium in a robot).

(relatively) neutral medium (i.e., an array of bytes and certain primitive operations on them) that can support a wide range of formal information processes (i.e., programs).

In the context of the form-matter dichotomy it is natural to think of matter as something fundamentally formless and simple, but form and matter are relative to each other and to an appropriate level of system analysis. In fact computational media are often quite complex. For example, while the concept of a bit is simple, a modern digital computer architecture is quite complex. Embodied computation, in particular, often makes use of complex matter, which exhibits a wide repertoire of complicated and interrelated, but not necessarily functional, behaviors. Computation recruits, organizes, and coordinates these complex behaviors to achieve the computation's purpose. Examples of such complex embodied computational media include neurons in the nervous system, social insects in colonies, cells in morphogenesis, and proteins in intracellular regulation [Tokuriki, Tawfik, 2009]. Many computational media belong to Wolfram's dynamical class IV, which resides on the border between static and periodic behavior (classes I, II) on one hand and chaotic behavior (class III) on the other [Wolfram, 2002]. As Wolfram has stressed, rich, complex behavior can emerge from very simple mechanisms [Wolfram, 2002, ch. 12]. This insight is summarized in Stuart Kauffman's slogan, "order for free."

6.2. Regulation and Causation

A principal goal of natural information processing is *regulation* of other physical processes to some end. That is, information is extracted from the larger physical system, processed formally, and used to control or influence physical processes. This includes the regulation of other systems (i.e., in the environment of the computational system), but especially self-regulation (homeostasis and development). Because computation is a formal process, and essentially independent of physical magnitude, it can regulate physical processes that involve more matter or energy than the computation itself.

Regulation is for some purpose or end, and therefore it is always future-directed. Its goal is either to maintain a current state into the future or to alter the current state in the future in order to pursue some goal. As a consequence, artificial computation, like natural computation, is functional; it is directed toward some *end* (in the sense of purpose, not final state; cf. Aris., *Phys.* 194b32–33). Teleology is unavoidable in computation, whether natural or artificial.

As a consequence, all four of the Aristotelian primary "causes" (Grk. *aitia*, Lat. *causa*) can be applied profitably to descriptions and explanations of computation and information processing, especially in nature (on the four causes, see Aris., *Phys.* II 194b–195a, *Met.* 983a–b, 1013a–1014a).[c]

The *formal explanation* appeals to "the form [*eidos*] or pattern [*paradeigma*]; that is, the essential formula [*logos*] and the classes that contain it" (Aris., *Met.* 1013a26–28). The form is correlative to the matter in the physical state of the computational system, and it is the form that governs the computational process, which is understood as a process of *transformation* (change of form). In some cases, such as morphogenesis and algorithmic self-assembly, the end and goal of transformation is the creation of some final form (structure, organization).

The *material explanation* accounts for computation in terms of its *matter*, that is the computational medium, whether specific to a particular realization, or generic for a class of computational systems. The medium must be able to support the formal structures and processes of the computation and be suited to the system's purpose.[d] Aristotle (*Phys.* 194b9) observes that "the conception of 'material' [*hulê*] is relative, for it is different material that is suited to receive the several forms." The material is the *substratum of form and its transformation*. The material aspects assume a much larger importance in embodied computation than they do in traditional computation.

---

[c] The conventional translation "cause" does capture the ancient terms' ranges of meaning, which include responsibility, motive, occasion, theme, category; i.e., explanation, answer to "how? and why?" (LSJ, OLD).

[d] "In the crafts, then, it is we that prepare the material for the sake of the function it is to fulfill, but in natural products Nature herself has provided the material. In both cases the material is commanded by the end to which it is directed." (Aris., *Phys.* 194b8–10, tr. Wicksteed & Cornford).

The *efficient explanation* appeals to the agent or mover (Grk. *kinoun*, Lat. *efficiens, movens*), that is, "to something to initiate the process of change or its cessation when the process is completed" (Aris., *Phys.* 194b29–31). This is both the initial *informing agent* (which physically imposes the initial formal state on the medium), and the *transforming agent* of the initiation and completion of each successive step of computation (each step imposing new form on the medium). Computational systems are dissipative physical systems and their state changes require energy. A few computational processes can be initialized in a nonequilibrium state and allowed to compute to equilibrium, but most computational processes must be fueled or powered so long as they continue. Energy issues, both its provision and its dissipation, are more important in embodied computation than they were in conventional computation.

The *final explanation* focuses on the function, purpose, end, or completion (Grk. *telos*, Lat. *finis*) of a process, and indeed the formal, material, and efficient causes together constitute the *means* to achieve the *end*, which is the final cause. The final explanation is relevant to artifacts, which serve our ends, as well as to organisms, which serve their own. In particular, we have seen that purpose is fundamental to the definition of natural and artificial computational systems, since their function is information processing, as manifest in multiple realizability.

In summary, all four of Aristotle's "causes" or kinds of explanation are relevant to computation and information processing, but in embodied and natural computation the material, efficient, and final aspects play a more important role than they do in traditional computation (for which the formal aspect dominates).

6.3. *Structure*

Conventionally we think of the physical realization existing for the sake of realizing an abstract computation. That is, we have some system of forms and transformations (an information process) in which we are interested, and we arrange (by construction or programming) the physical process to instantiate the abstract process of interest. However, as we have seen, sometimes the function of a computational process is regulation, that is, its purpose is to *inform* (impose a form on) matter, or to organize energy.

This is apparent in natural computation systems, where information processing is often devoted to the maintenance of an organism, colony, or species. For example, information-mediated regulatory processes control tissue growth and repair, embryological development and morphogenesis, social organization, and colony construction and maintenance. It is significant that in many of these cases the information process is modifying (transforming) its own physical realization or, to put it in other terms, the computation is recomputing its physical implementation. Embryological morphogenesis is a clear example, since information processes regulate the development of the embryo, and the structure of the embryo reciprocally governs the information process. Similarly social insects coordinate their behavior to construct a physical colony, which in turn conditions the collective behavior of the insects.

This sort of mutual determination of information processes and physical processes will be increasingly important in artificial systems as well, since we can use automatic information processing to fabricate or manufacture systems that are too small or too intricate for traditional techniques. For example, self-repairing or self-healing artificial systems, like natural systems, may use intrinsic information processes to detect damage, recruit repair resources, and coordinate (re-)construction. In various self-assembly processes, such as artificial morphogenesis [MacLennan, 2009 a, 2010], elementary physical components, with primitive information-processing capacities, organize into a physical substrate for further, more coordinated behavior, which creates more complex physical structures that in turn structure more complex information processes. Finally, radically reconfigurable computers and reconfigurable robot collectives can adapt themselves to changing requirements by disassembling themselves into neutral physical components and then reconfiguring themselves into a new physical structure, in a process analogous to the metamorphosis of a caterpillar into a butterfly. Thus information processes can reorganize matter and energy, including the physical substrate realizing the information processes, which is perhaps the best example of embodied computing.

7. A Mathematical Model of Embodied Computation

In this section I will provide a more precise, mathematical characterization of the difference between information processing and other physical processes. The key criterion, as previously discussed, is multiple realizability in a teleological context.

Before developing a mathematical model it is essential to recall that each model is suited to answering a certain class of questions, and therefore exists in a *frame of relevance* [MacLennan, 2003 b; MacLennan, 2009 b], determined by the model's intended use, and that in conformity to its frame, a model exists at a corresponding level of description, and that it incorporates factors relevant to these questions and excludes the rest for the sake of simplicity.

7.1. *States and Trajectories*

Therefore we will consider the set S of states for a closed system (which I'll also call S). Since computation is relative to a purpose, of an artifact, in an organism, in a colony, etc., we will decompose S into two subsystems, A an agent involving information processing, and E, its environment. In terms of the state space, $S = E \times A$.

However, A is typically only partially computational, and so as a first approximation, we might factor the agent into a body B and a computational part C, that is, $A = B \times C$. The computational part is devoted to information processing, as will be explicated shortly. This decomposition is suitable for conventional computation, which is internal to the agent, but in embodied computation the information is partially externalized to the environment. Therefore it is more accurate to factor the complete system into a physical part P and a computational part C, that is, $S = P \times C$. The computational state C has exterior and interior parts, C_E and C_A, which reside in the environment and agent respectively: $C = C_E \times C_A$.

An additional complication that arises in embodied computation is that the state spaces might not be fixed through time. Think of embryological morphogenesis; as cells proliferate, the state space of the embryo increases in dimension (degrees of freedom), including the computational state space, which increases to accommodate the information processing of the proliferating cells. Conversely, in embryological development *apoptosis* (programmed cell death) decreases the dimension of both computational and non-computational state spaces.

The easiest way to treat this possibility is by defining the state spaces (S, C, P, etc.) to be large enough to accommodate the highest dimension required. An increasing effective state space then corresponds to a state trajectory rising out of a lower dimensional subspace into higher dimensions. Conversely, a contracting state space corresponds to the trajectory confining itself to progressively lower dimensional subspaces.

Since we are concerned with information processes, which govern behavior, we must consider trajectories in state space over some defined time interval $T = [t_0, t_f]$. Thus we may consider the state $s(t) \in S$ at time $t \in T$, and its computational component $c(t) \in C$.

However, at the appropriate level of modeling the trajectories may be nondeterministic, and therefore each trajectory has a probability distribution over states at a given time. The probabilities of the trajectories themselves are conditional on their initial states and also, for open systems, on their boundary conditions, but for simplicity we restrict the presentation here to closed systems. Therefore we interpret a trajectory as a function $\tau : S \times T \times S \to [0,1]$ so that $\tau(s_0, t, \sigma) = \Pr\{s(t) = \sigma \mid s(t_0) = s_0\}$ is the probability that the trajectory beginning at s_0 is in state σ at time t. Of course probabilities are required to be normalized, $\int_S \tau(s, t, \sigma) \mathrm{d}\mu(\sigma) = 1$ for all $s \in S$ and $t \in T$, where a measure μ appropriate to the state space is chosen. In specific cases there will of course be other restrictions on the trajectories, but that is not relevant to our present discussion.

7.2. Multiple Realizability

With this background we can formulate the property of multiple realizability, which is fundamental to information processing. The idea we want to express is that all physical systems realizing the same abstract computational process will generate the same distribution of trajectories, but it is not so simple as this, because the computational state is part of the total state, and so any change of its realization will change the state space.

A certain subspace I of C constitutes the interface between computational system and the physical system P. Thus we write $C = I \times H$, where H is the "hidden" (non-interface) subspace of the computational state. Thus, I represents the physical inputs and outputs of the computational system, which must have a specific physical representation in order for the computation to fulfill its purpose. For example, its purpose may be to detect a gradient in the concentration of some particular chemical and move in the corresponding direction. In more conventional terms, the relation between I and H is that between the input/output transducers and the rest of the computational system.

Therefore consider a potentially alternative realization of C with physical state space $C' = I \times H'$. We are concerned with the trajectories generated by computations in C and C' on the visible state space $V = P \times I$. Each trajectory τ in S generates a projected visible trajectory $\upsilon : V \times T \times V \rightarrow [0,1]$ defined by:

$$\upsilon(v_0, t, v) = \int_H \int_H \tau[(v_0, h_0), t, (v, h)] \, d\mu(h) \cdot \Pr\{h_0 \mid v_0\} \, d\mu(h_0),$$

where v_0, $v \in V$ and $\Pr\{h_0 \mid v_0\}$ is the probability of initial state $s_0 = (v_0, h_0)$ given v_0; they are the initial states h_0 of the computation consistent with observable state v_0.

Then, if we have two computational realizations C and C', the condition for their realizing the same abstract computation (and hence serving the same purpose) is the equality of their visible projections: $\upsilon = \upsilon'$. This defines an equivalence relation on physical realizations of computations, and the corresponding equivalence classes correspond to abstract computations.

We have described how the same abstract computation can be realized in different physical state spaces C, C', C'', ... There are also abstract computational state spaces C^*, in which, in effect, all the components are dimensionless numbers as opposed to real physical quantities. All physical realizations C of this computation generate the same observable behavior as C^*, that is, $\upsilon = \upsilon^*$.

The foregoing are necessary conditions for multiple realizability, but what are the sufficient conditions? To establish them, we need to know something about the structure of the computation. To illustrate, we will restrict our attention to a system that can be specified by a simple differential or difference equation, $s(t') = F[s(t)]$, where t' represents the next "instant" of time: $t + \Delta t$ in the case of a difference equation, $t + dt$ in the case of a differential equation.[e] The initial state is $s(t_0) = s_0$. Next, we separate the non-computational from the computational components of the system:

$$v(t') = F_V[v(t), h(t)],$$
$$h(t') = F_H[v(t), h(t)].$$

F_V incorporates output transduction and F_H incorporates input transduction. Similarly, the abstract computation is described:

$$v(t') = F_V^*[v(t), h^*(t)],$$
$$h^*(t') = F_H^*[v(t), h^*(t)].$$

A sufficient condition for the physical system to realize the abstract computation is that there exists a mapping $r : H \rightarrow H^*$ satisfying the following homomorphism conditions [cf., MacLennan, 1994 a; MacLennan, 2004]:

$$F_V = F_V^* \circ (i \times r),$$
$$r \circ F_H = F_H^* \circ (i \times r).$$

---

[e] It is straight-forward to put these differential equations into standard form.

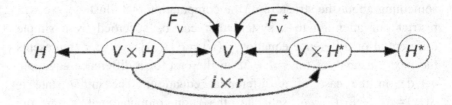

Fig. 1. Commutativity diagram for visible state.

where $i : V \rightarrow V$ is an identity function; see the commutativity diagrams (Figs. 1 and 2). For the initial state the condition is $h_0^* = r(h_0)$.

When stated in such abstract terms it is easy to mistake multiple realizability for a mathematical property, but it is not; it is physical property or, more properly, a property of physical systems in a teleological context. Therefore, it is helpful to consider an example.

Ants lay down pheromone trails when they return to their nests with food [Camazine, Deneubourg, Franks, Sneyd, Theraulaz, Bonabeau, 2001]. In addition to showing the way to the food source, these trails convey other information, such as the quality of the food source. The competition between reinforcement of the trail as the ants use it, and its disappearance as the pheromone dissipates and degrades, ensures that the path structure is adaptive and efficient in guiding the ants to and from their food sources. The primarily computational function of this system is evident in the fact that the pheromone could be replaced by other physical substances that would work as well. The transducers would have to be replaced appropriately; that is, the ants would have to be able to produce and detect the new signal substance. Of course, to fulfill its

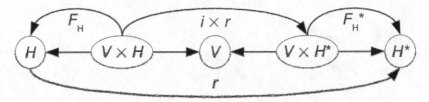

Fig. 2. Commutativity diagram for hidden state.

function adequately, the new substance would have to have the same rates of increase and decrease (although it is likely that any substance with the same ratio of increase rate to decrease rate would work as well). The ready availability of such a substance and the difficulty of ants producing or detecting it are not the important issues. What is important is that we can see that the functioning of the process does not depend in an essential way on any specific substance. The process is essentially formal not physical; it is information processing.

We may contrast this with a non-computational process that has some superficial similarities: the transport of food to the nest. If we think of it in purely mathematical terms it might seem to be multiply realizable. We can imagine a sort of input transducer that converts a portion of physical food into a number (encoding the food's quality and quantity in some way). This number is conveyed by a formal process (perhaps modeling the movement of the ants to the nest), where an output transducer converts the encoding into corresponding physical food.

Certainly, such a system could be constructed, but we can see that it would not fulfill the same purpose as the original transport process, which was to convey energy (stored in specific substances) from one physical location to another. In order to actually implement the alternative realization described, it would be necessary for the output transducer to be able to take the input signal (encoding the amount and kind of food) and use it to guide the synthesis of physical food that could be used by real ants. Naturally, this output transducer would consume energy and raw materials to fuel this synthesis, which would defeat the purpose of the transport process, which was to bring resources to the nest. Since the purpose of the transport process is to convey real, physical matter and energy from one place to another, we can see that a formal process is not suitable.

Therefore, when we are considering a supposed alternative realization, we must do so in the context of physical reality, not mathematical structure. It is an alternative realization only it fulfills the same physical function as the original system. There will, of course, be borderline cases, and we know that some systems may not be purely computational, but such complications do not invalidate the general concept. Categories may be useful even though neither nature nor engineering is compelled to conform exactly to them.

8. Design of Embodied Computation Systems

One of the challenges of embodied computation is that we have very little experience doing it. Much of our programming has been done in the idealized worlds of perfect logic and implementation-independent programming languages; unavoidable interactions with physical reality have been relegated to the periphery. Fortunately nature provides numerous examples of effective embodied computation, from intracellular genetic regulatory circuitry to the swarm intelligence of social insects and other animals. Therefore we can look to nature to learn how computation can cooperate with physics, rather than opposing it, and how information processing systems can fruitfully interact with the physical embodiment of themselves and other systems.

Since embodied computation is a new computing paradigm, it may be worthwhile to say a few words about how embodied computation systems might be designed. The first step is to *understand* how information processing occurs, and interacts with physical reality, in natural systems. We may benefit both from studies of specific systems relevant to some application of interest, but also from more general information about embodied computation in nature [e.g., Camazine, et al., 2001].

The second step is to *abstract* the process, so far as possible, from the specifics of its physical realization. In practical terms, this often amounts to developing a mathematical model of the relevant aspects of the system (i.e., the embodied information processing). This might seem like a return to disembodied, abstract models of computation, but it is not, for it incorporates physical processes in their essential form. For example, a natural system might exploit the diffusion and degradation of some pheromone, but its mathematical description would be in terms of the diffusion and degradation of *some* substance (with appropriate relative rate constants). That is, once we understand the computational principles, a *specific* quantity can be replaced by a *generic* quantity. Of course, some natural embodied computational systems will be more dependent on specific realizations (e.g., particular physical quantities) than others, and the more generically realizable ones will be the more generally useful to us.

The last step in developing an embodied computation system is to *realize* the abstract computational principles in an appropriate medium by selecting substances, forms of energy, quantities, and processes conformable to the mathematical model and the purposes of the system. This, of course, is more difficult than the disembodied computing with which we are familiar, but it will be necessary to master these techniques as we enter the post-Moore's Law era and attempt to apply computing principles more widely.

In the end, the process of designing an embodied computation system is not so different from designing a conventional computation system. The designer develops an abstract dynamical organization that will exhibit the required interactions with its environment. This is analogous to programming, the principal difference being that embodied computation makes use of different primitive processes and representations, namely those that have comparatively direct physical realizations. As a consequence, the physical environment and the physical realization of the computation will never be far from the designer's mind.

By looking at embodied computation in nature we may begin to isolate computational primitives that are generally useful and realizable in a variety of media. Because of its importance, I will focus here on embodied computation in morphogenesis (the self-organized development and metamorphosis of hierarchical form). Although there is some overlap and ambiguity, we may distinguish those primitives that pertain to the individual elements of the system and those that pertain to masses of them.

An embodied computation system, especially one organizing morphogenesis, will comprise a very large number of elementary units, such as cells or molecules. In the first case we are interested in physical processes involving single elements, which may respond passively or actively. Examples of such *individual primitives* include mobility (translation, rotation), adhesion and release, shape change, differentiation or state change, collision and interaction, and proliferation and apoptosis (programmed cell death, unit disassembly). Other processes pertain more to spatially distributed masses of elementary units, and they may be called *collective primitives.* Examples include elasticity, diffusion, degradation, fluid flow, and gradient ascent.

Finally, biological morphogenesis teaches us that embodied computation can orchestrate and organize complex, multistage processes operating in parallel at both the microscopic and macroscopic levels. For example, Bonabeau, Dorigo, and Theraulaz, in their investigations of swarm intelligence in wasp nest construction, recognized the concept of a *coordinated algorithm*, which leads to an organized nest structure [Bonabeau, Dorigo, Theraulaz, 1999]. Similarly, we need to discover how to design coordinated algorithms for embodied computation in artificial morphogenesis and similarly complex applications.

9. But Is It Computing?

The reader may allow that embodied computing, as described above, is interesting and potentially useful, but object to considering it a species of computing. After all, we have a precise definition of computation in the Turing machine and its equivalents (according to the notion of equivalence defined in Church-Turing computation theory). On the other hand, the notion of embodied computing may seem imprecise and difficult to discriminate from other physical processes.

If we consider "computation" and related terms, both in historical usage (which includes "analog computation") and in the context of contemporary discussions in philosophy and computer science, we can describe computation as *a physical process, the purpose or function of which is the formal manipulation (processing) of formal objects* [MacLennan, 1994 a; MacLennan, 2004]. As we have seen, a physical process may be considered computation (or information processing) if its purpose could be fulfilled as well by another physical system with the same abstract (e.g., mathematical) structure. In short, its purpose is *formal* rather than *material*.

This definition might seem to exclude embodied computation, or make it an oxymoron, but I do not think this is so, for there is nothing contradictory about embodied computation's greater reliance on physical processes for information processing. However, embodied computation may be directed also at the production of specific material effects; that is, its purpose may be physical rather than formal.

There are two answers to this. First, embodied computation's physical effects can often be understood abstractly (i.e., mathematically). For example, an activator-inhibitor system will produce characteristic Turing patterns, which can be characterized mathematically, independently of specific substances involved [Turing, 1952]. Second, we cannot expect all physical systems to fit neatly into categories such as *computational* and *non-computational*, but we should expect there will be degrees of essential embodiment and of independence from specific physical realizations.

Indeed, we must recognize that while artificial systems often have clearly specified purposes, and thus may be definitely computational or not, things are not so clear cut in nature, which often combines multiple functions into a single system. For example, ant foraging may simultaneously bring food to the nest and accomplish computational tasks such as adaptive path finding, path minimization, and exploration. Also, the circulatory system transports oxygen and nutrients, but also transmits hormonal signals.

Indeed, even well-engineered artificial systems obey the *Shanley Principle*, which says that multiple functions should be combined into single parts; orthogonal design is important for prototyping, but it should be followed by integration of function [Knuth, 1974, p. 295]. Thus, as we push the limits of computing technology and embed it more deeply into our world, we will have to combine functions, which will result in systems that are less purely computational and more essentially embodied.

10. Non-Turing Computation

It is important to remember that Church-Turing (CT) computation is a *model* of computation and that, like all models, it has an associated *frame of relevance* [MacLennan, 2003 b; MacLennan, 2009 b]. As previously remarked, a model's frame of relevance is determined by its simplifying assumptions — by the aspects and degrees to which the model is similar to the modeled system or differs from it — since these (often unstated) assumptions determine the sort of questions the model is suited to answer. It is important to understand a model's frame of relevance, since if we use a model to address issues outside its frame of relevance, we are apt to learn more about the model and its simplifying assumptions than about the modeled system. For example, from a highway map we may infer the travel distance between cities from the length of a line on the map, but we cannot infer the width of the road from the width of the line, nor conclude that many cities have circular boundaries and are colored either black or red!

Recall that the theory of CT computation was developed to address issues in effective calculability and formalist approaches to mathematics; the simplifying assumptions that it makes are well-suited to these issues and define its frame of relevance. Within this frame it makes sense to consider something computable if it can be computed in a finite number of steps (of finite but indeterminate duration) using a finite (but unbounded) amount of memory. It also makes sense to treat computation as a matter of function evaluation and to define computability in terms of sets of functions. (See [MacLennan, 1994 a, 2003 b, 2004, 2009 b] for more on the frame of relevance of CT computation.)

Unfortunately, the CT model is not well-suited to address issues in embodied computation or, more generally, natural computation, which lie outside its frame of relevance; its simplifications and approximations are bad ones for embodied computation systems. For example, the CT model ignores the real-time rates of the operations, but they are highly relevant in embodied computation. Similarly, the CT notions of equivalence and universality do not address the efficiency (in real-time, not asymptotic, terms) with which one system may simulate another.

Although it is premature to define a model of embodied computation, since we do not yet understand which issues are relevant and which are not, and premature formalization can impede the progress of a field, nevertheless we can produce a preliminary list of relevant issues. They include robustness (in the presence of noise, errors, faults, defects, and uncertainty), generality, flexibility, adaptability, morphological and steric constraints, physical size, consumption of matter and energy, reversible reactions, and real-time response [MacLennan, 2003 b; MacLennan, 2004; MacLennan, 2009 b].

11. Conclusions

In conclusion, we can see that embodied computation will play an increasingly important role in post-Moore's Law computing, but that we will need new models of computation, orthogonal to the Church-Turing model, that address the relevant issues of embodied computation and information processing. As a consequence we also expect there to be an ongoing fruitful interaction between investigations of embodiment in computation, psychology, and philosophy.

References

Abbreviations:

LSJ = Liddell, Scott, & Jones, *Greek-English Lexicon*, 9th ed., 1940.
OED = *Oxford English Dictionary*, 2nd ed., 1989.
OLD = *Oxford Latin Dictionary*, 1982.

Anderson, M. L. (2003). Embodied cognition: A field guide. *Artificial Intelligence*, 149, pp. 91–130.

Barish, R. D., Rothemund, P. W. K., and Winfree, E. (2005). Two computational primitives for algorithmic self-assembly: Copying and counting. *Nano Letters*, 5, pp. 2586–92.

Benzi, R., Parisi, G., Sutera, A., and Vulpiani, A. (1982). Stochastic resonance in climatic change. *Tellus*, 34, pp. 10–16.

Bonabeau, E., Dorigo, M., and Theraulaz, G. (1999). *Swarm intelligence: From natural to artificial systems*. New York: Oxford Univ. Press.

Brooks, R. (1991). Intelligence without representation. *Artificial Intelligence*, 47, pp. 139–59.

Camazine, S., Deneubourg, J.-L., Franks, N. R., Sneyd, G., Theraulaz, J., and Bonabeau, E. (2001). *Self-organization in biological systems*. New York: Princeton Univ. Pr.

Clark, A. (1997). *Being there: Putting brain, body, and world together again*. Cambridge: MIT Press.

Dreyfus, H. (1979). *What computers can't do: The limits of artificial intelligence*, rev. ed. New York: Harper & Row.

Hamann, H., and Wörn, H. (2007). Embodied computation. *Parallel Processing Letters*, 17 (3), pp. 287–98.

Haykin, S. (1999). *Neural networks: A comprehensive foundation*, 2nd ed. Upper Saddle River: Prentice-Hall.

Iida, F., Pfeifer, R., Steels, L., and Kuniyoshi, Y. (Eds.) (2004). *Embodied artificial intelligence*. Berlin: Springer.

Johnson, M., and Rohrer, T. (2007). We are live creatures: Embodiment, American pragmatism, and the cognitive organism. In J. Zlatev, T. Ziemke, R. Frank and R. Dirven (Eds.), *Body, Language, and Mind*, Berlin: Mouton de Gruyter, vol. 1, pp. 17–54.

Khatib, O. (1986). Real-time obstacle avoidance for manipulators and mobile robots. *International Journal of Robotics Research*, 5, pp. 90–9.

Kirkpatrick, S., Gelatt, Jr., C. D., and Vecchi, M. P (1983). Optimization by simulated annealing. *Science*, 220, pp. 671–80.

Knuth, D. E. (1974). Structured programming with **go to** statements. *Computing Surveys*, 6 (4), pp. 261–301.

MacLennan, B. J. (1994 a). Continuous computation and the emergence of the discrete. In K.H. Pribram (Ed.), *Rethinking neural nets: Quantum fields and biological data*, Hillsdale: Lawrence-Erlbaum, pp. 199–232.

MacLennan, B. J. (1994 b). Continuous symbol systems: The logic of connectionism. In D.S. Levine and M. Aparicio IV (Eds.), *Neural networks for knowledge representation and inference*, Hillsdale: Lawrence-Erlbaum, pp. 83–120.

MacLennan, B. J. (2003 a). Molecular combinatory computing for nanostructure synthesis and control. In *IEEE Nano 2003 (Third IEEE Conference on Nanotechnology)*, IEEE Press.

MacLennan, B. J. (2003 b). Transcending Turing computability. *Minds & Machines*, 13 (1), pp. 3–22.

MacLennan, B. J. (2004). Natural computation and non-Turing models of computation. *Theoretical Computer Science*, 317, pp. 115–145.

MacLennan, B. J. (2009 a). Computation and nanotechnology (editorial preface). *International Journal of Nanotechnology and Molecular Computation*, 1 (1), pp. i–ix.

MacLennan, B. J. (2009 b). Super-Turing or non-Turing? Extending the concept of computation. *International Journal of Unconventional Computing*, 5 (3–4), pp. 369–387.

MacLennan, B. J. (2010). Models and Mechanisms for Artificial Morphogenesis. In Hiroshi Umeo (Ed.), *International Workshop on Natural Computing*. Springer series, Proceedings in Information and Communications Technology (PICT). Berlin: Springer, pp. 23–33.

Miller, M. I., Roysam, B., Smith, K. R., and O'Sullivan, J. A. (1991). Representing and computing regular languages on massively parallel networks. *IEEE Transactions on Neural Networks*, 2, pp. 56–72.

Pfeifer, R., and Bongard, J. C. (2007). *How the body shapes the way we think — A new view of intelligence*. Cambridge: MIT.

Pfeifer, R., Lungarella, M., and Iida, F. (2007). Self-organization, embodiment, and biologically inspired robotics. *Science*, 318, pp. 1088–93.

Pfeifer, R., and Scheier, C. (1999). *Understanding intelligence*. Cambridge: MIT.

Rimon, E. and Koditschek, D. E. (1989). The construction of analytic diffeomorphisms for exact robot navigation on star worlds. In *Proceedings of the 1989 IEEE*

International Conference on Robotics and Automation, Scottsdale AZ. New York: IEEE Press, pp. 21–6.

Rothemund, P. W. K., Papadakis, N., and Winfree, E. (2004). Algorithmic self-assembly of DNA Sierpinski triangles. *PLoS Biology*, 2 (12), pp. 2041–53.

Rothemund, P. W. K, and Winfree, E. (2000). The program-size complexity of self-assembled squares. In *Symposium on Theory of Computing (STOC)*, New York: Association for Computing Machinery, pp. 459–68.

Steinbeck, O., Tóth, A., and Showalter, K. (1995). Navigating complex labyrinths: Optimal paths from chemical waves. *Science*, 267, pp. 868–71.

Stepney, S. (2004). Journeys in non-classical computation. In T. Hoare and R. Milner (Eds.), *Grand Challenges in Computing Research*, Swindon: BCS, pp. 29–32.

Stepney, S. (2008). The neglected pillar of material computation. *Physica D*, 237 (9), pp. 1157–64.

Ting, P.-Y., and Iltis, R. A. (1994). Diffusion network architecture for implementation of Gibbs samplers with applications to assignment problems. *IEEE Transactions on Neural Networks*, 5, pp. 622–38.

Tokuriki, N., and Tawfik, D. S. (2009). Protein dynamics and evolvability. *Science*, 324, pp. 203–7.

Turing, A. M. (1952). The chemical basis of morphogenesis. *Philosophical Transactions of the Royal Society*, B 237, pp. 37–72.

Winfree, E. (1998). *Algorithmic self-assembly of DNA*. Unpublished doctoral dissertation, California Institute of Technology, Pasadena.

Wolfram, S. (2002). *A new kind of science*. Champaign, IL: Wolfram Media.

CHAPTER 10

COMPUTATION ON INFORMATION, MEANING AND REPRESENTATIONS. AN EVOLUTIONARY APPROACH

Christophe Menant

Bordeaux.France
christophe.menant@hotmail.fr

Understanding computation as "a process of the dynamic change of information" brings to look at the different types of computation and information. Computation of information does not exist alone by itself but is to be considered as part of a system that uses it for some given purpose. Information can be meaningless like a thunderstorm noise, it can be meaningful like an alert signal, or like the representation of a desired food. A thunderstorm noise participates to the generation of meaningful information about coming rain. An alert signal has a meaning as allowing a safety constraint to be satisfied. The representation of a desired food participates to the satisfaction of some metabolic constraints for the organism. Computations on information and representations will be different in nature and in complexity as the systems that link them have different constraints to satisfy. Animals have survival constraints to satisfy. Humans have many specific constraints coming in addition. And computers will compute what the designer and programmer ask for.

We propose to analyze the different relations between information, meaning and representation by taking an evolutionary approach on the systems that link them. Such a bottom-up approach allows starting with simple organisms and avoids an implicit focus on humans, which is the most complex and difficult case. To make available a common background usable for the many different cases, we use a systemic tool that defines the generation of meaningful information by and for a system submitted to a constraint. This systemic tool allows to position information, meaning and representations for systems relatively to environmental entities in an evolutionary perspective.

We begin by positioning the notions of information, meaning and representation and recall the characteristics of the Meaning Generator System (MGS) that link a system submitted to a constraint to its environment. We then use the MGS for animals and highlight the network nature of the interrelated meanings about an entity of the environment. This brings us to define the representation of an item for an agent as being the network of meanings relative to the item for the agent. Such meaningful representations embed the agents in their environments and are far from the Good Old Fashion Artificial Intelligence type ones.

The MGS approach is then used for humans with a limitation resulting of the unknown nature of human consciousness.

Application of the MGS to artificial systems brings to look for compatibilities with different levels of Artificial Intelligence (AI) like embodied-situated AI, the guidance theory of representations, and enactive AI. Concerns relative to different types of autonomy and organic or artificial constraints are highlighted. We finish by summarizing the points addressed and by proposing some continuations.

1. Information and Meaning. Meaning Generation

1.1. *Information. Meaning of information and quantity of information*

Information, meanings and representations are part of our everyday life. We receive information from everywhere: environment, newspapers, other persons,... We interpret the received information to generate meanings that will be associated to it. The received information may be already meaningful or not, and the meanings that we generate are specific to ourselves.

Different persons will associate different meanings to the news on the radio. A thunderstorm noise will generate different meanings depending if we are on the beach or in our house. Thunderstorm noise is not meaningful by itself. It is the interpretation we make of it that generates a meaningful information. In addition to all these more or less conscious meanings, there is the world of our unconscious meanings that we cannot access directly.

Important work has been done on questions related to the meanings of signs, words, sentences or emotions (semiotics, linguistics, analytic philosophy, psychology, ...), and through the intentionality and aboutness of mental states (phenomenology).

Important work has been done also regarding the measurement of the quantity of information. C. Shannon has theorized in the middle of the xxth century on the calculation of the quantity of information in order to evaluate the transmission capacity of communication channels [Shannon, 1948]. Such measurement of information is widely used in today communication systems. But things are different regarding the meaning of information. We do not know how to measure a meaning. The quantity of information has no relation with the meaning of the information, "semantic aspects of communication are irrelevant to the engineering aspects."

Among animals also there is management of information and meaning. Ants build up paths toward food by depositing pheromones which are interpreted by other ants as indicating an already used path. The dance of a bee indicates a source of pollen to the other members of the hive, but it will not generate that meaning to a passing by butterfly also looking for pollen. There, the pheromones and the bee dance are already meaningful. Meaningful information is a key element in the relation of an organism with its environments. Jacob Von Uexkull (1864-1944) has introduced the notion of internal world for organisms as an Umwelt. All animals have their individual phenomenal world that characterizes the interpretation and meaning they give to their sensations. Von Uexkull work is being continued by Biosemiotics, an "interdisciplinary science that studies communication and signification in living systems", as a specialized branch of semiotics focusing on communications in living systems [Sharov, 1998].

These questions relative to meaningful information and representations are also to be looked at in the world of artificial systems. Can a computer attribute some meaning to the information it processes? And does a robot, designed to avoid obstacles, generate a meaning when facing an obstacle? All these subjects relative to information and meaning for different systems like humans, animals and robots bring us to consider that there may be some interest to look at meaning generation following a systemic approach. The meaning would be generated by and for a system in a given environment, taking into account the specificities of the system.

This would allow us to characterize a meaning as specific to a system with a common background usable for all systems.

1.2. *Meaningful information and constraint satisfaction. A systemic approach*

The above rapid overview highlights that meaningful information can be considered as related to some purpose and action for the system that uses it or creates it.

Meaningful information does not exist by itself, for free, but has a reason of being for the system that generates it or uses it. The sight of a prey creates a meaning for an animal. But this meaning will be of different value if the animal is hungry or not. The meaning associated to an outside entity depends of the entity and also of the internal state of the system.

But such a statement is very general. The purposes and actions can be very many. The actions of simple animals are mostly immediate on the quasi-reflex mode (a frog catching a fly with her tongue). The action can also be an alert signal for other members of the species. More complex animals will build up actions using the results of passed experiences, some may also simulate several options to compare the different outcomes and implement the best solution. There are also cases where there is no immediate action and where the memorized meaningful information is stored for further usage.

The case of humans is even more complex as conscious free will comes in addition to modify the biologic meanings inherited from our animal history. And we do not really know what free will is. As of today, the nature of human mind is a mystery for science and philosophy. Many researches are in process on this subject in various fields like philosophy, neurobiology, psychology, cognition and computer science. But the question is still to be answered. We do not know the nature of human mind.

In the case of robots, it looks natural to say that the actions implemented come from the designer of the robot and from its environment.

As introduced above, meaningful information is system dependant. Different systems can generate different meanings when receiving the same information. Incident information can be meaningful or meaningless[1].

An important characteristic of meaningful information is that it establishes a relation between the system that creates it and its environment. Such relation has two aspects. First the build up of the meaningful information which links the system to the information

---

[1] Our usage of meaningful information is different from the Standard Definition of semantic Information linked to linguistics where information is considered as meaningful data [Floridi 2003]. Our systemic approach brings a different perspective by introducing the possibility of meaningless information participating to the generation of meaningful information.

received from the environment. And second, the action implemented by the system on its environment. The action implemented is an interactive and dynamic link as it will modify the environment, and consequently impact the meaning generated by the system. Meaning generation creates an interactive relation between the system and its environment. Such creations of links by meaning generation are obvious in any social life where interactions between organisms are intertwined with creations of meanings. These meanings have effects on the environment, on other organisms, as well as on the organisms that generated the meaning. Meaning generation is a relational phenomenon.

Information and representations are tightly linked. We will show that a meaningful representation of an item for a system can be defined as made of meaningful information. Our focus will first be on the nature and origin of meaningful information from which we will deduce the nature and content of a meaningful representation.

We have introduced above that a meaningful information is related to the purposes and actions of the system that creates it or uses it. On an evolutionary standpoint, animal life brings us to consider that organisms generate meanings to satisfy constraints related to their nature, basically survival constraints for the animal itself or for the species. These constraints are internal to the organism. For humans, the subject is more complex. We can agree that the meanings that we humans deal with have some reasons of being, but identifying these reasons is not easy. The meaningful information we process are very many and are not always clearly related to constraints that are to be satisfied. What type of constraint do we satisfy when getting the meaning of a sentence in a book? Is it about knowing more on a subject in order to be more performant? Or is it only about implementing a needed Pascalian diversion? Whatever the answers to such questions, we will use as a background the idea that a meaning is generated by a system submitted to a constraint and that it is a meaning about an entity of the environment of the system.

The identification of the constraint will be addressed on a case per case basis depending on the nature of the system. We will use an already presented systemic tool on meaning generation [Menant, 2003]. It allows an evolutionary approach, starting with a very small organism that gives us a frame to define a Meaning Generator System (MGS) based on constraint satisfaction. We use the MGS for more complex organisms through evolution up to humans. Artificial systems are also taken into account with the MGS approach.

A system can be defined as a set of elements standing in interrelation. So we first identify the elements constituting the MGS in order to get clear enough an understanding of its functions. We will then be in a position to link it with other functions and integrate it in higher level systems.

2. Information, Meaning and Representations. An Evolutionary Approach [2]

2.1. *Stay alive constraint and meaning generation for organisms*

Our starting point for the introduction of a systemic and evolutionary approach to meaning generation is a simple organism. We choose a unicellular organism: a paramecium. Organisms have constraints to satisfy in order to maintain their nature. Life being "the sum of the functions by which death is resisted" [Bichat], the basic constraint that an organism has to satisfy is to resist death, to stay alive.

It has been shown experimentally that a drop of acid in the water at the vicinity of a paramecium will make her move away, looking for a less hostile location in water where there is less acid. This reaction of a paramecium moving away from a hostile environment brings us to introduce the notion of meaning for an organism. The acidity of the environment is an incident information received by the paramecium that will participate to some generation of meaning within the paramecium. A meaning that "has sense of", that "wants to say": "the environment is becoming hostile versus the satisfaction of vital constraints". And this meaning is going to trigger within the paramecium an action aimed at putting her at distance from the acid environment. It is clear that the paramecium does not possess an information processing system that allows her to have access to an inner language. But a paramecium has usage of sensors that can participate to a measurement of the

---

[2] This paragraph reproduces and complements the content of a 2003 publication [Menant, 2003] and of a 2005 presentation [Menant, 2005].

environment acidity. The information made available with the help of these sensors will be part of the process that will generate the move of the paramecium in the direction of less acid water.

So we can say that the paramecium has created a meaning related to the hostility of her environment, in connection with the satisfaction of her vital constraints. This example brings up several characteristics relative to the notion of meaning that we want to conceptualize. We can formulate them and bring up a "systemic aspect", more general than the small living organism that we have taken as example:

1) A meaning (the environment is becoming hostile versus the satisfaction of vital constraints) is associated to an information (level of acidity) received from an entity of the environment (drop of acid).
2) The meaning is generated because the system possesses a constraint linked to its nature (stay alive) that has to be satisfied for the system to maintain its nature.
3) A meaning is generated because the received information has a connection with the constraint of the system (too high an acidity level impacts the satisfaction of the vital constraints).
4) A meaning is a meaningful information generated by the system relatively to its constraint and to its environment (the environment is becoming hostile versus the satisfaction of the vital constraint).
5) The meaning is going to participate to the determination of an action that the system is to implement (move away from acid area) in order to satisfy its constraint and maintain its nature (stay alive).

These five characteristics lead to a systemic definition of a meaning for a system submitted to a constraint that receives an information from an entity of its environment:

"A meaning is a meaningful information that is created by a system submitted to a constraint when it receives an incident information that has a connection with the constraint. The meaning is formed of the connection existing between the received information and the constraint of the system. The function of the meaningful information is to participate to the determination of an action that will be implemented in order to satisfy the constraint of the system".

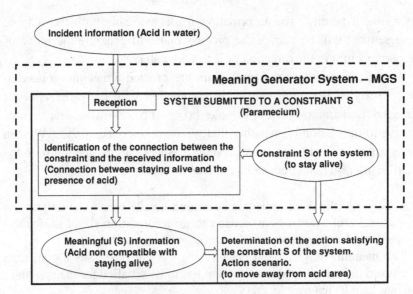

Fig. 1. The Meaning Generator System

This definition of a meaning tells what the meaning is and what the meaning is for. The definition is illustrated in Fig. 1.

In the following text, we will use indifferently the expressions "meaning" or "meaningful information".

2.2. *The Meaning Generator System (MGS). A systemic and evolutionary approach*

The above example of meaning generation in a simple organism makes available the elements needed for our systemic approach to meaning generation. The Meaning Generator System (MGS) is introduced as made of:

- A system submitted to a constraint and able to receive information from an entity of its environment.
- An information coming from an entity of the environment and incident on the system (that information can come from the natural presence of the entity (shape, color, ...) or be the result of an action of the system (displaced element, frightened animals,...). The incident information can be already meaningful or not).

- An information processing element, internal to the system and capable of identifying a connection between the received information and the constraint.

The generated meaning is precisely the connection existing between the received information and the constraint. It will be used to determine an action that will be implemented in order to satisfy the constraint of the system. The action implemented will modify the environment of the MGS and bring the generation of new meanings in order to coordinate the satisfaction of the constraint through time. The MGS participates to a sensori-motor coordination articulated on constraint satisfaction.

A MGS is represented in Fig. 1 where a system submitted to a constraint S generates a meaningful (S) information about an entity of its environment. It is to be highlighted here again that meanings do not exist by themselves. Meanings are generated by systems that have constraints to satisfy in order to maintain their nature (the nature of a system being what it does when it is functional. Stay alive for an organism, avoid obstacles for a robot). The meaning generation process is constraint satisfaction driven.

Meanings are generated by the systems and for the systems in their environments. Meanings link the systems to their environments. As the meaning generation process links the system to its environment by the received incident information and by the implemented action, it is natural to look at the grounding of the generated meaning. An overview of the information and functions related to the meaning generation brings to consider that the generated meaning is naturally grounded by the MGS.

The meaning is grounded in the MGS by the functions present in the MGS, and the meaning is grounded out of the MGS by the received information and by the action. The grounding by the action has two components: the action scenario and, on a dynamic standpoint, the consequences of the action in terms of receivable information. Fig. 2 illustrates this point.

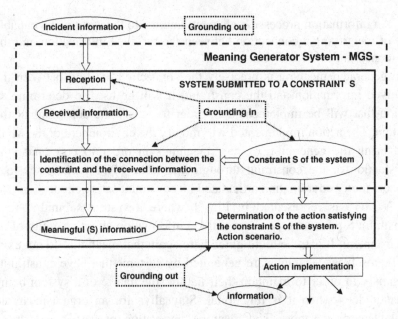

Fig. 2. Groundings of meaning by the MGS

Such groundings in and out of the MGS allow to present on a same picture the objectivist and constructivist aspects of perception. The incident information that will be received by the MGS is an objective component of the outside reality of the MGS, as is the action implemented on the environment. And the meaning generation process, by comparing the received information to the constraints of the system, brings the constructivist aspect of the generated meaning.

In real life, the MGS is most of the time part of a higher level system. Such integration of the MGS in a higher level system brings to highlight the following points:

a) The MGS is simple. It is a simple tool usable for a bottom-up approach to meaning generation. It is a building block for higher level systems capable of actions (agents) which have constraints to satisfy in order to maintain their nature (the constraint of the MGS can be considered as a subset of the constraints of the agent).

The nature of the agent can be biological or artificial. Biological constraints and biological meanings are intrinsic to the biological agent. In the case of artificial agents, the constraints are not intrinsic to the agent as they come from the designer. Artificial agents generate artificial meanings. In both cases, constraint satisfaction goes through meaning generation which links the agent to its environment.

b) The agent can contain other functions like memory, scenarios simulation, action implementation, other receivers, other MGSs. These functions are linked together as part of the agent. A memory will contain action scenarios coming from past experiences where different updatings can be compared through simulation. The receivers bring feedbacks from the results of actions and provide information on constraint satisfaction level. An agent will use its MGSs to interface directly with its environment by sensori-motor processes or indirectly by using higher level performances like simulation and optimization. The former is related to reflex and insect type situated behaviors. The latter covers cases involving a more centralized data processing. Both types have existed through evolution of organisms up to humans, and are still active. The MGS is usable with both types of agents where it participates to the sensori-motor coordination.

c) An agent submitted to constraints has a nature to maintain in an environment through the satisfaction of its various constraints. Constraints satisfaction is implemented by the actions resulting of the generation of meanings that link and adapt the agent to its environment in a permanent and dynamic process. The agent is naturally embedded in its environment by the generated meanings which bring it to be permanently coping with its environment.

d) The participation of the meaningful information to the determination of an action can be indirect. Several actions and meanings generations can be chained before the final constraint satisfaction. As the various action scenarios are linked to the entities of the environment and to the constraints, they are to be considered as meaningful (we call them indirect meanings).

Animal life gives examples of such combinations of meanings generations. When a group member receives information about the presence of a predator, she generates a meaning "presence of predator as incompatible with survival of the group". This meaning triggers an action (alert) to inform the group members about the threat. When the other members of the group receive the alert information, they generate a meaning "presence of predator incompatible with survival" which in turn triggers individual hiding or escape actions. The well known case of vervet monkeys alert process is an example [Manning, Stamp Dawkins, 1998]. Such chaining of meanings contributes to the build up of networks of meanings (see hereunder).

e) The actions implemented to satisfy the constraints of an agent can be of many types (physical, chemical, nervous, data processing, signalling, conscious or unconscious cognitive processes, ...). Actions will modify the environment of the agent and consequently modify the received information and the meaning generation. On a dynamic standpoint, the results of the implemented actions that can be received by the agent are part of the meaning generation process. As a MGS is internal to an agent, a generated meaning can participate to actions internal to the agent. A constraint satisfaction process can internally modify the agent.

Some of the relations of a MGS with higher level systems elements are represented in Fig. 3.

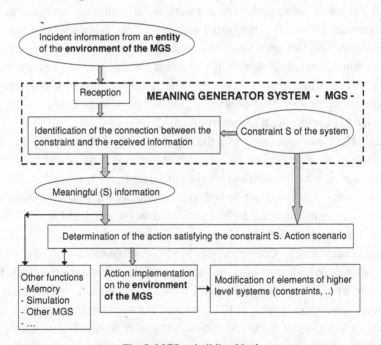

Fig. 3. MGS as building block

The definition of meaning proposed here above has been built up with an example coming from the animal world that has been formalized into a system. As said above, a meaning does not exist by itself. A meaning is a meaningful information about an entity of the environment, and it is generated by and for a system submitted to a constraint. Such approach is close to a simplified version of the Peircean theory of sign. Peirce's theory is a general theory of sign, and the present approach is centred on meaning. The element of this approach that can be related to the Peircean theory of sign is the MGS: the generated meaning combines an objective relation with the environment (the received incident information) and a specific build up of the system (the connection with the constraint). This can be compared to the Sign relating the Object to the Interpreter that will produce the Interpretant. The MGS can be compared to a simplified version of the Interpreter where the incident information is the Sign coming from the Object, and the meaningful information is the Interpretant. In the Peircean theory of sign, the Interpretant is also a sign available for another interpretation, and so on. The Interpretant is at the same time the third term of one triadic relation and also the first term of another triadic relation. This "necessarily involves chains of triads" [Queiroz, El-Hani, 2006].

On the same token, the meaning generated by a MGS can become an incident information on other MGSs. In terms of MGSs, the "chains of triads" are part of the networks of meanings (see hereunder).

Meaning generation by an organism as presented here has some similarities with the build up of a subjective world by animals as proposed by J. von Uexkull. Von Uexkull studied the problem of how living beings subjectively perceive their environment and how this perception determines their behaviour (with the key notion of "Umwelt" as an internal world). Umwelt has been re-actualized as a support for several studies on artificial life and artificial intelligence [Ziemke, Sharkey, 2001].The MGS is usable for meaning generation processes existing in the world of animals, humans or artificial systems, assuming we define precisely enough the agent with its constraints and the corresponding MGSs. Such generality is the purpose of a systemic approach.

2.3. Meaning transmission

We have seen that the action resulting of meaning generation may sometimes implicate other agents. The formal action that will satisfy the constraint comes after the transmission of the meaningful information and its reception by other agents. These other agents can also be submitted to specific constraints, different from the constraint of the transmitting agent. In order to take these cases into account, we need a new notion that can characterize the possibility for the transmitted meaningful information to participate to the determination of an action within other agents having possibly different constraints to satisfy. The notion of "efficiency of a meaning" has been introduced to address such cases [Menant, 2003].

2.4. Individual and species constraints. Group life constraints. Networks of meanings

A given agent can have different constraints to satisfy. In addition to individual vital constraints, most organisms are submitted to species vital constraints which bring them to reproduce and protect the young in order to maintain the species alive. Group life constraints are also to be considered as being constraints related to group life stability and not directly identifiable as individual or species constraints. Social hierarchy is a reality in animal group life where it generates specific constraints. Corresponding meanings generations will determine actions like access to food or mating. These different constraints are active at the same time and can be conflicting. The satisfaction of individual constraints can become incompatible with the satisfaction of species constraints. For an ant colony to cross water, several ants may sacrifice themselves and get drowned to allow the build up of a bridge usable for the ant colony. The species constraints are here stronger than the individual ones.

Regarding the environment of an agent, a given entity can make available different information to the agent (sound, odor, ...). As a result, the different information received by an agent and the different constraints that the agent has to satisfy bring the agent to generate many different meanings relatively to an entity, including the indirect meanings like action scenarios. These meanings will be spread around through the various MGSs or centralized, depending on the structure of the agent. All these meanings relative to a given entity are available to the agent for the build up of a network of meanings relative to the entity. These networks of meanings also contain the dynamic aspect of meaning generation with the consequences of implemented actions, as well the action scenarios with past experiences or simulations making available anticipation performances. These networks connect entities, constraints, scenarios, actions outcomes and are inter-related. Agents are permanently embedded in their environments by networks of meanings that link them to their environment by real time information exchanges as well as by past experiences or anticipated action scenarios. Human and animal societies are societies of communication that are organized and embedded in their environments by such networks of meanings.

Regarding artificial systems, meaning generation is simpler to analyze in its content as we, the designers, can decide of the constraints and of their interdependences.

Networks of meanings fit with the Peircean triadic theory of sign as a generated meaning can become an incident information for another MGS, and so on. These natural interdependencies of meaningful information show that a given meaning barely refers to a single entity but that meanings are naturally interrelated in networks of meanings. As the MGS is also a tool for an evolutionary approach to meaning generation, networks of meanings can be used in an evolutionary background. Understanding that species are linked through evolution from simple living organisms up to us humans, we can look at applying such continuity to networks of meanings. A given MGS at a stage of evolution can be considered as linked to MGSs of lower evolutionary stages. But the constraints of an organism at a given stage of evolution have to be clearly defined for the evolutionary network of meaning to be applicable (we again highlight here the problem related to the level of human in evolution where human mind with its constraints is still a mystery for today science and philosophy).

Networks of meanings link agents to entities of their environments through constraints that have to be satisfied. Such links limit the dimension of the networks. Networks of meanings based on constraints satisfaction is a subject which is to be developed beyond the scope of this paper.

2.5. *From meaningful information to meaningful representations* [3]

The generation of meaningful information for constraint satisfaction by organisms has become more elaborated through evolution. The increasing complexity of the organisms has allowed the built up of richer networks of meanings about entities of the environment, the purpose still being to satisfy constraints as well as possible.

We have seen that a network of meanings is relative to an entity for an agent submitted to constraints, and that it dynamically links the agent to the entity. Networks of meanings relative to entities populating the environment of an agent embed that agent in its environment and allow it to maintain its nature by the satisfaction of its constraints. We would like to use these networks of meanings to introduce the notion of MGS based meaningful representation.

A representation can be considered as being "any entity (object, property, state, event) that designates, denotes, or stands in for another" [Anderson, 2005]. Representations haves been initially introduced in AI as meaningless symbols processed centrally by computers. Such "traditional AI" has faced practical limitations in some applications. Philosophical analysis came up to bring anti-representationalism as a position supported by some researchers in AI and cognition. We feel that the notion of representation should not be put aside but needs to be re-addressed and reformulated in terms of meaningful element build up by an agent submitted to constraints.

We would like here to define a meaningful representation of an entity for an agent submitted to constraints as being the network of meanings relative to that entity for the agent. Such meaningful representation has the properties of a network of meaningful information as highlighted above:

---

[3] This paragraph is a continuation of a 2006 presentation, with adds relatively to the initial version of a meaningful representation [Menant, 2006, a].

- A meaningful representation is generated by an agent in order to maintain its nature in its environment by the satisfaction of its constraints. A meaningful representation of an entity for an agent is not an abstraction or a mirror image of the entity but it is made of constraint satisfaction oriented information about that entity.

- A meaningful representation contains the meaningful information that dynamically links the agent to its environment. It includes the dynamic aspect of meaning generation with the consequences of implemented actions, as well as the action scenarios with past experiences or simulations making available anticipation performances.

- Meaningful representations exist by and for the agent and embed it in its environment. As an example, the meaningful representation of a mouse for a cat can be imagined as containing the real time perception of the mouse when the cat is experiencing it, with also the past experiences of the cat with mice and action scenarios that can be used for simulation (action anticipation). As a consequence of our evolutionary usage of MGSs, we want to consider that meaningful representations of entities of the environment were progressively built up by organisms through evolution as needed relatively to the satisfaction of the constraints of the organism.

- A meaningful representation avoids the combinational explosion as the dimension of the meaningful network is limited by the relations to constraints satisfactions.

3. Meaningful Information and Representations in Humans

Meanings and representations are important parts of our human lives. They can be conscious or unconscious. We build internal mental representations by our thoughts and external ones like maps and paintings. We live in a society of communications where interacting by meanings and representations happens all the time, language being a key tool. But analyzing the content and nature of meaningful information and meaningful representations in humans is not an easy task.

We as humans are embedded in networks of meanings, in meaningful representations as defined above. And most of what has been said for animals does apply. But what comes in addition in terms of constraints specific to humans is difficult to define. These difficulties come from the fact that we do not know our own nature. As said, the nature of human mind is a mystery for today science and philosophy.

Strictly speaking, the analysis of meaningful information for humans can only be incomplete due to our lack of understanding of human mind. What is known today about meaningful information for humans can be investigated using constraints satisfactions in two directions at least:
List the constraints we know as belonging to today human being and take them as a base for deducing the possible generations of meanings, or take the animal constraints as a starting point and try to identify what evolution may have brought in addition or modified.

The first approach belongs to psychology and to philosophy of mind. It can be addressed in a very simplified way by the Maslow pyramid of needs: physiological needs, needs for safety and security, needs for love and belonging, needs for esteem and the need to actualize the self, in that order. Considering these needs as constraints that humans have to satisfy makes possible a usage of the MGS for humans in their environment. But we have to be careful with such a process and highlight its limits: all the interferences of free will actions and conscious feelings with the Maslow pyramid needs will have to be taken into account as they are: with a limited understanding of their meanings.

Regarding the second approach, an evolutionary scenario can be proposed where a constraint of anxiety limitation is introduced [Menant, 2006 b]. The scenario is about the coming up of self-consciousness during evolution. The performance of intersubjectivity that existed at pre-human primate level is used as a thread to explain the build up of a conscious self. But the resulting identification with conspecifics also led to identifying with endangered or suffering conspecifics which produced a significant increase of anxiety at these times of survival of the fittest. Such anxiety increase had to be limited. The hypothesis developed is that anxiety limitation came up as a key constraint for our pre-human ancestors and played a significant role as an evolutionary engine up to today human nature. The evolutionary scenario proposes that the actions implemented to limit anxiety have favored the development of empathy, imitation, language and group life which brought obvious evolutionary advantages and allowed a positive feedback in the evolutionary process.

In terms of meaning generation, the hypothesis is that an anxiety limitation constraint has been a high contributor through human evolution (and still is today, as shaping many of our thought and behaviors). More work in needed on this subject as anxiety generations and limitations are today beyond identification with suffering conspecifics. Following the same thread, other pre-human and human specific constraints are also to be identified.

Figure 4 gives a summary of the proposed scenario about the evolution of self-consciousness.

The proposed scenario positioning anxiety limitation as a key item in the coming up of self-consciousness during evolution opens a new path for an evolutionary approach to consciousness.

Self-consciousness can be defined as "the possession of the concept of the self and the ability to use this concept in thinking about oneself" [Block, 2002]. It is different from phenomenal consciousness which can be understood as "experience; the phenomenally conscious aspect of a state is what it is like to be in that state" [Block, 2002]. The presence of phenomenal consciousness has also to be taken into account in this type of evolutionary scenario. Work is in process on this subject [Menant, 2008].

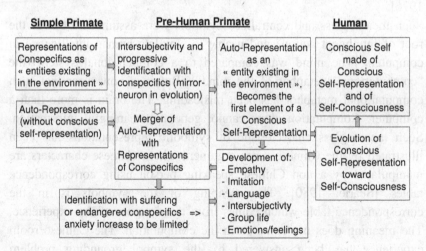

Fig.4. Evolution of self-consciousness

4. Meaningful Information and Representations in Artificial Systems

Our definition of meaning generation has been introduced as based on the performances of life (stay alive constraint) and has been generalized into a system (maintain a nature by constraint satisfaction). This approach allowed us to define a meaningful representation of an item for a system.

We want here to see how this systemic approach to meaning generation can be used for artificial systems. In that case, the systems and the constraints are artificial as coming from the designer. The constraints and meanings are not intrinsic to the system as they were in the case of organisms. We will look at the compatibility of the MGS approach with different stages of AI from traditional AI to the enactive approach.

4.1. *Meaningful information and representations from traditional AI to Nouvelle AI. Embodied-situated AI*

Representations were first introduced in traditional AI and cognitive sciences as meaningless symbolic elements standing for the represented entities and processed by a central system "A symbol may be used to designate any expression whatsoever. That is, given a symbol, it is not prescribed a priori what expressions it can designate." [Newell, Simon, 1976].

Such meaningless and centralized symbols were assumed to be "at the root of intelligent action" and usable to simulate human intelligence in computers. The mind was compared to a computational system (the "computational metaphor of the mind"). But it is now clear that such computational metaphor has been misleading. The brain is more than a computer. Computation alone cannot generate meaningful information. Such meaningless characteristic of symbolic representations has been illustrated by the Chinese room argument where Chinese characters are manipulated by a non Chinese speaking person using correspondence tables [Searle, 1980]. The meaning of the symbols is in the correspondence table which comes from the designer of the experience. The meaning does not come from the computation. The Chinese room experience has been answered by the symbol grounding problem (connecting the symbols to what they are about) [Harnad, 1990].

Traditional AI has been successful for computing on large numbers of symbols using precisely defined rules (chess playing, expert systems, trajectories simulations, ...). But besides important successes, traditional AI has encountered limitations due to its brittleness and limited flexibility, and also to the risk of combinational explosion when dealing with complex subjects. Traditional AI follows a Cartesian approach to problem solution where a complex problem is subdivided into smaller problems easier to solution ("divide each of the problems I was examining in as many parts as I could"). Following the same rule, entities to be represented are divided into sub entities down to a level where they are simple enough to be symbolized. Such process becomes highly consuming in computing power and lacks flexibility. Calculation overload is at risk by combinational explosion when the represented entities are complex. The limitations of traditional AI were the cost of looking for a detailed symbolic representation of the environment. Such traditional AI has been dubbed GOFAI (Good Old Fashion AI) [Haugeland, 1989].

To go beyond the limitations of GOFAI, new concepts had to be looked for. They came from the world of robotics through a "Nouvelle AI" where the symbolic model of the environment is replaced by multiple continuous sensing implemented by the agent when needed. Central control is not the rule any more. The agent has the possibility to continuously use its sensors to feel its environment rather than referring to a centralized model: "the intelligent system is decomposed into independent and parallel activity producers which all interface directly to the world through perception and action" [Brooks, 1991 a]. The construction of internal models of an outside reality is not needed any more. Intelligence is then considered as emerging from the interaction of simple behaviours. Symbolic representations are put aside. "It turns out to be better to use the world as its own model" [Brooks, 1991 a]. The agent is now "situated" and "embodied" in its environment. "The robots are situated in the world—they do not deal with abstract descriptions, but with the "here" and "now" of the environment that directly influences the behaviour of the system"..."The robots have bodies and experience the world directly. Their actions are part of a dynamic with the world, and the actions have immediate feedback on the robots' own sensations". [Brooks, 1991 b].

The situated and embodied approach does not use the notion of meaningful information because it is not needed for the functioning of the robots. Direct sensori-motor loops link the robot to its world without needing to explicit a meaningful aspect of the processed information. However, meaning generation could be introduced in each sensori-motor loop, bringing in information related to the local constraint satisfaction of each sensori-motor loop. Such add would not bring anything to the robot as it is now but it could make available spread meanings regarding environmental entities. These meanings could be used in a higher level system as meaningful representations of the environment for the robot. It may look quite surprising to propose reintroducing representations in Nouvelle AI. But these representations are not the symbolic ones that Nouvelle AI has put aside. We are talking about using meaningful information that link the system to its environment. As said, embodied-situated robotics does not need this meaningful information, we just note that the generation of such artificial meaningful information is possible in embodied-situated robotics. But it should be clear that these meanings are not intrinsic to the robot, they are artificial meanings generated with artificial constraints coming from the designer of the artificial agent.

On the same token, the performances of the sensori-motor loop of an artificial system, even if processing meaning generation, are far from covering the performances of life. Despite all the progress made by the AI field, we are still "not good at modelling living systems" [Brooks, 2001]. A possible reason for this may be that we are missing some important property or characteristic of life still to be discovered. In order to overcome this point, we may need to "find new ways of thinking about living systems to make any progress".

Among the performances of life that we are not successful modeling is autonomy. Autonomy is a performance of life that we have difficulties to describe. The nature of autonomy is not clearly understood and efforts are deployed to characterize it as constitutive (or intrinsic, as internally generated) or behavioural (or extrinsic, as externally imposed). It is agreed that the autonomy of today artificial systems is far from the autonomy of living systems: "despite all biological inspiration and self-organization, today's so-called "autonomous" agents are actually far from possessing the autonomy of living systems." [Ziemke, Sharkey, 2001].

4.2. *Meaningful representations versus the guidance theory of representation*

The guidance theory of representation (GTR) [Anderson, Rosenberg, 2008] is a theory of representational content which focuses on action. It proposes that "the content and intentionality of representations can be accounted for in terms of the way they provide guidance for action". The notion of representation is linked to what the representation does for the agent: "what a representation does is provide guidance for action". This focus on action goes with grounding the content of a representation in the action on the environment. "Representations come into existence and derive their content from their role supporting the basic intentionality of action". Constraints are considered as "associated with assigning motivating reasons".

The GTR and the MGS approach are close as they both take into account the action of an agent on its environment and are rooted in biological behaviour. There are some differences however. Differences are in the nature of the representations and in the level at which the action is taken into account.

For the GTR, a representation is mostly considered by what it does in terms of providing guidance for action. The GTR focuses on the usage of the representation more than on its nature or origin. "We ask first not what a representation is, but what it does for the representing agent, and what the agent does with it; what is a representation for? Our contention is essentially that representations are what representations do". The MGS approach, on its side, defines the nature of the representation as made of meaningful information. The representation is defined as resulting of meanings generations by a system submitted to constraints.

For the GTR, the action is the key contributor to the definition of the representation. The guidance theory presumes "that the intentionality of representation can be grounded in the intentionality of action". A percept becomes a representation because it provides guidance for action. For the MGS approach, it is first the presence of a constraint to be satisfied that generates the build up of meanings and representations. The action comes after.

Also, as the MGS approach is rooted in constraint to be satisfied as source of meaning generation, the organic or artificial nature of the constraint allows to differentiate the organic and artificial natures of the generated meanings and representations in the agent.

GTR and MGS approach are on the same ground as maintaining a role for representations in AI and cognition.

4.3. *Meaningful information and representations versus the enactive approach*

The enactive approach to cognition and AI has been initiated in the 1970s by the work of H. Maturana and F. Varela. The enactive approach is the baseground of significant current research activities. The word "enact" links cognition to action, to the doing and experiences of the agent. The knowledge that the agent has of its environment comes from the interactions that links it to its environment: "...enaction asserts that cognition is a process whereby the issues that are important for the continued existence of a cognitive entity are brought out or enacted: co-determined by the entity as it interacts with the environment in which it is embedded" [Vernon, Furlong, 2007].

This perspective introduced by enaction as linking agents to their worlds is applied to the field of cognition for organisms including humans and also to the field of AI with the new domain of enactive AI: "enactivism can have a strong influence on AI because of its biologically grounded account of autonomous agency and sense-making" [Froese, 2007].

We will look first at the compatibility of the MGS based meaningful information and representations with enaction, and then with the enactive AI.

The enactive approach can be characterized by five themes [Torrance, 2005]:

(a) Minds are the possessions of embodied biological organisms viewed as autonomous – self-generating and self-maintaining – agents.

(b) In sufficiently complex organisms, these agents possess nervous systems working as organizationally closed networks, generating meaning, rather than processing information as inner representations of the external world.

(c) Cognition, conceived fundamentally as meaning-generation, arises from the sensori-motor coupling between organism and environment.

(d) The organism's world is "enacted" or "brought forth" by that organism's sensori-motor activity; with world and organism mutually co-determining one another, in ways that have been analyzed by investigators in the continental phenomenology tradition.

(e) The organism's experiential awareness of its self and its world is a central feature of its lived embodiment in the world, and therefore of any science of the mind.

The compatibility of MGS based meaningful information with enaction is to be addressed first by looking at the compatibility with the two themes expliciting the notion of meaning generation.

Meaningful information is compatible with b): the MGS is part of a higher level system (an agent) where meaning generation exists for the system to maintain its nature in its environment. We however do not oppose meaning generation to information processing as meaning generation by the MGS is information processing (see Figs. 1, 2 & 3). And our meaningful representations, made of meaningful information, come from meaning generation.

Meaningful information is compatible with c) as the MGS links and couples the agent with its environment by a permanent interaction through perception and action.

This brief comparison based on the characteristics of the MGS brings to consider that MGS based meaningful information looks compatible with the two themes of enaction that explicitly deal with meaning generation. The compatibility with the other themes is difficult to address as they introduce concepts from phenomenology and science of the mind which are beyond a systemic approach to meaning generation. This brings us to limit the compatibility of the MGS approach with enaction to the generation of meaningful information. It should also be noted here that the five themes characterise enaction for organisms, not for artificial systems. The MGS on its side is a systemic approach that can apply to organisms as well as to artificial agents.

Regarding the compatibility of meaningful representations with enaction, one could assume that it can be deduced from the proposed compatibility of meaningful information generation with enaction, as meaningful representations are made of meaningful information. But several researchers and philosophers are reluctant to use the notion of representation in enaction. There are several reasons for that: one is the origin of representations in AI as meaningless and centrally processed symbols which limits their possible usage. Another reason goes with the rooting of enaction in phenomenology [Depraz, 2007] which brings several philosophers to argue that the notion of representation should not be used with enaction. H. Dreyfus has been holding for long that the usage of representation in AI is a mistake and that the importance of the body behavior should be taken as key : "Heidegger's crucial insight is that *being-in-the-world* is more basic than *thinking* and solving problems; it is not representational at all." [Dreyfus, 2007]. Francisco Varela also has been arguing against the notion of representation. When coining the word "enactive", he wrote [Varela and all, 1991]: "We propose as a name the word *enactive* to emphasize the growing conviction that cognition is not the representation of a pre-given world by a pre-given mind but is rather the enactment of a world and a mind on the basis of a history of the variety of actions that a being in the world performs".

Consistent with such positions, some today philosophers and researchers in the enactive area tend to reject the notion of representation: "there are certain ideas in cognitive science that the enactive approach clearly rejects, e.g., homuncularity, boxology, separability between action and perception, and representationalism" [Di Paolo and all, 2007].

We consider that such a rejection is mostly a rejection of the GOFAI type of representations (symbolic and meaningless) and that it should not apply to the meaningful representations as defined here. So we consider that the proposed compatibility of meaningful information generation with enaction can be extended to meaningful representations. Meaningful representations that embed agents in their environments by constraint satisfactions are to be considered as compatible with enaction in terms of meaning generation.

But the above sentence about enaction as rejecting boxology and separability between action and perception brings in some concern about the MGS compatibility with enaction in terms of building block. As said above, the MGS is a building block modelling meaning generation in agents. The fact that enaction is reluctant to use a building block approach has to be highlighted as it limits the compatibility of the MGS approach with enaction.

Enactive AI is a new and maturing domain proposing to go beyond some limitations of embodied AI. Among these is the fact that "the presence of a closed sensori-motor loop *does not* fully solve the problem of meaning in AI" [Di Paolo, 2003]. The MGS approach is compatible with such a position as the generated meaning comes from the connection existing between the sensed information and the constraint of the system, not from a closed sensori-motor loop alone.

Enactive AI is looking for a system having the capacity "to actively regulate its ongoing sensori-motor interaction in relation to a viability constraint." [Froese, Ziemke, 2009]. The MGS approach where the generation of a meaning is directly related to the satisfaction of a constraint is compatible with such linking of a system to its environment by a constraint.

Beyond these first elements of compatibility, enactive AI considers two "necessary systemic requirements": constitutive autonomy and adaptivity [Froese, Ziemke, 2009]. Enactive AI takes them both as necessary for meaning generation (sense making).

Constitutive autonomy is basically the autonomy of organisms as the applicability of the constitutive approach is "mainly restricted to actual organisms. " [Froese and all, 2007]; The MGS approach, as a systemic tool, is usable for organisms and for artificial systems. The performance of autonomy that applies to the MGS is the one of the agent hosting it. In the case of organism, the MGS will deal with the autonomy of organisms, which is compatible with constitutive autonomy.

The performance of adaptivity[4], "reflects the organism's capability – necessary for sense-making – of evaluating the needs and expanding the means towards that purpose" [Di Paolo, 2005]. There are tight links between adaptivity and meaning generation as "a careful analysis of sense-making shows that different properties of adaptivity (self-monitoring, control of internal regulation, and control of external

---

[4] Adaptivity is defined in Enactive AI as [Di Paolo, 2005] "a system's capacity, in some circumstances, to regulate its states and its relation to the environment with the result that, if the states are sufficiently close to the boundary of viability, 1. tendencies are distinguished and acted upon depending on whether the states will approach or recede from the boundary and, as a consequence, 2. tendencies of the first kind are moved closer to or transformed into tendencies of the second and so future states are prevented from reaching the boundary with an outward velocity".

exchanges) are implied by assuming that organisms have a meaningful perspective on their world". The MGS approach looks compatible with the performance of adaptivity as constraints satisfactions can go by internal or external actions from the agent.

As introduced above, the compatibility of the MGS approach with the phenomenological concepts used by enaction and by enactive AI still needs to be addressed. Phenomenology calls for first person point of view and lived experience that are significantly beyond the horizon of the proposed systemic approach on meaning generation. The MGS approach does not need first person point of view nor lived experience (which does not mean that it is incompatible with them). Also, regarding lived experience, we consider that there still may be a need to look for "something unknown" in our models for understanding the nature of life. Probably "we might be missing something fundamental and currently unimagined in our models of biology" [Brooks, 2001] in order to get clear enough an understanding of organic autonomy and corresponding intrinsic meaning generation. The MGS approach can be a thread for further investigations in this area by using constraints positioned between physico-chemical laws and biological ones. The introduction of "pre-biotic constraints" to be defined could open a path for the evolution of material constraints toward organic ones. (see Walter Riofrio, this volume).

5. Conclusion and Continuation

5.1. *Conclusion*

In this chapter we have extended to meaningful representations the existing systemic approach on meaningful information based on the Meaning Generator System (MGS) [Menant, 2003].

Our starting point is a meaningful information about an entity of the environment as generated by a system submitted to a constraint. The meaningful information (the meaning) is the connection existing between the constraint and the information received by the system from the entity. It is used by the system to produce an action that will satisfy its constraint. The generated meaning links the system to its environment. An agent having several constraints to satisfy and receiving different information from an entity will generate a network of meanings relative to the entity, including the actions scenarios. We call this network of meanings "meaningful representation of the entity for the agent". The meaningful representations of entities of the environment embed the agent in its environment.

The notion of meaningful representation has been applied to animals, humans and artificial systems. For artificial systems, the constraints and meanings are artificial and come from the designer. For animal and humans, they are intrinsic to the agents. Our lack of understanding about human mind highlights the existence of unknown items about human representations in terms of constraints satisfactions. Openings are proposed on this subject by an evolutionary scenario.

The MGS approach has been positioned relatively to embodied-situated AI, to the guidance theory of representations, and to the enactive AI.

It has been proposed that the MGS approach can be added to embodied-situated AI, and that it has some common grounds with the guidance theory of representations.

The comparison of the MGS approach with enaction has shown that meaningful information and representations, as embedding an agent in its environment by constraint satisfactions, are compatible with enaction in terms of meaning generation. Comparison with enactive AI has presented the MGS approach as compatible with constitutive autonomy and with adaptivity.

Some concerns have been highlighted relatively to the rejection of boxology by enaction that makes difficult the usage of the MGS as a building bock. Also, the compatibility of the MGS approach with phenomenological concepts like first person point of view and lived experience is to be analyzed.

5.2. *Continuation*

The positioning of meaningful representations within AI as introduced here brings up subjects that deserve some further analysis:

- Provide a more detailed description of networks of meanings as based on constraints satisfaction. Consider if it could be an entry point for ontologies based on systems having constraints to satisfy to maintain their natures

- Investigate the notion of constraint and look if it could be related to physico-chemical laws in order to position a link between artificial constraints and biological ones. (Introduction of pre-biotic constraints).

- See how a better understanding about the nature of life could shed some light on the nature of organic (intrinsic, constitutive) autonomy and make available a reference for the definition of artificial (behavioural) autonomy. (This may be related to the hypothesis [Brooks, 2001] that "there may be some extra sort of 'stuff' in living systems outside our current scientific understanding").

- Look at how the notion of autonomy could be related to the notions of constraint satisfaction and of meaning generation.

- See how the build up of an identity could be based on constraints that an agent has to satisfy in order to maintain its nature in its environment.

- Identify human specific constraints in order to relate them to an evolutionary approach on human consciousness.

- Investigate the evolution of the anxiety limitation process beyond the phylogenetic thread of identification with suffering or endangered conspecifics.

- Analyse the compatibility of the MGS approach with phenomenological concepts like first person point of view and lived experience.

References

Anderson, M. (2005). Representation, evolution and embodiment. Institute for Advanced Computer Studies. University of Maryland. *http://cogprints.org/3947/*.

Anderson, M. and Rosenberg, G. (2008). Content and Action: The Guidance Theory of Representation. *The Journal of Mind and Behavior* Winter and Spring *2008*, Volume 29, Numbers 1 and 2, pp. 55-86.

Block, N. (2002). Some Concepts of Consciousness. In *Philosophy of Mind: Classical and Contemporary Readings*, David Chalmers (ed.) Oxford University Press.

Brooks, R. (1991, a). Intelligence without representation. *Artificial Intelligence* 47, pp. 139-159.

Brooks, R. (1991, b). New Approaches to Robotics. *Science,* 13 September 1991: Vol. 253. no. 5025, pp. 1227-1232.

Brooks, R. (2001). The relationship between matter and life. *Nature*, Vol. 409, 18 Jan 2001. pp. 409-411

Depraz, N. (2007). Phenomenology and Enaction. *Summer school: Cognitive sciences and Enaction.* Fréjus, 5-12 september 2007.

Di Paolo, E. (2003). Organismically-inspired robotics: homeostatic adaptation and teleology beyond the closed sensori-motor loop. In: K. Murase & T. Asakura (eds.), *Dynamical Systems Approach to Embodiment and Sociality*, Advanced Knowledge International, pp. 19-42.

Di Paolo, E. (2005). Autopoiesis, adaptivity, teleology, agency, *Phenomenology and the Cognitive Sciences*, (4), pp. 429-452.

Di Paolo, E. Rohde, M. De Jaegher, H. (2007). Horizons for the Enactive Mind: Values, Social Interaction, and Play in: J. Stewart, O. Gapenne, E.A. Di Paolo (Eds.), *Enaction: Towards a New Paradigm for Cognitive Science*, The MIT Press, Cambridge, MA, in press

Dreyfus H. (2007). Why Heideggerian AI Failed and how Fixing it would Require making it more Heideggerian. *Philosophical Psychology*, 20(2), pp. 247-268.

Floridi, L. (2003). From data to semantic information. *Entropy*, 2003, 5, pp. 125-145. *http://www.mdpi.org/entropy/papers/e5020125.pdf.*

Froese, T. (2007). On the role of AI in the ongoing paradigm shift within the cognitive sciences; In: M. Lungarella et al. (eds.), *Proc. of the 50th Anniversary Summit of Artificial Intelligence*, Berlin, Germany: Springer Verlag, in press.

Froese, T. Virgo, N. Izquierdo, E. (2007). Autonomy: a review and reappraisal. *University of Sussex research paper.* ISSN 1350-3162.

Froese, T. and Ziemke, T. (2009). Enactive artificial intelligence: Investigating the systemic organization of life and mind. *Artificial Intelligence*, Volume 173 , Issue 3-4, pp. 466-500.

Harnad, S. (1990). The Symbol Grounding Problem *Physica*, D, pp. 335-346.

Haugeland, J. (1989). *Artificial Intelligence, the very idea*, 7th Ed. (MIT Press, USA).

Manning, A. and Stamp Dawkins, M. (1998). *An introduction to animal behaviour.* Cambridge University Press.

Menant, C. (2003). Information and meaning. *Entropy*, 2003, 5, pp. 193-204. http://www.mdpi.org/entropy/papers/e5020193.pdf.

Menant, C. (2005). Information and Meaning in Life, Humans and Robots. Foundations of Information Sciences. Paris 2005. *http://www.mdpi.org/fis2005/F.45.paper.pdf.*

Menant, C. (2006, a). Evolution of Representations. From Basic Life to Self-representation and Self-consciousness. TSC 2006 poster.*http://cogprints.org/4843/.*

Menant, C. (2006, b). Evolution of Representations and Intersubjectivity as sources of the Self. An Introduction to the Nature of Self-Consciousness. ASSC 10 poster. *http://cogprints.org/4957/.*

Menant, C. (2008). Evolution as connecting first-person and third-person perspectives of consciousness. ASSC 12 poster. *http://cogprints.org/6120/.*

Newell, A. and Simon, H. (1976). Computer Science as Empirical Inquiry: Symbols and Search. *Communications of the ACM.* March 1976, Vol 19, Number 3. 113-116.

Queiroz, J. and El-Hani C. (2006). Semiosis as an Emergent Process. *Transactions of the Charles S. Peirce Society* Vol 42, N° 1.

Searle, J. (1980). Minds, brains, and programs. *Behavioral and Brain Sciences*, (3): pp. 417-457.

Shannon, C. (1948). A mathematical theory of communication. *Bell System Technical Journal*, vol. 27.

Sharov, A. (1998). What is Biosemiotics? http://home.comcast.net/~sharov/biosem/geninfo.html#summary.

Torrance, S. (2005). In search of the enactive: Introduction to special issue on Enactive Experience *Phenomenology and the Cognitive Science.*, (4) December 2005, pp. 357-368.

Varela, F. Thompson, E. Rosch, E. (1991). *The Embodied Mind: Cognitive Science and Human Experience*. Cambridge, MA: MIT Press.

Vernon, D., Furlong, D. (2007). Philosophical Foundations of AI. In *50 Years of AI*. Lecture Note in Computer Science Vol. 4850, pp. 53-62.

Ziemke, T. Sharkey, N. (2001). A stroll through the worlds of robots and animals: Applying Jakob von Uexküll's theory of meaning to adaptive robots and artificial life. In: *Semiotica*, 134(1-4), 701-746.

CHAPTER 11

INTERIOR GROUNDING, REFLECTION,
AND SELF-CONSCIOUSNESS

Marvin Minsky

MIT
http://web.media.mit.edu/~minsky/

This is a slightly revised version of an essay published in 2005 in Brain, Mind and Society, Proceedings of an International Conference on Brain, Mind and Society, Tohoku University, Japan. See http://www.ic.is.tohoku.ac.jp/~GSIS/. Several parts of this also appeared in my 2006 book, The Emotion Machine.

1. Introduction

Some computer programs are expert at some games. Other programs can recognize some words. Yet other programs are highly competent at solving certain technical problems. However, each of those programs is specialized, and no existing program today shows the common sense or resourcefulness of a typical two-year-old child—and certainly, no program can yet understand a typical sentence from a child's first-grade storybook. Nor can any program today can look around a room and then identify the things that meet its eyes.

This lecture will suggest some ideas about why computer programs are still so limited. Some thinkers might say that this is because computers have no consciousness, and that nothing can be done about this, because it is in the nature of machines to only what they are programmed to do—and therefore they cannot be programmed to 'think'.

Citizen: I am convinced that machines will never have thoughts or feelings like ours, because machines lack vital ingredients that can only exist in living things. So they cannot have any feelings at all, no hopes or joys or fears or pains—or motives, ambitions, or purposes. They cannot have the faintest sense of pride or shame, or of failure, achievement, or discontent, because they simply can't care about what they do, or even know they exist.

It seems to me that we use such statements to excuse ourselves for our failures to understand ourselves. To do this, we collect the phenomena that we can't yet explain, and then pack them into such 'suitcase-like' words as sentience, spirit, or consciousness—and then describe these "vital ingredients" as entities with mysterious traits that can't be explained in physical ways.

However, here I will take an opposite view. Whenever some seemingly 'basic' aspect of mind seems hard to explain, I will try to depict it as the product of some more complex network of processes— whose activities may sometimes cooperate, but may also have ways to conflict and compete. Then in each of the examples below, a mystery that seemed inexplicable will then be replaced by a set of several different questions and problems, each of which may still be difficult, but at least won't seem so more intractable. We'll start by unpacking the set of phenomena for which we have come to use the word "consciousness." (This following section is condensed from chapter 4 of my forthcoming book, "The Emotion Machine.")

2. What is Consciousness?

Aaron Sloman: "It is not worth asking how to define consciousness, how to explain it, how it evolved, what its function is, etc., because there's no one thing for which all the answers would be the same. Instead, we have many sub-capabilities, for which the answers are different: e.g. different kinds of perception, learning, knowledge, ... self-control, etc."— From a message in comp.ai.philosophy, 14 Dec. 1994

To see how many things human minds do, consider this fragment of everyday thinking.

> *Joan is part way across the street on the way to deliver her finished report. While thinking about what to say at the meeting, she hears a sound and turns her head —and sees a quickly oncoming car. Uncertain whether to cross or retreat, but uneasy about arriving late, Joan decides to sprint across the road. She later remembers her injured knee and reflects upon her impulsive decision. "If my knee had failed, I could have been killed. Then what would my friends have thought of me?"*

It might seem natural to ask, "How conscious was Joan of what she did?" But rather than dwell on that 'consciousness' word, let's look at a few of the things that Joan actually "did."

> *Reaction: Joan reacted quickly to that sound.*
>
> *Identification: She recognized it as being a sound.*
>
> *Characterization: She classified it as the sound of a car.*
>
> *Attention: She noticed certain things rather than others.*
>
> *Indecision: She wondered whether to cross or retreat.*
>
> *Imagining: She envisioned some possible future conditions.*
>
> *Selection: She selected a way to choose among options.*
>
> *Decision: She chose one of several alternative actions.*
>
> *Planning: She constructed a multi-step action-plan.*
>
> *Reconsideration: Later she reconsidered this choice.*

In the course of doing those things, other 'parts' of Joan's mind did other things.

> *Recollection: She retrieved descriptions of prior events.*
>
> *Representation: She interconnected a set of descriptions.*
>
> *Embodiment: She tried to describe her body's condition.*

Emotion: She changed major parts of her mental state.

Expression: She constructed several verbal descriptions.

Narration: She heard them as dialogs in her mind.

Intention: She changed some of her goals' priorities.

Apprehension: She was uneasy about arriving late.

Reasoning: She made various kinds of inferences.

Many of these activities involved mental processes that used descriptions of some of her other mental processes.

Reflection: She thought about what she's recently done.

Self-Reflection: She reflected on her recent thoughts.

Empathy: She imagined other persons' thoughts.

Moral Reflection: She evaluated what she has done.

Self-Awareness: She characterized her mental condition.

Self-Imaging: She made and used models of herself.

Sense of Identity: She regarded herself as an entity.

That's only the start of a much longer list of aspects of how people feel and think— and if we want to understand how our minds work, we'll need explanations for all of them. To do this, we'll have to take each one apart, to account for the details of how it works—and then decide which of them to regard as aspect of what we call 'consciousness.'

3. The Mind Seen as an Organization of Multi-level Processes

This section outlines a model of mind that shows how a system could reflect (to at least some extent) on what it was recently thinking about. There is not enough room to describe the whole idea here, but the reader can find more details at http://web.media.mit.edu/~minsky/E5/eb5.html.

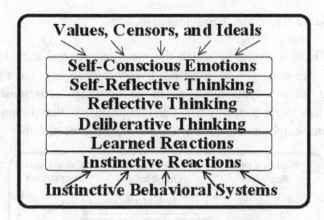

Fig. 1.

My associate Push Singh and I are at present developing a prototype of a system like this. We describe more details about this in http://web.media. mit.edu/~minsky/E4/eb4.html and in http://web.media.mit.edu/~push/ CognitiveDiversity.html

I should note that this model is consistent with some of the early views of Sigmund Freud, who saw the mind as a system for resolving (or for ignoring) conflicts between our instinctive low-level drives and our later-acquired goals and ideals:

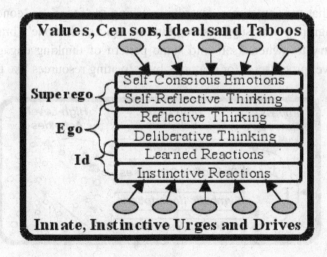

Fig. 2.

4. How do we Recognize Consciousness

Once we have a model in which the mind has several such layers of processes, we can start to construct hypotheses about what might be happening when a person claims to be thinking 'consciously'. For example, this might happen when a certain process in that person's brain detects some combination, such as this, of higher-level activities.

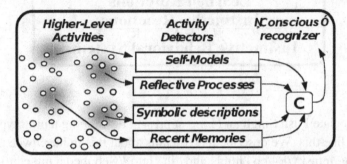

Fig. 3.

Similarly, we also could ask about what might cause a person to initiate such a set of activities. This might happen, for example, when a certain kind of 'critic-like' process detects that your thinking has got into trouble. The effect of such a critic might then help you to the sorts of things that we sometimes describe as trying to 'focus' or 'concentrate.' The diagram below suggests one kind of process that one's brain might use to try to switch itself into some pattern of thinking engages more high-level processes—for example, by activating resources like these:

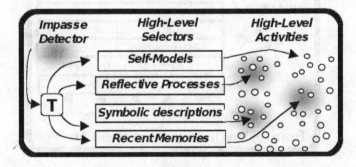

Fig. 4.

It is important to emphasize that each of those sets of activities can be extremely complex, and also are likely to differ significantly between different individuals. This is yet one more reason why no one should expect to be able to find a simple description of what we call consciousness.

5. How do Our Mental Levels Develop and Grow?

Over the past few centuries, our scientists have discovered far more about atoms and oceans and planets and stars than about the mechanics of feelings and thoughts. Those sciences progressed because those scientists were successful at discovering very small sets of "simple" and "basic" laws that explained many different phenomena in the realms of physics and chemistry.

Why did that strategy work less well for the science of psychology? It seems to me that one reason for this was an almost universal belief that such functions as emotions and feelings must be essentially non-mechanical— and that, therefore, they could not be explained in terms of physical processes. However, I suspect that the principal cause of this delay was the idea that psychologists, like physicists, should also seek simple "laws" of thought. In other words, it seems to me, that our psychologists and philosophers should not have tried so hard to use the methods that worked so well for those physical sciences. In fact, today we know that every human brain contains several hundred different, specialized kinds of machinery—each of which must have evolved different processes that helped our ancestors to solve the various problems that they faced in thousands of different ancient environments. So tens of thousands of different genes must be involved with how people think.

This suggests that modern psychologists should consider taking an opposite view, and reject the urge to base their ideas on discovering small sets of simple laws. Whenever some aspect of mind seems hard to explain (such as affection, fear, or pain), we could attempt, instead, to replace it by a more complex set of interconnected processes. In other words, we'll take each mental phenomenon and try to depict it, not as so 'basic' and 'elementary' that it is inexplicable, but as resulting from the complex activities of big networks of different processes—which sometimes cooperate and sometimes compete. Then each mystery will begin to disappear, because of having been replaced by a several new kinds of problems. Each of those problems may still be quite hard, but because they are far less mysterious, we'll be able to start to deal with them.

In other words, our main technique will be to demonstrate many seemingly separate 'features' of our minds are actually not single things but are aspects of what happens inside huge networks of different processes. To do this we'll need to accumulate ideas about how some of those processes work, and then we'll need to propose some ways that these might combine to produce the systems that we call our minds.

So now let us try to apply this idea to the question of how human learning works. It is easy enough to imagine machines with many levels of processes; indeed, many computer programs today are made of multiple layers of sub-programs. However, we still do not have good hypotheses about how our higher levels of brain-machinery come to do all the wonderful things that they do.

6. The Myth of "Grounding in Experience"

Today, the most popular theories of mental development assume that we begin by learning low-level reactions, and must wait for each stage to consolidate before we can learn to think more abstractly:

> *"Everything that we come to know—from the simplest facts to our most abstract concepts—is ultimately "grounded" on our experiences with the external world."*

More specifically, that 'standard theory' goes on to insist:

> *We begin by (somehow) learning to recognize particular sensory situations. Then we correlate our reactions with whether they lead to failure and success.*

> *Then, in subsequent stages of development, we learn increasingly abstract ways to represent the objects and their relationships in the situations that we perceive.*

However, this raises serious questions like these:

How do we recognize those "sensory situations"?

How do we represent them?

What determines how we react to them? ("Operants")

What constitute 'success' and 'failure'?

How do we make those correlations?

To answer such questions, it seems to me, we will need many new ideas about how to design such machinery. I doubt that it will ever suffice to assume (for example) that learning is basically a matter of statistical correlations, or that high-level concepts will spontaneously form in large neural networks with simple architectures—or that we will come to understand much of human cognition by making small extensions to traditional concepts about "association of ideas" or "operant reinforcement." One great philosopher clearly recognized that those ideas had serious deficiencies:

> *"That all our knowledge begins with experience there can be no doubt. For how is it possible that the faculty of cognition should be awakened into exercise otherwise than by means of objects which affect our senses, and partly of themselves produce representations, partly rouse our powers of understanding into activity, to compare, to connect, or to separate these—and so to convert the raw material of our sensations into a knowledge of objects?"*

> *"But, though all our knowledge begins with experience, it by no means follows that all arises out of experience. For, on the contrary, it is quite possible that our empirical knowledge is a combination of that which we receive through impressions, and [additional knowledge] altogether independent of experience …which the faculty of cognition supplies from itself, sensory impressions giving merely the occasion. [Immanuel Kant, Introduction to Critique Of Pure Reason, Second edition, April 1787]*

For although, as Kant remarked, sensations give us occasions to learn, this cannot be what makes us able to learn: in other words, it does not seem to explain how a person first could learn to learn. Instead, you need to begin with some 'additional knowledge' about how to produce representations and then to connect them. This is why, it seems to me, our human brains first had to evolve the kinds of complex architectures that our neuroscientists see.

For example, the traditional points of view do not begin to explain why the 'stages' of children's development so frequently seems highly abrupt; a child may spend an entire year expressing only "sentences" that contain no more than one or two words—and then, more complex expressions may quickly appear. This has led to a belief that has been popular for many years: that such capabilities must simply be "innate," and are actually not "learned" at all. Accordingly, that viewpoint holds that the child needs only to "tune up" or, in some way, adapt that machinery to the language of its culture, so that it can automatically speak properly when the developmental "time is right." The following section suggests, instead, that different levels of learning could have been proceeding simultaneously throughout that period, but do not usually appear in overt behavior until the resulting processes have become sufficiently competent.

7. A Theory of "Interior Grounding"

The old 'physical grounding hypothesis' assumed that no 'higher cognitive level" could start to learn before the levels below it have learned enough. In this view, mental development must begin with processes in which the child's lowest level reactive systems acquire some knowledge about that child's external environment:

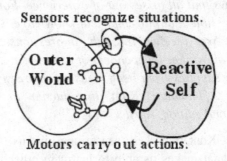

Sensors recognize situations.

Outer World

Reactive Self

Motors carry out actions.

Fig. 5.

Only then could the next level start to learn—because (in that traditional view) the construction of each new structure must be based on the foundations of what the levels below it have learned.

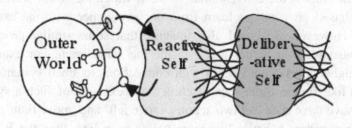

Fig. 6.

However, we can imagine a different kind of process in which each of several levels of the brain can, at the same time, learn some ways to predict and control some of the activities in the parts of the brain to which it directly connects. In other words, each part of the brain exists inside its own 'local world'. Then we can make a new hypothesis: evolution could have provided each of those local worlds with what we might call "mini-worlds" that genetically have been already each equipped with potentially useful kinds of behaviors.

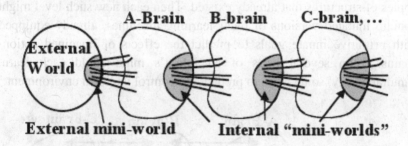

Fig. 7.

A typical external mini-world might consist of the system comprising some fingers and hand; then the reactive system can learn to predict how various combinations of finger-motions lead to different palm-sensations. Such a system could learn to predict that clenching the fingers will cause a sense of pressure on the palm. Similarly, an infant reactive level could learn to predict the effects of larger-scale motions of the limbs, or motions of the tongue in the mouth, or some visual effects of moving the eyes.

So far, this is the conventional view, in which all of our learning is finally based on what we learn from our experience with the external world. However, we could also imagine that some similar processes could also work at higher levels inside the same brain. For example, some higher levels could begin with connections to small systems that behave like simple finite-state machines. An example of such a system might have three state and two actions 'move left' and 'move right'.

If that system behaves like three points on a line, then the B-brain could learn to predict (for example) that performing 'move left' two or more times will always put the system into the leftmost state. There are many things that could be learned from this: that some actions are reversible, while other are not—and that this can depend, in various ways, on the situation that the system is in. There are many other important things that could be learned by such machines: for example, about how different sequences of actions can be combined, or about the effects of various kinds of such modifications.

How could such a system evolve? The simplest hypothesis would be the each of the major cognitive parts of our brains is based on mutated copies of structures that already existed. Then each new such level might contain mutated versions of older learning machines, already equipped with primitive innate goals to predict the effects of imagined action-chains. Then several parts of an infant's mind could each learn, simultaneously, some ways to predict and control its 'local environment.'

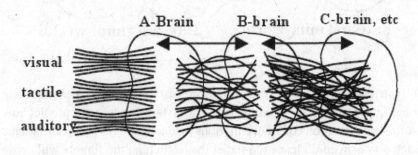

Fig. 8.

Eventually, these almost-separate systems would expand so that each of the levels inside that brain goes on to develop more powerful ways to exploit the abilities that its neighbors have learned.

8. Representations of Knowledge

Any theory of learning must try to include some ideas about how the learning machine might represent the knowledge information that it acquires. Most traditional theories assume that learning is somehow based on making connections—but only rarely go on to suggest the character of the things that are being connected. The situation is quite the opposite in the context of Computer Science, and practitioners frequently argue about what is the best way to represent knowledge. Sometimes such arguments go like this:

"It is always best to use rigorous Logic."

"No. Logic is too inflexible. Use Neural Networks."

"No, Neural Nets are even more rigid. They describe things with numbers, instead of abstractions. Why not simply use Natural Language."

"No, use Semantic Networks instead—where different ideas are connected by concepts! Such networks are better than sentences are—and have fewer ambiguities."

"No, Semantic Nets are too flexible—and can lead to inconsistencies. Only Logic protects us from paradox."

Chapter 8 of The Emotion Machine discusses this in more detail, and concludes that so far as human brains are concerned, we must use many different ways to represent different kinds of knowledge. That discussion concludes by imagining that human common sense knowledge must use a variety of different methods and processes that results in arrangements that might look like this:

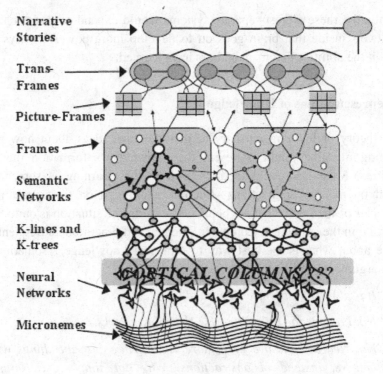

Narrative
Stories

Trans-
Frames

Picture-Frames

Frames

Semantic
Networks

K-lines and
K-trees

Neural
Networks

Micronemes

Fig. 9.

9. The Problem of Subjective Experience

Many philosophers have claimed that the hardest problem we need to face, both in psychology and philosophy, is to understand the nature of Subjective Experience. For example, here is one statement of this.

> *"The hard problem, in contrast, is the question of how physical processes in the brain give rise to subjective experience. This puzzle involves the inner aspect of thought and perception: the way things feel for the subject. When we see, for example, we experience visual sensations, such as that of vivid blue. Or think of the ineffable sound of a distant oboe, the agony of an intense pain, the sparkle of happiness or the meditative quality of a moment lost in thought. ... It is these phenomena that pose the real mystery of the mind." David Chalmers: http://eksl-www.cs.umass.edu/~atkin/791T/chalmers.html*

and http://consc.net/papers/puzzle.html. For more details, see Journal of Consciousness Studies 2(3): 200-19, 1995 or http://consc.net/papers/facing.html.)

Chalmers went on to propose an answer to this, by advocating a form of dualism, in which that sense of experience is regarded as a fundamental feature or property of the world.

> *"This leads to a natural hypothesis: that information (or at least some information) has two basic aspects, a physical aspect and a phenomenal aspect. This has the status of a basic principal that might underlie and explain the emergence of experience from the physical. Experience arises by virtue of its status of one aspect of information, when the other aspect is found embodied in physical processing. ... Of course, the double-aspect principle is extremely speculative and is also underdetermined, leaving a number of key questions unanswered." (Chalmers, ibid)*

Similarly, many thinkers have maintained that our sensations have certain 'basic' or 'irreducible' qualities that stand by themselves and can't be 'reduced' to anything else. For instance, in such a view, each color like Green and each flavor like Sweet has its own indescribable character, which is unique and can't be explained. For if such qualities do not have any smaller parts or properties, then there's no possible way to describe them.

Those thinkers call this the problem of 'Qualia", and argue that qualities of sensations cannot be explained in physical terms, because they have no physical properties. To be sure, it is easy to measure the amounts of Red light that comes a splotch of paint, or how much sugar is in each piece of a peach, but such comparisons (those philosophers claim) tells us nothing about the nature of the experience of seeing redness or tasting sweetness.

This subject might seem important because, if we cannot explain such 'subjective' things, that would undermine the whole idea that we can explain the human mind entirely in terms of such physical things as the machinery inside our brains. For, if the sensation of sweetness can never be measured or weighed, or detected in any physical way, then it must exist in a separate mental world, where it cannot possibly interact with any physical instruments.

Well, let's first observe that this claim must be wrong, because it is self-contradictory. For, if you can tell me that you have experienced sweetness then, somehow, that sensation has caused your mouth to move! So clearly, there must be some 'physical instrument' in your brain that recognized the mental activity that embodies your experience. In other words, we are simply facing, again, the same kind of problem that we solved in the previous section: we simply need another one of those internal "condition-detecting" diagrams, like the ones that we used above to account for why and how a person might talk about consciousness.

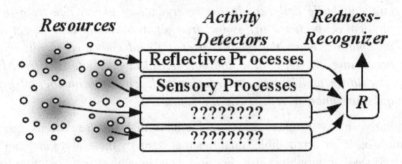

Fig. 10.

Similarly, Joan might first notice a change in her gait, or that she's been favoring her injured knee. Indeed, her friends may be more aware than she is, of how much that pain was affecting her. Thus, one's first awareness of pain may come after detecting signs of its effects—by using the kind of machinery.

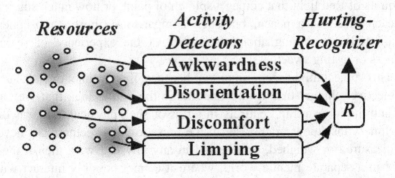

Fig. 11.

Of course, we do not yet quite know how to construct and connect those condition detectors. However, so far as I can see, this is merely another instance of where our popular psychology assumes that some mental phenomenon is far simpler than it actually is. Perhaps in just a few years from now we shall be able to ask a brave philosopher to enter a suitable scanning device so that we can discover which brain-cells best distinguish the conditions that we wish to detect.

In other words, to understand how feelings work in more detail, we'll have to stop looking for simple answers, and start to explore more complex processes. The sensory systems in human brains include dozens of different processors. So, when you try to tell someone else about the 'sensations' you 'experience', those pathways are so complex and indirect that you will be telling a story based on sixth-hand reports that have gone through many kinds of transformations. So despite what those philosophers claim, there is no basis to insist that what we 'experience' is uniquely 'direct'.

When a ray of light strikes your retina, signals flow from that spot to your brain, where they affect other resources, which then transmit other kinds of reports that then influence yet other parts of your brain. [NOTE: In fact, a single spot of red may not be sensed as being red; in general the colors we see depend, to a large extent, on which other colors are in its neighborhood. Also, some readers might be surprised to hear that the visual system in a human brain includes dozens of different processing centers.]

Also, at the same time signals from the sensors in your ears, nose, and skin will travel along quite different paths, and all these streams of information may come to affect, in various ways, the descriptions the rest of your mind is using. So, because those pathways are so complex and indirect, when you try to tell someone about what sensation you feel, or what you are experiencing, you'll be telling a story based on sixth-hand reports that use information that has gone through many kinds of transformations. So despite what some philosophers claim, we have no basis to insist that what we call our 'sense of 'experience' is uniquely direct.

The old idea that sensations are 'basic' may have been useful in its day, the way the four kinds of 'atoms' of antiquity were supposed to be elementary. But now we need to recognize that our perceptions are affected by what our other resources may want or expect.

Now some philosophers might still complain that no theory like this can truly describe or explain the experience of seeing that color or feeling that touch. Listen again to the best of those philosophers:

> *"When we visually perceive the world, we do not just process information; we have a subjective experience of color, shape, and depth. We have experiences associated with other senses (think of auditory experiences of music, or the ineffable nature of smell experiences), with bodily sensations (e.g., pains, tickles, and orgasms), with mental imagery (e.g., the colored shapes that appear when one rubs ones eyes), with emotion (the sparkle of happiness. the intensity of anger, the weight of despair), and with the stream of conscious thought.*

> *"[That we have a sense of experiencing] is the central fact about the mind, but it is also the most mysterious. Why should a physical system, no matter how complex and well-organized, give rise to experience at all? Why is it that all this processing does not go on "in the dark", without any subjective quality? Right now, nobody has good answers to these questions. This is the phenomenon that makes consciousness a *real* mystery." See David Chalmers: http://consc.net/papers/puzzle.html   or http://consc.net/papers/facing.html.*

Here is how I would deal with that 'mystery'. When you see your friend Jack react to things, you cannot see the machinery that makes him react in those ways—and so you have few alternatives to simply saying that, "he reacts to what he experiencing." But then, you must be using the word 'experience' as an abbreviation for what you would say if we knew what had happened inside Jack's—such as, "He must have detected some stimuli, and then made some representations of these, and then reacted to some of those by changing some of the plans he had made, etc."

In other words, if your brain can begin to speak about some 'experience' it must already have access to some representations of that event; otherwise, you would not remember it—or be able to say that you have experienced it! So your very act of discussing that 'experience' shows that 'it' cannot be a simple or basic thing, but must be a complex process that is involved with the high-level networks of representations that you call your Self.

When seen this way, the problem which Chalmers calls 'hard' is not really a single problem at all, because it condenses the complexity of all those many steps by squeezing them into the single word, 'experience' and then declares this to be a mystery. From this point of view, there should be nothing surprising about the fact that you find it so hard to talk about your sensations and feelings? You look at a color and see that it's Red. Something itches your ear and you know where to scratch. Then, so far as you can tell, that's all there seems to be to it; you recognize that experience—and nothing like "thinking" seems to intervene. Perhaps this is what leads some people to think that the qualities of such sensations are so basic and irreducible that they will always remain inexplicable.

However, I prefer to take the opposite view—that what we call sensations are complex reflective activities. They sometimes involve extensive cascades in which some parts of the brain are affected by signals whose origins we cannot detect—and therefore, we find them hard to explain. So, I see no exceptional mystery here: we simply don't yet know enough about what is actually happening in our brains. But when you think enough about anything, then you see this is also the case with everything.

References

Minsky, M. (2006). *The Emotion Machine*, Simon & Schuster, New York
http://www.amazon.com/exec/obidos/ISBN=0743276639/marvinminskyA

CHAPTER 12

A MOLECULAR DYNAMIC NETWORK: MINIMAL PROPERTIES AND EVOLUTIONARY IMPLICATIONS

Walter Riofrio

Complex Thought Institute Edgar Morin, University Ricardo Palma, Lima-Peru
Complex Systems Institute (ISC-PIF), Paris-France
walter.riofrio@iscpif.fr

Fundamental properties like robustness and evolvability are present in many dynamic systems. In biological systems, for instance, it seems that both properties are in continuous tension. However, this tension provokes throughout evolution the persistence of mutations and the existence of future evolutionary potential for changes.

The special characteristics of biological systems, tell us that its distinctive properties could have been developed in pre-biotic era. In other words, the basic properties of life would have been better comprehended if we had realized that they arisen much earlier than previously thought. Hence, it is needed to be aware that it would come when we would hardly be able to find a molecule remotely resembling DNA, RNA, or even proteins. Nevertheless, it seems that a grand evolution must have happened between the phases of protocellular and bacterial evolutionary history.

The design of this chapter is focus in proposing a working hypothesis, which addresses the problem of the emergence and self-maintenance of protocellular organization; and also the kind of evolutionary mechanism before life arose.

Some results concluded from recent researches indicate that the development of interconnected molecular processes from scratch is possible, which would evolve from random initial conditions.

At this point, it is shown that the most primary or basic properties of biological systems found in evolution are connected with new observations, and theoretical and practical implications. This happened due to how prebiotic protocells adapted and survived on that remote era. Moreover, the special self-organizing dynamics of biological systems suggests that its distinctive faculties could have been developed in prebiotic era much earlier than hitherto thought.

Keywords: bio-meaning; cohesion; constraints; evolvabilityprotocell; robustness.

1. Introduction

The application of informational concepts in biology was present for many of the decades in the twentieth century (for instance, Schrödinger 1944).

Although we can see arguments defending its validity (Williams 1992, Godfrey-Smith 2000, Griffiths 2001), other studies point out the importance that these concepts should be applied consistently (Sterelny et al. 1996). Obviously, some researches state that these uses are erroneous and they do not add knowledge to our understanding of the more essential aspects in biology (Kitcher 2001).

Nevertheless, the use of the term 'information' exists and is associated with the presence of contingencies and correlations between certain variables inside the phenomena. The Shannon's information notion could be applied to almost everything that has some alternatives stages in one specific moment (Shannon 1948).

It is clear that this specific use of information is not so problematic, due to its usefulness of quantifying facts about contingency and correlation. However, some new and special kinds of relation or property into biological phenomena are not introduced.

In this sense, it is avowed that genes contain information of proteins they make; but, in this case, it is concluded that no more than certain gene- stage are closely related with the production (synthesis) of certain proteins.

Despite, some researchers suspect there are some missing aspects in biology with information notion application in the sense of Shannon's information.

Recently, Kauffman and co-workers has published a paper on this topic. Initially, they proposed that while the Shannon theory is compelling, its scope is limited. Particularly, they stated that Shannon's information cannot describe information contained in a living organism. Subsequently, they introduced the notion of relativity of information and explained that the concept of information depends on the context of where and how it is being used. Finally, the authors examined the link between information and organization, showing that these two are intimately associated in biotic systems (Kauffman et al. 2008).

Furthermore, Maynard Smith & Szathmáry (1998) pointed out that several major transitions in the organization and transmission of genetic information from one generation to the next one occurred during evolution.

Alternatively, Jablonka worked to widen the notion of biological information developed by Maynard Smith. Not only she did not limit this notion to just genetic information but she also addressed other types of biological information, e.g. epigenetic information (Jablonka 2002).

On the other hand, there is a growing conviction concerning the information emerging role as a fundamental building block in physics and other sciences. Moreover leading researches in this field declare that this conviction is not a construction of mind instead it is a fundamental element of the physical world (Lloyd 2000, 2006, von Baeyer 2005, Seife 2006).

Subsequently, it seems that information has become an important issue in many sciences. On account of that, a study of what is involved in biological information and its role in the dynamics of living systems has turned into a timely and needed topic to address in biology.

Besides, research has been carried out for finding an answer to the question of whether some self-sustaining, autocatalytic networks have the capacity to emerge from random chemical systems once a determined threshold has been passed or, if on the contrary, some fine tuning of the underlying biochemistry is needed for these to be able to materialize (Mossel & Steel 2005).

2. Genetic Information and its Relatives

As previously considered, genetic information consists in information leading to proteins and is enclosed in sequence of DNA bases. Molecular mechanisms involved in these processes imply several coordinated molecular types and structures inside the cell, as well as, the existence of external signals (Ichinose et al. 2008).

In past decades, subsequent to one of the most famous molecular biology researches (Watson & Crick 1953), the immense quantity of laboratory experiments lead to the current notion of the implicated processes in the gene information transmission yielding proteins production.

The main steps in this issue are sketched in the well known "central dogma of molecular biology". Firstly, the information contained in DNA is transmitted to RNA (*Transcription*). Secondly, the information in RNA is used to construct proteins (*Translation*).

This schematic representation hides the intricate number of molecular mechanisms involved in each of these steps. For instance, the existence of pre and post processes of transcription and translation is found besides the complex concerted action between macromolecules in transcription and translation.

If deep problems in this study subject are sought, a question of how much it is known in regulatory processes guiding gene transcription would be asked. In particular, is the identification between a gene and its corresponding transcription factor already reached?

In a recent study is pointed out the difficulties to unwind the regulation of transcription for living-cell individual genes. It is proposed a method of imaging the transcriptional dynamics in Drosophila. A multiphoton microscopy imaging could provide an experimental ability to visualize the assembly and dynamics of individual transcription factors and regulators to target genes in living cells (Yao et al. 2008).

Going beyond, considering the importance of these results and this study subject suggest another kind of inquiry. Do the specific macromolecule action (e.g. DNA) and do the natural selection presence, both in the intertwined relation evolution among macromolecules had the role to fix like metaphorical architects in the process mentioned above?

In other words, how the process of transcription and the process of translation are initially constructed many millions of years ago. Furthermore, what causes such an impressive concerted macromolecular interaction inside each of these important processes and the connection precision of both parts?

Although it is crucial to identify the exact composition of the macromolecules involved in each biological function, it is even more important to provide an explanation for the natural dynamic assembly of the components found in a particular metabolic route.

Thus, it is clear that as long as it has the knowledge of all components in a particular metabolic route, and the understanding of molecular actions of each of these components, the best plausible interpretations is proposed. At the same time, this tentative explanation is expected in concordance with the main body of biological theory.

As a result, few of other researches related to the genetic information dynamics of transmission framework will be analyzed.

The studying the dynamics of individual ribosomes which translate single messenger RNA revealed that the translation occurs through successive translocation-and-pause cycles. Each translocation step contains at least three sub-steps. However, these researches do not clearly explain what causes these sub-steps. Conversely, they detected that the overall rate of translation would depend on the secondary structure of the mRNA (Wen et al. 2008).

The main idea exposed in that study which includes the use of techniques *in vitro* is impressive. Nonetheless, it is not confirmed if these phenomena are also produced *in vivo*. Moreover, do the intricate macromolecular interaction in cytoplasm and do the compounds forming ribosomes play any role in the timing of translocation sub-steps?

On the other hand, it is interesting the pleiotropy considering the analysis on the variety of effects perceived by the specific gene expression. It is known that Phenobarbital is a barbiturate that reduces brain and nervous system activity as well as triggering pleiotropic responses.

In another study, the use of a novel human hepatoma cell line (WGA) which expresses CYP2B6 gene is enlightened (Rencurel et l. 2005). That gene encodes a cytochrome P450 enzymes superfamily member which catalyzes many reactions involved in drug metabolism and synthesis of cholesterol, steroids, and other lipids.

In this research, the authors obtain insights into the regulation of gene expression by barbiturate drugs. They explained that AMP-activated protein kinase (AMPK) could mimic the Phenobarbital induction of CYP2B6. It was because the encounter AMPK activity which increases in cells cultured with Phenobarbital (PB). These findings strongly support a role for AMPK in the PB induction of CYP2B gene expression.

In view of more high levels, one connection among development and epigenetic phenomena would be mentioned.

The origin of cellular identity corresponds to the final product which results from multiple processes. These processes restrict transcription and replication of totipotent-cells-producing programs (Hyrien et al. 1995; Dazy et al. 2006). Some studies focused in totipotent-state nature hypothesize implicated epigenetic-modification deletions in the structure of chromosomes in somatic cells. Those studies also pointed that it can be induced to undergo dedifferentiation into pluripotent embryonic germ cells (Lemaitre et al. 2007).

In the studies cited above, some common themes are able to discern. Firstly, the phenomena addressed involve the presence of coordinated molecular mechanisms displayed in specific pathways; although, a metabolic pathway is only a network. It is important to consider scale-free and small-world networks as essential features of biological systems. For instance, it has been demonstrated that certain kinds of metabolic pathways shows small-world behavior (Wagner & Fell 2001).

Secondly, molecular species behave in certain mechanical ways depending on their dynamic spatial structures; their location and time in where their action is recorded. In presence of other conditions the behaviors or effects not always will be the same.

Thirdly, the intervention of external molecules, whose action is mediated by some structures able to 'recognize' its presence and concentration, exist.

Up to now, two issues could be inquired. Initially, how these networks are formed; and afterward, what could explain in the biology current knowledge the appearance of these kinds of networks emerging spontaneously in nature.

The experiments with Phenobarbital and AMPK directed our inquiries to more thoughtful questions. At first, how molecules match its specific location or how they are 'detected'. In biological systems, the needed short time between some cause and its answer is crucial. Does genetic information control all this dynamic organization? Was natural selection the only driving force which caused the appearance of an extraordinary coordination between biological networks and biological structures?

Moreover, terms such as signals, codes, information, computations, translations, decodes are part of nowadays terminology used in biological papers.

Why can it be concluded that only genetic information is what is called biological information? Or is biological information more than genetic information?

3. Minimal Complexity in Prebiotic Systems

Several authors have put forward the notion that biological information is not exclusively limited to genetic information (for example, epigenetic information in Jablonka 2002).

Nevertheless, there are certain aspects to the notion of biological information that would seem important to discuss if the purpose is to construct it in naturalistic terms.

Once it has been developed in those terms, it would be our guarantee of not using this concept to refer to any sort of adscription or to any type of epiphenomenon.

In other words, we are talking about an explanation that rests on an ontological proposal that defends the existence of emerging phenomena, understood in a strong sense (Holland 1998; Laughlin 2005; Chalmers 2006), an ontology that might explain the causal efficacy of a determined emerging phenomenon:

> "The ability to reduce everything to simple fundamental laws does not imply the ability to start from those laws and reconstruct the universe...The constructionist hypothesis breaks down when confronted with the twin difficulties of scale and complexity...at each level of complexity entirely new properties appear...Psychology is not applied biology, nor is biology applied chemistry..." (Anderson 1972, p. 393)

Living systems began a new level of complexity in terms of universal phenomena, and it is not possible to limit that complexity to just one chapter of applied chemistry. Even though biological phenomena do not run contrary to any law of physics, chemistry, or physical chemistry, it is, however, impossible to reduce them to a lower level of reality.

And this circumstance is owed to the fact that each new level of complexity materializing in the universe implies, by necessity, the emergence of new properties containing causal efficacy that will, in the end, produce new events in our universe.

This is the reason why we also have the certainty that normative emergence is necessary for any naturalistic account of biology. And only within a process metaphysics could the corresponding causally efficacious ontological emergence be defended (Bickhard 2004).

The case of the emergence of living systems implies efficacy to cause determined events, among them being the condition that makes it possible for the materialization of new levels of complexity (interaction with other living systems, the set of cognitive phenomena, human social experiences, etc.) which could not be produced by any event exclusive to physics, chemistry, or physical chemistry.

Therefore, it would seem important for us to study carefully that which made it possible for this new level of complexity to be produced in reality, known as the origin of living systems.

We will approach this issue starting with the time just before life appeared. Put differently, we will dedicate ourselves to the thesis and analysis of one kind of system that could have been present in what we will call the transition stage between inert phenomena (governed solely by the laws of physics, chemistry, and physical chemistry) and the appearance of the first forms of living systems.

This transition stage holds special interest for us since it is what we know as the prebiotic world; hence, we will establish a line of demarcation, separating the inert world from the prebiotic world. The latter is a section of road leading to the world of living systems, and so it might have fundamentally held determined types of systems that would have featured certain degrees of self-organization.

Moreover, we contend this prebiotic world might have been comprised by an almost continuous series of systems, and when we talk about continuous, it is in the sense that the most fundamental properties of these different types of systems – behaving as the details of a specific, self-organizing kind – would have been shared by all of them.

The trigger for all this movement or dynamic from the world of the inert to the world of living systems was the system that originated the prebiotic world.

We are calling it the **Informational Dynamic System** (Riofrio 2007), and it would have already contained within itself a certain degree of complexity that could not be reduced into its parts or constituents.

Expressed in another way, we assert the Informational Dynamic System is one that spurred the emergence of certain properties that will turn out to be grounds for the appearance of definite events concerning its surrounding environment as well as its dynamic internal milieu, events that would not be possible to generate by any phenomenon exclusive to physics, chemistry, or physical chemistry.

Therefore, we hold the Informational Dynamic System was already an autonomous agent and, at the same time, a kind of adaptive complex system.

In the words of Kauffman, an autonomous agent is:

"...the autonomous agent must be an open thermodynamic system driven by outside sources of matter or energy –hence "food"- and the continual driving of the system by such "food" holds the system away from equilibrium... [Then]...An autonomous agent is a reproducing system that carries out at least one thermodynamic work cycle..." (Kauffman 2000, p. 64).

Accordingly, an autonomous agent possesses a set of characteristics which needs to be underscored. First, it is an open thermodynamic system. Second, it is one far from thermodynamic equilibrium (since it is capable of obtaining matter or energy from its surroundings). Lastly, it can reproduce itself and carry out at least one thermodynamic work cycle.

We consider, then, our hypothetical system could have contained the minimum necessary capacities to lead us towards the first forms of life as well as have all characteristics of an autonomous agent.

Informational Dynamic Systems (IDS) are comprised of at least three classes of processes (Riofrio 2007, pp.235–240). The first of these enables the system to maintain itself in the far from thermodynamic equilibrium state, a micro-cycle that is capable of generating work (chemical work).

The second one is the spontaneous self-organization of a protoplasmic membrane – made of simple amphiphilic structures – which mimic, at least qualitatively, some of the basic processes displayed by the current plasma membranes (Segré et al. 2001).

The third group is a network of reactions that would perform the regeneration of the organizational dynamic, maintenance, and reproduction processes of the informational dynamic system.

The minimum complexity we have just pointed out is necessary for conditions to be ripe for the emergence of the most fundamental properties of life:

"…As the constriction maintaining them far from equilibrium is an intrinsic part of their dynamic organization, there are strategies they can develop that manage to keep this state in conditions compatible with the laws imposed on them by the material world… two new characteristics that emerge in the system – in the local interactions – and are directed at maintaining the far from equilibrium state… information and function….. Therefore, our proposal of the notion of information-function – as a characteristic emerging in the informational dynamic systems – is a relational concept that is strongly governed (ruled) by the far from thermodynamic equilibrium state…" (Riofrio 2007, pp. 240–241)

"…Everything taken together brings us to the thesis that starting the process from inanimate to animate could have been produced by the appearance of a type of dynamic system whose organization is an *informational and functional dynamic organization*…" (Ibid, p. 243)

On the other hand, the IDS is also a Complex Adaptive System (CAS) since it is reasonable to think a type of evolution can be found throughout the prebiotic era that (1) caused these systems to achieve a certain amount of adaptation to their surrounding environments and (2) brought about the existence of a sort of "inheritance" among different types of systems that materialized during that remote time period.

4. The Tree of Life

The three great domains on the tree of life are bacteria, eukarya, and archaea.

According to Woese, discovering the existence of Archae in different environments on planet Earth (Woese & Fox 1977; Woese et al. 1990; Theron & Cloete 2000; Pace 2006), together with uncovering the growing importance of Horizontal Gene Transfer (HGT) during early evolution (Gogarten et al. 1989; Hilario & Gogarten 1993; Gogarten et al. 2002; Huang & Gogarten 2009), impels us to review seriously and profoundly a topic that has not, until today, been broached in its real magnitude.

The upshot is, then, *the evolution of the modern cell* becoming one of the most important issues in biology when taken as a whole (Woese 2002; Woese 2004).

The following statement is known as Darwin's Doctrine of Common Descent, evolution's most primary assertion and the cornerstone of modern biology:

"Probably all of the organic beings which have ever lived on this earth have descended from some one primordial form . . . ." (Darwin 1859, p. 484).

Nonetheless, recent study results seem to have brought that claim into question:

"...There is evidence, good evidence, to suggest that the basic organization of the cell had not yet completed its evolution at the stage represented by the root of the universal tree. The best of this evidence comes from the three main cellular information processing systems. Translation was highly developed by that stage: rRNAs, tRNAs, and the (large) elongation factors were by then all basically in near modern form; hence, their universal distributions. Almost all of the tRNA charging systems were in modern form as well... But, whereas the majority of ribosomal proteins are universal in distribution, a minority of them is not. A relatively small cadre is specific to the bacteria, a somewhat larger set common and confined to the archaea and eukaryotes, and a few others are uniquely eukaryotic." (Woese 2002, p. 8742)

On one hand, outcomes from completed comparative studies seem to be suggesting the three great cellular designs we are currently managing did not simultaneously achieve the state of modern cells (a situation that would imply being in possession of the sufficient macromolecular arsenal required for replication, transcription, and genetic translation mechanisms):

"...A modern type of genome replication mechanism did not exist at the root of the universal tree... Virtually no homology (orthology) exists between the bacterial genome replication mechanism and that basically common to the archaea and the eukaryotes (although a number of bacterial and archaeal DNA polymerases, some of which serve repair functions, do show sequence homology). Modern genome replication mechanisms seem to have evolved twice... These fundamental differences in the genetic machinery constitute a *prima facie* case to the effect that the era of cellular evolution continued well into the evolutionary period encompassed by the universal phylogenetic tree. It would also seem that the order of maturation of the information processing systems was first translation, then transcription, and finally modern genome structure and replication..." (Ibid, p. 8743)

So, cellular entities that lacked the capacity to establish evolutionary lineages might have been the ones populating the epoch prior to the one in which materializing was the new cellular organization so called modern cells contain.

As a consequence, the most important evolutionary motor during that remote, previous time period could have been Horizontal Gene Transfer (HGT):

"...The degree of connectedness of the componentry of the cell has profound evolutionary implications... were that organization simple and modular enough, all of the componentry of a cell could potentially be horizontally displaceable over time. The organismal genealogical record would be ephemeral; *no stable record could exist*. Suppose that the primitive ancestors of modern cells were of this nature. That would mean that *at its beginning, cellular evolution would have been driven in the main by HGT...*" (Ibid, p. 8744)

What is more, on account of the fact there was no sort of heredity between parent and offspring cells, the time it took to pass through the stage of the origin of modern cells is also the time in which we can see the appearance of the capacity for possible species genesis.

Hence, that barrier becomes the Darwinian Threshold and turns out to be, at the same time, the Origin of Species since it is the origin of speciation:

"...In its subsequent evolution a primitive cell of this type would become ever more complex... In other words, there would come a stage in the evolution of cellular organization where the organismal genealogical trace (recorded in common histories of the genes of an organism) goes from being completely ephemeral to being increasingly permanent... This point in evolution, this transition, is appropriately call the "Darwinian Threshold." On the far side of that Threshold "species" as we know them cannot exist. Once it is crossed, however, speciation becomes possible... The Darwinian Threshold truly represents the Origin of Species, in that it represents the origin of speciation as we know it..." (Ibid, p. 8744)

Out of this entire, huge collection of studies, Woese suggests, in his most recent work, certain reasons that could allow him to make·a case for there being a time in which biological evolution was produced in a non-Darwinian manner:

"...The root of the universal tree is an artifact resulting from forcing the evolutionary course into tree representation when that representation is inappropriate... In the pre-Darwinian era the evolutionary course cannot be represented by an organismal tree topology. It is only after a more advanced stage in cellular evolution has been reached that tree representation begins to become useful. That stage is the Darwinian threshold, the critical point before which HGT dominates the evolutionary dynamic and after which it does not—thus allowing stable organismal genealogies to emerge... Only then can living systems finally be conceptualized in discreet, idiosyncratic species terms ..." (Woese 2004, p. 184)

Moreover, Woese deems we must respond to three fundamental questions in order to understand cellular evolution, and the most important of these makes reference to the origin of the great many novelties needed for constructing the incredibly coordinated, macromolecular scaffolding that constitutes modern cellular organization:

"Three questions are central to understanding cellular evolution: (i) when (under what circumstances) did the evolution of (proteinaceous) cells begin, (ii) how was the incredible novelty needed to create these first proteinaceous cells generated, and (iii) did all extant cellular life ultimately arise from one or from more than one common ancestor? The second of these questions, how the overwhelming amount of novelty needed to bring modern cells into existence was generated, is the central and most challenging question of the three..." (Ibid, p. 182)

5. Pre-Darwinian Evolution

Our intention here is not to analyze Woese's proposals in detail. Instead, it is to find a possible explanation to the second of the three questions raised above: "...the incredible novelty needed to create these first proteinaceous cells generated..." (Woese 2004, p. 182).

As stated above in the beginning, our proposal is set at the start up of the prebiotic world.

Hence, we hold (with greater conviction than does Woese) the kind of evolution in that ancient time, in this, the initial prebiotic era (from the origin of the Informational Dynamic System onward), was of a non-Darwinian nature (Riofrio 2008).

In that remote time, it is practically impossible to uphold the hypothesis that suggests existence of genetic information; neither genes nor any such other macromolecular component as RNA or proteins were part of reality then (Zimmer 2005; Bernstein 2006; Norris et al. 2007; Gleiser & Walker 2008).

We assume, then, it could be possible to think there was a type of cellular organization, separate from its environment, yet with the capacity to interact with its surroundings and its internal milieu.

The latter is a capacity the Informational Dynamic System possesses because the kinds of processes its "plasma membrane" exhibits.

In the same way, it is a system that maintains itself far from thermodynamic equilibrium because the connection between one exergonic process linked to an endergonic process and both linked to ancestral "energy currency" molecules is a type of process the IDS uses and that enables it to have sufficient amounts of needed free energy for doing some type of chemical, molecular work (Kauffman 2000, pp. 63–69).

It should be pointed out that both types of processes are also two types of constraints the IDS possesses (Riedl 1978; Schwenk 1995).

Besides, the third type of process regulates the connection among all three, thereby enabling this network of simple molecular compounds to perform well, to grow, and to reproduce.

Maintaining the far from thermodynamic equilibrium state is a fundamental characteristic enabling the IDS to be able to explore new connections and new compounds in respective processes as these allow and /or contribute to that state, i.e. the state of being far from thermodynamic equilibrium.

This will be the principal characteristic of the IDS (for more information, consult Riofrio 2007, particularly pg. 242 – 245).

So, all behaviors, happenings, mechanisms, components, etc. influencing the IDS will lead to one of two possibilities: maintaining / increasing its far from thermodynamic equilibrium state or, quite the opposite, reducing and weakening that state.

As with evolution prior to the appearance of the domains of bacteria, eukarya, and archaea, which was mainly governed by HGT, reproduction of these initial groups of prebiotic systems was dominated by some type of horizontal capacity and novelty exchange that enabled them to adapt to ever changing and completely hostile surroundings.

In other words, appearance of a prebiotic, adaptive evolution would have involved some type of component or process exchange (through direct protocell-to-protocell contact) that would have produced a benefit or maintained these systems in the far from thermodynamic equilibrium state.

It is also possible there might have been some form of asexual reproduction (similar a *binary fission* found in both bacteria and archaea).

Since it is not possible to talk about different "species" of prebiotic systems, we furthermore cannot bring up the idea of biological heredity as understood in Darwinian terms.

Indeed, during those distant times, evolution was a community based experience with no stable genealogical records:

> "...the primitive cell is a loose confederation of a relatively small number of rather simple modules. For cells of this type, most if not all cellular componentry would be open to HGT, making the combinatorics of gene transfer far and away the major factor in early cellular evolution..." (Woese 2004, p. 181)

6. Prebiotic Information

During a time period when it is not even possible to imagine a possible horizontal gene exchange between prebiotic cellular systems, we have to wonder what, reasonably, can be asserted.

Let us start, then, from the design of our Informational Dynamic System and focus on the self-assembly and self-organization logic of our proposal.

In essence, the protocell we are advocating is a dynamic structure containing three kinds of processes, each one relating to the other two.

And it is through a constraint which maintains the protocell in the far from thermodynamic equilibrium state that we find a condition which fundamentally defines our IDS at its most basic of definitions.

What our IDS will seek out at all times is to maintain or to increase its far from thermodynamic equilibrium state; therefore, each of its processes (or those it will gain) contribute (or will contribute) to the protocell expressing its fundamental nature.

This network of interconnected processes constituting the IDS is an informational and functional dynamic network.

This means information is transmitted and functions are performed at the same time in each particular IDS process.

Yet, before analyzing the notion of information in our protocell, it is important to discover if it would be possible to produce naturally some similar collection of processes, in accordance with the laws of chemistry and physics.

Specifically, what similar, prebiotic, dynamic structure (to our IDS) might have appeared in that distant past without necessitating prior existence and guidance from any type of genetic information.

A model of protocell self-assembly and replication was recently put forward that might demonstrate emergence of cellular structures where simple metabolism is linked to a protoplasmic membrane, something that is much easier than was before believed.

And what is even more revealing is this protocell is capable of reproduction, an expected outcome that likewise may be recreated at some point in lab experiments:

"...This result strongly suggests that the basic set of rules and the logic of the process (more than the exact parameters) is the key for finding a self-replicating protocell. Such positive result indicates that very simple mechanisms of micelle-metabolism coupling in a primitive Earth scenario might have been to trigger the proliferation of simple protocells...it fairly well illustrates how robust is the coupling between self-assembled amphiphiles coupled to an external source of precursors and displaying a simple catalytic reaction. The robustness of the observed results supports the view of cellular life as a likely event to happen provided that the basic molecular logic is in place.

Self-assembly is an essential component in the path towards cellular systems. The spontaneous generation of spatial order, allowing to easily define a container, is still at work at different scales of biological organization...the dynamics of many subcellular compartments take advantage of the physics of self-assembly..." (Solé 2009, pp. 282–283)

Our thesis does not just comprehend a protoplasmic membrane connected to simple metabolism, but also a very important process connected to these two, one that enables the Informational Dynamic System to maintain a thermodynamic state which makes possible and simplifies process correlation (Kosztin & Schulten 2004; Levine 2005).

So then, it seems that our dynamic protocellular structure might include an additional factor that would positively contribute to the possibility of it being simulated and even perhaps reproduced in future lab experiments.

On another point, the fact that the previously introduced model is "...within the context of information-free systems..." (Solé 2009, p. 279) has obliged this researcher to arrive at the conclusion that evolution of his protocells is not possible "...since no information is included in this system, no further evolution is expected to occur..." (Ibid, p. 282).

What type of information is this author referring to? It is evident he is thinking in terms of a blueprint or instructions containing information, whose expression in current cells is the DNA molecule.

To us, biological information is one of the most essential properties of living beings. In fact, we deem it to be of the utmost importance, so much so that we state without pause it can be found within the most basic aspects of the definition of a living entity.

For that reason, we believe this property emerged at the exact same point in time the door to the prebiotic world was flung open, and thus it produced not only biological information, but also biological function, these appearing at the absolute critical moment of the first protocell genesis on primitive earth:

"...information emerges in the biological world as 'information with meaning' or 'meaningful information'. To be exact, it emerges as information with biological meaning or what we like to call 'bio-meaning'..." (Riofrio 2008, p. 365)

But when we bring up the matter of information in protocells, we are not making exclusive reference to genetic information. As a result, we believe this is a type of information distributed within the interior of all Informational Dynamic Systems:

"...the information flow could be detected by the occurrences of mechanisms that are related to the execution of some function inside the dynamic organization of these systems..." (Riofrio 2008, p. 371)

Besides, what holds great importance to us is preparing a proposal on biological information that is developed in naturalistic terms; hence, the notion of information must be connected logically to something in the real world.

That is why our thesis includes relating the ideas of "information with meaning", a "sign", and "matter-energy variations":

"...It seems appropriate, in a naturalistic approach, to connect the matter–energy variations with the possible emergence of signs...whatever kind of energy variation may occur in a biological system, it will only turn into a sign...when the system has the capability to react accordingly. And this happens when the energy variation impacts something in the system and is incorporated into the system—as a variation—with the capacity of becoming part of the system's processes..." (Ibid., p. 365)

When a matter-energy variation is produced in the surrounding environment, it may have an effect on an Informational Dynamic System. First, the variation, whatever it might be, could be transmitted to certain protoplasmic membrane components. As the transmission process of this variation continues, the IDS will face one of these possibilities at some point in time: (1) variation will either help maintain or increase the far from thermodynamic equilibrium state or (2) variation could weaken, negatively influence, or destroy the far from thermodynamic equilibrium state.

The first possibility would be positive for the IDS. For the second, it will depend upon variation's degree of negative influence and the robustness of the group of IDS's experiencing the situation:

> "...Once these systems are confronted by a specific, environmentally-generated problem, the different possible solutions (strategies), produced in the system's protoplasmic membrane as a product of the reproduction of these systems, are nothing more than the maintenance of the integrity of their dynamic organization, i.e., the maintenance of the close interrelation between the three kinds of processes that would result in the physical expression of information, function, and autonomy at every moment and in each type of pre-biotic system. In other words, the system evolved by overcoming environmentally-generated problems through different ways of preserving the basic properties which characterized it..." (Ibid., p. 372)

Strictly speaking, since the IDS possesses both biological function and biological information and a strong connection exists between them, it therefore has the capacity to be an autonomous agent.

When it is time to start a reproductive cycle, a specific IDS will use components it finds to 'duplicate' its process network. This duplication does not refer to a specific series of components forming a determined type of process. Rather, it is a reference to the capacity of being a protocell, the dynamic organization of which is informational and functional, and this was the class of "heredity" produced during those beginning stages of the prebiotic world:

> "...The control property is distributed in the interdependence between the networks of processes so that the system's cohesion towards the far from the thermodynamic equilibrium is maintained by the intertwined correlation between biological functions and bio-meaning...preserving not so much the chemical structure of the

molecules as the interrelation between the three kinds of processes that make up the dynamic self-organization of the IDS. It is the environment that created conditions that were influencing—but not determining—the specific self-organization of the protocells. Faced with an environment filled with materials that could be used to build systems from scratch, the IDS would have developed ways to construct a network of processes that were maintaining the characteristic self-organization of Informational Dynamic Systems and their offspring..." (Ibid., p. 373)

This means each mechanism at work inside every process "contributes" to the entire system being in a state far from thermodynamic equilibrium.

Every process will accomplish its "biological function" as it carries out a specific action in these protocells' molecular dynamic and simultaneously participates in keeping or increasing the far from thermodynamic equilibrium state.

Likewise, every energy variation that accompanies a specific mechanism inside a molecular reaction that is part of a process type which increases, maintains, or weakens the far from thermodynamic equilibrium state of our protocell will be the biological information eliciting a response within the IDS, in accordance with variation itself.

References

Anderson, P. W. (1972). More is Different. *Science*, 177, pp. 393–96.

Bernstein, M. (2006). Prebiotic materials from on and off the early Earth. *Phil.Trans. R. Soc. B*, 361, pp. 1689–1702.

Bickhard, M. H. (2004). Part II: Applications of Process-Based Theories: Process and Emergence: Normative Function and Representation. *Axiomathes — An International Journal in Ontology and Cognitive Systems*, 14 (1), pp. 121–155.

Chalmers, D. J. (2006). Strong and Weak Emergence. In P. Clayton and P. Davies (eds.) *The Re-emergence of Emergence*. Oxford University Press.

Darwin, C. (1859). *On the Origin of Species*. Harvard Univ. Press Cambridge, MA, and London.

Dazy, S., Gandrillon, O., Hyrien, O. and Prioleau M. N. (2006). Broadening of DNA replication origin usage during metazoan cell differentiation. *EMBO Rep*, 7, pp. 806–811.

Gleiser, M. and Walker, S. I. (2008). An Extended Model for the Evolution of Prebiotic Homochirality: A Bottom-Up Approach to the Origin of Life. *Orig. Life Evol. Biosph.*, 38, pp. 293–315.

Godfrey-Smith, P. (2000). On the Theoretical Role of 'Genetic Coding'. *Philosophy of Science*, 67, pp. 26–44.

Gogarten, J. P., Doolittle, W. F. and Lawrence, J. G. (2002). Prokaryotic evolution in light of gene transfer. *Mol Biol Evol*, 19(12), pp. 2226–2238.

Gogarten, J. P., et al., (1989). Evolution of the vacuolar H+-ATPase: implications for the origin of eukaryotes. *Proc. Natl. Acad. Sci. U.S.A.*, 86(17), pp. 6661–6665.

Griffiths, P. E (2001). Genetic Information: A Metaphor in Search of a Theory. *Philosophy of Science*, 68, pp. 394–412.

Hilario, E. and Gogarten, J. P. (1993). Horizontal transfer of ATPase genes--the tree of life becomes a net of life. *Biosystems*, 31(2–3), pp. 111–119.

Holland, J. H. (1998). *Emergence: From Chaos to Order*. Basic Books.

Huang, J. and Gogarten, J. P. (2009). Ancient gene transfer as a tool in phylogenetic reconstruction. *Methods Mol Biol.*, 532, pp. 127–139.

Hyrien, O., Maric, C. and Mechali, M. (1995). Transition in specification of embryonic metazoan DNA replication origins. *Science*, 270, pp. 994–997.

Ichinose, N., Yada, T., Gotoh, O. and Aihara, K. (2008). Reconstruction of transcription-translation dynamics with a model of gene networks. *J Theor. Biol.*, 255(4), pp. 378–386.

Jablonka, E. (2002). Information: Its Interpretation, Its Inheritance and Its Sharing. *Philosophy of Science*, 69, pp. 578–605.

Kauffman, S., Logan, R. K., Este, R., Goebel, R., Hobill, D. and Shmulevich, I. (2008). Propagating organization: an enquiry. *Biology and Philosophy*, 23(1), pp. 27–45.

Kauffman, S. (2000). *Investigations*. Oxford University Press.

Kitcher, P. S. (2001). Battling the Undead: How (and How Not) to Resist Genetic Determinism. In R. Singh, C. Krimbas, D. Paul and J. Beatty (eds.), *Thinking about Evolution: Historical, Philosophical and Political Perspectives*. Cambridge University Press.

Kosztin, I. and Schulten, K. (2004). Fluctuation-driven molecular transport through an asymmetric membrane channel. Physical Review Letters, 93, p. 238102.

Laughlin, R. (2005). A Different Universe: Reinventing Physics from the Bottom Down. Basic Books.

Lemaitre, J. M., Gregoire, D. and Mechali, M. (2007). Replication, development and totipotency. *Med Sci (Paris)*, 23(3), pp. 245–247.

Levine, R. D. (2005). *Molecular Reaction Dynamics*. Cambridge University Press.

Lloyd, S. (2000). Ultimate physical limits to computation. *Nature*, 406, pp. 1047–1054.

Lloyd, S. (2006). *Programming the Universe*. Knopf.

Mossel, E. and Steel, M. (2005). Random biochemical networks: the probability of self-sustaining autocatalysis. *Journal of Theoretical Biology*, 233(3), pp. 327–336.

Norris, V., Hunding, A., Kepes, F., Lancet, D., Minsky, A., Raine, D., Root-Bernstein, R. and Sriram, K. (2007). Question 7: The First Units of Life Were Not Simple Cells. *Orig. Life Evol. Biosph.*, 37, pp. 429–432.

Pace, N. R. (2006). Time for a change. *Nature*, 441 (7091), p. 289.

Rencurel, F., Stenhouse, A., Hawley, S. A., Friedberg, T., Hardie, D. G., Sutherland, C. and Wolf, C. R. (2005). AMP-activated protein kinase mediates phenobarbital induction of CYP2B gene expression in hepatocytes and a newly derived human hepatoma cell line. *J Biol Chem.*, 280 (6), pp. 4367–4373.

Riedl, R. (1978). *Order in Living organisms: a systems analysis of evolution.* John Wiley & Sons.

Riofrio, W. (2007). Informational Dynamic Systems: Autonomy, Information, Function. In C. Gershenson, D. Aerts & B. Edmonds (*eds*), *Worldviews, Science, and Us: Philosophy and Complexity.* World Scientific, Singapore, pp. 232–249.

Riofrio, W. (2008). Understanding the Emergence of Cellular Organization. *Biosemiotics*, 1 (3), pp. 361–377.

Schrödinger, E. (1944). *What is Life?* Cambridge University Press.

Schwenk, K. (1995). A utilitarian approach to evolutionary constraint. *Zoology*, 98, pp. 251–262.

Segré, D., Ben-Eli, D., Deamer, D. W., and Lancet, D. (2001). The lipid world. *Origins Life Evol. Biosph.*, 31, pp. 119–145.

Seife, C. (2006). *Decoding the Universe.* Penguin Books.

Shannon, C. (1948). A Mathematical Theory of Communication. *Bell Systems Technical Journal*, 27, pp. 279–423, pp. 623–656.

Solé, R.V. (2009). *Evolution and self-assembly of protocells. Int J Biochem Cell Biol.*, 41 (2), pp. 274–284.

Sterelny, K., Smith, K. and Dickison, M. (1996). The Extended Replicator. *Biology and Philosophy*, 11, pp. 377–403.

Theron, J. and Cloete, T. E. (2000). Molecular techniques for determining microbial diversity and community structure in natural environments. *Crit. Rev. Microbiol.*, 26 (1), pp. 37–57.

von Baeyer, H. C. (2005). *Information: The New Language of Science.* Harvard University Press.

Wagner, A. and Fell, D. A. (2001). The small world inside large metabolic networks. *Proceedings of the Royal Society of London B*, 268, pp. 1803–1810.

Watson, J. D. and Crick, F. H. C. (1953). A Structure for Deoxyribose Nucleic Acid. *Nature*, 171, pp. 737–738.

Wen, J-D, Lancaster, L., Hodges, C., Zeri, A. C., Yoshimura, S. H., Noller, H. F., Bustamante, C. and Tinoco, I. (2008). Following translation by single ribosomes one codon at a time. *Nature*, 452, pp. 598–603.

Williams, G. C. (1992). *Natural Selection: Levels, Domains, and Challenges.* Oxford University Press.

Woese, C. (2002). On the evolution of cells. *Proc. Natl. Acad. Sci. U.S.A.*, 99(13), pp. 8742–8747.

Woese, C. (2004). A New Biology for a New Century. *Microbiol Mol Biol Rev.*, 68(2), pp. 173–186.

Woese, C. R., Kandler, O. and Wheelis, M. L. (1990). Towards a natural system of organisms: proposal for the domains Archaea, Bacteria, and Eucarya. *Proc. Natl. Acad. Sci. U.S.A.*, 87 (12), pp. 4576–4579.

Woese, C. and Fox, G. (1977). Phylogenetic structure of the prokaryotic domain: the primary kingdoms. *Proc. Natl. Acad. Sci. U.S.A.*, 74(11), pp. 5088–5090.

Yao, J., Zobeck, K. L., Lis, J. T. and Webb, W. W. (2008). Imaging transcription dynamics at endogenous genes in living Drosophila tissues. *Methods*, 45(3), pp. 233–241.

Zimmer, C. (2005). How and Where Did Life on Earth Arise? *Science*, 309, p. 89.

CHAPTER 13

SUPER-RECURSIVE FEATURES OF EVOLUTIONARY PROCESSES AND THE MODELS FOR COMPUTATIONAL EVOLUTION

Darko Roglic

Split, Croatia
E-mail: darko.roglic@st.t-com.hr

To build the systems that can adapt to their environments and learn from their experience is a long-standing goal and today it attracts researchers from many fields. But the power of evolutionary information processing that allows biological complex systems to adapt is still out of reach. With its extraordinary evolvable capabilities to adapt in rapidly changing and extremely hostile environment, brainless problem solvers such as bacteria successfully perform emergent computation for which they have no predetermined instructions or any *a priori* given referential or target values toward which they could converge. It is hard to capture adequately the adaptive efficiency of bacterial 'machines' within algorithmic notion of computation of Church-Turing thesis (CTT). With respect to different kinds of evolutionary information processing, presented in this paper, and in the direction of recently suggested study of computational evolution, we find it more adequate to exploit the diversity of algorithmic universe which has been revealed by the theory of super-recursive algorithms. According to CTT, in the current computational machines there is no place for mutations (mistakes in the genetic instruction set that survive actions of repair mechanisms and become possible source of inventions) which is one of the central concepts in the biology. Hence, emergent processes of evolution cannot even start by computation of Turing machine. The super-recursive algorithms are basis of a new paradigm for computation that changes computational procedures. Computation of Inductive Turing machines based on super-recursive algorithms presents transition from terminating computation to emergent computation. They work with the finite objects and obtain the results in a finite period of time without halting. Additionally, we may identify different characteristics in the processes of adaptation of bacteria which we discuss here as super-recursive features of evolutionary information processing. The model of evolutionary computer discussed here is the one we need to do experiments that specifically test for essential questions related to computational evolution and that could possibly lead to exploitation of physical ideas about the nature of evolution.

1. Introduction

To build the systems that can adapt to their environments and learn from their experience is the long-standing goal and today it attracts researchers from many fields. According to Turing biographer Hodges, during the war, Turing started to attach great importance to the ability of computers to modify their own programs and do what programmers could not have foreseen [Hodges, 2000]. In order to elaborate the goal of designing computers that can modify their own programs in the course of adaptation this study uses our knowledge of natural evolution of biological systems.

Generally we know that biological systems have many properties that are desired in computational systems. Biological systems are robust, in that if some processors (e.g. white blood cells, a single neuron in an organism) fail, the whole system does not come to a crushing halt like a traditional computer would, but is able to keep running viably. Then, biological systems are very good at adapting to changing circumstances. Such adaptability is essential for autonomy in the real world. Harnessing evolutionary processes, we may believe, could help us perform new computations which could not be performed without them.

Recently, the group of authors have exposed the research agenda to develop a new field: computational evolution (CE) [Banzhaf *et.al.*, 2006]. The authors suggest that the current artificial evolution (AE: evolutionary programming, genetic algorithms, evolutionary strategies and genetic programming) could be transformed into CE by incorporating algorithmic analogues of our current understanding of molecular and evolutionary biology that could solve previously unimaginable or intractable computational and biological problems. They uncovered the limitations of the current AE approaches which might be adequate for solving a single, specific optimization or design problem but solving more difficult problems will require a richer evolutionary understanding. "Complexity and robustness in nature", authors argue, "is proof that biologically inspired processes can be powerful algorithmic tools."

At a glance, one could find that computational evolution is related with the field of computational science i.e. scientific computing that uses computers to analyze and solve scientific and engineering problems. In practical sense, it is typically the application of computer simulation and other forms of computation to problems in various scientific disciplines. But additionally, we may find that CE could pose, for example, the question "whether it is possible to construct a program that functions like an organism, with interacting software objects (analogues of cells) that collectively perform a global function such as providing operating system services (such as file management), with the ability to respond gracefully to demand and damage (analogously to homeostasis)?" [Banzhaf *et.al.*, 2006] This question does not imply computer simulation of biological organisms but it rather describes computer programs that function like biological organisms or autonomous systems that can undergo computational evolution. If we want to consider such or similar questions in the future then computational evolution will guide us primarily to investigate whether CE justifies what it immediately and purely indicates – namely, the central issue in this context is whether evolution is a computational process.

From mathematical point of view, computers function under the control of algorithms so, to understand and explore the possibilities of computers and their boundaries, we have to study algorithms. Yet, the scrutiny of the concept of algorithm was not the subject of the CE guidelines in [Banzhaf *et.al.*, 2006] and it has been taken as granted. However, CE proposals encounter some essential questions: Is evolution algorithmic? Is Turing machine evolvable? By what kinds of evolutionary processes could a certain computable mechanism (program) arise without human assistance? Could a particular molecular mechanism, once developed (by evolution) and implemented into computers, have the computable power equivalent to the power it has within biological systems? Finally, is it possible that such biological-like computation has power beyond Turing machine and if so how to asses such a computation?

If we consider evolution in terms of information processing then we may define its intrinsic property that selection operates all the time over finite set of objects without halting and it achieves the results (say new adaptive functions) non-randomly in finite time. Accordingly, we may suspect that arbitrary computational machine capable of evolution is equivalent to an Inductive Turing Machine (ITM) for which it has been already shown that it possesses similar favorable properties and that it is more powerful than ordinary Turing machine. Namely, computation of ITM is based on super-recursive algorithms. [Burgin, 2005] Theory of super-recursive algorithms (TSRA) extends our notion of algorithms and according to the theory they allow us to compute what we held previously as non-computable. I suggest, with this paper, that study of computational evolution could take this into consideration.

Let only briefly consider here why someone would think that TSRA are more suitable formalism for evolutionary information processes of the living systems than Church-Turing thesis (CTT)? Let me discuss the following example. According to CTT, it is not possible to find a procedure or to write a program that allows us to repair all the bugs of computer programs. Generally, Turing machine cannot 'survive' (solve a problem of) randomly appearing mistakes. Additionally, this implies that mistakes of a TM cannot survive. This is obviously true but it has no sense in the current computational paradigm of CTT. In biology, this is of great importance because mistakes (nucleotide misinsertions) can survive actions of repair mechanisms and they become mutations. Mutations (changes of genetic instructions) are processed by emergent processes of evolutionary information processing systems (EIS). Without mutations there is no diversity and selection has nothing to select. Hence, evolution cannot even start by computation of TM. On the contrary, the super-recursive algorithms are basis of computation that changes computational procedures. They have been built by modifications of recursive algorithms which allow continuous development of variety of new algorithms. Computation of Inductive Turing machines (ITM) based on super-recursive algorithms present a transition from terminating computation to intrinsically emerging computation. The main advantage of ITM is that they work with the finite objects and obtain the results in a finite period of time.

Organization of this paper has the following order of general consideration: how biological systems perform information processing (computation), what are the characteristics of such evolutionary information processes, and how to use ideas from natural biological systems to develop new kinds of computational evolution systems. Hence, in the section 2. different kinds of evolutionary information inheritance processes are presented. In section 3. we discuss adherence of evolutionary processes to super-recursive features. In section 4. I suggest conceptual framework of the evolutionary computer model and propose directions for its development in the course of study of computational evolution. As Francis Bacon said: 'It would be an unsound fancy and self-contradictory to expect that things which have never yet been done can be done except by means which never have yet been tried.' - implying here that we will need to do experiments that specifically test for conceptual questions related to computational evolution.

2. Evolution – The Science of Changes

Evolution is the science of changes and the bacteria are champions of evolutionary change. In order to understand better how biological systems perform information processing, different kinds of information processing systems of evolution are presented. Their categorization includes genetic (GIS), epigenetic (EPIS), behavioral (BIS) and language (LIS) information systems. LIS is considered as a 'part' of BIS. This categorization is influenced by the work of Jablonka and Lamb [Jablonka, Lamb, 2005]. However, in comparison with the mentioned reference this paper primarily considers studies and results of bacteria since they are an essential material to study and design models of digital cell computation.

2.1.a) *The prevailing view of evolution – the changes on the fundamental level of the genetic information system (eGIS)*

The current prevailing view of evolution combines Darwinian concepts of gradualism and natural selection with random mutation and Mendelian segregation as the mechanisms of evolutionary variability.

Evolution affects all aspects of an organism's life: morphology (form and structure), physiology (function), behavior, and ecology (interaction with the environment). Underlying these changes are changes in the hereditary materials. Hence, evolution consists of changes in the organisms' hereditary makeup. [Ayala, 2007] The physical basis for heredity, are discrete units of inheritance called genes, or we may call it genetic information. The full set of genes are genome. The "set" is not mathematical term in this case because the DNA is more than just a passive information carrier – it is also an active participant in transcription, translation, packaging and organizing the genome [Shapiro, 2005]. Breaking things down further, we can recognize two causal roles of genes, and hence two potential explanatory roles of genetic information, within biology. Genes are crucial to both explaining the development of individual organisms, and to explaining the inheritance of characteristics across generations. Information has been invoked in both explanatory contexts.

However, we may consider genetic information as a complex set of instructions formed by the sequence of nucleotides. In biology, DNA sequences (and consequently genetic information) can change through mutations, producing new alleles. If mutation occurs within a gene, the new allele may affect the trait (particular characteristics of an organism) that the gene controls altering the phenotype of the organism. Phenotype is determined by the organism's genetic make-up (genotype) and the environment in which the organism lives.

In the computer science we often distinguish data from the set of instructions (programs). Generally, data are pieces of information from the computer's system environment in a form suitable for use by a computer. Simple definition of computer states: a computer is a machine that manipulates data according to the list of instructions. Following the evolution, the focus is on the changes of the instruction set. So, when we consider the bacterium-like evolutionary computer it has to comprise not only certain program that operates using data or information from the environment but also, it has to include capabilities to change their own basic instructions on its fundamental program level via evolution. Roughly speaking, by analogy, under evolutionary processing the changes of the computer program will affect the traits of the computer, or more basically, according to definition, the way of how computer manipulates with data and information.

When Turing discussed the idea of learning machine [Turing, 1950] (let's assume that the learning is one kind of adaptation) he realized that it may appear as a paradoxical one to some readers. He wrote: "How can the rules of operation of the machine change? They should describe completely how the machine will react whatever its history might be, whatever changes it might undergo. The rules are thus quite time-invariant." We shall discuss this paradox from the evolution perspective since it has found its own way, as far as we know, (at least in principle) how to solve this problem.

Simply put, the change on the level of instruction set reflects mistake whether we consider the biological system (genome level) or computational system (program level). But, there is an essential difference in the processing of these particular systems when the error occurs. Most of mutations are deleterious or neutral. Yet, some of them could be beneficial. However, in the present computer systems there is no room for mistakes.

Before we continue this discussion on how evolution processes mutations, we shall briefly consider the self-maintenance of the system. When speaking about the evolution of complex systems we must take into consideration that the perpetuation of life depends on fine dialectical tuning between conservation and change.

Let us not forget the full title of Darwin's famous book. Most of us remember the title, *On the Origin of Species by Means of Natural Selection*, but then forget the subtitle, *Or, the Preservation of Favoured Races in the Struggle for Life*. Whereas the former pertains to change and variation, the latter relates to stability and uniformity. Aside from this dualism, i.e. the fine balance between the maintenance of the memory of evolution (DNA sequence) and its variability necessary for adaptive mutation, the DNA repair systems' prime role is the maintenance of the physical integrity of genomic DNA strands. Neither dividing nor the non-dividing cells can function with DNA strand discontinuities or chemical blocks, because neither replication nor transcription can fully operate. Briefly, the basic strategies to conserve the DNA sequence and genetic stability involve: (i) The maintenance of the chemical purity of ingredients for DNA replication; (ii) the high fidelity of DNA replication machine; and (iii) the quality control of new strands [Friedberg *et.al.*, 2006]. The stability of gene structure thus appears not as a starting point but as an end-product, as highly orchestrated dynamic process requiring the participation of a large number of enzymes organized into complex metabolic networks that regulate and ensure both the stability of DNA molecule and its fidelity in replication. [Fox, 2000] In other words, the source of genetic stability was not to be found in the structure of static entity but that stability is itself the product of dynamic process. High precision of DNA synthesis (error rate about 10^{-5}) results from the selection of complementary units (dNTP) but only after the proofreading (excision of the misincorporated wrong nucleotide), DNA replication process achieves its error rate per site - about 10^{-7}. Some incorrectly paired bases escape even the proofreading activity of bacterial DNA synthesis. It has a substantial, but still finite inherent accuracy. Since the measured mutation rate can be as low as one mistake per 10^{10} or 10^{11} the final degree of accuracy (in E. coli) depends on mismatch repair system. [Watson, *et al.,* 2007]

Despite this high-fidelity errors are inevitable. In the computer science and engineering the prevailing attitude towards mistakes is based on the tacit strategy that I presented by abbreviation FAECT i.e. "find all errors and correct them". In contrast to it in evolution, number of errors is optimal to the environment of life and strategy is to use them by natural selection for the benefit of the life itself. Hence, in biology mistakes (nucleotide misinsertions) can survive and they become mutations [Radman, 1998]. That is, nucleotide misinsertions that are followed by elongation of DNA will become mutations if not removed by postreplicative mismatch correction system. Such mutations and sequence changes that are created during repair or result from the movements of genomic parasites provide the raw material on which selection ultimately acts.

Mutations are random or chance events because (i) they are rare exceptions to the fidelity of the process of DNA replication and because (ii) there is no way of knowing which gene will mutate in a particular cell or in a particular individual [Ayala, 2007].

However, the meaning of "random" that is most significant for understanding the evolutionary process is (**iii**) that mutations are unoriented with respect to adaptation; they occur independently of whether or not they are beneficial or harmful to the organisms. Some are beneficial, most are not, and only the beneficial ones become incorporated in the organisms through natural selection. In 1943, Luria and Delbruck [Luria, Delbrück, 1943] performed a cornerstone experiment to prove that random mutations (i.e. mutations that are not related to the environment) do exist. They exposed bacteria to a lethal selective pressure - bacteriophage T1. As this bacteriophage immediately kills non-resistant cells, only cells with a pre-existing specifc mutation to resist the bacteriophage could survive the treatment (the selective pressure). Luria and Delbruck exposed populations of bacteria to such lethal environment, and analyzed the number of surviving cells in the different populations (different petri-dishes). From the distribution of surviving cells, they concluded that relevant mutations in bacteria, as in other organisms, had occurred randomly before the bacteria were exposed to the selective pressure, i.e. the mutations arose randomly and were not induced by the environment. Their experiments were then taken as a crucial support for the claim of the Neo-Darwinian theory that *all* mutations are random and can occur during DNA replication *only* [Dawkins, 1972; 1976; 1986; Gould, 1977; Jacob 1993].

As such, mutations adhere to the paradox mentioned above. From the evolutionary perspective mutations are the source of inventions. Actually, mutation is not a category within computer science. We may consider mutations as a kind of input information that is processed by evolutionary information-processing system. The process of information transformation from mutation to adaptive set of instructions that is coded for a novel function is the adaptation process. Note that discussion from *i-iii* and specifically Luria-Delbruck experiment clearly distinguishes evolutionary adaptation process from the processes of non-evolutionary adaptation and intelligence processes. This distinction is often neglected or superficially evaluated in the technical literature of the computer science and in the number of current models of AE.

The adaptation comes about by the combined processes of mutation and natural selection. Adaptation is the evolutionary process, which takes place under natural selection, whereby an organism becomes better suited to live in its habitat or habitats. [Dobzhansky, 1968] As a practical term, adaptation is often used for the product: features of a species which result from the process.

The evolution is not governed by random mutations. Rather, there is a natural process (namely, natural selection) that is not random but oriented and able to generate order or "create". It is Darwin's fundamental discovery, that there is a creation, although not conscious. This is about design without Designer. [Ayala, 2007]

The synthesis

Organisms exhibit complex design, but it is not, in current language, "irreducible complexity", emerging all of a sudden in full bloom. Rather, according to Darwin's theory of natural selection, the design has been arising gradually and cumulatively, step by step, promoted by the reproductive success of individuals with incrementally more adaptive elaborations. We can readily understand that the accumulation of millions of small, functionally advantageous changes could yield remarkably complex and adaptive organs, such as the eyes.

Darwin penned a famous passage, anticipating that the evolution of the eyes would be a target for attacks on his theory because eyes are such "organs of extreme perfection and complication". He wrote:"... that the eye... could have been formed by natural selection seems, I freely confess, absurd in the highest possible degree". [Darwin, 1859] However, note that the marvelous design of the eye is the only input information system (like a camera) of the complex vision information processing system as a whole. When we consider the adaptation of entire (sub)system it is not enough to consider the adaptation of perceptible features of a certain individual (sub)system. Adaptations must include what physical laws define, i.e. how light can be collected, focused and represented as an image, setting the fundamental limits on the optical features of eyes. [Laud, Fernald, 1992, Fernald, 1997] In addition, considering VIS as a whole, it becomes clear that during evolution some systems that are not proximately observable must have developed and adapted enabling the eye to work on specific information and send it for further processing. When we see an object in the room it seems so direct and immediate that the process seems quite irreducible. But, if we consult the science in more detail about what it knows regarding VIS and the things VIS able to do but we do not know how (e.g. extremely difficult problem is extracting the three-dimensional motion of an object from two-dimensional retinal images), then we reveal fascinating structure and large number of complicated information conversions and transmissions.

From evolutionary perspective we do not ask ourselves how certain system works but how it came into existence that includes its specific functional capacity and functional purpose. Evolution as a process is not directly involved in regular operational processing of the biological systems. Once they have evolved these particular processes are governed by highly accurate mechanisms and number of them could be presented as well-defined algorithms. Hence, evolution could be viewed as the process of open-ended synthesis and biological "machine" with its complex program that governs its function, behavior and maintenance is the product of such a process.

In his famous paper [Turing, 1936], Turing compares the *man in the process of computing* (that person was called Computer) with the machine which is only capable of finite number of conditions. Basically, Turing *created* a formal model for the physical machine which is capable to perform the process of computing providing that we may install in it the operational procedure (program) which previously performed a person-Computer by manipulating switches and patch cables. One could notice that the development of program is not captured by the concept of Turing machine. Following the distinction between operational procedure and process that create operational procedure one could try with enthusiasm, imitating the Turing work, to extend TM by incorporating the procedure of the *man in the process of programming*. This could be accomplished but only once for a particular operational procedure. So, we may find out that it does not extend the power of TM and it is far from being the general purpose program that may create any operational program. Additionally, TM cannot create a new procedure by itself. The behavior of the machine in the first case is rule-based or algorithmic. What to say about the second case?

This is the problem of synthesis and we do not have a formal model of how synthesis can be done automatically. Engineering students learn about existing solutions and techniques for well-defined, relatively simple problems, and then – through practice – are expected to improve and combine these to create larger, more complex systems. Product design is still taught today largely through apprenticeship. [Lipson, 2005] Robert Willis, a professor of natural and experimental philosophy at Cambridge, wrote in 1841 [Willis, 1841]: *[A rational approach to synthesis is needed] to obtain, by direct and certain methods, all the forms and arrangements that are applicable to the desired purpose. At present, questions of this kind can only be solved by that species of intuition that which long familiarity with the subject usually confers upon experienced persons, but which they are totally unable to communicate to others. When the mind of a mechanician is occupied with the contrivance of a machine, he must wait until, in the midst of his meditations, some happy combination presents itself to his mind which may answer his purpose."*

Willis's reflection of synthesis echoes even today, almost two centuries later. Progress in systematic synthesis is very slow and it is not clear in many domains. Obviously, we have two views of how synthesis of complex systems occurs. One is the view of Darwinian process of evolutionary synthesis without designer in the loop. This approach is more controversial in engineering. [Ziman, 2003] The second is intelligent, the goal-oriented design, under control of the designer during the process of development. This is still dominant approach in engineering. However, there is an obvious distinction which results from these two types of design. The products which are results of conventionally intelligent design in comparison with evolutionary design products are evolutionary dead-ends - they are very limited in self-maintenance, they are not self-replicable, they cannot evolve. This study tries to include synthesis approach according to the following direction: Instead of using for a design a computational procedure that we have created once and ultimately, try to identify the processes by which the procedure has been created and then make it possible to create a new procedure pursuant to processes which have created the first one. (section 4)

The solution of the 'machine that can change the rules'-paradox via evolution

Once we have accepted the mutation as the category of computational evolution we must face another great principle as a challenge for the solution of the paradox that the system (as an organism) must be viable at all stages of its development and at all stages of its evolution. This is obviously true, and what follows is that there are constraints on the evolution of development, behavior and structure of organisms. The main constraint is the requirement that changes in the system during evolution should be relatively small changes, because the body systems are so complex and interlinked. This is a sound principle, though there may be rare exceptions (e.g. polyploidy, symbiosis). Finally, we may find that the development of living organisms turns time-independent rules (the genome as information source) into autonomously adaptive system (the organism) in which time is an essential variable. The resulting organism is a hierarchical collections of structures within structures, with interactions between each level which smooth out the effects of environmental fluctuations on the organism. [Ramsden, 2003]

These principles, exploited by natural evolution, correspond to the paradox of the *machine that can change the rules* discussed by Turing and represent the challenge for computational evolution study.

2.1. b) *Programmed mutations of adaptive mutational genetic information system (amGIS)*

Natural selections lead not only to the evolution of eyes or wings and their programs that run vision or flight 'machine', but also to the evolution of new evolutionary rules. Many of these rules undermine the assumption that variation is random. [Jablonka, Lamb, 2005; 1998] The idea that genes do not mutate at random, but 'adaptively', as though 'Directed' by the environment in which the organisms find themselves, is so heretical that most biologists simply dismissed it out of hand; particularly 30 or 20 years ago.

Max Delbrück first used the term 'adaptive mutations' to refer to mutations formed in response to an environment in which the mutations are selected [Delbrück, 1946]. The experiments that succeeded have clearly distinguished between mutations that pre-existed at the time a cell was exposed to a selective environment from those 'adaptive' mutations formed after exposure to the environment [Tlsty, 1989; Rosenberg, 2001].

Inducible mutagenesis

A variety of sources such as radiation, chemical mutagens and products of metabolism induce damage to the genomes of organisms. Damage can be fatal for the organism since it can prevent DNA replication, and thus cell division. Biological responses to DNA damage are the fundamental problem, so important for life. Cells require the signaling systems to monitor faithfully any DNA strand discontinuity, any change in the instruction set. The first such cellular response to DNA damage was discovered in bacteria – the SOS response [Radman, 1974; 1975].

By definition, the SOS-response is postreplication DNA repair system induced by the presence of single-stranded DNA that usually occurs from postreplicative gaps caused by various types of DNA damage. Although the basic logic of the SOS circuitry is fairly simple - *RecA protein becomes activated (stimulated by single-stranded DNA) and mediates the cleavage (inactivation) of LexA repressor protein, thereby leading to the increased expression of LexA repressed genes, hence, inducing the response* - the detailed studies of SOS regulation carried out thus far indicate that there is considerably more subtiety to the regulation of SOS response than simply the coordinated induction of a set of genes [Friedberg *et.al.*, 2006; Michel, 2005; Schlacher, Goodman, 2007; Janion, 2008].

The SOS system can exist in two extreme states, fully repressed and fully induced. However, it can also exist in other states which are intermediate between these two extremes. When bacterial cells are subjected to sufficient DNA damage to induce the SOS response, a key event is the collapse of replication forks as they encounter the multitude of newly introduced DNA lesions in the template DNA. The primary goal of the SOS system is to restart replication productively.

Upon encountering damage to their genomes, bacteria such as *E. coli* respond by activating the SOS network, consisting of about forty-three genes, [Friedberg *et.al.*, 2006], whose task is to repair/bypass the DNA damage, in order to enable DNA replication. The SOS genetic network deploys a variety of specific functions such as detecting damage, repairing it correctly with base excision repair (BER) or by nucleotide excision repair (the NER mechanism) or by recombination, and if these functions do not succeed, bypassing damage by mutagenesis. SOS genes are also involved in triggering cell division, which occurs only after the genome has been fully replicated and it is safe for the cell to divide. Among the SOS genes are those encoding the specialized DNA polymerases, Pols II, IV, and V. The SOS polymerases catalyze translesion synthesis (TLS) by replacing a replicative Pol III that stalls when encountering a damaged template base. Once past the damage site, Pol III takes over to restart normal DNA replication. TLS, which results in mutations targeted to the sites of DNA damage, appears to be the biological basis of SOS mutagenesis. The regulation of SOS is governed by the action of two key proteins, the LexA repressor and RecA.

Adaptive mutation

When non-dividing *E. coli* are placed under non-lethal selective pressure, mutations accumulate seemingly in response to the selective environment. This phenomenon is known as adaptive mutation. Considering the role of SOS inducible mutagenesis in adaptive evolution we may find that the Pol V does not appear to participate in causing adaptive mutations, but the other two SOS polymerases are clearly involved. Pol IV is upregulated during stationary phase and is required for most (80%) adaptive mutations. Small deletions are characteristic of Pol IV's mutational spectrum in vitro. In contrast, Pol II, through its 3'-exonuclease proofreading function, serves to regulate the level of adaptive mutations by causing an approximate 5-fold reduction in magnitude [Schlacher *et.al.*, 2006; see reference therein].

Much later than the SOS hypothesis had been proposed came the excitement, and controversy - the possibility that Luria and Delbrück's conclusion might not be universally true. The results of Cairns *et. al.* (1988) showed that when the lactose auxotrophs were plated onto a minimal medium containing lactose as the only sugar - circumstances that require that the bacteria must mutate into lactose prototrophs in order to survive - then the number of lactose prototrophs that arose was significantly higher than that expected if mutations occurred randomly. In other words, some cells underwent programmed mutation and acquired the specific change in DNA sequence needed to withstand the selective pressure. However, in a second assay published by Cairns and Foster (1991) they measure reversion of a *lac* frameshift allele carried on an F2 conjugative plasmid in *E. coli* that are starving on lactose-minimal medium. Mutations occur by mechanisms unlike spontaneous, growth-dependent mutation and adapt the cells to their environment. Shapiro found that one type of mutation in *E. coli*, *araB-lacZ* fusions, involves a multi-step process that is physiologically regulated [Shapiro, 1984]. Wright has shown that amino acid starvation of *E. coli* increases transcription of specific set of genes that enable them to survive and these genes have enhanced mutation rate [Wright, 1997]. It became increasingly clear that bacteria have evolved mechanisms enabling them to actively generate a new variation in conditions where survival depends on genetic change.

Natural genetic engineering

Shapiro also suggests that organisms respond to stress by activating their natural genetic engineering systems. He proposed "..thinking of genomes as complex interactive information systems, in many ways comparable to those involving computers." [Shapiro, 1992] There is biological and environmental feedback into the genome. This means that evolutionary change may be very rapid because mutation rate can be increased and coordinated changes may occur at many sites within a single genome. Furthermore, although the induced genetic changes may not be specifically those that solve the organism's immediate survival problem if similar stress episodes have been frequent in the past, the genome may have been modified to target variation to a subset of sites or to be of a type that is likely to provide useful variation. More recent work suggests that transposable elements can effectively reprogram the genome between replications [Shapiro, 1992; 1997; 2005; 2006; 2007].

2.2. *Epigenetic information systems*

Epigenetic alterations are set of inherited but reversible changes in genom without modification of DNA sequences that lead to metastable changes in gene expression [Karpinets *et.al.* 2006; see Bird, 2007].These alterations create an inherited pattern of gene expressions in the genome realized as a set of repeatedly executing cellular functions. Epigenetics includes the effects that are inherited from one cell generation to the next whether these occur in embryonic morphogenesis, regeneration, normal turnover of cells, tumors, cell culture, or the replication of single celled organisms. These changes may be induced spontaneously, in response to environmental factors, or in response to the presence of a particular allele, even if it is absent from subsequent generations. Epigenetic alterations provide an important mechanism of transcriptional control regulating genes expression in cells of most living organisms. Generally, three classes of EIS have been recognized: stationary-state, structural, and chromatin-modification. Stationary-state systems are based on positive feedback loops – gene produces a product that simulates further activity of the gene and hence further synthesis of the product. Once switched on by physiological or developmental events the cell lineage continues transcription unless the concentration of the product falls. Structural inheritance is the transmission of a trait in a living organism by self-perpetuating spatial structures. We may note that this is in contrast to the transmission of digital information such as is found in DNA sequences, which accounts for the vast majority of known genetic variation: (recent studies of prions provide good example that is Sup35.) Bacteria make widespread use of postreplicative DNA methylation for the epigenetic control of DNA-protein interactions. *DNA methylation* in bacterial cells primarily serves as a mechanism of defence against the invasion of a foreign DNA into the cells. It functions as a part of restriction-modification systems that are comprised of genes encoding a restriction enzyme and DNA methyltransferases (DNA MTases). Bacteria make use of DNA adenine methylation (rather than DNA cytosine methylation) as an epigenetic signal. DNA adenine methylation is important in bacteria virulence in organisms such as *E. coli, Salmonella* and others. For additional bacteria examples see for instance [Casadesus, Low, 2006].

Epigenetic alterations of gene regulation or phenotype generation that are subsequently consolidated by changes at the gene level constitute another class of mechanisms for evolutionary innovation.

2.3. *Behavioral information systems (BIS) and language information systems (LIS)*

We may generally consider that the certain heritable pattern of behavior in a population, its origin and maintenance cannot automatically be related with genetic variations. [see Jablonka, Lamb, 2005] However, in the course of computational evolution we are primarily interested in microbial behavior-the concept which encompasses complex adaptive behavior shown by single cells and cooperative behavior in populations like or unlike cells mediated by chemical signaling that induces physiological or behavioral changes in cells and influences bacteria colony structures.

The idea that bacteria are simple solitary creatures stems from years of laboratory experiments in which they were grown under artificial conditions. However, each single-cell bacterium is, by itself, a biotic autonomous system with its own internal cellular gel that possesses informatic capabilities (storage, processing and interpretation of information). [e.g. Ben Jacob, Shapira, Tauber, 2006; Ben Jacob, Shapira, 2005; Ben Jacob, 2003] These afford the cell certain freedom to select its response to biochemical messages it receives, including self-alteration and broadcasting output chemical messages to signal and initiate alterations in other bacteria. Such capabilities elevate the level of bacterial cooperation during colonial self-organization.

The majority of bacteria spend most of their life cycle in single or multi-species biofilms, complex collective structures formed when bacteria attach to surfaces, and in this form they display an extraordinary repertoire of coordinated behaviors and interactions. A biofilm is a structured community of microorganisms possibly composed of many different bacterial colonies. The bacteria organized in biofilms, produce effective substances which individual bacteria are unable to produce alone [Matz *et. al.*, 2008] One benefit of this environment is increased resistance to antibiotics. In some cases resistance can be increased 1000 fold. [Stewart, Costerton, 2001].

The colonies' complexity is reproducible. So, upon replication, the new cells will immediately have the proper internal gene expression states to fit the colonial behavior. The reproducible complexity goes hand in hand with high flexibility for elevated adaptability leading to the great variety of patterns generated during growth under different conditions. The cells thus assume newly co-generated traits and abilities that are not explicitly stored in the genetic information of the individuals. [Ben Jacob, 2008, 2003;] These capabilities have been illustrated by exposing the bacteria to non-lethal levels of antibiotics. [see Ben Jacob, 2008]

Organization and coordination of organism's behavior depends on successful communication. Language is a part of the behavioral inheritance system. Cell-to-cell communication involving the production and detection of extracellular signaling molecules is called autoinducers. [Miller, Bassler, 2001] These small signal molecules carry on the process called quorum sensing. It allows bacteria to count their numbers, determine when they have reached a critical mass, and then change their behavior in unison to carry out processes that require many cells acting together to be effective. We may distinguish between intra-species communication (small-talk) and interspecies message-passing of the type that probably occurs quite regularly in multi-species biofilms. [see Bassler 2002; Schauder *et.al.* 2001; Miller *et.al.* 2004]

Additionally, with thanks to W. Riofrio [pers.comm.], I would like to reconsider the nature of these capabilities, mentioned above and others, – actually, how they are encoded in evolution? It seems, they do not exclusively depend on the step by step improvements that are shaped by the 'omnipotent' forces of natural selection. There are interconnected networks of molecular processes provoking the emergence of each one of these capabilities, and evolution of cellular design (see also Riofrio, chapter in this book).

To this point in time, biologists have seen the universality of the genetic code as either a manifestation of the Doctrine of Common descent or simply as a 'frozen accident'. The evolutionary dynamic (the 'rules') involves communal descent and it is not strictly vertical evolution. The key element in this dynamic is innovation-sharing, an evolutionary protocol whereby descent with variation from one 'generation' to the next is not genealogically traceable but is a descent of cellular community as a whole [Vetsigian, Woese, Goldenfeld, 2006]. Innovation-sharing protocol involves horizontal gene transfer of genes and perhaps other complex elements among the evolving entities required to bring the evolving translation apparatus, its code, and by implication the cell itself to their current condition. According to the [Vetsigian, Woese, Goldenfeld, 2006] there are three distinct stages of evolution classified as (i) weak-communal evolution, which gave way via development of an innovation sharing protocol and the emergence of universal genetic code to (ii) strong communal evolution which developed exponential complexity of genes, finally leading via the Darwinian transition to (iii) individual evolution-vertical, and so, Darwinian [see also: Woese, Goldenfeld, 2009].

3. Super-recursive Features of Evolutionary Processes

Currently, computation is a general term for any information processing. This includes phenomena ranging from human thinking to calculations in the most strict sense. Computation is a process which follows a well-defined model that is understood and can be expressed in an algorithm, a protocol, a network topology etc. Computation is also a major subject matter of computer science: it investigates what can or cannot be done in a computational manner. From the perspective of computational evolution study the aim is to investigate whether that neologism justifies its indication – namely, whether evolution is computational from the perspective of computer science. In other words, are information processes of evolution we discussed previously computable? To make this more clear, to see where these questions direct our research, we may use more radical questions suggested by Kauffman [Kauffman, 2008; 2009]. Let us consider visible Darwinian preadaptations (exaptations) which describe a situation where an organism uses a preexisting anatomical structure inherited from an ancestor for a potentially unrelated purpose. So the Kauffman's question is: "*Do you think you could prestate all the possible Darwinian exaptations of all organisms alive now? You might respond that we do not know all organisms alive now. I simplify my question: Do you think you could prestate all possible Darwinian exapatations just for humans?*" The expected answer could be negative. Evolution is a ceaseless creativity and a natural open-ended system does not need outside intervention to be settled. No Designer in the loop, no Creator, just Creativity with its *freedom to err*. Without certain degree of freedom there is no room for creativity in a precise, clockwork universe. To contrast computer science and engineering approach, an excellent reflection comes from the famous Swiss computer scientist, Niklaus Wirth: "In our profession, precision and perfection are not a dispensable luxury, but a simple necessity". "Traditional software engineering breaks down a problem into highly constrained interactions between modules, until modules are simple enough to be implemented in a computer code. This approach abhors emergence and avoids surprises" [Banzhaf *et.al.*, 2006]. Present computational methodology looks like a safe way to avoid computational evolution. However, we may suspect that information processing of the natural evolution is more powerful than automatic processes captured by Turing machinery. Turing himself wrote [Turing, 1948]: "There is the genetical or evolutionary search by which a combination of genes is looked for, the criterion being the survival value." It is further implied that the machine should have the "freedom to make mistakes". (Turing did not specify in 1948 how the "genetical or evolutionary search" for solutions to problems should be conducted but he pointed it out in his 1950 paper [Turing, 1950].

There is another approach which follows constructivist paradigm. Namely, the assumption is that any organelle, cell, organ including the brain, as well as the whole organism, is in principle equivalent to, and thus may in principle be simulated by universal Turing machine. According to this paradigm, one could consider transformation of the biological machine B into distinctive new machine T as a process that can be simulated by a Turing machine. However, as we may predict by present theory, such process cannot be done by a B machine itself, as it needs an outside intervention. It seems that this paradigm favors Creator (say kind of non-computable Oracle machine) rather than Creativity (evolution) notion as we discussed. Ben Jacob has pointed the state that [Ben Jacob, Shapira, 2005] everyone agrees that even the most advanced computers today are unable to fully simulate even an individual, the most simple bacterium of some 150 genes, let alone more advanced bacteria having several thousands of genes, or a colony of about 10^{10} such bacteria. As he noted, within the current constructivist paradigm, the above state of affairs reflects technical or practical rather than fundamental limitations.

Ben Jacob introduced a kind of Creativity paradigm but he dismissed Darwinian picture. Creation means emergence of something new and unpredictable, something not directly derivable from the present. Hence, he argued, if we understand science as the ability to predict the future state and behavior of a system based on the present knowledge about the system, then a creative process contradicts the tenets of scientific description and that is a paradox. Ben Jacob has been inspired by observations of bacteria morphotype transitions. He recognized the bacterial potential to perform the transitions from one morphotype to another in response to environmental conditions and their capacity for "deciding" to go through the transition as the collective action of many bacteria in the colony. He suggests that adaptive mutagenesis requires self-organization and cooperation of the bacteria. Hence in this picture evolution is not a result of successful accumulation of mistakes in replication of the genetic code, but is rather the outcome of creativity-like processes. [Ben Jacob, 1998]

There are other views within Creativity paradigm. One of the pioneers of system biology is Denis Noble. System biology focuses on the complex interactions in biological systems, thus using a new perspective - integration instead of reduction. At the beginning of the career Noble investigated the mechanisms of heartbeat. Since this work, it has become clear that there was not a single oscillator which controlled heartbeat, but rather this was an emergent property of the feedback loops in the various channels. Finally, he wrote that 'music of life' does not have a player [Noble, 2008]. Even more, he pointed out, there is no genetic program or programs at any other level of multi-level biological functionality including the brain. He also explains that genes in fact work in groups and systems, so that the genome is more like a set of organ pipes than a "blueprint for life". The genome, he holds, is a passive database. Similarly, in this direction, according to Coen [Coen, 1999] organisms are not simple manufacturers according to a set of instructions. He argued that there is no easy way to separate instruction from the process. "Dear Mr Darwin" wrote Gabriel Dover: "We don't have a theory of interactions and until we do we cannot have the theory of development or theory of evolution. There are no genes for interactions." [Dover, 2000]

Interactive computation (IC) involves interaction with the external world during the computation – rather than before or after it, as in algorithmic computation. [Goldin, Smolka, Wegner, 2006; Eberbach, Goldin, Wegner, 2004; Eberbach, Wegner, 2003] Hence, models of interaction capture the notion of performing a task or providing a service, rather than algorithmically producing outputs from inputs. They are modeled in terms of observable behavior consisting of interaction steps and they include environment as an active part in the computation by dynamically supplying the computational system (e.g. agent) with inputs and consuming the output values the system produces. [Goldin, Smolka, Wegner, 2006 and reference therein]. Different models of interactive computation could possibly, according to authors, lead beyond the limits of Church-Turing thesis. Generally, interactive computation is inevitable in the study of computational evolution taking into account that evolution means the presence of many individual systems interacting in different ways and levels [Banzhaf *et.al.*, 2006]. Additionally, advanced models of IC could be crucial when we need to avoid genome-centered concept of biological information toward our efforts to simulate for example, innovation-sharing protocols discussed in subsection 2.3.

In the rest of this section I am going to argue that information processing systems of evolution possess super-recursive features. The term came from the theory of super-recursive algorithms (TSRA) developed by Mark Burgin. [Burgin, 2005]. Burgin abandoned the absolute concept of algorithm and found it more relevant to speak about algorithm in relation to some given conditions. Hence, any approach to algorithms that tries to restrict algorithms to a mathematical model is not efficient enough for study, design and utilization of algorithms. Burgin organized and systematized diversity of algorithms through classification divided into three big classes: sub-recursive, recursive (this class is taken as the base) and super-recursive algorithms. As Burgin presented, super-recursive algorithms can compute what has been considered as non-computable.

We may consider that natural evolution is a complex information processing system which is not algorithmic. For instance, nobody can design the computer program of evolutionary adaptation process or speciation. But we may consider and study evolution in terms of information processing and computation, and scientists actually do that as we have shown. Additionally, we may find that certain mechanisms as well as some complicated repair processes are algorithmic. Scientists are capable theoretically and experimentally to create certain molecular DNA models of computation. [Shapiro, Benenson, 2006; Benenson *et.al.* 2004; Regev, Shapiro, 2002]. However, as we know, such models are not by themselves more powerful than Turing machines and they are based on the class of recursive algorithms. Such algorithmic DNA or RNA sequences could be the subjects of evolution but only if they include the random or non-random changes in the original structure i.e. evolution deals with mutational genetic information of GIS and with higher-level, more flexible structures as the carriers of other information categories like epigenetic patterns. Hence, the cell computation includes processes that are algorithmic but also includes the non-algorithmic capabilities of change, actually the process that is governed by evolution.

If we consider information processing systems of the evolution as computation in general and variety of mechanisms and different multilevel interactions, different pathways of signal transduction in particular, (and we have discussed only the small portion) then we may suggest that they expose super-recursive features. The following remarks include several examples of this consideration.

Emerging processes of EIS and inductive computation. From evolutionary perspective biological systems frequently change on the genetic level. Therefore, it follows that the process of adaptation is never finally complete, [Mayr, 1981] selection operates all the time and, as we know, it achieves the product (adaptive trait for the bodily part or function) without stopping in the finite period of time. Van Valen thought that even in a stable environment, competing species had to adapt constantly to maintain their relative standing - known as the Red Queen hypothesis. [Van Valen, 1973] Adaptation is a genetic tracking process, which goes on all the time to some greater or lesser extent, respectively; for instance, when the population cannot or does not move to another, less hostile area. Hence, fitness (an organism's capacity to propagate its genes) is not a static predetermined property. [cf. Freeman, Herron, 2007]

Evolutionary adaptation is an emergent process. We may consider that cellular machines perform the type of inductive computation. The characteristic of such computations is that they produce result without halting. Results emerge through a sequence of intermediate results and they are carried on by processes of replication (of DNA, molecular level) and consequently by division (of the cell), and finally by reproduction (of the organism). Intermediate results appear during the process of replication or between the two replications (as we discussed previously in relation with EIS subsystems). In some cases results are predictable but in general, results emerge only in the corresponding EIS process. Accordingly, we may consider that biological systems, such as cellular machines perform computation that is equivalent to computation of an Inductive Turing machine (ITM) based on super-recursive algorithms.(Computation of ITM is formally described in [Burgin, 2005]).

Infinity concept, becoming infinity of EIS processing and inductive computation. Emergent processes of evolution could become infinite. Emergent processes of computation according to TSRA is represented by the model of inductive Turing machine. There are situations when the result is already obtained but the ITM continues functioning [Burgin, 2005]. One could find such situation a possible source of confusion but Burgin exposed clear distinction between non-halting inductive computation with infinite and infinite-time computation. However, infinite-time computations are potential processes (rather then emergent) in the sense that it is possible that they produce result only after an infinite number of steps. In comparison, by inductive computation (for instance, by taking Inductive Turing machine)

(i) there are situations when some computations halt (by giving the result or not-giving the result as in the case of conventional computation by a Turing machine);

(ii) there are situations when the result is already obtained but computation continues;

(iii) additionally, inductive computation while working continuously, can occasionally change its output.

Observing evolutionary processes as computation of the evolvable cell, or single-cell organisms like bacteria, we may find similar distinction. In other words, evolution exposes very clearly its emergent properties rather than infinity computation properties. We may consider several different examples.

(i) Specific feature inherent to inductive computation performed by ITM presents transition from terminating computation to intrinsically emerging computation. It is evident from the previous discussion that such a characteristic is typical of EIS. As particular mechanisms in the nature of evolvable cells and organisms we may emphasize once again the processes of translesion synthesis governed by specific polymerases (II, IV and V) of SOS response because they are evidently represent mentioned transition. (see section 2.1.b)

Such activities are inducible and they are turned on only under a strong selective pressure. But as soon as the normal base pairs are created, mutation and hyper-recombination activities could be repressed (by LexA repressor) and regular faithful and processive replicative polymerases would take over the replication process. Hence, we may find that these mechanisms represents inductive computation because the results obtained without halting the replication but once the results are achieved inductive mechanisms halt. This is equivalent to situation of inductive computation when some computations halt by giving the result. We may consider that these mechanism represent silent super-recursive apparatus.

(ii) a) Example when cell 'machinery' cannot stop functioning could be HeLa cells. They are termed "immortal" in that they can divide an unlimited number of times in a laboratory cell culture plate as long as fundamental cell survival conditions are met. So called, established or immortalized cell line has acquired the ability to proliferate indefinitely either through random mutation or deliberately by (experimental) modification (explant culture method). Hence, we may consider immortal cell line of the cells derived from tumors as a kind infinity computation of cell division but what precedes this kind of behavior is an emergent process. The becoming mode of infinity computation needs for certain kind of tumors seven mutations of the cell. Generally, such mutations have to capture inhibition of cell division control mechanisms and then activation of cell division acceleration. Typically, we may take that frequency of mutations is 10^{-6} and probability that one normal cell accelerates all seven mutation is 10^{-42}. If we take in consideration the fact that there are temporally no more than 10^{24} living human cells tumor will never appear. But we know it happens. However, mentioned probability is related to the picture of the cell that is not divided. So, when the first mutation randomly appears that cell will divide and grow little bit faster than the adjacent cells and at the end of the year there will be more cells with one specific mutation then the others cells in the population. When the selfish, unsocial cell beneficial to itself but harmful to the rest intact cells approaches to the million cells in population probability for new mutation is close to 1. Emergent process of evolution (mutation and variability, reproduction and selection) proceeds toward seven specific mutations and it lasts approximately twenty years.

b) Single-cell organisms-bacteria are much more efficient than the single cell from the illustrative example above. This is based on the fact that they are very generous among themselves in exchanging their genes and emergent processes including different genetic materials from different cells that possibly lead to their adaptation much faster. (see section 2.)

c) Similar example for infinity computation from the world of bacteria may be found among bacterial ribosomal mutants resistant to high concentrations of streptomycin that have acquired very high ribosomal fidelity in the process of protein synthesis. Such mutants cannot grow any more without streptomycin addiction – the drug that increases the ribosomal error rate. [e.g. Bjorkman *et.al.*, 1999].

d) Strong genetic mutators are particularly favored when adaptation requires several genomic mutations which may be the case of most adaptations to complex environmental changes. Selecting for the mutator (which has been generated by inactivation of antimutator function) can allow fast exploration of the fitness landscape. Mechanistically, the mutator increases in its frequency because of its genomic association (hitch-hiking) with favorable mutations generated by mutators activity. In this case mutators have advantage over the inducible mutators because these ones may not have had time to produce adaptive solutions [Radman *et.al.*, 2000 and ref. therein].

(iii) The immune system processes without stopping, constantly trying to produce better solutions. We may identified several processes that are functioning in the direction of avoiding solutions equivalent to deleterious mutations and favoring only adaptive solutions. This behavior is equivalent to the inductive computation based on the fact that inductive computation while working without halting, can occasionally change its output. The result could be good enough even if another (possibly better) result may arrive in the future. Interestingly, the structured memory Inductive Turing machine allows the storing of adaptive solutions [cf. Burgin 2005] in the way as the immune system "memorizes" solutions through the mechanism of dividing and proliferation of the cells. According to this capability in the nature the response of the immune system to the appearance of the same antigene is very quick.

Results of EIS processing and inductive computation. The above mentioned examples (as well as many others) point out a very important characteristic of evolutionary processes (as in the cases of inductive computation by ITM) that they always give results in finite time (in contrast to infinite and infinite-time computations) but for which it is not specified how the results are obtained. According to TSRA the result appears as a word (string) that is written on the output tape after a certain step and it is not changing although the machine continues to work. If this output stops changing, it is then considered to be the result of the computation.

Equivalently, we may find in the emergent processes of evolution that beneficial mutations favored by natural selection eventually become fixed as a newly incorporated string of DNA sequence. By any subsequent generation the process of replication gives the same output of the word (string) unchangeable for many generations within continuity of biological evolutionary processes.

It turned out that TSRA could help us change the mind in relation to question whether evolution is computable. It is also possible that it helps us to assess that natural processes of evolution are beyond computation of Turing machine.

4. The Model of Evolutionary Computer Capable of Computational Evolution

Can we extract the information processes out of the biology to help us build things like computer networks and robots? I suggest the construction of an evolutionary computer in order to use ideas from natural biological systems and apply it to computational evolution study. The inspiration for building EC and study material comes from bacteria. Roughly speaking, a machine called EC has bacterial level of evolutionary adaptation if EC has bacteria-like capabilities. According to previous discussion we may briefly summarize such capabilities. They are highly evolvable, great chemical programmers, picking up information from the environment, talking with each other, distributing tasks, generating collective memory, assigning existential meaning to information from the environment, learning from past experience and creating new genes to cope better with new challenges and finally they are even capable of resurrection (e.g. *D.Radiodurans* [Zahradka *et.al.*, 2006]).

Additionally, we may consider bacteria-like evolutionary computer (BL-EC) with its program as 'pattern' of an organism in the sense in which the biologist calls it 'the four-dimensional pattern', meaning not only the structure and functioning of that organism at adult, or at any other particular stage, but the whole of its ontogenetic development from replication of the string, gene expression, from the cell to the stage of maturity, when the organism begins to reproduce itself toward society of EC 'digital' organisms, without loss of organization that allows that complex unity to exist. Preliminary introduction into the structure of the model primarily focused on the program of a BL-EC machine as follows (Fig. 4.1)

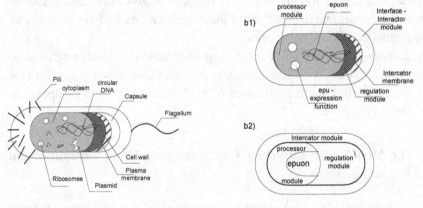

Fig. 4.1. a) Structure of Typical bacteria cell.   Fig. 4.1. b1,2) Simplified structure of bacteria-like EC-cell program.

BL-EC program includes two basic program modules Interactor program as a part of input and output information procesing system of the BL-EC and Processor program as a part of working information processing system of the BL-EC. Processor is divided into submodules of information processing programs, regulation, and reproduction programs. However, EC program in general and each executing program in particular have been developed from the basic program called *epuon*. *Epuon* is a set of basic program structures that undergo adaptation. They are **evolutionary processable units-*epu***. Single *epu* is a complex set of instructions and stays as an analogical equivalent to a single gene as a complex biological hereditary unit. *Epu* includes operational instructions (*s*) that encode for *proteator*-execution program, instructions for epu-interactions (*i*), instructions on the range of *epu*-variability (*v*) and instructions for replication (r). The replication may be integrated in the coding sequence (by analogy, as replicase that catalyses its own replication without the help from a protein) or separately added (by analogy, coding for the product with its enzymatic actions). The term *proteator* alludes to protein (peptide) sequences and their working role of biological molecules that arises after the process of protein folding, and it comes as abbreviation constructed from ***prot*ein-level-oper*ator***. Specific challenge is program development and growth of EC-program. However, before we proceed with elaboration of EC and its program synthesis I would like to introduce the notion of horizontal-vertical computation of an EC which also emphasizes certain analogies between gene and epu.

Horizontal-Vertical computation (HVC)

Genes are crucial to both explaining the development of individual organisms, and to explaining the inheritance of characteristics across generations. Hence, we may consider them in dual way. In the first case genetic information is a hereditary unit processed by replication. In the second case genetic information is a set of instructions to build and maintain the cells processed by transcription and translation. These processes of gene expression appear in the nature sequentially.

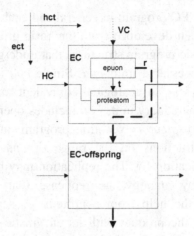

Fig. 4.2. EC incorporates paradigm of horizontal-vertical computation. **hct** stays for historical computational time by horizontal computation; **ect** stays for evolutionary computational time in correlation with steps of epuon changes by vertical computation.

In addition, these processes could be observed separately with certain degree of independence. Hence, I suggest that different processes on different levels of individual system development and functioning could be emphasized and easier to follow with the notion of horizontal-vertical computation (HVC). According to this notion, the replication processes information vertically, mutation produces new heritable alleles i.e. it is vertically transmitted variability, asexual reproduction is a vertical process of genetic information and so on. On the other side mentioned processes of genetic expression, recombination, different processes of genetic exchange, are all horizontal biological computations. In the present-day computing machines all processes are lateral. For instance, if we consider genome as a source code, it differs from programs as we know to be most common, we do not develop our computer programs in a way that we first make a replication of the source code. Common procedure includes direct transfer of sequence into the function. There are other very practical requests for introducing HVC. Actually, when we consider bacteria we find out that they exchange genetic information as well as signalling molecules. These are essentially different kind of information processed by different kind of information systems within single biological organism. Obviously, in the course of bacteria-like machine development, the EC-model has to incorporate two different "avenues" of information processing as well as two different kinds of information.

4.1. *Synthesis of evolutionary computer by Sequencer machine*

Evelyn Fox Keller emphasized that "There is one rather conspicuous point at which computers and organisms must definitively part ways, and that is the route by which the two kinds of systems came by such strikingly similar mechanisms...however much they may have been influenced by biological structures (computer networks built to resist errors and be reliable) computers nevertheless are built by human design, while organisms evolve without the benefit of a designer (or so it is generally presumed). The crucial question for biologists is therefore this: by what sort of evolutionary process did such complex self-organized beings come into existence?" Indeed, mechanisms that ensure developmental robustness have nonetheless evolved, and to such degree of sophistication that their operational principles have much to teach engineers. The question Fox left for engineers is: "By what kinds of evolutionary processes could such mechanisms have arisen without assistance from human ingenuity?"

Using Fox's approach we came to the point we have already reached in the 2.1 subsection about synthesis. The concept of evolutionary synthesis we are going to discuss here includes a certain machine, called Sequencer, by which we can try to build an evolutionary computer. Before we proceed, allow me to discuss an example that represents an obstacle we encounter, namely, a contradictory request at glance: the construction that tries to dismiss classical engineering design-approach and ultimately to extract human preconception and intentionality from the process of construction.

Richard Dawkins has conceived The Blind Watchmaker program that demonstrates effectively how random mutation followed by non-random selection can lead to interesting, complex forms. He tried to point out the power of micro-mutations and cumulative selection. [Dawkins, 1986] Graphical models of gene selection he used involving entities he called biomorphs. These are two-dimensional sets of line segments which bear relationships to each other, drawn under the control of "genes" that determine the appearance of the biomorphs. Dawkins started from a conventional recursive algorithm: for each iteration, a new connection is generated. The aim was to generate tree forms. Starting from a trunk, any new iteration corresponds to a sub-branch. The use of Biomorph program showed that it is not limited to the realization of different trees but could also generate many types of forms. Dawkins was therefore quite surprised to discover an insect-looking biomorph followed by planes, bats, branched candlesticks... He wrote with enthusiasm: *Nothing in my biologist's intuition, nothing in my 20 years' experience of programming computers, and nothing in my wildest dreams prepared me for what emerged on the screen.... With a wild surmise, I began to breed, generation after generation, from whichever child looked most like an insect. My incredulity grew in parallel with the evolving resemblance.... I still cannot conceal from you my feeling of exultation as I first watched these exquisite creatures emerging before my eyes. I distinctly heard the triumphal opening chords of Also sprach Zarathustra (the '2001 theme') in my mind.*

But, there are problems with using Dawkins program Biomorphs as an analogy for evolution. In 1994 Gell-Mann published a book, *The Quark and the Jaguar* where he briefly mentions Richard Dawkins's program Biomorphs without endorsing it. "In real biological evolution there is no designer in the loop". [Gell-Mann, 1994] Dawkins acknowledges that he uses artificial selection to guide the process:... *Our model, in other words, is strictly a model of artificial selection, not natural selection. The criterion for 'success' is not the direct criterion of survival, as it is in true natural selection. In true natural selection, if a body has what it takes to survive, its genes automatically survive because they are inside it. So the genes that survive tend to be, automatically, those genes that confer on bodies the qualities that assist them to survive.* However, the creatures are tightly constrained by Biomorph software and completely dependent on the computer's operating software. The ratio of actual to possible creatures in this genetic scheme is one to one: every sequence makes a viable creature. Mutations are not possible and program does not have any *freedom to err.* Hence, the only changes that occur in the creatures are those whose potential is already available in the program originally. From the perspective of computational evolution we may ask: How would biomorphs work if we allowed chance mutations to affect the "Blind Watchmaker" software, or the computer's operating programs?

Roughly, we may notice that human (programmer) intervention appeared on two levels. *A priori* it appears on program level as direct consequence of programming synthesis process governed by human preconceptions and desired purpose and tasks that certain program has to accomplish. *A posteriori*, intervention appears as intentional act (in this case artificial selection of the program properties or traits) which influences behavioral level of the program by changing certain parameters but not the program itself. In our conventional programming and engineering paradigm it doesn't seem that we may employ any trick to avoid preconceptions and intentionality in the process of synthesis. We may include randomness into the program but it will still have preconceptions of how to work and one, maybe, just won't know what those preconceptions are.

To overcome the problem of human intervention we may define our task as transformation of teleological paradigm into teleonomic (blind-teleological) paradigm. The idea that looks very simple pertains to the tracing and registering the process of program synthesis performed by human programmer which then allows rebuilding and evaluating the synthesis procedure. The machine capable of such computation can give us, in principle, the same result that human programmer can achieve by his conventional programming and that is the new program sequence. This idea stays behind the Sequencer machine – it allows simultaneous two-fold synthesis process execution and includes two outputs (Fig. 4.3) In this way we may achieve direction we posed previously (the synthesis in 2.1), that is, instead of using for a design a computational procedure that we created once and for all, we may identify the synthesis process by which the procedure was created and then make it possible to create a new procedure pursuant to processes which created the first one. Human capabilities of synthesis are based on brain processes highly unknown and this machine doesn't represent substitute for automated synthesis. Rather, it is a blind-machine and it could help us make first step toward a paradigm shift. In what follows, I will emphasize this step.

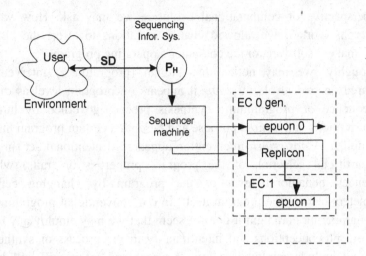

Fig. 4.3. 'Pictorial' framework of the 'man in the process of programming' applied into the concept of sequencing information system and EC synthesis.

I will briefly describe characteristics in relation to Sequencer machine, design processes and results. Human programmer (P_H) uses Sequencer as a tool for *epu*-programming. Sequencer is equipped with standard set of instructions and data structures (such as standard library of functions of programming language) as well as certain specialized operational, interactive and variation functions. We may deal with them all here using the name *program elements* (PE). Additionally, it includes specialized sequencer-functions by which programmer selects program elements in the course of program synthesis. Selection of sequencer functions during process of synthesis is supported by Main control structure or *Main-program* of the Sequencer machine. It controls and registers that every action of the programmer correlates with a certain steps and/or 'phases' of the cyclical pseudo-information-processing model (PIPM) of the 'brain in the process of the program synthesis'. PIPM models underline, in a certain way, our descriptions of different methodological procedures, for instance in the fields of scientific methodology, intelligence cycle management or software development. Such procedures are not recipes; they are more like guidelines in the complex process of synthesis which human brain, as we know, is capable to perform toward ultimate goals. According to our examples these goals are a scientific research report, an intelligence report or a computer program. The certain PIPM model is developed as Main-program designed within Sequencer machine and supports the programming process. However, brain and mind processes engaged in synthesis are far reaching goals of more advanced brain-computer interface study. There is no room here to elaborate this subject. The idea behind the Main-program is only partially related to the extraction of programmer's thoughts *out of brain* on the interface of the Sequencer machine but we are not directly focused on brain-computer interface techniques. Our aim is to put together a simple operational program and a program by which that operational program is created, and then let them evolve. This could be a crucial step toward teleonomic paradigm so let me emphasize this part by the following description. We may consider that a particular sequencer program simulates the process of how a human programmer synthesizes a particular operation program. Those programs correspond to each other and they become expressed as the finite procedures encapsulated into a single epu. Epu program allows a horizontal computation by operation program. (In our model operational program first has to be expressed in a proteator.) Now we may consider replication. Replication program uses the sequencer program and following the sequence pathway step by step performs mapping of epu program elements from the epu-store of the Sequencer machine into the novel epu sequence of an evolutionary computer. Epu by epu, Replication program automatically synthesizes a new epuon. By replication program vertical evolutionary computation starts. Epu encapsulated sequencer program of human synthesis is detached from Sequencer machine and human brain and it becomes the part of evolutionary information processing. Epu construction allows introduction of mutation category into computational processes and we may expect that an evolutionary computer is capable to processes different kinds of randomly appearing mutations. (see sec. 4.2). Mutation of the sequencer program of the epu will influence the replication of operational program of a new epu. This mutation may cause the stopping of replication function or such mutation can be replicated and consequently reproduced into the next EC offspring. Additionally, mutation of the sequencer program will influence the operational program and consequently program execution of a particular proteator. In this sense, program process of changes does not appear by human intervention which we may consider as the first step toward teleonomic paradigm. Additionally, we may consider that this process described above presents transition from terminating computation to intrinsically emerging computation, making a leap from the 'being' mode of recursive algorithms to 'becoming' mode of super-recursive algorithms.

Let's go back at the start of epu-programming. One by one epu is created by P_H. They are divided into particular epu-s for functional modules of regulation, interaction and operation but, as a rule they are uniform. Almost each epu consists of program sets: operational program (**o**), interaction program(**i**), sequencer program (**s**) and variation program (**v**). Operational program includes subprograms for proteator data structures and for proteator sequence conformation according to the particular task a proteator has to accomplish and predefined operational program for proteator functioning. Interaction program includes a program for interactions among the epu units (e.g.epistasis) and input subprograms acceptor (**a**) and operon (**o**). They allow incorporation of data (signals) from intracellular modules which then influence epu expression which is controlled by the operon. Sequencer program includes sequencer functions, data structures of sequence pathways, main control structures that are included in deployment of particular operational program. This program may additionally include replication function. Variation program includes possible range of changing parameters of each particular program of an epu. In some epu-units (e.g-mobile epu elements) this program includes recombination programs or mutation-prone programs.

Intended result of this synthesis by Sequencer machine is the epuon-program. Epuon is structured by system of interactive relations and functions that provide connections between the epu-units. After the whole epuon is generated operational programs of each particular epu start expression by transcription/translation program. The result is proteatom program (set of all proteators) which constitutes particular program modules of the cell/organism capable to exhibit a certain desired behavior. An epuon-sequence may embody information about one environment within which that sequence is functional. That environment is the one in which epuon replicates and in which its host 'lives'.

Additional synthesis that is performed during the synthesis done by programmer is automated by the Tracer program of the Sequencer. By this program epu-units of the generated epuon are disassociated and stored in the way that epuon cannot proceed with transcription. Instead this epu-program-store (EPS) becomes the source for extra epu units, programs and program elements on the disposition from which replication program (replicon) starts to generate new epuon (discussed above). The main role of Sequencer machine is to be the tool for epuon (evolutionary computer) development, but its additional role appeared to be the source for extra epu-elements for replication and hence to be the source that maintains the growth of BL-EC programs which possibly leads us naturally to the next step toward teleonomic paradigm. However, I left this step to the experiments of computational evolution that will possibly show that a certain BL-EC colony or biofilm conformation has separated from the Sequencer machine. That would imply according to the structure suggested in this paper that a metaepuon of BL-EC colony includes all information (knowledge about the environment) necessary for self-replication and furthermore that the domain knowledge of executive proteator level of digital bacteria is such that they can process the computational tasks for which they have been previously specialized between two reproductive cycles. This process implies acquisition of different further knowledge about the changes in the environment that are additionally processed within the following reproductive cycles.

4.2. *Functional decomposition of the BL-EC model*

Figure 4.4 presents functional decomposition of the BL-EC model to its second level. A different kind of biological information processing and mechanisms we discussed could possibly be simulated and supported by particular models of BL-EC. However, for the purpose of gaining general insight into the identity of the constituent components we will discuss functional relationship among the program modules of EC with its certain analogy toward biological structures, but detailed presentation of particular mechanisms and processing is omitted here.

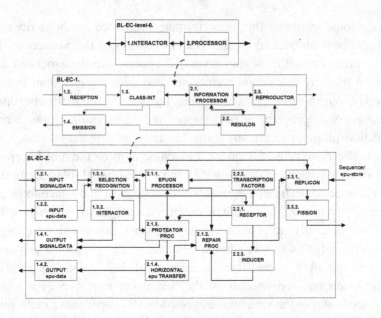

Fig. 4.4 Block-diagram of BLEC functional decomposition.

According to BL-EC model, 'mature' computation in the environment starts after the process of epuon expression. Epuon expression is the process that includes transcription from epu into proteator. Additionally, if we want to use different computational language for proteator programs then we have to include translation function. Epu-expression process in the first generation of 'digital bacteria' imitates information flow of the Central Dogma in molecular biology. It is important to note that only operational program of each particular epu of the epuon is the subject of transcription. Each particular program module represented by its block on the diagram 4.4 is the set of different proteator executive programs. We may recognize that a minimal epuon includes set of epu-s for interaction (Interactor), operational information processing (Operational processor), regulation (Regulon) and reproduction (Reproductor).

Input and output information processing systems of BL-EC are controlled by Interactor program module. It includes two different input and output information systems according to the working paradigm of H-V computation. (1.2; 1.4) Selection/recognition module (1.3.1) selects input data from different sources and proceeds them according to their specificites to the particular intracellular module. Interaction with environment could be based on the principles of interactive computation (discussed previously) by particular interactor module (1.3.2) in the diagram) and as such BL-EC model can perform certain information processing without engagement of central processing proteator-programs (2.1.3). One of the key requests in overcoming the constraints in the accepting power of computation is to choose data structures that by interacting, increase the number of internal degrees of freedom in the system. [cf. Banzhaf *et.al.*, 2006] Receptor (2.2.1) is the proteator program capable to receive data or signals from the environment and according to referent values regulation program of the receptor can produce the adequate data or signal response by which it selects particular proteator from the set of transcription factor(s) (2.2.2) Recruited factor influences the epu-expression by activation or repression (inactivation) of particular epu programs (see illustration 4.6) which ultimately change the proteator processing (2.1.3) toward particular behavioral response of digital bacteria. In the cases when such behavior is favored by environmental conditions the novel 'switch-order' of epu-expression pathway could remain unchanged and as such could be transferred to the next generation as epigenetic change.

Regular processes of replication are controlled by proteators of Replicon module (2.3.1). Replicon collects extra epu program elements from the Sequencer epu-store elements and synthesizes new epuon following the sequence pathway formed by previous synthesis (discussed previously). The quality of the replication is controlled by the proteator Quality of control (QC). QC compares the values of the new epu and its particular position in the new structured epuon memory according to referent values of existing epuon template. In the cases when mutation appear (misincorporated epu-program element) QC of the Replicon will activate repair system (2.1.2). Repair system removes misincorporated epu-PE and correct one can be interpositioned.

In particular cases, when 'digital bacteria' is exposed in the environment under constant pressures to novel data and signals for which they have not adequate response, then Receptor (2.2.1) could activate Inducer module (2.2.3) with its enzyme like regulation proteator program to turn on repair processes of the second order. These are proteators that simulate computation of translesion synthesis. They deliberately start to incorporate mutational epu elements and allow replication program to continue despite 'lesion' like epu-mutation fragments. This 'enzymatic' computation of change accelerates evolutionary processes (second-order selection) until the adaptive mutation—novel epu-function—is reached and Inducer becomes inactivated.

Horizontal epu transfers (2.1.4) computation is supported by different proteators for horizontal epu exchange among digital bacteria (e.g. recombination, conjugation like processes etc.). As well, this module includes proteators that control computation over 'mobile' epu elements (e.g.transponson like jumping epu units). Recombinations are included in the repair processes and they could contribute to adaptation. In general, HET module affects epuon alterations between two replication processes. After replication, new epuons are synthesized and Fission module starts with reproduction simulating bacteria asexual reproduction by binary fission proteators. Simply, it occupies new memory space and allows epu expression.

This presentation is very simplified in relation to realistic integrative models of cell computation but I believe that it clearly indicates that the concept of BL-EC model could span evolutionary information processing-EIS according to previously introduced categorization. EIS and EC models incorporate most of directions suggested by agenda of CE. Additionally, the suggestion is that computation of BL-EC could be based on the principles of interactive computation and diversity of super-recursive algorithms. For instance, model of BL-EC could be described by effective operations (as we informally presented above) but for the most of molecular mechanisms and behavioral patterns of EIS employed in the model it is not specified how the result is obtained. It means that a BL-EC is a machine governed by super-recursive algorithm.

4.3. *Evolution of evolvability – changes and possibility of improvement of the synthesis procedures*

Additional challenge for the models of evolvable computer appeared from the fact that evolution evolves and incorporates new mechanisms of evolutionary adaptation into the biological organisms. As we discussed above our engineering intelligent design approach didn't succeed to accomplish such a thing.

However, this process of change could be recorded to the certain degree of accuracy. Actually, any kind of mutation that occurred by base transition, transversion, insertion, deletion and so on, and which is then passed from one generation to another, from a mother cell to a daughter cell is implicitly recorded. One mutation occurs and then another one and so on. The mutations that pass many generations and obviously those that survive the selection could possibly create new sequence of mutations, actually, the novel functional sequence of instructions sufficiently adjusted toward environment of the cell i.e. it allows the cell to perform the computations and solve the problems for which it was not capable before.

Let's take into consideration sequence of mutations that is selected through many generations among uncountable number of mutations that occur in the process of evolutionary adaptation. We may consider such sequence not only as the ultimate result which is, as we know, a kind of a particular adaptation – but also as a certain trajectory of cell experience. Because such trajectory is recorded and finite we potentially have the algorithm that describes the process of adaptation which up to now existed in a purified algorithmic expression without harmful mutations. This algorithm could be incorporated as a copy among the rest of functional and regular algorithmic sequences and it could be silent. Additionally, this algorithm may appear in two epu-forms. In the first one we may consider it as a novel set of instructions used by existing proteator regulation program of epu-expression while the other more complex form is coded for new or improved proteators that can affect for instance, regular epuon-sequence during replication. In both cases we may consider that a certain cell has the programs that evolved as additional capability that can change its procedures. In certain cases, for example, we may expect that if some cell undergoes selective pressure the program could act by incorporating mispaired epu program elements and actually it starts to generate mutations along the line of the regular sequence during the process of replication precisely imitating the process from its own evolutionary past. This could be possibly equivalent computation to non-random adaptive mutation SOS-response mechanism. Accordingly, the cell becomes the active agent of evolution rather than its passive substrate.

5. Conclusion

Turing pointed out in 1947, [Turing, 1947], "the intention in constructing (computers) in the first instance, is to treat them as slaves, giving them only jobs which have been thought out in detail. Up till the present machines have only been used in this way." Then he asked "But is it necessary that they should always be used in such a manner?" Kugel [Kugel, 2005] tried to answer his question: "It isn't, if we are *willing* to allow them to carry out limiting computations" (super-recursive models of computation). He proceeded wondering "Who knows what, if anything, allowing programmers to think in terms of limiting-computable algorithms will do", and then finished encouraging "Let's try to find out." The authors of computational evolution (CE) vision [Banzhaf *et.al.*, 2006] emphasize similiar challenges: "The main difficulties will be psychological. CE practitioners and researchers must be *willing* to be patient.... patience will be necessary given the complexity and robustness of living systems compared with simplicity and brittleness of engineered systems;... they will also have to be willing to sacrifice precise specifications and full understanding of how individual components work."

Indeed, we cannot reflect on evolutionary computers from a typical engineer's point of view which only comprises intelligent design approach. We must let evolution take part in our design. It seems that bacteria and experimental evolution provide an excellent source of knowledge to create pioneer models of adaptive computers. Insights into and work on evolutionary models so far do not only provide new specification of knowledge needed for technical designing but they demand a different conception and approach in relation to computer models and applications developed. Instead of creationistic approach and conventional methods, evolutionary paradigm demands that we introduce decentralized approach and methods from which complex structures and behavior arise.

Software engineers and programmers up to now have got used to the fact that certain well known code lines are responsible for each segment of computer activity. However, we will not be able to understand the evolving program in the same way as we were able to understand the purpose of each code line in software that have been designed by human programmer so far. The new machines and application software will remain partly non-programmed. That other part of the program code will develop independently of the direct programmer's control depending on the environment in which this "young" computer will grow and develop (in a program sense of the word). Digital organisms will have no resemblance to those from biological world but they will maybe undergo their own evolution; serve us but taking care of their own reproduction at the same time. The life we know could be only the subset of all possible lives. This could, following our ideas of evolution, lead to completely new co-evolutionary relationship between a man and a computer.

Let me sum up insights and directions of this paper. Evolutionary information processes expose super-recursive features. Theory of super-recursive algorithms encourages us to change our mind in relation with question whether evolution is computational and help us to identify and extract different evolutionary information processes in order to build computer systems capable of computational evolution. If we reduce power of super-recursive algorithms to recursive ones an arbitrary evolutionary computer will lose the power of evolutionary adaptation. Finally, design and development of evolutionary computer has to be based on the super-recursive algorithms (the concept of Sequencer machine is proposed). Pursuing these directions the vision of computational evolution approaches its realization and the first experiments.

References

Ayala, F.J. (2007). Darwin's greatest discovery: design without designer. *Proc. Natl. Acad. Sci. U.S.A.* 104 Suppl 1: 8567–73.

Banzhaf, W.,Beslon, G., Christensen, S., Foster, A.J, Kepes, F., Lefort, V., Miller, F.J., Radman, M. and Ramsden, J. (2006). Guidelines: From artificial evolution to computational evolution: a research agenda. *Nature Reviews Genetics.* 7:729.

Bassler, B.L. (2002). Small talk: cell-to-cell communication in bacteria. *Cell* 109, 421–424.

Benenson Y., Gil B., Ben-Dor U., Adar R., Shapiro E. (2004). An autonomous molecular computer for logical control of gene expression. *Nature* 429, 423–429.

Ben-Jacob, E. (1998). Bacterial wisdom, Godel's theorem and creative genomic webs. *Physica A* 248, 57–76.

Ben Jacob, E. (2003). Bacterial Self-Organization: Co-Enhancement of Complexification and Adaptability in a Dynamic Environment *Phil. Trans. R. Soc. Lond. A*, 361:1283–1312.

Ben-Jacob, E., Becker, I., Y. Shapira. Y. (2004). Bacteria Linguistic Communication and Social Intelligence. *Trends in Microbiology*, Vol. 12/8 pp 366–372.

Ben Jacob, E. and Shapira, Y. (2005). Meaning-Based Natural Intelligence Vs. Information Based Artificial Intelligence. *Cradle of Creativity.*

Ben Jacob, E., Shapira, Y., Tauber, A.I. (2006). Seeking the Foundations of Cognition in Bacteria *Physica A* vol. 359; 495–524,.

Ben Jacob, E. (2008). Social behaviour of bacteria: from physics to complex organization. *The European Physical Journal B.*

Bird, A. (2007). Perceptions of epigenetics. *Nature* 447 (7143): 396–398.

Bjorkman, J.P., Samuelsson, D.I., Andersson & D. Hughes. (1999). Novel ribosomal mutations affecting translational accuracy, antibiotic resistance and virulence of *Salmonella typhimurium. Mol. Microbiol.* 31, 53:58.

Burgin, M. (2005). Monographs in Computer Science: Super-recursive Algorithms. *Springer.*

Cairns, J., Overbaugh, J. & Miller, S. (1988). The origin of mutants. *Nature* 335, 142–145.

Cairns, J. Foster, P. L. (1991). Adaptive reversion of a frameshift mutation in *Escherichia coli. Genetics* **128**, 695–701.

Casadesus, J., Low, D. (2006). Epigenetic Gene Regulation in the Bacterial World. *Microbiol Mol Biol Rev* **70** (3): 830–856.

Coen, E. (1999). The Art of Genes: How Organisms Make Themselves. *OUP* Oxford.

Darwin, C. (1859). On The Origin of Species by Means of Natural Selection *John Murray, London.*

Dawkins, R. (1986). The Blind Watchmaker. *W.W. Norton & Company*, New York.

Dawkins, R. (1972). The Extended Phenotype. *W.H. Freeman*, Oxford.

Dawkins, R. (1976). The Selfish Gene. *Oxford University Press*, Oxford.

Delbrück, M. (1946). Cold Spring Harbor Symp. Quant. Biol. 11, 154.

Dobzhansky, T. (1968). On some fundamental concepts of evolutionary biology. *Evolutionary biology* 2, 1–34.

Dover, G. (2000). Dear Mr. Darwin. *Weidenfeld & Nicolson*.

Eberbach E., Goldin D.,Wegner P. (2004). Turing's ideas and models of computation. In: Teuscher, Ch.(Ed.). Alan Turing Life and Legacy of Great Thinker. *Springer-Verlag* 159:194.

Eberbach E.,Wegner P. Beyond Turing Machines. (2003). *Bull. Eur. Assoc. Theor. Comput. Sci.(EATCS Bull)*. 81.

Fernald, R. D. (1997). The Evolution of Eyes, *Brain, Behavior and Evolution* 50 (4): 253–259.

Fox, E.K. (2000). The Century of the Gene. *Harvard University Press*.

Freeman S. & Herron J.C. (2007). *Evolutionary analysis*. Pearson Education.

Friedberg E.C., Walker G.C., Siede W, Wood R.D., Schultz R.A., Ellenberger T. (2006). DNA Repair and Mutagenesis, *ASM Press*. 2nd. ed.

Gell-Mann, M. (1994). The Quark and the Jaguar: Adventures in the Simple and the Complex, *W. H. Freeman and Company*.

Goldin D.,Smolka A.S.,Wegner P.(eds.) (2006). Interactive Computation – The New Paradigm. *Springer-Verlag*.

Gould, S.J. (1977). Ever Since Darwin. *W.W. Norton*, New York.

Hodges, A. (2000). The Nature of Turing and the Physical World. *A preface in The Collected Works of A. M. Turing*.

Jablonka, E., Lamb, M.J., Avital, E., (1998). 'Lamarckian' mechanisms in darwinian evolution. *Tree* vol. 13, no 5, 206–210.

Jablonka, E., Lamb, M.J. (2005). Evolution in Four Dimensions; Genetic, Epigenetic, Behavioral, and Symbolic Variation in the History of Life. *MIT Press*.

Jacob, J. (1993). The Logic of Life, A History of Heredity. Princeton University Press.

Janion, C. (2008). Inducible SOS Response System of DNA Repair and Mutagenesis in Escherichia coli. *Int. J. Biol. Sci.* 4(6):338–344.

Karpinets, T.V.,Greenwood3, D.J., Pogribny,I.P., Samatova, N.F., (2006). Bacterial Stationary-State Mutagenesis and Mammalian Tumorigenesis as Stress-Induced Cellular Adaptations and the Role of Epigenetics. *Current Genomics, 7*, 481–496.

Kauffman, S. (2008). Reinventing the Sacred: A New View of Science, Reason, and Religion. *Basic Books*.

Kauffman, S. (2009). Towards a Post Reductionist Science: The Open Universe *arXiv:0907.2492v1* [physics.hist-ph].

Kugel, P. (2005). It's time to think outside the computational box. *Communications of the ACM* Vol. 48, No. 11.

Land, M F., Fernald, R D (1992). The Evolution of Eyes. *Annual Review of Neuroscience* **15**: 1–29.

Lipson H. (2005). Evolutionary Design and Evolutionary Robotics. *Biomimetics*, CRC Press (Bar Cohen, Ed.) pp. 129–155.

Luria, S. E.; Delbrück, M. (1943). Mutations of Bacteria from Virus Sensitivity to Virus Resistance. *Genetics* 28 (6): 491–511.

Matz C, Webb JS, Schupp PJ, Phang SY, Penesyan A, et al. (2008). Marine Biofilm Bacteria Evade Eukaryotic Predation by Targeted Chemical Defense. *PloS ONE* 3(7).

Mayr, E. (1981). The growth of biological thought. *Harvard*. p481.

Michel, B. (2005). After 30 years of study, the bacterial SOS response still surprises us. *PLoS Biol* 3(7): e255.

Miller, M. B., Bassler, B. L. (2001) *Annu. Rev. Microbiol.*, 55, 165–199.

Miller, S.T., Xavier, K.B., Campagna, S.R., Taga, M.E., Semmelhack, M.F., Bassler, B.L., and Hughson, F.M. (2004). *Molecular Cell* 15:677–687.

Noble, D. (2008). The Music of Life – A view on nature and nurture. *OUP*.

Radman M. (1974). Phenomenology of an inducible mutagenic DNArepair pathway in *Escherichia coli*: SOS repair hypothesis. In: Sherman S, Miller M, Lawrence C., Tabor WH, eds. Molecular and Environmental aspects of mutagenesis. *Springfield IL:Charles C Thomas* publisher.: 128–142.

Radman, M., (1975), "Phenomenology of an inducible mutagenic DNA repair pathway in Escherichia coli: SOS repair hypothesis". *Basic Life Sciences* **5A**: 355–367.

Radman, M. (1998). DNA Replication: One strand may be more equal. *Proc.Natl.Acsd.Sci.* Vol. 95, pp. 9718–9719.

Radman M., Taddei, F., Matic, I., (2000). DNA Repair Systems and Bacterial Evolution. *Cold Spring Harbor Symposia on Quantitative Biology*. Vol LXV:11.

Ramsden, J.J. (2003). in Creatine Kinase and Brain Energy Metabolism (eds. Kekelidue, T. and Holtzmann, D.) *IOS Press*, Amsterdam.

Regev A.,Shapiro E. (2002). Cells as computation. *Nature*, Vol. 419, 343.

Rosenberg, S. M. (2001). Evolving responsively: Adaptive mutation. *Nature Reviews Genetics* vol2, 504–515.

Schauder, S., Shokat, K., Surette, M.G., and Bassler, B.L. (2001). *Molecular Microbiology* 41:463–476.

Schlacher, K, Pham, P., Michael M. Cox, M.M., Goodman M.F. (2006). Roles of DNA Polymerase V and RecA Protein in SOS Damage-Induced Mutation *Chem. Rev.*106, 406–419.

Schlacher, K., Goodman M.F., (2007). Lessons from 50 years of SOS DNA-damage-induced mutagenesis. *Nature Reviews Molecular Cell Biology 8*, 587–594.

Shapiro E., Benenson Y. (2006). Bringing DNA computers to life. *Scientific American*, 45:51.

Shapiro, J. A. (1984). Observations on the formation of clones containing araB–lacZ fusions. *Mol. Gen. Genet.* 194, 79–90.

Shapiro, J.A. (1992). Natural genetic engineering in evolution. *Genetica* 86, 99–111.

Shapiro, J. A. (1997). Genome organization, natural genetic engineering and adaptive mutation. *Trends Genet.* 13, 98–104.

Shapiro, J.A., (2005). A 21st century view of evolution: genome system architecture, repetitive DNA and natural genetic engineering. *Gene* 345, 91–100.

Shapiro JA. (2006). Genome informatics: The role of DNA in cellular computations. *Biological Theory* 1(3): 288–301.

Shapiro JA. (2007). Bacteria are small but not stupid: cognition, natural genetic engineering and socio-bacteriology. *Stud. Hist. Phil. Biol. & Biomed. Sci.* 38 807–819.

Siegelmann, H.T. (1995). Computation beyond the Turing machine. *Science*, 268:545.

Stewart P, Costerton J (2001). Antibiotic resistance of bacteria in biofilms. *Lancet* 358 (9276): 135–8.

Tlsty, T. D., Margolin, B. H. & Lum, K. (1989). Differences in the rates of gene amplification in nontumorigenic and tumorigenic cell lines as measured by Luria–Delbrück fluctuation analysis. *Proc. Natl Acad. Sci. USA* **86**, 9441–9445.

Turing, A. (1936). On computable numbers with an application to the Entscheidungsproblem. *Proc.Lond.Math.Soc.*Ser2, v, 42, 230–265.

Turing, A.M. (1950). Computing machinery and intelligence *Mind* **59** no 236, 433–460.

Turing, A. Lecture to the London Mathematical Society on 20 February 1947. In A.M. Turing's ACE Report and Other Papers, B. Carpenter and R. Doran, Eds. (1986). *MIT Press*, Cambridge, MA.

Turing A. Intelligent Machinery. (1948). In Collected Works of A.M.Turing: Mechanical Intelligence, ed.D.C.Ince. *Elsevier Science.* 1992.

Van Valen, L. (1973). A new evolutionary law. *Evolutionary Theory* 1: 1—30.

Vetsigian K, Woese C, Goldenfeld N (2006). Collective evolution and the genetic code. *Proc Natl Acad Sci U S A,* 103(28):10696–701.

Wagner A. (2005). Robustness and evolvability in living systems. (Princeton Studies in Complexity) *Princeton University Press.*

Watson, J.D., *et al.* (2007). Molecular biology of the Gene. *Benjamin Cummings*; 6th. Ed.

Werner, E. (2007). Systems Biology: How Central is the Genome? *Science* 10, 753–754.

Willis, R. (1841). Principles of Mechanism, London (available online at *http://kmoddl.library.cornell.edu*).

Woese CR and Goldenfeld N (2009). How the Microbial World Saved Evolution from the Scylla of Molecular Biology and the Charybdis of the Modern Synthesis. *Microbiol. Mol. Biol. Rev.* 73:14–21.

Wright, B.E. (1997). Does selective gene activation direct evolution? *FEBS let.* 402, 4–8.

Zahradka K., Slade D., Bailone A., Sommer S., Averbeck D., Petranovic M., Lindner B.A. and Radman M. (2006). Reassembly of shattered chromosomes in *Deinococcus Radiodurans. Nature.*

Ziman J, (2003). Technological Innovation as an Evolutionary Process. *Cambridge University Press.*

CHAPTER 14

TOWARDS A MODELING VIEW OF COMPUTING

Oron Shagrir

Department of Philosophy
Program of Cognitive Science
The Hebrew University of Jerusalem

The view that the brain computes is a working hypothesis in cognitive and brain sciences. But what does it mean to say that a system computes? What distinguishes computing systems, such as desktops and brains, from (arguably) non-computing systems, such as stones, stomachs and tornadoes? This question has generated an intense and lively discussion in recent years, and, as expected, there is no consensus over the answer. In fact, it is far from clear that there is only a single notion in play; it might well be the case that the term "computation" invokes very different notions in different contexts.

Most accounts of computing are "structural", in the sense that they take it that the difference between computing and non-computing has something to do with the structure of the mechanism, e.g., that computing processes have an algorithmic structure. I present the structural view of computing in section 1. As it turns out, however, the structural approach cannot account for much of the computational work in cognitive and brain sciences; I discuss this claim in section 2. There is thus a need for an alternative approach to computing, one that can take into account the current enterprises in computational cognitive neuroscience. My aim in section 3 is to sketch such an alternative, which is the modeling view of computing. The key feature of the modeling view is that computing consists in an isomorphism between the "inner" relations, defined over the representing states, and "outer" relations, defined over the represented states.

1. The Structural-Digital View

The claim that something computes goes beyond the use of computational models. Neuroscientists and cognitive scientists not only use computational models to study the nervous system but often claim, in addition, that the modeled system itself e.g., the brain, computes. What do they mean by this further claim?

Many hold that the distinction between computing and non-computing has something to do with the structure of the (computing) mechanism. Computing mechanisms have a special structure that is not shared by many of the non-computing mechanisms. Let us call this approach the *structural view* of computing. The proponents of the structural view tend to associate computing with types of digital structures. They take it that to compute a function is to follow some rule or algorithm or effective procedure; to execute a program; to implement an automaton; or to manipulate symbols (e.g., digits). This comes down to having the form of step-by-step, rule-governed, or discrete processes (this is, perhaps, in contrast to non-computing mechanisms that are often non-discrete, continuous, governed by dynamical equations, and so on).

The structural approach comes in different flavors. Newell and Simon (1976) famously associate a computer with a "physical symbol system", which "is capable of having and manipulating symbols, yet is also realizable within our physical universe" (Newell 1980: 138). This characterization of computing highlights two *non-structural* conditions. One is that the system is realizable in some physical structure that obeys the laws of physics. The other is that the system operates on symbols that are "interpretable" in one way or another. Yet when they come to elaborate on their notion they associate a physical symbol system with "a specific architectural" structure (1976: 42), which Newell, later on, describes in terms of five subsystems: memory, operators, control, input and output (Newell 1980: 142; see also Harnish 2002: 396-7).

Fodor characterizes computational processes as *formal*, namely, that "they apply to representations in virtue of (roughly) the *syntax* of representations" (1980: 309). Fodor does not say what exactly the syntactic properties are, but he very often associates them with certain "Classical" architectures: "The emphasis upon the syntactical character of thought suggests a view of cognitive processes... as occurring in a languagelike medium, a sort of 'language of thought'" (1994:9). Having this structure, computing systems are "automatic formal systems"

(Haugeland 1981b) in the sense that they reliably preserve truth (Fodor 1994: 8-9).

Cummins (1989) also emphasizes that computations operate on symbols, i.e., entities with semantic values. Yet he argues that there are mapping processes from symbols to symbols that compute the mapping functions, and there are mapping processes that only satisfy the functions but do not compute. Computations, according to Cummins, are those processes that involve program execution and, as such, have the unique structure of *step-by-step form*: "To compute a function g is to execute a program that gives o as its output on input i just in case $g(i) = o$. Computing reduces to program execution.... Program execution reduces to step-satisfaction" (Cummins 1989: 91-92).

More recently, Piccinini (2007, 2008a) advances a forceful structural account of computing. According to this account, computation "is the generation of output strings of digits from input strings of digits in accordance with a general rule that depends on the properties of the strings and (possibly) on the internal state of the system" (2008a: 34; see also 2007: 501). This account is "purely structural" in that it does not require a semantic condition. Computing processes operate on entities that could be interpreted in one way or another, but it is not essential for them to have semantic values (Piccinini 2008b). The only constraint on computing is structural: the condition being that computing processes manipulate inputs in accordance with a rule defined over the input types and their place within strings (2007: 521).

There is much to commend the structural-digital view of computing. It is in accord with the notion used in theoretical computer science, especially in computability and automata theory. It can be easily associated with central works in Classical AI (Newell and Simon) and in Cognitive Science (Chomsky 1957). It can be located within the current framework of functional explanations (Haugeland 1978; Cummins 1983) and mechanistic explanations (Craver 2007; Bechtel 2008). And, it is associated with the functionalist view that is so influential in philosophy of mind (Block 1995). Yet it has also one major defect: It is at odds with much of the work in connectionist cognitive science and computational neuroscience.

2. A Critique of the Structural-Digital View

The structural-digital view can be criticized on various grounds. One could argue that there is no precise definition of digitality, and thus of the digital/non-digital distinction (and does "non-digital" mean "continuous", "analog", or "dynamical"?); see discussion in Dodig-Crnkovic and Müller, (*this volume*, section 5). My criticism, however, is different. I do not think it is essential to have a precise definition of digitality. There are many useful notions in science – e.g., length, species, cells – for which there is no precise definition. It is enough to have a characterization of digital that makes sense of paradigm examples and excludes the obvious non-digital cases; and indeed there are such characterizations (see, e.g., Haugeland 1981c).

Another line of criticism is that the notion of digitality is vacuous, since, at one level or another, every physical system can be seen as a digital computer (Searle 1992; see also Putnam 1988). But, again, this is not my criticism against the structural-digital conception. In fact, I think that this line of criticism is not very effective, and I discuss it at some length elsewhere (Shagrir 2010). My criticism, rather, is that there is an important class of systems that are not seen as having digital structure yet are described as computing systems. As a matter of fact, I argue, structure – *any structure* –is not a necessary constraint on computing.

To make the point, let us consider a specific example of a computing nervous tissue that is in charge of holding the eyes still. The brain moves the eyes with quick saccadic movements. Between saccades, it keeps the eyes still (Leigh and Zee 2006). The brain can do this by storing a memory of eye-positions, known as *oculomotor integrator* (Robinson 1989). The brain's memory of horizontal eye-position appears to be implemented by a persistent neural activity, which is spread over several areas in the brainstem and cerebellum. Different experimental studies show that this system converts transient eye-velocity-encoding inputs into persistent eye-position-encoding outputs. It is concluded that the system locates the new eye-position by computing integration on the pulse saccadic inputs with respect to time. The motor neurons, reading out the memory, keep the eyes still in the new location.

In the language of state space analysis, the oculomotor integrator moves from one state, Si, which represents one eye-position, Ei, to another state, Sj, which represents another eye-position, Ej, by performing integration on eye-velocity-encoding inputs I (Fig. 1):

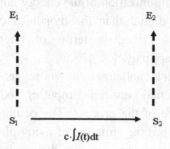

Fig. 1. The dynamics of the oculomotor memory: The system consists of stable states S_i, each representing a different eye-position E_i. The system moves from one state, say S_1, to another state, say S_2, by integrating on pulse saccadic inputs, I, which encode eye-velocity.

How does this system compute integration in arriving at a new position? The experimental findings show that when the eyes are still, the pattern of neural activity in the memory is constant in time, and that for every eye-position, the pattern of activity is different and persistent. This persistence is thus explained in terms of a multi-stable recurrent network with a *continuous line attractor* dynamics (Canon & Robinson 1985; Seung 1996, 1998); the continuity is required for consistency with the analog, graded encoding of the eye-position in the neural activity. Each point along the line encodes a horizontal eye-position. A novel input destabilizes the network, which gradually stabilizes at a new point along the attractor line; this point encodes the current eye position.

The theoreticians' work nicely exemplifies the difficulties confronting the structural-digital conception. Firstly, it challenges the element of digitality in the conception. The integrating mechanism is at odds with the idea that computing has to do with *digital* structure. It is true that the network consists of separable cells, but the activation of cells is continuous and is described in terms of differential equations. Moreover, the space of "states", S_i, is not discrete in the sense that they are "separable" attractors; the space, rather, is "dense" in that it is a continuous line attractor, whereas each point on the line represents a different eye-position. In addition, the dynamics of the network is not, in any obvious sense, algorithmic or rule-governed or step-satisfaction. The dynamics is a continuous relaxation on the next stable state, which is described in terms of minimization of the energy landscape. In short, the dynamics is no more digital than the dynamics of any other system whose dynamics is described in terms of interaction between its elements, e.g., elementary particles.

Secondly, the model challenges the more general structural idea, namely, that the distinction between computing and non-computing has to do with the structure of the process. The oculomotor integrator is a dynamical system that has the structure of many physical dynamics that we consider as non-computing, e.g., the dynamics of the volume of a flowing liquid into a container. It has no obvious structural property that distinguishes it from all the non-computing dynamics. Even the language used to describe the dynamics is not the language of automata or computability theory. The model describes the integrating process in the language of control theory and dynamical theory, which is the same language that is used to describe many non-computing dynamical systems. So, all in all, it is very difficult to see what could be a relevant structural difference between computing and non-computing. Structure, it seems, contributes nothing to the distinction between computing and non-computing.

3. The Modeling View

The modeling view starts with the observation that computation operates with information or on representations: "a physical system is considered a computer when its states can be taken as representing states of some other system" (Churchland, Koch and Sejnowski 1990: 48). But computation goes beyond this "semantic condition". It also has something to do with "formality", at least in the sense that computational descriptions are not sensitive to every difference in content. Our oculomotor integrator is a good example of the importance of the "formality condition". Some argue that the very same integrator also serves for another purpose. It serves to compute the desired eye-position from the velocity of the head-movement and as such serves as the computational basis of the VOR operation (Robinson 1989, Goldman *et al.* 2002). Still, we can notice that although the content of the representation is different, the computational description is the same. The content is different, since in one case the machine operates on representations whose content is eye-velocity and eye-position (oculomotor memory), whereas in the other case, the content of representations has to do with head-velocity and desired eye-position. Nevertheless, in both cases we count the operations as the performance of the same computation – namely, integration – regardless of the specific information content of the physical signals.

The modeling account, then, respects a formality condition. However, it does not conceive this formality condition as a structural constraint, i.e., that the process is algorithmic, rule-governed, and so on. The modeling account conceives of the formality constraint in terms of modeling. To see what modeling means here let us look again at the oculomotor integrator. We can observe that the term $\int I(t)d(t)$ describes two different relations: One is the mapping relation between the stable states of the neural network (oculomotor integrator), Si and Sj, and the other is between the eye-positions, Ei and Ej, that are being represented by these states. The term *I* refers, at one level, to the transient saccadic electrical inputs to the network and, at the other level, to the eye-velocity. In other words, the mathematical formula of integration describes relations at two different levels. It describes some cellular activity in the brain, but also some relations between the entities that are being represented by these cells (Fig. 2).

Another way to make this point is to state that the system models the physical world in a very special way: it models certain mathematical relations "in the world" by the mathematical relations defined over the electric cellular activity. There is, as it were, an "isomorphism" between mathematical relations among the states of the modeling system and the formal or mathematical relations between the states of the modeled system. The term "mathematical relations" means that what is being related are mathematical entities like real numbers, geometrical relations, set-theoretic structures and so forth. These entities are mathematical values, magnitudes that *abstract* from pertinent physical properties. At one level, the function relates numbers that abstract from the representations (e.g., electrical cellular activity). At another, it relates magnitudes that abstract from representational contents (e.g., position and velocity).

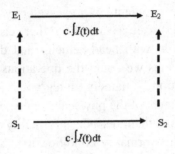

Fig. 2. Modeling by the oculomotor integrator: the expression $\int I(t)d(t)$ describes both the relations between two states of the neural memory, S_1 and S_2, *and* the relations between the two eye-positions, E_1 and E_2, which S_1 and S_2 represent.

This idea of modeling is not really new: we can trace it back to the old-fashioned analog computers. A paradigm example is the tide-predicting machine that was designed by Lord Kelvin and constructed in 1873. The machine determined the height of the tides by integrating (i.e., summation) of ten principal components. These components were made by means of teeth-wheels that simulated the motion of the sun, moon, earth and other factors that influence tides (see Kelvin's presentation at http://zapatopi.net/kelvin/papers/the_tides.html). We should notice, however, that the relevant sense of "analog" here is not continuous; computing, on the modeling account, can also be digital. The relevant sense of "analog" is that the mathematical function computed by the system is *analogous* to mathematical relations in other physical systems, one of which the system models.

This idea of modeling is widespread in computational neuroscience. In analyzing the Zipser and Andersen (1988) model of the response properties of the PPC cells in area 7a of macaque monkeys, Grush (2001) notices that the expression $(k_i^T e + b_i)\exp(-(r-r_i)^T(r-r_i)/2\sigma^2)$ refers to relations at two different levels. At one (abstract) level, it describes the activity of a certain group of PPC cells as a function of the activity of other, pre-synaptic, activity. At another (abstract) level, the formula refers to some complex mathematical relations between the things that are being represented, namely, eye orientation and stimulus retinotopic location, and the stimulus distance from the preferred direction relative to the head.

Another example is the Marr and Hildreth (1980) computational-level theory of edge-detection (see also Marr 1982, chap. 2). The relation between the activity of the retinal photoreceptors and the activity of cells in the primary visual cortex (V1) is described in terms of the zero-crossings of the formula $\nabla^2 G * I(x,y)$; I refers to the array of photoreceptors (retinal image), $*$ is a convolution operator, and $\nabla^2 G$ is a filtering operator: G is a Gaussian that blurs the image, and ∇^2 is the Laplacian operator $(\partial^2/\partial x^2 + \partial^2/\partial y^2)$ that is sensitive to sudden intensity changes in the image. The zero-crossings of this formula are precisely those places in the image that have sharp intensity changes. This formula, however, also describes relations between what is being represented by these cells. The formula states that the relations between light intensity values, signified by I, and the light reflectance along physical edges are those of derivation, i.e. that sudden changes in light intensities occur along physical edges such as object boundaries.

We can now characterize a computing system as follows. A computing system has two features: (a) the semantic feature: it is information-processing in the sense that it maps one set of representations to another; and (b) the formality feature: the functional, mathematical relations between its states are similar to the mathematical relations between the entities that are being represented by these states.

This is, of course, just a sketch. A detailed account is yet to be worked out, and the scope of the account is yet to be examined. But I hope that I have provided some indication that the modeling direction is more promising than the structural view, at least in the context of the current work in computational neuroscience.

Acknowledgement: Thanks to Gordana Dodig-Crnkovic for comments and suggestions. This research was supported by The Israel Science Foundation, grant 725/08.

Bibliography

Bechtel, W., (2008), *Mental Mechanisms: Philosophical Perspectives on the Sciences of Cognition and the Brain*, Routledge.

Block, N., (1995), The mind as the software of the brain, In D. Osherson, L. Gleitman, S. Kosslyn, E. Smith and S. Sternberg (eds.), *An Invitation to Cognitive Science, Volume 3: Thinking* (2nd), MIT Press, pp. 377-425.

Cannon, S.C., and Robinson, D.A., (1985), An improved neural-network model for the neural integrator of the oculomotor system: More realistic neuron behavior, *Biological Cybernetics*, 53, pp. 93-108

Chomsky, N., (1957), *Syntactic Structures*, Mouton.

Churchland, P.S., Koch, C., and Sejnowski, T.J., (1990), What is computational neuroscience?, In E.L. Schwartz (ed.), *Computational Neuroscience*, MIT Press, pp. 46-55.

Craver, C., (2007), *Explaining the Brain*, Oxford University Press.

Cummins, R., (1983), *The Nature of Psychological Explanation*, MIT Press.

Cummins, R., (1989), *Meaning and Mental Representation*, MIT Press.

Dodig-Crnkovic, G., and Müller, V. C., A Dialogue concerning two world systems: Info-computational vs. mechanistic, *this volume*.

Edelman, S., (2008), *Computing the Mind: How the Mind Really Works*, Oxford University Press.

Fodor, J.A., (1980), Methodological solipsism considered as a research strategy in cognitive psychology, *Behavioral and Brain Sciences*, 3, pp. 63-73. Reprinted in Haugeland (1981a), pp. 307-338.

Fodor, J.A., (1994), *The Elm and The Expert: Mentalese and Its Semantics*, MIT Press.

Goldman, M.S., Kaneko, C.R.S., Major, G., Aksay, E., Tank, D.W. and Seung, H.S. (2002), Linear regression of eye velocity on eye position and head velocity suggests a common oculomotor neural integrator, *Journal of Neurophysiology*, 88, pp. 659-665.

Grush, R., (2001), The semantic challenge to computational neuroscience, In P. Machamer, R. Grush, and P. McLaughlin (eds.), *Theory and Method in the Neurosciences*, University of Pittsburgh Press, pp. 155-172

Harnish, R., (2002), *Minds, Brains, Computers: The Foundations of Cognitive Science - An Historical Introduction*, Wiley-Blackwell.

Haugeland, J., (1978), The Nature and plausibility of cognitivism, *Behavioral and Brain Sciences*, 2, pp. 215-226.

Haugeland, J., (1981a), *Mind Design* (ed.), MIT Press.

Haugeland, J., (1981b), Semantic engines: An introduction to mind design, In Haugeland (1981a), pp. 1-34.

Haugeland, J., (1981c), Analog and analog, *Philosophical Topics*, 12, pp. 213–225.

Leigh, J.R., and Zee, S.D., (2006), *The Neurology of Eye Movements* (4th Edition), Oxford University Press.

Marr, D., (1982), *Vision*, Freeman.

Marr, D., and Hildreth, E., (1980), Theory of edge detection, *Proceedings of the Royal Society of London, Series B, Biological Sciences*, 207, pp. 187-217.

Newell, A., (1980), Physical symbol systems, *Cognitive Science*, 4, pp. 135-183.

Newell, A., and Simon, H., (1976), Computer science as empirical inquiry: Symbols and search, *Communications of the Association for Computing Machinery*, 19, pp. 113-126. Reprinted in Haugeland (1981a), pp. 35-66.

Piccinini, G., (2007), Computing mechanisms, *Philosophy of Science*, 74, pp. 501-526.

Piccinini, G., (2008a), Computers. *Pacific Philosophical Quarterly*, 89, pp. 32-73.

Piccinini, G., (2008b), Computation without representation, *Philosophical Studies*, 137, pp. 205-241.

Putnam, H., (1988), *Representations and Reality*, MIT Press.

Robinson, D. A., (1989), Integrating with neurons, *Annual Review of Neuroscience*, 12, pp. 33-45.

Searle, J. R., (1992), *The Rediscovery of the Mind*, MIT Press.

Sejnowski, T. J., Koch, C., and Churchland, P.S., (1988), Computational neuroscience, *Science*, 241, pp. 1299-1306.

Seung, H. S., (1996), How the brain keeps the eyes still, *Proceedings of National Academy of Science, USA*, 93, pp. 13339-13344.

Seung, H. S., (1998), Continuous attractors and oculomotor control, *Neural Networks*, 11, pp. 1253-1258.

Shagrir, O., (2010), Brains as analog-model computers, *Studies in History and Philosophy of Science A*, 41, pp. 271–279.

Zipser, D., and Andersen, R.A., (1988), A back-propagation programmed network that simulates response properties of a subset of posterior parietal neurons, *Nature*, 331, pp. 679–684.

CHAPTER 15

WHAT'S INFORMATION,
FOR AN ORGANISM OR INTELLIGENT MACHINE?
HOW CAN A MACHINE OR ORGANISM MEAN?

Aaron Sloman

School of Computer Science, University of Birmingham,
Edgbaston, Birmingham, B15 2TT, UK
http: // www. cs. bham. ac. uk/ ~axs

Words and phrases referring to information are now used in many scientific and non-scientific academic disciplines and in many forms of engineering. This chapter suggests that this is a result of increasingly wide-spread, though often implicit, acknowlèdgement that besides *matter* and *energy* the universe contains *information* (including information about matter, energy and information) and many of the things that happen, including especially happenings produced by living organisms, and more recently processes in computers, involve information-processing. It is argued that the concept "information" can no more be defined explicitly in terms of simpler concepts than any of the other deep theoretical concepts of science can, including "matter" and "energy". Instead the meanings of the words and phrases referring to such things are defined *implicitly* in part by the structure of the theories in which they occur, and in part by the way those theories are tested and used in practical applications. This is true·of all deep theoretical concepts of science. It can also be argued that many of the pre-scientific concepts developed by humans (including very young humans) in the process of coming to understand their environment are also implicitly defined by their role in the theories being developed. A similar claim can be made about other intelligent animals, and future robots. An outline of a theory about the processes and mechanisms various kinds of information can be involved in is presented as partial implicit definition of "information". However there is still much work to be done including investigation of varieties of information processing in organisms and other machines.

1. Introduction

The question "What is information?", like "What is matter?" and "What is energy?", cannot have a simple answer in the form of a non-circular definition. Answering such a question involves answering a host of related questions. Answers to the second and third cannot be given without presenting deep and complex theories about how the physical universe works. The theories, along with links to experimental methods, instruments and observation techniques, provide the only kind of definition possible for many of the concepts used in the physical sciences: implicit definition. Moreover, the answers are always subject to the possibility of being revised or extended, as the history of physics shows clearly: old concepts may be gradually transformed as the theories in which they are embedded are expanded and modified – sometimes with major discontinuities, as happened to concepts like "matter", "energy" and "force" in the work of Newton and Einstein, for example. Lesser transformations go with improved instruments and techniques for observation, measurement, and testing predictions. So concepts, have a continuing identity through many changes, like rivers, growing organisms, nations, and many other things (Cohen, 1962; Schurz, 2009).

1.1. *The need for a theory*

"Information" (in its oldest, and still growing, use), is another such concept. So answering the question "What is information?" will require developing a deep and complex theory of how parts of the universe that use or interact with information work, for instance entities (information users) that do various things with information: acquiring, manipulating, combining, deriving, storing, retrieving, comparing, analysing, interpreting, explaining, indexing, annotating, communicating, and above all *using* information for practical purposes. Information cannot play a role in any process unless there is something that encodes or expresses the information: an "information bearer" (B), and some user (U) that takes B to express information I (i.e. interprets B). The same bearer B may be interpreted differently by different users, and the same user, U may interpret B differently in different contexts (C). We need a theory that explains the different ways in which *a bearer B can express information I for U in context*

C, and what that means. I shall henceforth use "representation" to refer to any kind of information bearer, and will later criticise some alternative definitions, in Section 2.3.

Such a theory will have to mention different kinds of information-users and information-bearers (physical and non-physical), as well as different kinds of information content, and the different ways information-bearers can be related to the information they carry, often requiring several layers of interpretation, as we'll see. The theory will also have to survey varieties of information users, with different sorts of information processing architectures, interacting with different sorts of environment, using information-bearers (representations) that have different structures, and use different media (physical and non-physical).

Questions to be addressed include: What are the requirements for U to treat B as expressing a meaning or referring to something? What are the differences between things that merely manipulate symbolic structures and things that also understand and make use of information they associate with those structures, for example, deriving new information from them, or testing the information for consistency? Compare [Searle (1980)].

1.2. *Is biological information-processing special?*

Many of the questions have a biological context. In what ways do organisms acquire, store, extract, derive, combine, analyse, manipulate, transform, interpret, transmit, and use information? Which of these are, or could be, replicated in non-biological machines? If not all of them, then why not? Is there something special common to all forms of biological information processing?

1.3. *Questions seeking answers*

More general questions of a more philosophical kind that need to be answered include, whether "information" is as important a concept for science as "matter" and "energy", or just a term that is bandied about, with changing meanings, by undisciplined thinkers? Is it reasonable to think of the universe as containing matter, energy and information, with interdependencies between all three, or is there only matter and energy, in various static and changing configurations?

Why is a simple explicit definition for "information" impossible? Is it like some older scientific concepts, not explicitly definable, but implicitly definable by developing powerful explanatory theories that use the concept? Is information something that should be measurable as energy and mass are, or are its features mainly structures to be *described* not *measured* (e.g. the structure of this sentence, the structure of a molecule, the structure of an organism)? How does this (centuries old) notion of information (or meaning) relate to the more recent concept of information as something measurable? (Shannon, 1948) Are there conservation laws for information, or is that idea refuted by the fact that one user can give information to another without losing any? Moreover, it is even possible for me to say something that gives you information I did not have. (Compare the role of relay switches in electrical power circuits.)

This document attempts to give partial answers to these questions, and to specify requirements for more complete answers. I shall attempt to sum up what I think many scientists and engineers in many disciplines, and also historians, journalists, and lay people, are talking about when they talk about information, as they increasingly do, even though they don't realise precisely what they are doing. For example the idea of information pervades many excellent books about infant development, such as Gibson and Pick (2000), without being explicitly defined. I shall try to explain how a good scientific theory can implicitly define its main theoretical concepts, and will sketch some of the main features of a theory of the role of information in our universe. A complete theory would require many volumes. In several other papers and presentations cited below, I have presented some of these ideas in more detail.

2. Uses of the word "information"

2.1. *Confusions*

Unfortunately, there are many confusions about both the *content* of the notion of "information" (what we mean by it, how it should be defined, whether it can be given any precise definition) and its *status* (e.g. as a theoretical term in scientific theories, or as a loose and ill-defined, though currently fashionable, concept). The word may be a source of so much confusion that a better one is needed, but it is too late to propose a replacement, and there is no obvious candidate. "Meaning" is just as bad, or worse, since it often refers to an intention (what did you mean to do?), or the importance of some event or object (what's the meaning of the election result?), whereas information does not have to be the content of anyone's intention, and can be devoid of importance.

Some philosophers talk about "propositional content" but the normal interpretation of that phrase rules out information expressed in non-propositional forms, such as the information in pictures, maps, videos, gestures, and perceptual systems. So I shall stick to the label "information", and attempt to explain how it is used in many everyday contexts and also in scientific (e.g. biological) contexts. The word is also used in this sense in engineering, in addition to being used in Shannon's sense, discussed further in Section 2.2.

The phrase "semantic information" is as pleonastic as the phrase "young youths", since information, in the sense under discussion, is semantic. It is sometimes useful to contrast syntactic information with semantic information, where the former is about the form or structure of something that conveys information, whereas the semantic information would be about the content of what is said. ("Content" is metaphorical here.) For instance, saying that my sentences often have more than eight words gives syntactic information about my habits, whereas saying that I often discuss evolution or that what I say is ambiguous or unoriginal gives semantic information, or, in the latter case, meta-semantic information. Likewise, we provide syntactic information about a programming language (e.g. how it uses parentheses) or semantic information (e.g. about the kinds of structure and transformations of structure that it can denote). We can distinguish the "internal" semantics of a programming language (the internal structures and processes the programs specify) from its "external" semantics, e.g. its relevance to a robot's environment, or to a company's employees, salaries, jobs, sales, etc.

2.2. *This is not "information" in Shannon's sense*

There is another, more recent, use of the word "information" in the context of Shannon's "information theory" Shannon (1948). But that does not refer to what is normally meant by "information" (the topic of this paper), since Shannon's information is a purely syntactic property of something like a bit-string, or other structure that might be transmitted from a sender to a receiver using a mechanism with a fixed repertoire of possible messages. If a communication channel can carry N bits then each string transmitted makes a selection from 2^N possible strings. The larger N is, the more alternative possibilities are excluded by each string actually received. In that syntactic sense longer strings carry more "information". Likewise the information capacity of a communication channel can be measured in terms of the number of bits it can transfer in parallel, and the measure can be modified to take account of noise, etc. Shannon was perfectly aware of all this. He wrote

> "The fundamental problem of communication is that of re-
> producing at one point either exactly or approximately a
> message selected at another point. Frequently the messages
> have meaning; that is they refer to or are correlated according
> to some system with certain physical or conceptual entities.
> *These semantic aspects of communication are irrelevant to the*
> *engineering problem.*" (Shannon, 1948). [My emphasis.]

It is worth noting that although he is talking about an engineering problem of reproducing a message exactly, doing that is not what most human communication is about. If you ask me a question, my answer may fill a gap in your information, allowing you to make inferences that I could not make. Both of us may know that, and that could be the intention of my answer. On a noisy phone line that could happen if you knew in advance that the answer was either "elephant" or "fly". If I say "fly" and you hear "spy", the fact that my precise message was not transmitted accurately does not matter: you can tell that I did not say "elephant", and proceed accordingly. A pupil's questions or comments may give a teacher information that the pupil would not understand, e.g. about how to continue a lesson. So communication in intelligent systems depends on, but is far more than, mere signal transmission. It also uses context, general knowledge of the world, more or less sophisticated interpretation mechanisms, and reasoning capabilities. Shannon's work is summarised, with strong warnings about extending it beyond the context of electromechanical signal transmission in Ritchie (1986).

Having a measurable amount of information in Shannon's sense does not, in itself, allow a string to express something true or false, or to contradict or imply something else in the ordinary senses of "contradict" or "imply", or to express a question or command. Of course, a bit string used in a particular context could have these functions. E.g. a single bit could express a "yes" or "no" answer to a previously asked question, as could a "continue" or "stop" command. In some contexts, that single bit may indirectly convey a great deal of information. "Is everything Fred wrote in his letter true?" "Yes."

2.3. *Misguided definitions*

[Bateson (1972)] describes "a bit of information" and later "the elementary unit of information" as "a difference that makes a difference".[a] This is widely misquoted as offering a definition of "information" rather than "a bit/unit of information". He seems to be thinking of any item of information as essentially a collection of "differences" that are propagated along channels. This is far too simplistic – and perhaps too influenced by low level descriptions of computers and brains. An alternative approach is to define "information" implicitly by a complete theory, as happens for many scientific concepts. This paper attempts to present substantial portions of such a theory, though the task is not completed. Section 3.2 explains how theories can implicitly define the concepts they use and 6.1 relates this to defining "information".

What it means for B to express I for U in context C cannot be given any simple definition. Some people try to define this by saying U uses B to "stand for" or "stand in for" I. For instance, Webb writes "The term 'representation' is used in many senses, but is generally understood as a process in which something is used to stand in for something else, as in the use of the symbol 'I' to stand for the author of this article" citewebb06. This sort of definition of "representation" is either circular, if standing for is the same thing as referring to, or else false, if standing in for means "being used in place of". There are all sorts of things you can do with information that you would never do with what it refers to and vice versa. You can eat food, but not information about food. Even if you choose to eat a piece of paper on which "food" is written that is usually irrelevant to your use of the word to refer to food. Information about X is normally used for quite

---

[a] In at least two of the essays "The Cybernetics of 'Self': A Theory of Alcoholism" and in "Form Substance and Difference".

different purposes from the purposes for which X is used. For example, the information can be used for drawing inferences, specifying something to be prevented, or constructed, and many more. Information about a possible disaster can be very useful and therefore desirable, unlike the disaster itself.

So the notion of standing for, or standing in for is the wrong notion to use to explain information content. It is a very bad metaphor, even though its use is very common. We can make more progress by considering ways in which information can be used. If I give you the information that wet whether is approaching, you cannot use the information to wet anything. But you can use it to decide to take an umbrella when you go out, or, if you are a farmer you may use it as a reason for accelerating harvesting. The falling rain cannot so be used: by the time the rain is available it is too late to save the crops.

The same information can be used in different ways in different contexts or at different times. The relationship between information content and information use is not a simple one.

2.4. *The world is NOT the best representation of itself*

In recent years, an erroneous claim, related to confusing representing with standing in for, has found favour with many, namely the claim that "the world is its own best representation".

Herbert Simon pointed out long ago (Simon, 1969) that sometimes the changes made to the environment while performing a task can serve as reminders or triggers regarding what has to be done next, giving examples from insect behaviours. The use of stigmergy, e.g. leaving tracks or pheromone trails or other indications of travel, which can later be used by other individuals, shows how sometimes changes made to the environment can be useful as means of sharing information with others. Similarly if you cannot be sure whether a chair will fit through a doorway you can try pushing it through, and if it is too large you will fail, or you may discover that it can go through only if it is rotated in some complex way.

The fact that intelligent agents can use the environment as a store of information or as a source of information or as part of a mechanism for reasoning or inferring, does not support the slogan that the world, or any part of it, is always, or even in those cases the best representation of itself (a) because the slogan omits the role of the information-processing in the agent making use of the environment and (b) because it sometimes is better to have specific instructions, a map, a blue-print or some other information structure that decomposes information in a usable way, than to have to use the portion of the world represented, as anyone learning to play the violin simply by watching a violinist will discover.

In general, information about X is something different from X itself. Reasons for wanting or for using information about X are different from the reasons for wanting or using X. E.g. you may wish to use information about X in order to ensure that you never get anywhere near X if X is something dangerous. You may wish to use information about Xs to destroy Xs, but if that destroyed the information you would not know how to destroy the next one until you are close to it. It may then be too late to take necessary precautions, about which you had lost information.

[Dreyfus (2002)] wrote "The idea of an intentional arc is meant to capture the idea that all past experience is projected back into the world. The best representation of the world is thus the world itself." As far as I can make out he is merely talking about expert servo control, e.g. the kind of visual servoing which I discussed in Sloman (1982). But as any roboticist knows, and his own discussion suggests, this kind of continuous action using sensory feedback requires quite sophisticated *internal* information processing [Grush (2004)]. In such cases "the world" is not nearly enough.

2.5. *Disagreements about information bearers, representations*

Brooks also wrote a series of papers attacking symbolic AI, including (Brooks, 1991). He repeatedly emphasises the need to test working systems on the real world and not only in simulation, a point that has some validity but can be over-stressed. (If aircraft designers find it useful to test their designs in simulation, why not robot designers?) Moreover, he disputes the need for representations (information bearers constructed and manipulated by information users), saying: "We hypothesize (following Agre and Chapman) that much of even human level activity is similarly a reflection of the world through very simple mechanisms without detailed representations," and "We believe representations are not necessary and appear only in the eye or mind of the observer." A critique of that general viewpoint is presented in (Sloman, 2009c), which mostly deals with [Brooks (1990)], in which he goes further:

> "The key observation is that the world is its own best model. It is always exactly up to date. It always contains every detail there is to be known. The trick is to sense it appropriately and often enough."

That's impossible when you are planning the construction of a skyscraper using a new design, or working out the best way to build a bridge across a chasm, or even working out the best way to cross a busy road, which you suspect has a pedestrian crossing out of sight around the bend. The important point is that intelligence often requires reasoning about what might be the case, or might happen, and its consequences: and that cannot be done by inspecting the world as it is. Recall that information bearers and things they represent have different uses (Section 2.3).

2.6. *Computation and information*

It is sometimes suggested, e.g. in [Searle (1980)], that computation is concerned only with syntax. That ignores the fact that even in the simplest computers bit patterns refer to locations and instructions, i.e. they have a semantic interpretation. An extreme view in the opposite direction is expressed by [Denning (2009)]: "The great principles framework reveals that there is something even more fundamental than an algorithm: the representation. Representations convey information. A computation is an evolving representation and an algorithm is a representation of a method to control the evolution". A position close to Denning's will be developed here, though his view of computation (i.e. information-processing) is too narrow.

2.7. *Not all information is true*

Some people, for example the philosopher Fred Dretske, in his contribution to Floridi (2008), claim that what we ordinarily mean by "information" in the semantic sense is something that is true, implying that it is impossible to have, provide or use false information. False information, on that view can be compared with the decoy ducks used by hunters. The decoys are not really ducks though some real ducks may be deceived into treating the decoys as real – to their cost! Likewise, argues Dretske, false information is not really information, even though some people can be deceived into treating it as information. It is claimed that truth is what makes information valuable, therefore anything false would be of no value.

Whatever the merits of this terminology may be for some philosophers, the restriction of "information" to what is true is such a useless encumbrance that it would force scientists and robot designers (and philosophers like me) to invent a new word or phrase that had the same meaning as "information" but without truth being implied. For example, a phrase something like "information content" might be used to refer to the kind of thing that is common to my belief that the noise outside my window is caused by a lawn-mower, and my belief that the noise in the next room is caused by a vacuum cleaner, when the second belief is true while first belief is false because the noise outside comes from a hedge trimmer.

The observation that humans, other animals and robots, acquire, manipulate, interpret, combine, analyse, store, use, communicate, and share information, applies equally to false information and to true information, or to what could laboriously be referred to as the "information content" that can occur in false as well as true beliefs, expectations, explanations, and percepts, and moreover, can also occur in questions, goals, desires, fears, imaginings, hypotheses, where it is not known whether the information content is true. So in constructing the question "Is that noise outside caused by a lawnmower?", a speaker can use the same concepts and the same modes of composition of information as are used in formulating true beliefs like: "Lawnmowers are used to cut grass", "Lawnmowers often make a noise", "Lawnmowers are available in different sizes", as well as many questions, plans, goals, requests, etc. involving lawnmowers. Not only true propositions are valuable: all sorts of additional structures containing information are useful. Even false beliefs can be useful, because by acting on them you may learn that they are false, why they are false, and gain additional information. That's how science proceeds and much of the learning of young children depends heavily on their ability to construct information contents without being able to tell which are true and which are false. The learning process can then determine the answers. This will also be important for intelligent robots.

For the purposes of cognitive science, neuroscience, biology, AI, robotics and many varieties of engineering, it is important not to restrict the notion of "information" to what is true, or even to whole propositions that are capable of being true or false. There are information fragments of many kinds that can be combined in many ways, some, but not all, of which involve constructing propositions. Information items can be used in many other processes. The uses of information in control probably evolved before other uses of information in biological organisms, including, for example, microbes. Explaining how and why other uses evolved, such as forming memories, predictions, questions and explanations, along with increasingly sophisticated mechanisms to support them, is a task for another occasion. Some hypotheses are sketched in Sloman (2007a).

3. Is "information" as used here definable?

3.1. *The inadequacy of explicit definitions*

In order to understand how a concept like "information" can be used in science without being definable, we need to understand some general points from philosophy of science. Shannon's notion of information was defined precisely [Shannon (1948)] and has had important applications in science and engineering. Nevertheless, for reasons given above, that concept is not what we need in talking about an animal or robot that acquires and uses information about various things (the environment, its own thinking, other agents, future actions, etc.), even though Shannon's notion is relevant to some of the mechanisms underlying such processes. Can we define this older, intuitive, more widely used, notion of information?

After many years of thinking about this, I have concluded that "information" in this sense cannot be explicitly defined without circularity. The same is true of "mass", "energy" and other deep concepts used in important scientific theories. Attempts to define "Information" by writing down an *explicit* definition of the form "Information is ...." all presuppose some concept that is closely related ("meaning", "content", "reference", "description", etc.). "Information is meaning", "information is semantic content", "information is what something is about" are all inadequate in this sense.

This kind of indefinability is common in concepts needed for deep scientific theories. Attempts to get round this by "operationalising" theoretical concepts fail. For example, there are standard methods of measuring mass and energy, but those do not *define* the concepts, since the measuring methods change as technology develops, while the meanings of the words remain mostly fixed by their roles in physical theories. The measurement methods define what are sometimes called "bridging rules" or "correspondence rules", which link theories to observations and applications. [Carnap (1947)] called some of them "meaning postulates". All this was known to early 20th century philosophers of science, some of whom had tried unsuccessfully to show that scientific concepts are definable in terms of the sensory experiences of scientists, or in terms of "operational definitions" specifying how to detect or measure physical quantities (Bridgman, 1927).

The absence of any explicit definition does not mean either that a word is meaningless or that we cannot say anything useful about it. The specific things said about what energy is and how it relates to force, mass, electrical charge, etc., change over time as we learn more, so the concepts evolve. Newton knew about some forms of energy, but what he knew about energy is much less than what we now know about energy, e.g. that matter and energy are interconvertible, and that there are chemical and electromagnetic forms of energy. Growing theoretical knowledge extends and deepens the concepts we use in expressing that knowledge Cohen (1962); Schurz (2009). That is now happening to our concept of information as we learn more about types of information-processing machine, natural and artificial.

3.2. *Concepts implicitly (partially) defined by theories using them*

If concepts are not all defined in terms of sensory experiences or measurement operations, how do we (including physicists) manage to understand the word "energy"? The answer seems to be: such a word mainly acquires its meaning from its role in a rich, deep, widely applicable theory in which many things are said about energy, e.g. that in any bounded portion of the universe there is a scalar (one-dimensional), discontinuously variable amount of it, that its totality is conserved, that it can be transmitted in various ways, that it can be stored in various forms, that it can be dissipated, that it flows from objects of higher to objects of lower temperatures if they are in contact, that it can be radiated across empty space, that it can produce forces that cause things to move or change their shape, etc. (All that would have to be made much more precise for a physics text book.)

If a theory is expressed logically, and is not logically inconsistent, and its undefined concept labels are treated as variables ranging over predicates, relations and functions, then there may be a non-empty set of possible models for the set of statements expressing the theory, where the notion of something being a model is illustrated by lines, points, and relations between them being a model for a set of axioms for Euclidean geometry, and also certain arithmetical entities being a model for the same axioms. This notion of model was first given a precise recursive definition by Tarski but the idea is much older, as explained in [Sloman (2007c)]. I think the core idea can be generalised to theories expressed in natural language and other non-logical forms of representation including non-Fregean forms of representation, but making that idea precise and testing it are research projects (compare [Sloman (1971)]). The models that satisfy some theory with undefined terms will include possible portions of reality that the theory could describe. Insofar as there is more than one model, the meanings of the terms are partly indeterminate, an unavoidable feature of scientific theories. Chapter 2 of [Sloman (1978)] explains why it is not usually possible to completely remove indeterminacy of meaning. Compare [Cohen (1962)].

Adding new independent postulates using the same undefined terms will further constrain the set of possible models. That is one way to enrich the content of a theory. Another way is to add new undefined concepts and new hypotheses linking them to the old ones. That increases the complexity required of a piece of reality if it is to be a model of the theory. Other changes may alter the set of models and increase the number of things that are derivable from the theory, increasing the variety of predictions. Some changes will also increase the *precision* of the derived conclusions, e.g. specifying predicted processes or possible processes in more detail. Adding new "meaning postulates", or "bridging rules", linking undefined terms to methods of measurement or observation, as explained above, can also further constrain the set of possible models, by "tethering" (label suggested in [Chappell and Sloman (2007)]) the theory more closely to some portion of reality. As science progresses and we learn more things about energy. the concept becomes more constrained – restricting the possible models of the theory, as explained in [Sloman (2007c)]. This gradual increase in understanding would not be possible if the initial concepts were fully determinate. Far from requiring absolutely precise concepts, as normally supposed, some scientific advances depend on (partial) indeterminacy of concepts.

3.3. *Evaluating theories, and their concepts*

For concepts that are implicitly defined by their role in the theory, the evaluation of the concepts as referring to something real or not will go along with the evaluation of the theory. How to evaluate scientific theories is itself a complex and difficult question and there are many tempting but shallow and inadequate criteria. I think the work of Lakatos extending and refining Popper's ideas [Lakatos (1980)] is of great value here, in particular insofar as it draws attention to the difficulty of evaluating or comparing theories conclusively at a point in time. Instead it often takes time before we can tell whether the research programme associated with a theory is "progressive" or "degenerating". It always remains possible for new developments to resurrect a defeated theory, as happened to the corpuscular theory of light.

Doubt is cast on the value of a theory and its concepts if the theory does not enhance our practical abilities, if it doesn't explain a variety of observed facts better than alternative theories, if all its predictions are very vague, if it never generates new research questions that lead to new discoveries of things that need to be explained, if its implications are restricted to very rare situations, and if it cannot be used in making predictions, or selecting courses of action to achieve practical goals, or in designing and steadily improving useful kinds of machinery, In such cases, the concepts implicitly defined by the theory will be limited to reference within the hypothetical world postulated by the theory. Concepts like "angel" and "fairy" are examples of such referentially unsuccessful concepts, though they be used to present myths of various sorts, providing entertainment and, in some cases, social coercion.

These ideas about concepts and theories were elaborated in Chapter 2 of [Sloman (1978)], which pointed out that the deepest advances in science are those that extend our ontology substantively, including new theories that explain possibilities not previously considered. How concepts can be partly defined implicitly by structural relations within a theory is discussed further in [Sloman (1985, 1987)]. These ideas can be extended to non-logical forms of representation, as discussed in [Sloman (2008b)].

3.4. *The failure of concept empiricism and symbol-grounding theory*

Because a concept can be (partially) defined implicitly by its role in a powerful theory, and therefore some symbols expressing such concepts get much of their meaning from their structural relations with other symbols in the theory (including relations of derivability between formulae including those symbols) it follows that not all meaning has to come from experience of instances, as implied by the theory of concept empiricism. Concept empiricism is a very old philosophical idea, refuted by [Kant (1781)], and later by philosophers of science in the 20th century thinking about theoretical concepts like "electron", "gene", "neutrino", "electromagnetic field". (For more on Concept Empiricism, see: [Prinz (2005); Machery (2007)].)

Unfortunately, the already discredited theory was recently reinvented and labelled "symbol grounding theory" (Harnad, 1990). This theory seems highly plausible to people who have not studied philosophy, so it has spread widely among AI theorists and cognitive scientists, and is probably still being taught to unsuspecting students. Section 3.2 presented "symbol tethering" theory, according to which meanings of theoretical terms are primarily determined by structural relations within a theory, supplemented by "bridging rules". Designers of intelligent robots will have to produce information-processing architectures in which such theories can be constructed, extended, tested and used, by the robots, in a process of acquiring information about the world, and themselves.

Marvin Minsky in 2005 also talks about "grounding" but in a context that neither presupposes nor supports symbol-grounding theory. He seems to be making a point I agree with, namely that insofar as complex systems like human minds monitor or control themselves the subsystem that does the monitoring and controlling needs to observe and intervene at a high level of abstraction instead of having to reason about all the low level details of the physical machine. In some cases, this can imply that the information that such a system has about itself is incomplete or misleading. I.e. self-observation is not infallible, except in the trivial sense in which a voltmeter cannot be misled about what its reading of a voltage is, as explained in (Sloman, 2007b).

The rest of this paper attempts to outline some of the main features of a theory about roles information can play in how things work in our world. The theory is still incomplete but we have already learnt a lot and there are many possible lines of development of our understanding of information processing systems in both natural and artificial systems.

4. Information-bearers, information contents

4.1. *Users, bearers, contents, contexts – physical and virtual*

As explained in Section 1.1, an information-bearer B (a representation) can express information I for user U in context C. The user, U, can take B to express information about something remote, past, future, abstract (like numbers), or even non-existent, e.g. a situation prevented, or a story character.

The expressed information can be involved in many processes, for instance: acquiring, transforming, decomposing, combining with other information, interpreting, deriving, storing, inferring, asking, testing, using as a premiss, controlling internal or external behaviour, and communicating with other information-users. Such processes usually require U to deploy mechanisms that have access to B, to parts of B, and to other information-bearers (e.g. in U's memory or in the environment).

The existence of information-bearers does not depend on the existence of what they refer to: things can be referred to that do not exist. Mechanisms for this were probably a major advance in biological evolution. Example information-bearers explicitly used by humans include sentences, maps, pictures, bit-strings, video recordings, or other more abstract representations of actual or possible processes. At present little is known about the variety of information bearers in biological systems, including brains, though known examples include chemical structures and patterns of activation of neurons. In some cases the information-bearers are physical entities, e.g. marks on paper or acoustic signals, or chemicals in the blood stream. But many information-bearers in computing systems, e.g. lists of symbols, the text in a word-processor, are not physical entities but entities in virtual machines (see Section 6.3). The use of virtual machines in addition to physical machines has many benefits for designers of complex information processing systems. [Sloman (2009f)] argues that evolution produced animals that use virtual machines containing information bearers, for similar reasons. The problem of explaining what information is includes the problem of how information can be processed in *virtual machines*, natural or artificial. (In this context, the word "virtual" does not imply "unreal"[b].)

The bearer is a physical or virtual entity (or collection of entities) that encodes or expresses the information, for that user in that context. Many people, in many disciplines, now use the word "representation" to refer to information-bearers of various kinds, though there is no general agreement on usage. Some who argue that representations are not needed proceed to discuss alternatives that are already classified as representations by broad-minded thinkers. Such factional disputes are a waste of time.

4.2. *Changing technology for information-bearers*

Early general purpose electronic computers used only abstract bit-patterns as forms of representation, though the physical implementation of the bit-patterns varied. Over the years since the 1940s many more information-bearers have been developed in computers, either implemented in bit patterns, or in something else implemented in bit-patterns, e.g. strings, arrays, lists, logical expressions, algebraic expressions, images, rules, grammars, trees, graphs, artificial neural nets, and many more. These are typically constructed from various primitive entities and relationships available in virtual machines though they are all ultimately implemented in bit-patterns, which themselves are virtual entities implemented in physical machines using transistors, magnetic mechanisms in disc drives, etc. The use of such things as error-correcting memories and raid arrays implies that the bits in a bit pattern are virtual entities that do not correspond in any simple way to physical components.

This use of bit-patterns as a form of representation is relatively recent, although Morse code, which is older, is very close. Long before that, humans

---

[b] As explained in and in various papers and presentations available online [Sloman (1985, 1987, 2008b,c, 2009e)]

were using language, diagrams, gestures, maps, marks in the sand, flashing lights, etc. to express information of various kinds [Dyson (1997)]. And before that animal brains used still unknown forms of representation to encode information about the environment, their motives, plans, learnt generalisations, etc. [Sloman (1979, 2008b)]. It is arguable that all living organisms acquire and use information, both in constructing themselves and also in controlling behaviour, repairing damage, detecting infections, etc.[c]

Information-bearers need not be *intentionally* constructed to convey information. For example, an animal may hear a sound and derive the information that something is moving nearby. The original information-bearer is a transient acoustic signal in the environment produced unintentionally by whatever moved. The hearer constructs an enduring information-bearer (representation) that may be retained long after the noise has ended. The physical signal does not *intrinsically* carry that information, though for a particular user it may do so as a result of prior learning. However, in a different context, the same noise may be interpreted differently. So the association between bearer and information content can depend not only on user but on context: information (or meaning) involves at least a *four-termed relation* involving B, I, U, and C.

4.3. *A common error about bit patterns and symbols*

It is sometimes claimed that in Shannon's sense "information" refers to physical properties of physical objects, structures, mechanisms. But not all bit-strings are physical. For example, it is possible to have structures in virtual machines that operate as bit-strings and are used for communication between machines, or for virtual memory systems, especially when bit-strings are transmitted across networks in forms that both use data-compression and error correcting mechanisms based on redundancy. A similar mistake was made by Newell and Simon (Newell, 1980) when they proposed that intelligent systems need to use "physical symbol systems", apparently forgetting that many symbols used in AI systems are not physical entities, but entities in virtual machines (see Section 6.3).

---

[c]This is discussed in a presentation arguing that there is a sense in which life presupposes mind (informed control) http://www.cs.bham.ac.uk/research/projects/cogaff/talks/\#lifemind

4.4. *Many forms of representation*

There are many forms in which information can be expressed. Some are very general, including logic, human languages, and various structures used in computer databases. They are not completely general insofar as there may be some things, e.g. information about irregular continuous spatial or temporal variation, that they cannot express fully. Other forms of representation are more specialised, e.g. number notations, notations for differential and integral calculus, musical notation, and various styles of maps. What characterises a form of representation is a collection of primitives, along with ways of modifying them, combining them to form larger structures, transformations that can be applied to the more complex items, mechanisms for storing, matching, searching, and copying them, and particular uses to which instances of the form can be put, e.g. controlling behaviour, searching for plans, explaining, forming generalisations, interpreting sensory input, expressing goals, expressing uncertainty, and communication with others. The representing structures may be physical objects or processes, or objects or processes in virtual machines. The use of virtual machine forms of representation allows very rapid construction and modification of structures without having to *rearrange* physical components. In computers instead of physical rearrangements there are merely banks of switches that can be turned on and off, thereby implementing changes to virtual network topology and signals transmitted, in terms of which higher-level virtual machine representations can be implemented.

Humans often use forms that are Fregean [Sloman (1971)] insofar as they use *application of functions to arguments* to combine information items to form larger information items. Examples include sentences, algebraic expressions, logical expressions and many expressions in computer programs. Purely Fregean forms of representation use *only* function application, whereas impure forms also use spatial or temporal order, and other relationships in the bearer's medium, as [Bateson (1972)] noted. For example, the programming language Prolog uses ordering of symbols as well as the function-argument relationship, as significant.

The 1971 paper argued, against [McCarthy and Hayes (1969)], that non-Fregean forms of representation, e.g. analogical representations, are often useful, and should be used in AI alongside logic and algebra. For example, information may usefully be expressed in continuously changing levels of activation of some internal or external sensing device, in patterns of activation of many units, in geometrical or topological structures analogous to images or maps, in chemical compounds, and many more. Despite some partial successes, this has proved easier said than done.

Exactly how many different forms exist in which information can be encoded, and what their costs and benefits are, is an important question that will not be discussed further here. One of the profound consequences of developments in metamathematics, computer science, artificial intelligence, neuroscience and biology in the last century has been to stretch our understanding of the huge variety of possible forms of representation (Peterson, 1996), including some forms that are not decomposable into discrete components, as sentences, logical expressions, and bit strings are, and some which can also change continuously, unlike Fregean representations.

Besides analogical and Fregean forms of representation many others have been explored, including distributed neural representations and forms of genetic encoding. [Minsky (1992)] discusses tradeoffs between some symbolic and neural forms. There probably are many more forms of representation (more types of information-bearer) than we have discovered so far. Some philosophers use the misleading expression "non-conceptual content" to refer to some of the non-Fregean forms of representation – misleading because it presupposes that concepts (units of semantic content) can only be used in propositional formats. We can achieve greater generality by using the label "concept" wherever there are re-usable information components that can be combined with others in different ways whether in propositions, instructions, pictures, goal specifications, action-control signals, or anything else.[d]

Obviously, a representation may convey different information to different users, and nothing at all to some individuals (e.g. humans listening to a foreign language). Moreover, the very same information-bearer can

---

[d]See also the discussion of alternatives to logical representations in Chapter 7 of [Sloman (1978)]. [Sloman (2008b)] argues that non-communicative "languages" used for perception, learning, planning, etc., evolved before human languages, some of them using non-Fregean forms of representation.

convey different information to the same user at different times, in different contexts, for example, indexical expressions, marks in the sand, shadows, etc. (Further examples and their implications are discussed below in Section 5.9 and in Sloman (2006b).)

The continued investigation of the space of possible forms of representation, including the various options for forming more complex information contents from simpler ones, and the tradeoffs between the various options, is a major long term research project. This paper is mostly neutral as regards the precise forms in which information can be encoded.

4.5. "Self-documenting" entities

It is normally assumed that we cannot talk about the information expressed by or stored in a bearer B without specifying a user (or type of user) U. However, it is arguable that *any* object, event, or process is intrinsically a bearer of information about itself (a "self-documenting" entity), though not all users are equally able to acquire and use the information that is available from the entity. So a twig lying in the forest is a bearer (or potential bearer?) of information about its size, shape, physical composition, location, orientation, history, and relationships to many other things. Different information users can take in and use different subsets or impoverished forms of that information, depending on their sensory apparatus, their information processing architecture, the forms of representation they are able to use, the theories they have, and their location in relation to the twig.   (Compare the notion of "intrinsic information" in [Reading (2006)].)

Besides the "categorical" information about the parts, relationships, properties, and material constitution of an object or process that can be discovered by an appropriately equipped perceiver, there is also less obvious "dispositional" information about processes it could be part of, processes that it constrains or prevents, and processes that could have produced it. These are causal relationships. Intelligent perceivers make a great deal of use of such information when they perceive affordances of various kinds. Gibson's notion of "affordance" [Gibson (1979)] focuses on only a subset of possible processes and constraints, namely those relevant to what a perceiver can and cannot do: action-affordances for the perceiver. We need to generalise that idea if we are to describe all the different kinds of information a perceiver can use in the environment, including *proto-affordances*, concerned with which processes are and are not physically possible in the environment, *epistemic affordances*, concerned with what information is and is not available and *vicarious affordances*, concerned with affordances for other agents, all described in [Sloman (2008a)]. Some animals are able to represent *meta-affordances*: information about ways of producing, modifying, removing, or acquiring information about, affordances of various kinds.

Information-users will typically be restricted in the kinds of information they can obtain or use, and at any time they will only process a subset of the information they could process. They will typically not make use of the majority of kinds of information potentially available. For instance, detailed, transient, metrical information about changing relationships will be relevant during performance of actions such as grasping, placing, catching or avoiding, but only more abstract information will be relevant while future actions are being planned, or while processes not caused by the perceiver are being observed [Sloman (1982)]. States of an information-processing system (e.g. the mind of an animal or robot) are generally not just constituted by what is actually occurring in the system but by what would or could occur under various conditions – a point made long ago in [Ryle (1949)].

The information-processing mechanisms and forms of representation required for perceivers to acquire and use information about actual and possible processes and causal relationships are not yet understood. Most research on perception has ignored the problem of perceiving *processes*, and *possibilities for* and *constraints on* processes, because of excessive focus on perceiving and learning about *objects*.

5. Aspects of information

5.1. *Information content and function*

Items of information can have different aspects that need to be distinguished, of which three important examples are *content*, *function* (or use, or causal role) and the *medium* in which information is expressed, or represented, where each of those can be further subdivided.

It is possible for the same information content (e.g. that many parents abuse their children by indoctrinating them) to be put to different uses. E.g. it can be stated, hypothesised, denied, remembered, imagined to be the case, inferred from something, used as a premiss, used to explain, used to motivate political action, and many more. Those could all be labelled "declarative" uses of information. An item of declarative information can be true or false, and can imply, contradict, or be derived from, other items of factual information. It can also provide an answer (true or false) to a question, or a description of what needs to be achieved for an item of control information to be successful, e.g. for a command to be obeyed.

The same content can also occur in other information uses, e.g. "interrogative" and "imperative" uses: formulating requests for information and specifying an action to be performed (or modified, terminated, suspended or delayed, etc.), for instance asking whether it is the case or exhorting people to make it false by changing their ways. An important use that is hard to specify is in conditionalising some other information content, which could be a statement, intention, command, question, prediction. Examples: "If it's raining take an umbrella", "If it's raining, why aren't you wet?" There is usually no commitment regarding truth or falsity of the condition, in such uses.

Like questions, imperative uses of information are not true or false, though particular processes can be said to follow or not follow the instructions. Just as some declarative information contents are inconsistent, and therefore incapable of being true, likewise, some instructions are inconsistent, and therefore impossible to execute (e.g. "Put seven balls into an empty box and, put red marks on ten of them").

5.2. *Medium used for information bearer*

From the earliest days of AI and software engineering it was clear that choice of form of representation could make a large difference to the success of a particular information-processing system. Different expressive media can be used for the various functions: vocal utterances, print, internet sites, use of sign language, political songs, etc. The same content expressed in print could use different fonts, or even entirely different languages. But some information contents cannot be adequately expressed in some media, e.g. because, as J.L.Austin once quipped: "Fact is richer than diction" [Austin

(1956)]. Some kinds of richness are better represented in a non-Fregean medium, e.g. using static or moving images, or 3-D models.

A pre-verbal child, or a non-human animal, can have percepts whose content specifies a state of affairs in the environment; and can have intentions whose content specifies some state of affairs to be achieved, maintained or prevented. It is unlikely that toddlers, dogs, crows, and apes use only linguistic or Fregean forms of representation, though there are many unanswered questions about exactly which other forms or media are possible.

Many information-bearers use static media, like sentences, pictures, or flowcharts, whereas some use dynamic media, in which *processes* are information-bearers, e.g. audio or video recordings, gestures, play acting, and others. If the dynamic representation is repeatedly produced it may be represented by some enduring static structure that is used to generate the dynamic process as needed – e.g. a computer program can repeatedly generate processes. I suspect the role of dynamic information-bearers and static encodings of dynamic information-bearers, in animal intelligence, and future intelligent robots, will turn out to be far more important than anyone currently realises, not least because much information about the environment is concerned with processes occurring, and processes that could occur.

Earlier, in 4.5, we mentioned self-documenting entities, which potentially express information for various kinds of information user simply in virtue of their structure, properties and relations. These information bearers do not depend for their existence on users. They can be contrasted with the sensory signals and other transient and enduring information bearers constructed by information users. An element of truth in the view of Brooks criticised above (2.5) is that in some cases the presence of self-documenting entities reduces (but does not eliminate) the need for an information user to construct internal representations. Moreover, during performance of actions, force-feedback and visual feedback can be used to provide fine-grained control information that reduces the reliance on ballistic control, which may be inaccurate.

Another way of putting the point about control using feedback is that *the changing relationships* to external objects produced when performing physical actions can be useful *self-documenting* aspects of the environment, helping with control. They can also be useful for other observers (friendly or unfriendly!) who can perceive the actions and draw conclusions about the intentions and motives of the agent – if the viewers have appropriate meta-semantic information-processing capabilities. In that sense, intentional actions can serve as unintended communications, and it is conjectured in [Sloman (2008b)] that fact played a role in evolution of languages used intentionally.

5.3. *Same content, but different function*

Items of information with the same declarative content can be given different functional roles in an information user. For example, the same thing can be stated to be true and either asked about or commanded to be made or kept true. It can also be wondered about, hypothesised, imagined regretfully, treated as an ideal, etc.

The philosopher R.M. Hare (Hare, 1952) introduced the labels "Phrastic" and "Neustic" to distinguish the semantic content of an utterance and the speech act being performed regarding that content, e.g. asserting it, denying it, enquiring about its truth value, commanding that it be made true, etc. The concept of "information content" used here is close to Hare's notion of a "Phrastic", except that we are not restricting semantic content to what can be expressed in a linguistic or Fregean form: other media, including maps, models, diagrams, route-summaries, flow-charts, builders' blue-prints, moving images, 3-D models, and other things, can all encode information contents usable for different functions. Moreover, not all uses are concerned with communication between individuals: information is processed in perceiving, learning, wanting, planning, remembering, deciding, etc. [Sloman (1979, 2008b)]. We therefore need to generalise the Phrastic/Neustic distinction to contrast content and function in many different information media, including information expressed in diagrams, maps, charts [Sloman (1971)], and also whatever forms are used in animal brains or minds. In many cases the "neustic" is not expressed within the representation but simply by its role in an information processing architecture, as explained in [Sloman (2009a)], or in some aspect of the context, e.g. the word "Wanted" above a picture of a human face.

Questions, requests, commands, desires, and intentions, can all be described as examples of "control information", because their information-processing function (the *neustic* aspect), involves making something happen, unlike factual information, which, in itself, has no implications for action, although it can have implications in combination with motives, conditional plans, etc. Control information (and what should be done) is commonly found in kitchen recipes, computer programs, knitting patterns, legal documents, etc. There must be many forms implemented in animal brains.

Summing up: When information is used we can distinguish the content of the information (phrastic) from the use that is being made of it (neustic). The latter may be explicitly indicated in the medium, or implicitly determined by the subsystem of the user that the bearer is located in, or the context. We can also distinguish different information media, e.g. linguistic, Fregean, pictorial, hybrid, static, dynamic, etc. Each of these can be further subdivided in various ways, only some of which have already been explored in working artificial systems.

5.4. *Processing requirements for different media*

One of the achievements of AI research in the last half-century has been the study of different information media, and analysis of different information processing mechanisms required for dealing with them, including sentences, algebraic expressions, logical expressions, program texts, collections of numerical values, probability distributions, and a variety of analogical forms of representation, including pictures, diagrams, acoustic signals, and more. There are many ways in which information media can vary, imposing different demands on the mechanisms that process them.

One of the most important features of certain media is their "generativity". For example, our notations for numbers, sentences, maps, computer programs, chemical formulate, construction blue-prints, are all generative insofar as there is a subset of primitive information bearers along with ways in which those primitives can be combined to form more complex bearers, where the users have systematic ways of interpreting the complex bearers on the basis of the components and their relationships. This is referred to as a use of "compositional semantics", where meanings of wholes depend on meanings of parts and their relationships, and sometimes also the context [Sloman (2006b)].

If an organism had only six basic actions, and could only process bearers of information about complex actions made up of at most three consecutive basic actions, then it would have restricted generativity, allowing for at most 216 complex actions. Some organisms appear to have sensor arrays that provide a fixed size set of sensor values from which information about the environment at any time can be derived. In contrast, humans, and presumably several other species, do not simply record sensor values but interpret them in terms of configurations of entities and processes in the environment, e.g. visible or tangible surface fragments in various orientations changing their mutual relationships.

If the interpretation allows scale changes (e.g. because of varying distances) and sequential scanning of scenes, both of which are important in human vision, the user can construct and interpret information bearers of different kinds and degrees of complexity. The mechanisms involved may have physical limits without being limited in principle, in which case the animal or machine may have "infinite competence" (explained more fully in [Sloman (2002)]). Even when the competence is not infinite, compositionality implies the ability to deal with novelty, a most important feature for animals and robots inhabiting an extremely variable environment. Closely related to this are the ability to plan complex future actions and the ability to construct new explanations of observed phenomena.

A more complete exposition would need to discuss different ways in which information bearers can be combined, with different sorts of compositional semantics. One of the major distinctions mentioned in Section 4.4 is between and Fregean and other forms of composition. As explained in [Sloman (1971)], the systematic complexity of forms of representation can provide a basis for reasoning with information-bearers: deriving new conclusions from old information by manipulating the bearers, whether Fregean or not. Logical inference and geometric reasoning using diagrams two special cases among many.

5.5. *Potential information content for a user*

The information in B can be potentially usable by U even though U has never encountered B or anything with similar information content. That's obviously true when U encounters a new sentence, diagram or picture for the first time. Even before U encountered the new item, it was *potentially* usable as an information-bearer. In some cases, though not all, the potential cannot be realised without U first learning a new language, or notation, or even a new theory within which the information has a place.

You cannot understand the information that is potentially available to others in your environment if you have not yet acquired all the concepts involved in the information. For example, it is likely that a new-born human infant does not have the concept of a metal, i.e. that is not part of its ontology [Sloman (2009b)]. So it is incapable of acquiring the information that it is holding something made of metal even if a doting parent says "you are holding a metal object". In humans a lengthy process of development is required for the information-processing mechanisms (forms of representation, algorithms, architectures) to be able treat things in the environment as made of different kinds of stuff, of which metals are a subset. Even longer is required for that ontology to be extended to include the concepts of physics and chemistry. In part that is a result of cultural evolution: not all our ancestors were able to acquire and use such information.

5.6. *Potential information content for a TYPE of user*

It is possible for information to be potentially available for a TYPE of user even if NO instances of that type exist. For example, long before humans evolved there were things happening on earth that could have been observed by human-like users using the visual apparatus and conceptual apparatus that humans have. But at the time there were no such observers, and perhaps nothing else existed on the planet that was capable of acquiring, manipulating, or using the information, e.g. information about the patterns of behaviours of some of the animals on earth at the time. (This is related to the points made about self-documenting entities in 4.5.)

There may also be things going on whose detection and description would require organisms or machines with a combination of capabilities, including perceptual and representational capabilities and an information-processing architecture, that are possible in principle, but have never existed in any organism or machine and never will – since not everything that is possible has actual instances. Of course, I cannot give examples, since everything I can present is necessarily capable of being thought about by at least one human. Weaker, but still compelling, evidence is simply the fact that the set of things humans are capable of thinking of changes over time as humans acquire more sophisticated concepts, forms of representation and forms of reasoning, as clearly happens in mathematics, physics, and the other sciences. There are thoughts considered by current scientists and engineers that are beyond the semantic competences of any three year old child, or any adult human living 3000 years ago. If the earth had been destroyed three thousand years ago, that might have relegated such thoughts to the realm of possible information contents for types of individual that never existed, but could have.

5.7. *Information content shared between users*

It is sometimes possible for a bearer B to mean the same thing (convey the same information content I) to different users U and U', and it is also possible for two users who never use the same information-bearers (e.g. they talk different languages) to acquire and use the same information.

This is why relativistic theories of truth are false. It cannot be true for me that my house has burned down but not true for my neighbour. In principle we have access to the same sources of information in the world.

5.8. *Ambiguity, noise, and layers of processing*

Media can also vary in the extent to which they allow information to be expressed ambiguously. For example, some cases are totally unambiguous, e.g. the association between bit patterns and CPU instructions or memory addresses in a computer. In a virtual memory system, a bit pattern uniquely identifies a location in a virtual memory, but the mapping to physical memory locations is context sensitive. In natural languages and many forms of pictorial or map-like representation, local details are ambiguous and finding a global interpretation for a complex information-bearer can include searching and problem solving, possibly using constraint propagation and background knowledge, illustrated below in 5.9.

In some cases the medium requires several layers of interpretation, using different ontologies, to be coordinated, e.g. acoustic, phonetic, morphemic, syntactic, semantic and social, in the case of speech understanding systems. Other layers are relevant in visual systems, such as edge features, larger scale 2-D features, 3-D surface fragments, 3-D structures, layers of depth, 3-D processes involving interacting structures, intentions of perceived agents, etc. [Trehub (1991)] offers a theory about how such layers might be implemented neurally, but there remain many unknowns about how vision works.

In some cases, the requirement for layers of interpretation is the result of engineering designs making use of compression, encryption, password protection, zipping or tarring several files into one large file, and many more. In other cases, the layers are natural consequences of a biological or engineering information-processing task, e.g. the layers in visual information processing.

Some information-bearers include various amounts and kinds of noise, clutter, and partial occlusion, sometimes causing problems that require collaboration between interpretation processes at different levels of abstraction. Where multiple layers of processing are coordinated, ambiguities in some layers may be resolved by interpretations in other layers, possibly using background knowledge Chapter 9 of [Sloman (1978)]. This is sometimes described as "hierarchical synthesis", or "analysis by synthesis" [Neisser (1967)]. A related view of layers of interpretation is presented in [Barrow and Tenenbaum (1978)].

Although there has been much research on ways of extracting information from complex information-bearers, it is clear that nothing in AI comes close to matching, for example, the visual competences of a nest-building bird, a tree-climbing ape, a hunting mammal catching prey, a human toddler playing with bricks and other toys. In part, that is because not even the requirements have been understood properly [Sloman (2008a)].

5.9. *Information content for a user determined partly by context*

There are lots of structures in perceptual systems that change what information they represent because of the context. E.g. if what is on your retina is unchanged after you turn your head 90 degrees in a room, the visual information will be taken to be about a different wall even if retinal images are unchanged because the two walls have the same wallpaper. The new interpretation uses the information that the head was turned. Many examples can be found in (Berthoz, 2000). [Sloman (1971)] showed how a particular line can represent different things in a 2-D image of a 3-D scene, depending on its relationships to other fragments. Determining whether a vertical line in a picture represents a horizontal mark on the floor or a vertical line on a wall generally requires use of context. Similar problems arise in language processing, e.g. determining whether "with" introduces a prepositional or adverbial phrase in "He watched the boy with binoculars".

Some information-bearing structures express different information for the same user U in different contexts, because they include an explicit indexical element (e.g. "this", "here", "you", "now", or non-local variables in a computer program).

Another factor that makes it possible for U to take a structure B to express different meanings in different contexts can be that B has polymorphic semantics: its semantic function (for U, or a class of users) is to express a higher order function which generates semantic content when combined with a parameter provided by the linguistic or non-linguistic context. E.g. consider: "He ran after the smallest pony". Which pony is the smallest pony can change as new ponies arrive or depart. More subtly, what counts as a tall, big, heavy, or thin X can vary according to the range of heights, sizes, weights, thicknesses of Xs in the current environment and in some cases may also depend on why you are looking for something tall, big, heavy, etc.

There are many more examples in natural language that lead to incorrect diagnosis of words as vague or ambiguous, when they actually express precise higher order functions, applied to sometimes implicit arguments, e.g. "thin", "long", "efficient", "heap". Other examples include spatial prepositions and other constructs, which can be analysed as having a semantics involving higher order functions some of whose arguments are non-linguistic, discussed in [Sloman (2006b)].

A more complex example is: "A motor mower is needed to mow a meadow" which is true only if there is an implicit background assumption about constraints on desirable amounts of effort or time, size of meadow, etc. So a person who utters that to a companion when they are standing in a very large meadow might be saying something true, whereas in a different context, where there are lots of willing helpers, several unpowered lawnmowers available, and the meadow under consideration is not much larger than a typical back lawn, the utterance would be taken to say something different, which is false, even if the utterances themselves are physically indistinguishable. Moreover, where they are standing does not necessarily determine what sort of meadow is being referred to. E.g. they may have been talking about some remote very large or very small meadow.

The influence of context on information expressed is discussed in more detail in relation to Grice's theory of communication, in Sloman (2006b), along with implications for the evolution of language. The importance of the role of extra-linguistic context in linguistic communication can be developed in connection with indexicals, spatial prepositions, and Gricean semantics, into a theory of linguistic communications as using higher order functions some of whose arguments have to be extracted from non-linguistic sources by creative problem-solving. This has implications for language learning and the evolution of language. It also requires the common claim that natural languages use compositional semantics, to modified, to allow context to play a role. The use of non-local variables can have a similar effect in programming languages. It seems very likely that brain mechanisms also use context-modulated compositional semantics.

5.10. *Information-using subsystems*

An information-user can have parts that are information users. This leads to complications such as that a part can have and use some information that the whole would not be said to have. E.g. your immune system and your digestive system and various metabolic processes use information and take decisions of many kinds though we would not say that *you* have, use or know about the information.

Likewise there are different parts of our brains that evolved at different times that use different kinds of information, even information obtained via the same route, e.g. the retina or ear-drum, or haptic feedback. Input and output devices can be shared between sub-systems that use them for different purposes, possibly after different pre- or post- processing, as explained in [Sloman (1993)]. Some sub-systems are evolutionarily old and shared with other species, some are newer, and some unique to humans.

An example is the information about optical flow that is used in humans to control posture, without individuals being aware of what they are doing [Lee and Lishman (1975)]. More generally, it is likely that human information processing architectures include many components that evolved at different times, performing different functions, many of them concurrent, some of them surveyed in [Sloman (2003)]. The subsystems need not all use the same forms of representation, and individual subsystems need not all have access to information acquired, derived, constructed or used by others. In particular, some will use transient information that is not transferred to or accessible by other subsystems.

That is why much philosophical, psychological, and social theorising is misguided: it treats humans as unitary and rational information users. That includes Dennett's intentional stance and what Newell refers to as "the Knowledge level". For example, the philosophical claim that only a whole human-like agent can acquire, manipulate and use information is false. To understand biological organisms and design sophisticated artificial systems, we need what [McCarthy (2008)] labels "the designer stance". Unfortunately education about how to be a designer of complex working systems is not part of most disciplines that need it.

5.11. *Layers of interpretation in epigenesis*

There is a different kind of use of information: when the user is constructing itself! In that process there are not sensors and motors transferring information and energy between the organism and its environment. The processes by which genetic information is used in organisms are very complex and varied. The use of information provided genetically can be very indirect, involving many stages, several of which are influenced by the environment (e.g. maternal fluids, or soil nutrients), so that the interpretation process required for development of an organism, is highly context sensitive.

In many cases, much of the information from which the processes start is encoded in molecular sequences in DNA, specifying, very indirectly, how to construct a particular organism by constructing a very complex collection of self-organising components, which themselves construct more self-organising components. The interpretation of those sequences as instructions depends on complex chemical machinery assembled in a preceding organism (the mother) to kick-start the interpretation process. The interpreting system builds additional components that continue the assembly, partly influenced by the genetic information and partly by various aspects of the environment. During development, the ability to interpret both genetic and environmental information changes, partly under the influence of the environment. So the standard concept of information encoded in the genome is over-simple theory. (Many details are discussed in [Jablonka and Lamb (2005)]. The importance of cascaded development of layered cognitive mechanisms influenced by the environment is discussed in [Chappell and Sloman (2007)]. See also [Dawkins (1982)].)

The problems of interpreting and using visual and genetic information show that the role of the user U in obtaining information I from a bearer B in context C may be extremely complex and changeable, in ways that are not yet fully understood. That kind of complexity is largely ignored in most discussions about the nature of information, meaning, representation, but it cannot be ignored by people trying to design working systems.

6. Conclusion

In Section 3 it was claimed that it is not possible to define explicitly, precisely, and without circularity, what we mean by "information", in the semantic sense that involves not merely having some syntactic or geometric form but also having the potential to be taken by a user to be *about* something. So subsequent sections presented an *implicit* definition in the form of a first-draft informal theory about the role of information in our world.

6.1. *An implicitly defined notion of "information"*

What was said above in Section 3.2 about "energy" applies also to "information". We can understand the word "information" insofar as we use it in a rich, deep, precise and widely applicable theory (or collection of theories) in which many things are said about entities and processes involving information. I suspect that we are still at a relatively early stage in the development of a full scientific theory of information, especially as there are many kinds of information processing in organisms that we do not yet understand.

Some of the contents of a theory of information have been outlined in previous sections, elaborating on the proposition that a user U can interpret a bearer B as expressing information I in context C. Among the topics mentioned include the variety of sources of information, the

variety of information-bearing media (about which we still have much
to learn), the variety of structures and systems of information-bearers
(syntactic forms), the variety of uses to which information can be put
(including both communicative and non-communicative uses), the variety
of information contents, the variety of ways in which information contents
can change (e.g. continuously, discretely, structurally, etc.), the different
kinds and degrees of complexity of processes required for interpreting and
using the information in particular bearers, the variety of information-
using competences different users (or different parts of the same user)
can have, the potential information available in objects not yet perceived
by information users, and more. We already have broader and deeper
understanding of information in this sense than thinkers had a thousand
years ago about force and energy, but there is still a long way to go.

Unlike Shannon's information, the information content we have been
discussing does not have a scalar value, although there are partial orderings
of information content. One piece of information I1 may contain all the
information in I2, and not vice versa. In that case we can say that I1
contains more information. I1 can have more information content than
both I2 and I3, neither of which contains the other. So there is at most
a partial ordering. The partial ordering may be relative to an individual
user, because giving information I1 to an user U1, may allow U1 to derive
I2, whereas user U2 may not be able to derive I2, because U2 lacks some
additional required information. Even for a given user, the ordering can
depend on context.

Information can vary both discontinuously (e.g. adding an adjective or
a parenthetical phrase to a sentence, like this) or continuously (e.g. visually
obtained information about a moving physical object). More importantly,
individual items of information can have a structure: there are replaceable
parts of an item of information such that if those parts are replaced the
information changes but not necessarily the structure. Because of this,
items of information can be extracted from other information, and can be
combined with other information to form new information items, including
items with new structures. This is connected with the ability of information
users to deal with novelty, and to be creative. Moreover, we have seen
that such compositional semantics often needs to be context sensitive (or
polymorphic), both human language and other forms of representation.

It can be stored in various forms, can be modified or extended through various kinds of learning, and can influence processes of reasoning and decision making. Information can also be transmitted in various ways, both intentionally and unintentionally, using bearers of many kinds.

Some items of information allow infinitely many distinct items of information to be derived from them. (E.g. Peano's axioms for arithmetic, in combination with predicate calculus.) Physically finite, even quite small, objects with information processing powers can therefore have infinite information content. (Like brains and computers.)

There is a great deal more that could be said about our current theories about information, but that would take several volumes. Many additional points are in papers in the bibliography, and in other books and journals, as well as in human common sense.

6.2. *Life and information*

Some of the most important and least well understood parts of a theory about information are concerned with the variety of roles it plays in living things, including roles concerned with reproduction, roles concerned with growth, development, maintenance and repair, roles concerned with perception, reasoning, learning, social interaction, etc. The limitations of our understanding are clearly displayed in the huge gaps between the competences of current robots (in 2009) and the competences of many animals, including human infants and toddlers. For many very narrowly prescribed tasks it is possible to make machines that perform better than humans (e.g. repeatedly assembling items of a certain type from sets of parts arrayed in a particular fashion), but which are easily disrupted by minor variations of the task, the parts, or the starting configuration. Aliens who visited in 1973 and saw what the Edinburgh robot Freddy could do, as described in [Ambler *et al.* (1973)] and shown in this video `http://groups.inf.ed.ac.uk/vision/ROBOTICS/FREDDY/Freddy_II_original.wmv`, might be surprised on returning 36 years later to find how little progress had been made, compared with ambitions expressed at that time.

Every living thing processes information insofar as it uses (internal or external) sensors to detect states of itself or the environment and uses the results of that detection process either immediately or after further information processing to select from a behavioural repertoire, where the behaviour may be externally visible physical behaviour or new information processing. (Similar points are made in [Reading (2006)] and in Steve Burbeck's web site `http://evolutionofcomputing.org/Multicellular/BiologicalInformationProcessing.html`) In the process of using information an organism also uses up stored energy, so that it also needs to use information to acquire more energy, including the energy required for getting energy.

There are huge variations between different ways in which information is used by organisms, including plants, single celled organisms, and everything else. For example, only a tiny subset of organisms appear to have fully deliberative information processing competence, as defined in [Sloman (2006a)]. As explained in Section 5.10 there can also be major differences between the competences of sub-systems in a single information-user.

6.3. *Information processing in virtual machines*

A pervasive notion that has been used but not fully explained in this paper is the notion of a virtual machine. Our understanding of requirements for and possible ways of building and using them has gradually expanded through a host of technical advances since the earliest electronic computers were built.

Because possible operations on information are much more complex and far more varied than operations on matter and energy, engineers discovered during the last half-century, as evolution appears to have "discovered" much earlier, that relatively unfettered information processing requires use of a virtual machine rather than a physical machine, like using software rather than cog-wheels to perform mathematical calculations. A short tutorial on virtual machines and some common misconceptions about them can be found in [Sloman (2009f)]. See also [Pollock (2008)]. One of the main reasons for using virtual machines is that they can be rapidly reconfigured to meet changing environments and tasks, whereas rebuilding physical devices as fast and as often is impossible. It is also possible for a physical machine to support types of virtual machine that were never considered by the designer of the physical machine. Similarly, both cultural evolution and individual development can redeploy biological information processing systems in roles for which they did not specifically evolve.

In [Sloman (2009f)] I suggested that the label "Non-physically-describable-machine" (NPDM) might have been preferable to "virtual machine" (VM) because the key feature is having states and processes whose best description uses concepts that are not definable in terms of the concepts of the physical sciences. Examples are concepts like "winning", "threat", "rule", "pawn", "checkmate", relevant to virtual machines that play chess. These VMs/NPDMs are nothing like the old philosophical notions characterised by [Ryle (1949)] as referring to "The Ghost in the Machine", for we are not talking about mysterious entities that can continue existing after their physical bodies have been completely destroyed. The crucial point is that the nature of the physical world allows networks of causation to exist that support processes in such virtual machines that not only cause other virtual machine processes to occur but can also influence physical machines, for example when a decision taken by a running chess program causes the display on a computer screen to change [Sloman (2009e)]. A crucial step in evolution was the development of causal networks, including sub-systems running in parallel, in virtual machines that could be their own information-users.

This contradicts a number of common mistakes, such as the assumption that information-processing machines have to operate serially, that they have to use only programs installed by a designer, and that they cannot be aware of what they are doing, or why they are doing it, or decide to change their goals. Such mistakes might be overcome if more people studied AI, even if only designing relatively simple agents, as proposed in [Sloman (2009d)].

Although we (or at least software engineers and computer scientists, unlike most philosophers in 2009) understand current virtual machines well enough to create, modify, debug, extend and improve them, the virtual machines that have been produced by biological evolution are another matter: their complexity, their modes of operation, the best ways to describe what they do and how they do it, still defeat scientists, though many subscribe to various personal favourite theories of consciousness, or whatever. Some of them think the known phenomena cannot possibly be explained in terms of information-processing machinery, though in most cases that is because their concept of information-processing is too impoverished – e.g. because based on the notion of a Turing machine, whose relevance to this topic was challenged in [Sloman (2002)]. For example, Turing machines are limited to discrete operations, whereas there is no reason to assume that all information-processing has to be so limited, though it could turn out to be the case that no physical machine could support truly continuous information manipulation. Others take it for granted that brains are information-processing machines, but do not yet understand what information they process or how they do it. For instance, major features of human and animal vision remain unexplained.

6.4. *Finally: Is that everything?*

It is clear that what I have written so far does not come near exhausting our current notion of information, though it gives an indication of the diversity of phenomena and mechanisms involved. Moreover since most of this was not known a hundred years ago it shows that we are in the process of discovering more about information through scientific and engineering research, though progress has not been as fast as many hoped.

This is just the beginning of an analysis of relationships between information, bearers, users, and contexts. What is written here will probably turn out to be a tiny subset of what needs to be said about information. A hundred years from now the theory may be very much more complex and deep, just as what we know now about information is very much more complex and deep than what we knew 60 years ago, partly because we have begun designing, implementing, testing and using so many new kinds of information-processing machines. The mechanisms produced by evolution remain more subtle and complex, however.

I doubt that anyone has yet produced a clear, complete and definitive list of facts about information that constitute an implicit definition of how we (the current scientific community well-educated in mathematics, logic, psychology, neuroscience, biology, computer science, linguistics, social science, artificial intelligence, physics, cosmology, and philosophy) currently understand and use the word "information". But at least this partial survey indicates how much we have already learnt.

Some physicists seek a "theory of everything", e.g. [Barrow (1991); Deutsch (1997)]. However, it does not seem likely that there can be a theory that is recognisable as a *physical* theory from which all the phenomena referred to here would be derivable, even though all the information-processing systems I have referred to, whether natural or artificial, must be *implemented* in physical systems. I suspect that we are in the early stages of understanding how the physical world can support non-physical entities of which simple kinds already exist in running virtual machines in computers, including virtual machines that monitor themselves, and use information about what is happening inside them to take decisions that alter their internal and external behaviours.

My own view has been, for several decades, that as regards information processing our state of knowledge could be compared with Galileo's knowledge of physics. He was making good progress and laying foundations for future developments: including developments he could not possibly imagine.

One of the drivers of progress in science (and philosophy) is improved understanding of what is *not yet known*. I believe the ideas sketched here help us to focus more clearly on aspects of information processing that are not yet understood. Doing that in far more detail with far more specific examples, can help to drive advances that will produce new, deeper, more general explanations. But only time will tell whether this is what Lakatos would call a progressive or a degenerating research programme.

Acknowledgements

I am grateful to Gordana Dodig-Crnkovic and Christophe Menant for useful comments on an earlier draft. This is a much revised version of my attempt to answer a question asking what "semantic information" is, posted on the MINDMECHANISMS discussion forum. My original answer, posted on 20th Sep 2006, is available online at http://www.jiscmail.ac. uk/cgi-bin/webadmin?A2=ind0609&L=mindmechanisms&T=0&P=1717 as part of a thread with subject "Analysis of conscious functions". Comments and questions by several readers led to major improvements. Many of the points made here were previously also made piecemeal over several years in contributions to the Psyche-D discussion list, now archived at http: //www.archive.org/details/PSYCHE-D, and in papers and presentations on my web site, listed in the bibliography. Discussions by email and face to face with many colleagues have helped to shape the ideas presented here. It was Max Clowes who first introduced me to computational ways of thinking about philosophical problems.

References

Ambler, A. P., Barrow, H. G., Brown, C. M., Burstall, R. M. and Popplestone, R. J. (1973). A Versatile Computer-Controlled Assembly System, in *Proc. Third Int. Joint Conf. on AI* (IJCAI, Stanford, California), pp. 298–307.

Austin, J. L. (1956). A plea for excuses, in J. O. Urmson and G. J. Warnock (eds.), *Philosophical Papers* (Oxford University Press, Oxford), pp. 175–204.

Barrow, H. and Tenenbaum, J. (1978). Recovering intrinsic scene characteristics from images, in A. Hanson and E. Riseman (eds.), *Computer Vision Systems* (Academic Press, New York), pp. 3–26.

Barrow, J. D. (1991). *Theories of Everything: The Quest for Ultimate Explanation* (OUP, New York).

Bateson, G. (1972). *Steps to an Ecology of Mind: Collected Essays in Anthropology, Psychiatry, Evolution, and Epistemology* (Chandler Publishing, Bungay Suffolk).

Berthoz, A. (2000). *The Brain's sense of movement*, Perspectives in Cognitive Science (Harvard University Press, London, UK).

Bridgman, P. (1927). *The Logic of Modern Physics* (MacMillan, New York).

Brooks, R. A. (1990). Elephants Don't Play Chess, *Robotics and Autonomous Systems* **6**, pp. 3–15, URL http://people.csail.mit.edu/brooks/papers/elephants.pdf.

Brooks, R. A. (1991). Intelligence without representation, *Artificial Intelligence* **47**, pp. 139–159.

Carnap, R. (1947). *Meaning and necessity: a study in semantics and modal logic* (Chicago University Press, Chicago).

Chappell, J. and Sloman, A. (2007). Natural and artificial meta-configured altricial information-processing systems, *International Journal of Unconventional Computing* **3**, 3, pp. 211–239, URL http://www.cs.bham.ac.uk/research/projects/cosy/papers/\#tr0609.

Cohen, L. (1962). *The diversity of meaning* (Methuen & Co Ltd, London).

Dawkins, R. (1982). *The Extended Phenotype: The long reach of the gene* (Oxford University Press, Oxford, New York).

Denning, P. J. (2009). The profession of IT Beyond computational thinking, *Communications of the ACM* **52**, 6, pp. Pages 28–30, URL http://doi.acm.org/10.1145/1516046.1516054.

Deutsch, D. (1997). *The Fabric of Reality* (Allen Lane, The Penguin Press., London).

Dreyfus, H. (2002). Intelligence Without Representation, *Phenomenology and the Cognitive Sciences* **1**, pp. 367–83, URL http://www.class.uh.edu/cogsci/dreyfus.html.

Dyson, G. B. (1997). *Darwin Among The Machines: The Evolution Of Global Intelligence* (Addison-Wesley, Reading, MA).

Floridi, L. (ed.) (2008). *Philosophy of Computing and Information: 5 Questions* (Automatic Press /VIP, Copenhagen, Denmark), URL http://www.amazon.com/Philosophy-Computing-Information-5-Questions/dp/8792130097.

Gibson, E. J. and Pick, A. D. (2000). *An Ecological Approach to Perceptual Learning and Development* (Oxford University Press, New York).

Gibson, J. J. (1979). *The Ecological Approach to Visual Perception* (Houghton Mifflin, Boston, MA).

Grush, R. (2004). The emulation theory of representation: Motor control, imagery, and perception, *Behavioral and Brain Sciences* **27**, pp. 377–442.

Hare, R. (1952). *The Language of Morals* (Oxford University Pres, Oxford).

Harnad, S. (1990). The Symbol Grounding Problem, *Physica D* **42**, pp. 335–346.

Jablonka, E. and Lamb, M. J. (2005). *Evolution in Four Dimensions: Genetic, Epigenetic, Behavioral, and Symbolic Variation in the History of Life* (MIT Press, Cambridge MA).

Kant, I. (1781). *Critique of Pure Reason* (Macmillan, London), translated (1929) by Norman Kemp Smith.

Lakatos, I. (1980). Falsification and the methodology of scientific research programmes, in J. Worrall and G. Currie (eds.), *Philosophical papers, Vol I* (Cambridge University Press, Cambridge), ISBN 0-521-28031-1, pp. 8–101.

Lee, D. and Lishman, J. (1975). Visual proprioceptive control of stance, *Journal of Human Movement Studies* **1**, pp. 87–95.

Machery, E. (2007). Concept Empiricism: A Methodological Critique, *Cognition* **104**, pp. 19–46., URL http://www.pitt.edu/~machery/papers/machery_2007_concept%20empiricism.pdf.

McCarthy, J. (2008). The well-designed child, *Artificial Intelligence* **172**, 18, pp. 2003–2014, URL http://www-formal.stanford.edu/jmc/child.html.

McCarthy, J. and Hayes, P. (1969). Some philosophical problems from the standpoint of AI, in B. Meltzer and D. Michie (eds.), *Machine Intelligence 4* (Edinburgh University Press, Edinburgh, Scotland), pp. 463–502, URL http://www-formal.stanford.edu/jmc/mcchay69/mcchay69.html.

Minsky, M. L. (1992). Future of AI Technology, *Toshiba Review* **47**, 7, URL http://web.media.mit.edu/~minsky/papers/CausalDiversity.html.

M.Minsky (2005). Interior Grounding, Reflection, and Self-Consciousness, in *Brain, Mind and Society, Proceedings of an International Conference on Brain, Mind and Society* (Graduate School of Information Sciences, Brain, Mind and Society, Tohoku University, Japan), URL http://web.media.mit.edu/~minsky/papers/InternalGrounding.html.

Neisser, U. (1967). *Cognitive Psychology* (Appleton-Century-Crofts, New York).

Newell, A. (1980). Physical symbol systems, *Cognitive Science* **4**, pp. 135–183.

Peterson, D. (ed.) (1996). *Forms of representation: an interdisciplinary theme for cognitive science* (Intellect Books, Exeter, U.K.).

Pollock, J. L. (2008). What Am I? Virtual machines and the mind/body problem, *Philosophy and Phenomenological Research.* **76**, 2, pp. 237–309, URL http://philsci-archive.pitt.edu/archive/00003341.

Prinz, J. J. (2005). The Return of Concept Empiricism, in H. Cohen and C. Leferbvre (eds.), *Categorization and Cognitive Science* (Elsevier, Amsterdam), p. Part 6, URL (http://subcortex.com/PrinzConceptualEmpiricismPrinz.pdf).

Reading, A. (2006). The Biological Nature of Meaningful Information, *Biological Theory* **1**, 3, pp. 243–249, URL doi:10.1162/biot.2006.1.3.243.

Ritchie, D. (1986). Shannon And WEAVER: Unravelling the Paradox of Information, *Communication Research* **13**, 2, pp. 278–298, URL http://crx.sagepub.com/cgi/content/abstract/13/2/278.

Ryle, G. (1949). *The Concept of Mind* (Hutchinson, London).

Schurz, G. (2009). When Empirical Success Implies Theoretical Reference: A Structural Correspondence Theorem, *Brit. J. for the Philosophy of Science* **60**, 1, pp. 101–133, URL doi:10.1093/bjps/axn049.

Searle, J. (1980). Minds brains and programs, *The Behavioral and Brain Sciences* **3**, 3, (With commentaries and reply by Searle).

Shannon, C. (1948). A mathematical theory of communication, *Bell System Technical Journal* **27**, pp. 379–423 and 623–656, URL http://cm.bell-labs.com/cm/ms/what/shannonday/paper.html.

Simon, H. A. (1969). *The Sciences of the Artificial* (MIT Press, Cambridge, MA), (Second edition 1981).

Sloman, A. (1971). Interactions between philosophy and AI: The role of intuition and non-logical reasoning in intelligence, in *Proc 2nd IJCAI* (William Kaufmann, London), pp. 209–226, URL http://www.cs.bham.ac.uk/research/cogaff/04.html\#200407.

Sloman, A. (1978). *The Computer Revolution in Philosophy* (Harvester Press (and Humanities Press), Hassocks, Sussex), URL http://www.cs.bham.ac.uk/research/cogaff/crp.

Sloman, A. (1979). The primacy of non-communicative language, in M. MacCafferty and K. Gray (eds.), *The analysis of Meaning: Informatics 5 Proceedings ASLIB/BCS Conference, Oxford, March 1979* (Aslib, London), pp. 1–15, URL http://www.cs.bham.ac.uk/research/projects/cogaff/81-95.html\#43.

Sloman, A. (1982). Image interpretation: The way ahead? in O. Braddick and A. Sleigh. (eds.), *Physical and Biological Processing of Images (Proceedings of an international symposium organised by The Rank Prize Funds, London, 1982.)* (Springer-Verlag, Berlin), pp. 380–401, URL http://www.cs.bham.ac.uk/research/projects/cogaff/06.html\#0604.

Sloman, A. (1985). What enables a machine to understand? in *Proc 9th IJCAI* (IJCAI, Los Angeles), pp. 995–1001, URL http://www.cs.bham.ac.uk/research/projects/cogaff/81-95.html\#4.

Sloman, A. (1987). Reference without causal links, in J. du Boulay, D.Hogg and L.Steels (eds.), *Advances in Artificial Intelligence - II* (North Holland, Dordrecht), pp. 369–381, URL http://www.cs.bham.ac.uk/research/projects/cogaff/81-95.html\#5.

Sloman, A. (1993). The mind as a control system, in C. Hookway and D. Peterson (eds.), *Philosophy and the Cognitive Sciences* (Cambridge University Press, Cambridge, UK), pp. 69–110, URL http://www.cs.bham.ac.uk/research/projects/cogaff/81-95.html\#18.

Sloman, A. (2002). The irrelevance of Turing machines to AI, in M. Scheutz (ed.), *Computationalism: New Directions* (MIT Press, Cambridge, MA), pp.

87–127, URL http://www.cs.bham.ac.uk/research/cogaff/00-02.html\ #77.

Sloman, A. (2003). The Cognition and Affect Project: Architectures, Architecture-Schemas, And The New Science of Mind. Tech. rep., School of Computer Science, University of Birmingham, Birmingham, UK, URL http://www.cs.bham.ac.uk/research/projects/cogaff/03.html\ #200307(RevisedAugust2008).

Sloman, A. (2006a). Requirements for a Fully Deliberative Architecture (Or component of an architecture), Research Note COSY-DP-0604, School of Computer Science, University of Birmingham, Birmingham, UK, URL http://www.cs.bham.ac.uk/research/projects/cosy/papers/\#dp0604.

Sloman, A. (2006b). Spatial prepositions as higher order functions: And implications of Grice's theory for evolution of language. Research Note COSY-DP-0605, School of Computer Science, University of Birmingham, Birmingham, UK, URL http://www.cs.bham.ac.uk/research/projects/ cosy/papers/\#dp0605.

Sloman, A. (2007a). Diversity of Developmental Trajectories in Natural and Artificial Intelligence, in C. T. Morrison and T. T. Oates (eds.), *Computational Approaches to Representation Change during Learning and Development. AAAI Fall Symposium 2007, Technical Report FS-07-03* (AAAI Press, Menlo Park, CA), pp. 70–79, URL http://www.cs.bham. ac.uk/research/projects/cosy/papers/\#tr0704.

Sloman, A. (2007b). Why Some Machines May Need Qualia and How They Can Have Them: Including a Demanding New Turing Test for Robot Philosophers, in A. Chella and R. Manzotti (eds.), *AI and Consciousness: Theoretical Foundations and Current Approaches AAAI Fall Symposium 2007, Technical Report FS-07-01* (AAAI Press, Menlo Park, CA), pp. 9– 16, URL http://www.cs.bham.ac.uk/research/projects/cosy/papers/ \#tr0705.

Sloman, A. (2007c). Why symbol-grounding is both impossible and unnecessary, and why theory-tethering is more powerful anyway. URL http://www.cs. bham.ac.uk/research/projects/cogaff/talks/\#models.

Sloman, A. (2008a). Architectural and representational requirements for seeing processes, proto-affordances and affordances, in A. G. Cohn, D. C. Hogg, R. Möller and B. Neumann (eds.), *Logic and Probability for Scene Interpretation*, no. 08091 in Dagstuhl Seminar Proceedings (Schloss Dagstuhl - Leibniz-Zentrum fuer Informatik, Germany, Dagstuhl, Germany), URL http://drops.dagstuhl.de/opus/volltexte/2008/1656.

Sloman, A. (2008b). Evolution of minds and languages. What evolved first and develops first in children: Languages for communicating, or languages for thinking (Generalised Languages: GLs)? URL http://www.cs.bham.ac. uk/research/projects/cosy/papers/\#pr0702.

Sloman, A. (2008c). Virtual Machines in Philosophy, Engineering & Biology, in N. McCarthy and D. Goldberg (eds.), *Proceedings Workshop on Philosophy & Engineering WPE-2008* (Royal Academy of Engineering, London), pp. 31–33, URL http://www.cs.bham.ac.uk/research/projects/cogaff/08. html\#803.

Sloman, A. (2009a). Architecture-Based Motivation vs Reward-Based Motivation, *Newsletter on Philosophy and Computers* **09**, 1, pp. 10–13, URL http://www.apaonline.org/documents/publications/v09n1_Computers.pdf.

Sloman, A. (2009b). Ontologies for baby animals and robots. From "baby stuff" to the world of adult science: Developmental AI from a Kantian viewpoint. Online tutorial presentation: http://www.cs.bham.ac.uk/research/projects/cogaff/talks/#brown.

Sloman, A. (2009c). Some Requirements for Human-like Robots: Why the recent over-emphasis on embodiment has held up progress, in B. Sendhoff, E. Koerner, O. Sporns, H. Ritter and K. Doya (eds.), *Creating Brain-like Intelligence* (Springer-Verlag, Berlin), pp. 248–277, URL http://www.cs.bham.ac.uk/research/projects/cosy/papers/\#tr0804.

Sloman, A. (2009d). Teaching AI and Philosophy at School? *Newsletter on Philosophy and Computers* **09**, 1, pp. 42–48, URL http://www.apaonline.org/documents/publications/v09n1_Computers.pdf.

Sloman, A. (2009e). Virtual Machines and the Metaphysics of Science, URL http://www.cs.bham.ac.uk/research/projects/cogaff/talks/\#mos09,PDFpresentationforAHRCMetaphysicsofScienceConference.

Sloman, A. (2009f). What Cognitive Scientists Need to Know about Virtual Machines, in N. A. Taatgen and H. van Rijn (eds.), *Proceedings of the 31st Annual Conference of the Cognitive Science Society* (Cognitive Science Society, Austin, TX), pp. 1210–1215, URL http://www.cs.bham.ac.uk/research/projects/cogaff/09.html\#901.

Trehub, A. (1991). *The Cognitive Brain* (MIT Press, Cambridge, MA), URL http://www.people.umass.edu/trehub/.

CHAPTER 16

INCONSISTENT KNOWLEDGE AS A NATURAL PHENOMENON: THE RANKING OF REASONABLE INFERENCES AS A COMPUTATIONAL APPROACH TO NATURALLY INCONSISTENT (LEGAL) THEORIES

Kees (C.N.J.) de Vey Mestdagh and Jaap Henk (J.H.) Hoepman

Centre for Law&ICT, University of Groningen & TNO Groningen and Institute for Computing and Information Sciences, Radboud University Nijmegen
The Netherlands
c.n.j.de.vey.mestdagh@rug.nl

The perspective-bound character of information and information processing gives rise to natural inconsistency. Natural inconsistency poses a problem if a common perspective is needed, for example when a shared (consistent) decision has to be made (by humans, within logics or by computers). There are three main approaches to solving the problem of common perspective: universalism; utilitarianism; and contractarianism. However, none of these approaches has ever been made computationally tractable. Inconsistency as a natural phenomenon explains why this can never be achieved. The core of the problem is that natural inconsistency not only exists at the level of perspectives on the actual situation, but it also exists at the level of the principles used to decide on a common perspective. There is no universal preferential ordering of perspectives at either level because there is no known, let alone universally recognized, universal processor. Furthermore, there is no exhaustive or non-contradictory set of universal or utilitarian principles or contracts available. An analysis of the solution to the problem of common perspective found in the legal domain can probably be extended to solve this problem in other domains. In this chapter, we recapitulate the Logic of Reasonable Inferences, which formalizes the reduction of all actual legal perspectives in a case to all formally valid legal perspectives. Subsequently, we make an inventory of commonly used tentative legal decision principles and categorize them into three classes. The properties of the three classes are then used to define the semantics of meta-predicates, which can be used to rank the remaining perspectives computationally. Finally, we illustrate the behavior of the Logic of Reasonable Inferences in combination with the meta-predicates by means of an elaborate legal example.

1. Introduction: Inconsistent Knowledge as a Natural Phenomenon

The naturally distributed character of information processing renders both information processing (know how) and the resulting information (know what) inherently perspective bound. This contextual quality of knowledge is independent of the human or non-human nature of the processors and it will exist as long as there is variation amongst the different processors or between their information content prior to communication. In both human communication and in computer networks such variation is not only common but also natural[1], because communication (information exchange) between completely similar entities is impossible by definition. The perspective-bound character of information and information processing allows for natural inconsistency in the sense of inconsistency being the result of the different perspectives[2] as opposed to faulty perception or other forms of faulty processing such as processing on the basis of incomplete knowledge from a single perspective.

Natural inconsistency constitutes no general problem. It only generates a specific practical problem if a common perspective is needed. However, a common perspective is frequently required for a variety of reasons ranging from the demand to make a decision (on a common perspective or action) to the need for a decidable logic or for a finite algorithm. There are three main approaches to solving the problem of common perspective: universalism; utilitarianism; and contractarianism. Universalism claims that decisions can be made on the basis of universal principles (cf. Immanuel Kant's categorical imperative). Utilitarianism (cf. David Hume, Jeremy Bentham, John Stuart Mill) claims that a decisive cost-benefit analysis can be made (cf. Immanuel Kant's hypothetical imperative). Contractarianism avoids the semantic problems of utilitarianism by introducing a purely formal decision criterion (*pacta sunt servanda*). None of these approaches has ever been

---

[1] Natural in the sense of being a physical necessity: variation is a *conditio sine qua non* for communication

[2] Perspective is defined as a conviction based on a certain spatial and temporal position, individual characteristics of the perceptual and information processing apparatus, *a priori* knowledge and interests

made computationally tractable. As a matter of fact, the computational tractability of these approaches can never be achieved because inconsistency is a natural phenomenon. The core of the problem is that natural inconsistency not only exists at the level of perspectives on the actual situation, but it also exists at the level of the principles used to decide on a common perspective. There is no universal preferential ordering of perspectives at both levels because there is no known, let alone a universally recognized, universal processor. Furthermore, there is no exhaustive or non-contradictory set of universal or utilitarian principles or contracts available.

Each domain of knowledge is more or less affected by this problem, but this effect is particularly intense in the domain of legal knowledge, since it consists of the rules and procedures used to describe and solve legal conflicts, which presupposes contradictory and hence inconsistent perspectives. An analysis of the solution to the problem of common perspective found in the legal domain can probably be used to solve this problem in other domains. Human processors of legal knowledge follow formal and informal problem-solving methods in order to reduce the number of legal perspectives and eventually to decide, temporally and within a specific context, on a common perspective. The formal methods are based on universal properties of formally valid legal argument. The informal methods are based on legal heuristics consisting in tentative legal decision principles. The first category can be formalized by logic because it applies peremptorily to all legal perspectives. The second category cannot be fully formalized by logic because, although it is commonly applicable, it can always be refuted by a contradictory decision principle and even by the mere existence of an underlying contradictory argument.

In this chapter we recapitulate the Logic of Reasonable Inferences (LRI), which formalizes the reduction of all given legal perspectives to all formally valid legal perspectives. Subsequently, we make an inventory of commonly used tentative legal decision principles and categorize them into three classes. The properties of the three classes are then used to define the semantics of meta-predicates, which can be used to rank the remaining perspectives computationally. Finally, we illustrate the behavior of the LRI in combination with the meta-predicates by means of a complex legal example. Further research should elaborate on the formal properties of the three classes of meta-predicates and their applicability in other knowledge domains and in ranking algorithms.

2. Inconsistent Knowledge in the Legal Domain

Legal, or more broadly, normative knowledge[3] is used to infer the normative characteristics of actual social situations. Legal knowledge is a subdivision of normative knowledge that is used in the formal legal (judicial) subsystem of social systems, such as countries, organizations or coalitions. Normative knowledge encompasses both normative opinions (know what) and the normative procedures (know how) that are used to infer these normative opinions. The normative characteristics that are inferred represent the mutual expectations of people about the conduct of others (rules of conduct). In a formal legal context, these expectations are commonly labeled as 'rights' (to the realization of conduct of others) and 'obligations' (of others to behave in agreement with the expectations).

Normative opinions range from informal to formal. On the informal side we find moral principles, social scripts, protocols, (technical) instructions, rules of thumb, rules of play, etc. On the formal side we find legislation, legal principles, jurisprudence, policy rules, etc. Normative opinions can be of a general (uninstantiated) and of a specific (instantiated) character. Normative procedures consist of (1) procedures to list all the normative opinions about a given situation that can be inferred from the given situation combined with the set of pre-existing normative opinions of the parties concerned and (2) procedures to reduce the number of normative opinions about the given situation to a (local and temporal) common opinion for (not necessarily *of*) the parties concerned. Both procedures involve *legal reasoning*. The second

---

[3] The concept "legal" is commonly used to refer to an ideal world that actually does not exist. The world of the formal (e.g. statutory) introduction and application of formal regulations is just the tip of the iceberg of normative knowledge. Moreover, this formal tip itself is pervaded with the application of informal opinions and procedures. In order to maintain readability, we will generally use the concept "legal" instead of the broader concept "normative".

procedure also involves *legal decision-making*. Legal reasoning in the first class of procedures is concerned with the inference of normative opinions about the given situation. We will refer to this as "*the object level*". Legal reasoning in the second class of procedures is concerned with the inference of normative opinions about the reduction of normative opinions (e.g. "the judge is obliged to decide for a legally valid opinion"). We will refer to this as "*the meta level*". In the next two subsections, we will discuss the properties of legal knowledge that should be taken into consideration in order to be able to develop a tenable computational model.

2.1. *Legal reasoning: reasonable inferences and tentative decision-making*

Legal or normative reasoning has no unique qualities compared to reasoning in other domains of knowledge. Normative characteristics of social situations are inferred by plain logical deduction from (agreed or disputed) facts and normative opinions. Normative opinions can have facts (e.g. the conduct of others) or opinions as their subject. In the former case, expectations about the conduct of others in general are inferred (the object level). In the latter case, expectations about the application of opinions are inferred (the meta level). To be precise: at both levels, expectations about the conduct of others are inferred. At the object level this relates to conduct in general, while at the meta level it relates to conduct concerning the application of normative opinions. Consequently, there is no formal difference between legal reasoning at the two levels.

One could think that an idiosyncrasy of legal reasoning may be found in the above addition "agreed or disputed", but disagreements about facts and opinionated qualifications are part of every domain of knowledge. However, the representation of disagreements about facts and conflicting opinions and the (local and temporal) resolution of these disagreements and conflicts is the aim of, and therefore essential to, the practical application of legal knowledge. What is special about this particular aim is the local and temporal character of the resolution. The aim of the application of legal knowledge in a social situation is to decide on a common perspective in order to be able to act in a coordinated manner.

The decision does not (necessarily) cause facts or individual opinions to change; it simply introduces a new fact, that of the common perspective. It is even necessary for all the disputed facts and opinions to be represented permanently because they are not only part of the decision making process but remain part of the legitimation of the common perspective.

The continued representation of disputed facts and opinions, even after a decision regarding a common perspective has been made, is not only essential to the legitimation of the decision. Legal knowledge is ultimately dynamic, meaning not only that people can change their opinion sequentially over time but that they can also hold different opinions in parallel at any given time. Normative opinions change and differ with time and given context. A common perspective only holds for the given situation of the parties concerned. Furthermore, the parties need not merely maintain their individual opinions in parallel with the common, decided opinion, but they may also immediately renounce the common opinion either individually or in unison. It is not uncommon that parties decide to act *contra legem*, for example to maintain the status quo or just to avoid a bagatelle.

The world is not transformed into a consistent state as a consequence of the completion of the legal proceedings. Agreement is reached within one context, at one moment, in order to complete a singular legal transaction (e.g. a verdict). The judge and all other parties can stick to their original opinions in every other transaction, but they may and frequently will also change their opinions in the aftermath of legal proceedings. People may also continue to act in violation of a verdict. A verdict may be overruled or be revised. And even the law may change.

The preceding description of legal knowledge and legal reasoning renders any normative opinion relatively *legally valid* (i.e. legally valid within its own context) and thus allows the existence of contradictory opinions. Fortunately, there are some universal constraints that reduce the number of opinions that can be taken into consideration. These constraints are based on the legitimation principle, which is universally acknowledged in legal disputes and which comprises amongst others the principles of legal justification and legal rationality. The principle of legal justification demands that each derived normative opinion is based on a complete argument, meaning that the opinion reached is supported by facts and grounded opinions. The principle of rationality comes down to the demand that the derived opinion and the argument it is based on are non-contradictory. Psychologically, these demands amount to common characteristics of human cognition. Formally, they boil down to the requirements of valid deduction and consistency. A logic modeling legal reasoning should abide by these requirements. The formal demands of valid deduction and consistency of opinions and their justifications reduce the number of *formally valid* opinions (reasonable inferences), but in most cases they do not enable a reduction to a single common opinion. Unfortunately, there are no further formal (absolute) criteria to reduce all the remaining alternative formally valid legal opinions to a single common opinion.

In legal practice, tentative criteria are used to rank formally valid legal opinions. These criteria represent the arguments that the parties concerned normally accept as a basis for agreement on a common opinion. The ranking provides for a prediction of the relative probability that a common opinion will be agreed upon (by content or by procedure) and hold. So far, no statistical research has succeeded in yielding more than an ordinal ranking. Apart from that, the dynamic character of legal knowledge and the lack of available statistical data prohibit a model which includes more than an ordinal ranking. Conveniently, the parameters of the ranking are well-known as legal decision principles and policies, and they are a traditional subject of jurisprudential research.

2.2. *Legal decision-making: three classes of decision principles*

A jurisprudential and empirical analysis of the legal domain reveals the existence of three particular classes of principles used to evaluate the rules that are referred to in legal opinions [de Vey Mestdagh, 1997]. The first class of principles is that of (relative) legal validity. The second class of principles is that of legal exclusion, and the third class is that of legal preference. The application of these principles renders a rule legally valid or invalid (within a certain context) or entails the legal exclusion of one rule by another or the preference of one rule above another. All of these principles and the derived qualifications of the subjected rules are tentative. A legally invalid rule, a legally excluded rule or a rule that is legally not preferred is never absolutely legally invalid (i.e. invalid in any context). The inferences made with the aid of such rules are therefore not absolutely invalid either. The principles just provide for tentative ranking arguments. The principles of validity, exclusion and preference are expressed in a multitude of rules (at the meta level), concluding with the validity, exclusion or preference of other rules (at the object or at the meta level).

Legal validity (authority, competence and procedure)

Legal validity relates to the authority of legal rules at the object and at the meta level. Meta-rules of this class qualify rules as valid or invalid on the basis of (mainly) the legal authority of their source and of formal legal features of the process of their creation. For example, rules with statutory law, judicial decisions or administrative decisions as a source can be qualified as valid or invalid depending on whether they satisfy the requirements of formal law with regard to authority, competence, procedure, etc. Rules based on private decisions (such as contractual agreements) are valid if the contracting parties are authorized and competent to decide about the subject of the contract and act according to the agreed procedures. Even rules of play can be valid if they are introduced by the appointed games master or if agreed by the majority of the games participants. In the legal domain, an opinion based on a valid rule ranks above an opinion based on a non-valid or invalid rule and an opinion based on a non-valid rule ranks above an opinion based on an invalid rule.

Legal exclusion (applicability)

If one rule legally excludes another rule, then the first rule is legally preferred above the second rule, and their combination is *legally* invalid. Furthermore, if they contradict each other, their combination is also *formally* invalid. Meta-rules of this class relate rules on the basis of common subject on the one hand (which renders them *alternative* rules) but on the other hand different *space*, *time* or *specificity* dimensions. Legally valid rules are commonly applicable within a certain territory or on a certain territorial (organizational) level or to persons situated on or connected (by their nationality or acts) to a certain territory, within a certain timeframe and on a certain level of detail/specificity. Common examples of legal exclusion are based on *the legal principle of personality* (national/regional/municipal law is only applicable to nationals, etc.), *the legal principle of territoriality* (national/regional/-municipal law is only applicable to the national territory), *the superior principle* (higher laws, decisions of higher administrative bodies or courts overrule lower ones, etc.), *the posterior principle* (more recent laws, decisions, etc. exclude less recent ones) and *the specialis principle* (more specific laws, decisions, etc. exclude more general ones).

Legal preference (balancing interests)

If one rule is legally preferred to another rule, the first rule ranks above the second, but if they do not contradict each other their combination is legally valid and is preferred above the application of just one of the rules (the so-called *a fortiori* argument). In most cases, the preference of one rule to another is related to the *objectives* (c.q. the expected effects of the application) of the rules. The antecedents of meta-rules of this class will generally be involved with the interests and values associated with these objectives. In this class of meta-rules, not only legal principles but also legal policies play a part. Examples of legal principles that define legal preference are the principle of equality before the law (c.f. precedents in common law) and the principle of legal security. Examples of policies that define legal preference are public/administrative policies (e.g. preferring economic growth to environmental protection or private spending above public spending) and prosecution policies (e.g. against bagatelles or balancing the supply of cases with the available capacity).

3. The Extended Logic of Reasonable Inferences: A Formal and Computational Approach to Natural Inconsistency

One element of our past research has been focused on building legal knowledge-based systems. These knowledge-based systems have been used to model legal knowledge in order to be able to empirically test our theoretical assumptions about this knowledge. As we have seen in the previous sections, one of these assumptions is that natural inconsistency is an essential part of (legal) knowledge. This assumption poses a problem when it comes to formalization.

In order to be able to formalize natural inconsistency we have postulated that the theoretical principle of rationality holds universally, also in the legal domain, but that it holds separately from each possible perspective. The theoretical principle of rationality formally reduces to logical consistency. It demands that all formally valid opinions are internally consistent. This has forced us to define a logic that distinguishes all internally consistent opinions (*reasonable inferences*) that can be derived from a given situation and the full set of (*a priori*) known legal opinions, without discarding one of these *a priori* opinions, i.e. maintaining the natural (*meaningful*) inconsistency between alternative opinions. This formally associates our approach with inconsistency-tolerant or paraconsistent logics (cf. section 3.1.2. below). More important, it distinguishes our approach from other approaches to inconsistency that are aimed at permanently or temporally resolving the inconsistency by *retraction* of one or more of the conflicting opinions according to one or another criterion (constraint satisfaction, exhaustion (dialogue logics), logics of preference, most default logics, etc.) or at resolving the inconsistency by changing the semantics of the conflicting opinions (i.e. numerical representations that reduce conflicting opinions to a single opinion with a certain probability, etc.).

Retraction only works in simple domains where a complete inventory of all the relations between arguments for and against specific alternative opinions can be made in advance or where the relation with each newly introduced argument can be defined in advance. See, for instance [de Vey Mestdagh 2003; Dijkstra *et al* 2005 a; Dijkstra *et al* 2005 b; Dijkstra *et al* 2007], where we proposed a non-monotonic, dialogical approach using persuasion and negotiation to model data exchange in a network of distributed police databases where most arguments and their interrelations are known in advance.

Numerical reduction hides the arguments of the reduction behind numerals. In our approach, conflicting opinions cannot be retracted or reduced because they have to be present in the next phase (that of legal decision-making) and remain present after that to legitimize the tentative (local and temporal) decisions for a common opinion.

In most cases this still leaves us with a multitude of internally consistent, but mutually inconsistent, alternative opinions. We have not found other universal formal principles used in legal practice to reduce the number of opinions, but we have found three classes of tentative principles (heuristics) commonly used in legal practice to rank formally valid legal opinions. In this section we will summarize the features of the Logic of Reasonable Inferences (LRI) that formalizes the universal features of legal knowledge and we will describe the computational characteristics of the three classes of tentative principles added to the LRI in the form of meta-predicates and meta-rules. To illustrate the application of the extended LRI in this section, we will use the following example from Dutch environmental law.

An example from Dutch environmental law

The Dutch Waste Products Law (WPL) obliges industries which "handle waste" to do so following the directions of an environmental license (section 31 WPL). The ambiguous concepts "handle" and "waste" and their combination have caused a vast body of rules of interpretation, which in many cases contradict each other. These contradictions have been the subject of many subsequent legal disputes. This can be elucidated with the example of rubble. Until 1980, according to common legal opinion, rubble was designated as "waste" and any use of rubble was labeled as "handling of waste". In 1981, however, this interpretation was refined by the "Kroon" (the highest body of administrative appeal). Waste was defined as any product which is no longer used for a specific purpose (KB May 29 1981, BR 1982, p. 69), thus introducing an exception to the general rule. In a specific case, this meant that a farmer, who used rubble to fill up a ditch, thus not just dumping the rubble but using it to attain a purpose, did not need a WPL license. Some months later, the "Hoge Raad" (the highest body of civil appeal) decided that common parlance should be the criterion for the judgment of the waste property of any product (HR December 22, 1981, NJ 1982, 325). According to this interpretation, a WPL license was needed in any case concerning rubble, even if it was used to fill up a ditch. Since there are no hierarchical regulations which grant higher authority to the opinions of either of these bodies of appeal, both interpretations were valid within the legal system at the same time. Although, in this specific case, a **meta-rule** exists stating that a court of law should adhere to its own previous jurisdiction, this meta-rule is not coercive but tentative in nature. This provides us with one of the many clear cut examples of alternative legal opinions, which can be used at will in cases coming up before any court of law. This was confirmed by the refusal of the "Kroon" to obey a directive from the minister for the environment to adjust to the jurisdiction of the "Hoge Raad" (UCV 32, December 10, 1984, p. 12/13).

The conflict was finally resolved by legislation. Section 31 clause 3 WPL juncto "Werkenbesluit Afvalstoffenwet" declares that rubble is waste under any circumstance or use. In this case, a coercive **meta-rule** exists preferring legislation to jurisdiction. However, the conflict remains for any other material (except rubble) for which no specific definitions are included in the new legislation. So the interpretation rules of both the "Kroon" and the "Hoge Raad" are still valid except for rubble. This means that the rulings of the "Kroon" and the "Hoge Raad" cannot be removed from the rule-base. The introduced rule of law constitutes an exception to the present rules and calls for revision of some registered cases concerning rubble. Revision of registered cases is also needed if relevant factual circumstances change. In the case of rubble, the farmer can dump some material designated as waste, for instance wreckage, on top of the filled up ditch. This requalifies the rubble as waste according to common legal opinion (which should be comprised in the rule-base).

The Logic of Reasonable Inferences (LRI) and the extension with meta-predicates have been implemented to test their tenability empirically [de Vey Mestdagh 1997 a, de Vey Mestdagh 1997 b, de Vey Mestdagh 1998]. This research has shown that the implementation (and consequentially the extended LRI) models most of the examined legal decisions (425 out of 430). In section 4 of this chapter, we will illustrate the viability of the extended LRI by means of an elaborate example.

3.1. *The Logic of Reasonable Inferences*

The Logic of Reasonable Inferences (LRI), with which we have proposed to model legal reasoning as described above [de Vey Mestdagh, 1991], uses the language of predicate calculus, as this language seems powerful enough to express legal rules and factual situations without losing any relevant information. Section 3.1.1 lists our notational conventions and illustrates some predicate calculus concepts. In section 3.1.2 the LRI is defined, and in section 3.1.3 the LRI is compared with Reiter's Default Reasoning and with Poole's framework for Default Reasoning, both typical representatives of the approach that involves retraction as a decision making strategy. In section 3.2 we present a decision making strategy using meta-predicates as ranking arguments.

3.1.1. *Predicate Calculus Conventions*

This section describes those concepts of predicate calculus that we use to define the logic. This is intended to be a quick reminder rather than an exhaustive or precise introduction. We therefore presuppose some elementary knowledge of predicate calculus, and we assume that the more rigorous definitions will be used for the concepts we will only touch upon here.

$\mathcal{L}$ is the language of the logic containing all syntactically correct formulae, called the *well-formed formulae* (*wff*) of the logic. It will contain predicate symbols such as =, function symbols, and logic operators such as $\wedge$ (conjunction), $\vee$ (disjunction), $\neg$ (negation) and $\rightarrow$ (implication).

A theory Γ is a set of *wff* in $\mathcal{L}$. The semantic derivability relation denoted by $\vDash$ makes the distinction between correct and incorrect conclusions drawn from a theory. If a *wff* φ is semantically derivable from a theory Γ, we write $\Gamma \vDash \varphi$. The definition of $\vDash$ is the usual one.

If Γ is empty we write $\vDash \varphi$, which means that φ is universally valid. A theory Γ is called inconsistent if there exists some φ such that both $\Gamma \vDash \varphi$ and $\Gamma \vDash \neg\varphi$ hold. A theory is called consistent if and only if (*iff*) it is not inconsistent.

3.1.2. *Inconsistency and the Logic of Reasonable Inferences*

The predicate calculus definition of semantical derivability seems to be a fairly reasonable one, but it enjoys a peculiar property if theories are allowed to be inconsistent: anything can then be derived from them!

Thus, if Γ is an inconsistent theory, then $\Gamma \vDash \varphi$ for any $\varphi \in \mathcal{L}$. Theories like this are called *trivial*, and logics that render inconsistent theories trivial are called *explosive*. Explosiveness conflicts with any intuitive understanding of derivability. We surely do not want to conclude from an inconsistent theory on environmental law that the obligation to possess an environmental permit implies that one does not perform activities which concern the environment, or that all farmers are civil servants. One is not liable to accept any derivation of a formula containing concepts not present in the theory from which it was derived.

To describe this issue in a more formal framework, let Γ be an inconsistent theory in $\mathcal{L}$. Let α be a *wff* in $\mathcal{L}$ only containing variable, constant, predicate and function symbols that occur in some *wff* in Γ, and let β be a *wff* in $\mathcal{L}$ containing some variable, constant, predicate and function symbols **not** occurring in any *wff* in Γ. Then the intuitively undesirable property can be formally described by the observation that predicate calculus with its definition of $\vDash$ yields $\Gamma \vDash \alpha$ and $\Gamma \vDash \beta$ for any α and β defined as above, whereas one would more or less agree with a definition of $\vDash$ satisfying the constraint $\Gamma \nvDash \beta$ for any β as defined above (unless of course $\vDash \beta$ holds, in which case β is a universally valid formula).

Inconsistent theories, which model the body of rules of law, have their use in legal reasoning, as has been argued in section 2. Therefore, our definition of semantic derivability must surely avoid the property of predicate calculus derivability concerning inconsistent theories by responding to inconsistent theories along the lines described in the previous paragraphs. This can be achieved by demanding that every justification for a derived conclusion is internally consistent, where a justification is the set of rules and observations (facts) used to derive the conclusion. This demand is a straightforward observation taken from legal reasoning theory.

These constraints lead to the definition of a new (non-explosive) semantic derivability relation $\vDash_r$ for the Logic of Reasonable Inferences (LRI). The language of the LRI equals that of predicate calculus. The LRI can be classified as a paraconsistent logic (cf. [Priest, 2002]). A logic is paraconsistent *iff* its logical consequence relation is not explosive. Paraconsistent logics accommodate inconsistency in a manner that treats inconsistent information as informative. There are different systems of paraconsistent logic e.g. discussive logic, non-adjunctive systems, preservationism, adaptive logics, logics of formal inconsistency, many-valued logics and relevant logics. The LRI is closely related to the non-adjunctive systems, specifically to the non-adjunctive strategy proposed by [Rescher & Manor, 1970]. However, the LRI differs from these systems in its use of consistent subsets of premises instead of maximally consistent subsets of premises and structured premise-sets (axioms and hypotheses). These differences are required by legal domain specifics. An individual legal opinion is a consistent subset of all the axioms (ascertained facts and shared opinions) and a consistent selection of individually adhered hypotheses (non-shared opinions). Individual legal opinions (as opposed to maximal subsets) should be distinguished because they have to be compared in order for a legal decision to be made. In accordance with this demand, in section 3.2 we extend the LRI with meta-predicates, which can be used as ranking arguments in legal decision-making.

Definition (domain of rules)

A domain of rules in $\mathcal{L}$, or *reasonable theory*, is a tuple Δ defined as

$$\Delta = \langle A, H \rangle$$

where A and H are sets of *wff* in $\mathcal{L}$. A contains the *axioms*, and H contains the *assumptions* (hypotheses). A is required to be consistent. Δ

The *assumptions* model the rules of law that may or may not be applied in a given factual situation to derive a conclusion and contain all normative or subjective classifications of the factual situation. The *axioms* are intended to be valid in every justification and thus restrict the number of possible justifications. These axioms represent the ascertained facts and previously ascertained conclusions (the permanent database in any implementation).

Definition (position within a domain)

A *position* (or *conviction*) ϕ within a domain of rules $\Delta = \langle A, H \rangle$ is the set (or normal predicate calculus theory) defined as

$$\phi = A \cup H'$$

where $H' \subseteq H$ and ϕ must be consistent.
Δ

A position, then, is a set of rules taken from the domain of rules and represents a conviction. Note that all positions should at least contain all axioms of the domain of rules. A position is consistent by definition.

Definition (reasonable inference)

Let Δ be a domain of rules. Define a new semantic derivability-relation $\vDash_r$ as :

$$\Delta \vDash_r \varphi$$

iff there exists a position ϕ within Δ which satisfies

$$\phi \vDash \varphi$$

where $\vDash$ is the normal predicate calculus semantic derivability relation. If $\Delta \vDash_r \varphi$ holds, φ is said to be a *reasonable inference* from the **domain of rules** Δ.
Δ

We can paraphrase this definition by stating that a *wff* can reasonably be inferred from an inconsistent set of *wff iff* it is derivable (in the normal predicate calculus sense) from a consistent subset of this set which contains at least the axioms. Note that if a domain of rules $\Delta = \langle A, H \rangle$ is consistent (i.e. if $A \cup H = \Gamma$ is consistent), then $\Delta \vDash_r \varphi \Leftrightarrow \Gamma \vDash \varphi$ behaves exactly like $\vDash$ when applied to consistent theories.

In this setting, a **justification** for a conclusion φ derived from a domain of rules Δ is a minimal position (with respect to set-inclusion) J within Δ such that $J \vDash \varphi$. This definition is based on the more intuitive definition as a set of rules and statements about the factual situation used to draw the conclusion. Note that a justification needs not be unique but is always consistent, thus satisfying our constraints.

A **context** in Δ is the union of n simultaneously derived conclusions ψ_i and their justifications J_i derived from Δ, i.e. a context is the set of tuples $\{\langle J_i, \psi_i \rangle \mid 1 \leq i \leq n\}$. The J_i must however satisfy:

$$\bigcup_{i=1}^{n} J_i \text{ is consistent}$$

This guarantees that simultaneously derived conclusions are not based on mutually inconsistent positions, and that

$$\Delta \vDash_r \psi_1 \wedge \ldots \wedge \psi_n$$

holds. For a proof see the weak conjunction lemma stated below.

To clarify the behaviour of $\vDash_r$ we will consider an example.

Example 1:

Suppose we have the following domain of rules $\Delta = \langle A, H \rangle$ defined as

$$A = \{ WCP(A), USE(A) \}$$

where WCP refers to 'waste in common parlance' and USE to 'used for a specific purpose'

and

$$H = \{ \forall x(USE(x) \rightarrow \neg WAS(x)), \forall x(WCP(x) \rightarrow WAS(x)) \}$$

where WAS refers to 'waste'

From this formal structure, we can derive whether $WAS(A)$ or $\neg WAS(A)$, using the definition of reasonable inferences. This definition suggests that we should first of all find all possible positions within Δ. Using the definition of a position within a domain, we obtain the following positions:

$$\phi_1 = \{ WCP(A), USE(A), \forall x(WCP(x) \rightarrow WAS(x)) \}$$

$$\phi_2 = \{ WCP(A), USE(A), \forall x(USE(x) \rightarrow \neg WAS(x)) \}$$

Of course, all subsets of the above positions are also positions within Δ. These positions represent the possible ways (views) to tackle this legal problem. From these positions, we derive the contexts:

(1) $\phi_1 \vDash WAS(A)$
with justification: $\{ USE(A), WCP(A), \forall x(WCP(x) \rightarrow WAS(x)) \}$

(2) $\phi_2 \vDash \neg WAS(A)$
with justification: $\{ WCP(A), USE(A), \forall x(USE(x) \rightarrow \neg WAS(x)) \}$

From this we can conclude $\Delta \vDash_r WAS(A)$ as well as $\Delta \vDash_r \neg WAS(A)$. This result implies that further investigation of the justifications on which these contradictory conclusions are based must resolve whether $WAS(A)$ or $\neg WAS(A)$ must be concluded.
Δ

To demonstrate the viability of this logic formally, we will prove two lemmas stating important properties.

The first lemma states that the logic is safe in the sense that one cannot derive contradictions from it, thus representing the property that all contexts are contradiction-free.

Lemma (contradictions):

Let φ be a *wff* in $\mathcal{L}$. If φ is a contradiction, i.e. $\vDash \neg\varphi$, then

$$\Delta \nvDash_r \varphi$$

for any domain of rules Δ.
Δ

Proof:

Suppose that φ is a contradiction, and that $\Delta \vDash_r \varphi$ does hold. Then there exists a position ϕ within Δ which justifies φ, i.e. such that $\phi \vDash \varphi$. If $\Delta = \langle\{\},\{\}\rangle$ then $\phi = \{\}$ will suffice. But also $\phi \vDash \neg\varphi$, since $\vDash \neg\varphi$, which contradicts the fact that, by definition, ϕ is consistent.
Δ

The next lemma states that a *weak* conjunction rule holds if both conclusions are derived from mutually consistent justifications. This indicates that the conjunction rule only holds for mutually consistent justifications and not for mutually inconsistent justifications. The legal connotation of this lemma is that justifications which consist of conflicting opinions cannot be joined.

Lemma (weak conjunction):

Let α and β be *wff* in $\mathcal{L}$. Let Δ be an arbitrary domain of rules in $\mathcal{L}$. Suppose that

$$\Delta \vDash_r \alpha \text{ and } \Delta \vDash_r \beta$$

then

$$\Delta \vDash_r \alpha \wedge \beta$$

iff there exist positions A and B within Δ such that

$$A \vDash \alpha \wedge B \vDash \beta$$

and $A \cup B$ is consistent.
Δ

Proof:

If $\Delta \vDash_r \alpha \wedge \beta$, then there exists a position ϕ in Δ such that $\phi \vDash \alpha \wedge \beta$, implying that $\phi \vDash \alpha$ and $\phi \vDash \beta$. Since ϕ is a position in Δ, we also get $\Delta \vDash_r \alpha$ and $\Delta \vDash_r \beta$. For the *iff*-part of the proof, note that since $A \vDash \alpha$ and $B \vDash \beta$, we have $A \cup B \vDash \alpha$ and $A \cup B \vDash \beta$. From this we may conclude $A \cup B \vDash \alpha \wedge \beta$. Since $A \cup B$ is consistent, and both A and B are positions within Δ, $A \cup B$ is a position in Δ. This yields $\Delta \vDash_r \alpha \wedge \beta$.
Δ

To show that the general conjunction rule does not hold, i.e. that it is not the case that if $\Delta \vDash_r \alpha$ and $\Delta \vDash_r \beta$ we can conclude $\Delta \vDash_r \alpha \wedge \beta$, the following example should suffice.

Example 2:

Let Δ be the following domain of rules $\Delta = \langle\{\},\{\gamma, \neg\gamma, \gamma \to \alpha, \neg\gamma \to \beta\}\rangle$ with suitable α, β and γ, then we have $\Delta \vDash_r \alpha$, with $\Phi = \{\gamma, \gamma \to \alpha\}$ and $\Delta \vDash_r \beta$ with $\Phi = \{\neg\gamma, \neg\gamma \to \beta\}$ but not $\Delta \vDash_r \alpha \wedge \beta$.
Δ

This behaviour is caused by the mutual inconsistency of the justifications on which the conclusions are based.

3.1.3. Comparison to Default Reasoning

The Logic of Reasonable Inferences (LRI) is, in some important aspects, similar to Reiter's Default Reasoning when applied to normal default theories. However, there is a crucial formal difference as well as a difference in proposed use. In this section, we investigate the similarities, and indicate the essential points of difference. For a thorough description of default reasoning, we refer to Reiter's original article [Reiter, 1980].

Default reasoning was proposed as a model for reasoning with incomplete knowledge (e.g. birds can fly, ostriches are birds) and the retraction of previously derived conclusions (e.g. ostriches can fly) in the light of new information (e.g. ostriches can't fly). For this purpose *general default rules*

$$\frac{\alpha(\vec{x}): M\beta_1(\vec{x}), \dots, M\beta_n(\vec{x})}{w(\vec{x})}$$

are introduced, with the following interpretation: "if $\alpha(\vec{x})$ holds, then in the absence of any information contradicting $\beta_i(\vec{x})$ for any $i \in \{1,\dots,n\}$ infer $w(\vec{x})$". A default rule is called *normal iff* it has the following form:

$$\frac{\alpha(\vec{x}):M\ w(\vec{x})}{w(\vec{x})}$$

and *free iff* it has the following form:

$$:M \; w(\vec{x})$$
$$\overline{\phantom{:M \; w(\vec{x})}}$$
$$w(\vec{x})$$

Default rules are not part of the logical language as such, but are to be considered as rules of inference (like *modus ponens*).

A *default theory* is a pair *(D,W)* of a set of default rules *D* and a set of *wff W*. A *normal default theory* is a default theory in which all default rules in *D* are normal.

The first point of comparison between the LRI and default reasoning is that they are both non-monotonic logics. Let *Th(T)* be the set of *wff* derivable from theory *T* within a certain logic, then the logic is called *monotonic iff*

$$T \subseteq T' \Rightarrow Th(T) \subseteq Th(T')$$

and *non-monotonic* otherwise. This definition can be understood to mean that by using a monotonic logic, a conclusion derived from a given theory remains valid if new statements are *added* to the theory.

The non-monotonic nature of the LRI is stated in the following lemma (a similar lemma holds for default reasoning, see [Reiter, 1980, p.75 Theorem 3.2], and for Poole's framework, see [Poole, 1988, p.30 Lemma 2.5]):

Lemma (semi-monotonicity):

Let $\Delta = \langle A, H \rangle$ be a domain of rules, and define Th_r (the closure under reasonable inference) by

$$Th_r(\Delta) = \{\varphi \mid \Delta \vDash_r \varphi\}$$

then

(a) $H \subseteq H' \Rightarrow Th_r(\langle A, H \rangle) \subseteq Th_r(\langle A, H' \rangle)$

but not

(b) $A \subseteq A' \Rightarrow Th_r(\langle A, H \rangle) \subseteq Th_r(\langle A', H \rangle)$

for any A, A', H, H'.

Δ

Proof:

To prove **(a)**, let $H \subseteq H'$. Suppose $\langle A,H \rangle \vDash_r \varphi$. Then there exists a position ϕ in $\langle A,H \rangle$ such that $\phi \vDash \varphi$. This ϕ, then, is also a position within $\langle A,H' \rangle$, yielding $\langle A,H' \rangle \vDash_r \varphi$. This proves

$$\varphi \in Th_r(\langle A,H \rangle) \Rightarrow \varphi \in Th_r(\langle A,H' \rangle)$$

and thus

$$Th_r(\langle A,H \rangle) \subseteq Th_r(\langle A,H' \rangle)$$

To contradict **(b)** we only need to observe the counterexample $\langle \{ \}, \{ \alpha, \alpha \to \beta \} \rangle \vDash \beta$ and $\langle \{ \neg\alpha \} \rangle \{ \alpha, \alpha \to \beta \}, \nvDash \beta$.

Δ

This lemma shows that the logic is monotonic in H but non-monotonic in A. As pointed out above, the axioms A are intended to model some ascertained facts and previously ascertained inferences. The legal connotation of this lemma is that, if the axiom set is extended with an ascertained conclusion based on a choice of one of the alternative opinions, the number of derivations is restricted because contexts including the alternative conclusions are no longer constructed.

The similarity between the LRI and default reasoning becomes apparent if we consider the logical framework for default reasoning suggested by Poole [Poole, 1988] and applied to legal document assembly by Gordon [Gordon, 1989]. Poole defines a new semantic derivability relation $\Delta = \langle A,H \rangle$ which behaves like default reasoning with respect to free default theories, and which can be used to model general default theories [Poole, 1988]. We paraphrase his definition below, using our own notational conventions. Note that in Poole's framework defaults are explicit, whereas Reiter considers default rules as rules of inference.

Definition (Poole's semantics of default reasoning):

Let F and D be sets of *wff* in the language of predicate calculus. F is the set of facts (like W in default reasoning) and D is the set of default rules (like D in default reasoning, but the default rules are now denoted as ordinary *wff*). The new semantic derivability relation $\models_d$ is defined as

$$F,D \models_d \varphi$$

iff there exists a subset D' of all possible <u>ground instances</u> of *wff* in D such that $F \cup D'$ is consistent and

$$F \cup D' \models \varphi$$

where $\models$ is the normal semantic derivability relation of predicate calculus. A *ground instance* of a *wff* ψ is the *wff* resulting from renaming all bound variables to unique variable names in ψ, then removing all quantifiers in ψ (thus freeing all bound variables) from the result, and substituting constants for all free variables (i.e. all variables) after that.
Δ

Formal differences

The crucial difference between the definition of $\models_r$ and Poole's $\models_d$ is that Poole specifies that D' is a subset of all possible **ground instances** of *wff* in D, whereas we (if we equate A with F and H with D) specify H' (equated with D') as merely a subset of H.

Consequently, D' does not contain the default rules but only a subset of ground instances, whereas H' does contain the rules themselves. This reflects the formal difference between default rules and the formal representation of rules of law. Default rules represent general statements about reality which can be overridden by facts. Rules of law represent, possibly co-existing, opinions about the normative properties of reality, which only can be overruled by applying meta-rules. At a more concrete level this implies that the LRI insists that *all* consequences of a rule (representing an opinion) applied once within some context should hold within that context, that is to say no opposing opinions are allowed to co-exist within one context. We can clarify this by means of the example from Dutch environmental law introduced above.

Assume that we have the following set of facts, representing one case:

$$F=A=\{WCP(rubble),\ WCP(wreckage),\ \text{USE}(rubble),\ \text{USE}(wreckage)\}$$

in both systems, and the following set of rules

$$D=\left\{\frac{USE(x):\text{M}\neg WAS(x)}{\neg WAS(x)},\frac{WCP(x):\text{M}WAS(x)}{WAS(x)}\right\}$$

in default reasoning and

$$H=\{\forall x(USE(x)\rightarrow\neg WAS(x)),\ \forall x(WCP(x)\rightarrow WAS(x))\}$$

in the LRI, modelling the same rules.

Then in default reasoning the following ground instances are produced:

1. $USE(rubble)\rightarrow\neg WAS(rubble)$
2. $USE(wreckage)\rightarrow\neg WAS(wreckage)$
3. $WCP(rubble)\rightarrow WAS(rubble)$
4. $WCP(wreckage)\rightarrow WAS(wreckage)$

Combined with the facts, default logic produces four extensions:

1. $Th($ $WCP(rubble)$, $WCP(wreckage)$, $USE(rubble)$, $USE(wreckage)$, $USE(rubble)\rightarrow\neg WAS(rubble)$, $USE(wreckage)\rightarrow\neg WAS(wreckage)$, **¬WAS(rubble), ¬WAS(wreckage)** $)$

2. $Th($ $WCP(rubble)$, $WCP(wreckage)$, $USE(rubble)$, $USE(wreckage)$, $USE(rubble)\rightarrow\neg WAS(rubble)$, $WCP(wreckage)\rightarrow WAS(wreckage)$, **¬WAS(rubble), WAS(wreckage)** $)$

3. $Th($ $WCP(rubble)$, $WCP(wreckage)$, $USE(rubble)$, $USE(wreckage)$, $USE(wreckage)\rightarrow\neg WAS(wreckage)$, $WCP(rubble)\rightarrow WAS(rubble)$, **¬WAS(wreckage), WAS(rubble)** $)$

4. *Th(WCP(rubble), WCP(wreckage), USE(rubble), USE(wreckage),*
   WCP(rubble) → *WAS(rubble), WCP(wreckage)* → *WAS(wreckage),*
   WAS(wreckage), WAS(rubble))

whereas, the LRI will only produce two contexts.

The LRI defines the following positions:

Φ_1 = { *WCP(rubble), USE(rubble), WCP(wreckage), USE(wreckage),*
   $\forall x(USE(x) \to \neg WAS(x))$ }
Φ_2 = { *WCP(rubble), USE(rubble), WCP(wreckage), USE(wreckage),*
   $\forall x(WCP(x) \to WAS(x))$ }

From these positions, the following contexts will be produced:

(1) $\Phi_1 \vDash$ { $\neg WAS(rubble) \land \neg WAS(wreckage)$ }

with justification

{ *WCP(rubble), WCP(wreckage), USE(rubble), USE(wreckage),*
$\forall x(USE(x) \to \neg WAS(x))$}

(2) $\Phi 2 \vDash$ { $WAS(rubble) \land WAS(wreckage)$ }

with justification

{ *WCP(rubble), WCP(wreckage), USE(rubble), USE(wreckage),*
$\forall x(WCP(x) \to WAS(x))$}

These contexts are produced following the constraint that a rule, (representing an opinion) once used within a context, should hold within that context, thus discarding the contextual translations of extensions 2 and 3.

3.2. *Extending the Logic of Reasonable Inferences: meta-predicates as ranking arguments*

The Logic of Reasonable Inferences (LRI) reduces the set of all *a priori* known and deducible normative opinions to the set of all formally valid normative opinions. Formally, valid normative opinions (reasonable inferences) are internally consistent but can be mutually (meaningfully) inconsistent. As we have shown in the previous sections, there are no absolute criteria to retract (any but one of) these meaningful inconsistent opinions in order to reach a common opinion. In legal practice, three classes of tentative principles are used to rank these opinions. The meta-predicates **Valid**, **Exclude** and **Prefer** can be used in meta-rules from these three classes of tentative ranking principles.[4]

Formally, within the context of the LRI, a meta-predicate can be defined as a normal predicate calculus predicate with individual constants of object type 'rule' or variables of entity-type 'rule'. Variables can be informally typed by predication or they can be formally typed by means of the introduction of sorted predicate logic, which allows for the typing of variables [Gamut, 1991].

E.g.

$$\forall x \, [Rule(x) \land P(x) \rightarrow Q(x)]$$

or

$$\forall x/rule \, [P(x) \rightarrow Q(x)]$$

which can be denoted as the meta-rule

$$P(rx) \rightarrow Q(rx)$$

The meta-rules introduced in the example from Dutch environmental law above can be formally represented as follows:

$$Precedent(rx) \rightarrow Valid(rx)$$
$$Legislation(rx) \land Jurisdiction(ry) \rightarrow Prefer(rx,ry)$$

In section 2.2, three classes of legal decision principles were identified, which can be denoted by the unary meta-predicate Valid and the binary

---

[4] The LRI does not distinguish the formally valid inferences (opinions) at the object level from formally valid inferences at the meta level. Both are treated the same. As a consequence meta-predicates can be used to rank both the formally valid object level opinions and the formally valid meta level opinions. This recursive character of the extended LRI opens interesting and realistic possibilities that will be explored in further research. In this chapter we will restrict ourselves to the ranking of object level opinions by meta-predicates.

meta-predicates Exclude and Prefer. These classes of meta-predicates each play a distinctive role in legal decision-making by providing a class-specific type of rule-ranking arguments. These rule-ranking arguments can be defined by their semantic properties, which are based on the way they are actually applied in legal practice.

The following table contains the semantic properties of the three classes of ranking arguments. r1 and r2, represent two different rules at the object level. R12 means an opinion containing both r1 and r2. R1 means an opinion containing r1 but not r2. R2 means an opinion containing r2 but not r1. r1 and r2 do contradict if their consequents formally oppose. Rx>Ry and Rx>>Ry mean that Rx ranks higher than Ry, where >> is stronger than > (no quantification). Rx=Ry means that Rx ranks equally to Ry.

Valuation		*Ranking*	
		If r1 and r2 do not contradict	If r1 and r2 do contradict
Valid(r1)	**Valid(r2)**		
T	T	R12>R1 and R1=R2	R1=R2
T	Contingent	R12>R1 and R12>R2 and R1>R2	R1>R2
T	F	R1>>R12 and R12>R2	R1>>R2
Contingent	F	R1>R12 and R12 >R2	R1>R2
Contingent	Contingent	R12>R1 and R1=R2	R1=R2
F	F	R1=R2 and R2 >R12	R1=R2
Exclude(r1,r2)			
T		R1>R2 and R2>R12	R1>R2
Contingent		R12>R1 and R1=R2	R1=R2
F		R12>R1 and R1=R2	R1=R2
Prefer(r1,r2)			
T		R12>R1 and R1>R2	R1>R2
Contingent		R12>R1 and R1=R2	R1=R2
F		R12>R1 and R1=R2	R1=R2

To paraphrase the main properties: ˙

- *A fortiori* argument: combined, not invalid arguments (R12) rank highest;
- *Legal validity*: a legally valid argument outranks a non-valid or not valid argument;
- *Legal exclusion*: an exclusive argument takes priority, also over the combined arguments;
- *Legal preference*: a preferred argument takes priority, but not over the combined arguments.

The above semantic properties can be used by an external human or computer agent to compute a ranking as will be illustrated by example in the next section.

4. Application of the Extended Logic of Reasonable Inferences

To illustrate the discussed properties of normative reasoning and decision-making and to clarify the behavior of the proposed logic, we will now present a complex legal case that we will refer to as the *top-down* case. The facts of this case are hypothetical, but all the legal considerations are taken from real cases. An *attempt* is commonly defined as an uncompleted act in which circumstances independent of the will of the performer prevented the act from being completed. Section 45 of the Dutch penal code defines the concept of *criminal attempt* as follows: criminal *intent* should be revealed by a first act of execution (element) of a criminal offence. Suppose that during a conference visit to Pisa (Italy) we become involved in some heavy drinking one night. Furthermore, suppose that we wander over to the Tower of Pisa (*top*). To get rid of the strain of logical thinking, we decide to topple the *top* and we start shouting "we are going to get you *down*" and start pushing. Fortunately, what Shakespeare said in Macbeth was perfectly right. Drinking provokes the desire, but it takes away the performance. So our attempt is not very successful. Now, did we commit a criminal attempt under Dutch penal law? Of course not, you may respond. Literally there is a criminal attempt because there is intent (supposing that we drank enough to believe that we could succeed) and the intent is revealed by a first act of execution (pushing) of a criminal offence (section 141 of the

Dutch penal code: the public use of violence against persons or goods in conjunction with others), but the attempt is clearly unsound as it cannot result in the intended consequence, and nobody will think otherwise. Apart from that, Dutch penal jurisdiction is restricted by the principle of territoriality, so let us adapt the case slightly by bringing the Tower of Pisa into our own jurisdiction. As this is a formal discourse, we will gratefully leave the technical details of the transposition to the engineers. Furthermore, let us suppose that the poor condition of the Tower of Pisa has recently once again been brought to the attention of the public and that a (deviant) scientist has suggested publicly (in a scientific publication) that combined manpower is enough to topple the Tower of Pisa (but fortunately has not proven this experimentally). Things are becoming more complex now.

In this case there are more fish in the lake of jurisprudence and legal practice than you probably can imagine. Jurisprudence offers us at least three alternative ways of solving this legal problem. All of these have been applied (acted as concurring or dissenting opinions) in legal practice, but only the first two of them have been decisive in one or more cases. In the Dutch legal system thoughts are never punishable, so you can have as many mischievous thoughts as you like. The expression of thoughts as criminal intent, however, is punishable under certain circumstances. These circumstances are defined in different ways by three dominant opinions about the meaning of the concept of criminal attempt. These are the so-called subjectivist, objectivist and impressionist (eindrucks-) doctrines.

The *subjectivist view* states that the criminal intent of the suspect renders as a first act of execution (element) of a criminal offence any act he thinks fit to fulfil his criminal aims. Therefore, the mere wish of the suspect to destroy the tower, the fact that this would be a criminal offence and his belief that he can destroy the tower are sufficient to conclude that this is a criminal attempt. This subjectivist view has been repeatedly applied by Dutch courts in cases of unsound attempts. However, a distinction has been made between absolutely and relatively unsound attempts (by means and object). For example, murdering or raping a dead body or trying to poison someone with a substance that is commonly known to be non-poisonous are qualified as absolutely unsound, whereas robbing an empty bank or being caught approaching the border with goods that only turn into contraband when you cross the border are qualified as relatively unsound. The distinction is, of course, blurred and misguiding because both shooting a body and robbing a bank will generally have the intended consequences, while approaching a border is not the first element of the criminal act of smuggling. Sticking pins into Voodoo dolls is another example of the inadequacy of this distinction, since this act can have a physical effect on a true believer[5]. For the sake of the above example, however, we will presume that the subjective impression of the suspect and the chance of succeeding in general suffice. It is not absolutely (as 'in any case') impossible to topple a tower with human power and, moreover, in this case a scientific publication has proposed that such an event might be possible.

The *objectivist view* states that the first act really must be fit to cause the following elements in order for a criminal offence to take place. In this view, the unsoundness of an attempt prohibits it from being classified as a criminal attempt. Trying to topple the Tower of Pisa would not be a criminal attempt according to the objectivists if the (deviant) scientist proves to be wrong in his opinion. The objectivists will argue that the unsound attempt to destroy the tower of Pisa cannot possibly be an element of the criminal offence of public violence. However, in many cases the objectivist view would lead to bizarre results. This would be the case, for example, when the suspect intends to drown his victim by throwing him from a bridge only for the victim to die in the course of the action by bumping his head on the balustrade before hitting the water. Another example of a suspect who does not commit a criminal attempt according to the objectivists would be somebody who tries to poison his victim by mistakenly giving him sugar instead of the intended arsenic dose. However gruesome the intent may be, the attempt to kill or poison is not qualified as a criminal attempt in these cases. So in such cases the subjectivist view would make more sense.

Finally, the *impressionist view* states that the public alarm (the impact or *eindruck* on the public sense of justice) caused by an attempt can

---

[5] Emotional states and physical health. Salovey, Peter; Rothman, Alexander J.; Detweiler, Jerusha B.; Steward, Wayne T. American Psychologist. Vol 55(1), Jan 2000, 110–121.
Belief as Pathogen, Belief as Medicine: "Voodoo Death" and the "Placebo Phenomenon" in Anthropological Perspective. Robert A. Hahn and Arthur Kleinman. Medical Anthropology Quarterly, Vol. 14, No. 4 (Aug., 1983), pp. 3–19.

make it a criminal attempt. In the case of a robust tower, most people would laugh and maybe even try to 'help' you. In the case of the tower of Pisa, however, there is a possibility that your attempt would arouse so much public unrest that it would qualify as criminal (cf. someone shouting "I'll bomb this site" and waving an indistinct parcel at Ground Zero). If we had left the Tower of Pisa in Pisa, and thus under Italian jurisdiction, the local impressionist opinion would probably be absolutely positive about the criminality of the attempt. The impressionist view has not been decisive in criminal attempt cases. However, in other criminal cases, where the penal code could not keep pace with reality, it has been decisive, for example in extending the reach of the larceny section of the penal code to electricity and even to data. Finally, the Voodoo doll attempt case would probably not be a criminal attempt in Holland, but it possibly would be in Jamaica.

How may a case like this be decided? In this case there are many legal principles that can help. We will present four of them in order to illustrate the characteristics, specifically the tentative character, of the decision making process.

From case law we can conclude that the subjectivist and objectivist views are positively valid in the sense that they have been applied and have been decisive in a number of precedents[6], whereas the impressionist view has been applied as an alternative opinion (in most cases in support of the subjectivist view) more than once, indicating that its validity is contingent. Therefore, all three views can be used at will again in cases coming up in any court of law, but the first two views take precedence over the third (without excluding it).

The statutory principle of legality (section 1 of the Dutch Penal Code) demands that an explicit description of a criminal offence from a statutory law must be fulfilled for an act to be punishable. In cases of attempt, this principle is interpreted to mean that an explicit description of a criminal offence is fulfilled by the act of intent and its probable consequences.

---

[6] The prevalence of statutory law as the main source of legal decision-making in the continental system of justice as opposed to the prevalence of precedents in the common law system of justice is a coarse generalization. The formal principle of equality, amongst other things, introduces precedents in the continental system. For a more complete discussion see: Internet en de toegankelijkheid van het recht: van informatievoorziening naar kennisoverdracht. C.N.J. de Vey Mestdagh. Response, Jaargang 4, nr. 1, 1996.

This seems to favor the objectivist opinion, as it demands that at least the first element of a criminal offence has actually been performed. However, as we have seen, there are examples of the application of the other views in case law. Therefore, we must conclude that this interpretation of the legal principle of legality is tentative and not coercive by nature. In cases concerning criminal attempt, the principle only adds validity to the objectivist view, but does not decide the case.

The *lex specialis*-principle (*lex specialis derogat legi generali*) entails that specialized laws prevail over general laws (where *law* should be interpreted to mean *categorical normative statement*). The principle is not absolute in the sense that it should lead to retraction of the general law, but it strongly advocates the separate application of the specialized normative statement over the separate application of the general normative statement and the separate application of either statement over their combined application.

Finally, since the beginning of this century, the growing influence of terrorism-induced public policy means that legislators, governments and judges prefer opinions that soothe public alarm. Laws have been changed or reinterpreted, government policies have been adjusted and judicial decisions have been biased in order to allow the authorities to take action even in the phase of 'possible preparation of acts that possibly will disturb the public order'. The effectiveness of this policy unfortunately cannot be the subject of scientific research for lack of reliable data. However, the aforementioned effect on the legal system is certain. The fact that opinions that soothe public alarm take preference does not have the excluding effect as in the case of the *lex specialis*-principle described above. 'Taking preference' means that an opinion containing the preferred rule is preferred above an opinion that separately applies the non-preferred rule, whereas an opinion containing both rules is preferred above an opinion that separately applies the preferred rule. The non-preferred rule is not excluded by the preferred rule. It will even reinforce the application of the preferred rule if it is part of the same opinion.

The *top-down* case described above can be formalized as follows using the extended formalization of the Logic of Reasonable Inferences (LRI) from the previous section:

From the case description we have the following axiom set:

A(XIOMS)

A.1 Reveals_intent(One_of_us, Toppling_Top)
A.2 Aimed_at_offence(Toppling_Top)
A.3 ¬ First_element_offence(Toppling_Top)
A.4 Perceived_as_offence(Toppling_Top)
A.5 Recent_public_alarm(Toppling_Top)
A.6 Precedent(R1), Precedent(R2)
A.7 Complies_with_section_1_Penal_Code(R2)
A.8 Specialis(R2,R1)
A.9 Soothes_public_alarm(R1,Toppling_Top)
A.10 ¬ Soothes_public_alarm(R2,Toppling_Top)
A.11 Soothes_public_alarm(R3,Toppling_Top)

By shouting "We are going to get you down", and by actually pushing the *top*, we reveal intent to topple the *top* and that the intent is aimed at publicly using violence against a good, which is a criminal offence. As the attempt is clearly unsound, there is no first element of the offence of public violence, supposing the deviant scientist was not right after all. In this case, we assume that the nearby public perceived our action as an offence, and we assume that the opinion of our deviant scientist recently caused public alarm. Furthermore, we add the precedent status of the subjectivist and objectivist views (tagged as R1 and R2), the compliance of the objectivist view with the principle of legality and the specialis relation between the objectivist and subjectivist view, the objectivist view being the specialis because it shares all subjectivist clauses and has an extra clause. Finally, we express the fact that the subjectivist and impressionist (tagged as R3) views soothe public alarm whereas the objectivist view does not.

Furthermore, the case description provides us with the following (selection[7] of) hypotheses (i.e. opinions/(meta-)rules):

---

[7] A selection of hypotheses is presented to be able to keep track of the main argument. For instance, each doctrine consists of two complementary rules of which just one per doctrine is presented.

H(YPOTHESIS)

H.1   Reveals_intent(x,y) ∧ Aimed_at_offence(y) →
      Criminal_attempt(x,y)
      [*subjectivist view, tagged R1*]

H.2   ¬ (Reveals_intent(x,y) ∧ Aimed_at_offence(y) ∧
      First_element_offence(y)) → ¬ Criminal_attempt(x,y)
      [*complementary rule of the objectivist view, tagged R2*]

H.3   Reveals_intent(x,y) ∧ Perceived_as_offence(y) →
      Criminal_attempt (x,y)
      [*impressionist view, tagged R3*]

H.4   Precedent(rx) → Valid(rx)
      [*meta-rule precedent validity*]

H.5   Complies_with_section_1_Penal_Code(rx) → Valid(rx)
      [*meta-rule principle of legality*]

H.6   Specialis(rx, ry) → Excludes(rx,ry)
      [*meta-rule lex specialis*]

H.7   Recent_public_alarm(y) ∧ Soothes_public_alarm(rx,y) ∧
      ¬ Soothes_public_alarm(ry,y) → Prefer(rx, ry)
      [meta-rule terrorism induced policies]

The first hypothesis describes the subjectivist view. If the act reveals intent aimed at a criminal offence, then there is criminal attempt. The second hypothesis represents the complementary rule of the objectivist view. If the act does not constitute the first element of a criminal offence, then there is no criminal attempt. The third hypothesis expresses the impressionist view. If the act is publicly perceived as a criminal offence, then there is criminal intent. The fourth through seventh hypotheses denote the meta-rules of *precedent validity*, of *legality*, of *lex specialis* and of *terrorism induced policies*.

In this domain of axioms and hypotheses, a number of consistent positions can be distinguished. A selection of four of these[8] follows:

---

[8] The selection of certain positions by an external agent can also be based on the application of meta-rules (e.g. meta-rules preferring pure positions like the subjectivists, objectivists and impressionists positions).

P(OSITIONS)

P.1	Subjectivist	: A.1..A.11; H.1, H.4(R1), H.7(R1,R2)
P.2	Objectivist	: A.1..A.11; H.2, H.4(R2), H.5(R2), H.6(R2,R1)
P.3	Impressionist	: A.1..A.11; H.3, H.7(R3,R2)
P.4	Subjectivist+Impressionist	: A.1..A.11; H.1, H.3, H.4(R1), H.7(R1, R2), H.7(R3, R2)

The meta-rules comprised in these four positions (H.4-H.7) provide ranking arguments that allow for a variety of actual rankings depending on the actual local policies of (human- or computer-) decision-making-agents or agents involved in a dialogue. Meta-rule H.4 (*validity based on precedent*) can be used to rank the positions P.1, P.2 and P.4 above position P.3 if a local policy decides for positions containing inferences based on valid rules. Meta-rule H.5 (*validity based on legality*) can be used to rank position P.2 above the other three positions based on the same local policy. Meta-rule H.6 (*exclusion based on specificity*) can be used to rank position P.2 above position P.1 if a local policy decides for specialis positions[9]. Meta-rule H.7 (*preference based on the soothing of public alarm*) can be used to rank position P.4 above positions P.1 and P.3 and positions P.1 and P.3 above position P.2 if a local policy makes decisions on the basis of (the reduction of) public alarm (for example shortly after 9/11 or in a case that took place in the vicinity of Ground Zero, or by an agent that was hurt by the same peril or that has an audience of agents hurt in that way, etc.). Since there is no single/absolute ranking model (on the contrary, there are many competing local ranking models in most cases), the ranking process cannot be a part of the extended LRI[10]. A specific local policy could decide for position P.2 because it is up in three of the four rankings. This has actually been the dominant opinion of a majority of Dutch courts.

---

[9] The relativity or non-absoluteness of such a local policy can be easily understood. If a generalis is provable and a specialis is not, a specific type of local policies (e.g that applied by the DA) will decide for the generalis. The problem is that we cannot describe all the types of local policies and even less all the actual local policies of a type.

[10] Actually it could be part of the extended LRI if all the local ranking policies were known. However, in that case the number of positions would explode in another sense than in the case of inconsistency in classical logic.

From these positions, two contexts can be derived.

C(ONTEXTS) (showing only the dissimilar inferences)

C.1
Reasonable inference   : Criminal_attempt(One_of_us,Toppling_Top)
Justification   : P.1, P.3, P.4
C.2
Reasonable inference   : ¬Criminal_attempt(One_of_us,Toppling_Top)
                           Valid(R1), Valid(R2), Excludes(R2, R1)
Justification   : P.2

These contexts justify two (by definition) inconsistent reasonable inferences based on (by definition) mutually inconsistent positions and show the difference in behavior between the extended LRI and classical explosive logics. We can ask ourselves what an explosive logic, such as predicate logic, would do to the Tower of Pisa? Literally anything would be possible, such as letting the tower explode, bending it, etc. On the other hand, the extended LRI provides all reasonable inferences about the Tower of Pisa It presents these reasonable inferences in combination with their justifications as contexts. Furthermore, it provides the *ranking arguments* resulting in the four rankings as presented above. Since three of the four rankings prefer P.2, a human or computer agent using these ranking arguments will probably decide to C.2 (which is justified by P.2) as the common opinion. This means that a confusing multitude of positions is reduced to the minimum of consistent contexts and that each context provides the ranking arguments that can be weighed by a subsequent choice of local ranking policies.

The example shows that rather complex decision processes can be supported by the extended LRI. The extended LRI provides the global arguments (the coloration) for choosing a certain position but it does not cause retraction of positions, in perfect agreement with the theoretical demands for normative decision-making discussed in the first two sections.

5. Conclusions and Further Research

Information processing and information are naturally perspective-bound. This often results in naturally inconsistent opinions. Effective communication can demand the local and temporal acceptance of a common opinion by the parties concerned. Legal reasoning and legal decision-making are respectively aimed at deriving all alternative legally-valid opinions and deciding on a common opinion. Legal reasoning can be modeled by the *Logic of Reasonable Inferences* (LRI), which allows for internally consistent opinions, thus abiding by the principle of rationality and avoiding triviality without discarding mutually inconsistent opinions. The introduction and semantic definition of three classes of meta-predicates (legal validity, legal exclusion and legal preference) within the, thus *extended*, LRI allows for the derivation of ranking arguments that can subsequently be used computationally to model legal decision-making through the ranking of alternative opinions. Past research has confirmed that the extended LRI is a tenable model of legal reasoning and legal decision-making. Further research should elaborate on the formal properties of the three classes of meta-predicates (e.g. their applicability to positions and contexts as a whole instead of just to the rules that are part of the positions) and their applicability in other knowledge domains and in ranking algorithms.

References

Dijkstra, P., F.J. Bex, H. Prakken & C.N.J. de Vey Mestdagh (2005, a). Towards a multi-agent system for regulated information exchange in crime investigations. *Artificial Intelligence and Law* 13, 2005, pp. 133–151.

Dijkstra, P., F.Bex, H. Prakken & C.N.J. de Vey Mestdagh (2005, b). Outline of a Multi-agent System for Regulated Information Exchange in Crime Investigations. In Paul E. Dunne & Trevor Bench-Capon (red.), *IAAIL Workshop Series, Argumentation in Artificial Intelligence and Law.* Wolf Legal Publishers, 2005, pp 27–38. ISBN 90-5850-502-2.

Dijkstra, P., H. Prakken & C.N.J. de Vey Mestdagh (2007). An implementation of norm-based agent negotiation. *Proc. 11th International Conference on Artificial Intelligence and Law*, Stanford, 2007. New York: ACM Press 2007, 167–175.

Gordon, T.F. (1989). A Theory Construction Approach To Legal Document Assembly. *Pre-proc. Of The 3rd International Congress On Logica Informatica Diritto* (2 vols.),

Martino, A.A.(ed), Consiglio Nazionale Delle Richerge, Instituto Per La Documentazione, Giuridica, Florence, 1989, pp.:0485-0498.

Gamut, L.T.F. (1991). *Logic, Language, and Meaning: Introduction to logic.* University of Chicago Press, 1991. p166. ISBN 0226280853, 9780226280851

Poole, D. (1988). A Logical Framework For Default Reasoning. *Artificial Intelligence* 36, North Holland, Amsterdam, 1988, pp.:0027-0047.

Priest, G. (2002). Paraconsistent Logic. *Handbook of Philosophical Logic* (Second Edition), Vol. 6, D. Gabbay and F. Guenthner (eds.), Dordrecht: Kluwer Academic Publishers, pp. 287–393.

Reiter, R. (1980). A Logic For Default Reasoning. *Artificial Intelligence* 13, North-Holland, Amsterdam, 1980, pp. 0081-0132.

Rescher, N. & Manor, R. (1970). On inference from inconsistent premisses. *Theory and Decision*, vol. 1, nr 2. December, 1970, pp. 179–217.

Vey Mestdagh, C.N.J. de & G. Bos (1989). Conflicting legal opinions, a model for legal knowledge systems. *Martino, A.A.* (ed.). *Pre-proc. 3rd International Congress on Logica Informatica Diritto* (2 vols.), p. 217–241. Florence: Consiglio Nazionale delle Recerche, Instituto per la documentazione guiridica, 1989.

Vey Mestdagh, C.N.J. de, W. Verwaard & J.H. Hoepman (1991). The Logic of Reasonable Inferences. In Breuker, J.A., R.V. de Mulder & J.C. Hage (eds), Legal Knowledge Based Systems, Model-based legal reasoning, *Proc. 4th annual JURIX conference on Legal Knowledge Based Systems*, p. 60–76. Vermande, Lelystad, 1991. ISBN 90 6040 989 2/CIP.

Vey Mestdagh, C.N.J. de (1997). *Extended summary of Legal Expert Systems. Experts or Expedients?* PhD Thesis, 400 pp., Kluwer, Deventer, 1997, ISBN 90 268 3146 3.

Vey Mestdagh, C.N.J. de (1997). *Juridische Kennissystemen, Rekentuig of Rekenmeester?, Het onderbrengen van juridische kennis in een expertsysteem voor het milieuvergunningenrecht* (PhD Thesis), 400 pp., Kluwer, Deventer, 1997, ISBN 90 268 3146 3.

Vey Mestdagh, C.N.J. de (1998). Legal Expert Systems. Experts or Expedients? The Representation of Legal Knowledge in an Expert System for Environmental Permit Law. In Ciampi, C., E. Marinai (eds.), *The Law in the Information Society*, Conference Proceedings on CD-Rom, Firenze, 2–5 December 1998, 8pp.

Vey Mestdagh. C.N.J. de (2003). Administrative Normative Information Transaction Agents (ANITA): Legitimacy and Information Technology, the best of two worlds (abstract). *Access to knowledge and its enhancements*, Symposium bundle ToKeN2000 symposium, Delft University of Technology, February 21, 2003.

CHAPTER 17

ON THE ALGORITHMIC NATURE
OF THE WORLD

Hector Zenil[*,†,1] and Jean-Paul Delahaye[*,2]

*Laboratoire d'Informatique Fondamentale de Lille (USTL/CNRS)
†Institut d'Histoire et de Philosophie des Sciences et des Techniques
(CNRS/Paris I/ENS)

We propose a test based on the theory of algorithmic complexity and an experimental evaluation of Levin's universal distribution to identify evidence in
support of or in contravention of the claim that the world is algorithmic in nature. To this end we have undertaken a statistical comparison of the frequency
distributions of data from physical sources on the one hand–repositories of information such as images, data stored in a hard drive, computer programs and
DNA sequences–and the frequency distributions generated by purely algorithmic means on the other–by running abstract computing devices such as Turing
machines, cellular automata and Post Tag systems. Statistical correlations
were found and their significance measured.

1. Introduction

A statistical comparison has been undertaken of the frequency distributions
of data stored in physical repositories on the one hand–DNA sequences,
images, files in a hard drive–and of frequency distributions produced by
purely algorithmic means on the other–by running abstract computational
devices like Turing machines, cellular automata and Post Tag systems.

A standard statistical measure is adopted for this purpose. The Spearman rank correlation coefficient quantifies the strength of the relationship

---

[1]hector.zenil@lifl.fr
[2]delahaye@lifl.fr

between two variables, without making any prior assumption as to the particular nature of the relationship between them.

1.1. *Levin's Universal Distribution*

Consider an unknown operation generating a binary string of length k bits. If the method is uniformly random, the probability of finding a particular string s is exactly 2^{-k}, the same as for any other string of length k. However, data is usually produced not at random but by a process. There is a measure which describes the expected output frequency distribution of an abstract machine running a program. A process that produces a string s with a program p when executed on a universal Turing machine T has probability $m(s)$. As p is itself a binary string, $m(s)$ can be defined as being the probability that the output of a universal prefix Turing machine T is s when provided with a sequence of fair coin flip inputs interpreted as a program. Formally,

$$m(s) = \Sigma_{T(p)=s} 2^{-|p|}$$

where the sum is over all halting programs p for which T outputs the string s, with $|p|$ the length of the program p. As T is a prefix universal Turing machine, the set of valid programs forms a prefix-free set[3] and thus the sum is bounded due to Kraft's inequality. For technical details see [Calude (2002); Li and Vitányi (2008); Downey (2010)].

Formulated by Leonid Levin [Levin (1984)], m has many remarkable properties [Kirchherr and Li (1997)]. It is closely related to the concept of algorithmic complexity [Chaitin (2001)] in that the largest value of the sum of programs is dominated by the shortest one, so one can actually write $m(s)$ as follows:

$$m(s) = 2^{-K(s)+O(1)}$$

In a world of computable processes, $m(s)$ establishes that simple patterns which result from simple processes are likely, while complicated patterns produced by complicated processes (long programs) are relatively unlikely.

---

[3]No element is a prefix of any other, a property necessary to keep $0 < m(s) < 1$ for all s and therefore a valid probability measure

It is worth noting that, unlike other probability measures, m is not only a probability distribution establishing that there are some objects that have a certain probability of occurring according to said distribution, it is also a distribution specifying the order of the particular elements in terms of their individual algorithmic complexity.

2. The Null Hypothesis

When looking at a large-enough set of data following a distribution, one can in statistical terms safely assume that the source generating the data is of the nature that the distribution suggests. Such is the case when a set of data follows, for example, a Gaussian distribution, where depending on certain statistical variables, one can say with a high degree of certitude that the process generating the data is of a random nature.

When observing the world, the outcome of a physical phenomenon f can be seen as the result of a natural process P. One may ask how the probability distribution of a set of process of the type of P looks like.

If one would like to know whether the world is algorithmic in nature one would need first to tell how an algorithmic world would look like. To accomplish this, we've conceived and performed a series of experiments to produce data by purely algorithmic means in order to compare sets of data produced by several physical sources. At the right level a simplification of the data sets into binary language seems always possible. Each observation can measure one or more parameters (weight, location, etc.) of an enumeration of independent distinguishable values, a discrete sequence of values[4].

If there is no bias in the sampling method or the generating process itself and no information about the process is known, the principle of indifference [Thompson (2003)][5] states that if there are $n > 1$ possibilities mutually exclusive, collectively exhaustive and only distinguishable for their names then each possibility should be assigned a probability equal to $1/n$ as the simplest non-informative prior. The null hypothesis to test is that

---

[4]This might be seen as an oversimplification of the concept of a natural process and of its outcome when seen as a binary sequence, but the performance of a physical experiment always yields data written as a sequence of individual observations as a valid sample of certain phenomena.

[5]also known as principle of insufficient reason.

the frequency distributions studied herein from several different independent sources are closer to the experimental calculation of Levin's universal distribution than to the uniform (simplest non-informative prior) distribution. To this end average output frequency distributions by running abstract computing devices such as cellular automata, Post tag systems and Turing machines were produced on the one hand, and by collecting data to build distributions of the same type from the physical world on the other.

2.1. *Frequency distributions*

The distribution of a variable is a description of the relative number of times each possible outcome occurs in a number of trials. One of the most common probability distributions describing physical events is the normal distribution, also known as the Gaussian or Bell curve distribution, with values more likely to occur due to small random variations around a mean.

There is also a particular scientific interest in power-law distributions, partly from the ease with which certain general classes of mechanisms generate them. The demonstration of a power-law relation in some data can point to specific kinds of mechanisms that might underlie the natural phenomenon in question, and can indicate a connection with other, seemingly unrelated systems.

As explained however, when no information is available, the simplest distribution one can assume is the uniform distribution, in which values are equally likely to occur. In a macroscopic system at least, it must be assumed that the physical laws which govern the system are not known well enough to predict the outcome. If one does not have any reason to choose a specific distribution and no prior information is available, the uniform distribution is the one making no assumptions according to the principle of indifference. This is supposed to be the distribution of a balanced coin, an unbiased die or a casino roulette where the probability of an outcome k_i is $1/n$ if k_i can take one of n possible different outcomes.

2.2. *Computing abstract machines*

An abstract machine consists of a definition in terms of input, output, and the set of allowable operations used to turn the input into the output. They are of course algorithmic by nature (or by definition). Three of the most popular models of computation in the field of theoretical computer science were resorted to produce data of a purely algorithmic nature: these were deterministic Turing machines (denoted by TM), one-dimensional cellular automata (denoted by CA) and Post Tag systems (TS).

The Turing machine model represents the basic framework underlying many concepts in computer science, including the definition of algorithmic complexity cited above. The cellular automaton is a well-known model which, together with the Post Tag system model, has been studied since the foundation of the field of abstract computation by some of its first pioneers. All three models are Turing-complete. The descriptions of the models follow formalisms used in [Wolfram (2002)].

2.2.1. *Deterministic Turing machines*

The Turing machine description consists of a list of rules (a finite program) capable of manipulating a linear list of cells, called the *tape*, using an access pointer called the *head*. The finite program can be in any one of a finite set of states Q numbered from 1 to n, with 1 the state at which the machine starts its computation. Each tape cell can contain 0 or 1 (there is no special blank symbol). Time is discrete and the steps are ordered from 0 to t with 0 the time at which the machine starts its computation. At any given time, the head is positioned over a particular cell and the finite program starts in the state 1. At time 0 all cells contain the same symbol, either 0 or 1. A rule i can be written in a 5-tuple notation as follows $\{s_i, k_i, s'_i, k'_i, d_i\}$, where s_i is the tape symbol the machine's head is scanning at time t, k_i the machine's current 'state' (instruction) at time t, s'_i a unique symbol to write (the machine can overwrite a 1 on a 0, a 0 on a 1, a 1 on a 1, or a 0 on a 0) at time $t + 1$, k'_i a state to transition into (which may be the same as the one it was already in) at time $t + 1$, and d_i a direction to move in time $t + 1$, either to the right (R) cell or to the left (L) cell, after writing. Based on a set of rules of this type, usually called a transition table, a Turing machine can perform the following operations: 1. write an element from $A = \{0, 1\}$, 2. shift the head one cell to the left or right, 3. change the state of the finite program out of Q. When the machine is running it executes the above operations at the rate of one operation per step. At a time t the Turing machine produces an output described by the contiguous cells in the tape visited by the head.

Let $T(0), T(1), \ldots, T(n), \ldots$ be a natural recursive enumeration of all 2-symbol deterministic Turing machines. One can, for instance, begin enumerating by number of states, starting with all 2-state Turing machines, then 3-state, and so on. Let n, t and k be three integers. Let $s(T(n), t)$ be the part of the contiguous tape cells that the head visited after t steps. Let's consider all the k-tuples, i.e. all the substrings of length k from $s(T(n), t) = \{s_1, s_2, \ldots, s_u\}$, i.e. the following $u - k + 1$ k-tuples: $\{(s_1, \ldots, s_k), (s_2, \ldots, s_{k+1}), \ldots, (s_{u-k+1}, \ldots, s_u)\}$.

Now let N be a fixed integer. Let's consider the set of all the k-tuples produced by the first N Turing machines according to a recursive enumeration after running for t steps each. Let's take the count of each k-tuple produced.

From the count of all the k-tuples, listing all distinct strings together with their frequencies of occurrence, one gets a probability distribution over the finite set of strings in $\{0, 1\}^k$.

For the Turing machines the experiments were carried out with 2-symbol 3-state Turing machines. There are $(4n)^{2n}$ possible different n-state 2-symbol Turing machines according to the 5-tuple rule description cited above. Therefore $(4 \times 3)^{(2 \times 3)} = 2985984$ 2-symbol 3-state Turing machines. A sample of 2000 2-symbol 3-state Turing machines was taken. Each Turing machine's runtime was set to $t = 100$ steps starting with a tape filled with 0s and then once again with a tape filled with 1s in order to avoid any undesired asymmetry due to a particular initial set up.

2.2.2. *One-dimensional Cellular Automata*

An analogous standard description of one-dimensional 2-color cellular automata was followed. A one-dimensional cellular automaton is a collection of cells on a row that evolves through discrete time according to a set of rules based on the states of neighboring cells that are applied in parallel to each row over time. When the cellular automaton starts its computation, it applies the rules at a first step $t = 0$. If m is an integer, a neighborhood of m refers to the cells on both sides, together with the central cell, that the rule takes into consideration at row t to determine the value of a cell at the step $t + 1$. If m is a fraction of the form p/q, then $p - 1$ are the cells to the left and $q - 1$ the cells to the right taken into consideration by the rules of the cellular automaton.

For cellular automata, the experiments were carried out with 3/2-range neighbor cellular automata starting from a single 1 on a background of $0s$ and then again starting from a single 0 on a background of $1s$ to avoid any undesired asymmetry from the initial set up. There are 2^{2m+1} possible states for the cells neighboring a given cell (m at each side plus the central cell), and two possible outcomes for the new cell; there are therefore a total of $2^{2^{2m+1}}$ one-dimensional m-neighbor 2-color cellular automata, hence $2^{2^{(2\times3/2)+1}} = 65536$ cellular automata with rules taking two neighbors to the left and one to the right. A sample of 2000 3/2-range neighbor cellular automata was taken.

As for Turing machines, let $A(1), A(2), \ldots, A(n), \ldots$ be a natural recursive enumeration of one dimensional 2-color cellular automata. For example, one can start enumerating them by neighborhood starting from range 1 (nearest-neighbor) to 3/2-neighbor, to 2-neighbor and so on, but this is not mandatory.

Let n, t and k be three integers. For each cellular automaton $A(n)$, let $s(A(n), t)$ denote the output of the cellular automata defined as the contiguous cells of the last row produced after $t = 100$ steps starting from a single black or white cell as described above, up to the length that the scope of the application of the rules starting from the initial configuration may have reached (usually the last row of the characteristic cone produced by a cellular automaton). As was done for Turing machines, tuples of length k were extracted from the output.

2.2.3. *Post Tag Systems*

A Tag system is a triplet (m, A, P), where m is a positive integer, called the deletion number. A is the alphabet of symbols (in this paper a binary alphabet). Finite (possibly empty) strings can be made of the alphabet A. A computation by a Tag system is a finite sequence of strings produced by iterating a transformation, starting with an initially given initial string at time $t = 0$. At each iteration m elements are removed from the beginning of the sequence and a set of elements determined by the production rule P is appended onto the end, based on the elements that were removed from the beginning. Since there is no generalized standard enumeration of Tag systems[6], a random set of rules was generated, each rule having equal probability. Rules are bound by the number of r elements (digits) on the left and right hand blocks of the rule. There are a total of $(k^r + 1 - 1)/(k - 1)^{k^n}$ possible rules if blocks up to length r can be added at each step. For $r = 3$, there are 50625 different 2-symbol Tag systems with deletion number 2. In this experiment, a sample of 2000 2-Tag systems (Tag systems with deletion number 2) were used to generate the frequency distributions of Tag systems to compare with.

An example of a rule is $\{0 \to 10, 1 \to 011, 00 \to \epsilon, 01 \to 10, 10 \to 11\}$, where no term on any side has more than 3 digits and there is no fixed number of elements other than that imposed to avoid multiple assignations of a string to several different, i.e. ambiguous, rules. The empty string ϵ can only occur among the right hand terms of the rules. The random generation of a set of rules yields results equivalent to those obtained by following and exhausting a natural recursive enumeration.

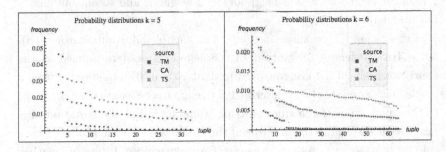

Fig. 1. The output frequency distributions from running abstract computing machines. The x-axis shows all the 2^k tuples of length k sorted from most to least frequent. The y-axis shows the frequency values (probability between 0 and 1) of each tuple on the x-axis.

As an illustration[7], assume that the output of the first 4 Turing machines following an enumeration yields the output strings 01010, 11111, 11111 and 01 after running $t = 100$ steps. If $k = 3$, the tuples of length 3 from the output of these Turing machines are: $((010, 101, 010), (111, 111, 111), (111, 111, 111))$; or grouped and sorted from higher to lower frequency: $(111, 010, 101)$ with frequency values

---

[6]To the authors' knowledge.

[7]For illustration only no actual enumeration was followed.

6, 2, and 1 respectively. The frequency distribution is therefore $((111, 2/3), (010, 2/9), (101, 1/9))$, i.e. the string followed by the count divided by the total. If the strings have the same frequency value they are lexicographically sorted.

The output frequency distributions produced by abstract machines as described above are evidently algorithmic by nature (or by definition), and they will be used both to be compared one to each other, and to the distributions extracted from the physical real world.

2.3. *Physical sources*

Samples from physical sources such as DNA sequences, random images from the web and data stored in a hard drive were taken and transformed into data of the same type (i.e. binary tuples) of the produced by the abstract computing machines. We proceeded as follows: a representative set of random images was taken from the web using the random image function available online at the Wikipedia Creative Commons website at *http://commons.wikimedia.org/wiki/Special:Random/File* (as of May, 2009), none of them larger than 1500 linear pixels[8] to avoid any bias due to very large images. All images were transformed using the *Mathematica* function *Binarize* that converts multichannel and color images into black-and-white images by replacing all values above a globally determined threshold. Then all the k-tuples for each row of the image were taken and counted, just as if they had been produced by the abstract machines from the previous section.

Another source of physical information for comparative purposes was a random selection of human gene sequences of Deoxyribonucleic acid (or simply DNA). The DNA was extracted from a random sample of 100 different genes (the actual selection is posted in the project website cited in section 5).

There are four possible encodings for translating a DNA sequence into a binary string using a single bit for each letter: $\{G \to 1, T \to 1, C \to 0, A \to 0\}$, $\{G \to 0, T \to 1, C \to 0, A \to 1\}$, $\{G \to 1, T \to 0, C \to 1, A \to 0\}$, $\{G \to 0, T \to 0, C \to 1, A \to 1\}$.

---

[8]The sum of the width and height.

To avoid any artificially induced asymmetries due to the choice of a particular encoding, all four encodings were applied to the same sample to build a joint frequency distribution. All the k-tuples were counted and ranked likewise.

There might be still some biases by sampling genes rather than sampling DNA segments because genes might be seen as conceived by researchers to focus on functional segments of the DNA. We've done however the same experiments taking only a sample of a sample of genes, which is not a gene by itself but a legitimate sample of the DNA, producing the same results (i.e. the distributions remain stable). Yet, the finding of a higher *algorithmicity* when taking gene samples as opposed to DNA general sampling might suggest that effectively there is an embedded encoding for genes in the DNA as functional subprograms in it, and not a mere research convenience.

A third source of information from the real world was a sample of data contained in a hard drive. A list of all the files contained in the hard drive was generated using a script, and a sample of 100 files was taken for comparison, with none of the files being greater than 1 Mb in order to avoid any bias due to a very large file. The stream was likewise cut into k-tuples, counted and ranked to produce the frequency distribution, as for DNA. The count of each of the sources yielded a frequency distribution of k-tuples (the binary strings of length k) to compare with.

One may think that data stored in a hard drive already has a strong algorithmic component by the way that it has been produced (or stored in a digital computer) and therefore it makes no or less sense to compare with to any of the algorithmic or empirical distributions. It is true that the data stored in a hard drive is in the middle of what we may consider the abstract and the physical worlds, which makes it however interesting as an experiment by its own from our point of view. But more important, data stored in a hard drive is of very different nature, from text files subject to the rules of language, to executable programs, to music and video, all together in a single repository. Hence, it is not obvious at all why a frequency distribution from such a rich source of different kind of data might end up resembling to other distributions produced by other physical sources or by abstract machines.

2.4. *Hypothesis testing*

The frequency distributions generated by the different sources were statistically compared to look for any possible correlation. A correlation test was carried out and its significance measured to validate either the null hypothesis or the alternative (the latter being that the similarities are due to chance).

Each frequency distribution is the result of the count of the number of occurrences of the k-tuples from which the binary strings of length k were extracted. Comparisons were made with k set from 4 to 7.

2.4.1. *Spearman's rank correlation coefficient*

The Spearman rank correlation coefficient [Snedecor and Cochran (1989)] is a non-parametric measure of correlation that makes no assumptions about the frequency distribution of the variables. Spearman's rank correlation coefficient is equivalent to the Pearson correlation on ranks. Spearman's rank correlation coefficient is usually denoted by the Greek letter ρ.

The Spearman rank correlation coefficient is calculated as follows:

$$\rho = 1 - ((6 \sum d_i^2)/(n(n^2 - 1)))$$

where d_i is the difference between each rank of corresponding values of x and y, and n the number of pairs of values.

Spearman's rank correlation coefficient can take real values from -1 to 1, where -1 is a perfect negative (inverse) correlation, 0 is no correlation and 1 is a perfect positive correlation.

The approach to testing whether an observed ρ value is significantly different from zero, considering the number of elements, is to calculate the probability that it would be greater than or equal to the observed ρ given the null hypothesis using a permutation test [Good (2005)] to ascertain that the obtained value of ρ obtained is unlikely to occur by chance (the alternative hypothesis). The common convention is that if the value of ρ is between 0.01 and 0.001 the correlation is strong enough, indicating that the probability of having found the correlation is very unlikely to be a matter of chance, since it would occur one time out of hundred (if closer to 0.01) or a thousand (if closer to 0.001), while if it is between 0.10 and 0.01 the correlation is said to be weak, although yet quite unlikely to occur by chance, since it would occur one time out of ten (if closer to 0.10) or a hundred (if closer to

$0.01)^9$. The lower the significance level, the stronger the evidence in favor of the null hypothesis. Tables 2, 3, 4 and 5 show the Spearman coefficients between all the distributions for a given tuple length k.

Table 1.   Examples of frequency distributions of tuples of length $k = 4$, one from random files contained in a hard drive and another produced by running cellular automata. There are $2^4 = 16$ tuples each followed by its count (represented as a probability value between 0 and 1).

CELLULAR AUTOMATA DISTRIBUTION			HARD DRIVE DISTRIBUTION		
rank	*string (s)*	*count* $(pr(s))$	*rank*	*string (s)*	*count* $(pr(s))$
1	1111	.35	1	1111	.093
2	0000	.34	2	0000	.093
3	1010	.033	3	1110	.062
4	0101	.032	4	1000	.062
5	0100	.026	5	0111	.062
6	0010	.026	6	0001	.062
7	0110	.025	7	0100	.06
8	1011	.024	8	0010	.06
9	1101	.023	9	1101	.06
10	1001	.023	10	1011	.06
11	0011	.017	11	1100	.056
12	0001	.017	12	0011	.056
13	1000	.017	13	1001	.054
14	1100	.016	14	0110	.054
15	0111	.016	15	1010	.054
16	1110	.017	16	0101	.054

When graphically compared, the actual frequency values of each tuple among the 2^k unveil a correlation in values along different distributions. The x and y axes are in the same configuration as in the graph 1: The x-axis plots the 2^k tuples of length k but unlike the graph 1 they are lexicographically sorted (as the result of converting the binary string into a decimal number). The table 6 shows this lexicographical order as an illustration for $k = 4$. The y-axis plots the frequency value (probability between 0 and 1) for each tuple on the x-axis.

---

[9]Useful tables with the calculation of levels of significance for different numbers of ranked elements are available online (e.g. at *http://www.york.ac.uk/depts/maths/histstat/tables/spearman.ps* as of May 2009).

Table 2. Spearman coefficients for $K = 4$. Coefficients indicating a significant correlation are indicated by † while correlations with higher significance are indicated with ‡.

k = 4	HD	ADN	IMG	TM	CA	TS
HD	1‡	0.67‡	0.4	0.29	0.5	0.27
DNA	0.67‡	1‡	0.026	0.07	0.39†	0.52†
IMG	0.4†	0.026	1‡	0.31	0.044	0.24
TM	0.29	0.07	0.31	1‡	0.37†	0.044
CA	0.5†	0.39†	0.044	0.37	1‡	0.023
TS	0.27	0.52†	0.24	0.044	0.023	1‡

Table 3. Spearman coefficients for $K = 5$.

k = 5	HD	ADN	IMG	TM	CA	TS
HD	1‡	0.62‡	0.09	0.31†	0.4‡	0.25†
ADN	0.62‡	1‡	0.30	0.11	0.39†	0.24†
IMG	0.09	0.30†	1‡	0.32†	0.60‡	0.10
TM	0.31†	0.11	0.32†	1‡	0.24†	0.07
CA	0.4‡	0.39†	0.24†	0.30†	1‡	0.18
TS	0.25†	0.24†	0.10	0.18	0.021	1‡

Table 4. Spearman coefficients for $K = 6$.

k = 6	HD	ADN	IMG	TM	CA	TS
HD	1‡	0.58‡	0	0.27†	0.07	0.033
DNA	0.58‡	1‡	0	0.12	0.14	0
IMG	0	0	1‡	0.041	0.023	0.17†
TM	0.27†	0.12	0.041	1‡	0	0
CA	0.07	0.14	0.023	0	1‡	0.23†
TS	0.033	0	0.17†	0	0.23†	1‡

2.5. *The problem of overfitting*

When looking at a set of data following a distribution, one can safely claim in statistical terms that the source generating the data is of the nature that the distribution suggests. Such is the case when a set of data follows a model, where depending on certain variables, one can say with some degree of certitude that the process generating the data follows the model.

However, a common problem is the problem of overfitting, that is, a false model that may fit perfectly with an observed phenomenon[10]. Levin's

---

[10]For example, Ptolemy's solar system model.

Table 5.   Spearman coefficients for $K = 7$.

k = 7	HD	ADN	IMG	TM	CA	TS
HD	1‡	0	0.091†	0.073	0	0.11†
DNA	0	1‡	0.07	0.028	0.12	0.019
IMG	0.091†	0.07	1‡	0.08†	0.15‡	0
TM	0.073	0.028	0.08†	1‡	0.03	0.039
CA	0	0.12	0.15‡	0.03	1‡	0
TS	0.11†	0.019	0	0.039	0	1‡

Table 6.   Illustration of the simple lexicographical order of the 2^4 tuples of length $k = 4$ as
plotted in the x-axis.

x-axis order	tuple	x-axis order	tuple
0	0000	8	1000
1	0001	9	1001
2	0010	10	1010
3	0011	11	1011
4	0100	12	1100
5	0101	13	1101
6	0110	14	1110
7	0111	15	1111

universal distribution, however, is optimal over all distributions [Kirchherr and Li (1997)], in the sense that the algorithmic model is by itself the simplest possible model fitting the data if produced by some algorithmic process. This is because m is precisely the result of a distribution assuming the most simple model in algorithmic complexity terms, in which the shortest programs produce the elements leading the distribution. That doesn't mean, however, that it must necessarily be the right or the only possible model explaining the nature of the data, but the model itself is ill suited to an excess of parameters argument. A statistical comparison cannot actually be used to categorically prove or disprove a difference or similarity, only to favor one hypothesis over another.

3. Possible Applications

Common data compressors are of the entropy coding type. Two of the most popular entropy coding schemes are the Huffman coding and the arithmetic coding. Entropy coders encode a given set of symbols with the minimum

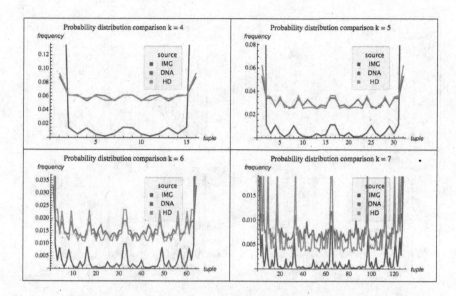

Fig. 2. Frequency distributions of the tuples of length k from physical sources: binarized random files contained in a hard drive (HD), binarized sequences of Deoxyribonucleic acid (DNA) and binarized random images from the world wide web. The data points have been joined for clarity.

number of bits required to represent them. These compression algorithms assign a unique prefix code to each unique symbol that occurs in the input, replacing each fixed-length input symbol by the corresponding variable-length prefix codeword. The length of each codeword is approximately proportional to the negative logarithm of the probability. Therefore, the most common symbols use the shortest codes.

Another popular compression technique based on the same principle is the run-length encoding (RLE)[11], wherein large runs of consecutive identical data values are replaced by a simple code with the data value and length of the run. This is an example of lossless data compression. However, none of these methods seem to follow any prior distribution[12], which means all of them are a posteriori techniques that after analyzing a particular image

[11]Implementations in different programming languages of the run-length encoding are available at *http://rosettacode.org/wiki/Run-length_encoding*

[12]The authors were unable to find any reference to a general *prior* image compression distribution.

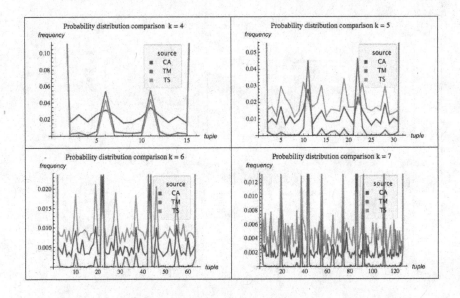

Fig. 3.   Frequency distributions of the tuples of length k from abstract computing machines: deterministic Turing machines (TM), one-dimensional cellular automata (CA) and Post Tag systems (TS).

set their parameters to better compress it. A sort of prior compression distributions may be found in the so-called dictionary coders, also sometimes known as substitution coders, which operate by searching for matches between the text to be compressed and a set of strings contained in a static data structure.

In practice however, it is usually assumed that compressing an image is image dependent, i.e. different from image to image. This is true when prior knowledge of the image is available, or there is enough time to spend in analyzing the file so that a different compression scheme can be set up and used every time. Effectively, compressors achieve greater rates because images have certain statistical properties which can be exploited. But what the experiments carried out here suggest for example is that a general optimal compressor for images based on the frequency distribution for images can be effectively devised and useful in cases when neither prior knowledge nor enough time to analyze the file is available. The distributions found, and tested to be stable could therefore be used for prior image compression techniques. The same sort of applications for other data sets

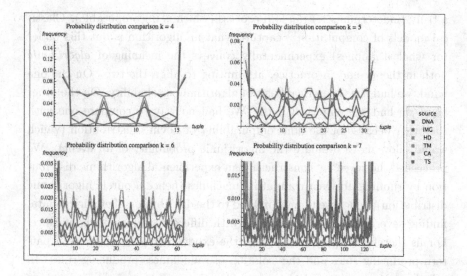

Fig. 4. Comparisons of all frequency distributions of tuples of length k, from physical sources and from abstract computing machines.

can also be made, taking advantage of the kind of exhaustive calculations carried out in our experiments.

The procedure also may suggest a measure of *algorithmicity* relative to a model of computation: a system is more or less algorithmic in nature if it is more or less closer to the average distribution of an abstract model of computation. It has also been shown [Delahaye and Zenil (2007)] that the calculation of these distributions constitute an effective procedure for the numerical evaluation of the algorithmic complexity of short strings, and a mean to provide stability to the definition–independent of additive constants–of algorithmic complexity.

4. The Meaning of *Algorithmic*

Perhaps it may be objected that we have been careless in our use of the term *algorithmic*, not saying exactly what we mean by it. Nevertheless, *algorithmic* means nothing other than what this paper has tried to convey by the stance we have taken over the course of its arguments.

In our context, *Algorithmic* is the adjective given to a set of processes or rules capable of being effectively carried out by a computer in opposition to a truly (indeterministic) random process (which is uncomputable). Classical models of computation[13] capture what an algorithm is but this paper (or what it implies) experimentally conveys the meaning of *algorithmic* both in theory and in practice, attempting to align the two. On the one hand, we had the theoretical basis of algorithmic probability. On the other hand we had the empirical data. We had no way to compare one with the other because of the non-computability of Levin's distribution (which would allow us to evaluate the algorithmic probability of an event). We proceeded, however, by constructing an experimental algorithmic distribution by running abstract computing machines (hence a purely algorithmic distribution), which we then compared to the distribution of empirical data, finding several kinds of correlations with different degrees of significance. For us therefore, algorithmic means the exponential accumulation of pattern producing rules and the isolation of randomness producing rules. In other words, the accumulation of simple rules.

Our definition of *algorithmic* is actually much stronger than the one directly opposing true randomness. Because in our context something is algorithmic if it follows an algorithmic distribution (e.g. the experimental distribution we calculated). One can therefore take this to be a measure of *algorithmicity*: the degree to which a data set approaches an experimentally produced algorithmic distribution (assumed to be Levin's distribution). The closer it is to an algorithmic distribution the more algorithmic.

So when we state that a process is algorithmic in nature, we mean that it is composed by simple and deterministic rules, rules producing patterns, as algorithmic probability theoretically predicts. We think this is true of the market too, despite its particular dynamics, just as it is true of empirical data from other very different sources in the physical world that we have studied.

5. Conclusions

Our findings suggest that the information in the world might be the result of processes resembling processes carried out by computing machines. That does not necessarily imply a trivial reduction more than talking about algorithmic simple rules generating the data as opposed to random or truly

---

[13] Albeit assuming the Church-Turing thesis.

complicated ones. Therefore we think that these correlations are mainly due to the following reason: that general physical processes are dominated by algorithmic simple rules. For example, processes involved in the replication and transmission of the DNA have been found [Li (1999)] to be concatenation, union, reverse, complement, annealing and melting, all they very simple in nature. The same kind of simple rules may be the responsible of the rest of empirical data in spite of looking complicated or random. As opposed to simple rules one may think that nature might be performing processes represented by complicated mathematical functions, such as partial differential equations or all kind of sophisticated functions and possible algorithms. This suggests that the DNA carries a strong algorithmic component indicating that it has been developed as a result of algorithmic processes over the time, layer after layer of accumulated simple rules applied over and over.

So, if the distribution of a data set approaches a distribution produced by purely algorithmic machines rather than the uniform distribution, one may be persuaded within some degree of certainty, that the source of the data is of the same (algorithmic) nature just as one would accept a normal distribution as the footprint of a generating process of some random nature. The scenario described herein is the following: a collection of different distributions produced by different data sets produced by unrelated sources share some properties captured in their frequency distributions, and a theory explaining the data (its regularities) has been presented in this paper.

There has hitherto been no way to either verify or refute the information-theoretic notion, beyond the metaphor, of whether the universe can be conceived as either the output of some computer program or as some sort of vast digital computation device as suggested by some authors [Fredkin (1992); Schmidhuber (2000); Wolfram (2002); Lloyd (2006)].

We think we've devised herein a valid statistical test independent of any bias toward either possibility. Some indications of correlations have been found having weak to strong significance. This is the case with distributions from the chosen abstract devices, as well as with data from the chosen physical sources. Each by itself turned out to show several degrees of correlation. While the correlation between the two sets was partial, each distribution was correlated with at least one distribution produced by an abstract model of computation. In other words, the physical world turned out to be statistically similar in these terms to the simulated one.

References

C.S. Calude, *Information and Randomness: An Algorithmic Perspective (Texts in Theoretical Computer Science. An EATCS Series)*, Springer, 2nd. edition, 2002.

G.J. Chaitin, *Exploring Randomness*, Springer Verlag, 2001.

R.G. Downey, D. Hirschfeldt, *Algorithmic Randomness and Complexity*, Springer Verlag, forthcoming, 2010.

J.P. Delahaye, H. Zenil, On the Kolmogorov-Chaitin complexity for short sequences, in Cristian Calude (eds) *Complexity and Randomness: From Leibniz to Chaitin*. World Scientific, 2007.

E. Fredkin, *Finite Nature*, available at http://www.digitalphilosophy.org/Home/ Papers/FiniteNature/tabid/106/ Default.aspx, 1992.

P.I. Good, *Permutation, Parametric and Bootstrap Tests of Hypotheses*, 3rd ed., Springer, 2005.

W. Kirchherr, M. Li, *The miraculous universal distribution*, Mathematical Intelligencer, 1997.

L. Levin, Universal Search Problems, 9(3):265-266, 1973 (c). (submitted: 1972, reported in talks: 1971). English translation in: B.A.Trakhtenbrot. *A Survey of Russian Approaches to Perebor (Brute-force Search) Algorithms*. Annals of the History of Computing 6(4):384-400, 1984.

M. Li, P. Vitányi, *An Introduction to Kolmogorov Complexity and Its Applications,* Springer, 3rd. Revised edition, 2008.

Z. Li, *Algebraic properties of DNA operations,*, BioSystems, Vol.52, No.1-3, 1999.

S. Lloyd, *Programming the Universe: A Quantum Computer Scientist Takes On the Cosmos,* Knopf, 2006.

J. Schmidhuber, *Algorithmic Theories of Everything,* arXiv:quant-ph/ 0011122v2, 2000.

W. Snedecor, WG. Cochran, *Statistical Methods*, Iowa State University Press; 8 edition, 1989.

E. Thompson Jaynes, *Probability Theory: The Logic of Science*, Cambridge University Press, 2003.

S. Wolfram, *A New Kind of Science*, Wolfram Media, Champaign, IL., 2002.